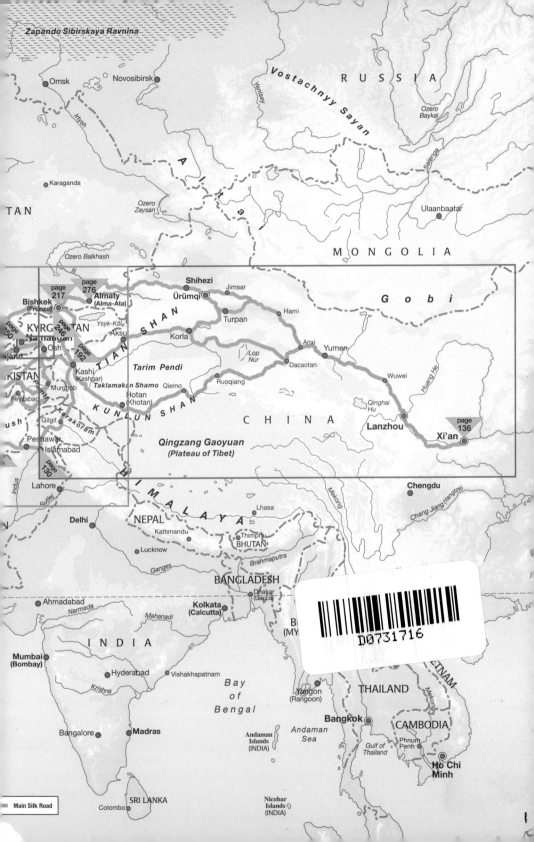

Zapando Sibirskaya Ravnina

RUSSIA

Vostachnyy Sayan

Omsk
Novosibirsk

Ozero
Baykal

Karaganda

Ulaanbaatar

TAN

Ozero
Zaysan

MONGOLIA

Ozero Balkhash

Gobi

Shihezi

page 217
Bishkek
(Frunze)
Almaty
(Alma-Ata)

page 276

Ürümqi
Jimsar

KYRG
Namangan
Osh

Ysyk-Köl

Aksu

Turpan

Hami

Korla

Anxi

Yumen

page 246

page 192

TIAN SHAN

Tarim Pendi

Lop
Nur

Dacaotan

Wuwei

Huang He

KISTAN

Murghob

Kashi
(Kashgar)

Taklamakan Shamo

Qiemo

Ruoqiang

Feyzabac

Hotan
(Khotan)

KUNLUN SHAN

Qinghai
Hu

ush

Gilgit

Karakoram

CHINA

Lanzhou

page 136

Peshawar
Islamabad

Qingzang Gaoyuan
(Plateau of Tibet)

Xi'an

Lahore

HIMALAYA

Chengdu

Indus

Sutlej

Delhi

NEPAL

Lhasa

Chang Jiang (Yangtze)

Mekong

Kathmandu

page 130

Lucknow

Thimphu
BHUTAN

Brahmaputra

Ganges

BANGLADESH

Ahmadabad

Narmada

Dhakar
(Dacca)

Kolkata
(Calcutta)

Mahanadi

B
(MY

Mumbai
(Bombay)

INDIA

Hyderabad

Vishakhapatnam

Krishna

Bay
of
Bengal

Yangon
(Rangoon)

THAILAND

Mekong

Bangalore

Madras

Andaman
Islands
(INDIA)

Andaman
Sea

Bangkok

CAMBODIA

Phnum
Penh

Gulf of
Thailand

SRI LANKA

Colombo

Nicobar
Islands
(INDIA)

Ho Chi
Minh

Main Silk Road

INSIGHT GUIDES
THE SILK ROAD

APA PUBLICATIONS L

Part of the Langenscheidt Publishing Group

✳ INSIGHT GUIDE
THE SILK ROAD

Editorial
Project Editor
Tom Le Bas
Series Manager
Rachel Lawrence
Designer
Ian Spick
Map Production
Original cartography Stephen Ramsay, updated by Apa Cartography Department
Production
Tynan Dean, Linton Donaldson and Rebeka Ellam

Distribution

UK
Dorling Kindersley Ltd
A Penguin Group company
80 Strand, London, WC2R 0RL
customerservice@dk.com

United States
Ingram Publisher Services
1 Ingram Boulevard, PO Box 3006,
La Vergne, TN 37086-1986
customer.service@ingrampublisher
services.com

Australia
Universal Publishers
PO Box 307
St Leonards NSW 1590
sales@universalpublishers.com.au

New Zealand
Brown Knows Publications
11 Artesia Close, Shamrock Park
Auckland, New Zealand 2016
sales@brownknows.co.nz

Worldwide
**Apa Publications GmbH & Co.
Verlag KG (Singapore branch)**
7030 Ang Mo Kio Avenue 5
08-65 Northstar @ AMK
Singapore 569880
apasin@singnet.com.sg

Printing
CTPS-China
© 2012 Apa Publications (UK) Ltd
All Rights Reserved
First Edition 2008
2nd Edition 2012

ABOUT THIS BOOK

The first Insight Guide pioneered the use of creative full-colour photography in travel guides in 1970. Since then, we have expanded our range to cater for our readers' need not only for reliable information about their chosen destination but also for a real understanding of the culture and workings of that destination. Now, when the internet can supply inexhaustible (but not always reliable) facts, our books marry text and pictures to provide those much more elusive qualities: knowledge and discernment. To achieve this, they rely heavily on the authority of experts.

How to use this book

Insight Guide: The Silk Road provides a comprehensive survey of this ancient trade route that stretched from China to the Mediterranean:

The Best of The Silk Road section at the front of the guide helps you to prioritise what you want to do.

The Features section, indicated by a pink bar at the top of each page, covers the fascinating history of the Road, from the early cultivation of silk in China to its spread west along the route, taking in the rise and fall of empires, life on the road and in the bazaars, the spread of ideas and the rediscovery of ancient treasures.

The main Places section, indicated by a blue bar, guides readers along the route from east to west and is divided into three sections: China, Central Asia and Western Asia, which are in turn divided into provinces (China) or countries.

The Travel Tips listings section, with a yellow bar, provides full information on transport, restaurants, hotels and activities, and an A–Z section of essential practical information.

who first visited the Silk Road in 1986 when China had just opened up to individual travellers; he also wrote the chapter on Pakistan. **Andrew Forbes**, a longtime Insight Guides contributor and the author of more than a dozen books on East and Southeast Asia, wrote the China section as well as most of the History and Features, plus the Introduction, The Incredible Journey and Talk of the Road.

Bradley Mayhew, who has been travelling and taking tours along the Silk Road for over 15 years and is the author of numerous guidebooks, wrote the bulk of the Central Asia section (Uzbekistan, Kyrgyzstan and Tajikistan), plus features including Rediscovering the Road, The Great Game, the Sogdians, Teahouse Culture, contributions to the Introduction and picture stories on Yurts and Treasures.

Author and lecturer **Chris Bradley** is a pioneering tour leader who took groups along the Chinese and Central Asian Silk Road during the 1980s and has since led many tours to Iran, Syria, Lebanon and Turkey. For this book he went back, to write and photograph the entire Western Asia section.

Laurence Mitchell wrote the Kazakhstan chapter and the Travel Tips for Central Asia; **Philippa Scott** wrote The Story of Silk; **Melissa Shales** wrote the Turkey chapter; **Andre Mann** penned the chapter on Afghanistan; **Michael Kohn**, wrote on Turkmenistan; and **Alan Palmer** the feature on Gandharan Art.

This second edition was copy-edited by **Scarlett O'Hara,** the picture researcher was **Tom Smyth**, and the book was proofread by **John King** and indexed by **Penny Phenix**.

The contributors

This new edition was supervised and edited by **Tom Le Bas**, a senior editor at Insight's London office, who commissioned **Sophie Ibbotson** and **Max Lovell-Hoare** to comprehensively update the content, and write a new chapter on People and their Environment, expand the Spread of Ideas chapter to include a section on architecture, and expand the Travel Tips with new Language sections. Sophie and Max run Maximum Exposure Productions, a company which provides logistics, investment and PR consultancy to businesses, NGOs and government agencies across Asia. They have raised the profile of a number of lesser-known countries through guidebooks, articles and photographic exhibitions.

The original book was commissioned and edited by **Tony Halliday**,

Map Legend

– ⋅ –	International Boundary
– – –	Province Boundary
– ⋅ –	National Park/Reserve
– – –	Ferry Route
Ⓜ	Metro
✈ ✈	Airport: International/Regional
🚌	Bus Station
❶	Tourist Information
✉	Post Office
🏠 † ✟	Church/Ruins
†	Monastery
∴	Archaeological Site
🏰 ⌂	Castle/Ruins
☾	Mosque
✡	Synagogue
∩	Cave
🗽	Statue/Monument
★	Place of Interest
³𐊢	Lighthouse

The main places of interest in the Places section are coordinated by number with a full-colour map (eg ❶), and a symbol at the top of every right-hand page tells you where to find the map.

Contents

Travel Tips

Maps

Inside front and back covers: the Silk Road.

THE BEST OF THE SILK ROAD: TOP ATTRACTIONS

Ancient cities, some in ruins, some still thriving; huge mountain ranges, deserts, oases; and buildings to take your breath away.

△ **Mogao Caves.** These caves near Dunhuang lay undiscovered for centuries. They contain one of the world's greatest collections of Buddhist art. See page 160.

◁ **Registan, Samarkand.** A spectacular architectural ensembles, with fantastic Islamic designs and calligraphy etched into the facades of its mosque and madrassahs. See page 255.

△ **Palmyra.** One of the most important cultural centres of the ancient world, Palmyra grew incredibly rich during Roman times thanks to its position right on the Silk Road. Its monumental ruins remain as a reminder of those past glories. See page 346.

△ **Isfahan**. This great city grew rich from the Silk Road trade linking with the Persian Gulf, resulting in some sublime architecture including the incomparable Imam Mosque. See page 325.

△ **Yurt living**. Experience the nomadic lifestyle amid the wilds of the mountain nation of Kyrgyzstan, at the heart of Central Asia. See page 214.

▽ **Poi Kalon ensemble**. Consisting of mosque, madrassah and minaret, this is the focal point of Bukhara, one of the great centres of trade and scholarship along the Silk Road. See page 264.

△ **The Turpan Oasis**. A sea of green surrounded by desert, is famous for its vineyards. The city of Turpan is also the base for excursions to ancient Silk Road sites and other attractions. See page 170.

◁ **Lake Issyk-Kul.** The world's second-largest saline lake has a dramatic mountain setting. Meaning "hot lake" in Kyrgyz, it does not freeze, even in the depths of the Kyrgyz winter. See page 220.

△ **Karakoram Highway**. One of the world's most awe-inspiring roads, linking Western China and Pakistan across the mighty Pamir and Karakoram mountain ranges. See page 282.

◁ **Terracotta Army**. A legacy of China's First Emperor, Qin Shi Huang, who had it built to protect him in the afterlife. See page 142.

THE BEST OF THE SILK ROAD: EDITOR'S CHOICE

Linking two continents across 8,000km (5,000 miles), the Silk Road has so much to offer, whatever your interests. The following selection will provide some food for thought and help you organise a trip.

BEST LANDSCAPES AND JOURNEYS

Mingsha Shan and Crescent Moon Lake. Get a taste of the Taklamakan Desert by taking a camel ride in these great dunes near Dunhuang. See page 161.

Flaming Mountains. This is a major landmark near Turpan, enshrined in Chinese folklore. See page 175.

Lake Karakul. Just off the Karakoram Highway, the lake has great views of the Kunlun peaks of Kongur and Muztagh Ata. See page 199.

Heaven Lake (Tian Chi). High in the Tian Shan to the east of Urumqi, at the base of Bogda Shan, this makes an invigorating escape. See page 201.

Kyrgyzstan jailoos. These are the upland pastures where the Kyrgyz nomads live during the summer. Visitors can stay in a nomad's yurt. See page 217.

Tajikistan's Pamir Highway. This is an amazing journey following the Silk Road across "the roof of the world", in the footsteps of some famous explorers. See page 231.

Iskander-Kul (Alexander's Lake) features on almost every trekking itinerary in Tajikistan's Fan Mountains. Legend has it that Alexander the Great appears riding on his horse through the water during a full moon. See page 241.

Hunza Valley, Pakistan. On the Karakoram Highway from China, this most beautiful of valleys is dominated by the enormous Rakaposhi. See page 282.

Syrian Desert. The classical desert route, between Dura Europos and Damascus via the ancient city of Palmyra, is what the Middle East section of the Silk Road is all about. See page 345.

ABOVE: the dunes of the Taklamakan Desert, near Dunhuang. **FAR LEFT:** Pakistan's Hunza Valley. **LEFT:** on a camel at the Flaming Mountains.

BEST CITIES

Xi'an. The ancient capital of China, the eastern terminus of the Silk Road, famous for its city walls, pagodas and the nearby Terracotta Army. See page 135.

Kashgar. Major market town at a busy Silk Road junction, a hub of travel for Western China. Buy your camels here. See page 193.

Samarkand. One of the most famous Silk Road cities of all, with fantastic Timurid architecture and a 2,500-year history. See page 253.

Istanbul. The meeting point of Europe and Asia, Christianity and Islam, is the vibrant starting point of the Silk Road in the west. See page 378.

Herat. Dominated by the remains of a citadel constructed by Alexander the Great, this ancient Afghan city could become a major Silk Road destination again. See page 295.

Shiraz. The city that gave its name to the grape variety, and a centre of Iranian poetry. See page 322.

Isfahan, Iran, once the showcase of Persian art and architecture, has some breathtakingly stunning buildings. See page 325.

Damascus, Syria. This great capital, one of the world's oldest cities, is home to the Umayyad Mosque and an ancient citadel. See page 350.

BEST BAZAARS

Sunday Market, Kashgar. Whether you want to buy a camel, a fat-tailed sheep or a horse, this is the place to come. An insight into the Silk Road of old. See page 195.

Peshawar, Pakistan. A maze of bazaars, the most authentic on the Silk Road. See page 286.

Siab Bazaar, Samarkand. A great place to meet the Uzbeks, and a bewildering array of produce. See page 257.

Aleppo, Syria. Famous for its labyrinthine souks. See page 358.

Bazaar-e Vakil, Shiraz. One of Iran's best markets. See page 323.

Grand Bazaar, Istanbul. The ultimate covered bazaar experience. See page 379.

LEFT: Kuntepa market near Margilan.

GREAT BUILDINGS

Jiayuguan Fort and the Great Wall. The Silk Road passes straight through this defiant building. See page 156.

Tash Rabat, Kyrgyzstan. A remote caravanserai in the wilds. See page 215.

Registan, Samarkand. The massive scale and intricate detail of the tilework is beyond compare. See page 255.

Gur-i-Mir, Samarkand. The tomb of the mighty ruler Timur (Tamerlane). See page 259.

Ismail Samani Mausoleum, Bukhara. An architectural gem of Central Asia. See page 263.

Khiva city walls. The 17th-century walls of this oasis town feel frozen in time. See page 270.

Baltit Fort in Karimabad, Pakistan. This mountain fort was a key site on the frontier of the Great Game and has spectacular views. See page 283.

Minaret of Jam, Afghanistan. Isolated 12th-century minaret. See page 294.

Friday Mosque, Herat, Afghanistan. This great mosque features stunning tilework. See page 295.

See-o-se Pol, Isfahan, Iran. This bridge with two rows of 33 arches was commissioned by Shah Abbas I in 1602. See page 327.

Umayyad Mosque, Damascus. A dazzling mosque. See page 352.

Ishak Pasha Palace, Dogubeyazit, Turkey. Dramatic sandstone palace at the eastern edge of the Ottoman Empire. See page 369.

ABOVE: the city of Bukhara. **BELOW:** the Kalta Minor in Khiva.

BEST MUSEUMS

Terracotta Warriors, Xi'an. An emperor's personal army – made for the afterlife. One of the great attractions of the Silk Road. See page 142.

Afrosiab Museum, Samarkand. A whole room of Sogdian murals has been recreated here; other rooms contain artefacts from the various periods in Samarkand's early development. See page 258.

Museum of the History of Uzbekistan, Tashkent. Some fine exhibits, including Buddhist remains from the Kushan era. See page 252.

Ulug Beg's Observatory, Samarkand. The underground chamber of the famous astronomer's great sextant can still be seen cut into the rock. See page 259.

National Archaeological Museum, Tehran. Some fascinating exhibits from all eras across the Iranian world. See page 320.

Carpet Museum, Tehran. Some of the finest Persian carpets collected from Iran's weaving centres, demonstrating a variety of designs. See page 320.

Azerbaijan Archaeology Museum, Tabriz. An astonishing wealth of fascinating archaeological exhibits from the region, plus the so-called "Chelsea rewoven carpet" on the upper floor. See page 331.

Palmyra Museum. Exhibits here include incredibly well-preserved silk fabrics used for wrapping mummies. See page 348.

Nationa Archaeological Museum, Damascus. World-class exhibits including the first complete alphabet of 30 cuneiform signs. See page 353.

Silk Museum, near Beirut. Dedicated enthusiasts run this museum and keep the Silk Road dream alive in the modern world. See page 366.

SHRINES, TOMBS AND MONASTERIES

Tomb of Bakhauddin Naqshband, Bukhara. The founder of the Naqshbandi order of Sufism. See page 268.

Tomb of Khoja Ahmed Yassawi in Turkistan, Kazakhstan. Local Muslims believe making three pilgrimages here is equivalent to going on Hajj. See page 279.

Shrine of Hazrat Ali, Mazar-e-Sharif. One of Islam's holiest shrines. See page 297.

Ismail Samani Mausoleum, Bukhara. Built for the founder of the Samanid dynasty.

See page 263.

Labrang. The most important Tibetan monastery outside Tibet. See page 150.

Tomb of Mevlâna Jelaleddin Rumi, Konya. Home of the Whirling Dervishes. See page 376.

FESTIVALS

Silk Road Festival. One of the main events in Syria, held annually in Damascus, Palmyra and Aleppo to celebrate Syrian heritage.

Nauroz (New Year). The spring equinox festival celebrated in Iran and Central Asian countries, deeply rooted in ancient Zoroastrian traditions.

Chinese New Year. The most important Chinese festival, which usually falls in late January or early February.

Central Asia Horse Festival, Kyrgyzstan. Watch the best of Central Asia's horsemen compete in horse races, horseback wrestling and kok boru – dead goat polo.

Muslim Festivals. The main ones are Id al-Fitr, held at the end of the fasting month of Ramadan; and Id al-Adha (the "Festival of the Sacrifice"), held to mark the culmination of the Hajj pilgrimage to Mecca.

TOP: prayer wheels at Labrang Monastery. **FAR RIGHT:** tomb of Ismail Samani, Bukhara. **RIGHT:** Iranian girl dressed up for the festival of No Ruz (New Year).

ANCIENT SITES

Maijishan Shiku. One of China's four most important Buddhist temple groups, in a dramatic location. See page 147.

Mogao Caves, Dunhuang. The source of the world's most extensive collection of Buddhist statuary, paintings and manuscripts. See page 160.

Jiaohe Ancient City. The best preserved of Xinjiang's ancient Silk Road cities. See page 172.

Bezeklik Thousand Buddha Caves. There are few murals left here, but the caves are in a dramatic location. See page 175.

Penjikent. One of the great lost Silk Road cities of Central Asia, beautifully situated in the Zerafshan Valley of northern Tajikistan. See page 242.

Toprak Qala. Spectacular ruins from the Kushan era in the desert of Khorezm, Uzbekistan. See page 272.

Merv. Once the world's largest city, Merv was never to recover from its sacking by Genghis Khan. Its impressive ruins rise from the Darvaza Desert in Turkmenistan. See page 298.

Taxila. One of Asia's great archaeological sites, at a very important crossroads in Pakistan. See page 286.

Persepolis. One of the great cities of antiquity, a capital of the Achaemenid Empire. See page 323.

Palmyra. The ruins of the ancient Syrian metropolis, spread across a vast area, are perhaps best visited on a camel. See page 346.

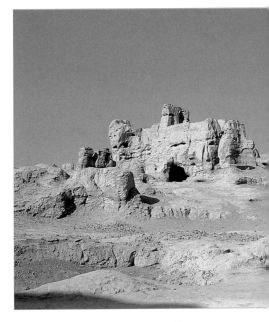

ABOVE: the ancient city of Jiaohe near Turpan.
BELOW LEFT: the griffin, a symbol from Persepolis.

PLACES TO STAY

Uzbekistan. There are some fine places to stay in both Samarkand and Bukhara, with many hotels occupying traditional houses. See page 410.

Turkey. Hotels cut into the rock are an unusual feature in Cappadocia. See page 437.

Kyrgyzstan and

Tajikistan. For those willing to rough it a little, homestays offer a viable alternative to hotels and in some areas may be all that is available. See page 407.

Yurts. Staying in a yurt is another exciting option, particularly on the jailoos of Kyrgyzstan. See page 217.

SILK ROAD AT A GLANCE

Where and how far?
The Silk Road starts in Xi'an in China and finishes at Antakya on the Turkish Mediterranean coast, or in Istanbul. It covers a distance of more than 8,000km (5,000 miles) and passes through 13 countries, which are (with their capitals): China (Beijing), Kyrgyzstan (Bishkek), Tajikistan (Dushanbe), Uzbekistan (Tashkent), Kazakhstan (Astana), Pakistan (Islamabad), Afghanistan (Kabul), Turkmenistan (Ashgabat), Iran (Tehran), Iraq (Baghdad), Syria (Damascus), Lebanon (Beirut) and Turkey (Ankara).

Geographical features
The Silk Road crosses some dramatic landscapes, including some of the world's harshest deserts like the Taklamakan and the Syrian Desert, and mountain ranges such as the Karakoram, Kunlun, Pamir, Hindu Kush and Tian Shan. The main rivers are the Huang He (Yellow River) in China, the Amu Darya (Oxus) and Syr Darya (Jaxartes) in Central Asia, and the Tigris and Euphrates in Iraq and Syria.

Why Silk Road?
Silk was one of its most valuable and important commodities, but the term Seidenstrasse (Silk Road) was only coined in 1877, by German geographer Ferdinand von Richthofen.

ANCIENT TRADE ROUTE

Dating back thousands of years, the Silk Road
refers to a series of overland routes from China
to the Mediterranean along which traders,
merchants and pilgrims would travel. Silk was
one of many luxuries traded along the way.

No highway in the world is as laden with romance
and adventure as the Silk Road. Yet for centuries
it remained little more than the stuff of dreams.
Today, however, with improved road, rail and air links
and an overall reduction in red tape, the Road has
become more accessible to ordinary travellers than at
any time in its history. No longer is the "Silk Road"
purely a historical reference to the overland trade route
of antiquity. It is now increasingly applied to a re-established network of highways stretching right across Asia,
linking East and West via harsh deserts and spectacular
mountains. The ancient cities through which they pass
bear names redolent with age, remoteness and mystery.

Viewed from a Western perspective, these fabled
settlements acquire an increased patina of romance
the further east they lie: Antioch (modern Antakya),
Palmyra, Balkh, Bukhara, Samarkand, Kashgar, Khotan,
Dunhuang and countless others en route to Chang'an
(modern Xi'an). This aura of the mystic Orient is epitomised in the verse of English poet James Elroy Flecker
(1884–1915):

Sweet to ride forth at evening from the wells
When shadows pass gigantic on the sand
And softly through the silence beat the bells,
Along the golden road to Samarkand.

The same, semi-mystic quality is attached to the Silk Road when viewed
from the East. Chang'an, the ancient Tang Dynasty capital, has long
been a familiar name for the Chinese to conjure with, and Jiayuguan,
the "Last Pass Under Heaven", traditionally marked the western limits of
civilisation. Beyond lay the jade fields of Khotan, the Heavenly Horses of
Fergana and – at the very edge of the western world – fabled Daqin, the
ancient Chinese name for Rome. In between lay boundless deserts and
insurmountable peaks inhabited by bandits and demons. An anonymous
Ming Chinese poet could not share the romantic view of Flecker:

PRECEDING PAGES: Jiayuguan Fort in Gansu province, China; Ala-Kol lake in the Tian
Shan mountains, Kyrgyzstan; the ruins of Palmyra in Syria. **LEFT:** the Sherdor
Madrassa on the Registan in Samarkand. **ABOVE:** in the heart of Bukhara.

Looking west, we see the long, long road –
Only the brave cross the Martial Barrier.
Who is not afraid of the vast desert?
Should not the scorching heat of heaven make him frightened?

Today, the restored Silk Road exercises an irresistible appeal on travellers from both East and West, as some sections of the journey become easier and more comfortable each year. The desert trip from Kashgar to Urumqi, which in 1940 took 40 days in an unsprung, camel-drawn cart, can now be accomplished in an air-conditioned sleeper bus in under 15 hours. The Chinese are proposing to build a high-speed-train line that would enable travel from London to Beijing in just two days. Moreover, as visitors bring new wealth, and long suppressed national pride burgeons, many ancient Silk Road sights and cities are being restored to their former glory.

At the time of its greatest use the Road was a series of trade routes connecting East with West. The name "Silk Road" was coined in the 19th century, when explorers and archaeologists began to rediscover long-lost cities. The German geographer Ferdinand von Richthofen was the first to use the word *Seidenstraße*, in 1877. He was describing the overland export of one of the earliest and most valuable commodities carried from China to the Mediterranean – the direction of travel followed in this book.

Silk was not the only costly product to be traded across Asia, but it was unknown in the West and therefore highly prized. For centuries it was the most celebrated and profitable item transported along the caravan trails. Other valuable products, such as lapis lazuli from Afghanistan and jade from China, were traded, but not all the way.

First produced in China 5,000 years ago, silk was symbolic of the link between continents as visionary rulers, explorers, merchants and pilgrims ventured further afield. Extending for around 8,000km (5,000 miles), the Road followed no single route – Central Asia in particular developed several branches – passing through different oasis settlements, depending upon the season and local political situation as much as the terrain. Water supply, earthquakes, desertification, or man-made events such as migration, wars and banditry all combined to make these intrepid

ABOVE: camels at the Flaming Mountains near Turpan. **TOP RIGHT:** Istanbul's Aya Sofia mosque. **BOTTOM RIGHT:** China's famous Terracotta Warriors.

merchants seek the safest and easiest course.

The Silk Road flourished throughout the first millennium AD, reaching its prime during the Tang Dynasty (618–907) and flourishing again in the 13th century under the Mongols. During the Ming Dynasty (1368–1644), land trade between China, Central Asia and the Middle East withered away, and by the time of the Ottoman and Qing supremacies, the Silk Road was little more than a memory, superseded by direct maritime trade between Europe and Asia and finally the arrival of the railways.

The Silk Road wasn't just a conduit for trade goods. As well as merchants, there were invaders, travellers, missionaries and pilgrims using the road and, crucially, spreading their ideas. The scientific knowledge, inventions, religions and foods that passed along the Silk Road transformed isolated countries into an interdependent global community. This made it the first, and perhaps the most important, information superhighway, helping to lay the foundations of the modern world.

Interdependence remains a vital theme. Travel along the Silk Road was never plain sailing: just as one route was cleared, another obstacle would arise. Today, most of the obstacles are not physical but ideological, and most people will think twice before travelling through countries such as Afghanistan and Iraq. On the other hand, new border crossings and passes have reconnected Central Asian states to their neighbours. Railway lines (the "Iron Silk Road"), oil pipelines, tour buses and even opium traders now follow former caravan trails.

The notion of the Silk Road is used to sell everything from home furnishings to tours of China. Musical collaborations such as YoYo Ma's Silk Road Ensemble also explore the cultural connections between East and West. Even the internet has been lauded as a "21st-century Silk Road". As researchers swap ancient documents online, it's clear that the idea of the Silk Road as a metaphor for international exchange is as valid today as it has ever been.

THE INCREDIBLE JOURNEY

From China to the West, the 8,000 km (5,000 miles) of trading routes known collectively as the Silk Road criss-cross some of the world's most spectacular terrain. But its mountains and deserts, which are such a delight for modern travellers, were perilous places for the early merchants.

The routes of the ancient Silk Road travel through more than a dozen countries between China and the Mediterranean, crossing some of the most challenging and inaccessible regions on earth. In classical times, the arid deserts and freezing mountains were incredibly hazardous to the long-distance travellers, who hastened to their journeys' end, pausing to rest only in the oases that had grown up along the way. Today, travelling the modern Silk Road, conditions are infinitely easier and more pleasant. The same fertile and hospitable oases remain, but the route between them is so greatly improved that the traveller is free to marvel at the natural beauty of endless, shifting sand dunes and serried, snow-capped mountains without fear of death through starvation, thirst, frostbite or attack by bandits (though modern hazards, notably motor accidents, may still pose a threat).

It took 20 days to travel the first stretch of the journey from Xi'an to Lanzhou by pony, which until the 1930s was the only way to go. Today, by coach or train, it takes eight hours.

The highway from Xi'an

The Silk Road starts life in the great city of Xi'an, formerly Chang'an, a modern metropolis, capital of China's Shaanxi Province, and home of the extraordinary Terracotta Army. From here, National Highway 312 and the railway

LEFT: Kyrgyz man on horseback.
RIGHT: donkey caravan at the Khyber Pass, Pakistan–Afghanistan border.

trace the old route west to Lanzhou, capital of Gansu province and the largest city in northwest China. Lying in a gorge, hemmed in by steep mountains, its strategic location has long made it an important garrison town. Surging through its centre is the Huang He, coloured a rich chocolate by the huge quantities of loess it carries downstream.

Beyond Lanzhou the route continues through the long, narrow Hexi Corridor in some of the most dramatic terrain in all of China. Extending for about 1,000km (620 miles) to Yumen near the frontiers of Xinjiang, China's westernmost province, this unwelcoming landscape is punctuated by fertile oases that form the basis for such old Silk Road towns as

Wuwei, Zhangye and Jiuquan. To the north stretch the barren wastes of the Gobi desert, and to the south the permanently snow-covered peaks of the Qilian Mountains. They mark the northern rim of the great Tibetan plateau, product of the cataclysmic collision between India and Asia some 200 million years ago – a process that continues today, as the Indian plate presses into the Asian land mass at the rate of about 20mm (0.8in) every year.

The limits of China "proper"

Following the Old Silk Road, National Highway 312 is paralleled by the Lanxin Railway, and

"Snow rests on them both winter and summer. There are among them venomous dragons, which spit forth poisonous winds, and cause showers of snow and storms of sand and gravel. Not one in 10,000 of those who meet these dangers escapes with his life."
Faxian (5th-century Buddhist) on the Pamirs

now carves its way west between these deserts and mountains, through a region that for centuries was seen by the Chinese as the limits of

THE TAKLAMAKAN

Of all the obstacles to progress along the Silk Road, the most fearsome was the Taklamakan desert. Its very name, *Takla makan*, means: "Go in and you will never come out". At 1,000km (620 miles) long and 400km (250 miles) wide, covering 270,000 sq km (105,000 sq miles), it is one of the world's largest sandy deserts.

The Taklamakan was a serious hindrance during the height of the Silk Road and it remains a perilous wilderness. The great Swedish explorer Sven Hedin (1865–1953) was nearly one of its victims when he spent two desperate weeks trudging through the sand only to realise he had been going round in circles. He was reduced to drinking camel urine and only had the

energy to crawl on all fours towards the forested edge of the desert. Two human companions and all but one camel died.

Winter temperatures can plunge to −20°C (−4°F). In 2008, snow was recorded right across the desert, reaching a depth of around 4 centimetres (1.6 in). With howling winds and desert ghosts, it is almost completely waterless, and comparable in terms of both harshness and beauty to Arabia's Rub' al-Khali or "Empty Quarter". Utterly uninhabited, the centre of the Taklamakan is filled with huge, shifting dunes, and it was only recently penetrated by two cross-desert highways built by the Chinese in their search for oil.

civilisation. Beyond Jiayuguan was alien territory, the home of wandering desert ghosts and fierce nomads, a land bitterly cold in winter and intolerably hot in summer, where a lack of water meant only a few hardy plants such as the desert tamarisk and sagebrush could survive. The oasis of Dunhuang, in Gansu Province, is the site of some of the greatest Silk Road discoveries. It marks the limits of China "proper" and the start of Central Asia, and is also where the route presents its first major division, offering three ways forward.

Highway 312 takes the Northern route, signposted with the ancient beacon tower at Yumenguan and heading for the oasis of Hami. The old Central Route goes via Loulan and a howling wilderness, the Desert of Lop, vividly described by Marco Polo. This route was abandoned more than 1,500 years ago and until 1996 China tested its nuclear bombs here. The third, Southern Silk Road heads southwest from the crumbling beacon tower of Yangguan, across the arid wastes of the Kum Tagh "Sand Mountains", home to China's only wild camel reserve.

The Chinese authorities are rapidly changing the ethnic map of their great western province of Xinjiang, the "New Frontier", allowing Han Chinese migrants to stream into the province where they now dominate Urumqi and the Dzungarian Basin in the north. But in the south, Uighur Turks and other related Turkic peoples are still predominant in many of the oasis towns that are strung like green jewels around the northern and southern rims of the Tarim Basin. This is impressive country, centred on China's largest desert, the incomparable Taklamakan (*see panel*).

Over the roof of the world

The Northern and Southern Silk Roads reunite at the old caravan city of Kashgar before climbing into the once-impenetrable Pamir Knot and leaving China via three routes. For centuries this transitional region marked the point where Chinese influence ended and the Silk Road passed into western Central Asia. The most dramatic of these routes is the Karakoram Highway, a Chinese-built metalled

ABOVE, FROM LEFT: a camel caravan crosses the Mingsha Shan desert; traveling the famous Silk Road, side-by-side on the Karakoram Highway.

road leading south and over the Khunjerab Pass (4,693 metres/15,397ft) to Pakistan. This is the highest paved international road in the world, and it descends through the awe-inspiring scenery of the Hunza Valley and within reach of Baltistan, home to five peaks in excess of 8,000 metres (26,000ft), including the world's second-highest peak, K2, and some of the world's longest glaciers.

Two other roads head north and west from Kashgar, going via the Irkeshtam and Torugart Passes respectively, to neighbouring Kyrgyzstan. At 3,752 metres (12,310ft), the Torugart Pass through the Tian Shan is lower

than the Khunjerab, but the road is narrow and difficult, often being blocked by heavy snow and avalanches. The easiest pass is the Irkeshtam, rising to 2,841 metres (9,321ft) before descending, via a narrow mountain valley, to the Kyrgyz city of Osh and the fertile Fergana Valley, most of which lies today within Uzbekistan. This is the heart of the Central Asian region known in antiquity as Transoxiana – the region beyond the Oxus River. In fact the region is watered by two great rivers, the Oxus and the Jaxartes, which the Uzbeks call the Amu Darya and Syr Darya. To the north lies the endless steppe of Kazakhstan, and to the south the jagged peaks of Afghanistan's Hindu Kush mountains, crossed by the army of Alexander the Great in 326 BC.

In classical times a branch of the Silk Road passed south of the Oxus, through the sandy wastes of northern Afghanistan, past the fabled city of Balkh – now little more than ruins – and Mazar-e-Sharif, the principal city of northern Afghanistan, before turning south to Herat and on to the great northeast Iranian city of Mashhad. There was another route to the north, via the Dzungarian Gate between northern Xinjiang and Kazakhstan, that avoided the Pamirs, but at the cost of travelling far to the north through territory controlled by fierce nomads.

the narrow defile called the "Iron Gates" in the Buzgala Gorge and on to the fabled Silk Road cities of Samarkand and Bukhara. Beyond Bukhara the old Silk Road left the banks of the Zeravshan River, crossing the Oxus near Chardzhou – now the city of Turkmenabat in Turkmenistan – and continuing over the black sands of the Karakum Desert to the old oasis city of Merv on the desert's southern edge. The Arab historian al-Muqaddasi, writing in the 10th century, described Merv as "delightful, fine, elegant, brilliant, extensive, and pleasant", but only the evocative ruins of the ancient city remain today.

Balkh in northern Afghanistan is one of the oldest Silk Road cities and is considered to be the first settlement to which the Indo-Aryan tribes moved from north of the Oxus River between 3,500 and 4,000 years ago.

So the main route continued west from Osh, through the settled Fergana Valley and the cities of Andijan and Kokand, to the former Sogdian centre of Chach – today the largely concrete city of Tashkent, the capital of Uzbekistan and the largest city in Central Asia.

From Tashkent the main branch of the Silk Road continued southwest, passing through

Persia and the Arab heartlands

Merv was where the southern spur of the Silk Road running through Balkh rejoined the main route. Beyond it, the route led southwest across the modern Turkmenistan-Iran frontier to the ancient Persian city of Mashhad, a holy city of the utmost importance to Shia Muslims and distinguished by some of the finest Islamic architecture in Iran.

West of Mashhad the Silk Road continued across the semi-desert plains of Khorasan and northern Iran before traversing the foothills of the Elburz Mountains, dominated by the snow-capped cone of 5,671-metre (18,605-ft) Mount Damavand. From here it passed through the old Zoroastrian centre of Rey, a city long since surpassed by nearby Tehran, though the latter was not insignificant when the Silk Road was in its prime. To the south, en route to the Persian Gulf, lay the wealthy cities of Shiraz and Isfahan.

Next came the wild Zagros Mountains, the last serious upland barrier before the Mediterranean Sea. The road passed through Hamadan, a city dating back to 3000 BC that was formerly the capital of the Achaemenids (559–330 BC) and, during the Silk Road's greatest period of prosperity, the summer capital of the Sassanids (AD 226–651). The surrounding mountains are home to Iran's

> *"One is not alarmed by robbers, but the road becomes unsafe by fierce tigers and lions who will attack passengers, and unless these be travelling in caravans of a hundred men or more, or be protected by military equipment, they may be devoured by those beasts."*
> Hou Han Shu (5th-century Chinese chronicle) on Ta Ts'in (Syria)

Bakhtiari tribe, many of whom are still pastoral nomads.

After leaving the Zagros, the road descended to the plains of Mesopotamia, passing through Ctesiphon and – after its foundation by the Abbasid Caliph al-Mansur in 761 – Baghdad, the modern capital of Iraq and second-largest city in the Arab world after Cairo. The route then led northwest, between the Tigris and Euphrates rivers, to Dura Europos and the eastern frontiers of Syria. Today much of this territory is desert, but in the Silk Road heyday it was forested, and we know from Arab and even Chinese accounts that it supported large numbers of wild animals, including lions.

The next major population centre was the Graeco-Roman caravan city of Palmyra, sometimes called the "Queen of the Desert". Here the road split, the southern branch leading to the capital, Damascus, while the main, northern branch led through the age-old mart of Aleppo,

a trading centre from 5000 BC, today remarkable for its Old City, Citadel and souks.

As it neared the Mediterranean, the Silk Road branched out, like the delta of a river, from the Levant to Anatolia. One of the main end points was Antioch, today's Antakya, a somnolent Turkish port – still claimed by Syria – that was the capital of the Seleucid Empire in the 4th century BC. Across the Anatolian plains, the Seljuks secured trade by building a series of *hans* (caravanserais). Here the Silk Road largely followed the ancient Persian Royal Road before reaching its ultimate destination, the great city of Constantinople.

ARCHITECTURAL GEMS

The Chinese Silk Road offers some awesome natural beauty, but rather less in the way of classical architecture. The ancient cities of the Tarim Basin are largely in ruins, and while Kashgar is justly proud of its great Id Gah Mosque it simply cannot compare with the architectural gems of Samarkand – the Registan, Bibi Khanum, Gur Emir and Shah-i-Zindah – or Bukhara (with its Poi Kolon complex, Ark citadel and Samanid Mausoleum), or indeed the picturesque cities of Iran like Isfahan. In the ruins stakes, Iran also has Persepolis, while further to the west the great city of Palmyra in the Syrian desert is one of the greatest sights of the Silk Road.

ABOVE, FROM LEFT: the new Silk Road, bringing oil, gas and other commodities; the northern Syrian city of Aleppo, a major Silk Road stop.

Talk of the Road

In the bazaars and on the road, dozens of languages would have been heard, but some were more dominant than others.

The Silk Road provided a cultural and commercial link between half of mankind, joining East and West and providing a constantly moving pathway for goods and ideas, peoples and entertainment. Between Chang'an and the

Mediterranean it passed through many diverse peoples and lands, which today include at least 13 countries, each with its own official language. How did people communicate with each other? Was there a universal *lingua franca*? Or did traders and cameleers employ interpreters, or resort to sign language?

The answer is, almost certainly, a bit of all three. Clearly merchants and caravaneers would have employed both sign language and the use of an interpreter, whenever and wherever it was necessary. And while there was no universal language employed between the Mediterranean and the Yellow River Valley (in the way that English is often used today), certain languages were more useful and more widely spoken than others.

Today, as in antiquity, China is the most unchanging political entity along the route of the Silk Road, and Chinese – generally the *putonghua* or "common speech" of Beijing and North China known as Mandarin in the West, as well as Xi'an and Gansu dialects – must have been, as they still are, the *lingua franca* of the Eastern Silk Road from Chang'an to Kashgar. Other languages spoken along the easternmost stretch of the Silk Road include Mongol and Tibetan, neither of which would have been much use to the west of the Pamirs, with the possible exception of Mongol during the Yuan Dynasty.

Yet, even as far to the east as the Hexi Corridor in Gansu, Chinese was soon to be challenged by a second major world language group – Turko-Altaic. The Turkic linguistic group constitutes at least 30 related languages spoken across Asia, from the Salar population of southeast Gansu in the east, to the Anatolian Turkish of Turkey, parts of Bulgaria and parts of Bosnia Herzegovina in the west. These languages are different and yet cognate, and with a little bit of Turkish acquired in Istanbul or Ankara, it is possible to gain some understanding of simple conversations in, for example, Kashgar or Urumqi.

Next, to the west of the Pamirs, in Tajikistan, Iran, north and west Afghanistan, and the predominantly Tajik-inhabited Uzbekistan cities of Samarkand and Bukhara, Farsi, Tajik or other dialects of Persian are widely spoken and have had a major impact on Urdu and related languages of South Asia. In times past, when the Silk Road was at its peak, Chinese, Turkish and Persian must all have served as common means of communication between people in Chang'an and the frontiers of Iraq.

Further to the west, in antiquity at least, Greek and later Latin were the *common tongues* of the Mediterranean world and the Levant. During the time of Alexander the Great, and under the Graeco-Bactrian Kingdoms in south and central Asia, no doubt Greek functioned as a language of trade – with Greek letters used on coinage minted in Bactria and other distant outposts of the Greek world.

Yet Greek and Latin were, after the 7th century AD, abruptly replaced by a fourth, quite different linguistic group to add to Chinese, Turkish and Persian. This was Arabic, a Semitic tongue related

LEFT: Uighur men in Kashgar. Uighur is a Turkic language which would be understood in Istanbul.

to Hebrew and Syriac, which had long been spoken as a language of commerce throughout historic Jordan, Syria and Iraq, but which burst forth from the Arabian Peninsula in 622 following the revelation of Islam. Most significantly, the immutable Word of God as revealed in the *Qur'an* was recited to Muhammad, according to Islamic belief, by the Archangel Jibril (Gabriel) in Arabic.

Within the short space of a hundred years, Arabic had become the dominant language of a huge swathe of territory extending from southern Spain and Morocco in the west to Iraq and the frontiers of Iran in the east. Most importantly, it was not just a language of trade, but also a language of religion. Although the Hanbali school of Sunni Islam, which predominates in the Turkic and Chinese Muslim worlds, permits the translation of Arabic texts, including *Qur'an* and *Hadith*, into languages other than Arabic, Arabic remains the chief identifying mark of the *umma* or universal Muslim brotherhood – the language of prayer and, to a considerable degree, of religious education. As such, it spread far to the east of the Arab-speaking lands, to Central Asia, China and even as far as distant Chang'an. At the same time it was spreading by sea, through maritime trade, to India, Southeast Asia and southern China, most notably in Guangzhou. By 800 AD, Arabic was probably the most universally established language along the entire Silk Road, from Antakya all the way to Chang'an.

To the main "indigenous" languages of the Silk Road – Chinese, Mongol, Tibetan, Turkic, Iranian and Arabic – may be added a plethora of less widely spoken languages. Some of these, such as Sogdian, Tokharian and Syriac, have all but disappeared. Others, such as Burushaski, spoken by about 90,000 people in the Hunza Valley in Pakistan, are "language isolates", not readily linked with any of the major world linguistic families such as Indo-European, Semitic or Sino-Tibetan. Although clearly never important in the multinational trade of the Silk Road, Burushaski and other little-spoken tongues – Monguor in Qinghai and Gansu, Nuristani in northeast Afghanistan, Circassian in the Caucasus and Aramaic in Syria – are indicative of the vast ethno-linguistic and cultural territory spanned by the Silk Road.

Finally, mention should be made of more recent additions to the languages of the Silk Road

– tongues which would have been little heard, or not at all, when the traditional Silk Road was at its peak, but which now serve as useful international languages the length of the route. Both are Indo-European, and both the result of European imperialism. The first of these is Russian, which now serves as a *lingua franca* in all the former Soviet Central Asian republics, as well as in Azerbaijan and the Caucasus. The second is English, which has already become the single most indispensable language of the entire modern Silk Road, as likely to be understood in the Muslim quarter of downtown Xi'an as in the antique souk of Aleppo or Damascus.

JOURNEY TIMES

Journeying along a section of the Silk Road was an epic undertaking: merchants spent months or even years waiting for the season to change or a war to end. Men couldn't travel faster than their feet, horse or camel could carry them, and steppe and mountains slowed their progress, forcing them to find navigable passes, food and watering holes.

On foot or by camel the journey from Kashgar to Urumqi took three months through the deserts of northwestern China. Men and camels died of thirst, lost among the dunes. When the railway arrived in the 1960s: the journey time fell to 24 hours. Today the flight time is 45 minutes.

RIGHT: a page from a very old Koran.

Decisive Dates

4000–3500 BC
Rise of civilisations in Mesopotamia and Egypt. First civilisations in the West.

3000–2500 BC
Early Chinese civilisation established on the Huang He (Yellow River); major urban developments in the Indus Valley.

3rd millennium BC
Lapis lazuli and rubies exported from Badakhshan west to Mesopotamia and Egypt. Sericulture is first developed in the Huang He valley.

2nd millennium BC
Phoenicians export cedar wood, gold jewellery, linen and purple Tyrian dye. Jade from Khotan is carried eastward to China.

1st millennium BC
Coastal shipping routes develop between China, Southeast Asia and southern India. Improvement in overland trade routes.

7th century BC
The Medes establish an empire which extending from Persia to modern-day Afghanistan, Tajikistan and northern Pakistan. They adopt the religion of Zoroaster.

c.550 BC
Persian Archaemenid Empire established by Cyrus the Great, who proceeds to rule over a vast region extending from the Hellespont to the Indus.

521–486 BC
Cyrus is succeeded by his son-in-law, Darius the Great, who extends the empire to the Black Sea and the Caucasus. Darius orders the construction of the Persian Royal Road.

333 BC
Alexander the Great defeats the Persians at the Battle of Issus, forcing Darius III to flee eastwards. Within five years Alexander crushes the Persian Empire and extends Greek power from the Hellespont to the Pamirs.

241–210 BC
Qin Shi Huang, the First Emperor, completes the unification of China and extends Chinese control south to the Pearl River Delta.

206 BC–AD 220
Qin Shi Huang's successor, Liu Bang, founds the illustrious Han Dynasty with its capital at Chang'an (modern Xi'an).

138 BC
Emperor Wu Di dispatches Zhang Qian to investigate the territories to the west towards Central Asia. He returns over 13 years later, having made the first recorded crossing of the Pamir-Tian Shan ranges.

119 BC
Zhang Qian leads a second, successful expedition to the west, establishing diplomatic relations with Ferghana, Bactria and Sogdiana. Chinese embassies eventually penetrate as far west as Rome.

83 BC
The Romans occupy Antioch, which becomes the capital of the newly formed Roman province of Syria, the third most important imperial city after Rome and Alexandria.

53 BC
The Romans are defeated by the Iranian Parthians at the Battle of Carrhae. This is thought to be the first time the Romans saw silk – in the banners brandished by the victors.

27 BC–AD 180
During the Pax Romana period a loose federation develops amongst the Decapolis (10 cities), in today's southern Syria and northern Jordan. Improved agricultural systems

552
Byzantine Emperor Justinian obtains silkworm eggs, smuggled to Constantinople across Persia by two monks. Silk gradually becomes a local Byzantine product.

618–907
The Tang Dynasty re-establishes full imperial control over the Eastern Silk Road.

c.610
Muhammad receives his first revelation from God, and begins teaching a strict monotheism aimed at driving idolatry from Arabia. This is the birth of Islam.

turn the land into a valuable source of grain and olives.

Turn of 1st century
The Italian explorer Maës Titianus leads a party of merchants as far east as Tashkurgan in the Pamirs, on the very western frontiers of China.

1st–3rd centuries AD
In Central Asia the Silk Road trade is dominated by the Kushans, whose empire extends across Afghanistan, Uzbekistan and Tajikistan and into northern India. Numerous monasteries are established in the Gandhara region, which becomes a centre of Buddhist pilgrimage and learning.

97
Ban Chao leads an army of 70,000 across the Pamirs and the Tian Shan in an effort to protect the Silk Road against the depredations of the fierce Xiongnu tribe.

CLOCKWISE, FROM LEFT: relief detail of Xerxes fighting a winged beast, Persepolis; portait of a Terracotta Warrior, Xi'an, China; a Roman mosaic from Bosra in Syria; female head on display at the Palmyra museum.

220
The fall of the Han Dynasty is followed by an era of internal division. China's old enemy, the Xiongnu, take advantage of the chaos to start a war.

274
Queen Zenobia claims Egypt for Palmyra before being defeated by the Emperor Aurelian and dragged off to Rome in golden chains.

476
The fall of Rome to the Germanic tribes leads to the ascendancy of Constantinople, or Byzantium, capital of the Eastern Roman Empire.

661–750
Under the Umayyad Caliphate, the Islamic Empire extends to Spain in the west and to the banks of the Indus in the east.

750–1258
Arab civilisation attains its classical Golden Age under the Baghdad-based Abbasid Dynasty, especially during the reign of the illustrious Harun al-Rashid.

751
At the Battle of Talas in modern-day Kyrgyzstan, the Arab forces of Ziyad ibn-Salih vanquish the Chinese forces of Gao Xianzhi, securing effective control over western Central Asia.

c.820
The Persian Samanids sever any direct Silk Road link between Tang China and the Abbasids. Samanid authority extends over Bukhara and Samarkand.

c.840
The Uighur are driven south by Kyrgyz raiders, and move into the Tarim Basin, settling in Kuqa and Aksu before spreading around the rim of the Taklamakan Desert.

907–960
As Tang power declines, outside interference in Silk Road traffic increases. The dynasty finally collapses and an era of disunity follows known as the "Five Dynasties and ten Kingdoms".

960
Rule of the Song Dynasty, the first government in the world to issue paper currency.

999–1211
The Karakhanid Turks take over the Tarim Basin. Islam gradually spreads across the region and into Gansu.

977–1186
The Samanids are replaced by the Turkish Ghaznavids, descendants of Turkic slave guards to the Samanids. The

Ghaznavids control most of Persia, all of Afghanistan and Transoxiana.

11th century
Renegade Shia Muslims – the Assassins – disrupt trade along the Silk Road. Led by their fanatical leader Hassan Saba, they establish fortified settlements in Iran, Iraq, Syria and Lebanon.

800–1200
Communication between Tang China and the West withers. Trade on the Silk Road is disrupted by political uncertainties.

1206–27
Mongol expansion under the rule of Genghis Khan.

1258
Baghdad falls to the Mongols under Hulagu Khan, marking

KEY PLAYERS

Abbasids second Muslim caliphate, based in Baghdad, AD 750–1000.

Achaemenids first Persian empire, created by Cyrus the Great.

Assassins murderous cult of Shia Muslims, 11th–13th century.

Assyrians ethnic group originating in Iraq, Iran, Turkey and Syria.

Bactrian Greeks successors to Alexander the Great, based in present-day Afghanistan and Tajikistan.

Byzantines successors to the Romans, based in Constantinople; became powerful silk brokers.

Han Chinese dynasty, 202 BC–AD 220.

Huns confederation of Central Asian nomads, 2nd–5th centuries AD.

Kushans branch of the Yuehzhi, ruled over Central Asia c. AD 100–250.

Mongols ruled over the world's largest contiguous empire in 13th century.

Ottomans rulers of a Turkish empire, 1299–1923.

Parthians Iranian civilisation and empire, 236 BC–AD 238.

Phoenicians ancient maritime civilisation based in what is now Lebanon.

Romans the first Western customers for Chinese silk.

Samanids Persian dynasty of Central Asia, AD 819–999.

Sassanids Persian empire which succeeded the Parthians.

Scythians nomadic, highly cultured people from the Central Asian steppe.

Seleucids Hellenistic successors to Alexander the Great.

Seljuks Turkish empire that united the eastern Islamic world, 1037–1194.

Sogdians people of Iranian stock who dominated trade in Central Asia.

Song Chinese dynasty, 960–1279.

Tang Chinese dynasty, 618–907.

Umayyads first Muslim caliphate, based in Damascus, 660–750.

Xiongnu feared nomads kept at bay by the Great Wall of China.

Yuezhi ancient Indo-European people from Chinese Central Asia who migrated west *(see Kushans)*.

the end of the Abbasid Dynasty.

1271
Marco Polo sets out on his journey to China together with his father and uncle, and spends 17 years in the service of the Great Khan.

1272
Kublai Khan founds Beijing.

14th century
The disintegration of the Mongol Empire brings about the collapse of Silk Road prosperity as the political and cultural stability of *Pax Mongolica* disappears.

1336–1405
Reign of Timur (known in the West as Tamerlane), the Turkic-Mongol conqueror and founder of the Timurid Dynasty.

1299–1922
The Ottoman Empire is the centre of interactions between the Eastern and Western worlds for more than six centuries.

1368–1644
China's Ming Dynasty pursues isolationist policies.

15th–16th centuries
New maritime trade routes diminish the importance of the Silk Road. Christopher Columbus' discovery of the New World, Vasco da Gama's forging of the sea route around the Cape of Good Hope and Ferdinand Magellan's successful voyage to the Philippines revolutionise global trade.

19th century
Opium wars are fought along the Chinese coast, officially in support of free trade. Tea planted in India breaks China's monopoly. Central Asian states fall under the influence of

Tsarist Russia as the Russian Empire expands south. Rivalry for the frontier lands between the Russian and British Empires is played out by spies, explorers and soldiers in the Great Game.

1900–79
Ottoman Empire collapses. Vast areas of Central Asia are swallowed up in the expanding but isolationist Soviet Empire. China turns Communist under the leadership of Chairman Mao. In 1979 the Soviets invade Afghanistan and the Shah of Iran is overthrown by Ayatollah Khomeini.

1979–91
Wars in Afghanistan and Lebanon paralyse both countries. Soviet Union tests hundreds of nuclear weapons in Semipalatinsk, Kazakhstan. In 1991 the Soviet Union collapses, bringing in periods of political and economic instability for the newly independent Central Asian Republics.

1991–Present
A booming Chinese economy and the development of oil and gas resources in Central Asia and the Caucasus are revitalising the Silk Road, with new roads, pipelines and rail links. US invasions of Iraq and Afghanistan in the early 2000s limits access for foreign tourists, as do revolutions in Kyrgyzstan (2005 and 2010) and civil unrest in Pakistan. A period of unrest in Syria begins.

CLOCKWISE, FROM LEFT: Han Chinese script; exquisite tilework at the Sheikh Lotfollah Mosque in Isfahan; Genghis Khan.

THE FIRST STEPS

The story begins with the first civilisations and the expansionist ambitions of their rulers. As trade followed conquests, multiple, inter-connecting routes began opening up, especially for such highly prized imperishables as lapis lazuli and jade.

It is impossible to state with any certainty when long-distance trade began, or indeed precisely where civilisations arose at each end of the Silk Road, but the west appears to have developed more significantly than the east, with both Damascus and Aleppo in Syria having substantial claims to be the oldest continually inhabited city on earth. They lie in the Fertile Crescent, an arc that stretches from the Persian Gulf to the Mediterranean, encompassing Mesopotamia and Egypt and producing the first civilisations in the west, from 4000 to 3500 BC, while those in the Indus Valley and China came later, between 3000 and 2500 BC.

Agricultural communities had already been active for several thousand years – the earliest granary yet discovered was built in the Jordan Valley around 9500 BC, and the granary at Mehrgarh just to the west of the Indus Valley in present-day Pakistan dates from 7500 BC. There was undoubtedly some limited bartering and communication between these Neolithic communities, who knew about weaving. But the later centres of civilisation had greater material needs, which meant trade links had to be established by land and sea. The former required domesticated, efficient pack animals, and none were better suited for crossing the deserts and vast steppes of Inner Asia than the horse and the camel, which became keys to the development of international relations and trade. High quality horses, necessary for both the military and for general transport, were in particularly short supply in China, and the need to ensure

regular deliveries from Central Asia led to the formation of the Tea and Horse Commission in the 10th century AD, a government monopoly that ensured the Chinese state first pick of all horses entering China.

The Silk Road was never static. Whilst policies such as the Pax Mongolica and infrastructure projects such as Darius' Royal Road (see below) brought certain routes to prominence, other roads fell out of use for protracted periods due to regional warfare, natural disasters, banditry and high taxation. Changing tastes, technologies and the availability of certain goods also dictated which cities flourished, while merchants, manufacturers and caravans turned their attention to places most likely to generate a profit.

LEFT: a stone relief at Persepolis in Iran showing offerings being brought to Darius. **RIGHT:** Stone Age granary from the Middle East.

Men of vision

Unlike local market trade, distant trade involved merchants and middlemen – entrepreneurs of vision, prepared to risk losses and endure delays in the hope of making a substantial return on their investment. Such speculative enterprises were dangerous, and goods carried ideally had to be small, light and as easily preserved as possible. In the 3rd millennium BC, for instance, caravans carried scarce lapis lazuli and rubies from the mines of Badakhshan west to Mesopotamia and Egypt; later precious jade from the rivers of Khotan was carried eastwards to China. Other goods included spices and perfumes, gold and silver ornaments, instruments in copper and bronze and, last but not least, rich textiles, the most valuable of which was silk – bringing with it strange rumours of the worm that spins silken threads.

exported cedar wood for ship and house-building, as well as such luxury goods as gold jewellery, glass, linen and purple Tyrian dye.

During the 1st millennium BC, coastal shipping routes also developed between China, Southeast Asia and southern India. Within a hundred years it is likely that a system of coastal commerce connected, however indirectly, the Mediterranean world with that of the Far East, but direct voyages, made possible by the seasonal monsoon winds, were not widespread for at least another three centuries. Graeco-Roman trade goods may have reached the Far East, and Chinese trade goods have been found in the

Coastal links

As well as overland trade, maritime trade also fostered links across the continents. In the west, the sophisticated civilisation of Mesopotamia had developed coastal shipping, and formed a link in a maritime chain connecting Egypt and the Mediterranean with the Indus Valley civilisation and South Asia. In the 2nd millennium BC the Phoenicians (from present-day Lebanon) dominated the Mediterranean; their merchants

The first major trade routes followed the great rivers that formed the agricultural bases for the earliest civilisations, on the Nile, the Tigris and Euphrates, the Indus and Huang He or Yellow River.

Mediterranean, but quantities were small, and the two centres of world civilisation knew little of each other.

The overland and maritime routes were not, however, separate entities. Cities such as Venice, Istanbul and Alexandria were meeting points for both types of traders. It was not until the discovery of the sea route around the Cape of

All the ultramarine paint in both Western and Eastern art came from the lapis lazuli mines of Sar-e-Sang, Afghanistan. The blue mineral has been prized and traded for more than 6,000 years.

Good Hope by Vasco da Gama in the 1490s and, later, the opening of the Suez Canal in 1869, that journeys from Europe to the Far East could be made entirely by sea.

The discovery of silk

With only these tentative links, China developed in virtual isolation from the rest of the world. The fertile valley of the Huang He (Yellow River) was the heartland of Chinese civilisation, and it was here, in the 3rd millennium BC, that the cultivation of silk, known as sericulture, first developed. Empress Xi Lingshi, wife of the Yellow Emperor Qin Shi Huang (2697–2598 BC, see panel) is traditionally seen as the person who first turned the fibrous excretions of a caterpillar into a prized material.

Although initially reserved for Chinese royalty, some silk made its way west. The grave of a Celtic chieftain dating from about 500 BC, at Hochdorf near Stuttgart, Germany, was found to contain silk garments – this is some 300 years before the "official" start of the Silk Road, at the end of the 2nd century BC when Roman and Chinese traders made contact. Traces of silk of probable Chinese origin have also been found in the hair of an Egyptian mummy dating from 1000 BC.

Throughout the 1st millennium BC trade routes and communications by land continued to improve. Along the Euphrates River, ancient cities such as Ur and Uruk (also known as Akkad) had been developed by the Sumerians. Sumer was to be followed by the rise of the Assyrian cities of the Tigris and Euphrates rivers, in particular the prosperous city of Babylon, where the "Hanging Gardens" became one of the Seven Wonders of the Ancient World.

In the 7th century BC the Medes from the east of Iran made incursions into the region to establish the first Persian Empire and introduce new levels of horsemanship and horse-breeding. By 550 BC the region came under Cyrus

ABOVE, FROM LEFT: Phoenician traders around 600 BC; the Yellow Emperor, Qin Shi Huang.

the Great, whose Persian Achaemenid Empire was the largest so far seen, stretching from the Hellespont to the Indus. Zoroastrianism, the world's first monotheistic religion, was established. It spread quickly along the early trade routes and was ultimately to have a massive influence on the development of Judaism, Christianity and Islam.

The Persian Royal Road

Cyrus was succeeded by his son-in-law, Darius the Great (521–486 BC), who extended the Persian Empire to the Black Sea and the Caucasus, venturing beyond the Oxus River.

TYRIAN PURPLE

Tyrian Purple, also known as Imperial Purple, is a dye that was first produced by Phoenician craftsmen in the Lebanese city of Tyre. It occurs naturally in *Bolinus brandaris* sea snails found in the Mediterranean. The dye was highly prized by the Romans, who used it to colour ceremonial clothing. Only emperors wore the full purple robe, while senators had a strip of purple on their white togas. Pliny the Elder noted: "The Tyrian hue is considered of the best quality when it has exactly the colour of clotted blood, and is of a blackish hue to the sight, but of a shining appearance when held up to the light."

> *"There is nothing in this world that travels more swiftly than the Persian couriers... Neither snow nor rain, nor heat nor darkness of night prevents them from accomplishing the task appointed to them with the uttermost speed."* Herodotus

In order to administer this region more effectively, subdue revolt and actively promote trade, Darius ordered the construction of the Persian Royal Road, which ran for almost 3,000km (1,900 miles) from the Persian capitals at Susa (in southwestern Iran) and Persepolis to the Lydian capital, Sardes, close to the eastern shores of the Aegean Sea. It also connected with other important trade routes into North Africa, Arabia and eastwards to both India and Central Asia. The Royal Road built by Darius was of such quality that it became a core section of the future Silk Road in the west, and was still in use in Roman times. Darius also revolutionised the Persian economy: he followed the Lydian tradition of minting coins with his own system of gold and silver coinage. Trade was encouraged and routes were improved, linking this overland route with the parallel sea trade, connecting to

the Persian Gulf and Euphrates and Tigris rivers.

THE LADY OF THE SILKWORMS

Once upon a time, Empress Xi Lingshi, chief wife of the Yellow Emperor Qin Shi Huang, observed the effect of hot liquid on a cocoon that accidentally dropped from a mulberry tree into her cup of tea. She deduced it would be possible to reel silk in a long, smooth unbroken filament. She is revered as the Lady of the Silkworms, and to this day, cocoons of *Bombyx mori* are immersed in hot water, a process that allows reeling. Sometimes she is also credited with inventing the loom, as one of a pantheon of deities connected with sericulture and silkworking, requiring propitiation and sacrifices to ensure good harvests.

Alexander the Great

The Greek states were united in the mid-4th century BC by Philip II of Macedon, but it was his son, Alexander the Great (336–323 BC), who conceived the ambitious idea of conquering all "the known world". For Alexander, a visionary and military genius, this meant, first and foremost, war with the Persian Empire. Soon after the death of his father, he crossed the Hellespont between Europe and Asia at the head of a 42,000-strong army that was to prove unstoppable. In 333 BC he defeated the main Persian army at the Battle of Issus, forcing Emperor Darius III to flee eastwards, abandoning his wife, mother and two daughters, as well as substantial treasure. He next drove south, capturing the Holy Land and seizing Egypt, before turning east against Mesopotamia. Here he again defeated Darius III, at the Battle of Guagamela in 331 BC, and captured the ancient city of Babylon. Next, following the Royal Road built by Darius I, he crossed the Zagros Mountains and captured the Persian royal capital at Persepolis.

Declaring his war against the Persian Empire over, Alexander adopted various Persian customs. As well as marrying into the former Persian royal family, he encouraged his Greek followers simi-

Hellespont to the Pamirs and the future frontiers of China.

Alexander's ambitions were boundless, and having married Princess Roxana of Balkh to cement his control over his newly conquered

About 70 cities and settlements were founded by Alexander. These include Alexandria in Egypt, Kandahar in Afghanistan, Alexandria on the Oxus, and Alexandria Eschate – "the furthest" – corresponding to Khojand in modern-day Tajikistan.

larly to take Persian wives to ensure the unity of the two peoples. Meanwhile, he began a new campaign against Bessus of Bactria, advancing as far into Central Asia as the western flanks of the Pamir Massif, conquering Bactria, Sogdiana and all of present-day Afghanistan.

At the height of his advances into Central Asia, Alexander seized control of the Fergana Valley in present-day Uzbekistan, in the foothills of the Tian Shan. Within just five years Alexander had crushed the Persian Empire and extended Greek power all the way east from the

ABOVE, FROM LEFT: a gold Daric coin from the late 5th century BC, showing King Darius I; Alexander the Great riding into battle at Issus (333 BC).

SYMBOLIC LANDMARK

Carved into the spectacular rock outcrop at Bisotun in western Iran, around which traders and invaders have had to pass for thousands of years, there is a life-sized bas-relief of Darius, attended by two servants, with his left foot on the chest of his opponent, the prostrate Gaumata. To the right stand ten 1-metre-high figures, with hands tied and rope around their necks, representing conquered peoples. The winged symbol of the Zoroastrian God, Ahura-Mazda, hovers above. The accompanying cuneiform inscription devoted to Darius' achievements is written in three different languages – Old Persian, Elamite and Babylonian.

Central Asian Empire, he turned his attention towards India. Marching south into the Hindu Kush and then east across the Khyber Pass, he conquered southern Kashmir – the Kingdom of Gandhara – before attacking the Hindu King Porus (Raja Puru) in the Punjab. Again, Alexander was victorious, but his army of Greek and Persian mercenaries had had enough, and mutinied by the Beas River in the eastern Punjab – the furthest point east of all Alexander's conquests.

Returning to Babylon, Alexander died suddenly of a fever on 10 June 323 BC, one month before his 33rd birthday. In an unparalleled explosion of energy, he had conquered a vast swathe of land, linking Libya and Greece in the west with Transoxiana and the Punjab in the east. He knew little or nothing of distant China, and so he was in effect, and in his own eyes, a world-conqueror.

Alexander's campaign had forged new and strong links between Greece and Central Asia that were both cultural and commercial, including the spread of the Greek language and monetary system. Although his invading forces temporarily decimated regional markets and the political instability damaged overland trade, in the longer term the movement of troops spread knowledge and taste for a vari-

JADE-CARVERS LOOK TO SCYTHIANS

The Scythians were a nomadic Indo-European people who dominated a vast area stretching from the Ukraine to Mongolia during the 7th–1st centuries BC. They developed highly skilled metalworking techniques, executed in bronze and gold with great skill. Designs featured bearded men, horses, stags and eagles, as well as griffins and other mythical creatures. From about the 3rd century BC they were increasingly influenced by contact with the neighbouring Greeks, producing a syncretic style which spread to the east, where Chinese jade-carvers began to adapt and borrow from Graeco-Scythian motifs.

ety of consumer goods, many of which had to be transported east from the Mediterranean. His generals subsequently divided up the conquered lands, and each set about forging their own small empires, establishing the Antigonid Empire in Greece (301–168 BC), the Ptolemaic Empire in Egypt and Palestine (305–30 BC) and the Seleucid Empire in Persia and Mesopotamia (323–63 BC). The Alexandrian territories furthest east formed the Graeco-Bactrian Kingdom of Bactria and Sogdiana (250–140 BC), the Indo-Greek Kingdom of Gandhara centred on Taxila, and the Punjab (189 BC–10 AD). This unlikely but fruitful union of Greek and Indo-Buddhist civilisations would produce some of the most spectacular syncretic art forms of the ancient Silk Road, particularly when Indo-Greek influences were extended north, across the Pamir Massif, into the heart of Central Asia.

Alexander's Bactrian successors continued to expand eastwards, especially under King Euthydemus (230–200 BC), who extended his control into Sogdiana on the Kazakh and Kyrgyz

Qin Shi Huang is famous not just for uniting China's warring clans; such was his ego that the First Emperor had a terracotta army of life-size warriors to guard him in the afterlife.

Manchurian Plains in the north to the Yangtze River in the south. The unification process was completed by Qin Shi Huang (241–210 BC), who became First Emperor, extending Chinese control south as far as the Pearl River Delta.

It was a question now of where else to expand: to the north was the barren desert where the hostile Xiongnu nomads had been held back since the 4th century BC by the construction of defensive fortifications that would eventually be combined to form the Great Wall. But another alternative existed in the direction of little-known Central Asia – source of precious jade.

frontiers with present-day Xinjiang. The Bactrians crossed the Tian Shan into Chinese Central Asia, marking the earliest known direct contacts between China and Europe, around 220 BC.

China heads west

Meanwhile, far to the east and beyond the Pamir Massif, nascent Imperial China was similarly flexing its muscles. For the first two millennia of its existence, the Chinese state had gradually coalesced, establishing its control over an area extending from the Gobi Desert and

ABOVE, FROM LEFT: map showing the conquests of Alexander the Great; the First Emperor's famous Terracotta Warriors at Xi'an.

Qin Shi Huang was succeeded by Liu Bang, founder of the illustrious Han Dynasty that lasted from 206 BC to AD 220, and with his accession as Emperor Gaozu in 202 BC, the stage was set for China's imperial expansion westwards – and the first recorded crossing of the Pamir Massif to Central and Western Asia.

The Silk Road could not become a single thoroughfare linking east and west until the barrier of the Pamir Massif and the steppes of Central Asia were breached, linking the antique lapis lazuli trade routes west of the Pamirs with the almost equally venerable jade routes to the east. Once this was achieved, the path was open for direct trade between the Chinese and Mediterranean worlds.

THE OPENING OF THE ROAD

The extraordinary adventures of the imperial envoy Zhang Qian, despatched west by the Han emperor Wu Di, breached the inhospitable lands of Central Asia to open up an eager market for the luxurious silk trade.

S ome 200 years after Alexander's adventures eastward, there was still no sign of China in the classical world. It was not until the ascendancy of the Han Dynasty that a unified and powerful Chinese state turned its attentions west. In 138 BC, Emperor Wu Di (141–87 BC) despatched his imperial envoy Zhang Qian to investigate the territories to the west, via the Hexi Corridor, towards Central Asia. If possible, he was to seek a military alliance with the Yuehzhi (the Indo-European Tocharians of the Tarim Basin and Bactria) against the powerful nomadic Xiongnu of the north. It was to be an epic journey, marking the first real beginning of the Silk Road.

Zhang Qian set out at the head of a delegation of around 100, mostly military officers, and one Xiongnu guide. A mural dating from the 8th century AD in the Mogao Caves at Dunhuang represents his departure, while another from the same era shows his patron, the Emperor Wu Di, venerating images of Buddha before starting his campaign against the Xiongnu.

Despite Zhang Qian's best efforts, he was captured by the Xiongnu and detained by them for 10 years before making his escape. He crossed over the Tian Shan into present-day Uzbekistan (which he called Dayuan), where he discovered many things unknown to the Chinese. There was the mundane (turnips), the intoxicating (wine), but above all were the legendary "heavenly horses" of the Fergana Valley (see panel), which the Han Chinese were eager to obtain to help transform their cavalry for the wars against the nomads of the north.

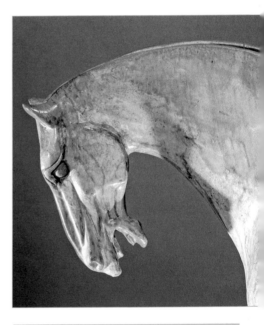

HEAVENLY HORSES

The "heavenly horses" of the Fergana Valley were prized above all other by the ancient Chinese. The Han Dynasty began the custom of importing great numbers of horses from Bactria and the western regions, frequently in exchange for silk. At other times the Chinese used military invasions to secure supplies. In AD 102 they attacked Bactria and demanded that the defeated forces should supply the Han Empire with 100 of their finest horses for breeding purposes, and a further 3,000 to use as war mounts. According to Chinese tradition, the finest of the heavenly steeds sweated blood, earning them the sobriquet "blood-sweating horses".

LEFT: exotic fruits depicted at the Temple of Bel, Palmyra.
RIGHT: green-glazed tomb figure of a Fergana horse.

Eventually Zhang Qian reached the long-sought kingdom of the Yuehzhi in Bactria, but they were not interested in joining a Chinese campaign against the fierce Xiongnu. After a stay of one year, the intrepid Zhang Qian set out on a voyage for home, but was once again captured and held prisoner by the Xiongnu. He managed to escape again two years later and eventually returned to the Han court at Chang'an in 125 BC.

After an absence of more than 13 years, he had long since been given up for dead by Wu Di, who was delighted by his return. The mission to form an alliance with the Yuehzhi may have failed, but Zhang Qian had succeeded in

Wu Di was the seventh Han emperor and one of the greatest rulers in Chinese history. He is remembered for the vast territorial expansion China attained under his reign, as well as for organising a strong, centralised Confucian state.

making the first recorded crossing of the Pamir-Tian Shan ranges and brought back much valuable information about the regions to the west.

According to the Han annals: "The Emperor Wu Di learned of Dayuan (Fergana), Daxia (Bactria), Anxi (Parthia) and other lands, all great states rich in unusual products where people cultivated the land and made their living in much the same way as the people of Han. All these states were weak militarily, and prized Han goods and wealth."

Zhang Qian's reports also made reference – apparently second-hand – to even more distant regions, including Liuxuan (Turkmenistan), Yancai (Kazakhstan), Tiaozhi (Iraq) and Shendu (India). Finally, in the furthest west, lay the almost mythical land of "Lijian", thought to be the earliest reference in Chinese literature to the distant territories of Rome.

Diplomatic missions

Zhang Qian was heaped with praise and honours before leading a second, successful expedition in 119 BC to the west of the Tian Shan, effectively establishing diplomatic relations with Fergana, Bactria and Sogdiana, all of which sent ambassadors to Chang'an, beginning a process of regular diplomatic missions to the Chinese capital.

DUNHUANG – THE BLAZING BEACON

Famous for its Buddhist art, the desert town of Dunhuang began life as a key command post built as part of Emperor Wu Di's massive programme of wall-building to defend China's outer frontiers against the forays of nomadic tribes. Built between 121 and 110 BC, this part of the Great Wall stretched across the mouth of the Hexi Corridor, the narrow strip of fertile land sandwiched between the Qilian Mountains to the south and the Ala Shan and Gobi deserts to the north. Dunhuang's strategic importance at this natural gateway was thus clear; the name means "Blazing Beacon", and it was one of a series of beacons used to warn the Chinese of enemy encroachment.

Dunhuang continued as a garrison town for around 1,000 years. Once the Silk Road opened up, its location made it an important commercial and cultural centre, as well as a military hub. Early Buddhist monks arrived via from Kashgar, and Dunhuang became a centre of pilgrimage and learning. A vast repository of Buddhist and other manuscripts was collected in the nearby Mogao Caves. Manuscripts and murals painted by the monks remained hidden in the caves. They were rediscovered by a Taoist monk in 1900 and then looted by international archaeologists such as Aurel Stein in the early years of the 20th century.

Zhang Qian returned via the southern rim of the Tarim Basin, bringing with him a gift of exquisite Fergana horses for Emperor Wu Di. About a decade later another Chinese emissary returned the favour when he visited the kingdom of Anxi or Parthia, bearing with him gifts of fine silks.

The basis of future trade along the great Silk Road was thus put in place, with commerce portrayed in contemporary Chinese annals as gifts going west and tribute travelling east to the Han court at Chang'an. In this way Chinese embassies eventually penetrated as far west as Rome, perhaps during the reign of Emperor Augustus (27 BC–AD 14). According to the historian Florus

of his remarkable achievements he still remains one of China's most revered national heroes, seen by many as the father of the Silk Road – the man who first opened the long route to Central Asia and the West.

Between 121 and 110 BC, Emperor Wu Di followed up his successful diplomatic and commercial initiative to the West by establishing military garrisons along the Hexi Corridor, thus ensuring control of the only practical road between Chang'an and the Tarim Basin. It also served to bind the future province of Gansu to "China proper" once and for all. Future generations of Chinese would make this distinction

"even those countries of the world not subject to imperial sway" sent embassies to Rome, "the great conqueror" of nations: "Thus even the Scythians and the Sarmatians sent envoys to seek the friendship of Rome. Nay, even the Seres came likewise, and the Indians who dwell beneath the vertical sun, bringing presents of precious stones and pearls and elephants... In truth it needed but to look at their complexions to see that they were people of another world than ours."

Zhang Qian died around 104 BC, but because

ABOVE, FROM LEFT: Emperor Wu Di welcoming a man of letters, from a history of Chinese emperors; mural of Zhang Qian serving as an ambassador to the West located in the Mogao Caves at Dunhuang.

– as they still do today – by referring to the area east of Dunhuang as "the region within", while to the west lay "the region without". The new garrisons were designated prefectures, and to ensure Han Chinese hegemony of the previously sparsely populated region, large numbers of convicts were sent west to settle them.

The area between Dunhuang and the Pamirs, corresponding to today's southern Xinjiang, was dominated by the vast Taklamakan Desert, around which a number of oases were strung. The choice was to go north or south. The southern route left China proper via Yangguan, the Pass of the Sun, while the more northerly route left via Yumenguan, the Jade Gate Pass. Later a third route would develop still further to the

"In the time of the Western Han there was Zhang Qian,
In the Eastern Han there was Ban Chao."
Chinese saying

north, running around the north rim of the Tarim Basin via the oases of Hami and Turpan, in the lee of the Tian Shan. Wu Di's control of this vast region was essential to hold back the nomads of the north – the Xiongnu and their successors – while maintaining the increasingly prosperous trade route with the west.

The conquests of Ban Chao

By the time of his death in 87 BC, Wu Di had almost doubled the size of Han territories, making China the largest and most powerful empire in the world – surpassing even contemporaneous Rome. Yet it fell to his successors, the Emperors Ming (AD 58–75), Zhang (76–88) and He (89–105) to truly consolidate Chinese control over the Tarim Basin and modern-day Xinjiang. These Western Han rulers all benefited from the services of one of China's truly great soldiers, General Ban Chao (AD 32–102), who crushed the Xiongnu and pushed west into the Tarim, eventually bringing the whole

THE CELTS IN CHINA

Although the Chinese were not to come west until the 1st century AD, there is significant archaeological and DNA evidence that Bronze Age Celts had already somehow made their way to Xinjiang's Tarim Basin. Burial pits unearthed in the Taklamakan Desert contain a significant number of mummies of European origin.

Dating back some 3,000 years, one of the earliest mummies is a 6-ft-tall male with reddish hair, high cheekbones, a long nose and a ginger beard. He was buried in a twill tunic and tartan leggings. Now preserved in the Urumqi museum, the mummy has been DNA tested and is undoubtedly of Caucasian heritage. His DNA and his dress link him strongly with the Celts

of France and Britain, but sadly offer no clue as to how or why he and his family might have reached China.

More than 400 such mummies have been discovered in the Tarim Basin, and there are also thousands of skulls. Thanks to the dry climate and alkaline soils, they are well-preserved: hair styles and make-up are still visible. Clothing is also in a sufficient state to be analysed, and some cloth samples have been shown to be of the same weave as those found on the bodies of salt miners in Austria. They date from 1300 BC.

These may not have been the only Europeans to find their way into China. There are accounts of Roman soldiers being taken as captives to Yongchang.

Tarim Basin under Chinese control.

In AD 97, Ban Chao led an army of 70,000 across the Pamirs and the Tian Shan to protect the now strategically vital Silk Road against the continuing depredations of the Xiongnu. Making an alliance with King Pacorus II of Parthia (AD 78–105), he advanced as far as the shores of the Caspian Sea, where he despatched an envoy to Rome – though he only reached the shores of the Black Sea before turning back. Nevertheless, with the advance of Ban Chao's armies to the borders of Europe and the Middle East, Chinese power, influence and prestige reached a high point in Inner Asia. The "Seres" (see panel), for so long

Mediterranean city of Antioch and it became the capital of the newly formed Roman province of Syria. Such territories at the eastern end of the Mediterranean acted as a buffer zone against troublesome Parthians of Persia and the Nabataeans further south around Petra. Semi-independent client kings such as Herod the Great (37–4 BC) carved out mini-empires within a creaking Hellenistic structure, though always with an eye on developments in Rome.

During the stable *Pax Romana* period, a loose federation developed amongst 10 cities known as the Decapolis, in what is today southern Syria and northern Jordan. Improved agricul-

mysterious and distant from the West, were now neighbours who had come to stay.

At the same time, the Great Wall of China, first established as a series of defensive walls against the nomads of the north, was extended west towards Lop Nur in the Tarim Basin. China's current claims to these far-flung territories are based on their conquest and settlement in Han Dynasty times – fully 1,000 years before the Uighur Turks, Xinjiang's main "indigenous people" in modern times, moved into the region.

Pax Romana

As the Chinese expanded westwards, the Roman Empire was spreading its influence east. In 83 BC, they occupied the eastern

tural systems, particularly the use of traditional Persian methods of collecting and distributing water, turned the land into a valuable source of grain and olives. Some of these underground water channels remain in use today and are still known as *qanat romani*.

In the expanding world of trade, silk began to arrive in Rome, and though some of this may have slipped through from China, much of it came from a people called the "Seres", about whom little is known (see panel). Despite Ban Chao's advances to the west, Rome remained largely ignorant of China. Romans believed that

ABOVE, FROM LEFT: the Great Wall near Jiayuguan; Roman colonnade at the city of Apamea in Syria.

silk was somehow "combed off leaves", while some contemporaneous Chinese sources state that asbestos cloth – obtained from the west – was "woven from the wool of sea sheep". It would not be long, however, before many of these misconceptions disappeared, for East and West were about to discover each other, not by coastal maritime trade, but much more directly, across the Pamir Massif and the steppes of Central Asia.

Silk banners show the way

Other great empires lay between Rome and China, most notably that of Parthia, which dominated the lands of Iran, Mesopotamia

> "I do not see how clothes of silk, material that does not hide the body, nor even one's decency, can be called clothing... Wretched seamstresses labour that the adulteress may be visible through her transparent dress, that her husband has no more knowledge than any outsider or foreigner of his wife's body."
> Seneca the Younger (3 BC–AD 65)

and Eastern Anatolia from 247 BC to AD 220. When the Parthians defeated the Romans at the Battle of Carrhae in 53 BC, survivors reported that the victorious Parthians had unfurled shimmering banners of an unknown material, embroidered with gold, which flashed like fire in the sunlight. This is widely interpreted as the first sighting of silk by Romans.

These three powerful empires finally enabled the Silk Road to operate effectively from around 100 BC. Though allied with Ban Chao against the nomads of the north, the Parthians were determined to maintain their role as middlemen between China and Rome, controlling all silk that came out of China and reselling it at fabulous prices.

As a consequence, no Roman armies penetrated beyond Parthia to China, and few Roman traders made it across the Iranian plateau to the Pamirs. One exception, however, was Maës Titianus, who at the end of the 1st century AD sent a party of merchants as far east as Tashkurgan on the very western frontiers of China. Almost nothing is known of Maës Titianus, but he was probably seeking to maximise his profits in the incredibly lucrative silk trade.

Silk was a mystery to the Romans, but it had captured the heart of the fashionable elite. The Senate, deeply troubled by the outflow of money to the east, tried several times to stem this trade through edicts prohibiting the wearing of silk. Yet Rome was gradually learning more about this desired material. Pliny the Elder (AD 23–79) had already established the fact that silk did not grow on trees, but that moths "weave webs, like spiders, that become a luxurious clothing for women, called silk". As this knowledge slowly spread westwards, China's monopoly on the rich silk trade would gradually begin to diminish.

PARTING SHOT

At the Battle of Carrhae, the Parthians employed their trademark military tactic known as "the Parthian shot". Mounted archers would feign retreat, then turn around in the saddle and shoot at the pursuing enemy while galloping at full speed. The manoeuvre required skilled horsemanship, since the rider needed both hands to shoot the arrows. The gambit entered the English language as a "parting shot" – scoring points by having the last word or gesture. It is referred to by the satirist Samuel Butler in *An Heroical Epistle of Hudibras to His Lady* (1678):
> You wound, like Parthians, while you fly,
> And kill with a retreating eye.

LEFT: Roman fresco from Pompeii depicting a silk-clad *maenad* (follower of Dionysus).

Roman Ancestry

Today, the citizens of Yongchang wonder if they are descended from a group of Romans who by a quirk of fate reached China.

I t had always been understood that until the time of Augustus, Rome and China had barely been aware of each other's existence. However, in 1957, American sinologist Homer Hasenpflug Dubs published a book suggesting that a group of captive

Roman soldiers had been resettled at the modern town of Yongchang, near Wuwei, in the remote reaches of Gansu.

According to Dubs, these lost legionaries were the last remnants of an army commanded by the Roman general Crassus that was defeated by the Parthians at Carrhae in 53 BC. Crassus' army of 42,000 was decisively routed, with 20,000 dead and more than 10,000 taken prisoner. According to the Roman historian Pliny, these captives were resettled in Sogdiana where they were employed as Parthian mercenaries.

ABOVE: a green-eyed man from Yongchang.
RIGHT: Roman defeat at Carrhae had an improbalble knock-on effect.

In 36 BC, a Chinese army led by General Kan Yanshou made a punitive raid against the Sogdian settlement of Zhezhe. The Han Dynasty annals record that the Chinese forces came up against a group of foreign soldiers who formed an unusual defensive formation like a tortoise, interlocking their shields above their heads – a military tactic of the Roman legions quite unknown to the Chinese. Despite the unfamiliar tactics, the attackers were victorious, and took around 150 of the defeated soldiers with them to Chinese Central Asia.

Four decades later, in AD 5, Chinese chronicles mention a newly established settlement named Lijian – a contemporaneous Chinese name for Rome – which was populated by assorted captives and convicts. Dubs suggests that the Roman soldiers captured at Carrhae, or their immediate descendants, were forcibly resettled at Lijian to help populate and defend the strategically vital Hexi Corridor. Such an action would have been very much in line with frontier policy of the time, which had long sought to "use barbarians to control barbarians". Dubs's hypothesis is fascinating but not entirely convincing. Unfortunately, DNA tests conducted at Yongchang, the modern town near Lijian, in 2007 found no genetic evidence to support claims of Roman ancestry among the town's overwhelmingly Han population.

Unconcerned with the findings, Yongchang remains proud of its supposed Roman heritage. Statues of a Chinese mandarin, together with two "Romans" – one male and one female – have been erected near the southern entrance of the town. These figures are more of a curiosity than a genuine attraction, but may well represent the easternmost limits of Roman penetration along the ancient Silk Road.

THE MIDDLEMEN

The peoples between the great powers in the West and East were vital in keeping trade flowing along the Silk Road. After the fall of both Rome and the Han Dynasty, it was the commercially savvy followers of Islam who kept business brisk in Asia's heartlands.

By the 1st century AD trade in both directions along the new Silk Road linking China with the Mediterranean was already well established, as were the diplomatic and tributary missions sent, with increasing frequency, between East and West. But China and Rome remained far apart, and few if any merchants would have made the long journey all the way from Chang'an to Antioch or to Rome itself. Local people took the caravans over the most dangerous and difficult sections of the journey. But, of course, this trade route was not just for silk. Towards Europe came exotic

Remote from the Greek heartlands, Bactria had a high level of Hellenic sophistication. Balkh and Ai Khanoum in northern Afghanistan had theatres, gymnasia and buildings with Corinthian columns.

animals, furs, ceramics, jade and, most importantly, spices – cinnamon, balsam, cardamom and pepper. In the other direction went gold, ivory, pearls and precious metals.

Trade was dominated by Central Asian middlemen, who bought goods from the Chinese at Dunhuang or Kashgar, and from Mediterranean caravan merchants in Mesopotamia, Iran or Transoxiana. Central Asian trade was dominated by Tocharian and South Asian traders to the east of the Pamirs, and by Bactrian and Sogdian merchants to the west of the Pamirs.

LEFT: Buddha preaching the law, in a painting from Dunhuang. **RIGHT:** Buddha in Greek garb from the monastery of Takht-i-Bahi in northern Pakistan.

The Kushans

The most important new Central Asian state to emerge during this period was the Kushan Empire (1st–3rd centuries AD), which is linked by historians with the peripatetic Yuehzhi, thought to have been the Indo-European Tocharians of the Tarim Basin, who were driven westwards to settle in Bactria by the Xiongnu in the 2nd century BC. In the 1st century BC the Yuehzhi began to absorb Graeco-Bactrian territories to the south of the Pamirs, adopting elements of Greek culture.

At its height in the 2nd century AD, the Kushan Empire sat squarely astride the Silk Road, as well as the southern extension via Kashmir to India, controlling all Bactria, the western Tarim Basin and northern India, and dominating Silk Road commerce. Besides trade goods, the ever-expanding network of Central Asian trade routes also carried art and ideas between distant centres of civilisation. The Kushans were nothing if not eclectic, adapting the Greek alphabet to suit their own language. They also borrowed the minting of coins from the Greeks, combining texts in Greek with South Asian Pali written in the Kharoshthi script. Their religion they took initially from Persia, embracing the heterodox ideas of Zoroaster, only to add a veneer of Buddhism from South Asia.

The Kushans established their summer and winter capitals at Bagram (Kapisa) in Afghanistan and Peshawar (Purushapura) in Pakistan, at the heart of the ancient Buddhist kingdom of Gandhara. They used part of the enormous wealth they derived from the Silk Road to sponsor the creation of Buddhist monasteries and stupas right across the territory, lavishly adorned with statues of Buddha and bodhisattvas (future Buddhas) and narrative scenes both from the life of Siddharta, the historical Buddha, and from the Jatakas, his previous births. From their position on the Silk Road the sculptors were able to draw on a range of artistic influences, and it was the particular fusion of Graeco-Roman and Indian styles that produced

the distinctive and much acclaimed Gandhara art form. Significantly, it was at this time that a new form of Buddhism developed called Mahayana Buddhism, in which the image of the Buddha himself came to be worshipped, and a revolutionary feature of the Gandhara School was the successful representation of the Buddha in human form, often wearing a Greek-style toga. Kanishka, the greatest of the Kushan kings, appeared to have given his full support to the new ideas. The message of Buddhism was sent out to the world. Missionaries were despatched westwards into Central Asia and eastwards into China and Tibet via the Karakoram. The extraordinary flowering of Gandharan Graeco-Buddhist art that would stun Silk Road archaeologists in the late 19th century dates from this imaginatively syncretic period of Kushan rule.

Nomads of the north

The great settled empires – Chinese and Roman, Persian and Kushan – were not alone in dominating the Eurasian land mass. To the north of the Silk Road, extending from Manchuria and the Gobi Desert in the east to Dzungaria and the Kazakh Steppe in the west, the great, empty open spaces were dominated by very different peoples. These were the wandering nomads, who migrated seasonally and whose wealth lay in livestock, not grain or the precious goods of the cities. Yet this very peripatetic existence made the nomads of the north into fine horsemen and fierce fighters, unpredictable warriors who could move vast distances in short periods of time, difficult – almost impossible – to control and almost equally impossible to predict.

Decline of the Han Dynasty

Ban Chao's advance into Central Asia at the turn of the 1st century AD had projected Chinese power far west along the Silk Road to encompass the small independent kingdoms of the Tarim Basin. By the 2nd century AD, however, Han power was rapidly disintegrating. When the dynasty fell, in AD 220, a period of internal division began, with Chinese imperial power effectively ending at Dunhuang. In the face of this weakness, China's old enemy, the Xiongnu, although divided into northern and southern sections, once again took up the cudgels of war, capturing the ancient Chinese capital of Luoyang in AD 311, and the Silk Road capital of Chang'an five years later. By the mid-4th century, all of northern China was under Xiongnu control.

During this period the petty oasis kingdoms of the Tarim Basin succeeded in restoring their autonomy, but as vassals to a branch of the Xiongnu nomads known in the West as the Hephthalites – and soon to become more

> Lokaksema was a Buddhist Kushan from Gandhara. He is the earliest known monk to have translated Mahayana Buddhist scriptures into Chinese.

widely known and feared as the Huns, particularly under Attila (AD 406–53), the "Scourge of God". To the south and west, the Kushan Empire was similarly in decline, losing western territories to the Persian Sassanids (AD 226–651), as well as to the Xiongnu in the north.

Palmyra's ascendancy

The extremities of the Roman Empire were always under pressure as rivals sought to regain territory. The Parthians, based at Ctesiphon on the Tigris, were almost continually at war with Rome. By a quirk of nature, the route from Dura Europos ("Fortress of Europe" in Aramaic), on the Euphrates, through Syria to Emesa (Homs) was dramatically shortened by a natural spring at Palmyra, enabling the Silk Road to run straight through the inhospitable Syrian Desert. By charging huge taxes, the city of Palmyra became extremely wealthy and formed a useful barrier between the Romans and Parthians. So wealthy did it become that many of the exotic goods never reached Rome, but furnished the ever-expanding demands of its own population. This independent state built a huge imperial city in the middle of the desert, much of which still lies buried, but the funerary objects and mummified silk remains testify to its great wealth.

The Parthians were replaced by the Sassanids in the Second Persian Empire (AD 226–651), who in AD 260 under King Shapur defeated the Roman Emperor Valerian, and held him in captivity in Bishapur where he died. Palmyra's King Odainath, siding with Rome against this Persian dominance

in the region, then defeated the Sassanids. His wife and successor was Queen Zenobia, who in AD 274 went on to claim Egypt for Palmyra before being defeated by Emperor Aurelian and dragged off to Rome in golden chains.

All this disruption in trade across the desert resulted in the development of another route further up the Euphrates, which made it only a short journey to Aleppo. This vibrant city had always been an important trading centre of the Levant, being on the edge of Asia, the Middle East, Europe and Africa. Silk and other luxury goods flowed naturally through its ancient souks and *khans*.

PAPER TRAIL

The art of papermaking is thought to have developed in China during the 2nd century AD. One of the "Four Great Inventions of Ancient China" (other are the compass, gunpowder and printing), the Chinese kept the process a secret for hundreds of years, though it appeared in Korea in the 7th century. After the Battle of Talas in 751, the technology spread to Baghdad and Damascus, then east and south to Iran and India. The first paper mill in the Islamic world was founded in Samarkand; the first paper mill in Europe was established at Valencia in Spain in 1120, probably as a direct result of the Battle of Talas, by way of Islamic Spain.

ABOVE, FROM LEFT: mural depicting Sogdian traders, at the Rudaki Museum in Penjikent, Tajikistan; a camel carved in stone at Palmyra.

This branch of the Silk Road ended at Seleucia Piera, the port of Antioch, which became wealthy enough to indulge in the decadent pleasures of silk even before it became popular in Rome. St Paul had set sail from here for Cyprus on his first missionary journey around AD 48, and when emerging Christian sects were outlawed by the Romans during the first few centuries AD, Christianity also moved east.

The secret is out

The fall of Rome to Germanic tribes in AD 476 led to the ascendancy of Constantinople

(modern Istanbul), capital of the Eastern Roman Empire, which had been founded by Constantine I (AD 306–77), the first emperor to convert to Christianity. By the mid-6th century, Emperor Justinian I (AD 527–65) had recovered Italy, southern Iberia and parts of North Africa, but the nature of this new Byzantine state had changed completely, with Latin abandoned and Greek adopted as the language of government. Justinian was also keen to strengthen his empire by expanding long-distance trade, and, in doing so, overcoming the Chinese and Persian Sassanid monopoly on silk.

For at least two millennia, even from the time of the legendary Yellow Emperor, Qin Shi Huang, China had managed to maintain a successful ban on the export of silkworms and the knowledge of sericulture. But no monopoly is foolproof, and no technology can be kept

> When Nestorian Christianity was outlawed by the Roman Church in AD 432, merchants took this faith along the Silk Road. The first Nestorian church in Chang'an was consecrated in AD 638.

secret forever. The industry was defended by imperial decree, which imposed a mandatory death sentence on anyone attempting to export silkworms or their eggs, but this security was breached by the 2nd century BC, when knowledge of sericulture reached Korea and Vietnam. During the first half of the 1st century AD, the technology is thought to have reached the

THE SOGDIANS, CONSUMMATE MIDDLEMEN

For centuries the cosmopolitan Sogdians dominated trade along the Central Asian Silk Road. As the route's consummate middlemen, their language became the *lingua franca* of trade for a thousand miles, as Sogdian communities enjoyed influential positions in cities from Samarkand to Xi'an. Masters of the production of iron armour and chain mail, they introduced the Chinese to the art of making coloured translucent glass and kept the Tang court supplied with its exotic delicacies.

The Sogdians lived mainly in the lands between the Amu Darya and Syr Darya, in modern Uzbekistan and Tajikistan. Much of what we know about them has come from archaeological finds and friezes unearthed in the cities of Penjikent (east of Samarkand), Varakhsha (near Bukhara) and Afrosiab. Their palaces had some of the region's most sophisticated decoration, mixing Graeco-Bactrian, Sassanian and even Indian artistic influences. We know they used the Aramaic alphabet and were religiously tolerant, promoting Zoroastrianism alongside pockets of Manicheism and Nestorian Christianity. Much of what we know of their political life comes from a cache of Sogdian documents discovered by Aurel Stein in a Great Wall watchtower near Dunhuang.

Copies of the Sogdian friezes can be seen at museums in Penjikent and Afrosiab.

Han Chinese-dominated oasis of Khotan in the Tarim Basin – a centre of silk production today.

From Khotan, silkworms and knowledge of sericulture is thought to have travelled south to India and west to Sassanid Persia, then inevitably further to the west. But the Sassanids still had a monopoly on production. The breakthrough for Justinian came in AD 552, when he first obtained the elusive silkworm eggs. These were smuggled to him in bamboo tubes across Persia by two Nestorian monks. With their safe arrival in Constantinople, silk would gradually become a local Byzantine product.

The Eastern Silk Road

Nearly a century later the first Byzantine ambassador arrived at the Chinese court at Chang'an (Xi'an) and presented himself to the Tang emperor. Just as Rome had entered a period of decline so had the Han Empire, following repeated nomadic invasions from the north. The Huns – a western branch of the same Xiongnu tribes troubling China far to the east – penetrated as far as the Alps and the central Balkans.

So it fell to the great Tang Dynasty (AD 618–907) to re-establish full imperial control over the Eastern Silk Road. The second Tang emperor, Taizong (AD 626–49), mounted campaigns against the Eastern and Western Turks

> A Chinese princess given in marriage to a Khotan prince is said to have carried the eggs of silkworms to her new husband concealed in her hair.

to the north, before sending his forces into the Tarim Basin and re-establishing control over Turpan, Kashgar and Yarkand as well as Kuqa and Khotan.

However, even under the Tang Dynasty, China's control over the Eastern Silk Road was to prove tenuous. With the northern nomads temporarily at peace, a new challenge to Tang power arose from an unexpected source – Tibet. It had no previous history of expansionism in Central Asia; indeed, it is hardly mentioned

in the Chinese annals until this time. In AD 608–9, however, a Tibetan nobleman named Namri Lontsan united the fledgling Tibetan state and sent emissaries to the Chinese court. For the next four centuries the Tibetan Empire would play a decisive military role in Central Asia, its armies issuing forth from the Tibetan plateau to challenge Chinese control over the Silk Road in Gansu and, especially, in the Tarim Basin, where Tibetan forces seized control of the Southern Silk Road between Dunhuang and Khotan.

Meanwhile, to the north of the Hexi Corridor and in the Gobi steppe and

ANCIENT TRIO OF CARAVANSERAIS

Perhaps the oldest trade route in the Middle East runs north from the Hejaz and Sinai through Jordan and Syria to the former Silk Road port of Antakya. Here it was joined by a desert route linking up with Mesopotamia and the Persian Royal Road. As well as the great cities of Damascus and Aleppo, three historic entrepôts straddle these routes, symbolic of an entrepreneurial past. Petra, Jordan's "Rose Red City half as old as Time" flourished 2,000 years ago and traded across the Syrian Desert with the city of Palmyra. Further to the east, on the banks of the Euphrates, Dura Europos formed the third of these famous desert caravanserais.

ABOVE, FROM LEFT: *The Beginning of the Silk Industry in Europe*, engraved by Philip Galle, c.1600; *The Story of the Silk Princess*, a wooden panel painting from the Khotan oasis, 6th century.

Dzungaria, a new power, the Gökturk Empire, arose to replace the Xiongnu. Between AD 552 and 745 the Gökturks succeeded in unifying the disparate Turkic tribes of Central Asia into a single powerful entity, playing the same role to the north of the Hexi Corridor as the Tibetan Empire to the south. By the mid-8th century, however, the power of the Gökturk khans was on the wane, and in AD 744 a new Turkic power, the Uighur Khaganate, took control of Mongolia and proclaimed itself leader of all the Turkic peoples of Central Asia.

The rise of Islam

By the 7th century Chinese power and prestige were once again established over much of the Eastern and Central Silk Road, with restive Turkic tribes to the north, and expansionist Tibetans to the south. The Middle East was generally under the control of the Sassanids, while Byzantium ruled much of the Mediterranean. But this established relationship would not survive much longer.

Sometime around 610, Muhammad, a prosperous Mecca-born merchant and trader, received his first revelation from God, and began teaching a strict monotheism aimed at driving idolatry from Arabia. In 622 he and his followers left Mecca on *hejira* or "migration"

for the relative safety of nearby Medina; the Islamic Era is dated from this event. By the time Muhammad died a decade later, in 632, most of Arabia had converted to the new faith of Islam, or "submission" to the will of God.

The new religion expanded at a phenomenal rate. Arab Islamic armies swept out of Arabia, conquering the great trade routes and cities of the Fertile Crescent, before advancing as far as Libya in the west and Afghanistan in the east. The emerging Arab civilisation chose Damascus as its first capital, and the Umayyad Mosque became the latest in a long line of religious buildings on this sacred site. Under the Umayyad Caliphate (AD 661–750) the frontiers of the Islamic Empire were extended to Spain in the west, while Bactria and Samarkand were conquered in Central Asia, and Muslim armies reached the banks of the Indus. The world had seen nothing like it before – Sassanid Persia was swept away in just over a dozen years.

In 750, the unpopular Umayyad Dynasty was replaced by the powerful Abbasid Dynasty. While the Umayyads were studiously Arab in their make-up, the new Abbasid rulers enjoyed a much wider power base in Baghdad that rested not just on Arab aristocrats, but on poor Arabs, non-Arab converts and even sectarian Shia dissenters.

The rise of the Abbasids brought a Golden Age for the Islamic Caliphate, lasting for just over five centuries until the Mongol conquest of Baghdad in 1258. Islam was a religion based on trade and wedded to both overland and maritime commerce. But before commercial, cultural and religious exchange between Tang China and the emerging Islamic Empire could be established, spheres of influence had to be sorted out. The testing ground would be Central Asia, as both sides sought to take control of the opulent Silk Road traffic.

Tang versus Abbasid

The first clash occurred in 715, when Alutar was installed as king of Fergana with the reported backing of both Arab and Tibetan soldiers – a combination of enemies guaranteed to anger the Tang ruler, Xuanzong. Ikhshid, the deposed

ABOVE, FROM LEFT: the tale 'Journey to the West', depicting the travels of Xuanzang; tilework on the Jameh Mosque in Yazd, Iran.

"The house that contains pictures will not be entered by angels." This saying is attributed in the Hadith to the Prophet Muhammad, who believed that only God could bestow life. It explains the absence of figures in Islamic art, which instead produced stunning geometric patterns.

Fergana king, fled to Chinese-controlled Kuqa, where he appealed for aid. Xuanzong sent a force of 10,000 men under Zhang Xiaosong to restore Ikhshid to his throne, a task he accomplished successfully. Two years later Arab and Tibetan armies cooperated in besieging Aksu in the Tarim Basin. Once again the Chinese, led by General Tang Jiahui, were victorious.

China had successfully asserted its might over the Arabs on two occasions without effectively projecting its control to the west of the Pamir Massif in the vitally important Fergana Valley and across western Central Asia. In AD 751 Xuanzong determined to change this by challenging the first Abbasid caliph, Abu al-Abbas Abdullah, for control of the Syr Darya (Jaxartes) River and, more particularly, the Fergana Valley – home to those valuable "heavenly horses". The Arab forces of Ziyad ibn-Salih and the Chinese forces of Gao Xianzhi eventually met by the banks of the Talas River in present-day Kyrgyzstan. The Arabs won the day and they now had effective control over western Central Asia. The Chinese inflicted heavy losses on their adversaries, however, and these rare Sino-Arab clashes helped to establish clear

spheres of influence, based on mutual respect and in no way hindering Silk Road traffic or the exchange of ambassadors between the Tang and Abbasid courts.

As a result of the Chinese defeat at the Battle of Talas, an important technological transfer between East and West is thought to have taken place. After the battle, large numbers of Chinese prisoners of war were sent to Samarkand, where they taught their Muslim captors the art of making paper. By 794 this new skill had reached Baghdad, where a paper mill was set up, and eventually the technology of papermaking reached the West.

XUANZANG, THE FAMOUS SILK ROAD PILGRIM

The peripatetic Buddhist monk Xuanzang (AD 602–64) remains the best-known and best-loved of all Chinese travellers on the early Silk Road, not least because of his fictional reincarnation in the celebrated 16th-century novel *Xiyouji* or "Journey to the West". The novelist Wu Chengen created a magical version of the Buddhist pilgrim's travels, accompanied by his companions Monkey, Pigsy and Sandy, to the realm of the "Queen Mother of the West".

The real Xuanzang set out from Chang'an (Xi'an) for India in AD 629, at a time when unauthorised travel to the western regions was forbidden. Travelling mainly by night to avoid soldiers and officials, he crossed the

Jade Gate Pass at Yumenguan and set out for the oasis of Hami, where he almost died of thirst in the desert. After a period of recuperation at Turpan, Xuanzang continued along the Northern Silk Road via Kuqa and across the Tian Shan to Transoxiana, before turning south to India. Here he studied at the Buddhist University of Nalanda for several years before continuing to visit historic Buddhist centres, spending a total of around 15 years in the subcontinent.

Later he returned to Chang'an, bringing with him 22 horses burdened with Buddhist manuscripts, written mainly in Sanskrit, as well as religious relics and precious Buddha images.

GLORY AND DECLINE

As the cities of the Silk Road prospered, so did trade. In China, Xi'an reached its zenith, while Arab culture also enjoyed a Golden Age. But the rise of silk manufacturing in Persia and Byzantium began to have an effect on Silk Road traffic.

Between its inception in AD 618 and its ultimate fall in 907, Tang China came to epitomise the prosperity, sophistication and power most associated with the ancient Silk Road. Through judicious use of the overland and maritime trade routes – and in particular the Silk Road – the Tang grew wealthy and gained access to new technologies. From India, Central Asia, Persia, the Middle East and the Mediterranean world they acquired new ideas of fashion, glass-making, ceramics, medicines, perfumes, incense, spices, wines and new techniques of metalworking. Foreign ideas crept in – from sitting on benches and chairs to new forms of dancing and musical entertainment.

The Tang state wasn't always militarily successful, yet during the halcyon days of the late 7th and early 8th centuries the capital at Chang'an (Xi'an) was unsurpassed in wealth and style. At its peak in around AD 750 it was probably the

> *"Seek Knowledge, even though it be in China" Hadith (Traditions of the Prophet)*

largest and most populous city in the world. An estimated 800,000 to 1 million people lived within its walls, with another million or so living outside in the greater metropolitan area. The city walls were massive, rising 5.5 metres (18ft) in height, and extending for 35 km (22 miles) to form an elongated square with sides 8km (5 miles) by 9.5km (6 miles). As many as 25,000

LEFT: detail of an anonymous painting, *Banquet and Concert*, showing life at the Tang court.
RIGHT: the Tang emperor Wudi and his entourage.

foreigners, including Turks, Persians, Arabs, Mongols, Indians, Koreans, Malays, Japanese and Armenians lived there too, congregated mainly around the Western Market. Although the Tang state functioned as a Confucian bureaucracy, other religions were widely tolerated, and Chang'an had Buddhist and Taoist temples, as well as places of worship for Manicheans, Nestorians, Zoroastrians, Christians and Muslims. It was a sophisticated, fun-loving city, with entertainers and courtesans from far and wide – though the dancers, tumblers, singers and musicians from the Tarim Basin city-states of Kuqa and Aksu were particularly popular.

Secondary trade routes branched off in all directions along the full length of the main Silk

Road: north to Mongolia, south to Guangdong and the Chinese colony of Annam, southwest to Yunnan and the Tibetan plateau, and east to the fertile plains of the Yellow River. At the western end a route developed which ran northwest from Rey (now a suburb of Tehran) on a more direct route through Tabriz to the Black Sea and Constantinople.

Continued demand for silk

By the mid-8th century, China's monopoly on silk production had been definitively broken, but the best silks in the world still originated in China, and demand for them continued. Moreover, from

Tang times China began to develop a new and important export to Central Asia, Tibet and India – tea, which was easily carried when compressed and valuable enough to exchange for the warhorses that China always greatly desired.

During the Tang era, maritime trade also flourished and expanded. Chinese goods were

> "Uighurs are the best among Turks. Their language is called King's Turkish"
> Mahmud al-Kashgari, Dictionary of Turkic Languages (1072)

THE TEA-HORSE ROAD

China's ancient Tea-Horse Road was a collection of tracks and trails leading from the tea-producing regions of Yunnan and Sichuan westwards to Central Asia and Tibet. Tea was in great demand among Mongols and Tibetans, for whom it represented an important dietary supplement, usually drunk with yak butter and salt. In exchange, the Chinese required swift and powerful steeds that they could not easily breed at home. The main Tea-Horse Road led from Yunnan, across the Chamdo region of Tibet, to Lhasa and Nepal. Other similar "tea for horse" roads paralleled the ancient Silk Road through Gansu and Qinghai provinces.

shipped from Guangdong and the south China coast to India and the Middle East, generally aboard Arab and Persian ships. The same merchant navigators carried wine and incense, pearls and precious glass back to China.

The Turkic Uighur

Around AD 840 a group of Turkic people known as the Uighur were displaced from their ancestral homelands in the Mongolian Steppe and driven south by Kyrgyz raiders. The Uighur moved into the Tarim Basin, settling in the old oasis cities of Kuqa and Aksu before gradually spreading around the rim of the Taklamakan Desert. Here they underwent a major transformation, turning from pastoral nomads into settled oasis dwellers and cultivators.

The newly settled Uighur seem to have practised Manicheism and Buddhism at this time, as well as writing in an adapted Sogdian script. It seems that they intermarried with the original Tokharian inhabitants of the oases, gradually giving the Tarim Basin the overwhelmingly Uighur nature of its indigenous population today.

The Songs of China

As Tang power and prestige declined, nomadic attacks on outlying garrisons and interference in the Silk Road's traffic increased. In AD

meritocracy, administering what became an increasingly free-market economy encompassing a massive population – for the times – of about 100 million people that produced abundant food surpluses and other goods for trade. The Song was the first government in the world to issue paper currency (known as *jiaozi*). It also maintained the first standing navy of any Chinese state, introduced gunpowder warfare, new techniques of hydraulic engineering and the first movable-type printing machines.

For most of the Song Dynasty's three centuries, China was prosperous and relatively powerful – but unlike in Tang times, the Song polity looked

907, after almost three centuries in power, the dynasty finally collapsed and was followed by a period of disunity known as the "Five Dynasties and Ten Kingdoms" (907–60). The nation was only reunified in 960 with the accession of the Song Dynasty that would rule all China under the Northern Song (960–1127) and the southern part of the country under the Southern Song (1127–1279).

Song China was both wealthy and sophisticated. The state rested on a Confucian

ABOVE, FROM LEFT: Tang-dynasty horseman; the Kizil Caves near Kuqa, one of many Buddhist sites abandoned as Islam began to spread into the northwestern part of China.

south and east, sending ships to the Indian Ocean and trading with Southeast Asia, India and beyond, but not exercising great control over Central Asia. Indeed, for most of the Song period, Gansu's Hexi Corridor represented the western limits of Chinese control, while in the Tarim Basin the scattered Uighur city-states came under the control of the Karakhanid Turks (999–1211).

It was during this period that Islam gradually extended its control across the Tarim Basin and into Gansu, changing the character of the northwest completely. No longer was Chinese Central Asia – the area today known as Xinjiang – a region inhabited by Tokharian Buddhists and Uighur Manicheans, but instead it became firmly Turkish-Muslim in culture.

Arabic Golden Age

To the west of the Pamirs, Arab civilisation attained its classical Golden Age under the Abbasid Dynasty during the 8th and 9th centuries, most particularly during the reign of the fifth Abbasid caliph, the illustrious Harun al-Rashid (763–809). Harun was a learned scholar and poet who promoted science and the arts, and encouraged wise men and scholars to settle at his court in Baghdad. He maintained diplomatic relations with India and China, as well as with the Holy Roman Emperor Charlemagne (768–814). Relations between these two near-contemporaries seem to have been very good. Harun sent envoys

bearing silks, brass, perfumes, slaves and ivory, as well as an elephant and a water clock, which made a great impression at Charlemagne's court in Aachen. In return he received fine Spanish horses, Frisian cloth and trained hunting dogs.

Harun was also a good soldier, and his relations with Eastern Christendom at Constantinople were by no means as good as his relations with Charlemagne and the Holy Roman Empire. Between AD 780 and 806 he led several large armies against Byzantium, which only prevented the capture of Constantinople by paying the Abbasids a substantial tribute in gold.

Following Harun's death, the Abbasid Caliphate entered on a long, slow period of decline. The rival Umayyads maintained their dynasty in Spain, and the North African provinces from Morocco to Egypt acquired de facto independence. Next, in about 820, the Persian Samanids asserted their control over Transoxiana and Khorasan, severing any direct Silk Road link between Tang China and the Abbasids. Samanid authority extended over Bukhara and Samarkand – the Mausoleum of Ismail Samani (892–907) in Bukhara was built during this time – and the Tajik people generally date their emergence as a nation from the Samanid period.

The Turkic-Muslim states

After nearly two centuries, the Samanids in turn were replaced by the Turkish Ghaznavids, descendants of Turkic slave guards to the Samanids who, ultimately, overthrew their Persian masters. The Ghaznavids controlled most of Persia, all of Afghanistan and Transoxiana, and northern India as far as the Punjab during the period of their primacy (975–1187). The Ghaznavid state was the first major Muslim empire in Central Asia, and definitively marked the end of Arab and Abbasid influence in the region. By the mid-11th century, however, the Ghaznavids found themselves challenged to the west by the emergence of yet another Turkic-Muslim state, the Seljuk Empire (1037–1194), which established control over all the territory between Anatolia and Afghanistan, reducing the Ghaznavid state to the North Indian plains.

The Assassins

During the 11th century a small group of renegade Shia Muslims began to disrupt trade along the Silk Road. They established a number

---

FORBIDDEN SILK

Under the Abbasids the Arabs, too, were desirous of fine silks, despite the Prophet Muhammad's injunction against wearing silk clothes – at least for Muslim men. According to the Hadith or "Traditions of the Prophet", Muhammad addressed a group of his companions while holding a silk garment in one hand and gold in another, saying "These are prohibited to Muslim men, but permitted to Muslim women." The Koran states that those believers who enter paradise will be "adorned with gold bracelets and pearls, and their clothing will be of silk" (Sura al-Hajj), and believers "will wear green garments of fine silk and rich brocade" (Sura al-Insan).

"The best-preserved and most wholly admirable castle in the world" T.E. Lawrence describing Krac des Chevaliers castle in Syria, built around 1030 to control the Homs gap, on one of several routes to reach the Mediterranean shore

of fortified settlements in Iran, Iraq, Syria and Lebanon, embarking on drug-crazed murdering sprees from their mountain hideouts, as instructed by their fanatical leader Hassan Sabah. These *Hashisheen* (meaning "hashish-users"; from which we also get our word "assas-

of contending Persian and then Turkish states did little to promote trade along the Silk Road with China. During this period, between AD 800 and 1200, the direct contacts that had been established between Tang China and the West withered. While caravans continued to traverse the Silk Road, trade was disrupted by political uncertainties, with the sea routes to China via the Indian Ocean prospering as a consequence.

Nor was silk the important commodity it had once been. Both the Tang and their successors, the Song, continued to produce and export millions of bolts of fine silk, but they were increasingly rivalled by Persian and Byzantine production.

sin") threatened the safety of locals and traders alike, and even launched suicide murderers against their Sunni foes (see also page 329.) They also formed alliances for territory with Christian Crusaders who arrived to free the Holy Land from Sunni Muslim control.

China in decline

To the east of the Pamirs, China was in absolute decline, and a series of petty states and fierce nomad entities developed to disrupt trade. To the west, Abbasid decline and the emergence

ABOVE, FROM LEFT: Harun al-Rashid; three assassins being prepared for their mission by the Old Man of the Mountain in Syria, from the *Travels of Marco Polo*.

THE LAST OF THE ABBASIDS

Hulagu Khan (1217–65), the grandson of the Mongol founder Genghis Khan, captured and sacked Baghdad on 10 February 1258. It was an event that marked the end of the Abbasid Caliphate and the Arab Golden Age. Muslims warned the victorious Hulagu that disaster would befall the Mongols if the blood of al-Musta'sim, the last Abbasid Caliph, were to be spilled. Hulagu took the warning to heart and had al-Musta'sim rolled in a carpet and trampled to death by horses to avoid bloodshed. Al Musta'sim's family were also executed, with the exception of the youngest son and daughter, despatched to Mongolia to become slaves to Hulagu's court.

THE MONGOL ERA AND THE RISE OF EUROPE

The ruthless genius of Genghis Khan brought a large proportion of the Silk Road under Mongol control, bringing it security and giving it a new lease of life. In later centuries, overland trade declined as new sea routes opened up.

In the 13th century a new and unexpected power exploded onto the scene, rapidly conquering the entire length of the Silk Road from Chang'an in the east to Antakya (Antioch) in the west, bringing the whole of the passage under the umbrella of a single empire for the first time in history. This produced the last great flourishing of Silk Road trade before its final decline and gradual disappearance in the 15th and 16th centuries. The engine for this new empire was the drive for Mongol expansion, and the man who made it happen was a nomadic ruler called Temujin, who would later assume the title Genghis Khan (1206–27). His name is remembered with a shudder by all the settled peoples from Chang'an to Baghdad, and with fierce pride by the nomadic Mongols themselves.

He was born around 1162 not too far from Ulaanbaatar, the present capital of Mongolia. Despite enduring a difficult childhood and relative poverty, he showed remarkable will-power and military ability, gradually defeating his clan enemies until, in 1206, he united the feuding Mongol tribes under his sole leadership as Great Khan. He lived for a further 21 years, during which time his armies conquered the greater part of Asia, including the Silk Road between China and the Caspian Sea. On his death in 1227, the Mongol Empire is estimated to have encompassed 26 million sq km (10 million sq miles), an area about four times the size of the Roman or Macedonian empires at their peak. It covered 22 percent of the earth's land surface and lorded over 100 million people.

Despite his ruthless efficiency as a military commander, Genghis was remarkably enlightened in matters of religion and culture, allowing his many conquered subjects considerable

RUSSIA'S CAPITAL DESTROYED

In 1246 Giovanni de Plano Carpini, papal envoy to the Mongols, gave an eyewitness account of the khan's ruthless methods: "The Mongols attacked Russia, where they made great havoc, destroying cities and fortresses and slaughtering men; and they laid siege to Kiev, the capital of Russia; after they had besieged the city for a long time, they took it and put the inhabitants to death. When we were journeying through that land we came across countless skulls and bones of dead men lying about on the ground. Kiev... has been reduced almost to nothing... and the inhabitants are kept in complete slavery."

The highly efficient Mongol shuudan or postal service used horse-relay stations similar to the US Pony Express. As most Mongol officers were illiterate, orders were communicated in verse to ensure that instructions were transmitted correctly.

freedom. He also set the seal on another aspect of Mongol policy – the encouragement of trade relationships between the increasingly far-flung corners of the empire. His rule generally brought destruction to most of Persia, includ-

hundreds, perhaps thousands of Western merchants to travel the Silk Road to China, the most celebrated of whom was Marco Polo (see page 68.)

Division of the spoils

Genghis Khan was succeeded by several wise and highly competent rulers, notably his third son Ogedei Khan (1229–41) and his grandson Kublai Khan (1260–94). Kublai, who had studied Chinese culture, became the first emperor of China's Yuan Dynasty in 1271, and under his rule Mongol power and prosperity reached new heights. Yet the seeds of future imperial decline were already sown before Kublai attained manhood. In his will,

ing the removal of the Assassins, but spared certain centres, including the city of Tabriz, close to the border with Azerbaijan and Turkey.

This enlightened policy caused a brief but dazzling resurgence of the ancient Silk Road, as all merchants and ambassadors carrying proper documentation and authority were permitted, and indeed encouraged, to travel throughout the vast Mongol realm under imperial protection. As a consequence, overland trade between Asia and Europe greatly increased. During the 13th and early 14th centuries this policy encouraged

LEFT: 14th-century portrait of Genghis Khan (1162–1227), founder of the Mongol Empire. **RIGHT:** Mongol mounted archer.

Genghis had ordered the Mongol Empire divided into four separate, notionally allied khanates. In fact, four rival kingdoms emerged. In the east, the greatest of all was the Empire of the Great Khan, soon to become the Yuan Dynasty of China. The greater part of Central Asia, including both Kashgar and Samarkand, became the Chagatai Khanate. Most of Persia and the Middle East became the Ilkhanate, centred on their capital at Tabriz. Finally the vast Russian steppe stretching from the Altai Mountains to Kiev was incorporated in the fabled Golden Horde.

This political division of the Mongol realms was soon to become a cultural divide as well. Quite simply, the Mongols were overwhelmingly outnumbered by the settled peoples they now ruled, and they were also deeply influenced by the more sophisticated cultures they had conquered. Thus Kublai Khan, who founded Beijing in 1272, was an enthusiastic student of Chinese culture and rapidly became sinicised. The rulers of the Chagatai Khanate adopted Islam and were soon absorbed into Central Asian Turkic culture. To the west, the Ilkhans similarly converted to Islam and, renouncing all loyalty to the Great Khan, became deeply influenced by Persian and Arab mores.

Timur's glories

Meanwhile, to the north and west the Golden Horde fell increasingly under Tatar influence and Ardebil. They also set their capital at Tabriz, but it was always too close to the border with the emerging Ottoman Empire, so they moved to Isfahan.

Decline and demise

The gradual disintegration of the Mongol Empire also brought about the collapse of Silk Road prosperity as the brief political and cultural stability of *Pax Mongolica* disappeared. The eastern part of the Silk Road passed from the short-lived Yuan Dynasty (1271–1368) to the sphere of the Ming Empire (1368–1644). At the same time, to the west of the Pamirs, the old Silk Road came under the control of various decentralised Turkic

abandoned its Mongol allegiance before being fatally weakened by the great Turkic-Mongol conqueror Timur (Tamerlane, 1336–1405). Timur was not only a military genius, but also a patron of the arts, and his rule inspired the creation of some of the greatest works of architecture ever built, including the Registan, the Bibi Khanum Mosque and his own tomb of Gur-i-Mir in Samarkand, as well as buildings in Bukhara, Shakhrisabz and elsewhere in Central Asia.

Timur's descendants would go on to found the Mughal Dynasty in India (1526–1867), while the Golden Horde finally succumbed to Muscovite Russia in the 16th century. The later Safavids, who established the first lasting Shia state in Iran, emerged from the northern Iranian city of

"In all the other parts of the world light descends upon earth. From holy Samarkand and Bukhara, it ascends." Tajik saying

kingdoms, including the Chagatai, Timurid and subsequently Uzbek khanates, while the Middle East and Anatolia unified under the new power of the Ottoman Empire (1299–1922), which would become the centre of interaction between the Eastern and Western worlds for more than six centuries. But the great trans-Asian highway that had for so many centuries served as a link between East and West was already fatally ruptured. Trade flourished in the East under the

Ming, and in the West under the Ottomans, but overland trade between the two was never fully re-established, due both to Central Asian instability and to two seminal changes that would irreversibly change the nature of commerce between Europe and China.

The first of these was the isolationism of the Ming Dynasty, which turned its back on Central Asia and fixed the limits of its territorial ambitions within the traditional Chinese cultural sphere. China increasingly became inward-looking, despite being the richest, most populous and – for a time – the most powerful state in the world. Eventually the empire lost touch with reality and failed to keep pace with the startling changes beginning to sweep the West.

Exploration by sea

Secondly, an emerging Europe was hungry for spices and trade with the Orient, but often cut off from China by a Muslim world that treasured its trade monopoly and drove prices ever higher. The resultant European search for new routes to the Orient led to Christopher Columbus's discovery in 1492 of the New World, which he mistakenly thought was "The Indies". Just six years later, Vasco da Gama reached Cochin on the Kerala coast by sea, establishing a direct link for the first time between Western Europe and India. Both the Ottoman and the Chinese empires were about to be outflanked by merchant navigators from Spain and Portugal, closely followed by the Dutch and British.

In 1521 Ferdinand Magellan completed the work of Columbus when he reached the Philippines, establishing a direct link between Europe and Asia across the Pacific for the first time. With two direct maritime routes established between Europe and the Far East, it was not long before Chinese waters were dominated by aggressive European sailors, while China had no effective naval response.

The demise of the overland Silk Road owes much to the development of the silk route by sea, where it became easier and safer to transport goods in ships that were stronger and more reliable. Over the following couple of centuries trade centres were established along the Indian Ocean coastal route, opening up opportunities

ABOVE, FROM LEFT: Gul-i-Mir, the sumptuous mausoleum of the Central Asian Conqueror Timur (Tamerlane), in Samarkand, Uzbekistan; Chinese ships at anchor.

for the Europeans and making new contacts. The new Safavid capital at Isfahan, for example, prospered on a trade route that connected the Persian Gulf with the Black Sea.

China refused any trade with the British, and in 1793 Emperor Qianlong informed the Macartney embassy that "We possess all things. I set no value on objects strange or ingenious, and have no use for your country's manufactures". The emperor made it clear that he regarded the embassy as a tributary mission, and sent a message to King George III warning that British vessels putting ashore at any point other than Guangzhou would be immediately expelled.

The great powers at play

Less than half a century later, in 1842, China was resoundingly defeated by Britain in the First Opium War; maritime trade in the Far East was securely in European (and later American) hands. The great, ancient Silk Road, long ago abandoned and remembered only at the best-surviving oases, was all but forgotten.

Rivalry for these forgotten territories of Central Asia and western China resurfaced throughout the 19th century when Britain wanted to prevent Russia expanding its territories southward. Britain's manoeuvrings for control to halt this threat to India, its Jewel in the Crown, became known as the Great Game (see following page). At a time when boundaries

Marco Polo

The description of the Italian's
adventures to the court of
Kublai Khan is one of the Silk
Road's greatest historical records.

During the 13th and 14th centuries, Venetian merchants dominated much of the trade in rare and exotic goods trafficked between Europe and Asia by way of the Mediterranean and Red seas. It was a source of great wealth to the tiny

but prosperous Venetian Republic. But the lure of the Silk Road still attracted the interest of ambitious Venetian merchants who sought to profit overland as well as by maritime trade. Two such merchants were brothers Nicolo and Maffeo Polo, who set out to trade in the region of the Volga steppes.

Depending on one's interpretation, their luck was either bad or exceedingly good, as their venture coincided with the wars of conquest of the expanding Mongol Empire, which prevented the brothers' return home. Instead, in 1264, they decided to accompany a tributary mission from the Volga region to Khanbaliq, the seat of Kublai Khan, near present-day Beijing. They were well received and hospitably treated by the Great Khan, who enjoyed religious and philosophical debate. At the

end of their visit Kublai Khan sent them back to Venice under his protection with a request that they should return to China together with "one hundred learned Christians" able to debate and argue the cause of their religion at the Mongol court.

In 1271 the Polo brothers set out on their return journey to Beijing accompanied by Nicolo's 17-year-old son, Marco, who would find especial favour with the Great Khan. The Polos travelled overland, by way of Central Asia, passing through Persia and staying three years in Bukhara before crossing the Pamirs into present-day Xinjiang. Here they took the Southern Silk Road via Kashgar and Khotan before passing through the much-feared "Desert of Lop", which Marco describes as a howling wilderness inhabited by malevolent demons intent on luring men and beasts into the sandy wastes of the Taklamakan Desert.

Marco Polo spent 17 years in China, much of it in the service of the Great Khan, before returning to Europe, by sea, in 1291. He reached Venice in 1295, reportedly laden with concealed rubies and other jewels, but was captured and briefly imprisoned by the Genoese in 1298, during a short war between Venice and Genoa. While in prison, he dictated an elaborate account of his travels to a fellow prisoner, Rustichello da Pisa, which was subsequently published as *Il Milione*, known in English as *The Travels of Marco Polo*.

The veracity of Marco Polo's account of his travels in China and beyond has been called into question by some authorities. Why, for example, does he not mention the use of chopsticks, or the Great Wall? Yet these apparently glaring omissions fade to almost nothing when compared with the information Marco did bring back, much of it arcane and arbitrary, but also clearly verifiable today. *Il Milione* was an immediate success, stimulating interest in the Orient across Europe. Christopher Columbus, who would discover the New World in his quest for a western maritime route to Asia, is known to have owned a heavily annotated copy.

TOP: the family of Marco Polo (1254–1324) travelling by camel caravan. **LEFT:** Nicolo and Marco Polo before the Great Khan.

> "Do not say that you were not warned in due time! Tremblingly obey and show no negligence!" Emperor Qianlong's message to King George III

were becoming increasingly important, much of the area remained unmapped, which added to the uncertainty, but also offered opportunities to seize land regardless. The impasse was superseded by the onset of World War I, as Russia and Britain found themselves allied against Germany.

freeing the Central Asian states and creating a complex jigsaw of new nation-states and nationalisms in the process.

For almost 1,500 years, the Silk Road had held a unique role in Asian foreign trade and political relations, but today the story is far from over. Like a disused railway line given a new lease of life, a booming Chinese economy is giving the modern Central Asian republics an opportunity to reuse the Silk Road, with new roads, pipelines and rail links. They continue to carry the latest commodities such as oil and gas from one region to another, which has always been the main reason for the Silk Road.

At the beginning of the 20th century vast areas of Central Asia were swallowed up in the expanding but isolationist Soviet Empire: the lands of the former Golden Horde and the khanates of Bukhara, Khiva and Kokand were divided up on ethnic rather than cultural lines, ensuring ongoing instability. But the end of World War I also saw the break-up of the Ottoman Empire, and the emergence of new identities such as Lebanon, Syria and Iraq. Equally momentous changes occurring at the end of the century led to the collapse of the Soviet ideal, once again

ABOVE, FROM LEFT: Ambassador George Macartney and his delegation grovelling before Emperor Qianlong in 1793.

CHINA TAKES THE SEA ROUTE

The third Ming emperor, Yongle (1402–24), was unique in the annals of Imperial China in that he pursued an active maritime policy, sending his favourite admiral, the Yunnanese Muslim eunuch Zheng He (1371–1433), to explore Southeast Asia and the Indian Ocean as far as the Red Sea and the East African Coast. Starting in 1405, Yongle sent Zheng He on six major naval expeditions at the head of a fleet of hundreds of "treasure ships". His purpose was to extend Chinese control over Nan Yang, the "southern seas", by imposing imperial control over trade and overawing the peoples of the littoral into paying tribute to the Ming throne.

The Great Game

As Britain and Russia headed towards each other in Central Asia, spies, skulduggery and derring-do brought tales of high adventure.

The 19th century saw the Russian Empire reach southwards towards India, Britain's "Jewel in the Crown", just as the British Empire expanded its grip into the northwest frontier and Afghanistan. As the two empires inched ever

closer, the need to map out the little-known areas between them and to gain influence with the various rulers in this buffer zone became imperative. The British in particular were terrified that the Russians would advance through Central Asia and into India in search of a warm-water port. The result was the Great Game, an imperial play of cat and mouse, incursions and espionage set in the deserts and mountains of Central Asia. It ranks as one of the most colourful periods of Silk Road history.

As listening posts in places such as Kashgar and Mashhad sent back reports to London and St Petersburg, a series of pundits, explorers, spies, diplomats and military officers (supposedly on "hunting leave") slipped into Central Asia, some in disguise, others in uniform at the head of armies. Those that returned brought reports of dastardly emirs, terrible deserts and ripping tales of derring-do. It was irresistible propaganda, and the public lapped it up in newspapers and at public lectures organised by the likes of the Royal Geographic Society.

Early disasters

The initial Russian forays south into Central Asia were disastrous. In 1717 a detachment of 4,000 Russian troops sent to Khiva were slaughtered to a man. In 1839 another winter march, this time to Khiva to free Russian slaves, was again forced to turn back, with the loss of 1,000 men and 8,500 camels and not a single shot fired.

In the meantime a series of intrepid British traveller-spies began to brave the deserts and slave-raiders of Central Asia, including William Moorcroft, Arthur Connolly (who travelled under the alias "Khan Ali") and Alexander "Bokhara" Burnes. Using charm and flattery, well-versed in local languages and dressed in local cloaks and turbans, these players of the Great Game wrote secret reports, reconnoitred military routes and (if they were lucky) returned home to publish a best-selling memoir.

It was a dangerous job. The Emir of Bukhara threw Captain Connolly and Colonel Charles Stoddart into a vermin-infested pit for two years before killing them. Alexander Burnes was hacked to death by an Afghan mob in Kabul and numerous others perished in remote valleys from disease or poisoning. All knew they would be coolly disowned by their governments should they be caught.

Russia advances

Russia's attempt to create a defendable southern border began with a line of forts across the Kazakh steppe, from Orenburg to Ak Mechet, and spread quickly as railway lines and steamer routes pressed deeper into Central Asia, bringing with them the double-edged sword of Russian trade and "protection".

The Russian conquest was gradual but unstoppable, largely because the emirates and khanates of Bukhara, Kokand and Khiva were too busy

LEFT: Alexander Burnes. **TOP:** Approaching Yarkand at a strategically important crossroads southeast of kashgar, from a sketch by R.B. Shaw (1868).

squabbling with each other to worry about the Russians. Russian troops took Shymkent (1864), Tashkent (1865), Samarkand (1868), Krasnovodsk (1869), Khiva (1873) and Kokand (1875) within a decade. St Petersburg's assertion that the towns of Turkestan would be returned to local rule was a farce.

As the Russians pushed south, the political temperature spiked. Russian troops crushed the Turkmen tribes at Gök-Tepe (1881) in a massacre that left 14,500 Turkmen dead. Three years later they took the oasis of Merv (1884), creating a panic that the British press wittily dubbed "Mervousness". The subsequent Russian advance to Pandjeh, the gateway to Herat, pushed the two sides to the brink

The focus of the Game now shifted to the Pamirs, a strategic vacuum where the Russian, British and Chinese empires converged. A string of Russian and British explorers (including Lord Curzon, Colonel Francis Younghusband, John Wood, T.E. Gordon and Ney Elias) mapped the rivers and passes in an attempt to pin down a border. Every now and then the two sides came face to face: Younghusband met his Russian counterpart General Gromchevsky in Hunza in 1889. Whatever their political affiliations, meetings required fine dinners accompanied by port, crystal and linens. The Great Game was, after all, a gentlemen's affair.

of war, and 25,000 British troops rushed to Quetta. The sabres were only put away with the establishment of a Joint Afghan Boundary Commission in the border town of Sarakhs.

Afghanistan

The British endured an even rougher time in Afghanistan. The 1838 invasion ended in the massacre of 16,000 British troops, with just one man surviving to limp back through the Khyber Pass. The second Anglo-Afghan War, a result of an 1878 Russian mission to Kabul, was almost as disastrous as the first. The message was as clear then as it would be to the Russians more than a century later; no one invades Afghanistan and wins.

The British solution to their ongoing military failures in Afghanistan was to create a tripartite frontier: a directly controlled British territory in the Punjab; a belt of vassal states (the Pashtun-dominated Federally Administered Tribal Areas – FATA); and then the independent buffer state of Afghanistan. Britain's foreign minister, Sir Mortimer Durand, met with Amir Abdur Rahman in Kabul in 1893 to discuss which areas of the FATA should fall under their respective influences. The dividing line they identified became known as the Durand Line.

ABOVE: the Russians engaging the Emir of Bukhara's forces. **RIGHT:** Colonel Francis Younghusband.

End game

Eventually the Joint Afghan Boundary Commission (1887) and Anglo-Russian Convention (1907) defused border tensions. Concerns over Russian influence on India lingered (and even prompted the Younghusband invasion of Tibet in 1903), but the height of Anglo-Russian rivalry was over. The Soviet army did not cross the Oxus until 1979, and Russian troops never even made it close to the thresholds of India. The Durand line marks a de facto border today, though it is still disputed. Some historians contend that the Great Game was more fiction than fact, owing more to Kipling's Kim than to historical events. The Russians themselves never used the phrase, referring only to a "Tournament of Shadows". But if parts of the Game were fiction, what a ripping yarn it was.

REDISCOVERING THE ROAD

Another Great Game broke out at the end of the 19th century. This time the players were not diplomats and spies, but explorers and archaeologists in search of the long-lost Silk Road cities and their vanished treasures.

A s Silk Road trade withered and China withdrew behind its wall, the ancient oasis towns of Chinese Central Asia grew increasingly isolated. Glacier-fed streams retreated, irrigation channels collapsed and the desert began to reclaim abandoned settlements. Half-buried temple complexes, garrison towns and Buddhist stupas were left to crumble undisturbed for centuries, preserved only in local legends of buried cities protected by desert demons.

Little by little, rumours of these lost cities began to funnel back to the listening posts of the British Empire. As the finds became more impressive, the trickle of interest turned to a flood, and soon archaeological teams from seven nations were involved in a frantic race to carve out spheres of influence in a rivalry that carried clear echoes of the Great Game.

The archaeologist-explorers who braved the fearsome Taklamakan Desert first unearthed walls, then houses, monasteries and entire cities,

> The Finnish Baron Carl Gustav Mannerheim (who later became president of Finland) passed by Dunhuang in 1907 but decided to go pheasant shooting instead, thus missing out on one of the greatest treasures of the Silk Road.

all spectacularly preserved in the dry desert air. Paintings in a hitherto unseen blend of Greek, Iranian, Indian and Chinese styles resurfaced as fresh as the day they were painted, alongside

LEFT: expedition in the Taklamakan, pictured by Aurel Stein. **RIGHT:** sculptures and murals inside the Mogao Caves, Dunhuang.

documents in Sogdian, Tokharian and a dozen unknown scripts.

Over a period of 25 years, caravan-loads of booty were carted out of China and, for better or worse, ancient libraries, frescoes, statues, relics and entire temples were removed by the tonne. Slowly but surely, the forgotten commercial and cultural crossroad towns of Turpan, Kuqa, Miran and Niya were resurrected after 1,500 years of slumber.

The first steps

Long before the archaeological teams launched their assaults on Turkestan, individual spies, explorers, scientists and travellers had begun to pick up fragments of the past coughed up by the desert. In 1876–7 Nikolai Przhevalsky, Russia's greatest Central Asian explorer, wrote of finding a large deserted city in the deserts of Lop Nur. The following year the Russian botanist Albert Regel became the first foreigner to lay eyes on Karakhoja near Turpan, before the Chinese threw him out as a spy. In 1890 the French explorer Dutreuil de Rhins picked up

terracotta figures and scriptures, and four years later was murdered on the Tibetan plateau.

The first reliable reports of Turkestan's lost cities had come from the *pundits* or *munshis*, Indian spies employed by the British Raj, but it was the arrival of the Bower Manuscripts in 1890 that really excited the British. Lieutenant Bower had purchased 51 pieces of birch bark in Kuqa (they were discovered by local treasure-hunters in a nearby stupa), while investigating the murder of Scottish trader Andrew Dalgleish. The eventual realisation that the Sanskrit documents dated from the 5th century – and thus were one of the oldest pieces of writing ever found – was a revelation. What were 1,500-year-old Buddhist documents written in an Indian

script doing in the heart of Central Asia?

It was the Russians, led by Dimitri Klementz in 1898, who were first, with a purely archaeological expedition to the region. Klementz's haul of manuscripts, frescoes and photographs from the cave temples of Karakhoja (Khocho), Astana and Yarkhoto in the Turpan oasis set the archaeological community alight, giving birth to the brand-new academic field of Central Asian studies.

Sven Hedin

The true trailblazer of Silk Road rediscovery was the Swede Sven Hedin, perhaps the greatest of all the explorers to Central Asia. Fluent in seven languages and tutored by Ferdinand von Richthofen, the German geographer who in 1877 had coined the phrase "Silk Road" (Seidenstrassen), it was Hedin's three ground-breaking expeditions in the 1890s into the heart of the Taklamakan that proved travel in Chinese Turkestan was possible. But his expeditions regularly left a trail of dead camels, ponies and assistants in their wake.

Hedin's first expedition was a disaster that claimed several lives, and nearly his own. In February 1895, after a winter crossing of the Pamirs that included a failed summit attempt on 7,546-metre (24,75-ft) Muztagh Ata, 29-year-old Hedin travelled to the Yarkand River and set off into the desert equipped with a mobile larder of animals and more than 1,000 photographic plates tied to the sides of several camels. Two weeks later the expedition was dying of thirst, jettisoning baggage left and right in a desperate race to find water. One guide lost consciousness after drinking camel's urine, while Hedin himself became temporarily paralysed after drinking primus fuel. After six days without water, two men and all the camels except one were dead and all the surveying equipment lost.

Not one to let a near-death experience slow him down, Hedin set out again in 1899 for three months through the Taklamakan Desert on a boat up the Yarkand and Tarim rivers, before continuing on foot for three weeks across the desert to Cherchen and Lop Nur. Here he unearthed the Chinese garrison town of Loulan (Kroraina), lost to barbarians in the 4th century and already under the sands for a millennium by the time Marco Polo passed through in 1275.

Hedin returned to a knighthood, gold medals from the Royal Geographical Society and a fame that was compounded by subsequent trips across the Trans-Himalaya to map the headwaters of the Indus and Bhramaputra in western Tibet. By the time of his death in 1952, however, his achievements were largely forgotten, replaced by notoriety for his pro-German stance in both world wars.

For all his achievements, Hedin was an explorer and a geographer – "The scientific research I willingly left to others." The detailed unearthing of the Silk Road was left to the archaeologists, foremost among them Marc Aurel Stein.

Aurel Stein

In many ways Marc Aurel Stein is the father of Central Asian archaeology. Inspired by the journeys of Alexander the Great and Xuanzang (see page 57), the British-Hungarian scholar, archaeologist and cartographer mounted three great expeditions to Chinese Turkestan over the course of 16 years, racking up an estimated 40,000km (25,000 miles) of travel. His first journey, from Kashmir in 1900, was described as "the most daring and adventurous raid upon the ancient world that any archaeologist has attempted".

Accompanied by his terrier Dash, he battled sandstorms and frostbite (the toes of his right foot were amputated after a surveying trip to the Kunlun Mountains), navigating the Taklamakan sands with the aid of Hedin's maps and excavating at remote sites for weeks at a time. Hedin proved you could travel to Turkestan, and Stein proved you could excavate there.

After an inauspicious start in Khotan where he found nothing but "complete decay and utter desolation", the incredible first trip revealed the cities of Dandan Oilik, Niya, Endere, Karadong and Rawok. At Dandan Oilik he dug through 2 metres (8ft) of sand to unearth Gandharan-style temple frescoes and a 5th–6th-century Buddhist library. At Niya his discovery of Greek-influenced images of Athena, Heracles and Eros proved cultural links with Bactria, while documents in Kharoshthi script tied the Southern Silk Road sites firmly to the Indian cultural sphere. Writing up notes in his tent late into the night until the ink in his pen froze, it was Stein who invented the term "Serindia" (from Seres, or Land of Silk) to describe the unique mix of Chinese, Indian and Gandharan styles that characterised Southern Silk Road art.

ABOVE, FROM LEFT: Sven Hedin on a camel; Aurel Stein in the field together with his guide and his terrier Dash.

At Rawok, north of Khotan, he discovered a huge stupa half-buried in 8 metres (25ft) of sand. Over nine days he unearthed 91 Gandharan-style statues, only to rebury them. Five years later he returned to the site to find that tomb-raiders had smashed the statues in the hope of finding gold inside.

Stein sent his treasures back to George Macartney, the British Consul-General in Kashgar. Over the years Macartney's residence, Chini Bagh, became a clearinghouse for Serindian art, arranging discrete shipment and logistical support for Stein and others. Eight ponies carried the 12 crates of treasure over the mountain passes to Osh

THE FORGER OF KHOTAN

One of the great archaeological hoaxes in history was perpetrated by Islam Akhun, an Uighur from Khotan. After years of duping European experts with his forged documents and scripts, Akhun came clean only after being confronted by Aurel Stein in Khotan in 1901. The enterprising forger would stain his documents with local tree dye and hang them over a fire to age them, finally adding sprinkles of sand for authenticity. Demand became so great that he had to block-print entire texts. By the time Stein exposed the fraud the documents were in museums across Europe, fooling the finest philologists and orientalists in their fields.

and Andijan, where they were placed on a train to Russia. News of Stein's finds preceded him, and by the time he returned to Europe the secret of Turkestan's lost cities was out.

The Germans

Spurred on by Stein's success and Klementz's reports, in 1902 the Germans launched the first of four expeditions to the relatively accessible oasis of Turpan. Over the next decade the expedition leaders Albert Grünwedel and Albert von Le Coq would send back 34 tonnes of antiquities to Berlin in 423 crates, including over 40,000 fragments of manuscripts.

At the time of the first expedition (1902–3) even getting to Central Asia took more than seven months, first by Trans-Siberian train, then steamer up the Irtysh River, and then by carriage to Urumqi, with von Le Coq sitting astride 12,000 roubles in gold (the expedition funds), brandishing a shotgun. The first expedition worked on Karakhoja (modern Gaochang), with modest results. Grünwedel was ill for the second expedition and leadership passed to von Le Coq, a museum volunteer and former wine merchant who had changed careers in mid-life to study Arabic, Turkish, Persian and Sanskrit. The string of breathtaking finds that followed included a Nestorian church and a 1.8-metre (6-ft) fresco of Manes (the founder of Manichaeism), the first

such portrait ever found. Other finds included cloth paintings, further frescoes, illuminated manuscripts (including a Christian prayer book in Persian) and manuscripts in 24 different scripts, as well as the murdered corpses of 100 Buddhist monks.

It was Bezeklik ("Place of Paintings") that yielded the greatest finds, including six wall-sized Buddhist portraits and 15 giant murals of the Buddha. The chance discovery of the Bezeklik murals was a classic moment of Silk Road rediscovery. Von Le Coq's response to such splendour was to hack away at the straw-and-mud walls, cutting the largest frescoes into pieces and packing them with reeds and cotton wool to transport them back to Germany. It was a move that would later make the blood of Chinese scholars "boil with indignation".

By the time of the second German expedition in 1906 the race was really heating up, as rival international groups staked their claims. Stein was about to return, and the Russians and French (relative latecomers due to their excavations at Angkor in the French Protectorate of Cambodia) were both planning expeditions. Such was the heightened rivalry that Russian and German archaeological teams almost came to blows over the division of excavation rights in Kuqa.

The Germans headed straight for the Ming-oi or "1,000-chambered" cave temples of Kumtura and Kizil, on the Muzart River near Kuqa. At one stage, scraping off an inch of white mould, the team revealed a row of incredible 1,500-year-old Hellenistic images painted in a distinct Kuqan style. To this day the Kizil frescoes remain a highlight of Central Asian art and the Germans' greatest discovery. "What I have seen here", Grünwedel was moved to declare, "goes beyond my wildest dreams."

Tensions grew between von Le Coq and Grünwedel, who disagreed strongly over the cutting and removing of frescoes, but the expedition was immensely successful, amassing some 128 cases of treasures. It was such a haul that it was to be six years before they returned to Central Asia.

The discovery of Dunhuang

Back in Kashgar in 1907, a departing von Le Coq missed the arrival of his rival Stein by less than a week. For his second expedition Stein entered Central Asia through the Pamirs on what would be a two-and-a-half-year expedition, recounted in his book *Ruins of Desert Cathay*.

Stein's first target was Loulan, remotest of the desert sites. Travelling by night to avoid the heat, his caravan included 50 labourers and 25 camels, most of which were to carry huge blocks of ice for drinking water. Stein's analysis of documents and rubbish at Loulan revealed it as an outpost so remote that it was still paying a tribute in the name of an empire that had ceased to exist 14 years previously. Stein also found Hedin's measuring tape, which he returned to him at an RGS dinner in London.

From Loulan, Stein headed to Miran to uncover some fabulous murals, including one of classical winged angels signed by the Roman-sounding artist "Titus". He packed these off to Kashgar, two months' travel away, and headed for his most important discovery yet.

Rumours had long been echoing down the Silk Road about the cave complex at Dunhuang. Stein had heard of it from a Hungarian geological expedition who visited in 1879. Albert von Le Coq had considered visiting from Hami in 1905 and spun a coin to decide; it landed tails up and he returned to Kashgar. Stein arrived at Dunhuang in March 1907 to find the self-appointed guardian Abbot Wang (Wang Yuanlu) away. While killing time he discovered a series of watchtowers that he believed formed an extension of the Great Wall, and located the famous Jade Gate, or Yumen, through which all Silk Road traffic had passed for centuries. Stein had to tread slowly to placate the nervous Abbot Wang, but finally won him over with their shared appreciation of Xuanzang. As Wang revealed the walled-up cave (Cave 17), filled with texts and hidden for 1,000 years, Stein wrote:

"The sight disclosed in the dim light of the priest's oil lamp made my eyes open wide. Heaped up in layers, but without any order, there appeared a solid mass of manuscript bundles rising to a height of nearly 10 feet and filling, as subsequent measurement showed, close on 500 cubic feet."

Stein bundled up 24 cases of documents and five cases of rare Tang paintings and secured the purchase of the priceless documents for £130. Among the 13,000 documents brought back to the British Museum was the *Diamond Sutra*, a giant scroll dating back to AD 868, making it the world's oldest dated printed book. Linguists

ABOVE, FROM LEFT: Albert von Le Coq on an expedition; Abbot Wang of Dunhuang.

"Suddenly, as if by magic, I saw on the walls bared in this way, to my right and left, splendid paintings in colours as fresh as if the artist had only just finished them."
Von Le Coq on the Kizil frescoes

spent the next 50 years translating the estimated 32km (20 miles) of scrolls. It was an archaeological scoop that would later be compared with the discovery of the Dead Sea scrolls.

Stein's finds in Dunhuang were incredible, but his inability to read Chinese was a

severe hindrance. The brilliant (and Chinese-speaking) 29-year-old French linguist Paul Pelliot faced no such handicap when he arrived at the caves a year later, unaware that Stein had already visited. He spent three weeks in the tiny cave reading by candlelight through the remaining 20,000 manuscripts and sifting out the cream of the crop, which he then purchased for £90. Amongst Pelliot's finds was a 14-page section of *The Record to Five Indian Kingdoms*, a hitherto lost text by Hwi Chao, the Korean equivalent of Xuanzang who travelled through Turkestan to India from AD 713 to 741. Back in Beijing at the end of his two-year trip on horseback, Pelliot revealed some of the documents to local Chinese scholars, and orders were finally sent to seal up the caves. Pelliot had effectively closed the door on Dunhuang.

End games

As news of the spectacular finds from Dunhuang reached Europe, great rivalry came to the fore, and the race turned into an archaeological free-for-all. The British labelled their rival Japanese archaeologists as spies and shadowed them for more than a year. The Russians were also back, rediscovering the fortress citadel of Karakhoto (Black City) in 1908, while the 1909 and 1914 expeditions of Sergei Oldenburg, Russia's foremost Buddhist expert, explored more sites around

Turpan and Kuqa. Moreover, by 1913 the Germans had returned, excavating once more at Kuqa and the important artistic centre of Kumtara. The following year Stein returned to Dunhuang to grab another five cases of documents, before continuing to Karakhoto, Bezeklik and finally the 5th-century tombs of Astana, where he carefully removed silks from dozens of 1,000-year-old corpses in an attempt to date them and trace the spread of silk designs across Central Asia.

Yet the times were changing. The Germans were forced to return early in 1914 due to the threat of war in Europe, and never returned to Central Asia. Hedin and Stein (then aged 67) both returned to Central Asia after World War I, but their expeditions were largely failures. China was by this time racked by political instability (every member of Hedin's team was issued with 800 rounds of ammunition), and foreign archaeologists were no longer welcomed. Only the American Langdon Warner, the Harvard professor who was a model for Indiana Jones, scored some success, travelling in 1923–4 to Karakhoto and Dunhuang, where he removed a dozen 8th-century cave murals in their entirety. But the world was now quite a different place, and the Chinese were about to slam shut the door. The race for Turkestan's treasures was over.

Soviet archaeology

Unknown to most Westerners, archaeologists from the newly formed Soviet Union were quietly unearthing some spectacular sites. One highlight was the discovery of the ancient Parthian capital of Nissa, in modern-day Turkmenistan,

COUNTRIES WITHIN COUNTRIES

Although Tsarist Russia had begun colonising Central Asia in the 1890s, it was Stalin whose political policies were to have greatest regional impact. In creating new Soviet Socialist Republics (SSRs), he implemented a set of borders based on ethnic lines rather than cultural or geographical ones, and these ultimately became the borders of the new independent republics in 1991.

In practice this made no sense: ethnic communities did not live in discreet blocks and often intermarried. Consequently, the border lines wriggled between villages, including some fields and houses but not others. Enclaves and exclaves were created, regardless of whether or not they were entirely surrounded by

someone else's sovereign territory. There are four Uzbek exclaves in Kyrgyzstan alone, and another two belonging to Tajikistan. Kyrgyzstan too has exclaves in Uzbekistan and Tajikistan.

Stalin's border policy in Central Asia was one of divide and rule: he understood that constant border skirmishes between the various states would ensure ongoing instability in the region, preventing the states joining together (for example on the grounds of shared culture or religion) and challenging Moscow. In this respect, the policy was a great success: the Fergana Valley, where most of the enclaves are found, is the least stable part of Central Asia.

where digs revealed 40 ivory *rhytons* (drinking horns) and fragments of a marble Aphrodite.

Sergei Tolstov's later excavations in the wasteland of Khorezm between 1948 and 1957 revealed a rich oasis culture dating from the 7th century BC and centred around the desert castles of Toprak Qala and Koy Krylgan Qala. Focus then shifted to the spectacular Sogdian friezes of Penjikent, Varakhsha and Afrosiab.

In Turkmenistan the Greek-Russian archaeologist Victor Sarianidi has been excavating for half a century to reveal the civilisation of ancient Margiana. In the sun-baked mud flats of Gonur Tepe he brought to light a 5,000-year-old temple, palace and necropolis that may mark the birthplace of the Zoroastrian religion.

Unearthing Afghanistan's past

Archaeology in neighbouring Afghanistan had a relatively late start. Aurel Stein had long wanted to excavate in Balkh, but it was the French Archaeological Delegation in Afghanistan (FADA) that finally gained permission in the 1920s to excavate the country's rich trove of Bactrian and Kushan sites. Their most famous discovery was the 2,000-year old Begram Treasure, unearthed in 1937–9. At the junction of the Indian, Chinese and Greek worlds, the Kushan-era court epitomised the cosmopolitanism of the Silk Road, with finds ranging from Indian ivories and Hellenistic bronzes to Graeco-Roman glassware.

The French followed this 30 years later with the Greek city of Ai Khanoum ("Alexandria on the Oxus"); the 2,300-year-old palace complex revealed Corinthian capitals and a statue of Heracles.

Recent finds

One of the great finds of recent years was the discovery in 1978 of six royal Bactrian/Kushan tombs at Tillya Tepe, near Sheberghan on the bank of the Oxus (Amu Darya). Over the course of nine years archaeologist Victor Sarianidi's "Golden Hoard of Bactria" has totalled 22,000 gold objects, from necklaces and bracelets to buckles and brooches in Greek and Scythian styles, alongside Indian ivories, Parthian coins and Chinese mirrors. The find was rushed to Kabul Museum in 1979 to an uncertain future.

ABOVE, FROM LEFT: Paul Pelliot inspecting scrolls at the Mogao Caves, Dunhuang (Cave 17); Russian archaeologist Sarianidi at work in Afghanistan.

Remarkably it survived, though Afghanistan's quarter-decade of civil war has taken a terrible toll on its museums and cultural heritage. The Taliban destruction of the Buddhas of Bamiyan in 2001 marked a low point in Silk Road archaeology, but Afghan archaeologist Zemaryali Tarzi claims to have found the fabled third Buddha of Bamiyan, a 300-metre (1,000-ft) -long sleeping Buddha mentioned by Xuanzang and thought to be east of the destroyed Buddhas.

The 1994 discovery of Djumbulak Kum, an unknown 2,000-year-old fortified city, showed that even the deserts of Xinjiang have yet to reveal all of their secrets.

HEROES OR THIEVES?

While fêted at home as heroes, archaeologists like Stein, Pelliot and von Le Coq are viewed by most Chinese scholars as thieves. Accusations of exploitation are hard to avoid. At one point von Le Coq swapped rotten berries for a pile of priceless manuscripts, claiming the berries held rejuvenative powers. Even Stein privately described von Le Coq and his assistant as "little more than treasure-hunters". Archaeologists' claims to be safeguarding finds for posterity suffered a direct hit in World War II when seven Allied bombs struck Berlin's Ethnographical Museum and 28 of the Bezeklik murals were destroyed.

TREASURES OF THE SILK ROAD

A treasure-trove of manuscripts, murals and artefacts reveals a great deal about daily life centuries ago.

A century of excavations along the length of the Silk Road have resulted in a spectacular array of finds, from stirringly beautiful 1,000-year-old desert murals to glittering caches of gold.

The Buddhist frescoes of Xinjiang and Gansu remain perhaps the most visually impressive, with frescoes from Bezeklik, Kyzil and especially Dunhuang most clearly illustrating the quintessential Silk Road blurring of styles – Greek, Indian and Chinese – that would eventually be termed Serindian or Gandharan art.

Less visual but perhaps more important historically are the contemporary documents that remain so vital in dating and contextualising the surrounding finds. The earliest documents were on birch bark or wooden tablets (paper did not find its way from China until AD 100). Equally fascinating are the mundane scraps recovered from ancient rubbish tips (everything from bills of sale and correspondence to ancient mousetraps), that offer revealing insights into daily life two millennia ago.

The spectacular caches of gold that signify royal tombs across the continent remain something of a mixed blessing. Though beautiful, it was the lure of these highlights of applied art that drove tomb-raiders and looters to ransack so many stupas and tombs in their search for treasure.

The real work of deciphering the Silk Road finds began back at home. Academics at the British Museum took 50 years to work their way through Stein's Dunhuang documents, and some silks were so fragile that it took seven years to open them! Research continues to this day.

TOP: a griffin-headed bracelet from the Oxus Treasure, a 5th-century BC collection of gold and silver discovered on the borders of modern Tajikistan and Afghanistan in 1877.

TOP: mural from the caves at Bezeklik depicting Uighur princes wearing Chinese-style robes and headgear, dating from 8th–9th centuries.

ABOVE: the Mogao Caves at Dunhuang represent the richest collection of Buddhist statuary, paintings and manuscripts ever discovered. This coloured-ink illuminated manuscript shows Marici, the Buddhist Goddess of Light, and her two servants.

LEFT: the Buddhas at Bamiyan were long one of the great treasures of the Silk Road, despite defacement by iconoclasts. They were finally toppled by the Taliban in 2001.

ONLINE TREASURES

It's surprisingly difficult to view the major art collections of the Silk Road. London's British Museum and British Library, Paris' Guimet Musée, Berlin's Museum of Indian Art, Tokyo's National Museum and Stockholm's Ethnographical Museum all have excellent collections, but only a fraction of these are on view at any one time.

Digital technology is now at the forefront of Silk Road research, and online collections present the best opportunity to view Central Asia's treasures up close.

Visitors to the British Museum's website (www.british museum.org) can view an online collection of paintings from Dunhuang. The British Library website (www.bl.uk) also has an online Silk Road feature, and even offers a 3D viewing of the Diamond Sutra (click on "Turning the Pages"). The new Silk Road Museum in Jiuquan has an excellent online collection showing artefacts excavated along the Silk Road dating from pre-history to the Ming and Qing dynasties (www.silkroutemuseum.com/).

The website of Silk Road Seattle (http://depts.washington.edu/silkroad) is particularly useful for its links and overview of all the major Silk Road collections, including the wonderful Turfan (Turpan) collection.

Other sites include the Digital Silk Road Project (http://dsr.nii.ac.jp) the groundbreaking International Dunhuang Project (http://idp.bl.uk), which has a database of 100,000 digitised documents.

ABOVE: Bactrian gold from Tillya Tepe. Uncovered in 1979 in Northern Afghanistan, the Bactrian Hoard (1st century BC) was presumed looted until it resurfaced in Kabul in 2003.

TOP: frontispiece of the Diamond Sutra, the world's oldest book. Dating from 868 AD, it was discovered in Dunhuang and is now in the British Library.

LEFT: murals found at the Sogdian city of Penjikent in Tajikistan include this depiction of Rustam, the supreme hero of Firdausi's *Shahnameh*.

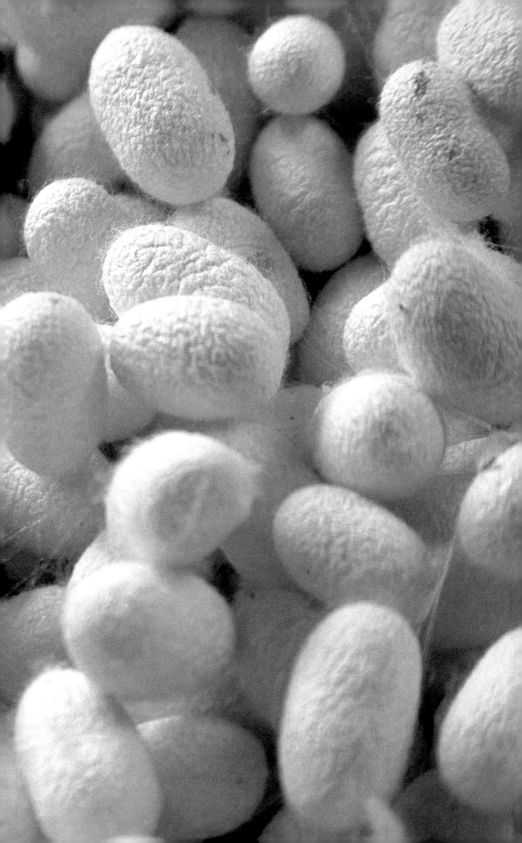

THE STORY OF SILK

The luxurious material that gave its name to the Silk Road has been in high demand for thousands of years. Who would have thought a tiny caterpillar, the *Bombyx mori*, could have created such a fuss?

No matter where you travel, you can find silk, a fabric that is as luxurious and desirable today as when it was discovered in China thousands of years ago. It is one of nature's most remarkable creations, and no man-made fibre has ever been found to challenge its supremacy.

Silk is a protein fibre produced by silkworms and akin to the spun filaments of spiders' webs, which are produced in a similar way. Silkworms are caterpillars of the order Lepidoptera (butterflies and moths). All Lepidoptera produce silk, but none can match the lustrous, long fibre created by *Bombyx mori*, a Chinese domesticated species that dominates silk production worldwide. Selectively bred over thousands of years, *Bombyx*

> "Patience is power; with time and patience the mulberry leaf becomes a silk gown."
> Chinese proverb

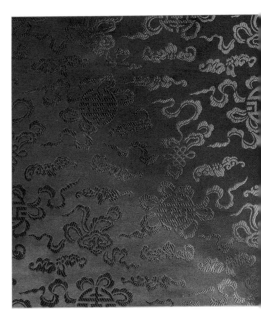

mori has evolved into a species of blind moth that can flap its wings but cannot fly. Its only impulse is to reproduce. The female moth waits for her suitors to scent her pheromones and trundle towards her to fulfil their destiny, ensuring the next generation of silk-producing caterpillars.

All Lepidoptera pass through the same stages of metamorphosis: egg (also called grain), caterpillar, chrysalis and adult. The eggs require an initial period of cold incubation, and usually hatch 6–12 weeks after being laid. Normally this coincides with the freshest supply of mulberry leaves,

PRECEDING PAGES: cocoons, the source of all silk.
LEFT: drawing of a silk workshop, China, 18th century.
RIGHT: Chinese silk.

but scientists have also engineered other methods to bypass nature and maximise production.

Once hatched, the caterpillars start eating: cultivated silkworms increase their body weight 10,000 times in their 25- to 28-day lives. Their principal foodstuff is white mulberry, to which they are attracted by the odorant cis-jasmone, but they will also eat other plants of the Moraceae family such as Osage-orange. At first, the caterpillars spend more or less their whole lives eating. Periodically they sleep for about a day, wake up, wriggle out of their old skin and start eating again. After the final skin shedding, they cast a light web to anchor themselves. The caterpillar then rears up and moves its head in a figure-of-eight, as a liquid is extruded from two pairs of spinnerets or silk glands located below its mouth. The effect of air on the liquid solidifies it into a continual silk filament. Spinning a silk cocoon takes two to three days, and then the silk is secured by a gum called sericin. Once cocooned, the caterpillar can rest; its final caterpillar skin slips away and a chrysalis is formed.

When the adult moth is ready to emerge it will make a hole in the cocoon, but silk-makers do not want *Bombyx mori* cocoons to be broken, so the insects are stifled inside the cocoon either by steaming, baking or soaking in salt water. Then the sericin is removed by immersing the cocoons in hot water, while stirring constantly, to allow the unbroken silk filament to loosen. Then the cocoons are gathered, usually with revolving brushes, which pick up the end thread as it comes loose.

Depending on the thickness needed, the silk thread is twisted or plied with several others, and reeled for the next stage. Other silks have

THE EXTRAORDINARY QUALITIES OF SILK

- Silk is highly absorbent, which makes it easy to dye. This also means that it is an ideal material to wear, as it conducts moisture away from the body.
- Silk is nature's strongest natural fibre and has a high tensile strength. It is stronger than a filament of steel of equivalent dimensions. This means that silk threads do not yield to breaking and are even stronger if twisted (plied) round each other. Silk was used in making Concorde's nose, and the Tour de France spins along on silk tyres, which give a smoother ride and better traction.
- Silk threads can be stretched to 20–25 percent of their length, which makes them ideal for stockings.

Provided it is not overstretched, silk will recover its former shape immediately.
- Silk will fold or crush to extraordinary degrees. It can also be worn multi-layered.
- Woven, silk falls and drapes in ways particularly flattering to the human form, making it the fashion fabric par excellence.
- Pure silk is difficult to burn.
- Silk is hypo-allergenic. There are no known allergies to silk, which makes it extremely useful for surgical and medical purposes.
- Silk is a good insulator, and has been used for the insulation of electric wires.

different qualities and textures, but *Bombyx mori* silk is unique in that it can be reeled in this way, as a long, strong, continual filament.

Ancient silk production

Lady Xi Lingshi, chief wife of the Yellow Emperor, Qin Shi Huang, is revered as the Lady of the Silkworms and the inventor of sericulture. This was during the reign of the Yellow Emperor (2677–2597 BC). However, we know that silk-making was long established by then, as the oldest surviving silk fabric has been dated to the middle of the 4th millennium BC.

Cocoons were one of many natural fibres

and embroidered silks survives in the surface corrosion of ritual bronze vessels from the Shang period (*c.*1766–1400 BC), which were wrapped in precious silk. Shang literary sources are full of references to silk and sericulture; they even mention human sacrifices to a pantheon of silkworm deities to ensure good harvests of cocoons.

China guarded the secrets of sericulture for hundreds of years, and many colourful stories explain the dissemination of this knowledge, involving beautiful and resourceful princesses hiding silkworm eggs or cocoons in their hair when despatched to marry foreign princes. Chinese emigrants took sericulture to Korea around 200

explored to see what practical use they may have; the Chinese realised that one particular type of cocoon, made by the wild ancestor of *Bombyx mori*, had superior qualities, being smoother, finer and rounder than that of other silk moths, which produce irregular, flattened filaments. Flatter threads tangle easily, and break if unwound, whereas the rounder filament can be reeled as a long, continuous, stronger thread.

Archaeologists in China have found silkworms made of jade, inscribed oracle bones, and tools for all stages of textile production, including fine bone embroidery needles. Evidence of woven

ABOVE, FROM LEFT: the silk moth, *Bombyx mori*, emerges from a cocoon; silk is ideal for dyeing.

BC, and Chinese annals record silk fabrics in Japan from about 28 BC. A series of Japanese envoys visited the Chinese court, and in AD 188 the Japanese emperor received a gift of silkworm eggs, evidently not the first, from a Chinese ruler.

India's wild silks

India's history of silk production is also thousands of years old. Very early references to Indian silk usually indicate native moths, which produce silks of different textures and qualities from that of *Bombyx mori*. Silk found in the hair of an Egyptian mummy from the Ptolemaic period (around 300–30 BC) proved to be from one of the Indian Saturnidae moths, suggesting early export from the subcontinent, albeit on a small scale. Assam's Muga moths produce a distinctive golden-yellow silk, used undyed as embroidery threads, while silk woven from Assam's Eri moths is warm and durable, but it has short staple, which must be spun like cotton or wool. A certain amount of farming and domestication has been achieved to commercialise these silks, but they are not as easy to dye or bleach as *Bombyx mori*, and their rougher, more robust texture is referred to generally as "wild silk". But India also has truly wild silk, produced by huge caterpillars guarded in the forests by little boys with big sticks, who protect them against birds. Silk was deemed by Hindus to be a pure substance; the Jains, who abhor the taking of life, produce silk from broken cocoons.

Commercial silk trading

The earliest known exports of silk from China were gifts from the emperor to those who had served him well or with whom he wished to form an alliance. The beauty and exclusivity of the product quickly made it much sought after, and a commercial industry was born.

The first silk workshops were set up during the Han Dynasty (206 BC–AD 220); from the Han capital, silk was traded as far as Antioch on the Mediterranean, and eventually onwards by sea to Rome, where laws were enforced to try to control overspending on this luxury. Queen Zenobia founded the breakaway city-state of Palmyra around AD 270 to try to wrest control of the lucrative silk trade from Rome – surviving funerary statues of Palmyran high society, draped in jewels and swathed in silks, are reminders of this. Not all the silk that found its way west was woven. Silk yarn, to be dyed, woven and used as the ultimate embroidery thread, was also transported and traded.

By the beginning of the 3rd century AD, the Parthian Dynasty (in what is now Iran) was making huge profits from customs duties levied on silk and other goods transported along the Silk Road. The Parthians were defeated in AD 224 by the Sassanians, whose weavers developed their own highly distinctive silk designs. These so impressed the Tang Chinese (AD 618–906) that they began to imitate them. Preserved Tang silks display typically Sassanian designs, such as repeated registers of single or confronting birds or animals, often with a central tree or flowering element. Variations on this distinctive motif were echoed by Sogdian weavers in Central Asia.

Byzantine silk

Sassanian-ruled Persia provided Byzantium with its silk, but political problems around AD 550 obliged Roman Emperor Justinian to seek other solutions to fulfil Byzantine silk requirements. By this time, a chain of Nestorian monasteries stretched as far as China's heartland, so he despatched two monks whose mission was to return with whatever was necessary to start independent Byzantine sericulture. The monks returned carrying silkworm eggs packed in bamboo staves. At this time, Byzantine territories included Greater Syria, and it was here, and in the Morea (in modern Greece – *moria* is Greek for mulberry) that sericulture was established.

Silk and the Church

Silk production and trade in Byzantium and Christian Europe had a close connection with the Church, and was closely regulated by government decree. Clerics would wear silk garments, and altar cloths were made of silk. Sumptuary laws (which determined what people were entitled to wear according to their status) were important in maintaining the hierarchies of the imperial court and Church, and colour and design were an integral part of silk's symbolic status. "Royal purple" was the colour of Byzantium, a silk-ruled empire, and the best was obtained by Syrian dye masters from the murex shellfish, an industry developed by the Phoenicians. Syrian silk merchants were always accorded special privileges by the Byzantines. Byzantine rulers are depicted wearing silk garments with huge patterns, roundels containing lions, eagles, mounted heroes and heroic images, symbols seen also in older Near Eastern images.

Islamic influence

Following the tide of Islam that flooded out of the Middle East, sericulture and silk weaving was introduced into Spain in the 8th century, where new forms and patterns of silk weaving and embroidery developed. Sicily's conquest (*c.* 880) made it another centre of excellence for silk weaving. After the defeat of the Tang army by a Muslim army at the Battle of Talas in AD 751 (in present-day Kyrgyzstan), many skilled Chinese craftsmen and master weavers taken prisoner were sent to Iraq, where they taught local weavers their skills. The first dynasties of Islamic rule,

RIGHT: embroidery on silk.

> *"A silkworm spins all its silk until it dies, and a candle won't stop its tears until it is burnt out."* Tang poem.

the Umayyads in Damascus and the Abbasids in Baghdad, adopted the Sassanian *tiraz* system of textile production. This involved elegant calligraphy, and it became a feature of court silks and embroideries. Although under Islam the wearing of silk was not as restricted as in Byzantium or China, the *tiraz* robes of honour were made for caliphs and high-ranking nobles.

The Crusades brought exotic Near Eastern silks into European courts and churches. But the Fourth Crusade's sack of Constantinople (1202–4) ended the great silk tradition in Byzantium, although silks continued to be woven in Nicaea (present-day Iznik in northwest Turkey).

Pax Mongolica and Italian silks

Under the *Pax Mongolica* of the Yuan Dynasty (1260–1368), when the Silk Road was under the control of the Mongol Empire, Venetian explorer Marco Polo brought back "Tatar Cloths" from the Far East. The most sumptuous of these silks were embellished with gold thread manufactured by gilding fine strips of membrane or parchment. An important Mediterranean trading centre for these cloths was Ayas, on the coast of Turkey, then in Greater Armenia. They became readily available to Italian merchants, and later featured in Quattrocento paintings and sculptures. They inspired Italian weavers to incorporate Far Eastern motifs.

As the Silk Roads approached the eastern

> Information technology owes a lot to silk. Joseph-Marie Jacquard's silk-weaving loom, invented in 1801 using punchcards to make patterns, is seen as an important step in the development of computers.

Mediterranean, they multiplied – across Anatolia there were five main routes, and some 22 beautiful early Ottoman caravanserais still mark their transit. The Turkish tribes that settled in Anatolia were traditionally weaving cultures, and motifs from further east – dragons, phoenixes, lotus palmettes, sinuous cloudbands – infiltrated Seljuk, and subsequently Ottoman, patterns.

Genoa and Venice competed energetically for the eastern luxury trade, and the availability of raw silk and the inspiration of glorious woven fabrics during the Pax Mongolica gave fresh impetus to the fledgling Italian silk industry, which seems to have begun in Lucca. Skills and techniques were jealously guarded, and workers were forbidden to travel in case they revealed weaving secrets to a competitor. The city-states developed their own styles and specialities. Venetian silks, which reached their peak in the 15th century, can sometimes be identified by ship or boat designs. Undulating patterns with pomegranates and pine cones, bifurcating stems and small blossoms gave drama to silks woven in rich colours.

Silk designs

Under the Ottomans, Bursa in northwest Turkey became an important centre for imported silk, weaving, and eventually sericulture. After their conquest of Constantinople, the Ottomans adopted the Byzantine guild system to regulate all aspects of silk production and commerce, and produced a wide range of glorious silks, many worked with gold thread.

In Persia, under the Safavid Dynasty, the palette of silks was one of tender shades of pale peach, pinks, almond greens, ivory and shades of blue, silver and gold, in delicate

floral designs, with birds, butterflies and figures. Safavid silks include extraordinary figurative velvets and carpets.

Persian influence is also apparent in India, where Mughal looms adopted existing Indian techniques and patterns. Some Mughal rugs, with silk warps and wefts and pashmina pile, are so fine that they have been mistaken for velvets. Mughal style is predominantly floral, with underlying geometry. Though sharing common roots, each culture developed highly individual silks.

The most spectacular silks during this period incorporated gold and silver thread, and the most sumptuous are velvets woven in large-scale pat-

terns. Richest to the touch, the most extravagant velvet was a Venetian speciality, *alto-e-basso*, velvet cut in two or more levels. To make these lavish textiles required huge quantities of raw silk.

French fashion seasons

Sericulture in France began round the papal city of Avignon, and flourished in the nearby hills of the Cévennes until the mid-1850s when disease devastated the silkworm stock. Tours was an important early centre, but Lyons became the silk-weaving heart of France. In 1667 Colbert, Louis XIV's Minister of Finance, directed manufacturers to produce new patterns on a regular basis, and by the end of the 17th century fresh designs were introduced twice a year. This led directly to the development of the fashion trade, and the twice-yearly showing of collections, which continues today.

Religious strife in Europe resulted in the arrival in England of Huguenot refugees. Many were weavers, and attempts were made to introduce sericulture, as well as silk weaving, to Britain. Silk weaving flourished, and Spitalfields silks, known as "flowered silks", became fashionable.

Silk production today

The first imperial silk workshops were established in Sichuan and Shandong. These tra-

Silk today is produced and processed by more than 30 countries, and despite its high value accounts for just 0.2 percent of the global textile fibre market. Como is the silk centre of Italy, Europe's main producer country, processing raw material imported from the East. China produces more than 80 percent of the world's silk, employing more than a million workers. The country's silk production is around US$10.88 billion a year, and silk exports exceed US$4 billion. Both China and Japan are the main suppliers for *Bombyx mori* eggs, and silkworm technology is a thriving science.

ditional Chinese silk-producing regions have retained importance but whereas once, vast mulberry orchards were needed to furnish supplies of fresh leaves to feed the voracious caterpillars, and production was restricted and seasonal, now genetically modified bushes produce four consecutive harvests of fresh leaves. Japanese scientists have also produced a synthetic diet, based on powdered mulberry leaves, soya beans and cornstarch, which contains the necessary ingredients for nourishment and growth, so that caterpillars, and thus silk, can be produced year-round.

ABOVE, FROM LEFT: spools of shiny silk; weaving silk on a handloom.

SILK MUSEUMS

China National Museum of Silk, Hangzhou, the largest silk museum in the world.
France Musée des Tissus, Lyon, www.musee-des-tissus.com
India Silk Museum of India, Navsari. www.silkmuseumnavsari.com
Italy Museo Didattico della Seta, Como, at the centre of modern silk manufacture. www.museosetacomo.com
Japan Yokohama Silk Museum, silkmuseum.org.jp
Lebanon B'sous Museum www.thesilkmuseum.com
UK Silk Museum, Macclesfield, Cheshire. www.silkmacclesfield.org.uk

SILK PRODUCTION

How extraordinary it is that the filament spun by an unprepossessing caterpillar should be responsible for the world's favourite fabric.

Nowadays the majority of silk is made in large factories and most of these are in China. However, it is still possible to see traditional methods of weaving along the Silk Road. The two best-known places are at Khotan in Xinjiang, where there are a number of small factories spinning and weaving silk, and Margilan in the Fergana Valley, where visitors are welcome to tour the Yodgorlik Factory. In addition to these, from Xi'an to Istanbul there are numerous small-scale producers – artisan cooperatives in Bukhara and Khiva, for example, that produce beautiful hand-made silk carpets.

Whether large or small scale, the same fundamental principles are used to produce a silk item. The cocoon is produced by the *Bombyx mori* silkworm (see page 85) after it spends its short life munching mulberry leaves. The cocoon itself consists of a single filament of raw silk up to 1,000 metres (3,000ft) long. However, the individual filaments are very thin, and so they must be twisted together with other filaments to produce a silk thread. To draw out the silk successfully, the thread must be reeled smoothly and consistently – too fast and the silk breaks, too slow and it sticks to itself and becomes tangled. A form of Chinese exercise called "silk reeling" involves movements made in continuous, cyclic patterns performed at a steady speed with the same light touch needed to reel silk.

It takes approximately 5,000 silkworms to produce a pure silk kimono (the traditional garment of Japan, which literally translates as "something worn" in English). Roughly 110 cocoons are needed to make a man's tie, and 630 for a woman's blouse.

TOP: the mulberry tree provides food for the voracious *Bombyx mori*.

ABOVE RIGHT: the silk worm in its fourth instar (stage of development), now about 10,000 times heavier than when it first hatched.

ABOVE: cocoons being harvested from mulberry branches in Uzbekistan. They will be taken to the factory to be sorted according to quality, size and colour. The actual cultivation of silkworms in Uzbekistan and elsewhere is a cottage industry, with individual farmers selling their produce on to massive state-run factories.

ABOVE: an Uighur woman completes the reeling process in Khotan.

LEFT: this is the start of the reeling process at the traditional Yodgorlik Silk Factory in Margilan, Uzbekistan, where the cocoons are immersed in hot water to kill the silkworms and make the cocoons easier to unwind. The filaments from several different cocoons are then combined to produce a silk thread.

ABOVE: ikat-weaving with pre-dyed warp, very popular in Uzbekistan.

NOT THE REAL THING

As the world's most expensive fabric, silk has long had its imitators. It was not until the 19th century that these began showing any signs of success, with such inventions as the electric light filament developed by Joseph Swann. In 1892, a patent was taken out for viscose made from wood or cotton fibres by the French Count de Chardonnet, and in the 1920s viscous rayon, the first man-made fibre, was produced in France from polymers derived from wood pulp. The technology was bought a decade later by the DuPont Company of America, who went on to develop nylon, made from polymers, which became a substitute for silk stockings. Cut off from Asian silk during World War II, the Americans also put nylon to military use, as a substitute material for silk in tyres and parachutes.

Today, artificial silks can be made in a variety of ways. Fake silk rugs are often made from cotton that has been mercerised, a process that strengthens the fibre and adds lustre. To tell the genuine article from an artificial one takes a practised eye. Real silk is warmer to the touch, is more tightly woven and, if you care to set fire to a piece, will turn into an ashen ball and smell like burning hair.

BELOW: the start of silk production in a modern factory.

LIFE ON THE ROAD

Silk Road travel took place in stages, with goods changing hands from local merchant to local merchant. Yet journeys were still long and comforts few, factors which helped to make the bazaars and caravanserais – oases of life amid the barren desert – among the most exciting places on earth.

Trading along the Silk Road in either direction was no small undertaking, whether for small-scale trader or merchant prince. The road was tough, often beset by bandits or dangerous animals, and suffered extremes of weather.

Along the road there was greater safety in numbers, and travellers would wait in urban centres or even at remote caravanserais to join major caravans that might include hundreds or even thousands of camels and horses, perhaps accompanied by armed guards. As well as merchants, possibly with their families, servants and translators, there were many specialists, including camel-drivers, doctors and vets, local guides, cooks and guards. Journeys could last for weeks or months, with the precise distance covered per day liable to the availability of water and the exigencies of the weather, nomadic raiders and local politics.

Merchant caravans were often joined by private individuals, whether itinerant traders, monks and religious teachers, entertainers moving between urban centres, adventurers or even criminals and escaped slaves. Musicians would travel east from Persia and Sogdiana, Khotan and Kuqa, while some travelled west from China into Central Asia, adding to the sounds of the journey, and though their songs are lost to us, we can see from murals and paintings the kind of instruments they played. Because of this mix of people, as well as for purposes of taxation, regulation and promoting peaceful

commerce, passports and other forms of *laissez passer* were issued by various authorities, notably at times of dynastic strength. Again, only under the Mongols would a single pass, issued by the appropriate authority, have sufficed for the entire length of the Silk Road – and then only briefly. Examples of such bronze passports *(paizi)*, looking rather like medals, survive today; engraved in a special Mongol script called Phags-pa commissioned by Kublai Khan in 1269, these passports guaranteed unimpeded passage for diplomats and other official travellers throughout the vast Mongol realm. Marco Polo was issued with one of these on his journeys in the service of the Great Khan.

LEFT: The Departing Caravan, by Herman David Salomon. **RIGHT:** Samarkand's golden peach was highly valued at the Tang court.

Merchandise

Although the Silk Road owes its name to the most significant article of merchandise to travel its entire length, in fact hundreds of different products were constantly on the move, carried on pack animals and traded at the markets en route. Other exports heading westwards included ceramics, bronze artefacts, spices and medicinal herbs. This meant that the caravaneers needed something similarly valuable to carry back in the other direction. Due to the difficulty and expense of long-distance commerce, and because of the challenging terrain, such goods needed to be light, compact, rare and

GOLDEN PEACHES OF SAMARKAND

The American Sinologist Joseph Fletcher (1934–84) made the "Golden Peaches of Samarkand" symbolic of the trade in Tang exotica, choosing them as "deputies and proxies of all exotic goods in medieval China" because "they suggest, simultaneously, the Golden Apples of the Hesperides, the Peaches of Immortality believed by Chinese tradition to flourish in the far west, and James Elroy Flecker's poem *Golden Journey to Samarkand*. The peaches were sent by the Kingdom of Samarkand as gifts to the Chinese court. According to the Tang annals, "They were as large as goose eggs, and their colour was like gold."

valuable. Ideally, to suit such sophisticated and demanding tastes as those of the Tang court, they also needed to be both precious and exotic.

Exotic food

The Golden Peaches of Samarkand may have been deemed "royal", but they were far from the only exotic fruits and foodstuffs valued by the emperors' court. Dates, unknown in China, were brought dried and sugared from the Middle East, while watermelons from Khorezm (in what is now Uzbekistan) and honeydew melons from Hami were transported east, preserved in lead containers packed with ice from the Tian Shan. Still more valued were the "mare-teat grapes" of Kuqa, brought east and planted at Chang'an in around AD 640. Grapes were a novelty to the Tang, a society that produced many types of alcohol from rice and other grains, but which soon learnt to plant vineyards and produce wine.

Pine seeds were imported, peeled and eaten as exotic snacks, as were pistachio nuts, which were not only deemed tasty, but thought to enhance male sexual vigour. Little cakes of sugar known as "stone honey" came from Bukhara and Samarkand, while both black pepper and long peppers, known by their Sanskrit name *pippali*, travelled overland from India. In the case of the latter, the annals comment: "Westerners bring it to us; we use it for its flavour, to put in food." Quite different was the betel pepper, also a highly valued product from the West, considered by Tang pharmacists to be "a tonic for loins and legs, and a digestive aid to abolish coldness in the stomach".

Aromatics, too, were carried to Chang'an. These included a scented resin called storax from Parthia – long thought by the Chinese to be dried lion's dung – gum guggul and benzoin from Gandhara, and myrrh and frankincense from southern Arabia and distant Somalia. The value of these rare substances was greatly increased by traversing the Arabian Incense Road between Yemen and Damascus even before starting the long journey east along the Silk Road to Chang'an.

Caravans travelling from west to east took gems, gold and other precious metals, ivory, amber and coral, as well as opium from the Middle East, which was introduced as a medicine in China 1,500 years before the West began pushing it as a narcotic.

> "When I drink this wine, I am instantly con-
> scious of harmony suffusing my four limbs.
> It is the true Prince of Grand Tranquillity."
> Emperor Muzong (821–4)

Distant Khorezm (Uzbekistan) exported to China prized furs including sable, ermine, fox and marten. Rhubarb, too, came from the northwest; its root was highly regarded as a bowel tonic. Less valuable, but also transported east from the Hexi Corridor and Mongolia, came horsehides for use in making armour, and small coracle-like craft

Beasts of burden

Goods moved slowly across Asia, travelling about 40km (25 miles) a day, the distance typically covered by a fully loaded camel in about eight hours, depending on the terrain. On the flatter sections, camel-drawn carts would also be used. Few caravans – if, indeed, any – would have completed the entire journey between Chang'an and the Mediterranean. Instead, goods were moved in stages, passing through the hands of different caravan-drivers and on the backs of different beasts of burden from oasis to oasis, each transfer of ownership increasing the cost to the purchaser and enrich-

used on the Huang He and other rivers of north China. Sacred objects, such as Buddha images, relics and, of course, religious treatises and books of secular knowledge also entered China by caravan from the west and especially, via the passes across the Pamirs, from India to the south.

Among the most extraordinary examples of imported Tang exotica were ostrich eggs, sometimes set in precious metal and used as drinking vessels. The Chinese regarded ostriches – which they called "camel-birds" – with awe, believing they could run 500km (300 miles) in a day, fuelled by a diet of copper and iron.

ing local merchants and transport guilds.

Perhaps the most important beasts of burden employed in the caravan trade were camels, which could be ridden by merchants and caravaneers, as well as being used to carry valuable trade goods. Far to the west, in the warmer lands of Syria and Mesopotamia, the single-humped dromedary was preferred, while in Central Asia and western China, harsh landscapes that endure long and bitter winters, the double-humped Bactrian was the camel of choice.

Caravans also employed asses, mules and even cattle to carry goods, depending on the nature of the terrain. Large, fierce caravan dogs were valued, both to help drive off predatory

ABOVE, FROM LEFT: dates from the Middle East; a halt in the desert.

wildlife such as leopards and cheetahs, and to deter sneak-thieves or warn of approaching groups of bandits. In the coldest and highest regions yaks might also be used as beasts of burden, notably in the mountains of Badakhsan and the Pamirs, across the Qinghai tablelands and on the icy Tibetan plateau.

Domestic animals

Domestic animals also formed an important part of the trade between west and east. The Chinese particularly valued the horses of Central Asia, and especially of the Fergana Valley (see page 247), which they exchanged for silk, but they

> "On large roads guards were posted at junctions to safeguard communications. Travellers and merchants had the right to demand that their wealth and belongings should be escorted by these guards, who were held responsible for any loss." Amir Timur.

also imported Bactrian camels, asses and sheep from the plains of Central Asia. Particularly swift and dependable camels were assigned to an official called "Emissary of the Bright Camel", and used to carry the imperial mail. Other highly

CAMELS, THE ESSENTIAL TRANSPORT

There are two kinds of camel. The dromedary, also known as the one-humped or Arabian camel, has a single hump and is native to the dry desert and upland areas of Western Asia. It was domesticated in the 3rd millennium BC and traditionally plied the trade routes in Iran, Iraq and Syria. The two-humped Bactrian camel is from Central Asia, where its long hair insulates it from the cold during the night and reflects the sunlight by day. The Bactrian, which was domesticated about 2,500 years ago, was preferred along the Chinese section of the Silk Road from Xi'an to Kashgar, as well as to the west of the Pamirs in Transoxiana. In fact Bactrians were not known in the West until

Islamic traders began using the Silk Road. Dromedary-Bactrian hybrids are raised in Kazakhstan where they are called *bukhts*. They are larger than either parent, have a single hump, and make good draft animals.

Camels can go for four or five days without water (they can drink up to 60 litres/13 gallons in 10 minutes) carry heavy loads, and sustain speeds of up to 40kph (25mph), but they also produce milk and wool, and their dung can be used to make fires. There are an estimated 14 million dromedaries in North Africa and the Middle East, with a further 1.5 million Bactrians in Central Asia and Western China. They live for between 40 and 50 years.

esteemed Bactrians were designated "flying dragon camels" and kept in the imperial stables.

Camels were not just used for transport, but also prized for their long manes, which made excellent cloth, while camel hump was considered a delicacy. Similarly yaks, as well as being used in transport, were valued for their milk, cheese and meat, as well as dung, which could be burnt as fuel. Their hair was spun into yarn for knitting warm clothing.

Maintaining the road

Even at the height of its prosperity, the Silk Road was not a single track, except where it was forced

Great empires and rulers of vision who appreciated the value of trade ordered the construction of garrisons and caravanserais at regular intervals, for example in the West under the Abbasids and Ottomans, in the East, again, under the great Tang Dynasty. At other times imperial control collapsed and chaos ensued, with caravans threatened by bandits and natural hazards. Only under the Mongols in the 13th and early 14th centuries was the entire length of the Silk Road briefly united under a single, efficient system, best exemplified by the Mongol shuudan or postal relay service, in which fast horses were maintained in prime

through narrow defiles such as the Iron Gates at Tiemenguan near Korla and its namesake at the rather wider Buzgala Gorge in Uzbekistan, or across narrow passes in the Pamirs or Tian Shan. Rather, it was an interconnecting network of tracks, established over the centuries and familiar only in parts to experienced caravaneers who knew and understood the terrain. In sections and at times of imperial strength it was well maintained, for example the Persian Royal Road under the Achaemenids, and the Hexi Corridor under the Han and Tang dynasties.

ABOVE, FROM LEFT: caravanserai at Mylasa, Turkey, 1845; the caravanserai at Qasr al-Hayr a-Sharqi, Syria.

condition at regular stations, ready to speed military orders and political news from one end of the empire to the other.

Most caravan transport was carried by road, but there were instances when boats, ferries or rafts were necessary – as, for example, in crossing the Oxus at Chardzhou or the great rivers of Mesopotamia, the Tigris and the Euphrates, in present-day Iraq. Elsewhere river transport could be a useful and economic way of transporting goods through difficult terrain where roads were poor or dangerous, for example eastwards on the Wei River or the Huang He in Gansu, where rafts of inflated goatskins are still used today, or westwards on the Oxus in the region of Termiz.

Bazaars and caravanserais

A series of overnight halts known as caravanserais or khans was established to provide food, water and security for the travellers and to promote and protect the trade that enriched their kingdoms. The word "caravanserai" comes from the Persian *karvan*, meaning a company travelling together, and *sara*, a living place, though in Persia it was also called a *khan*, in Turkey a *han*. Ideally these were roadside inns placed a day apart where travellers could eat, sleep and recover from the day's journey, with their animals securely tethered, watered and fed, and their precious goods safely within

A few caravanserais, such as the atmospheric Hotel Shah Abbas in Isfahan, have been turned into hotels. Others serve as markets or have been restored to provide service as restaurants.

walls. Of course, the harshness of the terrain and the great distances involved meant that inns of such quality were the exception rather than the rule, especially in the wilder reaches of the Middle Eastern deserts and Central Asian mountains.

THE RELIGION OF TRADE

It is no coincidence that some of the great bazaars of the world are in Muslim countries, for much of the ethos of Islam revolves around commerce. Soon after the initial Arab conquests, it became advantageous for the conquered peoples to embrace Islam, both to avoid paying the tax levied on infidels, and to benefit from Islam's extended trade links. Muslim traders helped each other in ports, oases and city bazaars. Caravanserais sprang up along trade routes to serve the travellers, while mosques acted as places for Muslim travellers to rest, store goods safely and exchange information. In Islamic law, a mosque should be established in any community where there are at least 40 believers. Resident Muslims, whether restaurateurs and innkeepers or religious teachers, required wives and readily intermarried with local women, bringing up the children of such unions as Muslims.

In this way Islam spread rapidly along the Silk Road – indeed along most trade routes – establishing small, self-propagating Muslim communities just about everywhere trade caravans or sailing dhows might stop. Islamic law requires that Muslims should only eat permitted, halal food, while non-Muslims, too, would happily consume Muslim fare. It's hardly surprising, then, that Muslims gradually acquired a monopoly in the accommodation and catering businesses.

> *"When such a wind is about to arrive, only the old camels have advance knowledge of it, and they immediately stand snarling together, and bury their mouths in the sand. The caravan men always take this as a sign, and they too immediately cover their noses and mouths by wrapping them in felt. If the men did not protect themselves in this way, they would be in danger of sudden death." Bei Shi – Northern History (Chinese Annals)*

Typically, caravanserais were built within a square or rectangular wall to give protection from attack as well as from the elements, excessive heat and cold, rain and snow, dust storms and hail. They were entered by a single, easily defended gate that was wide enough and high enough to permit fully laden camels to pass through. The central courtyard was open to the sky and lined with stalls for beasts of burden and rooms to accommodate travellers together with their merchandise. Well-organised caravanserais provided washing facilities, cooked food and fodder for animals, and sometimes contained small shops. In Muslim areas – which, by the 8th century AD, meant most of the Silk Road – there were rooms for prayer, orientated towards Mecca.

Bazaars, by contrast, were not established at regular intervals in the wild, but were naturally found in towns and oases, especially at large commercial crossroads such as Lanzhou, Dunhuang, Yarkand, Kabul, Bukhara, Mashhad, Rey and Palmyra. The very best were at Xi'an in the East, at Kashgar and Samarkand in the centre, and at Baghdad, Damascus and Aleppo in the West. Today, remarkably, the great souks of Damascus and Aleppo survive almost unchanged, 1,500 years on. It seems entirely possible that a time traveller from Abbasid Aleppo could find the spice bazaar or the gold market of Aleppo's walled and covered souk in exactly the same location as it was during his or her lifetime.

In contrast to the simplicity of the cara-

ABOVE, FROM LEFT: 19th-century sketch of the main bazaar in Kabul; Sabz Bazaar (vegetable market) in Peshawar, Pakistan.

vanserai, essentially a transit stop where men and beasts rested overnight, layovers in the great bazaars could easily extend into weeks or even months. Trade was carried out in these locations, goods sold, purchased and exchanged for onward carriage or for local consumption. Specialists services such as money-changing, banking, interpreting and, of course, a gamut of entertainments ranging from music and theatre through to drinking and sex were also available to caravaneers and merchants.

The most difficult stages on the old Silk Road were those that crossed the Tarim Basin circling

the barren central Taklamakan Desert and the passes across the Pamir and Karakoram ranges. Caravans would generally halt for a longer rest, perhaps for a week or two, before setting out to face these natural obstacles. An ingeniously crafted pair of goggles currently on exhibit at the Xinjiang Autonomous Region Museum in Urumqi, cut from metal a thousand years ago to permit tiny eye-slits, and lined with felt to keep out the driven sand, confirms the ever-present threat of sand-storms.This imparted particular importance to the bazaars at Dunhuang, Kashgar and Samarkand, all key bazaar towns on the Central Asian Silk Road, and further to the west at Palmyra and Petra in the Syrian and Jordanian deserts.

BAZAARS

Bazaars are the economic and social hubs of villages, towns and cities throughout Asia. They are also great fun for visitors.

One of the modern thrills of travelling through any of the Silk Road countries is to experience the cut and thrust of shopping within the bazaars and souks. Traders along the Silk Road would traditionally stay overnight in caravanserais, which provided food, water and shelter for both man and beast. In the major towns and cities there would be a number of warehouses, each specialising in a particular item, such as gold, silk, leather, metal or spices, from which the local merchants would purchase their raw goods. It was then up to the merchant to work that raw material into a desirable item.

The system of each trade having its own section within a souk or bazaar is still obvious in some of the older souks such as Aleppo, Isfahan, Samarkand and Kashgar. It is still possible to see these central warehouses with the shops of the local merchants clustered nearby.

Most towns and cities have permanent bazaars open for five or six days a week, but there are some places that have special weekly markets attracting people to buy and sell. The most famous would probably be the Sunday market in Kashgar with traders even today travelling from other countries to attend. Simply observing is not an option as everyone gets carried along with the massive swell of people around the temporary stalls. The most interesting, chaotic and dusty area is the trading of animals, as goats, sheep, donkeys and camels are all systematically prodded, poked and inspected by potential buyers.

ABOVE: bazaars are organised by the products they sell; this trader is selling Chinese silks in the bazaar at Shiraz, Iran. Most silks sold on the Silk Road are still from China.

LEFT: to see how animals are traded in Central Asia, head for the Sunday farmers' market in Kashgar, China.

CHAIKHANA CULTURE

Perhaps the best place to soak up the local culture along the Silk Road is in a *chaikhana*, or teahouse. Although they vary across Asia, these crowded roadside meeting places are always part social club, part café, and provide respite from the modern world. In many Islamic countries, drinking alcohol is frowned upon and so tea is at the hub of the community's social life.

A *chaikhana* is to the Uzbeks, Uighurs and Iranians what a pub is to the British. Seats are generally on a *tapchan*, or "tea bed", with a low table placed on it. Green tea is the norm and *shashlyk* (kebabs) and local bread are generally available, though sadly the storytellers and jugglers of the past are now long gone. If you do partake in the local tipple, remember the following golden rules of tea etiquette: pour the first two *pialas* (cups) back into the pot to aid brewing; don't blow on your tea to cool it; and always keep a guest's teacup full. From Syria to Xi'an, identical scenes are played out each day, amid shouted orders, the clicking of dominoes and the drifting smoke from the waterpipes or hookahs.

ABOVE: spices are usually sold together in one section of the main bazaar. In Istanbul, there is a separate Spice Market, with an astonishing array of products in all the colours of the rainbow.

ABOVE RIGHT: no self-respecting bazaar would be complete without a decent selection of gold, like this gold jewellery on display in Damascus.

TOP RIGHT: taking tea in a *chaikhana*, sitting on "tea beds".

BELOW: Uzbek bazaars tend to be dominated by women, most of whom wear the long silk dresses seen throughout the country.

THE SPREAD OF IDEAS

It wasn't just goods that travelled along the Silk Road. Ideas were on the move, too. As communities and peoples came into contact with each other, culture, religious beliefs, architectural styles and technical developments were all soon passed on.

In the courtyards of the caravanserais, around the sociable oases and in the excitable bazaars, conversations would have turned to many things. There would be a thirst for news of events and upheavals, a need to know the latest market prices of goods and the desire to learn of any bargains. People would tell of the adventures they had endured and enjoyed, and the extraordinary sights, both natural and man-made, they had seen. But perhaps it was during the long, monotonous days on the road in awe-inspiring landscapes and beneath vast empty skies that they would spend time mulling over the state of the world, what it should look like, who and what it was governed by, and where their destinies lay.

RELIGIONS AND PHILOSOPHIES

Not surprisingly, it was the proselytising religions that travelled furthest. Flowing east were the monotheistic religions of Judaism, Christianity and Islam. Persian religious traditions such as Manichaeism and Zoroastrianism found audiences, too. South Asian religions, including Buddhism and some aspects of Hinduism, cut off from China by the Tibetan plateau, passed east along the Silk Road, and reached the Far East by sea.

In the other direction, Daoism and Confucianism made no real progress west along the Silk Road, except as practised by Chinese migrants – officials, troops and settlers – in the western regions. Daoism is a philosophical tradition based on abstract concepts such

as the "flow of the universe", and Confucianism approximates more closely to a moral, ethical and philosophical social system. Neither offered a personal path to salvation in the way that Buddhism, Christianity and Islam did. Yet, perhaps because of the dominant cultural role played by China in East Asia, Daoism and Confucianism did spread east and south from the Middle Kingdom to the kingdoms of Korea, Japan and Vietnam.

Zoroastrianism

This is a late 19th-century term for the religion based on the teachings of the Persian prophet Zoroaster, who was active around the 5th century BC. Also known as Mazdaism, it

LEFT: *Sufis in Ecstasy*, a Persian watercolour from the mid-17th century. **RIGHT:** entrance to the Kukeldash Madrassa in Tashkent.

acknowledged one universal and transcendental god called Ahura Mazda. The best-known Zoroastrian symbol is fire, which is kept burning in Zoroastrian temples and represents radiance and purity. For this reason Zoroastrians have often been styled "fire worshippers" by proponents of other religions. At one time this monotheistic belief dominated much of the greater Iranian world, and had a significant impact on both Greek and Roman thought.

Under the Sassanids (AD 226–651), Zoroastrianism spread north to the Caucasus and east to Sogdiana, then along the Silk Road to Xinjiang and China. Zoroastrianism in the

East centred on communities of Sogdian traders. Remains of their temples have been found in the Tarim Basin, notably at Dandan Uilik, and further to the east at Dunhuang, Kaifeng and Zhenjiang in China. Significantly, there were at least four Zoroastrian temples in Tang Dynasty Chang'an (Xi'an).

Manichaeism

Derived from the dualistic teachings of the Persian prophet Mani (AD 210–77), who postulated the existence of two natures, lightness and dark, Manichaeism decrees that the universe is the temporary result of an attack from the realm of darkness on the realm of light. Mani proclaimed himself the last in a line of

> *"Now have I seen him with my own eyes, knowing him in truth to be the wise Lord of the good mind and of good deeds and words."* Zarathustra (Zoroaster)

prophets that included Zoroaster, Buddha and Jesus – a position that won him no friends among the Zoroastrian Persian establishment, who had him killed.

Mani's teachings spread with remarkable speed, reaching Egypt in AD 244 and Rome by 280. But in AD 296 the Roman emperor Diocletian ordered his followers "be condemned to fire along with their abominable scriptures". Persecuted and proscribed in the West, Manichaeism fared rather better in the East, arriving in China by the mid-6th century. Manichaean churches were established at numerous locations along the Eastern Silk Road, including at Chang'an. The Uighur ruler Bugug Khan (AD 759–80) adopted Manichaeism, which became the state religion of the Uighur Empire for the following century. The last organised Manichaean communities seem to have died out in southern China in the 16th century.

The sacred texts of Manichaeism were originally composed in Syriac Aramaic, but as they spread west were translated into Greek, Coptic and Latin. To the east their history serves well to illustrate the multicultural nature of Silk Road society, as they passed through Iranian, Parthian, Sogdian, Uighur and Chinese translations.

Buddhism

This developed from the teachings of Siddhartha Gautama, the future Lord Buddha, who was born around 563 BC, a prince of the Shakya clan in the Kapilavastu Kingdom on the Indo-Nepal borderlands. Although raised amid the comforts of the royal court, Siddhartha was deeply troubled by the misery and poverty he encountered beyond the palace gates, and embarked on a long quest to identify the cause of suffering. Eventually, he discovered the Middle Way, a path of moderation that lies between indulgence and mortification, and results in enlightenment. The philosophy that he taught gradually spread across northern India and, under the Buddhist emperor Asoka (260–218 BC), beyond to Sri Lanka, Burma and Bactria. From Bactria it gradually spread along the Silk Road west to the shores of the Black Sea and Mediterranean, and east to the Tarim Basin and China.

Buddhism reached China around the 1st century AD, but extensive contacts date from the 2nd century, with the establishment of the Buddhist Kushan Empire (see page 51). The earliest Buddhist missionaries to follow the Silk Road to China were Parthian, Sogdian and, later, Kuqan. This cultural traffic became a two-way exchange from the 4th century, when Chinese monks travelled west to the Tarim Basin and south, across the Pamirs to India, seeking Buddhist scriptures. The Silk Road

transmission of Buddhism began to decline from about the 8th century, with the rise of Islam in Transoxiana and, subsequently, the Tarim Basin.

Once in China, Buddhism began to acquire broadly Mahayana characteristics, eventually spreading to Korea, Japan and Vietnam. In Southeast Asia it re-encountered Theravada Buddhism, which had been established in Sri Lanka and Burma during the reign of Emperor Asoka. Meanwhile, in Tibet and Mongolia, a third variant, Vajrayana, emerged.

ABOVE, FROM LEFT: the Cube of Zoroaster at Naqsh-e-Rustam in Iran; an embroidered silk banner of the Buddha Sakyamuni, with an almond-shaped aureole.

Judaism

Judaism may have existed in China for as long as two millennia. A stele preserved in the city of Kaifeng in Henan Province suggests that Jews settled there as early as 231 BC, though there is no record of a synagogue until 1163. It is believed that the ancestors of this community migrated along the Silk Road from Central Asia, where a small community still survives in Bukhara. Over the centuries, the Kaifeng Jews became integrated within Chinese society and, in particular, with the local Chinese Muslim community.

Intermarriage and isolation from both Ashkenazi and Sephardic Jewish communities far to the west led to a loss of religious and ritual customs, as well as social and linguistic tradition. The Kaifeng synagogue collapsed in the mid-19th century, but by this time, it is said, all that survived of Jewish tradition were the injunctions to circumcise sons and to abstain from eating pork. So it is quite probable the last Kaifeng Jews were subsumed in the local Hui Muslim population.

Nestorianism

It is thought that Nestorianism penetrated China by way of the Silk Road as early as the 3rd century AD; a metropolitan see was established there by representatives of the Assyrian Church in 411, when Christianity was known as *Jingjiao* or the "Luminous Religion". The Syrian monk Nestorius (AD 386–451) taught that Christ exists as two persons, the human (Jesus) and the son of God (Logos). This view was condemned at the Council of Ephesus in

HALOS FROM THE EAST

The halo that first appears in Christian art in the 5th century is probably derived from the much older circular sun symbol associated with the Egyptian Sun God Ra. It was also used in Persian representations of kings and divinities. The symbol was carried east, perhaps by the Greek armies of Alexander the Great, and was subsequently used in Graeco-Buddhist representations of the Buddha from the 1st century AD, before spreading back west along the Silk Road to Christendom. The crown is merely a more sophisticated version of the halo, designed to represent the idea of light emanating from the head of a superior being.

431, leading to the separation of the Assyrian Church of the East from the Byzantine Church.

Condemned as heretics in the West, Nestorians migrated east along the Silk Road, spreading their variant of Christianity to Central Asia, China, Mongolia and ultimately Japan. The Nestorian missionary Alopen arrived at Chang'an in AD 635 and was given a warm welcome by the Tang emperor Taizong (AD 626–49). The famous Nestorian stele was erected at Chang'an in AD 781 celebrating the accomplishments of the Assyrian Church in China. Murals from a Nestorian monastery at Khocho in Xinjiang from the 7th century also survive.

Islam

Islam, along with Buddhism, was one of the most successful of the great world religions to pass east along the Silk Road to China. The first Arab missionaries to Chang'an caused something of a stir, refusing to *ketou* ("kowtow" or "knock the head") except to the One God. They soon established communities across the empire, intermarrying and eventually becoming so Chinese that the only distinction between them and their Han neighbours was their religion. Today, officially recognised as the Hui minority, Chinese-speaking Muslims are to be found all over China, often still working in transport-related businesses like trucking and catering.

Other, non-Chinese minorities within China converted to Islam as it spread east, including the Uighur, Kazakh, Kyrgyz and Salar Turks, the Bao'an and Dongxiang Mongols, and the Persian-speaking Tajiks. Almost all, including the Hui, are Sunni Muslims of the Hanafi *madhhab*, the sole Islamic school of law to permit translation and recitation of the Holy Koran in languages other than Arabic – clearly a factor in the successful proselytising of Islam in Chinese and – in Turkic-speaking lands. Only the tiny Tajik minority in Xinjiang's far west are Shia, followers of the Ismaili Aga Khan.

SCIENCE AND TECHNOLOGY

Unlike religion and philosophy, which flowed chiefly from west to east, the transfer of science and technology was very much a two-way traffic. In antiquity, and independent of Persian, Greek or Roman discoveries, Chinese scholars made significant advances in mathematics, medicine and astronomy, recording the earliest observations of solar eclipses, supernovae and comets, and developing acupuncture, herbal medicine and their own traditional Chinese pharmacopoeia.

The "Four Great Inventions" of ancient China are defined as the compass, gunpowder, papermaking and printing, all of which spread west along the Silk Road, making an immense contribution to both the Muslim world and medieval Europe. The Tang era (AD 618–906), in particular, was a time of great innovation, while technological and scientific exchanges continued along the Silk Road up to the end of the Yuan Dynasty, in 1368, and into the early Ming period.

Tang innovations included woodblock printing. The *Diamond Sutra*, discovered at Dunhuang and dating from AD 868, is the world's first known printed book, and it has both illustrations and text. The Buddhist monk Yixing (AD 683–727) developed an astrolabe powered by a waterwheel to be used in astronomical calculations as a rotating celestial sphere; the device had a mechanical bell that chimed the hours and a mechanical drum that beat the quarter-hours, becoming effectively the world's first astronomical clock.

More frivolous, but equally impressive in technical terms, was a mechanical wine pourer installed at the Tang court that used a hydraulic pump to siphon wine from dragon-headed taps, as well as tilting bowls that dipped when filled into a central wine lake – an interesting

In AD 589 the Arab Muslim traveller Yan Zhitui recorded the use of toilet paper, noting with disapproval that the Chinese, unlike Muslims, used paper rather than water to clean themselves after visiting the bathroom.

example of imperial indulgence serving scientific discovery.

Tang pharmacologists and doctors spared no effort in classifying all manner of herbs and drugs used in Chinese medicine. In AD 657 Emperor Gaozong commissioned a comprehensive *materia medica*, complete with full descriptive text and illustrations listing more than 800 medicinal substances derived from herbs, vegetables, fruit, animals and minerals. Alchemists, too, were active, compounding different chemical formulae for waterproofing, fireproofing and even repelling dust.

Cartography was another field in which the Tang made great advances. Chinese map-makers developed grid systems and graduated scales, and in AD 785 Emperor Dezong commissioned the geographer Jia Dan (AD 730–805) to draw up a map of China together with its Central Asian territorial possessions – effectively the first complete map of the Eastern Silk Road. On completion, the map – now lost – measured 9 metres (30ft) in length and 10 metres (33ft) in height.

Chinese contributions to military technology that spread west along the Silk Road included gunpowder and cannon, as well as a kind of brass flame-thrower that forced incendiary material known in the West as "Greek fire" through a nozzle.

The Muslim contribution

Just as Chinese scientific discoveries were transferred to the Muslim world and, subsequently, to Europe via the Silk Road, so many Muslim inventions and discoveries passed the other way, from the Middle East and Central Asia to China and Japan. This was an ongoing process from the Arab conquest of Transoxiana in 706, but as China enjoyed a time of great innovation under the Tang, so the Arabs went through a truly astonishing scientific and philosophical

ABOVE, FROM LEFT: tomb of the 12th-century Sufi mystic Farid ud-Din Attar in Nieshapur, Iran; paper being made traditionally in China today.

Golden Age at the time of the Baghdad-based Abbasid Caliphate (AD 750–1258).

When the Arabs first burst out of the Arabian Peninsula in AD 637 they were a desert people of relatively little sophistication. Over the next century, however, their conquests made them heirs to the accumulated knowledge of the ancient Middle East, Greece, Persia and India. Under the Abbasids, they systematically translated and classified this knowledge, developing and adding to it, transferring it east along the Silk Road, as well as ultimately, helping to fuel the European Renaissance. Without six centuries of Arab science and learning, it is quite pos-

sible, for example, that Greek philosophy might have been lost following the European "Dark Age" (*c.*476–1000).

In astronomy the great Tajik philosopher Abu Rayhan al-Biruni (973–1048) first proposed that the Milky Way was a collection of thousands of nebulous stars, while Ibn Bajjah (Avempace, 1095–1138) devised a new post-Ptolemaic model of planetary motion (without any epicyles) long before Galileo. Muslim scientists laid the foundations for later telescopic astronomy, developing astrolabes and other astronomical instruments to enquire into the position of the sun, planets and stars. In chemistry, Muslim scholars invented steam distillation and produced the first kerosene and solid soap, while in geography they developed techniques of triangulation to measure the radius of the earth, as well as the topographic coordinates of towns and other important localities.

In mathematics al-Khwarizmi (780–850) established algebra as an independent discipline in his treatise *al-Jabr wa-l-Muqabala* ("The Compendious Book on Calculation by Completion and Balancing"), a compilation and extension of known rules for solving quadratic equations and other problems. The mathematician al-Kindi (801–73) wrote a pioneering work on cryptology, while al-Karaji (*c*.953–1029) introduced the theory of algebraic calculus.

In mechanics Ibn Sina (980–1037), better-known in the West as Avicenna, discovered the concept of momentum as a precursor to Sir Isaac Newton's laws of motion, while in 1115, al-Khazini first proposed that the gravity of a body varied depending on its distance from the centre of the Earth, a phenomenon subsequently described by Newton's law of universal gravitation in 1687.

In medicine and pharmacology Muslim scientists made many ground-breaking advances, developing a mathematical scale to quantify the strength of drugs, pioneering urinalysis and stool analysis, and identifying smallpox

SUFISM

It was not just trade that propelled Islam along the Silk Road, nor the invasions of Muslim armies. Just as important for the spread of the religion was the missionary activity of Sufi *pirs* (preachers), named for the clothes of wool *(suf)* that they wore as a badge of their having renounced the world to pursue a path of mystical realisation. These wandering mystics had a tolerant, sometimes revolutionary message, often scornful of authority. They taught that it was possible to attain a special closeness to God – sometimes described as unity with the divine – even during life. The idea caught on and spread widely along the Silk Road into Turkey, Central Asia and China, as well as southwards into India, and it continues

to thrive in all four areas today. The famous "whirling dervishes" of Turkey are Mevlevi Sufis, while the greatest of the Sufi orders all remain active.

The most enduring Sufi discipline has been the practice of listening to the singing of mystical poetry in the strongly rhythmic style called *qavvali*. Particularly encouraged by the Chishti order, this devotional music has always had immense popular appeal. The venue for *qavvali* performances will often be the courtyard of the shrine built over the tomb of a Sufi master, or saint. The musical tradition of the Uighurs has been particularly strongly influenced by *qavvali*; it is also a vital part of the cultural life of Pakistan.

and measles. Abu al-Qasim (936–1013) compiled a 30-volume medical encyclopaedia and invented numerous surgical instruments, including the first designed specifically for gynaecology. His encyclopaedia, together with Avicenna's *Canon of Medicine* (1025) and *Book of Healing* (1027) remained standard textbooks in both Muslim and European universities until the 17th century.

Ibn Zuhr (1091–1161) performed the first known medical dissections and post-mortem autopsies, as well as being the first physician known to have used vivisection and animal testing. In 1242, towards the end of the Abbasid

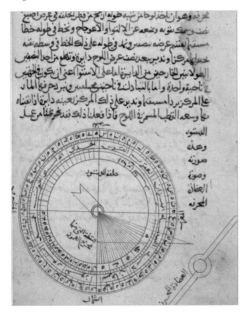

Golden Age, Ibn al-Nafis was the first to describe pulmonary circulation and coronary circulation.

Other Muslim medicinal discoveries include the immune system, the invention of injection by syringe, and the identification of more than 2,000 medicinal and chemical substances.

ARCHITECTURE

The materials, engineering techniques and latest fashions for architecture were also passed along the Silk Road. Architects, engineers and

ABOVE, FROM LEFT: the alchemist, Avicenna, born in Bukhara in AD 980; text and diagram from al-Biruni's treatise on the construction of the astrolabe.

skilled craftsman travelled to cultural centres – often the capital city – where wealthy patrons indulged every aspect of the creative arts. Architecture was particularly important as impressive buildings enabled a ruler to project his power to his subjects and rivals: construction flourished when a ruler was at his peak, and his buildings were the first thing to be significantly altered or razed and reconstructed once he fell from grace.

Artisans brought with them the skills and tastes of their respective homelands and, consequently, when they worked together on a structure, numerous influences brought a fusion of styles. The same thing happened when the building's patron changed. Exemplary is the Hagia Sophia in Istanbul. It began life as a Roman church but later builders added Hellenistic columns, the Byzantine dome and mosaics, four new buttresses, calligraphic inscriptions and Islamic minarets. The Hagia Sophia's structure mirrors the cultural shifts in each era of Istanbul's history.

Byzantine

Early Byzantine architecture was a continuation of Roman architecture, but it developed to incorporate features found within the new territories of Constantine's Eastern Roman Empire: Asia Minor and the Near East. Churches began to be built in a cross shape (a tradition drawn from Greek Orthodoxy), and engineers developed the techniques necessary to support a dome on top of a square structure. Pillars taken from classical buildings were re-incorporated in both religious and secular buildings, most notably in Istanbul's Basilica Cistern.

Exposure to the decorative conventions of Islamic architecture is evident in Byzantine design from at least the 11th century. The exteriors of buildings began to be decorated with geometric patterns, either executed in polychrome brickwork or through the addition of coloured tiles. Ornamental scripts, in imitation of Islamic calligraphy, also came into vogue.

Persian

The Islamic conquest of Persia in the 7th century AD brought the early Islamic design of the Middle East first to Iran and then to Afghanistan and Central Asia. In each of these regions it encountered indigenous artistic traditions, and evolved into new, syncretic forms.

Out of these encounters, two important developments emerged: elaborate funerary architecture, and the technical innovations that would enable the construction of giant domes. Improvements in dome buildings under the Ilkhanate, founded by Genghis Khan's grandson Hulagu Khan in 1255, included the creation of double-layered domes. Arches between the layers reinforced the structure, ultimately enabling the construction of a dome 50m high and 25m in diameter in Zanjan, Iran by 1312.

Persian architecture experienced a renaissance in the 16th century under the Safavid Emperor Shah Abbas. Designating Isfahan as

"Proclaims Xerxes the King: By the favor of Ahuramazda I built this Gateway of All Nations. I built many other beautiful things in Persia. I built them and my father built them. All beautiful things we built, we have built by the favor of Ahuramazda." Inscription at Persepolis by Xerxes I (r. 486-65 BC)

his new capital, Shah Abbas set about constructing a city with dozens of colourful domes. The turquoise blue tiles were a tradition inherited

ABU RAYHAN AL-BIRUNI, SILK ROAD POLYMATH

Abu Rayhan al-Biruni was born near Khiva in present-day Uzbekistan in AD 973, and died at Ghazni in Afghanistan in 1048. A Persian-speaking Tajik, he ranks as one of the greatest universal geniuses of all time, a true Muslim "man for all seasons". Although less well known in the West than such great Muslim scholars as Ibn Sina (Avicenna) and Ibn Rushd (Averroes), in the past century the full extent of his extraordinary contribution to human knowledge has become increasingly appreciated, and a geological feature on the moon, the Al-Biruni Crater, has been named in his honour.

As a young man, al-Biruni studied mathematics and astronomy under Abu Nasr Mansur. One of his

colleagues was the great philosopher and physician Ibn Sina. He was a member of the court of Mahmud of Ghazni (971–1030), accompanying the latter on his campaigns in India where he developed an enduring passion for Indian science and philosophy. In addition to his native Persian, al-Biruni mastered Arabic, Greek, Sanskrit and Syriac. During his long and active life he wrote no fewer than 146 works in Arabic and Persian on many subjects.

He was the first Muslim scholar to study India and the Brahmanical tradition, and is remembered as the father of Indology, as well as the founder of experimental mechanics and experimental psychology.

from the Seljuks, but the Safavids were also able to glaze tiles in gold, white, dark blue and a myriad of patterns, having recently invented the *haft rangi* (seven colours) technique for colouring and firing tiles.

Mughal

The Mughal emperors were Timurids, and their familial lands were in the Fergana Valley. Various attempts to control Samarkand, and a lengthy exile with the Safavid Shah Tahmasp in Herat, had exposed them to masterpieces of Persian architecture and this was to heavily influence the structures they built across Afghanistan, Pakistan and northern India.

The Mughals were, however, a religious and ethnic minority within their empire, and under the leadership of Akbar (r.1556–1605) they began to integrate the local elite and project themselves as the legitimate rulers of not only their Muslim subjects, but Hindus, Jains and other religious groups as well. The archi-

> "Over the grave is erected a dome on four supports, each of them flanked with twin marble columns of green, black, white and red colours. The walls of the mausoleum are decorated with multicoloured gilded inlay; its roof is covered with lead; the tomb is made of inlaid ebony, with silver-studded corners, and three silver lamps are hung inside."
> Ibn Battuta describing the tomb of Sheikh Kusan ibn-Abbas in Samarkand

tecture they created in this period consciously drew from a variety of architectural influences, including Hindu and Jain temples.

A prime example of Mughal syncreticism is the Badshahi Mosque in Lahore, built by Emperor Aurangzeb in 1671. The red sandstone of its construction was a popular building material for mosques and temples across the subcontinent, but was rarely used further west. Whilst the onion domes show Persian influence, the cupolas and arches atop the minarets are an Indian design. The ornamental merlons have their origins in Roman battlements, and

the lotiform motifs are derived from Hindu and Buddhist sources.

Indo-Saracenic

From the late 18th century, British imperial architects pioneered the Indo-Saracenic or Mughal Gothic style. It took aspects of Mughal and Hindu architecture and combined them with Gothic revivalism and neoclassicism. There was a belief that although architectural forms originating in the colonies had a certain charm, they could be significantly improved with the application of European forms and engineering.

Structures built in the Indo-Saracenic style were predominantly those associated with the state: railway stations, courthouses, government colleges and public museums. Their grand scale and impressive facades were intended to remind colonial subjects of the superiority of their British masters.

It was not only in the colonies that Indo-Saracenism took off, however. Asian exoticism was a hot topic in the fashionable drawing rooms of London and Paris, where wealthy patrons commissioned homes and pleasure gardens styled with an oriental twist. The Royal Pavilion in Brighton, with its bulbous domes, minarets and chinoiserie interiors, is an excellent example.

ABOVE, FROM LEFT: Sheikh Lotfollah Mosque (built in 1615), Isfahan; Badshahi Mosque, Lahore, Pakistan.

PEOPLE AND THE ENVIRONMENT

The population of the Silk Road has never been static. The availability of water, land and resources has always dictated the best places to live, and political demands, environmental degradation and climate change continue to force migration.

The history of the Silk Road is a history of peoples on the move. Traders journeyed along the road as they transported their goods, but at some time or other almost every community living along the Silk Road has moved in pursuit of land, food and opportunities, or been driven into new territories by natural disasters, war or political upheaval. The movements of these people transcends the boundaries of modern nation states, and the decisions (political, economic or environmental) made in one country often have repercussions felt far beyond their borders.

PEOPLES OF THE SILK ROAD

The peoples of the Silk Road can be categorised in numerous ways – by their ethnic roots and languages, their religions or their cultural traditions. The identification of a specific group can often be a challenge, not least because of their

> Ethnographic research suggests that the Kyrgyz and Native American peoples have the same ancestors, a group of people who lived in Siberia at a time when the region was still linked to the Americas by a land bridge, between 12,000 and 20,000 years ago.

migrations, the many different historical names used for them both by themselves and by outsiders and, of course, because of intermarriage and assimilation. That said, two umbrella groups have been identified, through their common

ancestry, related languages and customs and also, more recently, through DNA testing. These groups are the Turks and the Kurds.

The largest group of peoples along the Silk Road are Turkic: they speak languages belonging to the Turkic group and, to a greater or lesser extent, share some historical background and cultural traits. Although it is the Turkish in Turkey who most readily bear the Turkic name today, Kazakhs, Kyrgyz, Turkmen, Uzbeks and Uighurs are all part of the same ethno-linguistic group, as were past civilisations such as the Seljuks, Ottomans, Mamluks and Timurids.

Though now spread across Europe and Asia, it is thought that the first Turkic people lived in the Altay Mountains (between modern Kazakhstan

LEFT: young Kazakh hunter with his falcon.
RIGHT: a Uighur man enjoys a cigarette.

and China) and spread as far as Siberia. They were nomadic herdsmen with a clan-based society. These nomadic tribes were united under the Göktürk Empire (AD 552–745) but the unity was undermined by dynastic conflicts. When the empire finally collapsed, the competing groups migrated to different territories including Eastern Europe, Iran and Anatolia in the west, Russia in the north, and Mongolia in the east. Recent DNA studies have confirmed the shared Siberian origins of these migrants' modern descendants.

A second significant ethno-linguistic group is the Kurds, whose 30 million members are found in significant numbers in Armenia,

Iran, Iraq, Syria and Turkey but are most concentrated in Kurdistan, a historical region not widely recognised by modern nation states. The Kurds are rooted in tribes at least 4,000 years old, including the Lullubi, Guti and Medes.

Kurdish nationalism arose after World War I and the collapse of the Ottoman Empire. During the war Kurds had been victims of ethnic cleansing and deportations, and more conservative members of the community deeply opposed Ataturk's secularism. Some Kurdish groups sought political autonomy and although a number of Kurdish states existed for brief periods in the 20th century (notably the Republic of Ararat in Turkey, the republic of Mahabad in Iran, and the Kingdom of Kurdistan in Iraq), all were short-lived.

Modern migrations

Josef Stalin was responsible for the greatest upheaval of people that the Silk Road has ever known – the so-called Soviet "purges". In the late 1930s and '40s as many as 6 million people were deported from their homelands: they were not only political dissidents and those he wished to punish but also groups who might sympathise with Nazi Germany or Japan, farm labourers to cultivate the "Virgin Lands", and Russians and Eastern Europeans who might "civilise" the nomads of the steppe.

Between 1941 and 1949 alone, some 3.3 million people were deported to Siberia and the Central Asian republics. An estimated 43 percent of this resettled population died from malnutrition and disease, but those that survived had to start new lives in an unfamiliar and

THE 40 TRIBES OF MANAS

The legendary hero Manas (see page 212) is at the heart of Kyrgyz national identity for unifying 40 tribes against the Khitans. The very name "Kyrgyz" recalls this event – it is derived from the Turkic word for 40.

Although the government espouses that the Kyrgyz are one people, this origin myth proclaims the opposite: tribal or clan-based allegiances remain exceptionally strong. There are three main clan groupings in Kyrgyzstan today: the Ong (from southern Kyrgyzstan), the Sol (from northern and western Kyrgyzstan) and the Ichilik (who are from the south but also include some non-Kyrgyz groups). The Sol incorporates seven clans including the Buguu and the Sarybagysh, the

clan from which the country's first President, Askar Akayev, was drawn.

Clan affiliation plays a significant role in both business and politics and has the power to topple governments: regimes in Kyrgyzstan have been strongest when there has been a balance of clan power, perception of an external threat, a legitimate power broker and a pact between the clans of the north and the south. Clan alliances make introducing a functional democracy in the country a considerable challenge: block voting is common, it is hard to reach a consensus and each side is accused of promoting their protégés and rotating them continually between key political posts.

often hostile land. Ironically, the deportations meant that the Central Asian capitals became amongst the most cosmopolitan cities in the USSR: in a single marketplace you'd find not only ethnic Russians and local people, but also Volga Germans, Crimean Tartars, Poles, Greeks, Chechens, Lithuanians and Koreans – and so on. Significant numbers of indigenous communities fled the Soviet Union, migrating to China and Afghanistan. The Kyrgyz nomads in the Wakhan Corridor are one such group: they fled Stalin's purges only to be trapped permanently in Afghanistan once the USSR's borders closed.

Despite the USSR's attempt to indoctrinate these disparate groups with a single, Soviet culture and identity, this was only ever a limited success. Ethnic communities continued to live separately from one another, preserving as best they could their languages and traditions. When the Soviet Union fell and these ethnic minorities had the opportunity to return to their homelands, many of them chose to do so despite half a century in exile. They had never fully integrated in Central Asia and were afraid of cultural, political and economic repression under rising nationalism in the newly independent states.

The most politically significant migration of recent times is that of the Han Chinese into Xjinjiang and, more recently, into southern Russia and Central Asia. Since 1949, the percentage of Han Chinese in the population of Xinjiang has risen from just 6 percent to as much as 45 percent. The majority of this population influx occurred since the 1990s as the Chinese government sought to rapidly industrialise the province.

ENVIRONMENT

The geography of the Silk Road encompasses everything from glaciers and alpine lakes to some of the most arid landscapes on earth. Whilst the need for resources has always kept people on the move, man's interference in his environment (sometimes deliberate, sometimes accidental) has put more pressure than ever before on water supplies, land, food and mineral resources.

Water

From the *New Statesman* to the BBC, environmental commentators agree that the bitterest conflicts of the 21st century will be fought over

ABOVE, FROM LEFT: Kurd farmers on Mount Nemrut, Eastern Anatolia; Uighur woman in costume, China.

water: the Silk Road may well be their battleground. Melting glaciers cause first dramatic floods and then drought; misuse of water supplies creates saline soils where nothing can grow, sinking water tables and disappearing seas.

The Aral Sea disaster dates back to the early 1960s. It had been the fourth-largest inland sea in the world, fed by the Amu Darya and Syr Darya rivers. Soviet planners, keen to expand Central Asia's cotton production, ordered the building of canals across Uzbekistan and Turkmenistan, diverting the rivers' water into the fields. Cotton output boomed, but the Aral Sea began shrinking.

By the mid-2000s the inland sea was a quarter of its original size. The fishing industry was decimated because ports were cut off from the sea; the water's salinity increased to a level at which the fish could no longer survive; biological warfare agents dumped on islands in the sea were now exposed; and dust and sandstorms ripped across the region, often carrying with them the toxic pesticides and fertilisers used in the cotton fields. Whereas the sea once played a moderating role on the local climate, now summers are shorter and drier, winters longer and colder. Rainfall has decreased and growing seasons are significantly reduced, leading to a fall in agricultural output.

To the east about 5,000km (3,000 miles), the Hexi Corridor (see page 151) has begun suffering from the opposite problem: sudden floods are wreaking havoc, washing away villages and crops. The glaciers above the corridor are melting because of climate change and are expected to have disappeared entirely by 2050. In the short term this means that the springs on which people depend for drinking water have swollen, particularly during the winter months. More than 1,000 families have had to evacuate in the past five years, and both Zhangye and Jiuquan have flooded repeatedly.

Perhaps even more concerning is what will happen once the glaciers have gone. There are 26 million people living in the Hexi Corridor

and, as precipitation in the region is so low (an annual average of just 125mm/5ins), when the glacier-fed springs dry up, there will be no alternative source of water. The competition for water resources is not without its political consequences, particularly as water consumers in one country are often dependent on water supplies in another country. In 2009 the Russian government gave the Kyrgyz $2 billion in loans to build hydroelectric stations and water-management systems. The Kremlin was confident the Kyrgyz would default on their repayments (which they duly did), putting the new infrastructure under Russian control. Kyrgyzstan's rivers flow directly

Radiation tourism is on the rise in Kazakhstan. Local companies offer tours to the Polygon, but in order to participate you must bring your own radiation suit and Geiger counter.

into Uzbekistan, and the hydroelectric power generated is not only a key power source for Kyrgyzstan but is also exported to Uzbekistan and thence to Afghanistan. The ability to turn off the tap is a powerful bargaining chip indeed.

Minerals

Lapis lazuli has been mined in northern Afghanistan for at least 5,000 years, and the mountains of Central Asia are rich in gold, copper, uranium, rare earth metals and precious stones. Soviet geologists mapped mineral deposits in the mid-20th century and their exploitation makes up a significant proportion

KYRGYZSTAN'S KOREANS

In 1935 there was one known Korean living in Kyrgyzstan – a middle-aged woman named Pak. Two years later Stalin began mass deportations from the far east of Russia to Central Asia, displacing almost 40,000 families. An unknown number of people died on their forced march west, but today some 200,000 Koreans are living in Kyrgyzstan, the descendants of these same refugees.

Unlike other countries that established policies to repatriate their nationals after the fall of the Soviet Union, South Korea had no such programme. Instead, the Korean government has encouraged ethnic Koreans to learn about Korean culture through local

institutions (such as the Korean Center for Education, opened in Bishkek in 2001) but also to fully integrate with other communities in Kyrgyzstan. There are several popular Korean restaurants and grocery stores; and marriage between Koreans and other ethnic groups is increasingly common.

In recent years, Koreans in Korea have taken an interest in Kyrgyzstan. South Korea opened a full diplomatic mission in Bishkek in 2008, Korean missionaries have established a number of small churches for Korean Christians, and Korean businesses are investing in a variety of Kyrgyz industries including potato processing, shoe making and mobile phone assembly.

of the region's economies. A single gold mine in Kyrgyzstan, Kumtor, accounted for 55 percent of the nation's industrial output in 2011 alone.

Though gold and other metals are valuable commodities and other minerals have vital industrial applications, their extraction is not without significant environmental impact. Open pit mines leave vast craters in the earth; highly toxic chemicals are used to leach metals from their ores; and huge quantities of waste products (known as tailings) are generated in the process.

The gold-mining industry in Kyrgyzstan makes an ideal case study. Though the country's main mines are run by fairly reputable international companies and strict environmental controls are observed, mines still have a detrimental effect on the environment. Sodium cyanide is used in large quantities to extract the gold from granular ore. In 1998 a truck transporting the cyanide to the mine plunged into a river, contaminating the water supply and poisoning 2,500 people downstream. Spills of nitric acid and ammonium nitrate have also been recorded. It is estimated that the mining sector in Kyrgyzstan has generated 100 million m3 of waste products, 2 percent of which are radioactive. Though currently stored behind dams, there is constant concern

Kazakhstan's President Nazarbayev has regularly spoken out against nuclear testing, first preventing the USSR expanding the Polygon in the late 1980s and, more recently, encouraging the UN's General Assembly to establish August 29th as International Day Against Nuclear Tests.

that if any one of these dams were to rupture (which is relatively likely given that the region is prone to earthquakes), the waste would pour down into the valleys below.

Nuclear testing

The Silk Road has the unenviable distinction of being home to two of the world's largest nuclear-test sites: the Chinese site at Lop Nur, and the Soviet site at Semipalatinsk in Kazakhstan (called the Polygon). Around 500 nuclear tests took place at the two sites between 1949 and 1989.

The Polygon, which lies in northeast Kazakhstan, covers around 190,000 sq km (70 sq miles) of steppe land. The city of Semipalatinsk is 150km (90 miles) to the west, and a number of small villages are even nearer. Until 1991 the full impact of radiation exposure was kept hiddens; it has even been alleged that populations were not evacuated from the fallout zone so that scientists could observe the long-term effects of radiation poisoning. Health studies since the test site was closed suggest that the test site has had a direct and detrimental impact on the health of 200,000 people, many of whom are suffering with cancers and thyroid abnormalities.

ARALSK: KAZAKHSTAN'S GHOST PORT

The Aral Sea has shrunk to such an extent that the waters are up to 100km (60 miles) from harbour of the once-rich fishing port of Aralsk. The roach, bream, sturgeon and carp that were once caught by the thousand are but a distant memory, the empty canneries and rusting cranes seem to mock their former workers, and the skeleton ships sit rotting into the sands.

There are still 35,000 people living in Aralsk, largely supported by NGOs. The young have left in search of work, and the old sit on steps around the town and wait in the forlorn hope that the waters will one day return.

ABOVE, FROM LEFT: playing soccer in the desert that was once the Aral Sea; Lapis lazuli in close-up.

THE SILK ROAD EXPERIENCE

With the advent of modern transport, travel along the Silk Road has undoubtedly become easier. However, the sense of adventure is not diminished, even if the journey covers just a short stretch.

Most of the silk trade flowed in an east–west direction, the route followed by this guide, which covers the whole road and some of its most important tributaries from Xi'an to Antakya (ancient Antioch) on the Mediterranean coast, ending at the western hub, Istanbul.

Just as travel along the Silk Road would have been divided into sections, so is this book, with the first section devoted to China, the second to Central Asia and the third to Western Asia. The borders of modern nation states are a relatively new construct, but for ease of planning, the three main sections correspond to countries, and within China, provinces. Each chapter includes information about border crossings, so that readers wanting to cover whole stretches of the route can still see what's involved. It isn't always easy: getting the required visas to travel from one Central Asian country to another can be particularly difficult. But negotiating local bureaucracy was always a requirement for Silk Road travellers (except during Mongol times when you were given a passport good for the whole route), and the challenges of dealing with border guards, for example, are part and parcel of the Silk Road experience.

There are a number of countries on the route that are considered dangerous for visitors from the West. Travellers should think twice before heading into war-torn Iraq, Afghanistan, Syria or even Pakistan, for example. However, all countries share that same vital ingredient without which the Silk Road could never have blossomed, namely hospitality. A mural found at the ancient site of Penjikent in Tajikistan depicts the rituals of hospitality as practised by the Sogdians back in the 7th century AD. Most places will still give the traveller an equally warm welcome today.

PRECEDING PAGES: camel train in the desert near Dunhuang, China; the Karakul river wends its way past the Fan Mountains, Tajikistan. **LEFT:** a Mongolian camel breeder relaxes in his yurt in the Gobi Desert. **ABOVE, FROM LEFT:** entering a mosque in Bukhara, Uzbekistan; a donkey cart drives through the ruins of an ancient Buddhist town along the Silk Road, northwest China.

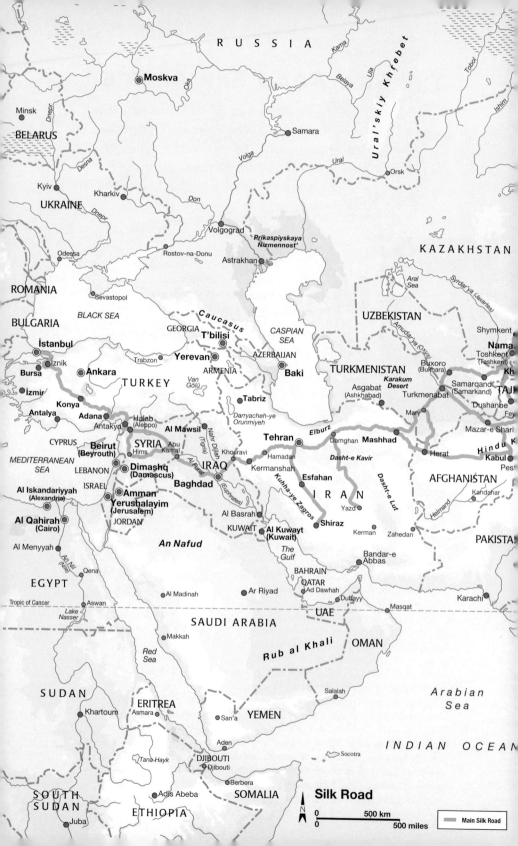

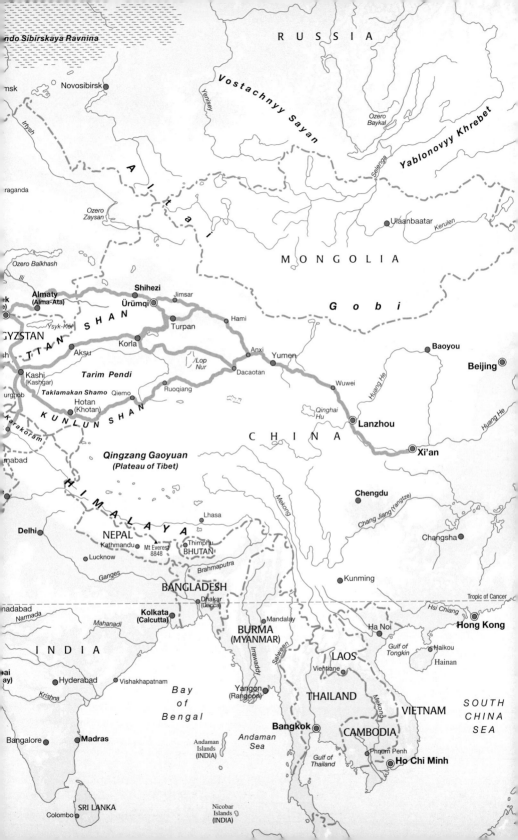

CHINA

The journey through China, from Xi'an to the
western frontiers of Xinjiang, covers almost half
of the Silk Road, across vast and varied landscapes,
taking in an extraordinary cultural heritage.

Sericulture, or silk cultivation, was first developed
between 3,000 and 5,000 years ago in the Yellow
River region that forms China's traditional heartland. From here, it spread east to Korea and Japan, and
south to Vietnam, but most famously west, along the
ancient trade route that would come to bear its name.
China lies at the eastern extremity of the Silk Road, but
was always of central importance in this long-distance
link between East and West. Today, the section of the
Silk Road that lies within Chinese frontiers encompasses almost half of the fabled caravan route that
joined ancient China with Greece and Rome, and passes
through some of the wildest and most spectacular scenery on earth.

Through deserts, mountains and oases

The Silk Road starts in old Chang'an, today the great city
of Xi'an, capital of Shaanxi Province. From here it heads
west through the spectacular gorges of the Wei River and
the rich yellow soil of China's vast loess region to the old
garrison city of Lanzhou, at the eastern end of the Hexi
Corridor. To the north are the barren wastes of the Gobi Desert and
to the south the snow-covered peaks of the Qilian Shan, and the road
passes from oasis to oasis through Gansu Province until it reaches
Yumenguan, the "Jade Gate" that traditionally marked the western limits of China proper.

Here the Silk Road splits into northern and southern branches as it
enters China's largest province, once known as Chinese Turkestan or
Eastern Turkestan, but today designated Xinjiang, the "New Frontier".
This vast and inhospitable region, bitterly cold in winter and baking
hot in summer, and the size of Western Europe, comprises a sixth of
China's territory, but is home to less than a sixtieth of its population.
The Silk Road continues west, passing along the northern and southern
rims of the Tarim Basin, which forms one of the most extraordinary
geographical features on earth. At its centre lie the shifting sands of

LEFT: camels by Lake Karakul. RIGHT: a figure next to the grottoes at
Maijishan Shiku.

the Taklamakan Desert, while to the south, north and west stand the snow-capped mountain ranges of Kunlun Shan, Tian Shan and Pamir.

Around the Tarim Basin lie a series of fertile, poplar-lined oases, fed by the icy runoff from distant glaciers. Linked by the Silk Road, they have served for millennia as halting places for long-distance caravans and are home to a succession of different peoples: Indo-European, Turkic, Mongol, Tibetan and Sinitic. At the Tarim Basin's western extremity, the two branches of the trade road again conjoin at the venerable oasis city of Kashgar, the pivot of the antique Silk Road at the heart of Central Asia.

Kashgar lies at the foot of the Pamir and Tian Shan ranges and marks the western limits of Chinese territory. To the south the Karakoram Highway leads past the glaciers and ice-covered peaks of Kongur Tagh (7,650 metres/25,100ft) and Muztagh Ata (7,550 metres/24,760ft) to

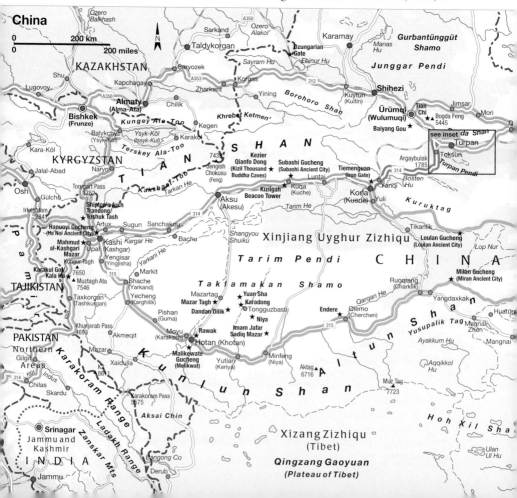

the high Tajik settlement of Tashkurgan and across the Khunjerab Pass to South Asia. To the west the main branch of the old Silk Road crosses a lower but formidable spur of the Pamirs, passing into Western Turkestan and the fabled caravan cities of Samarkand, Khiva, Bukhara and Balkh.

Peoples, cultures and religions

China has always been a land-based rather than a maritime power. From the time of unification under Qin Shi Huang in 221 BC, its major territorial imperative has been westward, towards Central Asia and away from the sea. Through more than two millennia of conflict, Han civilisation has been pitted against the primarily nomadic peoples of the northwest – Turkic, Tibetan and Mongol. At times of Chinese strength, notably under the Han (206 BC–AD 220), Tang (618–907) and especially Qing (1644–1912) dynasties, Chinese imperial power has been projected into western Central Asia.

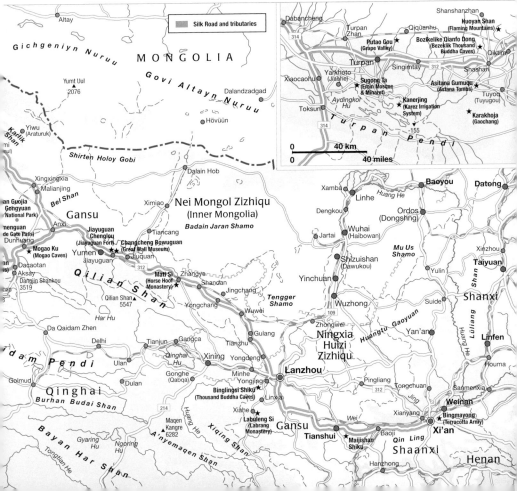

At times of Chinese weakness – notably during the Tibetan Empire in the 7th and 8th centuries and under the Mongols during the 13th century – the nomads surged back, retaking the northwest and briefly conquering China itself. This back-and-forth process culminated in the Manchu conquest of China in 1644, but the resultant Qing Dynasty, like the Mongol Yuan Dynasty before it, soon became sinicised and adopted a Han policy of conquest and control across the northwest.

This constant mixing of peoples and cultures, augmented by the transfer of religions, ideas and settlers from South Asia and the West, eventually made China's great northwest into an ethnic and cultural melting pot. The establishment of the People's Republic in 1949 and subsequent large-scale Han migration into the region, coupled with major improvements in transport, has strengthened the links between the northwest and the rest of the country. Nevertheless, Han Chinese cultural influence diminishes the further west one travels. Hui Muslims, so distinctively different in Xi'an, begin to appear almost Han as the traveller crosses onto the high Tibetan plateau, and still more so in distant, as yet distinctly Turkic cities like Yarkand and Khotan.

Travelling China's Silk Road today

In large part because of Chinese control and Beijing's determination to bind its distant western provinces ever more closely to the centre, it has never been easier to travel the length of the ancient Silk Road between Xi'an and Kashgar. New roads and railways are under construction, in particular the addition of a high-speed passenger line between Lanzhou and Xinjiang, and even the much-feared Taklamakan Desert,

once considered quite impassable, has now been penetrated by surfaced, cross-desert highways. Meanwhile Chinese settlement continues apace. In Inner Mongolia, Han now outnumber Mongols by at least eleven to one, while in Xinjiang their numbers have risen from fewer than 5 percent in 1949 to over 50 percent today.

As elsewhere in China, prosperity has increased rapidly in recent years. Once-isolated oasis settlements of single-storey mud-and-brick buildings are rapidly being replaced by towering high-rise cities, and for every kebab restaurant or itinerant *samsa*-seller there are now two Sichuan or Beijing restaurants, while Western and international cuisine, too, is increasingly available. In predominantly Han cities such as Urumqi and Aksu, felt boots and sheepskins have long since been replaced by Gucci and Armani – even if most are illegal copies – and the bazaars are filled with more DVDs and computer games than rare spices and hand-woven carpets.

There are practical advantages to counter the shock of unexpected globalisation in the backstreets of Chinese Central Asia. The visitor can travel in a comfortable minibus along a carefully maintained, surfaced highway between Kashgar and Lake Karakul in a few hours. The scenery is magnificent, and the glaciers and snow-capped peak of Muztagh Ata, the "Father of Ice Mountains", are still reflected in translucent waters. If you venture this far, you may see a noble Kyrgyz horseman clad in furs edge his mount into the shallows to allow it to drink – just before his mobile phone rings.

PRECEDING PAGES: landscape around the Kizil caves near Kuqa; Tibetan prayer wheel at Labrang. **TOP LEFT:** lunchtime in Khotan. **LEFT AND ABOVE:** contrasts in kashgar.

SHAANXI

Xi'an, known previously as Chang'an, or "Enduring Peace", capital of Shaanxi province and the ancient capital of China, is the start of the Silk Road, and what a send-off: it offers iconic city walls, pagodas, a characterful Muslim quarter and the world-famous Terracotta Warriors.

L ying near the geographical heart of China, Shaanxi has also long been at the centre of Chinese civilisation. The Huang He or Yellow River, traditional cradle of Chinese civilisation, forms the eastern frontier with Shaanxi province, and its principal city and current capital, Xi'an, or "Western Peace", is one of the four great ancient capitals of China (together with Beijing, Nanjing and Luoyang). Even today Shaanxi lies near the centre of China's vast communications network, linking Beijing with the Southwest, and Shanghai with Xinjiang. It is a province whose political, cultural and historical significance can scarcely be overstated or overlooked.

XI'AN

Xi'an served as China's capital for more than a thousand years, most notably under the illustrious Tang Dynasty (618–907). Located near the heart of China's traditional Yellow River and Wei River valleys, yet far enough to the west to exercise effective control over the great overland trade routes between East and Central Asia, the city emerged as the western gateway (or eastern terminus, depending on geographical perspective) of the fabled Silk Road.

As early as 5000 BC a sophisticated agricultural society had developed in the area, firing clay pots and domesticating animals. Relics of this early civilisation, called the Yangshao Culture, can best be seen at Banpo, to the east of today's city.

Xi'an became the political and cultural centre of China in 1027 BC, when the Western Zhou Dynasty established its capital at Fenghao, about 15km (9 miles) southwest of the present-day city centre. Next, under the short-lived Qin Dynasty (221–206 BC), Emperor Qin Shi Huang (246–210 BC) ordered the construction of a great tomb, guarded

Main attractions
XI'AN:
CITY WALLS
MUSLIM QUARTER
GREAT MOSQUE
FOREST OF STELAE MUSEUM
PAGODAS
SHAANXI MUSEUM OF HISTORY
TERRACOTTA WARRIORS

LEFT: the Little Wild Goose Pagoda.
RIGHT: Hui walnut vendor.

ENTERING AND LEAVING SHAANXI

Xi'an, the capital of Shaanxi and eastern terminus of the Silk Road, is readily accessible by air, train and bus from Beijing and most Chinese provincial capitals. (See Travel Tips, page 383, for more information on transport in China.)

Deluxe and express trains run between **Beijing** and Xi'an via Shijiazhuang and Taiyuan, on a daily basis, as do express bus services. The simplest and most comfortable way to reach Shaanxi from Beijing overland is by overnight sleeper, though a daytime bus journey through the middle Huang He area is an interesting experience.

Deluxe and express trains run between Xi'an and Lanzhou in **Gansu** province several times a day, as do express bus services. The journey by train is swift and comfortable, and the new super-highway, opened in 2010, allows motorists to complete the journey in around four hours.

Soft- and hard-sleeper express trains run between Xi'an and Chengdu in **Sichuan** province on a daily basis, as do express bus services. The bus journey is spectacular as it climbs through the Qin Ling range to the south of Xi'an, and across the easternmost outriders of the Tibetan plateau.

A similar range of rail services operates between Xi'an and Chongqing on a daily basis, as do express bus services. Both the railway line and Highway 210 run directly between the two great cities, cutting through the forested Qin Ling Mountains to reach the vast Sichuan Basin.

by a Terracotta Army, befitting the founder and "Commencing Emperor" of the first unified Chinese state. The magnificent tomb survives at Xianyang, the location of the former Qin capital, 36km (22 miles) to the east.

Xi'an prospered greatly under the Han Dynasty (206 BC–AD 220), and began to develop as a great cosmopolitan city, the capital of China and also the chief beneficiary of the developing Silk Road, the overland corridor connecting the Chinese heartlands with Central Asia and the distant Mediterranean world. The city prospered further under the magnificent Tang Dynasty (618–907), when Xi'an, now renamed Chang'an, emerged as the largest and most culturally diverse city in the world, attracting businessmen, traders, artisans, courtesans, mendicants and holy men from all over Asia and beyond. Xi'an lost its position of national prominence after the fall of the Tang Dynasty in 907, with subsequent imperial capitals moving to Kaifeng and, under the Mongols, to Dadu – later renamed Beijing. Xi'an prospered under the Ming Dynasty

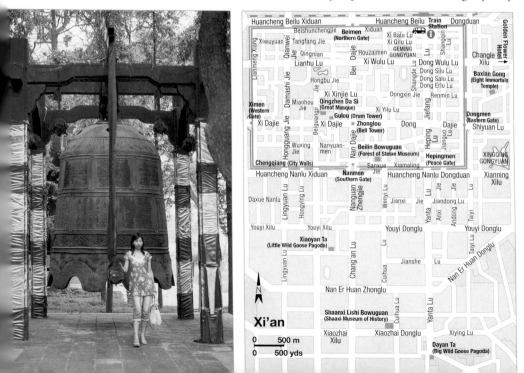

(1368–1644), when a new city wall was built by Emperor Hongwu in 1370. Tellingly, however, the new wall enclosed a much smaller city than the earlier Tang city at Chang'an. Despite its former size and pedigree, Xi'an would remain something of a western outpost, removed from the power and influence of Beijing, until the completion of the strategic east–west Shanghai–Lanzhou Railway in the 1930s.

Since that time Xi'an has expanded as a major industrial centre. The walled central area contains most of the more interesting sights, while the extensive suburbs conceal such historic locations as the remains of the former Weiyang Palace to the north, the complex of religious buildings such as Little Wild Goose Pagoda and Big Wild Goose Pagoda to the south, and the presumed "Start of the Silk Road" near the current junction of Zaoyuan Lu and Daqing Lu to the west of the city walls – this latter supposedly corresponding to the site of the former Western Market, once the terminus of the ancient Silk Road in Tang Dynasty Chang'an.

Within the walled city

Perhaps the most distinctive feature characterising present-day Xi'an is its iconic walls. Known in Chinese as **Chengqiang** (City Walls; open daily 7am–10pm, shorter hours in winter; admission fee), they date back more than six centuries and extend for more than 14km (8 miles), creating one of the largest defensive systems in the ancient world. The walls are in truly remarkable condition – the best and most complete medieval city wall anywhere in China. They are 12 metres (40ft) high and up to 18 metres (60ft) across at the base, quite wide and smooth enough to permit a comfortable four-hour stroll around the perimeter. It is also possible to hire bikes by the hour to cycle the same route. The 5,984 crenellations and periodic watchtowers, as well as **Nanmen** (the Southern Gate), are illuminated at night with rows of red lanterns and spotlights that reflect attractively in the waters of the surrounding moat.

Near the very centre of the walled city, the 14th-century **Zhonglou** (Bell Tower; open daily 8am–9pm, shorter

TIP

Easier and faster than walking around the walls is to rent a bicycle, and there are some available at the city gates, especially the Southern Gate. Alternatively, electric buggies operate on top of the walls, and will carry passengers along the parapets for a small fee.

BELOW LEFT: giant bell at the Little Wild Goose Pagoda. **BELOW:** the Bell Tower.

Life in Old Xi'an

In the 8th century, at the height of its power, the Tang capital was one of the greatest and most sophisticated cities in the world.

Xi'an lived and prospered by trade during the Silk Road's heyday, and naturally attracted communities of merchants from all over the known world. Many such traders from groups as diverse as Arabs and Turks, Sogdians and Persians, Tibetans, Mongols and South Asians settled within the city walls, often close to the great Western Market where most long-distance trade occurred.

The city was known as Chang'an until the start of the Ming dynasty and at its peak it had a population of more than 2 million. Contacts with Central Asia and the Far West meant that troops of musicians and dancers from the Tokharian Oases of Xinjiang and celebrated "tumbling dancers" from Sogdiana performed nightly in the city's entertainment area. Restaurants and teahouses served delicacies and cuisines from regions as diverse as Guangzhou and Bukhara, while wine shops were well stocked with intoxicating liquors from the four quarters of the known world.

Hardly surprisingly, Chang'an catered to the sexual needs of its itinerant merchant population, as well as to the foibles of its local citizens, rich and poor. There were recognised brothel quarters and taverns with friendly serving girls, and there was even a gay quarter in the northwest of the city where those who enjoyed "the way of the cut sleeve" (as homosexual love in China was called) could indulge themselves.

Many musical traditions were represented in the singing houses of Chang'an, but perhaps the most famous and most admired was that of Kuqa, characterised by four-stringed lute and drum-playing orchestras. The Emperor Xuanzong (712–56) was particularly fond of Kuqan music, and is reported to have maintained 30,000 musicians and dancers at the imperial palace. Kuqan dance seems to have been strongly influenced by Indian traditions, placing emphasis on hip movements and hand gestures, flashing eyes and stylised facial expressions. Dance troops from India, Burma, Sogdiana and Southeast Asia competed with the popular Kuqans for custom.

In addition to music and dance, Chang'an was famous for its poets, painters and other artists. Two of China's most prominent classical poets, Du Fu (712–70) and Li Bai (701–62) lived in Chang'an during its primacy. Other, less intellectual pastimes and entertainments included cockfighting, horseriding and polo. We know from painted pottery figures that women paid great attention to fashion, in terms of their clothing, make-up and elaborate hairstyles.

The people of Chang'an celebrated many holidays and festivals, the most important of which then (as now) was Lunar New Year. This was a seven-day festival characterised by the ritual consumption of "Killing Ghosts and Reviving Souls Wine", which was believed to guard against illness during the coming year. Particularly beautiful was the Lantern Festival, held on the 14th, 15th and 16th days of the first lunar month, when the city's night-time curfew was lifted and citizens could stroll through the streets, competing with each other in the size and splendour of their lanterns. Three-day carnivals were also frequent, with much merrymaking involving eating, drinking, street parades and sideshows. Such carnivals were not tied to fixed events, but were called to celebrate good harvests, military victories and other auspicious events.

LEFT: ladies of the court enjoying a banquet.

hours in winter; admission fee) was restored under the Qing Dynasty in the 18th century and is today in excellent condition, offering fine views across the city's central junction and busy Drum Tower Square. Also dating from the 14th century and having benefited from an 18th-century Qing restoration, the nearby **Gulou** (Drum Tower; open daily 8am–9pm, shorter hours in winter; admission fee) is open to the public and offers good views, as well as a chance to examine some of the biggest drums you are ever likely to see. Musical performances featuring – hardly surprisingly – bells and drums are held at both the Bell Tower and the Drum Tower each morning (9–11.30am) and afternoon (2.30–5.30pm, variable).

Immediately to the north and east of Drum Tower Square lies Xi'an's sizeable **Muslim Quarter**, a direct link with the city's culturally diverse Silk Road past when itinerant Muslim merchants and religious teachers settled in the city from the time of the Tang Dynasty onwards. Today some 50,000 Chinese-speaking Muslims, officially recognised as the Hui minority nationality, live within the narrow streets of the Old City. A prosperous community, easily recognised by the simple white caps of the men and the modest head veil worn by some – but by no means all – of the women, the local Muslims have converted **Beiyuanmen**, to the north of the Drum Tower, into an "Islamic Walking Street", where street stalls and restaurants serve a wide range of halal (Chinese: *qingzhen*) foodstuffs, ranging from the ubiquitous *rouchuan* kebabs (beef, mutton or chicken) and toasted Hui flat breads called *bing*, to fresh fruits, raisins, walnuts and pistachios. Other shops offer an eclectic selection of souvenirs aimed chiefly at local tourists (including apparently endless models of Terracotta Warriors as chess pieces or bookends), different varieties of specialist teas and tea-related

paraphernalia, and Islamic sign-writing in both Chinese and in the unusual and rather eccentric Arabic script favoured by the Hui.

A left (west) turn along bustling Xiyangshi Jie gives onto a narrow alleyway leading to Xi'an's **Qingzhen Da Si** (Great Mosque; open daily 8am–7pm, shorter hours in winter; admission fee for non-Muslims). One of the oldest and most unusual mosques in China, it was originally founded in 742 during the Tang Dynasty, though in its present form most of the buildings date from Ming or Qing times. Much of the charm of this lovely building lies in its apparent heterodoxy, featuring a large spirit screen to the west of the main gateway, as well as representational art forms in the shape of huge stone tortoises hunched unexpectedly in the carefully maintained mosque gardens. Eaves are sharply upturned, and the pillars and interior of the Five Room Hall and the Phoenix Pavilion are lacquered in deep red and gold. The minaret – in fact a three-storey pagoda-like structure – owes little

TIP

Visitors can climb the stairs inside the Little Wild Goose Pagoda, but it's difficult to see or to take photographs from the small and rather inaccessible windows.

BELOW: birdcages in old Xi'an.

Almost completely Chinese in design, the Xi'an Great Mosque is somewhat reminiscent of a Confucian Temple of Literature, but built along an axis facing west, towards Mecca, rather than south.

indeed to Islamic architecture. But over doors and gateways, in curvilinear Arabic script, the Oneness of God and the Prophethood of Muhammad are constantly proclaimed as reminders to the faithful. The prayer hall is closed to non-Muslims.

Also within the city walls, the **Beilin Bowuguan** (Forest of Stelae Museum; open daily 8am–6.30pm; admission fee), once a Confucian temple, is located just to the east of **Nanmen** (Southern Gate). The main attraction here is the collection of more than 1,000 inscribed stone stelae, including the earliest extant Nestorian Christian tablet, dating from AD 781. A sculpture gallery featuring Buddhist images dating from the Tang Dynasty and before is similarly evocative of Xi'an's former position as the beginning – or end – of the Silk Road.

The western section of the city walls houses the **Xi'an Tang Hanguang Entrance Remains Museum** (open 8am–5.30pm; entrance fee), is a pleasant place to visit. Some of the oldest and most fragile sections of the city wall are preserved within the museum,

BELOW: stone figure in the garden at the Little Wild Goose Pagoda.

protected from the elements, alongside stone tablets, oracles, clay seals and Chinese calligraphy.

Beyond the walls

Immediately south of the city walls, about 1.5km (1 mile) beyond Nanmen, **Xiaoyan Ta** (Little Wild Goose Pagoda; open daily 8am–6pm; admission fee) stands in the grounds of **Jianfu Si** (Jianfu Temple). Dating from AD 684, this temple was dedicated to the deceased Tang Emperor Gaozong (649–83). Between 707 and 709 Gaozong's successor, Zhongzong, ordered the construction of the Xiaoyan Ta to house Buddhist scriptures brought back from India and Srivijaya by the itinerant Chinese monk Yi Jing (635–713). In all, Yi Jing is reported to have collected more than 400 Buddhist manuscripts over 25 years of travel, and these were lodged in the Little Wild Goose Pagoda for safekeeping and translation.

In its original form, the ochre-yellow pagoda rose through 15 storeys, though an earthquake in 1487 is said to have split the pagoda in half. A subsequent earthquake brought the two halves of the pagoda back together again – in fact no signs of the former split are visible – but the top two storeys were destroyed, reducing the pagoda to its current 13 levels. There is a small *stelae* garden to the east of the pagoda.

About 2km (1.2 miles) to the southeast, on Yanta Nanlu, **Dayan Ta** (Big Wild Goose Pagoda; open daily 8am–6.30pm; admission fee) is an iconic landmark for the City of Xi'an that was constructed in AD 652 on the orders of Emperor Gaozong. Like the slightly more recent Little Wild Goose Pagoda, it was built to house Buddhist sutras and texts brought back to Xi'an by the Buddhist monk Xuanzang (602–64). Xuanzang is said to have asked the emperor for a solid stupa of the kind he had seen on his travels in India, but Gaozong built a hollow wood-and-stone structure,

which was originally called Scripture Pagoda. Initially five storeys high, it was raised to 10 storeys in 703, then subsequently reduced to the current seven storeys by fire. The pagoda stands in the grounds of **Daci'en Si** (Temple of Grace; open daily 8am–6.30pm; admission fee included with Dayan Ta), also established by Gaozong in 647.

Just to the northwest of Big Wild Goose Pagoda on Xiaozhai Donglu, **Shaanxi Lishi Bowuguan** (Shaanxi Museum of History; open daily 8.30am–5pm; admission fee) is one of the better museums in China. The 300,000 exhibits follow Chinese history from the earliest semi-legendary period on the ground floor, via Han Dynasty (206 BC–AD 220) artefacts on the second floor, to significant Sui and Tang Dynasty (581–907) displays in the last section of the museum. Characteristic Silk Road objects include bronze bells, murals and ceramic figurines of braying camels, dancers, musicians and local Xi'an women with elaborate Tang Dynasty hairstyles.

Weiyang Palace

North of the Walled City, about 2km (1.2 miles) northwest of Xi'an West Railway Station, are sections of wall and moat that mark the site of the former **Weiyang Gugong** (Weiyang Palace), built by the first Han Emperor Gaozu (247–195 BC) to grace his new capital at Chang'an. Originally extending over 5 sq km (3 sq miles), and with a wall 8,800 metres (5.5 miles) in circumference, this area was at the heart of Han and subsequently Tang Chang'an. Said to have been the largest palace ever constructed on earth, historic sources claim it was 6.8 times the size of Beijing's Forbidden City, or 11 times the size of Vatican City, though there is little to see there today. Instead, with the massive local tourist market very much in mind, a huge 67-hectare (165-acre) **Tang Paradise Theme Park** (Datang Furongyuan; open daily 9am–10pm; admission fee) seeks to recreate an idealised version of Tang Dynasty Chang'an for enthusiastic Chinese visitors. Everything from the food to the music fits with the park's theme.

Hui man outside the prayer hall of the Great Mosque.

BELOW: the Big Wild Goose Pagoda.

AROUND XI'AN

There are many historic sites in the Wei and Jing river valleys around Xi'an, and it is quite common (as well as practical) for visitors to take the readily available day tours that are on offer at hotels and travel agencies across the city. The most popular tour is the **Dongxian Youlan** or Eastern Circuit, which takes in the Tomb of Qin Shi Huang, Banpo Neolithic Village, Huaqing Hot Springs and – most impressive of all – the Army of Terracotta Warriors. Less popular but still very entertaining is the **Xixian Youlan** or Western Circuit, which includes visits to Famen Temple, the Imperial Tombs, the Tomb of Emperor Jingdi and Xianyang City Museum (Xianyang Shi Bowuguan).

From a Silk Road perspective, the most significant of these outer sites are those associated with **Qin Shi Huang** (r. 221–210 BC), the first emperor of a unified China who, despite his ruthless and autocratic rule, also introduced far-reaching improvements in administration and infrastructure. He also sought to protect China from the restless nomads of the Northwest, ordering the construction of a single defensive wall – Changcheng, the fabled "Great Wall"

Terracotta Warriors

The most impressive memorial to Qin Shi Huang, a site that has made Xi'an internationally celebrated and also earned the city a UNESCO World Heritage Listing in 1987, is undoubtedly **Bingmayong** (The Terracotta Army; open daily 8.30am–5.30pm; admission fee). Although it was widely believed that Qin Shi Huang was entombed in the area, no trace of the celebrated Terracotta Army was known to exist until March 1974, when local farmers digging a well to the east of Li Mountain uncovered traces of terracotta soldiers and horses. Subsequent archaeological excavations have revealed a total (to date) of 8,099 life-sized terracotta figures arranged in ranks, as well as 130 terracotta chariots and more than 600 terracotta horses. It's now generally accepted that their function was to help Qin Shi Huang continue his autocratic rule over a spirit empire in the imperial afterlife.

The statistics behind the Terracotta Army are impressive enough to be somewhat mind-boggling. Building of the mausoleum began in 246 BC and is supposed to have taken an army of 700,000 workers four decades to complete. Qin Shi Huang was interred after his death in 210, amid great pomp and expense. According to the historian Sima Qian (145–90 BC), the First Emperor was entombed with great quantities of treasure amid a jewelled model of the universe complete with flowing rivers of mercury and assorted crossbows and other booby traps designed to repel tombraiders. Despite these precautions, it seems likely that General Xiang Yu, who looted the tomb just five years after Qin Shi Huang's death, started a conflagration that lasted for three months and destroyed large parts of the complex.

BELOW: ranks of terracotta warriors.

Nevertheless, large numbers of terracotta figures, of both men and horses, survived, although their wooden weapons and most of their chariots have by and large burnt or rotted away. From these figures it is apparent that their production was almost on an industrial scale, with specific body parts being manufactured and fired before being arranged in subterranean vaults in careful order of rank and duty. The completed figures were both life-sized and lifelike, and it is famously claimed that no two figures look exactly the same.

Seeing the Terracotta Warriors requires a degree of patience because of the sheer numbers of visitors queuing to share the experience. In fact the authorities have made an excellent job of preserving the serried ranks of warriors in three separate covered pits, the largest of which – **Pit 1** – contains nearly 6,000 equine or human statues in various states of repair, their original brightly coloured lacquer finish on faces and clothing now having almost completely faded. **Pit 2** contains around 1,800 warriors, as well as several perfect specimens that have been preserved in glass display cases at room level to permit visitors an opportunity to get "up close and personal" with some of Qin Shi Huang's warriors and their mounts. **Pit 3**, the smallest yet excavated, is thought to represent the army headquarters, with 72 warriors believed to be of senior rank, together with weapons and horses.

The actual **Tomb of Qin Shi Huang** (Qin Shi Huang Ling; open daily 7am–6pm; admission fee) is located about a mile to the west of the Terracotta Warriors complex, and remains unexcavated pending, perhaps, the development of more sophisticated archaeological preservation techniques in the future. A distinct low hill marks the spot where, according to legend, the deceased emperor was entombed together with all the artisans and workmen who had helped in its construction, buried alive to take their secrets with them, quite literally, to the grave.

TIP

A small air-conditioned museum at Bingmayong displays important finds from the Terracotta Army and surrounding area, most notably two fine bronze chariots and horses, as well as examples of Qin Dynasty weaponry.

BELOW: a close-up of one of the warriors.

The First Emperor

The first emperor of a united China, Qin Shi Huang, inherited the throne of the State of Chin in 247 BC and set about conquering the surrounding states with a view to uniting all China under his leadership. He attained this goal in 221 BC and announced himself "Commencing Emperor". A tyrant who burnt books and persecuted Confucianism, sometimes burying his opponents alive, he nevertheless assumed colossal status after his death in 210 BC. Among his monumental achievements were the building of the Great Wall, the foundation of a network of roads and canals, the standardisation of weights, measures and currency, and the establishment of a national legal system. He remains a central figure in Chinese history and culture.

GANSU

Gansu, with its colourful peoples and dramatic landscapes, marks the first leg of the journey to the West: from Tianshui and Lanzhou, through the Hexi Corridor and culminating in the great Jiayuguan Fort and caves of Dunhuang.

The long, narrow province of Gansu, shaped like a cartoon drawing of a dog's bone, extends northwest from the Shaanxi frontier all the way to Yumenguan, the "Jade Gate Pass" that marks the western limits of China proper and the start of China's vast Central Asian province of Xinjiang, the "New Frontier".

Gansu is the very essence of the Eastern Silk Road. A narrow corridor created by the tectonic upheaval of India's collision with Asia, it passes between the high mountainous Tibetan plateau to the south and the bleak Gobi of the Mongolian Steppe to the north, growing harsher and less "Chinese" with each stage further west. In times past it offered merchants and long-distance caravaneers the opportunity to grow rich and prosper. Yet to officials who were exiled here far from the central plain around China's capital, the distance was measured in despair; after all they were almost halfway to the Jade Gate Pass and total banishment from China.

Modern times

Today Gansu remains one of China's poorer provinces, with an economy based largely on agriculture and mining, and a population that is about 75 percent rural. Unlike Shaanxi, which is almost entirely Han Chinese, Gansu is home to numerous minority nationalities including Hui, Tibetan, Dongxiang, Mongol, Kazakh and Salar, comprising almost 10 percent of the population. This ethnic diversity, combined with the province's ancient archaeological treasures, make Gansu an essential destination in following the ancient Silk Road. Here, at the end of the narrow Hexi Corridor, is the mighty fortress of Jiayuguan, which marks the "first and greatest pass under heaven", and the ancient oasis town of Dunhuang,

Main attractions
MAIJISHAN SHIKU
BINGLINGSI SHIKU
LABRANG
ZHANGYE
SILK ROUTE MUSEUM, JIUQUAN
JIAYUGUAN FORT
OVERHANGING GREAT WALL
FIRST BEACON TOWER
DUNHUANG
MOGAO CAVES
MINGSHA SHAN
YUMENGUAN
YANGGUAN
YARDANG NATIONAL PARK

LEFT: camels at the giant sand dunes of Dunhuang. **RIGHT:** fearsome clay figure at the Buddhist grottoes of Maijishan Shiku.

ENTERING AND LEAVING GANSU

Gansu is a long and narrow province and, as such, most visitors not flying directly into Lanzhou or Dunhuang will enter from Shaanxi to the east or Xinjiang to the west. There are no direct links with the Mongolian People's Republic to the north. (See Travel Tips, page 383, for more information on transport in China.)

Deluxe and express trains run between Lanzhou and Xi'an in **Shaanxi** province several times a day, as do express bus services. Improved road links thanks to the new superhighway have reduced the journey time to a little over eight hours, making it directly comparable to travelling by train.

The celebrated Lanxin railway links Xi'an with Urumqi and Kashgar in **Xinjiang**, passing through most of the main Eastern Silk Road destinations en route. Regular buses ply National Highway 312 between Lanzhou and Urumqi, but given the distances involved it's still faster and more comfortable to travel by train.

It's possible to reach Chengdu in **Sichuan** province directly by train from Lanzhou, but it's much more interesting and popular to travel by bus or car across the mountainous Tibetan-inhabited uplands via Linxia, Langmusi and Songpan, making a side visit to the important Tibetan monastery of Labrang, at Xiahe, en route.

Hard- and soft-sleeper carriages (equipped with oxygen) travel regularly from Lanzhou to Lhasa in **Tibet** on the Qingzang Railway, via Xining and Golmud. Long-distance buses are a convenient and easy way to reach Xining, but are not a terribly comfortable option for onward travel to Tibet (20–25 hours between Golmud and Lhasa).

where the Mogao Caves – also dubbed the "Caves of a Thousand Buddhas" – are a major Silk Road highlight.

SOUTHEASTERN GANSU

Despite the incredible importance of the Eastern Silk Road in the past, communications across China's great northwest have always been poor, and notwithstanding titanic feats of engineering currently under way, the road across Gansu between Shaanxi and Xinjiang remains slow and difficult in many places. Until a motor road was built between Xi'an and the Gansu capital of Lanzhou in the 1930s, this 720km (447-mile) stage of the Silk Road took about 20 days to traverse by mule track. Communications were further improved with the completion of the Xi'an–Lanzhou Railway in 1954, and the new superhighway along the same route, opened in 2010, has significantly reduced travelling times.

Taking the old and more photogenic road route, the first half of the journey westwards to Tianshui is fast and easy along the dual carriageway of Route 310 as far as the industrial

The Lanxin Railway

The Lanxin Railway (Lanzhou–Xinjiang) is the only rail link joining Xinjiang to the rest of China. It was constructed in 1952–62 and runs for 1,904km (1,183 miles) from Lanzhou, closely following the route of the old Silk Road via Turpan to Urumqi. In the 1980s a 477-km (296-mile) extension was added to reach the Kazakh frontier at Alashankou, the link-up with Kazakhstan Railroads forming a route across Central Asia. In 1999, the South Xinjiang Branch of the Lanxin Railway was completed between Urumqi and Kashgar, again closely following the route of the Silk Road. Future projects may include extensions to Osh in Kyrgyzstan and also to Pakistan via the Karakoram Highway, an ambitious plan that would link the Chinese and South Asian rail systems for the first time.

town of Baoji near the western frontier of Shaanxi. Beyond this point the Wei Valley narrows dramatically as the river is forced through a steep defile between the Qin Ling and Liupan ranges. Here the road is reduced to a single carriageway, winding precariously through the gorge in marked contrast to the Xi'an–Lanzhou Railway, which drives through tunnel after tunnel and crosses soaring viaducts in an almost straight line.

Maijishan Shiku

Tianshui or "Heavenly Waters" is the second-largest city in Gansu, with a population of almost 400,000. Confusingly, it is divided into two urban areas connected by a freeway. The industrial area in the east is the place from which to catch a minibus or taxi to **Maijishan** or "Wheat Stack Mountain", about 35km (22 miles) southeast of town.

Maijishan Shiku (Maijishan Grottoes; open daily 8am–6pm; admission fee) are one of China's four most important Buddhist temple groups (the others being Datong, Luoyang and the famous Mogao Caves at Dunhuang, further west along the Silk Road). Starting during the Northern Wei (386–535) and Northern Zhou (557–81) dynasties, pious Buddhists cut caves into the sides of a startling red outcrop rising from the surrounding foliage-covered hills. Figures of the Buddha, bodhisattvas and disciples were carved in harder rock brought from elsewhere, and installed in the caves; it is thought that well-to-do merchants involved in the Silk Road trade acted as patrons, putting a percentage of their profits into endowing and expanding the cave complex, both to give thanks for their good fortune and to ensure future success in the material and spiritual worlds. At their height, the Maijishan Grottoes are believed to have numbered almost 800, but they suffered serious damage during an earthquake in 734. This event, combined with the exigencies of time, has reduced the number of

extant caves to 194 – still no small number, making a visit to Maijishan a very worthwhile day trip.

A great part of the attraction of visiting Maijishan lies in the striking setting of "Wheat Stack Mountain", which rises unexpectedly out of the surrounding hills. The red rock face is pitted with caves and grottoes large and small, as well as two large carvings of the Buddha attended by bodhisattvas. The entire complex is reached by a confusing and apparently precarious (though in fact quite safe) series of steps and catwalks set into the side of the cliff – this is no place for sufferers from vertigo – leading through or past series of caves, many of which are locked, though it is possible to peer in. The surviving sculptures and murals reflect a wide range of artistic styles, with some of the earlier images clearly reflecting South Asian influences, while later images are more distinctively Chinese.

Lanzhou

West of Tianshui, Route 316 continues through hilly countryside for about 250km (150 miles) to **Lanzhou**, the

EAT

Lanzhou is one of the better towns on the Chinese Silk Road for dining out, and with lots of fine restaurants and fascinating street stalls it's the best place to sample the exceptional Gansu school of cuisine. It's also famous for its Lanzhou *lamian* (Lanzhou beef noodles). Behind the Lanzhou Hotel, on busy Nongmin Xiang you can find a number of good, moderately priced restaurants serving local favourites.

BELOW LEFT: the Lanxin Railway.
BELOW: Lanzhou on the Yellow River.

TIP

Most people leaving Binglingsi return directly by boat to Yongjing, but it is also possible to take a small speedboat down the Yellow River and across the Liujiaxia Reservoir to the pier at Lianhuatai, where it's easy to catch a taxi for the short, 50-minute trip to Linxia, a convenient place to overnight on the journey south to Xiahe.

BELOW: Xuanzang and his companions on their Journey to the West.

largest city and provincial capital of Gansu. Due to its strategic location by the Huang He (Yellow River) in a narrow gorge dominating all traffic between central China and the northwest, Lanzhou has long been a vital garrison town that has expanded rapidly in recent decades to become a major city of more than 3 million people. With an economy based on heavy industry and petrochemicals, Lanzhou isn't a particularly appealing town, but it sits squarely astride east–west communications, and remains as vital a transport hub today as it was during the Silk Road era. Long and narrow by virtue of its geography, sandwiched between steep hills, it is a very cosmopolitan city, with a noticeable Hui Muslim presence.

As well as good hotels and restaurants, Lanzhou has a few attractions to appeal to visitors, not least of which is the fast-flowing Huang He, already a major river though still about 1,500km (900 miles) from the East China Sea. The best way to see the Yellow River is to take the cable car across the chocolate-coloured, loess-rich waters up **Baita Shan** (White Pagoda Hill;

open daily 6.30am–8.30pm; admission fee), where fine views across the city can be augmented by a cold drink and a snack. Near the cable-car station, by the bank of the Yellow River and facing westward towards Central Asia, stand the **Journey to the West** *(Xiyouji)* statues featuring the celebrated Buddhist monk Xuanzang and his legendary companions, Monkey, Pigsy and Sandy. Nearby is **Waterwheel Park** (Shuicheyuan; open daily 6.30am–8.30pm; admission fee), where two giant, reconstructed waterwheels revolve in the waters of the Yellow River. Introduced as an irrigation technique from Yunnan in the 16th century, these two wheels are all that remain of an estimated 250 waterwheels in the Lanzhou area in the early 20th century. Also in the same downtown area, the Daoist **Baiyun Guan** (White Cloud Temple; open daily 7am–5.30pm; admission fee) offers a tranquil and attractive retreat from the city bustle.

Finally, in the northwest of the city not far from the West Train Station, the **Gansu Provincial Museum**

(Gansu Sheng Bowuguan; open Tue–Sun 9am–5pm; admission fee) is definitely worth visiting for its unsurpassed collection of Silk Road artefacts including, most famously, the "Flying Horse of Gansu" found at Wuwei in 1969, and a 2ndcentury silver plate showing Dionysus, the Greek god of wine, found near Lanzhou but clearly originating far to the west and carried overland to China at some stage during the early Silk Road era.

Thousand Buddha Caves

Lanzhou may have relatively few attractions, but the city serves as a gateway to some of the most interesting Silk Road sites in eastern Gansu.

Binglingsi Shiku (Thousand Buddha Caves; usually accessible June–October; admission fee) is a remarkable collection of caves and grottoes set in an inaccessible canyon by the Yellow River about 80km (48 miles) upstream from Lanzhou. To reach them, take a bus or car to the small town of Yongjing, then catch a ferry (four hours) or a speedboat (90 minutes) along the Liujiaxia Reservoir to Binglingsi. There is no direct road access, and during winter months – approximately November to May – water levels in the Yellow River fall, making access by boat impossible.

Yet it is this very isolation that has protected and preserved Binglingsi, not least from marauding Red Guards during the Cultural Revolution (1966–76). The first Buddhist grottoes at Binglingsi date from the Eastern Jin Dynasty (c.317–420), and construction continued for well over 1,000 years throughout the Tang, Song, Ming and Qing eras. As was the case with nearby Meijishan, the Binglingsi Caves were often sponsored by wealthy patrons investing some of their Silk Road profits and accruing merit for this life and the next. A total of 183 caves, together with nearly 700 carved stone statues and 82 terracotta sculptures, survive, many showing very clear evidence of South Asian Buddhist artistic

influences – indeed, art experts agree that Binglingsi is a stylistic midpoint between the former monumental Buddhas of Bamiyan in Afghanistan and grotto complexes further east within China at Datong and Longmen.

The setting is indeed spectacular. Travellers arrive by boat at a steep dock by the banks of the Yellow River in extraordinary eroded sandstone country, with tall peaks hemming in the cave complex in a narrow valley known as **Dasi Gou** or "Big Temple Gully". The caves are dominated by a giant carving of Maitreya, the Buddha of the future, which is almost 27 metres (90ft) tall. Green-painted wooden catwalks lead up the cliff to a point above the image's head, but these are generally closed to visitors, both for reasons of safety and to protect the images. A one-hour hike up the narrow canyon (or 15 minutes by jeep, apparently specially brought in by boat) leads to a small but active Tibetan monastery, together with a Tang Dynasty cave sheltering a Buddha image holding the *dharmachakra* or "wheel of life".

Carving of Maitreya, the Buddha of the future, at Binglingsi.

BELOW: transport options on the Liujiaxia Reservoir to Binglingsi.

Pilgrims in the prayer-wheel corridors around the perimeter of Labrang.

BELOW: the beautifully situated Labrang Monastery.

Detour to Labrang

Linxia, formerly known as Hezhou, is a little-visited but economically significant town on a southern spur of the former Eastern Silk Road leading to the Tibetan plateau and, ultimately, to Lhasa. Nowadays a city of 300,000 people, it is a predominantly Muslim town, the capital of **Linxia Hui Autonomous Prefecture** and home to an Islamic-majority population comprising Chinese-speaking Hui Muslims, Mongol-speaking Dongxiang Muslims, and a few Turkic-speaking Salar Muslims who may have originally migrated from distant Uzbekistan. The town is an important Sufi centre for Muslim mystics (recognisable by their six-cornered hats), as well as a cultural meeting point for Han Chinese, Hui Muslims, Tibetan Buddhists and Dongxiang Mongols. Most visitors staying overnight in Linxia will be en route from Binglingsi to the great Tibetan monastery at Labrang. There's not a great deal to see, but there are a number of adequate hotels, and it's easy to find cheap and good Muslim food – lamian noodles, lamb and beef kebabs, toasted *bing* (flat breads) and the like – at the night market on central Minzu Square.

The countryside beyond Linxia is densely populated by Dongxiang Muslims – in fact they look very much like Hui, with whom they have lived and sometimes intermarried for many centuries – living in small, prosperous agricultural settlements raising livestock (but not pigs) and growing wheat, millet and a luscious selection of fruits including grapes, pomegranates, melons, apples and pears. Each village has at least one mosque surmounted by a row of three crescent moons, and the relaxing, pastoral atmosphere makes for a very pleasant drive.

After about an hour the road passes through two long tunnels linking Linxia Hui Autonomous Prefecture with **Gannan Tibetan Autonomous Prefecture**. Minarets give way to Buddhist *chorten (stupas)*, and the deep magenta and purple of Mahayana Buddhist monks' robes replace skullcaps and veils. This cultural frontier marks the beginning of the Tibetan plateau, and although part of Gansu province, local Tibetan residents make it quite apparent that they, at least, consider this to be a part of Tibet. The road rises steadily, and after about two hours enters a beautiful mountain valley. Here, attached to the predominantly Tibetan town of **Xiahe**, stands **Labrang Monastery** (Labuleng Si; admission fee), one of the six major **Gelug** "Yellow Hat" monasteries in Tibetan Buddhism, and a major pilgrimage centre, attracting Tibetans from as far afield as Lhasa and even Dharamsala (the Dalai Lama is a member of the "Yellow Hat" order).

Labrang, which is the most important Tibetan monastery outside the Tibetan Autonomous Region, was established in 1709. At its peak it held as many as 4,000 monks. Today numbers of monks is around 2,000 and crowds of Tibetan pilgrims throng the prayer-wheel corridors in their very colourful best clothing. Increasing numbers of Han Chinese visitors also come to

worship here, some even painstakingly completing the full 6km (4-mile) *kora* or pilgrimage circuit, constantly prostrating themselves full length as they go.

The large complex dominates the western part of the village. The white or ochre walls and gilded roofs are predominantly Tibetan in architectural style, though the occasional Chinese dragon also graces the eaves. In all there are 18 halls, six colleges, the **Gongtang**, a magnificent golden stupa bearing gilded bas-reliefs of the goddess Tara, and miles of prayer-wheel corridors.

The modern town of Xiahe, where the best accommodation and some surprisingly good restaurants are to be found, lies to the east. It's here that the Han Chinese and Hui Muslims have their shops, with many Hui shopkeepers selling all kinds of religious paraphernalia, including Buddha images and prayer wheels, to the visiting Tibetan faithful.

HEXI CORRIDOR

West of Xiahe, old trade routes extended Silk Road traffic across the Tibetan plateau and beyond, as well as

south to Sichuan and Yunnan. But the main route continues to the northwest from Lanzhou, through the Hexi, or Gansu, Corridor. This long, narrow strip of land, sandwiched between the snow-capped Qilian Mountains to the south and the Ala Shan and Gobi deserts to the north, has always provided China with its main overland access to Central Asia and the West. Compared to the harsh terrain to the north and south, travel was always relatively easy along the Hexi, with its series of interconnected oases.

Wuwei

Almost 280km (175 miles) due north of Lanzhou on Route 312, the city of **Wuwei** is "small" only by Chinese standards, with a population of around 500,000, mainly Han Chinese, but with visible numbers of Hui as well as Mongols and Tibetans. In earlier times it was called Liangzhou. Dominating the eastern end of the Hexi Corridor, it has long played a significant role on this major trade route.

Wuwei's most famous historic artefact, the celebrated Han Dynasty (206

BELOW: a sprightly Flying Horse of Gansu in downtown Wuwei.

The Flying Horse of Gansu

In 1969 archaeologists were excavating at a tomb beneath Leitai Temple in Wuwei when they discovered, among more than 200 other relics, a 25-cm (10-in) -high bronze sculpture of a horse at full gallop, its raised head neighing and its rear right hoof resting lightly on the head of a startled swallow in flight. Believed to represent the "heavenly steed" of Central Asian tradition so greatly desired by the ancient Chinese, the "Flying Horse of Gansu" soon became an icon for the province and, increasingly, for China as a whole. Widely considered to be an artistic masterpiece, representing Chinese bronze work at its most sophisticated and elegant, the "flying horse" was cast by an unknown artist at the time of the Eastern Han Dynasty around 2,000 years ago.

Musician in Wenhua Square, Labrang.

BELOW: a Buddhist monk alone with his thoughts.

BC–AD 220) bronze horse known as the **Flying Horse of Gansu**, was discovered here in a tomb beneath **Leitai Temple** (Leitai Si; admission fee) in the north part of town. Although the original is now on display in the Gansu Provincial Museum at Lanzhou, the horse's likeness is everywhere, most notably at the centre of Wuwei's downtown Wenhua Square.

Other sights to visit include the impressive and tranquil **Wen Miao** (Confucius Temple and Museum; open daily 8am–6pm; admission fee), where stelae recording past academic achievements adorn well-tended gardens; and **Dayun Si** (Dayun Temple; open daily 8am–6pm; admission fee), the ancient Bell Tower located on the northeast of the city. Just beyond the restored Bell Tower, in an undistinguished courtyard, Daoist rites are often performed, with mediums covering supplicants with red cloths, ringing bells and shaking censers, vigorously casting out spirits and diseases in the heart of People's China. Finally, and related directly to the old Silk Road, **Luoshi Si Ta** (Kumarajiva Pagoda; admission fee) dates from the

7th century, when it was built to honour the Buddhist monk Kumarajiva (Jiumoluoshi, AD 344–413). Born into a royal household in Kuqa, he travelled to Kashmir and parts of India before returning to translate the Mahayana Buddhist sutras and other writings he had collected. He lived at Wuwei from 386 to 403, and is remembered as one of the city's most illustrious residents. The temple, which is currently undergoing very extensive renovation and which will be quite splendid when complete, centres on the 1,300-year-old yellow brick pagoda dedicated to Kumarajiva.

Zhangye

Just 56km (36 miles) northwest of Wuwei, Highway 312 passes through the undistinguished little town of **Yongchang**. In 1957 an American sinologist, Homer H. Dubs, advanced the theory that a group of 145 Roman centurions captured by the Chinese in 36 BC were settled here (see page 49).

A further 250km (150 miles), or half a day's bus ride northwest of Wuwei, **Zhangye** is an important light industrial and agricultural centre at the

Kumarajiva, the Great Translator

The renowned Buddhist monk and translator Kumarajiva, known to the Chinese as Jiumoluoshi, was born into the Kuqan aristocracy in AD 344, the son of a South Asian nobleman, Kumarayana, and a Kuqan princess, Jiva. His father was an Indian Buddhist monk who had crossed the Pamirs to Xinjiang before settling in Kuqa, where he became the royal priest, while his mother entered the Buddhist nunnery of Tsili near Kuqa when Kumarajiva was just seven years old.

Even by this age, the young Kumarajiva is said to have mastered several Buddhist texts and committed many sutras to memory, and during the two years his mother spent in the nunnery his studies continued apace. Aged 9, he returned to Kashmir to further his religious education. He spent three years in India before returning to Xinjiang, where he continued his studies at Kashgar, ordaining the son of the king of Yarkand while studying the Hindu Vedas.

Subsequently he moved to the Chinese capital at Chang'an where he eventually died in 413. During his long life Kumarajiva translated many texts, including the *Amitabha Sutra*, the *Lotus Sutra*, and the *Diamond Sutra*, but he is best remembered for his peerless rendering of the great *Maha Prajna Paramita Sutra*, or "Heart of Perfect Wisdom" Sutra into Chinese.

heart of the Hexi Corridor, with a population of about 200,000. Like Wuwei, it was originally an important garrison town designed to protect Silk Road traffic and keep the troublesome nomadic invaders out of China proper.

Everything narrows in central Gansu as the northern **Longshou Shan** or "Dragon's Head Mountains" press south from the Gobi to sandwich all – the former Silk Road, the modern road, railway lines and the **Great Wall of China** itself – into a narrow corridor facing the mighty **Qilian Shan** or "Sky Mountains" further south. The Great Wall, which is mainly of compressed earth in these remote western reaches, stretches to the north of Highway 312 for about 150km (90 miles) before cutting across the road at Shandan and continuing, like a crumbling mud serpent, south of the highway towards Zhangye.

Zhangye is a more attractive town to stay in than either Wuwei or, further to the west, Jiayuguan. There are adequate shops and hotels, as well as Mingqing Jie, a reconstructed "Ming and Qing Dynasty" walking street that is lined with reasonably priced, clean restaurants. Cultural attractions tend to be clustered in the southwest of town, around Zhongxin Square, a large, paved walking area where local people gather to drink beer, chat or fly kites in the cool of the evening. Dominating the west of the square is Mu Ta (Wooden Pagoda; open daily 7.30am–6.30pm; admission fee), a carefully restored octagonal pagoda dating originally from the 6th century. A short distance south is Xilai Si (open daily 7.30am–6.30pm; admission fee), a small but active Buddhist temple with a resident population of monks.

To the southeast of the square stands – or rather, lies – a 34-metre (20-ft) -long Reclining Buddha, said to be China's largest. The image is housed in the main building of **Dafo Si** (Great Buddha Temple; open daily 7.30am–6.30pm; admission fee), which is currently being restored. The Buddha image is impressive, but photography is forbidden. Further to the east in the temple grounds stands Tu Ta (Earthen Tower), a 20-metre (65-ft) -high Tibetan-style stupa.

BELOW: the entrance to Dafo Si, the Great Buddha Temple, in Zhangye.

Marco Polo in downtown Zhangye.

BELOW: Ta Ta (Earthen Tower) in Zhangye.

Away from southeastern Zhongxin Square, the geographical centre of the city is marked by a fine **Gulou** (Drum Tower; open 7am–8pm; admission fee) that dates from 1507 and holds a large Ming Dynasty bronze bell. Finally and rather unexpectedly, in the northwest part of town near Ganquan Park, there stands a robed and distinctly Occidental statue representing the Venetian traveller **Marco Polo** (1254–1324), who is said to have spent a year here, together with his father Niccolo and his uncle Maffeo, towards the end of the 13th century.

Around Zhangye

Southwest of Zhangye a narrow road climbs into the foothills of the Qilian Shan, approaching a series of permanently snow-capped peaks rising to Mt Qilian at 5,547 metres (18,199ft). The road leads to **Mati Si** (Horse Hoof Monastery; admission fee), carved into sandstone hills some 65km (40 miles) from Zhangye. The monastery was once an important religious centre, but suffered badly at the hands of iconoclastic Red Guards during the Cultural Revolution. It is sobering to think that, had Binglingsi been more accessible, it too might have suffered irreparable damage. As things are, Mati Si is being restored, and in any case is worth visiting if time permits, as the countryside round about is wild and appealing for hikers, as well as being home to the Buddhist Yugur minority who are embracing tourism with some enthusiasm, offering horse-riding and accommodation in Yugur yurts together with such delights as *chang* (barley wine) and *shouzhua yangrou* or "hand-eaten lamb".

Beyond Zhangye Route 312 runs northwest for a further 250km (155 miles) to Jiuquan, passing through pleasant, fertile countryside sheltering poor, but not impoverished, villages of mud-walled, inward-looking domestic compounds. Few rural buildings are more than one storey high because of the threat of earthquakes. Grapevines hang in front of many houses to provide shade in the heat of the day, while flat roofs are covered with firewood or straw to guard against the bitter cold of winter. Livestock includes numerous sheep, goats and cows, but fewer pigs in this increasingly Islamic region. Everywhere are small trucks packed with tomatoes, big red chilli peppers, apples, melons, grapes and pears, tended by local people who – especially the high-cheek-boned Gansu women – all seem to sport rosy cheeks as a result of the strong, sometimes sandy wind and the hot Central Asian sun. The predominant colours of the surrounding countryside are green where irrigated fields and lines of poplars define the outskirts of villages, and a sere, dusty yellow reflected in the surrounding hills, scrubland and the surviving entrails of the Great Wall, still staggering towards the "Last Pass under Heaven" at Jiayuguan, the traditional terminus of the Ming Great Wall.

Jiuquan

Just half an hour before Jiayuguan, the old Silk Road city of **Suzhou** (not to be confused with Suzhou

in Jiangsu province) has been reinvented around **Jiuquan** (population 350,000). Jiuquan is another old Silk Road garrison town, said to derive its name *jiu quan* or "wine spring" from a legendary incident that took place in around 120 BC, during the Han Dynasty's long wars with the Xiongnu nomads of the Northwest. The Han commander, Huo Qubing (140–117 BC) was sent a flagon of wine by the emperor, and deciding to share it with all his men, tipped the wine into a nearby spring, which was subsequently named Jiuquan. The spring – officially called Jiuquan Yuan or "Wine Spring Park" – still exists, and Jiuquan artisans still produce "night-glowing cups" of green Qilian Mountain jade which are said to glow when filled with wine and set in the moonlight. A nice story, but *caveat emptor* – they don't!

The modern town of Jiuquan is centred on a **Drum Tower** (Gulou) established in the 14th century when Suzhou was an important Ming garrison town guarding the western end of the Hexi Corridor, but dating in its present form from 1905. The original structure was praised by Marco Polo in his writings. Aligned with the cardinal directions, above each of its gates are inscriptions in Chinese proclaiming that "East is Huashan" (in distant and desirable Shaanxi), "North is the Great Desert" and "South are the Qilian Mountains". Chinese soldiers stationed here over the centuries would hardly have needed the fourth reminder that: "West is Yiwu", the old name for Hami Oasis in Xinjiang, distant some 650km (390 miles) across some of the most bleak and arid desert anywhere in the world.

The town's newest attraction is the **Silk Route Museum** (www.silkroutemuseum.com; open daily; admission fee), which opened in 2009 and is spread out across a huge site of 280 hectares (700 acres) The museum houses over 35,000 artefacts including well preserved frescoes from the Wei Jin tomb, fossils, Buddhist temple carvings and a large selection of jade figurines. The museum has a large fund at its disposal for ongoing acquisitions and has regularly changing exhibitions.

Most of the people of Gansu speak a dialect of Mandarin Chinese. In outlying areas Tibetan, Mongol, Kazakh and Salar – the latter a Turkic language – are also spoken, but Mandarin, also called putonghua or "common speech", is understood by just about everyone.

BELOW: reaching for the sky at the Jiuquan Satellite Launch Centre.

Jiuquan is widely known as China's aerospace city, although the massive Jiuquan Satellite Launch Centre, which covers an estimated 2,800 sq km (1,081 sq miles) and may house up to 20,000 scientists and technicians, is in fact located in the nearby Alashan region of Inner Mongolia.

Around Jiuquan

There are two sites of interest shortly outside Jiuquan city, 3km (2 miles) to the west. The **tomb chamber** at Dingjiazha houses some of China's earliest wall paintings, dating from the East Jin Dynasty (317–430 AD). The tomb is thought to belong to a nobleman, and the murals include scenes of hunting and banquets, as well as an attractive depiction of the heavens.

The **Jiuquan Satellite Launch Centre** (Shuang Cheng Tzu) was China's first ballistic missile and satellite launch pad. The Centre is a part of **Dongfeng Space City**, which features test-flight facilities and a small museum.

Jiayuguan

Much closer to hand, just 20km (12 miles) or so from Jiuquan, stands the great fortress of **Jiayuguan**, the "First and Greatest Pass under Heaven", completed in 1372 on the orders of Zhu Yuanzhang, the first Ming emperor (1368–98), to mark the end of the Ming Great Wall – or, more specifically, the very limits of

Chinese civilisation, and the beginnings of the outer "barbarian" lands. For centuries, the fort was not just of strategic importance to Han Chinese, but of cultural significance as well. This was the last civilised place before the outer darkness – those proceeding beyond, whether disgraced officials or criminals, faced a life of exile among nomadic strangers, before which they had to cross the ghost-infested wastes of the Gashun Gobi, a wind-blasted, arid wasteland hundreds of kilometres across where hapless travellers faced extremes of heat and cold by day and night. Jiayuguan was quite properly feared, and even today many Chinese associate the pass with exile and despair, bringing to mind the exiles' poem:

Looking westward, we see the long, long road.

Only the brave cross the Martial Barrier Who is not afraid of the vast desert?

Should not the scorching heat of heaven make him frightened?

Soldiers stationed at Jiayuguan took a similarly bleak view of the location, but one that was perhaps rather more sanguine, as befits military men. In the mid-8th century the Tang poet Liu Zhongyong summed up their feelings in his verse "The Troopers' Burden":

For years, to guard the Jade Pass and the River of Gold

With our hands on our horse-whips and our sword-hilts

We have watched the green graves change to icy snow

And the Yellow River ring the Black Mountain forever.

Today **Jiayuguan City** is a modern, prefecture-level town of about 150,000 people – almost all Han Chinese – that makes a living from transport and heavy industry, and has little to recommend it other than its proximity to the great fortress, and a spectacular natural setting at the western end of the Hexi Corridor beneath the permanently snow-covered peaks of the great Qilian range. There's really nothing of interest to the visitor in the town itself,

BELOW: a young artist at Jiayuguan.

though there's adequate accommodation and even a couple of rather good restaurants. In other words, it's a good base to visit the nearby fortress and various remains of the Great Wall, as well as the rather superior Great Wall Museum that opened in 2003.

Jiayuguan Chenglou (Jiayuguan Fort; open daily 8.30am–7.30pm; admission fee) stands in the desert about 6km (4 miles) west of Jiayuguan City, overlooking the narrow entrance to the Hexi Corridor, at this point about 15km (9 miles) across, dominated by the icy Qilian to the south and the bleak, wind-blasted Mazong Shan, or "Horse-Mane Mountains" to the north. The fort, which has been fully restored and is in fine condition, is surrounded by walls 11 metres (36ft) high and about 750 metres (2,500ft) in length, being trapezoid in shape and pierced by three gates, the eastern **Guanghua Men** or "Gate of Enlightenment", the inner **Rouyuan Men** or "Gate of Conciliation" and the outer, western gate, sometimes imaginatively called the "Gate of Sighs", but in fact bearing the Chinese characters

Jiayuguan Men, or "Gate of the Pass of the Pleasant Valley". Each of the three main gates has 17-metre (10-ft) -high towers with curving, upturned eaves. Within the main courtyard, the restored **Residence of General Rui Neng** is a Ming Dynasty structure with realistic waxwork figures of the general's family, soldiers and domestic servants going about their business. The whole complex is surrounded by a lesser, outer wall, and the crumbling remains of the Great Wall itself march west from the fort's southwest corner to the nearby Taolai River, where it stops suddenly above a steep gorge.

Outside the fortress, but within the grounds of the park that surround it, **Changcheng Bowuguan** (Great Wall Museum; open daily 9am–5pm; admission fee included with fort) features many aspects of the history of the Great Wall, as well as Silk Road exhibits and painted tiles from the **Wei and Western Jin Tombs** (AD 220–420) that lie scattered in the desert about 25km (16 miles) east of Jiayuguan. Outside the museum stand busts of **Feng Sheng**, the Ming general who drove

BELOW: Jiayuguan Pass, with the Qilian Mountains in the distance.

First Pass under Heaven

For Han Chinese the great fortress at Jiayuguan marked – symbolically, at least – the westernmost limits of civilisation. Beyond lay only the demon-inhabited wastes of the Gashun Gobi and Taklamakan deserts, as well as the fierce and unpredictable nomadic tribes that posed a constant threat to China's settled security. Jiayuguan was the harshest and least popular station in the entire empire for those troops sent to guard the western frontier and the all-important Silk Road that lay beyond. It was also a place of terror and anguish for those banished from the realm, whether disgraced officials or common criminals, who were forced, unwillingly, through the "Gate of Sighs".

Those passing through the gateway, whether into exile or on imperial service in some distant "barbarian" oasis, would often leave despairing poems and other graffiti on the walls of the narrow passage leading to Jiayuguan Gate. Small pebbles were thrown at the wall to see if they bounced back or simply fell to the ground – a sign of whether the traveller would eventually return to the safety and civilisation of China, or might languish forever in a realm of malevolent spirits and "barbarian" nomads "stinking of rancid mutton". For merchant venturers, however, Jiayuguan represented a gateway to opportunity and the possibility of immense wealth.

The impressively restored Overhanging Great Wall.

BELOW: a red flag flutters from the Overhanging Great Wall.

the last Mongol armies westwards out of the Hexi Corridor in 1368, and of **Yi Kaizhan**, the legendary master engineer who oversaw the construction of the fortress soon thereafter.

Two other Silk Road-related sites worth visiting in the vicinity of Jiayuguan are the **Overhanging Great Wall** (Xuanbi Changcheng; open daily 8.30am–7pm; admission fee) and the **First Beacon Tower** (Wanli Changcheng Diyi Dun; open daily 8.30am–7.30pm; admission fee). The former is an impressively restored section of wall to the northwest of the fort, connecting its ramparts to the outliers of the Mazong range. The wall climbs straight up the mountain flank in a manner reminiscent of the Great Wall north of Beijing, offering fine views across the surrounding countryside. The latter marks the point where the Great Wall meets the Taolai River Gorge, and is marked by an abandoned beacon tower. A balcony of reinforced glass projects from the cliff and offers dizzying views of the waters of the Taolai River swirling through the gorge below.

WESTERN GANSU

The fortress at Jiayuguan represents the end of the Hexi Corridor, but not quite the end of Gansu province and of China proper. The proximity of Central Asia is palpable, in the faces and clothing of the people, the aroma of grilling kebabs and spiced naan breads pervading the markets, even the dust storms that blow in all too frequently from the Gashun Gobi and Taklamakan deserts. Yet there is still some distance – nearly 400km (250 miles) – to the unprepossessing truck stop of Xingxingxia on the Gansu–Xinjiang frontier, and Western Gansu, freed from the crushing embrace of the Qilian Mountains now far to the south, opens out to embrace the antique oasis town of Dunhuang, as well as the celebrated Mogao Caves and two long-abandoned Han Dynasty passes, Yumenguan and Yangguan, that marked the traditional start of the Northern and Southern Silk Roads, respectively, via the Tarim Basin oases that skirt the unforgiving Taklamakan.

Yumen and Anxi

About 60km (37 miles) west of Jiayuguan, Highway 312 skirts north of the old city of **Yumen** or "Jade Gate", a name that hangs heavy with evocative nostalgia, but is today a rather uninspiring oil town. Continuing northwest, the road leaves the Qilians behind and enters bleak and arid wasteland. After a further 230km (140 miles) the town of **Anxi** or "Pacified West" marks an important junction on the former Silk Road, but was badly damaged during the 19th-century Muslim rebellions, and holds little appeal for the visitor today. The Silk Road divided here, with a northern branch heading across the Gashun Gobi to the oasis city of Hami in Xinjiang, and thence to Turpan and the northern Tarim Basin, while a southern branch led first to Dunhuang, and then across the dry Kum Tagh, or "Sand Mountains", to the remote oases of the southern Tarim Basin. Both routes would rejoin at the distant caravan city of Kashgar, near China's westernmost extremity.

Dunhuang

Yumen and Anxi may be little more than transit points today, but **Dunhuang**, or "Blazing Beacon", more than makes up for this deficiency. As early as 117 BC, Dunhuang was made a prefecture by the Han Emperor Wu Di (141–87 BC). Wu Di recognised the strategic location of the oasis, both as the last major watering hole before the Taklamakan Desert, and because it sat astride the three main Silk Road routes running west. The Great Wall was extended into the desert to the west of Dunhuang, linking the settlement with the two main Silk Road gates, **Yumenguan** and **Yangguan**. By the 3rd century AD, Dunhuang dominated Silk Road traffic in the region and had become a prosperous town, with merchants and pilgrims sponsoring the construction of the nearby Buddhist **Mogao Caves**. Subsequently the town enjoyed mixed fortunes, being occupied by Tibet in the 7th century but prospering under the Tang Dynasty (618–907) before being occupied, in turn, by the Xixia (1036) and the Mongols (1227). The city was re-established by the Qing in 1760, and once again became prosperous, enjoying – according to missionary sources – the Silk Road sobriquet "Little Beijing".

Today **Dunhuang** is a busy and, once again, prosperous little frontier town of about 100,000, mainly Han but also Hui, Uighur, Mongol and Tibetan citizens. Laid out in a simple grid pattern around a central traffic circle, the town is small enough to explore on foot. The atmosphere is relaxed and friendly. Busy **Shazhou Night Market** on Yangguan Donglu sells excellent food, while a string of small restaurants on nearby Mingshan Lu, near the main bus station, offer Sichuan and other regional cuisines often accompanied by – luxurious surprise – English-language menus! Accommodation is both plentiful and reasonably priced. All in all, Dunhuang is an excellent place to break a Silk Road trip for at least a

BELOW: the oasis of Dunhuang, with the Mingsha Shan (Singing Sand Dunes).

TIP

Dunhuang town is small enough to get around on foot, and the lake and dunes to the south of town can be reached by bicycle or taxi. To get to the Mogao Caves you can take a regular bus, minibus or taxi for the 30-minute journey. From the centre of town it's easy enough to find transport. Once you reach the caves you are obliged to join a guided tour to see a selection of the caves.

BELOW: the entrance to the Mogao Caves.

couple of days; as well as being congenial, there's plenty to see in the surrounding area. Not that there's much in town itself, beyond **Dunhuang County Museum** (Dunhuang Xian Bowuguan; open daily 8am–6pm; admission fee), where rather average collections of Silk Road-related artefacts and Mogao Caves scrolls are displayed.

Around Dunhuang

The most important attraction in northwest Gansu, and the main reason most Silk Road travellers and Buddhist pilgrims visit Dunhuang, is the **Mogao Caves** (Mogao Ku; open daily 8.30–11.30am, 2.30–6pm; admission fee). Located about 25km (15 miles) southeast of the town centre and accessible by taxi or minibus, the caves were cut into the soft rock face of the **Mingsha Hills** over a period of more than 1,000 years, from the 3rd to the 14th centuries. They represent China's – and probably the world's – most extensive collection of Buddhist statuary, paintings and manuscripts, though many of the original materials

are now in foreign museums, especially in Europe.

Having suffered many depredations at the hands of robbers, warlords, iconoclastic Muslims and Red Guards over the years (but none so damaging to the Mogao Caves, at least, as their late 19th–early 20th-century discovery by archaeologist-explorers such as Aurel Stein – see page 75 – and Paul Pelliot) the cave complex is now extremely well cared for. Visitors cannot enter without a guide, photography is forbidden and generally the only illumination will be the guide's flashlight – to prevent the murals fading over time.

Almost 500 caves survive, set back against and cut into the cliff face, and connected by a series of ramps and walkways. Not all the caves are open to the public – even accompanied by an obligatory guide – and it may be necessary to make special arrangements (and payment) with the Mogao authorities to explore further such off-limits grottoes. An estimated 45,000 sq metres (148,500 sq ft) of murals and more than 2,000 painted stucco figures can be seen (though it would take considerable dedication and several days to try to visit all of them). The years of darkness have kept the generally pastel colours fairly bright, and it is a wonderful experience, even to the lay person with limited knowledge of Buddhist art, to wander through the caves as the torchlight reveals image after image derived, variously and distinctively, from South Asian, Gandharan, Turkic, Tibetan and of course Chinese traditions. A well-presented museum in front of the caves features examples of the astonishing number of scripts found on manuscripts and other documents preserved at the caves, including writings not just in Chinese and Sanskrit, Tocharian and Tibetan languages, but also in various Turkic dialects, Persian and even Hebrew.

Less spectacular, but also less well known, the **Western Thousand Buddha Caves** (Xi Qianfodong; open daily 7am–5.30pm; admission

fee), located 35km (22 miles) west of Dunhuang City, are also worth visiting. The supervision by guides is much less strict, and visitors can generally explore the six caves (of a total of 16) that are open to the public. The caves date from the Northern Wei Dynasty (4th century) through to the late Tang and beyond.

Also reminiscent of the Silk Road, about 4km (2.5 miles) due west of Dunhang, the nine-storey **White Horse Pagoda** (Baima Ta; open daily; admission fee) is dedicated to the memory of the Buddhist monk Kumarajiva's horse, which died here in 384. The 12-metre (40-ft) –high, dun-coloured pagoda is made of baked clay decorated with stucco overlay.

After Mogao Caves, and perhaps even more popular with local tour groups, the biggest attractions at Dunhuang are the **Mingsha Shan** (Singing Sand Dunes; open daily 6am– 9pm; admission fee). Dominating the horizon about 4km (2.5 miles) south of town, these are the largest and most impressive sand dunes in China. The main dunes, which rise to between 250 and 300 metres (820ft–1,000ft), would not look out of place in the Grand Erg dunes of Algeria, and are truly impressive. They're called "Singing Sands" because the shifting grains reportedly make a humming noise in powerful winds.

Set in the lee of the great dunes, **Crescent Moon Lake** (Yueyaquan; admission included with Mingsha Shan) is – as the name suggests – a small, crescent-shaped stretch of water that can look very blue at the right time of day and in good weather. The entire (admittedly lovely) area has become a kind of Silk Road theme park and funfair, with long teams of Bactrian camels carrying Chinese tourists wearing orange sand-boots and carrying mobile phones up the sand dunes. It's a great photo opportunity, but also rather deflating to find that – just off lens from that perfect sand dune and camel train image shot at sunset – there are another 250 camels carrying similar, long lines of tourists! Other very popular activities in the area include quad biking, paragliding and sand-surfing down the steep dunes.

BELOW: reclining Buddha at the Mogao Caves.

Camels make a popular photo opportunity.

BELOW: the oasis at Crescent lake.

Further afield, and directly related to the former Silk Road, are the remains of the two Han Dynasty gates marking the various Silk Roads running west, beyond Dunhuang, to Kashgar and beyond.

Yumenguan

Yumenguan (Jade Gate Pass; open daily; admission fee) is about 90km (56 miles) to the west of Dunhuang City. It was established by the celebrated Han Emperor Wu Di around 120 BC to defend the western reaches of the empire and control trade and taxes. The Silk Road passing through Yumenguan divided west of the gate, a long-lost central route leading via Lop Nur and the former city of Loulan to Korla, and thence following the southern foothills of the Tian Shan around the northern Tarim Basin to Kashgar. An alternative northern route avoided Loulan altogether and swung northwest, across the Gashun Gobi to Hami, and then on to Turpan and Korla, where it rejoined the central route. Due to progressive desertification and the shifting of Lop Nur Lake,

the pass at Yumenguan – really a kind of ancient toll gate – was probably abandoned by the 6th century, as traffic increasingly followed the present northern route via Xingxingxia and Hami to Turpan.

Today Yumenguan is an isolated rectangular watchtower of rammed earth some 10 metres (33ft) high. It has two gateways, in the west and the north. A *ma dao* or horse ramp once allowed soldiers to lead their horses onto the tops of the crenellated battlements. The admission fee includes a small but worthwhile museum detailing Yumenguan's former importance on the Silk Road and postulating that the name "Jade Gate Pass" originated from the fine jade brought back to China via the toll gate from Khotan and beyond.

The Tang Dynasty poet Li Bai (701–62) immortalised Yumenguan in his poem "The Moon over Jade Gate Pass", which remains familiar to many Chinese and evocative of exile far from home:

A bright moon rises above the Mountains of Heaven,

Lost in a vast ocean of clouds.
The eternal wind, across thousands
upon thousands of miles,
  Blows past Jade Gate Pass.

Yangguan

Near Nanhu village, about 60km (37 miles) south of Yumenguan and a similar distance west of Dunhuang, stand the remains of **Yangguan** (Sun Pass; open daily; admission fee). Like its twin at Yumenguan, Yangguan was erected by Wu Di in around 120 BC to control the Southern Silk Road to Kashgar, striking west through the arid wastes of the Kum Tagh "Sand Mountains" before reaching the ancient Silk Road settlement and fortress of Miran, some 75km (46 miles) northeast of Charklik. From here the southern route continued via the oases to the south of the Taklamakan Desert, and via Khotan and Yarkand, to rejoin the northern and former central routes at Kashgar.

Like Yumenguan, Yangguan is remembered in a famous verse of parting and exile, penned by the Tang poet Wang Wei (701–61):

A morning rain has settled the dust in Wei City.
Willows are green again by the tavern door.
Do not leave until we have drained one more glass of wine together –
To the west of Yangguan you will meet no more old friends!

Today the remains of Yangguan stand atop a low hill in the desert. In recent years it has been joined by a Silk Road Exhibition Hall at Yangguan Museum (Yangguan Bowuguan; open daily; admission fee). Nanhu Village offers opportunities for snacks and cold drinks, as well as delicious locally grown grapes.

Finally, in the desert beyond, **Yardang National Park** (Yadan Guojia Dizhi Gongyuan; admission fee included with Yumenguan) is an extraordinary terrain of steep, wind-eroded outcrops on the edge of the Gashun Gobi. Set in an isolated, eerie wasteland, it's no wonder the local people traditionally considered it an "abode of demons". At twilight or in a dust storm the natural formations do indeed look strangely like the time-worn buildings of an abandoned, ancient city.

Yangguan was once the major gateway to the west and an important toll point on the Chinese Silk Road. In the 7th century the eminent Buddhist monk Xuanzang passed through on his return to Xi'an from India, when Yangguan was a military strongpoint set in a small but flourishing oasis.

BELOW: the remains of Yangguan.

Yardangs

Yardangs are strange-looking, wind-eroded outcrops formed by the elements over many millennia. The name is Turkic in origin, meaning "steep banks". Yardangs form in areas where water is scarce and prevailing winds are strong and abrasive. These harsh winds erode low-lying areas into parallel ridges and distinctive mounds that take on a unique shape reminiscent of the upturned hull of a ship. The process gradually yields a field of yardangs of roughly the same size, commonly referred to as "a fleet" due to their uniquely characteristic shape. Yardangs occur most commonly in Xinjiang, the Tibesti region of the central Sahara, and in Arizona in the American West. Recently, huge yardang formations have also been discovered on Mars.

XINJIANG

For many, Xinjiang is archetypal Silk Road terrain: endless desert, mountains, colourful bazaars, abandoned ancient cities. It's all here, from the vineyards of Turpan to the silk looms of Khotan, while Kashgar brings you to the edge of Central Asia.

Xinjiang is China's largest province, accounting for one-sixth of the nation's territory and, at 1,660,000 sq km (640,000 sq miles), equalling almost exactly the land areas of France, Germany, Spain and the UK combined. At a mere 20 million, the population is sparse but demographically diverse. In 1949, the inhabitants of this part of China were mainly Turkic Muslim, with Uighurs predominating in the south and Kazakhs in the north. Han Chinese, almost all of whom were officials or merchants from China proper to the east of the Jade Gate, numbered between 3 and 4 percent of the total population.

Since 1949, Han Chinese have migrated to Xinjiang in large numbers, and are now the second-largest ethnic group in the province, comprising around 41 percent of the total, compared to the Uighur at 45 percent. Smaller groups – ranging from the Kazakhs at 7 percent and the Hui at 5 percent down to the Persian-speaking Tajik minority at Tashkurgan in the far west, numbering a mere 0.2 percent of the population – are numerically less significant.

Xinjiang has been of immense strategic significance to China for more than 2,000 years. From about the 2nd century BC, when Han China first began to extend its influence over the area, it was called Xiyu or "Western Region". For centuries it was known in the West variously as Eastern Turkestan or Chinese Turkestan. Following the Qing re-conquest of the area in 1884, it was renamed Xinjiang or "New Frontier" and given provincial status, before becoming the Xinjiang Uighur Autonomous Region in 1955.

The vast area is dominated by some of the highest mountains and most arid deserts in the world. In the east, the area around Hami and Lop Nur

Main attractions

HAMI
TURPAN:
  TURPAN MUSEUM
  GRAPE VALLEY
  JIAOHE ANCIENT CITY
  ASTANA TOMBS
FLAMING MOUNTAINS
BEZEKLIK
TIEMENGUAN
KUQA
KHOTAN
YARKAND
KASHGAR:
  SUNDAY MARKET
SHIPTON'S ARCH
LAKE KARAKUL
XINJIANG AUTONOMOUS REGION
  MUSEUM
HEAVENLY LAKE

LEFT: Lake Karakul, south of Kashgar.
RIGHT: the Flaming Mountains near Turpan.

ENTERING AND LEAVING XINJIANG

Travellers leaving China via Xinjiang for points further west on the Silk Road should apply for onward visas in their home country or in Beijing. It is not possible to get visas for any of the neighbouring countries on arrival at the land border. (See Travel Tips, page 383, for more information on transport in China.)

Entering Xinjiang from **Gansu** is easy via either the Lanxin Railway, or National Highway 312 between Lanzhou and Urumqi.

Highway 219 runs south from Karghalik before heading across the **Tibetan plateau** towards Lhasa. This is one of the most difficult roads in the world, and reaches exceptionally high altitudes. It remains officially closed to foreign visitors in China, though increasing numbers of independent motorists and bus passengers do manage to take it.

The difficult, largely unpaved route from Dunhuang, via the Dangjin Pass and the hellish mining town of Magnai Zhen, leads across remote northwest **Qinghai** to Charklik on the Southern Silk Road in Xinjiang, but this route is not recommended and is often snowbound in winter.

There are efficient overland crossings between Xinjiang and **Kazakhstan** at Korgas and Tacheng, as well as a rail link at Alashankou to Druzba and on to Almaty in Kazakhstan.

Two roads lead to **Kyrgyzstan**, the relatively easy Irkeshtam Pass to Osh and the less-frequented Torugart Pass to Naryn and Bishkek. It is only possible for foreigners to cross the Torugart Pass with private transport.

The spectacular Karakoram Highway via the mighty Khunjerab Pass leads to Baltit (Hunza), Gilgit and Islamabad in **Pakistan**. A regular bus service plies this route from May to October.

has long been strongly influenced by nearby China proper, and is dominated by Han and Hui Chinese with a scattering of Uighurs. North of the Tian Shan, Urumqi is an overwhelmingly Han Chinese city, while the Dzungarian Steppe and Altai Mountains are home mainly to the province's Kazakhs. The Tarim Basin in the southwest, distinguished by a series of oasis towns surrounding the central Taklamakan Desert like beads on a necklace, is dominated by Uighur, though both Han and Hui continue to settle throughout the area, especially in the larger cities.

The Silk Road has defined Xinjiang for millennia, dividing into three main routes near Dunhuang and traversing the province before coming together again in Kashgar and continuing to Central Asia. The very transient nature of Silk Road commerce has forged Xinjiang's character as a marginal land, a meeting place of peoples and cultures as diverse as Chinese and Arab, Tibetan and Turk, Mongol and Manchu. The religions they brought – Buddhism, Manichaeism, Nestorian

Christianity, Judaism and Islam, all left their mark and have contributed to the fascinating cultural and artistic heritage of the province.

THE FORMER CENTRAL ROUTE

Until the 4th century AD, the main Silk Road route west from Dunhuang led through Yumenguan, across the incredibly inhospitable Gashun Gobi, to the almost legendary city of Loulan on the shores of a lake called Lop Nur, before following the waters of the Konqi River northwest to the oasis town of Korla. By about AD 400, increasing desertification and the wandering nature of Lop Nur – dependent on the Tarim River system and the run-off of glacial waters from the Tian Shan, Pamir, Kunlun and Altun ranges – had combined to make this Central Route impracticable. It became easier to follow either the old, long-established Southern Route via Yangguan and Miran to Khotan, or the Northern Route, via the oases of Hami and Turpan, to Korla. Both routes converged in the west at Kashgar before continuing west to Samarkand, or south to Ladakh and Kashmir.

Ancient Loulan was rediscovered by Sven Hedin in 1899, then excavated more thoroughly by Aurel Stein in 1906 and 1914. It was rediscovered by the Chinese authorities in the 1970s, and desultory excavations have continued in the area since that time. The best of the finds are on display at the Xinjiang Autonomous Region Museum in Urumqi (see page 200), and include a manuscript outlining the military strategies of the Warring States period, mummies and a 10-metre (33-ft) -high pagoda. The archaeological site at **Loulan Gucheng** (open 8am–4pm daily; admission fee) remains off-limits to ordinary Silk Road travellers. Four-wheel-drive vehicles and camels are necessary to visit, as well as a professional GPS system and – crucially – an expensive permit from the appropriate Chinese authorities.

One reason such permits are not readily obtained is the damage that has been done to the site over the years by robbers, vandals and others.

BELOW LEFT: a balcony in Khotan.
BELOW: Loulan ruins in Lop Nur.

Lop Nur, the Wandering Lake

Lop Nur lake was the key to the flourishing caravan city of Loulan and the Central Silk Road between Yumenguan and Korla. When the lake began to dry up around 2,000 years ago, Loulan gradually declined and was eventually abandoned in the 5th century AD. Soon, as Silk Road traffic was redirected via the Northern and Southern routes, Loulan – together with other former caravan cities lost to the advancing sands of the Taklamakan – became little more than a legend, a rumour of lost splendour and wandering ghosts.

The ancient city was rediscovered by the Swedish explorer Sven Hedin in 1899. Hedin was the first to understand and explain how Lop Nur had "wandered", changing its location apparently at random over the centuries, but in fact due to the changing course of glacial rivers losing themselves in the heart of the Tarim Basin. In the 1920s Lop Nur dried up almost completely, and today there is little more than a small, seasonal salt marsh to indicate the presence of the former lake.

In the 1960s Lop Nur once again emerged from obscurity, when China exploded its first nuclear device, codenamed "596", in the area. China is now observing a de facto moratorium on nuclear testing, and has begun a project to divert water from Korla's Kongque River in an attempt to bring Lop Nur back to at least partial life.

BELOW: Hami
melons.

Another, which should also discourage thought of a casual journey to Loulan, is that apart from its extreme aridity the **Lop Desert** has been extensively irradiated. China's first nuclear bomb test took place at Lop Nur in 1964, and was followed by a further 44 nuclear explosions until testing was halted in 1996. Today the town of **Yuli** (Lop Nur), about 85km (53 miles) south of Korla on Highway 218 to Charklik, remains an important centre of China's nuclear industry, and is consequently not commonly a part of the Silk Road itinerary.

THE NORTHERN ROUTE

With the decline of Lop Nur and the Central Silk Road, the importance of the longer – but better-watered – Northern Silk Road increased, until by the time of the Tang Dynasty (618–907) it also came to overshadow the older, Southern Silk Road. Since that time the road northwest via Hami and Turpan to Korla and Kashgar (followed by today's highways 312 and 314) has remained the most important east–west route across southern Xinjiang. It's no coincidence, also, that the railway from Jiayuguan to Kashgar, completed in 1999, also follows this route.

Hami

It's a long 621km (386 miles) from **Jiayuguan** to the isolated oasis of **Hami**, the first settlement of any size along the Northern Route in Xinjiang. At first Highway 312 crosses the bleak **Bei Shan** or Northern Mountains – in fact, little more than blackened, sun-blasted slag heaps – to reach the Xinjiang frontier post at **Xingxingxia**. There's little to see in this unprepossessing truck stop, but several of the hills overlooking the road where it passes through a narrow ravine are topped by old fortifications dating from the warlord era that characterised the Republican period (1911–49). Beyond Xingxingxia the highway becomes, if anything, still more bleak, as it passes through the endless flat wastes of the windswept Gashun Gobi, while the arid, saw-toothed peaks of the **Karlik Shan** range dominate the northern horizon.

The ancient oasis settlement of **Hami**, also known in Uighur as **Kumul**, sits in a fault depression 155 metres (510ft) below sea level and, like nearby Turpan, experiences extremes of temperature ranging from a scalding 45°C (113°F) in summer to a freezing -30°C (-22°F) in winter. Clearly, Silk Road caravans didn't visit Hami for its appealing climate – rather they stopped there for its fresh springs and water run-off brought by *karez* (underground canals) from the distant Karlik Tagh, for its fabled fresh fruit – Hami melons are famous across China today – and perhaps, if Marco Polo is to be believed, for the ready appeal and easy morals of its women. More importantly still, they stopped there because there simply was nowhere else to go. Hami was, and still remains, the only significant oasis in the Gashun Gobi, an essential stop on the long and difficult desert stages between Anxi and Turpan.

Hami's association with China goes back at least as far as 73 BC, when the great Han general **Ban Chao** first conquered the oasis and established a settlement there. Chinese rule was far from continuous, however, and between the 9th and 17th centuries Hami passed at various times under Turkic and Mongol control. During the Ming Dynasty (1320–1644) the local Uighur rulers of Hami generally paid tribute to Beijing, a practice that was continued under the Qing whenever circumstances allowed, eventually making Hami the most "Chinese" of all the Uighur oases. The local ruling family survived until 1930, when Maqsud Shah – known to his Uighur subjects as Khan Maqsud, to the Chinese as the Hami *wang* or king, and to his occasional European visitors as the "King of the Gobi" – died, leading Jin Shuren, the avaricious Chinese governor of Xinjiang between 1928 and 1933, to annex the khanate. The resultant rebellion led to the destruction not just of any vestigial Uighur power in the area, but also left most of the oasis in ruins.

Today Hami is a prosperous agricultural prefecture with about 500,000 people, around 70 percent Han Chinese, with less than 25 percent Uighur, the balance being mostly Hui Muslims. Although there isn't a great deal to see of historic interest, it remains an essential (and very convenient) stopping point along Highway 312, about equidistant between Dunhuang to the east and Turpan to the west. The main attraction, **Hami Wangling** (Tombs of the Hami Kings; open daily 9am–8pm; admission fee), is located in the southern part of town on Tuanjie Lu. A large complex encompassing the attractive old wooden tombs of the former rulers, the royal mosque, and what the Hami tourist office describe in English as "King Hui's Palace" – a misleading description both because the hereditary ruling house was Uighur and because the current building, a modern restoration designed to replace the palace destroyed in the 1931 rebellion, is very much a Han Chinese creation, owing little to authentic Uighur history or culture.

BELOW: colourful corridor in "King Hui's Palace".

Last King of the Gobi

Sometimes called "The King of the Gobi", Maqsud Shah was the last of the hereditary Uighur rulers of Hami, enjoying semi-autonomous powers under Chinese suzerainty, not unlike the contemporaneous Princely States in British India. In fact Maqsud was very sinicised for an Uighur Muslim, speaking Turkic with a Chinese accent, dressing in Chinese robes, and being proficient in the use of chopsticks. He also liked a drink or two, and the German archaeologist Albert von Le Coq was "astonished to find in the house of a Muhammedan prince an enormous quantity of Russian liqueurs and excellent French champagnes. He was continually drinking our health and seemed quite hardened against any of the ill effects of alcohol". Maqsud died in March 1930.

The centre of modern Hami, together with the best accommodation and restaurants, lies further to the north, near Renmin Park. There are several good hotels with Muslim, Chinese and "Western" restaurants available, while the bustling **Night Market** on Aiguo Beilu serves tasty and reasonably priced fare.

Turpan

On leaving Hami, Highway 312 runs through rich oasis farmland supporting orchards and extensive melon fields before, after about 15km (9 miles), re-entering unremittingly harsh, flat, stony desert – there are no graceful sand dunes here. To the north, the Karlik Tagh gradually give way to another eastern outlier of the Tian Shan, the **Bogda Shan**, dominated by the snow-crowned summit of 5,445-metre (17,860-ft) **Bogda Feng**. After a short climb into the Bogda Shan foothills, the road descends sharply into another basin, the Turpan Depression, before reaching the lush and attractive oasis of Turpan some 400km (250 miles) from Hami.

Turpan (called Tulufan by the Chinese) is about the same size as Hami, with a similar population of around 500,000, but in almost inverse ethnic proportion – about 70 percent Uighur and 20 percent Han, the remainder comprising mainly Hui Muslims. Long an economic backwater, its relative isolation to the south of the main Silk Road (and today of Highway 312) has helped to protect both the local Uighur culture and a considerable bucolic charm. Yet in times past Turpan Oasis was a strategically significant centre on Xinjiang's Northern Silk Road, site of the ancient cities of Yarkhoto (Jiaohe) and Karakhoja (Gaochang).

Chinese armies first entered Turpan in the 2nd century BC, during the reign of Han Emperor Wu Di (141–87), when the oasis was a centre of Indo-European Tocharian culture. From about this time the city of Yarkhoto, known to the Chinese as Jiaohe, functioned as the capital until the 5th century AD when it was replaced by Karakhoja, called Gaochang by the Chinese, some

BELOW: vineyard in the oasis village of Tuyok near Turpan.

45km (28 miles) further to the east. From the mid-9th century the oasis became increasingly dominated by Uighur Turks migrating from the northern steppe, but Turpan retained a Buddhist character until the time of the Chagatai Khanate in the 13th century, when Islam gradually became the dominant religion. The Venetian Marco Polo passed through here in about 1271, and reported that the people of Karakhoja were "idolaters [Buddhists], but they include many Christians of the Nestorian sect and some Saracens [Muslims]".

A side road leads south from Highway 312 to Turpan, running through fertile fields watered, like those of Hami, by run-off brought by many *karez* (canals) from the mountains to the north. Important crops are wheat, cotton, vegetables and fruit of all kinds including mulberry, apricot, apple, pomegranate, fig and walnut. There's no doubt, however, that here the grape is king, as widely celebrated across China as Hami melons or Korla pears. The oasis is set in the **Turpan Basin**, at 155 metres (509ft) below sea level the second-lowest depression in the world (after the Dead Sea), and experiences great variations in temperature, ranging from 40°C (104°F) in summer to well below zero (32°F) in winter. Officially, it's the hottest place in China, once known as **Huozhou** or "Region of Fire", and the **Huoyan Shan** or "Flaming Mountains" to the northeast (see page 175) have long been infamous as a furnace-like wasteland. The lowest point in the depression is **Aydingkol Hu** (Moonlight Lake), a bleak, salt-encrusted pan where temperatures in midsummer can reach as high as 60°C (140°F).

Modern Turpan is a pleasantly relaxed small town centred on the downtown junction of Laocheng Lu and Gaochang Lu. Most attractions are located well out of town in the surrounding oasis, but **Turpan Museum** (Tulufan Bowuguan; open daily 9am–7.30pm; admission fee) on Gaochang Lu is worth visiting. The second-largest museum in Xinjiang, it houses an intriguing collection of funerary goods, mummies, silks and painted figurines excavated at the Astana Tombs, some 40km (25 miles) to the east. Well enough known to have become a symbol of the city, the 18th-century **Sugong Ta** (Emin Mosque and Minaret; open daily 7am–7pm; admission fee), the largest minaret in Xinjiang, is located just 2km (1.2 miles) southeast of the town centre and also merits a visit. One of the most impressive Islamic monuments in China – and very Central Asian in style – the mosque, made of simple, dun-coloured brick arranged in attractive geometric patterns, is dominated by its 44-metre (144-ft) -high minaret, built on the orders of the Turpan ruler **Emin Khoja** in 1777–8.

There's a good range of comfortable, reasonably priced accommodation in town, as well as restaurants serving Uighur, Chinese and an approximation of Western fare. A busy Night Market sells mainly Uighur and Hui

DRINK

As befits a famous wine-producing area, good Turpan wines (dry red and sweet white dessert wines) are widely available in the town and a reasonably priced alternative to the local beer. "Loulan" is one of the better reds, while the strangely named "Scent of a Woman" dessert wine is also very refreshing.

BELOW: Turpan's Emin Mosque and Minaret.

food by the junction of Gaochang Lu and Wenhua Lu.

Grape Valley

There's a lot to see and do around Turpan, and it makes sense to spend a day or two here exploring either by local taxi or by one of the many private tours that just about every hotel and travel agent is happy to arrange. Some of the closer sights are easily accessible by bicycle, but others – notably the Flaming Mountains and Tuyoq – are rather too distant for biking, at least in the hot summer months.

To the northeast of town, **Putao Gou** (Grape Valley; open daily; admission fee) is the most celebrated of Turpan's extensive vineyards and a must on every tour-group itinerary. Turpan has been cultivating grapes for more than two millennia, and today more than 100 varieties are grown, accounting for around 90 percent of China's seedless grape production. In times past the most valued variety of grape, known as *manaizi* or "mare's nipple" grapes, formed part of Turpan's tribute to the Chinese court at Xi'an and later Beijing. Today the grape harvest contributes substantially to the wealth of the oasis and its people, and vines are cultivated just about everywhere they can be grown, for fruit, wine and indeed shade. To celebrate this bounty, an annual **Turpan Grape Festival** is held each August and includes grape-eating competitions, folk dances and live music.

Yarkhoto

To the west of town the ruins of **Yarkhoto** or **Jiaohe Gucheng** (Jiaohe Ancient City; open daily; admission fee) are perhaps the best-preserved and most accessible of the ancient Silk Road cities anywhere in Xinjiang. Located just 10km (6 miles) west of Turpan town at the confluence of two small rivers, the ruins stand on a raised loess bluff. Yarkhoto was developed as an administrative centre and garrison town by the Chinese following the Han conquest of the area in the 2nd century BC and the city flourished under the Tang Dynasty (618–907), before eventually being abandoned early in the 14th century. The extensive

BELOW: the ruins of the abandoned city of Yarkhoto (Jiaohe).

ruins that remain today date mainly from the Tang era, when the population numbered in excess of 7,000, mainly Buddhist Uighurs.

The entire city is made of sun-baked loess soil, prompting the contemporary Chinese authorities to describe it as "the largest, oldest and best-preserved earthen city in the world". Overall, the city is 1,650 metres (1 mile) long by 300 metres (1,000ft) wide, with a main avenue leading north from the South Gate. In total it was home to about 700 households supporting 6,500 residents and 1,000 soldiers. The city was divided into three quarters, one for the common people to the west, one for the ruling aristocracy to the east, and one for religious observances to the north. At the end of the main avenue stands a Buddhist complex comprising a monastery, stupa and monks' cells. At the northern end of the city there is another, well-preserved stupa surrounded by tombs.

Yarkhoto was partially excavated by the Chinese authorities in the 1950s, and remains in excellent condition.

Wooden boardwalks allow the visitor to explore the streets, private dwellings and temples without damaging the site. There are fine views from the top of the bluff across the valley; on the clifftops opposite stand numerous grape-drying houses used for producing Turpan's famous raisins. Guides are informative and many of the information boards are in English as well as Chinese.

On the way back to town, drivers will encourage you to visit an ancient underground canal or *karez* system (**Kanerjing**; open daily; admission fee). Although heavily commercialised, this is an attraction worth seeing. For centuries Turpan has owed its lush agricultural produce and green oasis setting to an elaborate system of underground canals called *karez* that bring water from the nearby mountains. Turpan is watered by more than 400 such underground canals, with a total length of almost 5,000km (3,000 miles). In a complex and sophisticated process, water run-off from the mountains is carried by gently sloping tunnels accessed every few hundred

BELOW: photo opportunity in the Flaming Mountains.

metres by vertical maintenance shafts, substantially reducing evaporation by the blazing sun.

Karakhoja

Like Yarkhoto, the ruins of **Karakhoja** or **Gaochang Gucheng** (Gaochang Ancient City; open daily; admission fee) date from the initial Han Chinese conquest of the area in the 2nd century BC. Located about 46km (29 miles) southeast of Turpan on the edge of the Lop Desert, Karakhoja is larger than Yarkhoto, but rather less well preserved. Originally established as a garrison town, it developed into a prosperous city by Tang times, before being eventually abandoned in the 14th century, probably due to a combination of endemic warfare and desertification. In its prime, Karakhoja was divided into three sections – an outer city, inner city and palace area. It was surrounded by a 5.5-km (3.5-mile) -long, 11-metre (36-ft) -high defensive wall of tamped earth, pierced by nine city gates, the best-preserved of which are to the west. Over the centuries local people have carried away much of the crumbling loess buildings to use in new construction work but a fairly substantial Buddhist monastery remains in the southwest part of the city. A row of covered restaurants serving kebabs and other Uighur foodstuffs, as well as cold drinks, is situated by the Karakhoja ticket office, and you can explore the site on foot or by donkey trap.

Astana Tombs

The **Astana Tombs** (Asitana Gumuqu; open daily; admission fee) are located a short distance north of Karakhoja, about 40km (25 miles) from Turpan. Both rulers and citizens of Karakhoja were buried here, sometimes in elaborate splendour, in sealed subterranean burial places. Astana was excavated by the Chinese in the 1970s, and over 1,000 tombs were identified. The arid climate had preserved the bodies and many elaborate accompanying artefacts and murals almost perfectly, and the Xinjiang Autonomous Region Museum in Urumqi (see page 200) has a particularly fine collection of painted terracotta figurines showing

BELOW: steps from the Astana Tombs.

Journey to the West and the Flaming Mountains

Written in the 1590s and ascribed to the writer Wu Chengen, *Xiyouji* or "Journey to the West" is considered one of the four great novels of traditional Chinese literature. In the West, it is better known by the title *The Adventures of Monkey* or, more simply, *Monkey*. It presents a fictionalised account of the travels of the Buddhist monk Xuanzang (see page 57). On the instructions of the bodhisattva Guanyin, he is accompanied by three bodyguard-disciples, Sun Wukong or "Monkey", Zhu Bajie or "Pigsy" and Sha Wujing or "Sandy". Xuanzang is also provided with a celestial mount in the form of a dragon prince disguised as a horse.

As they progress westwards, the pilgrims are faced with all kinds of obstacles, including the Flaming Mountains near Turpan. They are unable to cross them because of the burning heat, until Monkey procures a magical palm-leaf fan from Princess Iron Fan, wife of the Ox Demon King, with which he extinguishes the flames. As an allegory, satire and travelogue, the text is deeply rooted in Chinese folk tradition. A large part of its continuing appeal is that it is also a great adventure story that has been adapted innumerable times for the stage, movies, comics, television soap operas and, most recently, computer games.

scenes from contemporaneous everyday life. Little remains on display in Astana, however, though visitors can descend into three of the tombs via narrow flights of steps to view three mummified figures, as well as murals depicting auspicious Confucian figures.

Highway 312, leading back towards Hami, is the best and quickest way to reach both Astana and Karakhoja. En route, to the immediate north of the highway and running for a distance of about 90km (60 miles), the **Flaming Mountains** (Huoyan Shan; open daily; admission fee) dominate the horizon. Charging an entry fee to a range of mountains that few people in their right mind would wish to enter may seem an unlikely business venture, but these are no ordinary barren hills. The Flaming Mountains are known throughout China as the place where the 7th-century Chinese Buddhist monk Xuanzang almost died of thirst, a story immortalised by **Wu Chengen** in his 16th-century allegorical account *Xiyouji* or "Journey to the West". As a consequence, a stream of predominantly Chinese tourists queue to enter not the mountains themselves, but an elaborate subterranean *Xiyouji* Disneyworld featuring Xuanzang and his companions, Monkey, Pigsy and Sandy. Above ground – where it is indeed generally blazing hot at noon – the serrated, ochre-coloured flanks of the Flaming Mountains make a startling backdrop against which tourists can be photographed perched astride Bactrian camels.

Bezeklik

The celebrated **Bezeklik Thousand Buddha Caves** (Bozikelike Qianfo Dong; open daily; admission fee) are set above the Murtuk Darya Gorge in the side of the Flaming Mountains some 60km (40 miles) from Turpan, and are easily accessible by road. "Bezeklik" means "place where there are paintings" in Uighur, with reference to a series of 77 caves once lined with pious Buddhist murals dating from the 4th to the 10th centuries. Sadly the surviving murals are but a shadow of what Bezeklik must once have been. Many of the finest were

BELOW: the spectacularly located Bezeklik Caves.

Detail of a mural at Bezeklik, the "place where there are paintings".

removed by the German archaeologist Albert von Le Coq at the beginning of the 20th century and subsequently sent to Berlin; others were reportedly damaged by iconoclastic Red Guards during the Cultural Revolution (1966–76). The caves and their mud-brick porticos are still worth visiting, however, not simply for a glimpse of the surviving murals, but for the caves' spectacular setting in the side of a cliff overlooking a narrow but lovely gorge.

Tuyoq

About 30km (19 miles) southeast of Bezeklik and 70km (44 miles) east of Turpan, near the eastern rim of the Turpan Basin, the traditional Uighur village of **Tuyoq** (Tuyugou; open daily; admission fee) offers a fasci-nating opportunity to visit a remote and traditional Uighur village set in a narrow valley in the southern outliers of the Flaming Mountains. There are numerous caves set high into the steep mountainside above the village, but they are all but inaccessible, and such artistic treasures as they once held have mainly either been destroyed or

dispersed to museums in China and Europe. Yet the appeal of Tuyoq is less these caves than the village's idyllic setting and bucolic charm. The **Tomb of the Seven Sleepers** dominates the hillside above the settlement and its green dome is an attractive feature on the otherwise low-rise skyline. The local Uighur people do not per-mit non-Muslims to enter either the shrine or the dusty cemetery that abuts it, but will grant permission to take photographs outside.

WEST OF TURPAN

West of Turpan, Highway 312 fol-lows the former Northern Silk Road for a further 46km (29 miles) before branching off north to Urumqi and ultimately, via the Dzungarian Route, to Kazakhstan on an old northern spur of the Silk Road that passes by the shores of the Issyk-Kul, to rejoin the main Silk Road near Samarkand. The main Northern Route to Kashgar branches off from Highway 312 near Toksun, becoming Highway 314 and heading west all the way to Kashgar and, beyond, to Pakistan via

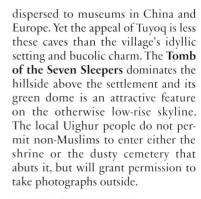

Climbing Tiemenguan

Located 7km (4 miles) northeast of Korla, the ancient strongpoint of Tiemenguan has now been bypassed by the 21st-century tarmac of Highway 314. Set amid incredibly barren, harsh and crumbling mountains that would not seem out of place in J.R.R. Tolkien's vision of Mordor, it's possible to under-stand the immense strategic signifi-cance of the "Iron Gate" pass by climbing the exhausting 1,497 steps to the summit. Here the tomb of Tzuhola and Tayir is set high above the narrow defile that once channelled the old Silk Road between two impassable rocky outcrops. A small path winds by a stream, far below – nowadays all but unused, but for at least two millennia a narrow artery for men, goods and cam-els passing between east and west.

the Karakoram Highway. After crossing the bleak Argaybulak Pass (1,785 metres/5,856ft) it descends through the arid, 60-km (37-mile) -long **Gan Gou** or "Dry Ditch" gorge before reaching the eastern fringes of the Tarim Basin by **Bagrash Kol** (Bosten Hu). This 1,000 sq km (386 sq mile) freshwater lake, located in **Bayingolin Mongol Autonomous Prefecture**, seems remarkably lush when set against the surrounding Gobi, and is home to many species of fish and birds. Nearby is the small settlement of **Yanqi**, today an unremarkable town, but during the Han Dynasty (206 BC–AD 220) it was better known as **Karashahr** or "Black City", capital of an independent Buddhist kingdom located between Turpan to the east and Korla to the west. Little remains to be seen today other than some tamped-earth city walls.

Beyond Yanqi the road enters another rocky defile, leading to the former stronghold and toll gate of **Tiemenguan** or "Iron Gate" (open daily; admission fee). Because of its strategic location controlling the Silk Road as it passed south of the Tian Shan and into the Tarim Basin, Tiemenguan was easily defended by garrison troops and almost impossible for merchants and other travellers to avoid. The gate was destroyed during the Cultural Revolution (1966–76) but has since been rebuilt. Its significance for Han Chinese and Uighur is rather different, though it carries sad associations for both peoples. Han Chinese, understandably, considered a posting here akin to being banished to outer darkness. A traditional verse laments:

Iron Gate at the edge of the world
Few travellers are to be seen
One lowly official guards the gate
All day staring at stone walls
A mountain pass, a thousand dangerous steps
A narrow road winding between sharp cliffs
I climb West Tower to take a look
One glance and my hair turns white!

For Uighurs, however, the narrow pass is associated with tragedy in love. Long ago Tzuhola, an Uighur princess, fell in love with Tayir, a simple shepherd. Her father, the king, had intended the princess to marry a prince, and was greatly displeased. The two lovers fled into the mountains pursued by the king's troops, who had orders to bring them back. They fell to their deaths near Tiemenguan and the king, who was heartbroken, ordered the building of a twin tomb so they could be together in the afterlife. A statue of the two lovers in flight on horseback has recently been erected near the tomb.

Uighur tragedy: the two lovers in flight on horseback.

Korla

The city of **Korla** (Kuerle) about 7km (4 miles) southwest of Tiemenguan is today one of Xinjiang's wealthiest cities, with a rich agricultural economy (in particular for the production of mulberries, white apricots, figs and musk melons) boosted by heavy industry and, in recent decades, oil production from the nearby Taklamakan Desert. Although it has a long history

BELOW: the modern skyline of Korla.

– it was occupied by the Han general Ban Chao in AD 94, and the head of the Korla king, together with the head of the king of neighbouring Karashahr were sent to be displayed in distant Luoyang – there is little of historical interest to see in town.

As in historical Silk Road times, Korla remains an important communications centre sitting astride the main road and rail links between Urumqi, Kashgar and Lanzhou, as well as Highway 218 south to Charklik, while Korla's Hualing Bus Station is the northern terminus for Desert Highway 312 to Niya on the Southern Route. Besides its significance as a transport hub, Korla is a pleasant enough place to stay. The Konqi River (*konqi* is Uighur for "abundant waters") flows through the centre of town on its way south from the Tian Shan, making for abundant greenery, while the nearby presence of oil ensures that Korla has some of the best hotels and restaurants in Xinjiang.

West of Korla, Highway 314 runs through arid desert in the lee of the Tian Shan, passing through vast wind

BELOW: making *samsa* in old Kuqa.

farms, for 310km (190 miles) to the oasis of Kuqa. About halfway, at the small town of **Luntai** (Uighur name Bugur), the **Shamo Gonglu** (Desert Highway 312) branches off south across incredibly inhospitable shifting sand dunes to Niya, 522km (324 miles) distant. This modern road, opened in 1995, offers an opportunity to take a shortcut to the old Southern Silk Road, as well as to see the endless sand dunes of the much-feared Taklamakan Desert.

Kuqa

The ancient oasis town of **Kuqa** (Kuche), though now overshadowed by Korla to the east and Aksu to the west, was once a key stop on the Northern Silk Road. It first came under Han Chinese control when it was conquered, in AD 91, by the indomitable General Ban Chao. By the 4th century it had emerged as an important centre of Tocharian civilisation, sitting astride not just the Northern Silk Road, but also lesser routes to Dzungaria in the north and Khotan in the south. The celebrated Buddhist monk Kumarajiva (see page 152) was born here, and travelled west on the Silk Road to study in Kashmir before returning east, to Wuwei, where he taught and translated Buddhist texts for 17 years.

The oasis reached its zenith during the Tang Dynasty (618–907), when the royal court at **Qiuci** was famed for its pious Buddhist monasteries with more than 5,000 monks, as well as its rather less pious musicians, singers and dancing girls, who were much appreciated in the distant Tang court at Xi'an. Kuqa took on an increasingly Uighur character from the mid-9th century, abandoning Buddhism in favour of Islam during the 13th century. For many centuries Kuqa was the most populous oasis in Xinjiang, but today only about 100,000 people live here, about 75 percent Uighur, with Han Chinese and Hui Muslims making up the balance.

Modern Kuqa is divided into two parts, the overwhelmingly Uighur **Old City** to the west, and the predominantly Han Chinese **New City** to the east. The former, a warren of twisting, narrow alleys, is both picturesque and home to the city's most interesting sights. The latter, a typical small, grid-system Chinese town, is the centre for transport, accommodation and dining. The two are separated by the narrow Kuqa River and an open area given over to the important **Friday Market**, which sells local foodstuffs including iced yoghurt and giant *naan*. Also lying between the two are the remains of **Qiuci Gucheng** (Qiuci Ancient City), though there is little to see apart from an ancient mud wall.

Most visitors will stay in the New City, but spend their time exploring in the Old City. It's a 40-minute walk or 10-minute drive between the two, heading west along Wenhua Lu past **Maulana Ashidin Khoja Mazar**, the tomb of an early Muslim missionary still venerated by local Uighurs. Little enough is known of Ashidin Khoja, said to have been an itinerant Arab teacher, except that some time after his arrival in Kuqa, probably in the mid-13th century, he killed a pigeon and subsequently dropped dead – surely a story rooted in Qiuci's ancient Buddhist past rather than in Islam! The simple wooden shrine, which was restored in the mid-19th century, stands next to a green-roofed mosque. As is common in Central Asian Islam, strips of cloth are attached to a tree outside the shrine, indicating the presence of the tomb of a *pir* or Muslim holy man.

Wenhua Lu continues west through the open market area to the Old City. The market brims with all manner of fresh produce, and some sections of the market are given over to clothing of all kinds, others to Uighur hats, equine equipment, knives, tools, rugs and carpets, toys and even jewellery.

Beyond the market, an old bridge leads over the Kuqa River and enters the Old Town via **Laocheng Shihchang**, the Old City Bazaar. Watch out here for open-air barbers and hairdressers, kebab and naan bread sellers – Kuche is famous in

BELOW: Kuqa's Jama Masjid (Great Mosque).

Kizilgah is just one of many beacon towers built by the Chinese to warn of imminent invasion. Watchmen manned the towers at all times, lighting a blazing fire at night or a smoking fire by day to alert other beacon towers down the line to the east.

BELOW: the Silk Road passes Subashi Gucheng.

Xinjiang for its unique wholemeal naan (flat breads), much larger than elsewhere in the province and covered with toppings of chopped carrot, onion and sesame. Immediately to the west of the bazaar stands an old Qing Dynasty mosque with Uighur elders known locally as *aqsaqal* or "white beards" selling religious tracts and Islamic paraphernalia. One block further to the west is Kuqa's **Great Mosque** (**Jama Masjid**; **Qingzhen Da Si**; open daily; admission fee for non-Muslims), an attractive building dating from 1923 with an imposing gateway flanked by two tall minarets leading to a large, green-domed prayer hall. The mosque is entirely Central Asian in style, with none of the Chinese Islamic characteristics seen further to the east (and especially at Xi'an's Qingzhen Da Si). Beyond the Great Mosque, on Linji Lu, the **Kuqa Museum** (**Kuche Bowuguan**; open daily; admission fee) houses an interesting collection of artefacts from old Qiuci and the nearby ruins of ancient Subashi.

While fresh and good street food is available in and around the Old City

Bazaar, the best restaurants and hotels are to be found back in New Kuqa, clustered along central Wenhua Lu and on nearby Tianshan Lu. There is also a busy **Night Market** by the junction of Youyi Lu and Xinhua Lu that serves all the usual Uighur specialities as well as freshly squeezed juices – a welcome source of vitamin C.

Around Kuqa

Kuqa's once flourishing Buddhist past is best appreciated by visiting two ancient Silk Road-related sites that are readily accessible by taxi. About 20km (13 miles) northeast of town, the ruins of **Subashi Gucheng** (Subashi Ancient City; open daily; admission fee) are all that is left of the ancient capital of the Kingdom of Qiuci from the 4th century AD until it was abandoned sometime in the 12th century. After Yarkhoto and Karakhojo in Turpan Oasis, Subashi is one of the better preserved and more easily accessible abandoned ancient cities of the Tarim Basin. The city walls and a row of once-inhabited caves are all that remain, but they're spectacularly situated beneath snow-covered peaks.

Most impressive are the ruins of **Zhaoguli Buddhist Temple**, dating from the 5th century AD. The site was first excavated by Count Otani Kozui of Kyoto in the early 20th century. His most important find, a 6th-century *sarira* or relic box now held in the Otani Collection at Tokyo National Museum, shows paintings of Tocharian men in long robes. Another noted archaeological discovery from the city is the so-called "Witch of Subashi", a desiccated female mummy found wearing a tall and pointed black hat, now on display at the Xinjiang Autonomous Region Museum in Urumqi (see page 200).

Located 75km (47 miles) to the northwest of Kuqa, the **Kizil Thousand Buddha Caves** (**Kezier Qianfo Dong**; open daily 7am–7pm; admission fee) is a Buddhist cave temple complex dating from the 3rd to

13th centuries AD. Accessible only by taxi or private car, the road to the caves leads through **Yanshui Gou** or "Saltwater Gulley", an extraordinary landscape of eroded rock formations. The caves are set in the cliff face of a narrow gorge sometimes optimistically styled "Tian Shan Grand Canyon" by Kuqa travel agents. At its height, during the Tang Dynasty, the complex numbered 236 caves, though the travails of time and the destructive impact of Islamic iconoclasm and both Western and Japanese archaeologists have reduced the number to just 80 caves containing mural fragments – no statuary survives. The researches of Japanese Count Otani and German von Le Coq show that the caves once contained particularly fine examples of Gandharan Indo-Greek art, with some Persian but almost no discernible Chinese influence, but fully to appreciate this it is necessary to travel to Berlin's Ethnology Museum (*Museum für Völkerkunde*). Only nine caves are open to visitors at Kizil today, and these contain mere fragments of frescoes.

On leaving Kuqa, Highway 314 (as well as the Urumqi–Kashgar Railway) passes the isolated, 16-metre (52-ft) -high **Kizilgah Beacon Tower** about 6km (4 miles) west of Kuqa. This imposing structure, dating from the Han Dynasty (206 BC–AD 220), marks an antique Chinese garrison point on the former Northern Silk Road. Goats are the tower's most common visitors.

Aksu

Like the other oasis towns of southern Xinjiang, **Aksu** – which means "White Water" in Uighur – has a long history, though little survives to suggest this today. Like Kuqa and Korla to the east, it was conquered by the Chinese general Ban Chao in the 1st century AD, and visited by the monk Xuanzang in the 6th century. In the 14th century Tughlugh Timur, Khan of Moghulistan (1347–63), briefly made Aksu his capital, a position the city temporarily regained under the Mughal Khan Esan Buqa II (1429–62). After this time Aksu slipped into political obscurity, though it remained

Having a haircut in Old Kuqa.

BELOW LEFT: a modern symbol of Aksu. **BELOW:** the Kizilgah Beacon Tower west of Kuqa.

Uighur cuisine, found throughout Xinjiang, is characterised by mutton, beef, tomatoes, aubergines, onions, naan bread and a variety of dairy products such as yoghurt. Although the camel is still an important means of transportation, it is also sometimes used as a food source.

a significant caravanserai on the Northern Silk Road.

Today **Aksu** (Akesu) is an industrial city of about 400,000 inhabitants, the great majority of whom are Han Chinese; another 200,000 or so ethnic Uighurs farm the surrounding oasis. There is really nothing of historical significance for the visitor to see, but Aksu remains a convenient stopping place on the long road west from Kuqa to Kashgar, with a good choice of hotels and restaurants, as well as plenty of Uighur and Chinese street food in and around **Aksu Bazaar** (Aksu Shihchang). In October 2007 a **second desert highway** was opened, leading directly across the barren wastes of the Taklamakan to Khotan, 424km (264 miles) to the southwest. This has greatly increased Aksu's importance as a communications hub – but still, it seems few Silk Road travellers will choose to do more than stay overnight here.

Beyond the green fields and poplar-lined lanes of Aksu, arid, windswept desert resumes. Highway 314 continues west along the track of the old

Northern Silk Road, hemmed in by the bare, rugged outliers of the Tian Shan to the north and the great sand dunes of the Taklamakan to the south. There are no major oases along the route between Aksu and Kashgar, but 214km (133 miles) west of Aksu, at the small oasis of **Sanchakou**, a small junction marks an old road south, following the Yarkand River through the traditional Uighur farming centres of Bachu and Markit, to **Yarkand** (see page 192) on the Southern Road. West of Sanchakou, Highway 314 continues for a further 213km (132 miles), passing through the small towns of Sugun and Artux, before terminating at the fabled Silk Road city of **Kashgar**.

THE SOUTHERN ROUTE

As we have seen, the antique Southern Route between Dunhuang and Kashgar started at Yangguan or "Sun Pass", near today's Nanhu village, about 60km (37 miles) west of Dunhuang. Probably older than the Northern Route, and still more arid and remote, it nevertheless had certain advantages, including being further

BELOW: downtown Aksu, a convenient stopping place on the road west from Kuqa to Kashgar.

from the nomadic raiders of Mongolia and the Dzungarian Steppe – though the Tibetans were nearer at hand, a people also not averse to raiding caravans or direct military conquest.

Having rested up and watered their beasts in Dunhuang, the caravaneers would leave China proper through the watchtower and toll gate at Yangguan and head straight into open desert, leading their camels through the waterless **Kum Tagh** or "Sand Mountains" on the southern edge of the Gashun Gobi through a wind-blasted, lifeless wilderness in the lee of the mighty Altun Shan range. This route passed through the last, most remote fringes of western Gansu province before crossing into a still more barren corner of Xinjiang. Nobody, indeed nothing, could live here, except perhaps a few wild camels. Marco Polo passed this way in the 13th century, and noted: "Beasts and birds there are none, for they find nothing to eat." There were legions of ghosts, however, who would call out in spirit voices to lure travellers into the void, where they would inevitably perish:

Yes, and even by daylight men hear these spirit voices, and often you fancy they are listening to the strains of many instruments, especially drums, and the clash of arms. For this reason bands of travellers make a point of keeping very close together. Before they sleep they set up a sign pointing the direction in which they have to travel.

In fact travellers have posted "signs" to indicate direction along the Southern Route for centuries, using the skeletons of dead camels and other beasts of burden as markers. Over the intervening centuries the inexorable advance of the desert southwards has made this section of the route still more inhospitable. This is the most difficult and inaccessible stretch of the former Silk Road anywhere in China, and to all intents and purposes it is closed, both because of its poor condition and because of its proximity to the Lop Nur nuclear testing site. As if in confirmation of this, a short distance west of Dacaotan, Highway 313 is blocked by a police guard post. Just about the only way to reach Miran and Charklik via this

BELOW: domesticated cousins of the threatened wild Bactrian camel.

Wild Camel Reserve

Wild Bactrian camels survive only in the central Taklamakan Desert, the Lop Nur region and a remote part of the Gobi Desert on the China–Mongolia border. Experts estimate their total number at less than 1,000. In 1998 plans were put forward to establish the Arjin Shan Wild Camel Reserve in the inhospitable Kum Tagh Desert near Lop Nur, and in 2002 this reserve, covering 78,000 sq km (30,000 sq miles) was completed. Scientists based in the reserve were subsequently astonished to find the camels surviving on salt water bubbling up from beneath the sands, and are currently investigating whether these Kum Tagh Bactrians are a new sub-species of camel, or have adapted over the millennia to resist levels of salinity that would kill any other known mammal.

route is to arrange a four-day jeep safari with a specialist company in Urumqi – though this is an expensive option by any standards.

Dunhuang to Charklik

There are at present two alternative ways of reaching Charklik from Dunhuang – neither authentically part of the Southern Route, but until and unless the Chinese authorities improve and open the western section of Highway 313 between Dacaotan and Charklik, there are no other options.

The first alternative involves following the Northern Route from **Dunhuang** as far as **Korla** (see page 177). From here Route 218 runs south past China's nuclear research centre at Lop Nur (Yuli), following the rapidly diminishing waters of the Tarim River as it is gradually swallowed by the eternal sands. After the small desert settlement of **Tikanlik**, 216km (134 miles) south of Korla, the last waters disappear, and the road continues between the Taklamakan and Gashun Gobi deserts for a further 227km (141 miles) to Charklik. It's a long way round, but

the road is good and there are regular buses between Korla and Charklik.

The second route between Dunhuang and Charklik involves travelling south along Highway 215 from Dunhuang to **Aksay**, then climbing into the vast, snow-capped Altun Shan and crossing into Qinghai province via the spectacular 3,519-metre (12,840-ft) **Dangjin Pass**. The road – now Highway 315 – continues across the bleak Qaidam Basin, through starkly magnificent scenery about as different to the Tarim Basin as might be imagined, to the ugly mining town of **Huatugou**. Although this route crosses some very harsh terrain and is often closed during winter months, buses ply between Dunhuang and Huatugou twice a day, and the journey is not as difficult as it sounds. Things becomes worse at Huatugou, a gritty, unappealing settlement where it is, nevertheless, generally necessary to stay overnight. Hotels and restaurants exist, but they are basic.

Huatugou may feel like the end of the world, but it isn't. That distinction should be reserved for the next

BELOW: barren scenery nearing Charklik.

stopover, **Magnai Zhen** or "Asbestos Mine", located about 70km (44 miles) further west on the Qinghai–Xinjiang border. Local minibuses run between Huatugou and this least attractive of places on a regular basis when full, covering the distance in about two hours. The route onwards to Charklik crosses the high Altun Shan, with the horizon to the left dominated by the 6,062-metre (19,890-ft) **Yusupalik Tag** ("Yusuf Ali Mountains"), before descending via narrow valleys and generally dry river beds to the small settlement of Yandaxkak and, ultimately, to the isolated – but very welcome – oasis.

Charklik

Once at **Charklik** (Ruoqiang), whether by way of Korla or Qinghai, the traveller is back on the authentic Southern Route. The isolated oasis has an overwhelmingly Uighur population of around 30,000. There's nothing to keep the visitor in Charklik, which centres around the long-distance bus station providing links north to Korla and west to Khotan. About 110km (68 miles) east, back along the original Southern Silk Road (Highway 215), the ancient site of **Miran** (Milan Gucheng; admission fee) is one of the more accessible "lost cities" of the Taklamakan – the ancient ruins are set in the desert about 15km (9 miles) southwest of the new town. To visit, a permit (fee) must be obtained from the local Charklik Cultural Relics Bureau, or – more expensively – can be purchased in advance in Urumqi. Travellers should take a bus to New Miran, 96km (60 miles) distant, then hire a taxi to Old Miran; alternatively, a taxi can be hired for the return trip in Charklik.

Miran was a flourishing trade centre on the Southern Silk Road between about AD 100 and 400. In the 8th century it was occupied and fortified by the Tibetans. The site was rediscovered by the American Ellsworth Huntington in 1905, and first excavated by Aurel Stein in 1907. Stein discovered rich examples of Gandharan art, the most easterly evidence of Graeco-Buddhist influence yet found. He took away many of the tempura murals he unearthed, some of which were richly gilded, and the best are now held in the National Museum in New Delhi. He also discovered numerous documents in Tibetan, Kharoshthi and Turkic scripts in a 1,000-year-old midden by the Tibetan fort, of which he wrote: "I have had occasion to acquire rather extensive experience in cleaning ancient rubbish-heaps, and know how to diagnose them. But for intensity of sheer dirt and age-persisting smelliness I shall always put the rich 'castings' of Tibetan warriors in the front rank". Today the main relics viewable at Miran include the 8th-century Tibetan fort, the remains of a 2nd-century Buddhist stupa and the foundations of several Buddhist monasteries.

Cherchen

Highway 315 runs southwest from Charklik through sandy wastes for

BELOW: luscious pomegranate from Niya.

The ancient city of Endere (Endere Gucheng), dating from the 2nd–7th centuries, is buried in the desert to the northwest of Cherchen, but is currently inaccessible except to authorised archaeological expeditions.

350km (220 miles) to **Cherchen** (Qiemo). The oasis, which is predominantly Uighur, supports a population of 60,000, and is watered by the Cherchen Darya with snowmelt from the Altun Shan to the south. The most significant Silk Road site is at the village of **Zaghunluq**, 5km (3 miles) southwest of the town centre. More than 1,000 ancient tombs were discovered here in the 1980s, and one tomb, containing 14 mummified corpses that date back 2,600 years, is open to the public. Other finds from the tombs, including Zaghunluq grave artifacts, are preserved in the **Cherchen Museum** (Qiemo Bowuguan; open daily; admission fee), located in a the former home of an Uighur warlord. About 10km (6 miles) to the northwest of town, **Old Cherchen** (Qiemo Gucheng; open daily; admission fee) is accessible by taxi, but little remains for the casual visitor to see.

Niya

West of Cherchen, Highway 315 continues to follow the ancient Southern

Silk Road for 314km (195 miles) to the small town of **Niya** (Minfeng), a predominantly Uighur oasis supporting a population of about 10,000. The southern terminus of the Desert Highway 312 from Luntai joins Highway 315 to the east of town, and the opening of this route in 1995 transformed remote Niya into an important communications hub. There is little to see in Niya itself, and the ancient town of **Old Niya** (Niya Gucheng), lost in the shifting sands of the Taklamakan some 130km (81 miles) to the north, is only accessible by camel caravan with special permission from the Chinese authorities. Niya has adequate hotels and restaurants, however, and is an ideal base for making a short excursion into the Taklamakan without crossing the entire 522km (324 miles) of the Desert Highway.

Around Niya

It is possible to make a fascinating day trip from Niya by taking a minibus or taxi north into the desert, to the tiny and isolated Uighur village of

XINJIANG Maps on pages 130, 192 187

Kapakaskan (Padishayimu) to see the **Imam Jafar Sadiq Mazar** (open daily; admission fee), the so-called "Mecca of Turkestan". While the shrine is of interest, in particular its impressive brick entrance gate, it's the journey itself that really makes the trip worthwhile. To get to Kapakaskan head east along Highway 315 for 21km (13 miles) to the junction with Highway 312, then head north along the Desert Highway for a further 50km (31 miles), before turning west, into the desert, near kilometre marker 512. Kapakaskan is 12km (7 miles) to the west.

While more than 500km (300 miles) of Desert Highway – in fact a black ribbon of tarmac stretching through and around endless drifting sand dunes – can easily become tedious, the 50km (30-mile) journey to the Kapakaskan turning is ample to witness the extraordinary feats of engineering and desert control techniques employed by the Chinese in building this extraordinary road. It also allows the traveller to see something of the Taklamakan Desert without arranging a special caravan expedition. There are blue buildings with red roofs every 5km (3 miles). These are irrigation stations that pump water from aquifers beneath the desert to water the desert reeds and grasses planted to stabilise the sands in the immediate vicinity of the road. Each is manned by a single person or couple whose job it is to maintain the irrigation system – surely one of the loneliest jobs in the world.

Kapakaskan is a tiny oasis, watered by the rapidly diminishing flow of the Niya Darya, which loses itself in the desert sands about 35km (22 miles) further north. Surrounded by a veritable *shamo* or "sea of sand", the hamlet is an entirely Uighur settlement of mud-brick houses, with a single, concrete school. The shrine is a further 5km (3 miles) north of the village, set amid shifting sands. It's not clear who exactly is buried here, but it's not the celebrated Imam Jafar Sadiq, the sixth

Shia imam and direct descendant of the Prophet Muhammad, whose tomb is in Medina, Saudi Arabia (though some local Uighur will tell you that it *is* his final resting place). Rather a simple structure, decorated with branches, skins, feathers and tied pieces of cloth, it is typical of similar small tombs, often of Sufi mystics, that can be found across Central Asia.

Keriya

Highway 315 continues from Niya through endless sandy desert to the oasis of **Keriya** (Yutian) 120km (75 miles) to the west. Another predominantly Uighur oasis, Keriya supports a population of around 160,000. Marco Polo visited in the late 13th century and noted that the oasis was "amply stocked with the means of life", with rich estates including orchards, vineyards and cotton, as indeed it is today. Even so, there's not a great deal to see here, though there are several reasonable hotels, as well as restaurants serving Chinese and Uighur cuisine. The oasis is watered by the Keriya Darya, which rises in the high Kunlun Shan

BELOW: the fruit market in Keriya.

to the south and flows through Keriya before disappearing into the sands of the Taklamakan far to the north.

Around Keriya

A number of antique, sand-smoth-ered sites lie to the north of Keriya, including the former Buddhist cen-tre of **Dandan Oilik** (Dandan Oilik Gucheng), thought to have been aban-doned in the 8th century; **Karadong** (Karadong Gucheng), thought to have been abandoned in the 4th century; and still further north, about 220km into the shifting sands, the former settlement of **Yuan Sha** (Yuan Sha Gucheng), abandoned as early as 130 BC. Like ancient Niya further to the east, these former settlements are generally only accessible with special permission, and using special equipment, including four-wheel-drive vehicles, camel caravans and global positioning systems. The tiny Uighur settlement of **Tongguzbasti**, 170km (102 miles) north of Keriya beside the rapidly diminishing Keriya Darya, must rank as one of the most remote places in Xinjiang. It is said to

stand on the ruins of the lost city of Keladun, and artefacts dating from the Han Dynasty (206 BC–AD 222) have been found here. Today about 50 families of Keriya Uighur live here in almost complete isolation, and they are known as the "lost tribe of the Taklamakan". It is possible to visit their undecorated wooden homes and also the village school.

Khotan

Highway 315 heads west from Keriya for 180km before reaching the sub-stantial oasis of **Khotan** (Hotan), the first sizeable town (and first ATM or money-changing facilities) since Korla or Dunhuang. Here the minor oases of the Southern Route are at an end, and both facilities and accessible sights of interest increase markedly.

The Buddhist Kingdom of Khotan traces its history back at least as far as the 3rd century BC, when the eldest son of the Indian emperor Asoka is said to have settled there. It was long of great importance on the Silk Road, and is claimed to have been the first place outside China to have cultivated

BELOW: silk drapery at the market in Khotan.

Fruits of the Loom

Khotan has long been famous for its hand-woven carpets, and while qual-ity may have declined over the past 50 years, it's still worth visiting the Carpet Factory (Gillam Karakhana/Ditang Chang) over the bridge on the east side of the Yurungkash River where women artisans weave by hand on looms. Another work-shop of special significance for this old Silk Road city is Shatuo Silk Factory (Shatuo Sichou Chang; open daily; fee for tour) in Laksui District, a short distance north of town. Here the visitor can see the entire process of silk manufacture before being led into a silk showroom and encouraged to make purchases. Less organised but perhaps more authentic is the Atlas Silk Workshop (Atlas Karakhana) in Jiya Village, about 13km (8 miles) northeast of Khotan.

silk. It sits astride the Karakash or "Black Jade" and Yurungkash or "White Jade" rivers, which here conjoin to form the Khotan Darya, and has been famous for its jade for well over two millennia. In times past trade routes crossed the desert to the north all the way to Kuqa, and as recently as 2007 this link has been re-established for the first time in centuries with the opening of a second Desert Highway leading to Aksu, some 424km (264 miles) to the north.

In 1006, Khotan was conquered by Uighur Muslims from Kashgar, and since that time the city has remained a very Uighur place indeed – seemingly the more so since the increased sinicisation of Kashgar in recent decades. It has an urban population of 114,000, good communication links with Aksu, Yarkand and Kashgar, plenty of good hotels and restaurants, and a great deal to see. The city – which in itself is ordinary enough – centres on **Tuanjie Square** (Tuanjie Guangchang), with Beijing Lu running north–south and Tanaiyi Lu running east–west. Most hotels and restaurants are in the central area, and this makes it a good base for explorations further afield.

There isn't much left of old Khotan, though a few hundred metres of the crenellated city wall (Chengqiang) survive immediately to the northwest of the huge central square. Just to the south of Tuanjie Square – which is dominated by a statue of Chairman Mao Zedong shaking hands with an elderly Uighur man – is the excellent **Khotan Museum** (Hetian Bowuguan; open daily; admission fee). The ground floor is devoted to regional archaeology and includes a fascinating diorama of the site of Old Niya, as well as two well-preserved 1,500-year-old mummies, jewellery, cooking utensils and remnants of silk. The second-floor exhibits are more recent, and include examples of local manufactures (jade, carpets, silk, musical instruments) and regional costumes.

Just south of the museum at the junction of Gujiang Bei Lu and Jiamai Lu is the **Khotan Jade Factory** (Hetian Yuqichang; free tours, but naturally visitors are encouraged

"Khotan is a pleasant and prosperous kingdom, with a numerous and flourishing population. The inhabitants all profess Buddhism, and join together in its religious music for their enjoyment. The monks amount to several myriads, most of whom are students of the Mahayana School."

Fa Xian, 5th century AD

BELOW: extracting silk fibre from boiling cocoons, Khotan.

Remains of Melikawat near Khotan.

BELOW: an assortment of nuts and dried fruit at the market.

to make a purchase). The ground floor is a workshop where skilled jade carvers are at work, while the second floor is a large showroom filled with all kinds of jade sculptures for sale. Jade enthusiasts will also find a street of **jade shops** on nearby Beijing Lu, while a 4km (2.5-mile) walk or taxi ride east along Beijing Donglu leads to **Yurungkash River** where, during the winter months when the water level is low, you can join local jade prospectors in raking through the pebbles hoping to strike it lucky. Across from the jade factory is Jianshe Lu, leading to **Khotan Night Market**, a good place to find cheap and tasty Uighur food – just follow the aroma of grilled kebabs.

Slightly further afield, in the northeast of town by the attractive Jama' Masjid or Friday Mosque, **Khotan Bazaar** is a good place to watch local artisans – tinsmiths, silversmiths, goldsmiths, carpenters – at work, as well as to shop for fruit, spices, clothing, knives, carpets, silk and other handicrafts. The bazaar is at its busy best on Fridays and Sundays. Khotan also holds a celebrated **Sunday Market** (Xingqitian Shihchang) which is similar to, but less touristy than, its celebrated Kashgar equivalent.

Carpet hunters should head to **Khotan Carpet Factory** (free) on the outskirts of the city (accessible by bus 5 or 10). The factory celebrates 2,000 years of carpet weaving in Khotan and features tours of the hand-weaving workshops and the option to purchase direct from the artisans.

Around Khotan

The Jiya township 23km (14 miles) northeast of central Khotan is home to the **Atlas Silk Workshop** (open 9am–4pm daily). Tours are in Chinese only but visitors are welcome to wander around and watch the hand-weaving. Whilst in Jiya, also visit the **Tomb of Imam Asim** (open daily). In April and May pilgrims come here from across Xinjiang and it is possible to watch traditional storytelling, wrestling and music.

A number of ancient sites are scattered around Khotan and further to the north in the Taklamakan Desert. The former Buddhist centre of **Melikawat** (Malikewate Gucheng; open daily; admission fee) is just 28km (17 miles) south of the city and readily accessible by taxi, but there's much less to see than at Yarkhoto or Karakhoja in Turpan. Much more impressive is **Rawak**, site of a relatively well-preserved Buddhist stupa rising 9 metres (30ft) out of the desert sands about 32km (20 miles) northeast of Khotan. The site is open to visitors, but visits must be arranged ahead of time through the Cultural Relics Bureau at Khotan Museum. Similarly the old Tibetan fort at **Mazar Tagh**, 180km (112 miles) north of Khotan in the heart of the Taklamakan, may be visited, but only with the appropriate permit from the Cultural Relics Bureau. A visit to either of these sites, and especially the latter, requires special transport and can be expensive.

Highway 315 continues northwest from Khotan, following the Southern Silk Road through the towns of Karakash (Moyu) and **Guma** (Pishan), to **Karghilik** (Yecheng), a distance of 226km (140 miles). In earlier times this small oasis was a stopover for trade caravans heading south from Yarkand to Ladakh and Kashmir by way of the difficult 5,575-metre (18,290-ft) Karakoram Pass. Today this route is decisively closed, as the Karakoram Pass lies in an area disputed by China and India, as well as close to the Siachen Glacier, the world's highest battlefield, where India confronts Pakistan.

Highway 219 follows part of the old trade route as it heads south from Karghilik, through Akmeqit, Mazar and Xaidulla, across the disputed Aksai Chin to Ali (Senge Khabab) in western Tibet. Although it is still officially closed to visitors, Chinese security has relaxed and it is becoming a popular (if difficult) way for travellers to reach Tibet from Xinjiang. Karghilik itself is a quiet little place with an attractive 15th-century Friday Mosque, a bustling bazaar and several reasonable hotels, making it a possible stopover on the journey between Khotan and Kashgar.

BELOW: the entrance to Yarkand.

Queen of Yarkand

Queen Amannisahan (1526–60) was a noted poet in the Uighur language, penning two celebrated collections of poetry, which are both still widely read in this part of China – *Virtue* and *Poems of Amannisahan*. She also collected the "Twelve Muqam" of traditional Uighur music that follow the astronomical almanac and take around 20 hours to perform. Queen Amannisahan died prematurely in childbirth at the age of 34, and lies entombed in the blue-and-white-tiled mazar that bears her name in Old Yarkand. In 2005 her achievement was recognised when UNESCO designated the Twelve Muqam "a masterpiece of the Oral and Intangible Heritage of Humanity". She also features as the heroine of the popular 1994 Chinese movie *Amannisahan*.

BELOW: tomb of Abakh Khoja.

Yarkand

Just 52km (32 miles) north of Karghilik, the important oasis of **Yarkand** (Shache) was once the seat of an ancient Buddhist kingdom and an important caravanserai on the Southern Silk Road. It was of particular importance as the northern terminus for the trade route over the Karakoram Pass to Ladakh, *and* by the 19th century its population outstripped even that of Kashgar. Today it is a predominantly Uighur city with a population of 375,000 producing cotton, wheat, corn and fruit (notably pomegranates, pears and grapes), as well as oil and natural gas. Modern Yarkand is divided into a mainly Han Chinese New Town and an overwhelmingly Uighur Old Town or **Altyn Shahr**. Most visitors will stay and eat in the former, which lies to the west along Xincheng Lu or "New Town Road", while exploring the narrow lanes and busy bazaar of the latter, which lies east of the town centre along – appropriately enough – Laocheng Lu, or "Old Town Road". A small section of the former **City Wall** (Chengqiang) survives in the west of town, but there's little else of interest here. To the northeast, however, there is a large and busy bazaar, packed with goods and businesses of every kind, as well as hole-in-the-wall places to eat and food stalls. Once a week this expands into Yarkand's picturesque Sunday Market. A short distance further east, in the heart of the Old Town, is the Friday Mosque, the 16th-century **Altyn Masjid** (Aqindian Qingzhen Si), as well as the **Amannisahan Mazar**, a blue-and-white tiled tomb that is the last resting place of Amannisahan, poet, musician and queen of Yarkand in the 16th century, who was a celebrated composer of Uighur *muqam* music. The adjacent **Cheeltanlireem Cemetery** houses the tombs of a number of Yarkand's former kings, including that of Amannisahan's husband.

Yengisar

Highway 315 continues for another 120km (75 miles) to the small Uighur-dominated oasis of **Yengisar** (Yingjisha), known throughout

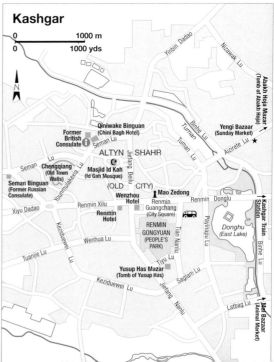

Kashgar

0 — 1000 m
0 — 1000 yds

N

Ymbin Dadao
Nizawak Lu
Abakh Hoja Mazar (Tomb of Abakh Hoja)

Qiniwake Binguan (Chini Bagh Hotel)
Yengi Bazaar (Sunday Market)
Former British Consulate
Seman Lu
Binhe Lu
Tuman Lu
Tuman
Aizirete Lu

ALTYN SHAHR
Seman
Chengqiang (Old Town Walls)
Seman Binguan (Former Russian Consulate)
Jiefang Beilu
Masjid Id Kah (Id Gah Mosque)
Youmulakexia Lu
(OLD CITY)
Xiyu Dadao
Wenzhou Hotel
Mao Zedong
Renmin Donglu
Kashgar Train Station
Renmin Xilu
Renmin Hotel
Renmin Guangchang (City Square)
Tian Nanlu
Payinapu Lu
Kezidewei Lu
Wenhua Lu
RENMIN GONGYUAN (PEOPLE'S PARK)
Donghu (East Lake)
Binhe Lu
Tuanjie Lu
Tuanjie Lu
Tiyu Lu
Yusup Has Mazar (Tomb of Yusup Has)
Saglam Lu
Jiefang Nanlu
Kezidewei Lu
Latbag Lu
Mal Bazaar (Animal Market)

Xinjiang for its production of hand-made knives. It's worth stopping off to visit the **Small Knife Factory** (Pichak Chilik Karakhana/Xiadaochang) to see skilled local craftsmen producing fine knives with inlaid handles. Just about every Uighur man carries a knife, both as a sign of manhood and for the more utilitarian purpose of cutting up melons, and the most valued (and expensive) come from here. Beyond Yengishar, just 58km (35 miles) to the north, lies the important oasis and city of Kashgar, the western terminus of the Southern Silk Road, and also the point at which the Southern and Northern routes meet, having encir-cled the Taklamakan Desert.

Kashgar

Kashgar (Kashi) has been a key centre on the Silk Road for well over two mil-lennia. The Northern and Southern roads that separated at Dunhuang rejoin here, linking up with mountain passes leading west to Samarkand and Bukhara, as well as south to Kashmir. In times past, when caravans reached Kashgar, men and beasts alike drew

breath and rested, secure in the knowledge that they had reached a safe haven near the very centre of the Silk Road.

Kashgar's physical centre may be the vast (and relatively empty) main square (**Guangchang**), dominated by a huge statue of Chairman Mao Zedong, but the city's spiritual heart lies a few hundred metres further to the north, at the **Id Gah Mosque** (Masjid Id Kah/Aiti Gaer Qingzhen Si; open daily; admis-sion fee for non-Muslims). "Id Gah" means "Place of Festival" in Farsi, and it is here that the city's Uighur Muslims congre-gate to worship every Friday, and also to celebrate the twin festivals of Id (or Eid) – Id al-Fitr, or "the celebra-tion of the breaking of the fast" at the end of the holy month of Ramadan, and Id al-Adha, or "the celebration of sacrifice" marking the Hajj, or annual pilgrimage to Mecca.

Probably the largest mosque in China, the Id Gah Mosque was built in 1442 but it incorporates a structure

Yengisar is famous for its high quality knives.

BELOW: the Sunday Market in Kashgar.

Muhammad Yakub Beg

Yakub Beg was a Central Asian potentate at the height of the Great Game, when the British and Russians were vying for the region.

During the 19th and early 20th centuries a fierce, if clandestine, competition for political and military influence in Central Asia was played out between the British and Russian empires. As Britain extended its control across South Asia from the shores of Sri Lanka to the Himalayas, imperial Russia pressed south and east, across the great plains of Central Asia, to threaten the venerable khanates of Bukhara and Khiva. By the early 19th century only a few hundred kilometres of desert and mountains separated British from Russian forces, and both Afghanistan and Xinjiang emerged as unlikely settings for the Great Game between the Russians and the British in India.

In 1862 the great Northwestern Muslim Rebellion spread across China between Shaanxi and Gansu. Hui Muslims living in eastern Xinjiang and Dzungaria soon joined in the general rising, cutting the Uighur oasis towns of southern Xinjiang off from China proper. The Uighurs, though Muslims, had very different aspirations to their Hui co-religionists, looking to Central Asia rather than to China as their natural spiritual home.

At a time of Chinese imperial weakness, there were opportunities for Central Asian adventurers, and one of the most interesting, Muhammad Yaqub Beg, was to make himself emir of the "independent" Kingdom of Kashgaria. An Uzbek from the Kokand Khanate, he became commander-in-chief of the Khan's armies and fought against the Russians, albeit unsuccessfully, at Ak Mechet in 1853. On being defeated, his thoughts turned eastwards, and he crossed the Pamirs, making himself master first of Kashgar and Yarkand, then gradually of all the oasis towns as far east as Turpan and Hami.

Yakub Beg was able to benefit from the *realpolitik* of the Great Game, appealing for British aid and recognition to act as a buffer state between the British, Russian and Chinese Empires. He issued his own currency, recognised the spiritual authority of the Ottoman Caliph in Istanbul, and sought arms from both Turkey and British India. He was not popular with his Uighur subjects, however, and as an Uzbek remained something of an outsider.

Yaqub Beg did not long enjoy the fruits of his conquests. By 1877 the great Chinese general Zuo Zongtang had fought his way across Gansu and was engaged on a reconquest of the far west for the Qing authorities. Yakub Beg was preparing to resist the Chinese from his advance base at Korla, when he was either poisoned or died of a stroke on 30 May 1877. After his death all resistance in Kashgaria ceased, and Zuo Zongtang claimed the entire region, including Urumqi and Dzungaria in the north, for China. Zuo also gave this vast tract of land a new name: Xinjiang, or "New Frontier".

Yakub Beg's death and the re-establishment of Chinese power over Xinjiang didn't lead to the end of the Great Game, but rather drove it underground. Between the late 19th century and the Chinese Communist seizure of power in 1949, rival British and Russian consuls based at Kashgar alternately spied and schemed against each other on behalf of their imperial masters, or shared drinks and played cards together in this most remote of diplomatic destinations.

ABOVE: Muhammad Yakub Beg.

500 years older. It is said to be able to accommodate as many as 10,000 worshippers during the Id festivals (known as Bairam and Qurban in Turkish/Uighur). Yellow-tiled and very different to the Great Mosque in Xi'an (see page 139), the architectural style is definitively Central Asian and not Chinese, although – while impressive – it does not match up to the mosques of Samarkand and Bukhara. Still, this is clearly a cultural frontier, the end of China and the beginning of Islamic Central Asia.

Non-Muslim visitors may enter the mosque at will (except during prayers), but should dress modestly and observe the usual strictures such as removing shoes and (in the case of women) covering their hair. Tellingly, Han Chinese are far less likely to observe these restrictions than are Westerners, much to the bemused and frustrated disdain of the Uighur custodians.

Kashgar is a city that is changing fast. Once ringed by crenellated walls and staunchly Muslim, today it is increasingly Han Chinese, as waves of settlers from the east – from "China proper" – follow the newly con-structed railway from Lanzhou (1999) to seek their fortune in China's "Wild West". Much of the Old City (Altyn Shahr/Laocheng) has been demol-ished in recent years.Old Kashgar is best seen to the west of Id Gah Square – where parts of the Old City wall (**Chengqiang**) are still extant to the west of Seman Lu; alternatively, another section of the Old Town has been preserved to the east of Id Kah Square and is now actively promoted as a (paying) tourist attraction.

The Old City aside, Kashgar's main attraction is undoubtedly the **Sunday Market** (Yengi Bazaar/Xinqitian Shichang). In fact the market is open daily, though at its busiest on Sundays – if you have time and opportunity, head out west of the Tuman River to Aizirete Lu early on a Sunday morn-ing for the most authentic Kashgar market experience. Overwhelmingly Uighur (though Han Chinese, Hui, Kazakh, Kyrgyz and Tajiks are also pre-sent), expect everything from locally manufactured hats, furs and knives to carpets, clothing, boots and traditional aphrodisiacs – the dried scorpions look particularly appealing. Uighur food-stuffs, from kebabs to *naan*, are also ubiquitous. You'll see plenty of tourists as well, but – interestingly – most will be Han Chinese, who seem to know little of their Uighur fellow citizens, but are clearly fascinated by them.

Also best visited on a Sunday, the **Animal Market** (Mal Bazaar/Dongwu Shichang) is great fun and uniquely "Kashgari". Located in the southeast of town, some distance beyond the confines of urban Kashgar, it's packed with Uighur men buying and selling livestock of all kinds, from fat-tailed sheep to camels and yaks. This is seri-ous business for the locals, and tour-ists are all but ignored as Uighurs in leather boots and *chapan* (long-sleeved Central Asian coats) weigh up and discuss the relative merits of livestock of all kinds, or "test ride" horses, camels and even yaks in the

In traditional Uighur society much respect is paid to the opinions of elderly and experienced men generally known as aqsaqal or "white beards".

BELOW: the Id Gah Mosque in Kashgar.

Carpets for sale in Kashgar.

BELOW: Chini Bagh, the former British Consulate in Kashgar.

dusty surroundings of the vast, open market.

Roughly 5km (3 miles) from the city centre, on the northern outskirts of town, is the **Tomb of Abakh Hoja** (Abakh Hoja Mazar/Xiangheimu; open daily 10am–7pm; admission fee for non-Muslims), also known locally as the **Tomb of Xiangfei**. Dedicated to the memory of Xinjiang's most celebrated Sufi mystic – a member of the Naqshbandi order and reputed *sayyid* or descendant of the Prophet Muhammad – the 17th-century sage is entombed here together with many members of his family, as well as Abakh Khoja's granddaughter, the Uighur woman Iparhan – better known in Chinese as Xiang Fei, the "Fragrant Concubine" – who was given as a wife to the Emperor Qianlong (1735–96) and immortalised in a painting by Giuseppe Castiglione (1688–1766).

Another important Uighur site is the **Tomb of Yusup Has** (Yusup Has Mazar; open daily 10am–7pm;

admission fee for non-Muslims). Yusup Has was the author of the Uighur text *Qutatu Bilik* or "Benefical Lore", one of the greatest works of Uighur literature, and together with Mahmud Kashgari (see below) remains among the most respected and revered of Uighur intellectuals.

During the late 19th and early 20th centuries, Kashgar was at the very centre of the Great Game (see 70) for power and influence in Central Asia, with both the British and the Russians maintaining consulates in the remote but strategically significant oasis. The former British Consulate, known as Chini Bagh or "Chinese Garden", is located behind the **Chini Bagh Hotel** (Qiniwake Binguan) on Seman Lu, while the former Russian Consulate survives at the **Seman Binguan** (also now a hotel), also on Seman Lu. It's extraordinary to think that the diplomatic representatives of these two great powers lived and competed with each other in this remote oasis, plotting and planning each other's downfall while at the same time meeting for dinner and drinks on a regular

basis, driven to friendship by isolation, while at the same time serving the interests of their different, distant masters in London and Moscow.

Around Kashgar

About 35km (21 miles) northeast of town lies the remains of **Hanuoyi Gucheng** (Ha Noi Ancient City) and **Mu'er Fota** (Mor Pagoda), both dating from the pre-Islamic period when Buddhism flourished in Xinjiang, and contemporaneous with other abandoned cities in the Taklamakan Desert like Niya and Karahoja. Thought to have flourished between the 7th and 12th centuries AD, there's little enough to see nowadays, though the remains of the Mor Pagoda are indicative of the Buddhist civilisation that once flourished here.

More interesting (and harder to get to) is the natural phenomenon known as **"Shipton's Arch"**. Remote, unique and astonishing – yet only 40km (24 miles) from downtown Kashgar – this is considered to be by far the largest natural rock arch anywhere in the world, rising to the same height as the

Empire State Building. Discovered by British mountaineer and Kashgar-based diplomat Eric Shipton (1907–77), it is located in the heart of the remote slot canyons of the inaccessible **Kara Tagh** or Black Mountains. Known in Turkic as **Tushuk Tash** or "Pierced Rock", and in Chinese as **Tiandong** or "Heavenly Gap", its location was completely forgotten in the troubled years following the Chinese Communist seizure of power in 1949, and the arch was only rediscovered (and permanently located using GPS technology) by a National Geographic expedition as recently as May 2000. It is possible to climb the arch, and ladders have been added to the lower section to make the scramble easier.

Leaving Kashgar

Beyond Kashgar, the old Silk Road continues westward to Kyrgyzstan and Uzbekistan via the **Torugart Pass** (3,752 metres/12,310ft) as well as the somewhat easier **Irkeshtam Pass** (2,841 metres/9,321ft) leading to Osh and the Fergana Valley – this is the poet James Elroy Flecker's

BELOW: camels at Lake Karakul on the Karakoram Highway.

Local Kyrgyz at Lake Karakul.

BELOW: Ghez River landscape.

Golden Road to Samarkand. The Irkeshtam Pass is the main route following the old Silk Road, and remains the main link between western China and the former Soviet Central Asian republics – the so-called "Stans".

Buses leave Kashgar for Osh, the first major town in Kyrgyzstan, twice a week from the **International Bus Station** (Guoji Chichezhan on Jiefang Beilu), or a taxi will take you to the Irkeshtam international frontier (250km/155 miles, about five hours). Crossing the Torugart Pass is more complex and requires a special permit or *xukezheng* from the Chinese authorities, and it isn't always easy to find onward transport from the Kyrgyzstan border to Naryn or Bishkek. It's best to make arrangements beforehand with one of the Kashgar travel agencies such as the Caravan Café, John's Café or CITS.

An alternative route following the old Southern Silk Road spur to South Asia leads via the Khunjerab Pass (4,693 metres/15,397ft) to Pakistan.

This is the Zhongba Gonglu or **Karakoram Highway**, an engineering marvel that was opened in 1986 and remains the highest paved road in the world. Even if you're not going all the way to Pakistan, it's well worth travelling the 280km (175 miles) to Tashkurgan or "Stone Castle", the last town in China before the Khunjerab Pass. Fans of the 2007 film The Kite Runner may recognise the castle as many scenes were shot on location here in place of Kabul Fort.

An hour distant from Kashgar is the small town of **Upal** (Wupaer). On a bluff above the town is the **Mausoleum of Mahmud al-Kashgari** (Mahmud al-Kashgari Mazar; open daily; admission fee). This renowned 11th-century linguist, poet and historian compiled the first comprehensive dictionary of Turkic languages. A statue of the great man stands in front of the actual mausoleum.

Lake Karakul

Beyond Upal, the highway climbs through stunning scenery, following the valley of the Ghez River (Ghez

Darya) before passing through the weird Kum Tagh or "Sand Mountains", strange formations that look as though they are made of wet sand. Before long the permanently snow-capped peaks of the Pamirs come into view, with **Kongur Tagh** (7,649 metres/25,100ft) and **Muztagh Ata** (7,546 metres/24,760ft) dominating the skyline. At an altitude of 3,900 metres (12,800ft), **Lake Karakul** (Karakul Gol/Kala Hu) must be one of the loveliest stretches of water in Asia. Renowned for its clarity and tranquillity, the huge mass of Muztagh Ata is clearly reflected in the waters. It's possible to see no fewer than 14 separate glaciers from the lakeshore. Two small settlements of Kyrgyz nomads lie by the side of the lake, and visitors can stay overnight in one of their mobile homes or yurts – Kyrgyz men will approach travellers as they arrive at the lake and offer to arrange this accommodation. It's cold at this height even in summer, so travellers intending to stay overnight should ensure that they bring sufficient warm clothing.

Those staying overnight will be able to experience the peace and tranquillity of Lake Karakul at dusk and at dawn, when the increasingly common tour buses have left or not yet arrived, and when the majestic scenery surrounding the lake is at its best. Yet despite its remoteness, Lake Karakul is changing fast as its fame percolates through to eastern China. The influx of tourists both here and at Tian Chi or "Heaven Lake" in the Tian Shan to the northeast of Urumqi has inevitably had an impact on the local herdsmen, and it's now common to see local tribesmen, richly clad and sitting astride magnificent horses, chatting with their neighbours across the waters by mobile phone.

Beyond Lake Karakul the road descends slightly to reach the small Tajik town of **Tashkurgan** (Taxkorgan), 260km (162 miles) distant from Kashgar. This ancient settlement was mentioned by Ptolemy in the 2nd century AD as the western-most point in the "Land of Seres" or China. Xuanzang passed this way in the 7th century laden with precious Buddhist sutras he was carrying back from India to Xi'an. Today Tashkurgan is a quiet little place with a couple of fairly basic hotels and restaurants for travellers. Out of season the hotels may not have heating. The remains of a 6th-century stone fort – from which the settlement derives its name – stand just north of the town.

The Chinese border post of Pir Ali (Hongqilapu) is a further 54km (32 miles) beyond Tashkurgan, though the actual frontier is 50km (30 miles) beyond this point. The road climbs over the **Khunjerab Pass** via the Karakoram Highway before continuing to Sost and, eventually, to Gilgit in Pakistan.

The Dzungarian route

In times past a northern spur of the Silk Road led north of the Tian Shan crossing the Dzungarian Basin of northern Xinjiang before entering what is now Kazakhstan by way of the Dzungarian Gap. Today China's only

BELOW: Mausoleum of Mahmud al-Kashgari.

The Khunjerab Pass, at 4,693 metres (15,397ft), is the highest paved international frontier crossing in the world. Completed in 1982, it takes its name from the local Wakhi language, meaning "Valley of Blood" – though it is often snowcovered.

BELOW: mosque in Urumqi.

rail link with Kazakhstan, as well as Highway 312 to Almaty, pass the same way. Truth to tell, there is little of Silk Road interest in the area today, though it's a convenient and relatively easy way of travelling between China and Kazakhstan – certainly more straightforward than using either the Torugart or Irkeshtam routes from Kashgar.

Xinjiang's capital and main city, **Urumqi** (Wulumuqi) lies this way, and while it's a relatively new city with few sites to see, it is a convenient hub for onward journeys by road, rail or air. The airport is well connected to other cities in China, and to most of the Central Asian capitals. In marked contrast to the Uighur oases of southern Xinjiang, it's a very Han Chinese city, with a population of 3.1 million, with Han making up 75 percent of the residents while Uighurs constitute a mere 12 percent. The balance is made up of Hui Muslims and Kazakhs.

Good hotels, restaurants and communications links aside, there is one very good reason to visit Urumqi. The **Xinjiang Autonomous Region Museum** (Xinjiang Zizhiqu

Bowuguan) is one of the finest museums in China and has some truly outstanding Silk Road exhibits, including the most famous of all, the Taklamakan Desert mummies, the 4,000 year old "Beauty of Loulan", "Cherchen Man" and the "Witches of Subeshi". The museum has undergone extensive renovation in recent years, including the addition of 10 new halls at a cost of $13 million, and new exhibits include dioramas of some of the lost desert cities, a fine display of Buddhist frescoes from Kizil near Kuqa, and a stunning collection of artefacts from the Astana Tombs at Turpan, including remarkably preserved brocades. It's easy to spend a whole day here, and there's really nothing else to match it anywhere in the province.

Beyond Urumqi it's possible to follow the old northern spur of the Silk Road to Kazakhstan by either road or rail. Trains depart Urumqi for Almaty twice a week, but it's a slow journey, with long delays at the international frontier – reckon on six hours going through both sets of customs.

Alternatively, sleeper buses run between Urumqi's **North Bus Station** (Changtu Qichezhan) and the border town of Korgas (12 hours); from here it takes a further 12 hours by bus to Almaty.

Around Urumqi

There are two outstanding natural beauty spots near Urumqi, and it's worth visiting at least one of them to see the Tian Shan or "Heavenly Mountains" up close, as well as to meet some of the region's nomadic Kazakhs who inhabit the high mountain pastures. **Tian Chi** or "Heaven Lake" is 110km (66 miles) east of the city and can be reached in about 2.5 hours by bus or taxi. It makes an excellent day trip, though it's also possible to stay overnight in a Kazakh yurt – you'll certainly be approached with offers of accommodation on arrival, and it's also possible to book overnight accommodation through a travel agent in Urumqi.

The long, blue lake is at an altitude of 2,000 metres (7,000ft) and lies in the lee of permanently snow-capped **Bogda Feng**, "The Peak of God", at 5,445 metres (17,864ft) the highest mountain in the eastern Tian Shan. During the summer months Kazakh yurts cluster by the lakeshore, and there are plenty of tourists and day-trippers from Urumqi taking advantage of the truly beautiful scenery. In winter, however, it's simply too cold to visit, and even the hardy Kazakhs move down to lower pastures. It's difficult to overstate the pristine beauty of Tian Chi, though purists will cavil at the chairlift that now whisks passengers from the lower parking area to the shores of the lake several hundred metres above.

Also appealing are the "Southern Pastures" at **Baiyang Gou**, about 48km (30 miles) south of Urumqi. The main attractions are a 20-metre (66-ft) -high waterfall, the wooded slopes of White Poplar Valley and – once again – the distinctive circular yurts of the Kazakh nomads who live here. It's a popular day trip from Urumqi, and Chinese tourists enjoy themselves riding horses or camels and drinking *kumis*, the fermented mare's milk for which Xinjiang's Kazakhs are famous.

BELOW: Heavenly Lake.

CENTRAL ASIA

Through Central Asia the Silk Road crosses
several countries, and travel here is a mix of
real adventure and high culture in cities such as
Samarkand, Bukhara and Herat.

Whether you call it Central Asia, Inner Asia, Tartary, Turkestan or Transoxiana, the lands between the Caspian and the Tian Shan – today's "Stans" – have always formed the heartlands of the Silk Road. This meeting point between Europe and Asia forms the middle leg of the route, a resting spot and a place of transfer, whose spectacular cities have long attracted traders and invaders in equal measure.

Mountains, steppe and desert

With a huge land area of 6.45 million sq km (2.5 million sq miles), Central Asia is subcontinental in its scope. Kazakhstan alone is roughly the size of Western Europe. Mountains, steppe and desert characterise much of the scenery. To the north is the endless Kazakh steppe, the reason for 19th-century Russia's relentless drift south in search of a permanent defendable border. South of here, steppe turns to sand in the wastes of the Karakum (Black Sands) and Kyzylkum (Red Sands) deserts of Uzbekistan and Turkmenistan. Between the two threads is the Amu Darya (Oxus), Central Asia's great river of antiquity and the life source of the Khorezm oasis and the Aral Sea.

The southeast is dominated by the high mountains of the Tian Shan, Pamirs and Hindu Kush, whose remote, snow-capped ranges reach to 7,000m (23,000ft) and higher. Wrapped in the spurs of these mountains is the Fergana Valley and the great lake of Issyk-Kul. North of here, heading back towards the steppe, the regions of Semireche and Dzungaria provide the major route into Chinese Turkestan.

In the far south the plains, mountains and deserts of Afghanistan mark the transition from Central Asia to the Indian subcontinent, with the northern regions of Herat and Afghan Turkestan oriented towards Central Asia and the Pashtun areas of the east and south pointed to Pakistan.

PRECEDING PAGES: siesta time near Shakhrisabz, Uzbekistan. **LEFT:** doorway at the Kalon complex in Bukhara. **ABOVE:** family in the Fan Mountains, Tajikistan.

Empires and invaders

Central Asia's spectacular history is overwhelming in its richness and could fill several books of its own. The stars of the past stretch from the enigmatic settled cultures of the Sogdians and Bactrians to the nomadic lands of the Scythians, Kazakh hordes and Turkmen tribes, and the almost global empires of Alexander the Great, the Kushans, Tamerlane and Genghis Khan.

One major theme you'll recognise early on is that of the settler versus the nomad; the horsebound traditions of the Kazakhs and Kyrgyz versus the settled trading cultures of the Tajiks and Uzbeks. Central Asian history has been shaped for millennia by the cyclical nature of its empires: from growth, expansion and brilliance to decadence, invasion and, ultimately, destruction. The region has been fought over by everyone from the Mongols and Arabs to the Persians and Russians.

Perhaps the most colourful period of history was that of the Great Game, the 19th-century imperial stand-off between the Russian and British empires. Central Asia formed a critical gap in the imperial chessboard of the day and provided the principal setting for the game. The Russians were, of course, to prevail and their successors, the Soviets, changed the face of the region faster than anyone else since the Mongols.

Since the fall of the Soviet Union and the disappearance of such icons as Lenin, Central Asian leaders have been keen to promote new indigenous heroes to fill the ideological vacuum. Uzbekistan has rehabilitated its hero Tamerlane, Tajikistan has closely allied itself with the Persian-speaking Ismail Samani (Ismoil Somoni in Tajik) and Kyrgyzstan has rallied around its epic hero Manas. Statues of Kazakh bards have popped up across Kazakhstan, and Turkmenistan has been turned into a shrine to its recently deceased leader Turkmenbashi. One set of myths has replaced another.

Silk routes

The silk routes criss-crossed Central Asia like a web. There were three main options: the northern route through the Dzungarian Gap from the Ili Valley into modern Kazakhstan; the central mountain routes over the Tian Shan to the Fergana Valley (the modern Torugart and Irkeshtam crossings); and the Wakhan route, from the Stone Tower at Tashkurgan to Ishkashim, Faizabad, Kunduz and Balkh in modern Afghanistan. The northern route offered the easier terrain but longer stages and more brigands. The southern route required a transfer from camels to donkeys to climb from the desert sands to the snowy passes but offered a more direct route to Fergana and Persia beyond.

The central routes joined at Samarkand and continued west to Bukhara and Merv, and on to Persia. It was in the great clearinghouses of Samarkand, Bukhara and Merv that caravans from Baghdad and Aleppo handed over their goods to merchants from Turpan, Kashgar, Yarkand and Khotan.

Above: visitors to Shakhrisabz, with Timur's White Palace and statue.
Top Right: Timur's mausoleum, the Gur-i-Mir, in Samarkand. **Bottom Right:** Tash Rabat Caravanserai, south of Naryn.

Travel today

These days modern travellers can once again retrace Silk Route crossings over the Torugart and Irkeshtam passes, and savour the Silk Road cities of Samarkand, Bukhara and Herat. As with all worthwhile trips, obstacles do remain. The modern borders of the ex-Soviet "Stans" remain a largely artificial Soviet invention. The Soviets created nationalities and their homelands where there was previously only settler and nomad, or Persian- and Turkic-speaker. The oddly-shaped modern republics are only now disentangling themselves after 70 years of enforced Soviet brotherhood, resulting in a bewildering array of visa regulations, travel permits, currencies and border crossings. The meeting point of this bureaucratic tangle is the Fergana Valley, which remains a political and security hotspot after violence in summer 2010.

The Soviet era has taken its toll on the romance of the region. You are more likely to find a Kazakh in a tracksuit than on a horse these days, and the road to Samarkand is now black tarmac, not golden sands. Much of neighbouring Afghanistan lies shattered after a generation of war, though a number of areas in the north of the country remain accessible and relatively safe.

Still, a visit to Central Asia promises some marvellous moments. You can stay overnight at the Tash Rabat caravanserai in the high mountains of the Tian Shan, wander Tamerlane's ruins in Samarkand and track down ruined forts and ancient cities in the Wakhan Corridor or the deserts of Karakalpakstan. The spirit of the Silk Road can still be felt on a horse trek to a Kyrgyz yurt or while taking tea with a turbanned Uzbek in a *chaikhana*. The very names of cities such as Samarkand, Balkh, Herat and Merv still resonate with association, unequalled in their romance, centuries after their heyday.

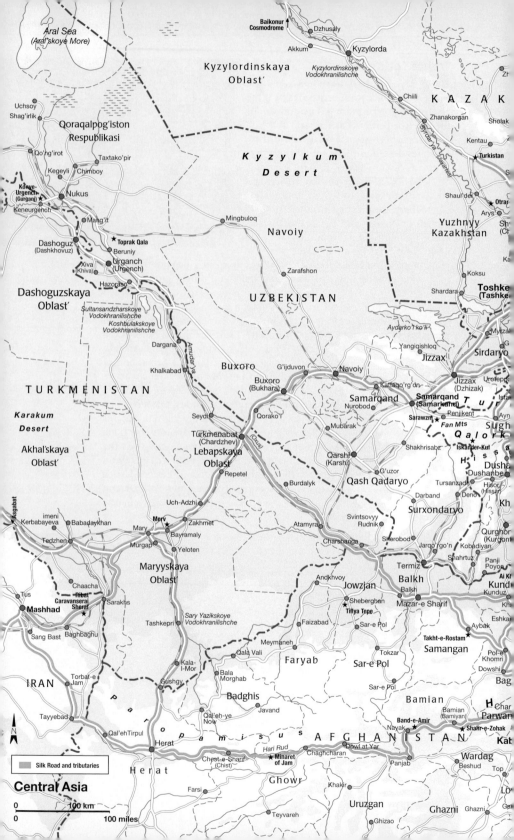

Central Asia

Silk Road and tributaries

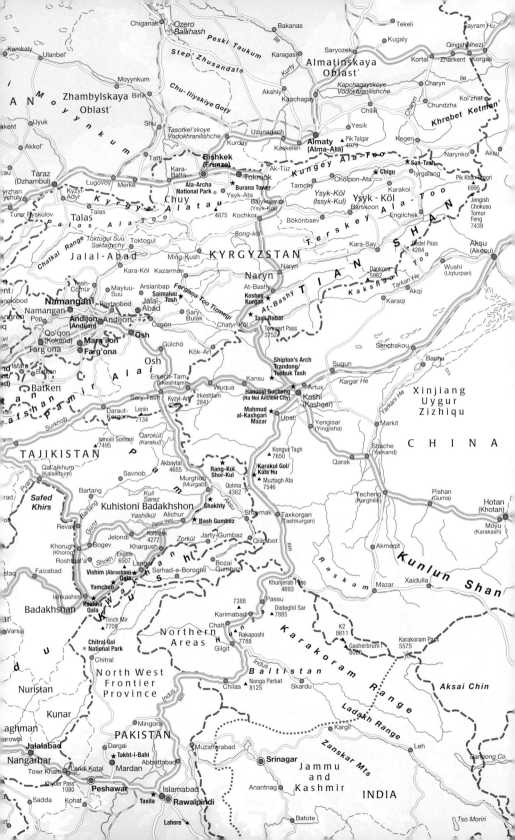

KYRGYZSTAN

Life in this mountainous country is hard but exhilarating. Visitors can enjoy the dramatic scenery, experience the nomadic lifestyle on the high pastures, and seek out the many historical sights connected with the Silk Road.

The small mountain republic of Kyrgyzstan is often dubbed the "Switzerland of Central Asia" for its alpine valleys, flower-filled meadows and snow-capped peaks. Lake Issyk-Kul may indeed rival Lake Geneva, but the similarities end abruptly with the eagle hunters, yurts and nomads that make Kyrgyzstan a distinctly inner Asian country. Like its many lakes, it is a jewel hidden high in the mountain valleys of Central Asia, and more than amply rewards those who make the effort to explore it.

The Kyrgyz Republic is defined by its geography, specifically its mountains, which make up over 94 percent of the country. The north is dominated by the wild valleys of the Tian Shan – the "Heavenly Mountains" – or Tengir-Too in Kyrgyz, whose valleys offer some of the world's loveliest alpine scenery: a trekkers' paradise of rushing streams, juniper forests and glaciated peaks.

To the south, forming the southern wall of the Fergana Valley, are the remote towers of Turkestan and Pamir Alai, spurs of the great Pamirs. In between are the central highlands – rolling hills dotted with yurts and mountain lakes – Issyk-Kul, Song-Kol and Sary Chelek to name just three.

Life for the Kyrgyz

The Kyrgyz people arrived here in the 16th century, after migrating across inner Asia from homelands in the Yenisey Valley of Siberia. Today around 60 percent of the people are Kyrgyz, who remain close ethnic kin to their neighbours the Kazakhs. There are also significant numbers of Uzbeks and Russians, as well as pockets of Dungans, Koreans and others.

Despite years of Soviet collectivisation and modernisation, the remnants of a Kyrgyz nomadic culture remain.

Main attractions

TASH RABAT
SAIMALUU TASH PETROGLYPHS
LAKE SONG-KOL
KOCHKOR
BISHKEK:
  ALA-TOO SQUARE
  STATE HISTORICAL MUSEUM
ALA-ARCHA NATIONAL PARK
BURANA TOWER
LAKE ISSYK-KUL
KARAKOL
ALTYN ARASHAN VALLEY
IRKESHTAM ROUTE
ALAY VALLEY
OSH:
  HISTORICAL MUSEUM
  JAYMA BAZAAR
  OZGON MAUSOLEUM

LEFT: riding out into the Ak-Su Valley in the Pamir-Alay. **RIGHT:** horseplay in a *jailoo* (pastureland).

ENTERING AND LEAVING KYRGYZSTAN

Roads in Kyrgyzstan are often poor and the terrain difficult. (See Travel Tips, page 405, for more information on transport in Kyrgyzstan.)

Buses and taxis run between Bishkek and Almaty in **Kazakhstan**, a journey that can take as little as three hours (excluding border formalities). In summer, frequent buses also run between Almaty and Cholpon-Ata.

Bus services from Bishkek to **Uzbekistan** travel via Kazakhstan and terminate at the Uzbek border, from where a taxi or minibus can be taken on to Tashkent. A Kazakh transit visa is necessary. Minibuses and taxis run from Osh to the Uzbek border, from where local transport can be taken to reach Andijan and other towns in the Fergana Valley.

A public bus runs twice a week from Osh to Kashgar in **China** by way of the Irkeshtam Pass. Tour operators in Bishkek and Kashgar can arrange travel up to the Torugart Pass, although this is not technically an authorised crossing point for foreigners, and travellers may be left stranded for hours at a freezing-cold frontier post waiting for a lift on the other side.

A rough road crosses the Kyzyl-Art Pass south of Sary-Tash to reach Murgab in **Tajikistan**, for which a GBAO (Gorno-Badakhshan Autonomous Oblast) permit is required. Shared taxis run between Batken in southwest Kyrgyzstan to Isfara in Tajikistan. However, reaching Batken itself may require an Uzbek transit visa and a multiple-entry Kyrgyz visa, as public transport between Osh and Batken travels through an Uzbek enclave. Private taxis can be persuaded to travel around the enclave, however.

All along the roadside in grazing areas you'll see locals selling Coke bottles full of *kymyz*, fizzy and bitter fermented mares' milk. The country's literary heritage rests largely in the memory of itinerant bards called *akyn*, and nomadic-inspired horse games are still played out annually in the summer pastures. Less desirable nomadic hangovers remain too, from the custom of bride-kidnapping to the system of clan-based politics. Islam remains a relatively thin veneer, especially in the north and centre of the country.

Central to the Kyrgyz definition is the *Manas* (see panel), an oral epic poem 20 times longer than the *Odyssey* and *Iliad* combined. The epic chronicles the history of the formation of the Kyrgyz people through the exploits of the hero Manas, his wife Kanykei and son Semetei. A tomb, the Manas Gumbez, was built for the fictional hero in 1334, just southeast of the modern town of Talas.

Tulip Revolution

During the Soviet era the mountains of "Kyrgyzia" remained off-limits

The Father of Kyrgyzstan

The *Epic of Manas* is a traditional poem of more than 500,000 lines that has been transmitted orally for hundreds of years. Its exact origins are unknown, but what is certain is that in the 1920s and '30s the text was changed to reinforce a link between the hero, Manas, and the Kyrgyz people. The text is key to Kyrgyz national identity as it describes the unification of seven tribes into a single people. Consequently, the Kyrgyz government has promoted the epic heavily, celebrating its highly-debatable 1,000th anniversary in 1995 and building a Manas-themed park in Talas. The official line also claims it is the world's longest poem; it may have the most verses, but the Indian *Mahabharata* has more words.

thanks to its uranium mines, hydro-electric dams and prickly mountain border with China. Reluctant independence brought great economic hardship to the country, a problem compounded by the ensuing exodus of most of Kyrgyzstan's skilled and educated Russian population. President Akayev pushed through early reforms to turn the Kyrgyz economy into the most liberal in Central Asia. Increasingly corrupt and authoritarian, he was overthrown a decade later in the popular Tulip Revolution of March 2005.

The 2010 revolution and violence

Akayev's successor, Kurmanbek Bakiyev, came to power with significant support from the US, but he proved no better as a leader and corruption sky-rocketed. In 2009 he announced the eviction of the US from their Manas airbase near Bishkek, purportedly in exchange for a $2 billion loan from Moscow, but the US was then able to renegotiate the lease and Bakiyev kept the Russian's money, losing him vital support from the Kremlin. The Russian media, influential in Kyrgyzstan as well as at home, ran an anti-Bakiyev campaign, culminating in protests, bloody riots and an eventual coup in April 2010. Along with his son, Maxim, Bakiyev is alleged to have stolen more than $3 billion from Kyrgyzstan. Both men are wanted by Interpol.

Ousted from power, Bakiyev fled first to Osh and then with his family to Belarus. The vacuum of power was seized upon by the mafia to settle old scores, and the drug lords to pressurise the interim government into awarding them more favourable transit rates through the country. Under the guise of inter-ethnic violence, labourers in the south of the country were paid 2000 som (approximately $43) to kill both Uzbeks and Kyrgyz indiscriminately in a bid to destabilise the region. Violence between the communities

inevitably escalated. At least 200 people died, 300,000 were internally displaced and 100,000 crossed the border into Uzbekistan as refugees.

Despite this, with its welcoming people, spectacular scenery and few of the visa and permit hassles that so dog tourism in the other Central Asian republics, Kyrgyzstan has huge tourism potential. Its network of fantastic community tourism projects unlocks the door to a unique world of yurts, nomads and mountain hospitality.

To experience fully the nomadic half of the schizophrenic Central Asian psyche you have to head up into the *jailoos* (pasturelands) of central Kyrgyzstan. Here the jagged northern Tian Shan soften into a landscape of rolling corduroy hillsides, rocky bluffs and high-altitude lakes that forms the border with China's Xinjiang province.

THE ROAD FROM KASHGAR

The classic Silk Road route from Kashgar to Kyrgyzstan crosses the Torugart Pass. Logistically more complex than the other high road from

BELOW LEFT: the Manas Gumbez tomb.
BELOW: Kyrgyz herder in the local headgear.

Community-Based Tourism

The best way to experience the nomadic flavour and natural hospitality of Kyrgyzstan is to stay with a mountain community.

The network of homestays, herders, yurt-owners and others that make up the Community-Based Tourism (CBT) organisation offers a unique chance to experience rural Kyrgyzstan. It was established a decade ago with Swiss assistance as part of measures to improve living conditions in remote mountain communities, by developing small-scale sustainable ecotourism initiatives. The family-based initiatives are not only sustainable but perfectly suited to the hospitality-rich but infrastructure-light nature of tourism in Kyrgyzstan. The CBT umbrella organisation provides training and marketing, but the bulk of the money (80–90 percent) goes directly to the service providers.

Given some warning, the various branches of the CBT organisation can arrange everything from transport, homestays, yurt-stays and English-speaking guides to multi-day horse treks. For larger groups they can arrange workshops on yurt construction or felt-making, and can even arrange concerts of traditional Kyrgyz music.

Don't expect this to be a pampered, top-end experience. Your bed is likely to be a pile of duvets and a sheet: clean but simple. Transport will be a Soviet-era Zhiguli that's unlikely to start at the first attempt, and you may have to wait a few hours for your horses to arrive from the local pastures.

One of the great things about the yurt-stays is the opportunity to try fresh dairy products, such as fantastic yoghurt, *kaimak* (fresh cream) and *airan* (yoghurt drink). For dinner expect such staples as *laghman* (noodles), *manti* (mutton dumplings) or *shorpo* (potato, carrot and mutton soup), plus plenty of *kok chai* (green tea) and snacks like *boorsuk* (fried dough pieces) and *kurut* (dried yoghurt balls). If you're lucky, you might get to try the traditional Kyrgyz dish *besh barmak* (noodles, meat and sauce), named "five fingers" because it is traditionally eaten with one's hands.

There are branches of CBT in almost every corner of the country, in Kyzyl-Oi (Suusamyr Valley), Arslanbob, Jalalabad, Kara-Suu (for Lake Sary-Chelek), Kazarman, Kochkor, Naryn, Aral, Kupuro Bazar, Talas, Bokonbayevo, Karakol, Tamchy, Batken, Alay, Kerben, Sary-Moghul and Chong-Kemin. Enquiries and bookings are best made online as the level of English spoken in the regional offices is sometimes limited.

CBT offers horse-riding through the walnut forests of Arslanbob, horse and foot treks to the alpine lakes of Sary-Chelek and Song-Kol, hikes into the Tian Shan mountains behind Karakol, jeep safaris through Central Kyrgyzstan and bike tours of Issyk-Kul. In rural areas their homestays are almost always the best places to stay. And with prices as low as $10 per night for accommodation and $10 for a day's horse hire, this is one of the Silk Road's best travel bargains. For detailed descriptions of the various options check out www.cbtkyrgyzstan.kg.

LEFT: traditional living in a yurt. **ABOVE:** a boy and his horse.

China via Irkeshtam, though undoubtedly more photogenic, this crossing is one part of your trip that you need to arrange in advance through a travel agency. For one of Central Asia's most enthralling adventures, add overnight visits to Tash Rabat, Song-Kol and Kochkor and then arrange a yurt-stay excursion through the community-based organisation there (see page 214).

Torugart to Kochkor

Flush from the relief of clearing Kyrgyzstan immigration, you'll soon pass the beautiful lake and nature reserve of **Chatyr-Kol** before ascending to the Tuz-Bel Pass. After the desert scenery of Xinjiang, the rolling green hills and mountains come as quite a shock. The surrounding hills are often covered in snow as late as June, which makes for challenging driving conditions. The road crosses one final border-zone checkpoint to crest the Ak-Beyit Pass before descending into the Kara-Koyuk Valley. The only traffic you are likely to see along this stretch is the occasional truckload of scrap metal headed for China.

The one unmissable Silk Road site in central Kyrgyzstan is **Tash Rabat** (Stone Caravanserai), a fantastically atmospheric 15th-century caravanserai hidden up a side valley, 7km (4 miles) off the main highway. Restored in the 1980s, the stone interior includes stables and two dungeons. There is also basic accommodation, sleeping on the wooden benches that visitors sit on by day. Two yurt camps at the base of the site offer simple but cosy accommodation. It's possible to arrange a horse trek up to the pass behind the caravanserai for views over Chatyr-Kol, or you can continue over the pass to overnight in a CBT yurt on the silent shores of the lake.

About 20km (12 miles) past the turn-off to Tash Rabat the road temporarily expands into a three-lane superhighway, a former military airstrip, before passing the small fortress of Koshoy Kurgan to the left. The lonely ruins are connected to the great warrior-hero Manas, who allegedly built the site for his companion Koshoy.

The views north to the At-Bashy range open up as the highway bypasses

TIP

The CBT offices in Kochkor and Naryn can arrange transport, yurt-stays at Song-Kol lake and two- or three-day horse treks into the Song-Kol basin. They can also organise *jailoo* trips; two of the most popular locations are *Sarala-Saz*, 64km (38 miles) northwest of Kochkor, and the two- to four-day horse trek to *Kol Ukock* lake, to the east.

BELOW: yurts at Song-Kol.

the small settlement of At-Bashy and climbs up to the Kyzyl-Bel (Red Saddle) Pass, before finally descending into the Naryn Valley.

Naryn

Naryn is a popular overnight stop for Torugart travellers, though the long, strung-out Soviet town is fairly grim. On the western edge of town, past the army base, is a garish new mosque financed in the 1990s by Saudi Arabia. The regional museum is worth a quick look for its examples of yurts and *shyrdaks*, as is the art gallery on the main square displaying work from contemporary Kyrgyz artists. The Naryn River that flows through town is a major branch of the Syr Darya (Jaxartes).

From Naryn the main highway continues north to Bishkek, but a little-travelled dirt road branches west directly to the Fergana Valley, via Kazarman. It's a rough route that demands a reliable car. Along the route is a very remote collection of over 10,000 petroglyphs, at **Saimaluu Tash**. The 3,000-year-old petroglyphs (*saimaluu tash* means "Embroidered Stones" in Turkic) date from the Bronze Age to the Saka era, depicting ibex, shamanic ceremonies and warfare, and are a proposed UNESCO World Heritage Site. The local CBT office can arrange a three-day return trip to the site on horseback, and this is undoubtedly the best way to see it.

A major highlight of central Kyrgyzstan is **Song-Kol**, a large and remote high-altitude lake cradled in a large bowl halfway between Naryn and Kochkor. Every year between June and August herders bring their flocks here to graze the lush pastures, and mushroom-like yurts sprout along the lakeshore. Visitors can reach the lake by road from the south or east, though the best way to visit is to follow the herders' example and make your way here on horseback. The views of the lake and mountains are unparalleled, and the overnight stay here in a simple yurt is a highlight of any trip to Kyrgyzstan.

Kochkor

Further north along the main highway, the town of **Kochkor** is the hub of tourism in central Kyrgyzstan. It's

BELOW: the colourful *shyrdaks*, or felt rugs made by Kyrgyz women are used to decorate yurts and are given as wedding gifts.

Souvenir Shyrdaks

If you only pick up one souvenir in Kyrgyzstan, make it a *shyrdak*, the felt carpets that are handmade in the highlands of central Kyrgyzstan. Kochkor, Bokonbaev and Bishkek are all good places to find a *shyrdak*, though purists claim the best examples come from Naryn.

Felt-making has long been an important summer activity for Kyrgyz women. The wool is first cleaned by beating it with sticks and is then spread over reeds as boiling water and soap are poured over it. The soggy wool is then rolled up into a tight tube and repeatedly rolled back and forth using opposing sets of ropes. The procedure is then repeated, before the felt is laid out to dry.

Shyrdaks are made from appliqué, not pressed, felt so the designs are cut out from the felt and then hand-stitched together, with a border sewn onto the sides as a final touch. The carpet motifs have their origins in the natural environment, with ibex horns, rams' horns, bird tracks and plant designs among the most popular. Brightly coloured Soviet chemical dyes supplanted traditional muted browns and greys in the 1970s, but these days natural dyes are making a comeback, particularly among NGO-supported *shyrdak* co-operatives. Crimson cochineal comes from the insect of the same name, and dark greens are extracted from motherwort.

the epicentre of a remarkable experiment in community-based tourism (see page 214) that has spread like wildfire throughout the country, even into the neighbouring republics.

The CBT organisation can put you in touch with the town's 20 local homestays and also the **Altyn Kol** organisation, a co-operative of over 200 Kyrgyz women that produces and markets traditionally and locally made *shyrdak*s (Kyrgyz felt carpets). The quality is top-notch, and the association provides a much-needed additional source of income to a community that was hit particularly hard by the demise of the Soviet Union.

One of the best things you can do in Kyrgyzstan is take a trip out to the *jailoo*s, summer pastures at an elevation of around 2,500–3,000 metres (8,200–9,800ft), where you can get a real taste of traditional Kyrgyz life. There are half a dozen locations around Kochkor where you can visit local herders, stay overnight in a yurt and ride horses. If you want, you can even take part in herders' chores, from milking and making yoghurt to herding

the animals. You can string together locations to make a foot or horse trek of anywhere from two days to a week or more, visiting en route high-alpine lakes, petroglyphs, waterfalls and some dramatic scenery. You can also observe traditional horse games, especially in late July or August. Most exciting is *ulak-tartysh*, similar to the Afghan *buzkashi*, in which two teams compete on horseback to capture and then carry a 20kg (44lb) goat carcass into a designated goal. It's a wild, exciting game that takes great skill. Also popular is *kish-kuumai*, a form of kiss-chase, in which a male rider tries to catch a female opponent, despite her advantage of a head start and a faster horse. Rooted in the practice of bride-kidnapping, these days the race provides plenty of opportunities for flirting on the grasslands.

BISHKEK

Kyrgyzstan's capital, Bishkek, is a pleasant, homely city of around 1 million people. It is often described as the polite younger brother of the Kazakh capital Almaty, just a couple of hours'

BELOW: on parade in Ala-Too Square, Bishkek.

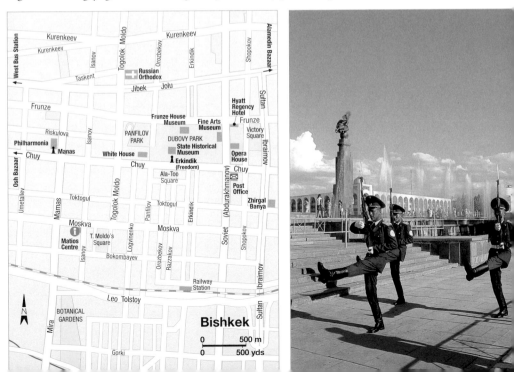

drive to the north, and it certainly retains a relaxed, small-town feel. Unlike many of Central Asia's settlements, it's not a great city of antiquity. It started life as a fort guarding the trade routes at the fringe of the Kokand Khanate before becoming the Russian garrison town of Pishpek in 1878. Renamed Frunze in 1926 by the Soviets after the leader of the Red Army who was born here, it was only after independence in 1991 that it took on the name Bishkek.

Bishkek's physical centre is **Ala-Too Square**, where locals gather to picnic and have their photos taken amongst the flowers and fountains, or protest in more trying times. The central Lenin statue is gone, replaced by a statue of Erkindik (Freedom), but the capital has seen little of the mass-scale whitewashing of the Soviet era that is so apparent in neighbouring Uzbekistan. Lenin is still hanging around, after all; he's just been demoted to the back of the building, a short skip away from fellow ideologue Karl Marx.

Facing the square to the north is the **State Historical Museum** (open Tue–Sun 9am–6pm), worth a visit as an introduction to Kyrgyz culture and also for the mural of an American cowboy riding astride a Pershing missile. Fans of Lenin will not be disappointed – this was once the Lenin Museum, and many of the original exhibits remain. On the west side of the square is the Kyrgyz government building known as the White House, from where snipers shot protestors during the 2010 coup.

To the east is leafy Dubovy (Oak) Park, where a second statue of Erkindik has replaced the far more sinister image of Felix Dzerzhinsky, founder of the Soviet secret police. Another Soviet construction to the north is the **Frunze House Museum** (open Wed–Mon 10am–6pm), built around the supposed childhood home of the Red Army general. As the man who led the Soviet capture of Bukhara and Khiva and smashed the local *Basmachi* rebel movement, Frunze is not a likely hero of Bishkek, but locals still maintain the museum and his statue opposite the railway station on Erkindik nonetheless.

BELOW: wooden bucket for making paper pulp.

The Defining Battle

Few pivotal moments in world history are as little-known as the Battle of Talas, in AD 751, when Arab and Chinese armies fought each other for five furious days near the modern border of Kazakhstan and Kyrgyzstan.

In the end the Chinese armies were routed after their allies switched allegiances mid-battle. The clash defined the limits of Arab and Tang Chinese expansion and shaped the Islamic face of Central Asia for centuries to come. Samarkand became a great centre of papermaking thanks to skills learnt from Chinese prisoners of war. The spilled secrets of paper and silk production spread along the Silk Road from Samarkand to Baghdad and on to Europe, where they sparked an intellectual revolution.

Other buildings worth checking out include the Philharmonia to the west, fronted by a large statue of Manas, the World War II monument and the **Russian Orthodox Church**, the spiritual centre of Bishkek's large Russian population. The **Fine Arts Museum** on Abdurakhmanov has a permanent collection of Kyrgyz folk art, including textiles, and also hosts temporary exhibitions of work from modern Russian artists. Top off a long day's sightseeing across the road with a performance at the charming neo-classical **Opera House** (admission fee) or, alternatively, a shot of vodka and a brief flogging with birch branches at the sauna **Zhirgal Banya** (open 8am–9pm) on Toktogul Street.

Around Bishkek

Wherever you stand in Bishkek the snow-capped range of the Kyrgyz Alatau frames the horizon to the south. Several travel agents in town can arrange treks, climbs, heli-skiing or picnics in the fine alpine valleys, just a short ride from the city.

The most popular trekking area is the **Ala-Archa National Park**, where trails lead up to a dilapidated ski centre or up the Ak-Say Canyon into a stunning mountain amphitheatre of snow-capped peaks. Climbers head here to ascend peaks Korona (4,860 metres/16,038ft) and Uchityel (4,572 metres/15,088ft). Other parallel canyons worth exploring to the southeast are the **Alameddin Canyon**, with its hot-springs sanatorium, and the **Kegeti Canyon**, where travel agents offer horse-riding and hiking trips.

The Chuy Valley

The most popular excursion from Bishkek is to the **Burana Tower** (open 8am–5pm; admission fee), Kyrgyzstan's only major Silk Road site, 80km (48 miles) east of the capital. The ruins have been identified as the 11th-century Karakhanid city of Balasagun, though the Mongols called it Gobolik when they passed through in 1218.

The collection of Nestorian crosses, Chinese coins and Buddhist carvings on display in the site museum point to the cosmopolitan nature of the city, though all that remains today is the heavily restored minaret, now half its original height of 44 metres (140ft). Climb the minaret for views of the city walls. Surrounding the site is a fine collection of 1,500-year-old *balbal*s, man-shaped stone grave markers or totems.

Several other minor settlements litter the Chuy Valley, which once formed a popular side branch of the Northern Silk Road. Though little remains, they point to an intriguing meeting of the Sogdian, Turkic and Chinese worlds. Xuanzang recorded several of the sites during his trip through the valley in AD 620, and Chang Chun passed through in 1220 en route from China to the court of Genghis Khan.

Ak-Beshim, 7km (4 miles) southeast of Tokmok, is thought to be the ancient settlement of Suyab, a capital of the Western (Blue) Turks. Excavations have revealed a Buddhist temple and Nestorian church, along with a Chinese fortress raised here in AD 679, but there

The Burana Tower near Bishkek is all that remains of the city of Balasagun, once an important trading centre on the Silk Road.

BELOW: one of the many *balbals* surrounding the Burana Tower.

is sadly little to see today. The city was later eclipsed by Balasagun.

The 6th- to 12th-century remains of **Navekat** (modern Krasnaya Rechka) have recently come under UNESCO protection. Modern excavations have unearthed a golden burial mask, an 8-metre (26-ft) -long reclining Buddha, the remains of a Zoroastrian fire temple and also artefacts suggesting the presence of Manicheans and Nestorian Christians. Clearly, Navekat was once a cosmopolitan settlement, though the key discoveries made here have been removed to museums in St Petersburg and Bishkek.

The nearby town of **Tokmok** carries a certain infamy as the centre of a 1916 revolt against Tsarist Russian rule (and attempts at conscription) that resulted in 120,000 Kyrgyz deaths. Another 120,000 fled over the Tian Shan to Xinjiang, with thousands more dying en route. The event is now known as the *Urkhun*, or Exodus. You may want to stop for a photo alongside the **MIG fighter jet** on the outskirts of the town, and there is also a small **archaeological museum** with labels in Russian.

LAKE ISSYK-KUL

The pearl of the Tian Shan is **Issyk-Kul** (Ysyk-Köl in Kyrgyz), a great turquoise inland sea dusted with sandy shores and framed on both sides by snow-capped peaks. At 180km (108 miles) long, it is the world's second-largest alpine lake, after Bolivia's Lake Titicaca, and the second largest saline lake after the Caspian Sea. The local Kyrgyz named it "Warm Lake" because, despite the altitude, it never freezes, due to its slight salinity. Unusually, over 80 streams flow into the lake but none flow out. To the north rises the Kungey (Sunny) Ala-Too range; to the south is the Terskey (Dark) Ala-Too.

The lake's scenic shores have long been popular with visitors. The submerged Saka-Usun settlement of Chigu on the northern shore dates from the 2nd century BC, and Saka (Scythian) burial mounds dot the northeastern shoreline. Genghis Khan and Timur both led their armies nearby. Russian and Ukrainian settlers built their gingerbread Tsarist buildings on the lakeshore in the late 19th century, and Soviet apparatchiks flocked here in the 1970s to soak in its sanatoria.

It was near Issyk-Kul that Xuanzang came across the magnificent tented court of the Blue Turks, surrounded by lush summer pasturage. He described "riders mounted on camels or horses, dressed in furs and fine woollen cloth and carrying long lances, banners and straight bows". The multitude "stretched so far that the eye could not tell where it ended". It was the last-ever description of the great nomad confederation, which fragmented soon afterwards.

The northern shore

The northern shore of the lake is easily the more developed, with more frequent transport, sandier beaches and better tourist facilities. There are simple homestays at the villages of Tamchy and Cholpan-Ata, and the upmarket hotels and renovated sanatoria appeal to wealthy Kazakhs and Russians as well as domestic tourists.

BELOW: Lake Issyk-Kul and the snow-capped peaks of the Tian Shan.

Trekkers will want to explore the network of trails that lead up the northern valleys, past verdant meadows and glaciers and over the high passes to Almaty in Kazakhstan.

One site worth a visit is the collection of 2,000-year-old **petroglyphs** at Cholpon-Ata. The hundreds of Scythian-era rock carvings depict ibex, wolves and hunting scenes.

Perhaps the most intriguing site on the northern shore is **Svetly Mys**, the location of eight Nestorian, Armenian, then Russian Orthodox monasteries, all built around the alleged burial site of St Matthew. Although little of the original buildings remain (the last monastery was burned and the monks killed in 1916), the church and almshouses have been restored for use as a children's home. There is also a craft workshop on site.

Karakol and the Tian Shan

Founded in 1869 by Tsarist military officers, the pleasant settlement of **Karakol**, at the southeast corner of the lake, is the biggest town in the region and an increasingly popular base for adventure tourists headed into the surrounding Tian Shan mountains. Time your visit for a Sunday and you'll get to catch both of the town's highlights – the bustling weekly animal market and the morning liturgy at the wooden **Holy Trinity Cathedral**. The town's excellent tourist information centre and network of homestays can help smooth out the logistics of your visit.

Worth checking out in the north of town is the Dungan mosque, built in 1910 by the town's community of Dungans, Muslim Chinese who crossed the border at the end of the 19th century, and also the **Regional History Museum** (open daily 9am-5pm; admission fee) with its display of stuffed wildlife, musical instruments and, most interestingly, old photographs of the area.

One easy excursion from Karakol is to the Tsarist-era **Przhewalsky Memorial**, 7km (4 miles) northwest from town. Famed for his expeditions to Mongolia, Tibet, Xinjiang and the Gobi between 1870 and 1885 and for the discovery of the diminutive brand of wild horse that still bears his name, Przhewalsky died in a nearby hospital after contracting typhus during the final preparations for an upcoming expedition. Lord Curzon wrote of Przhewalsky that he "deserved to be ranked with Livingstone and Stanley in this century as a pioneer of scientific exploration in an unknown and perilous continent". The interesting Soviet-era museum overlooks a former secret torpedo research centre.

Karakol's real draw is its proximity to the wild valleys of the Tian Shan. Local travel agencies and the local CBT office can arrange transport, accommodation and yurt-stays, though nothing beats camping in these achingly beautiful valleys. The most popular destination is the **Altyn Arashan Valley**, a bone-shaking drive to the southeast, where you can soak in a hot spring while savouring views over alpine meadows and pine forests to the peaks of the Tian Shan. Equally good for trekking is the **Karakol Valley**, just behind Karakol town.

A large pile of sun-bleached stones at San-Tash in the Karkara Valley, northeast of Karakol, gets its name from a story relating to Timur. As he crossed the pass in pursuit of the enemy, he ordered his soldiers each to place a stone there. After the battle, to see how many troops he had lost, he ordered each soldier to remove a stone from the pile. The huge mass of "counting stones" (san tash) that remains stands as a memorial to Timur's lost troops.

BELOW: ornate porch in Karakol.

Another good overnight excursion is the **Jeti-Oghuz (Seven Bulls) Valley**, southwest of town. Neither the Soviet-era sanatorium or the eroded rock formations that name the valley are really worth the fuss, but the yurt camps further upstream in the Valley of Flowers offer an opportunity for non-trekkers to get a taste of the fine alpine scenery.

The road east of Karakol winds over the mountains into the Engilchek (Inylchek) Valley, opening up trekking routes to the Engilchek Glacier and Khan Tengri base camp. This region offers some of the world's most spectacular trekking, but you need to arrange the trip well in advance with an experienced trekking company.

The southern shore

The southern shore of Issyk-Kul remains wilder, rockier and less visited than the northern route, but it offers a useful loop route back to the eastern shore, and local travel companies offer some intriguing activities here, from local food festivals to displays of eagle hunting and multi-day horse treks.

The Kyrgyz village of **Barskoon** is perhaps the most interesting stop along the southern route. Here you can shop for a yurt at the Ak Orgo Yurt Workshop on Lenina, track down ancient Tibetan rock inscriptions at nearby Tamga Tash or, best of all, arrange a multi-day horse trek through the company Shepherds Way (www.kyrgyztrek.com), which is based in the village. It's also possible to be put up at one of several local yurt-stays, if arranged in advance. The company Ecotour (www.ecotour.kg) has several eco-friendly yurt camps in the region, and the CBT can arrange accommodation. Silk Road fanatics can follow the paved road that leads south of town up the Barskoon River to a local waterfall. The road follows an ancient Silk Road branch that led over the Yshtyk Pass into the Ak-Shyrak region and then over the **Bedel Pass** (4,284 metres/14,136ft) into China. Xuanzang crossed this pass from Chinese Turkestan during his epic 7th-century voyage. Centuries later, thousands of Kyrgyz died along the route fleeing Russian troops in July 1916. Today the

BELOW: an eagle hunter in action.

Eagle Hunting

For millennia the Kyrgyz and Kazakhs of the Tian Shan, Altai and Western Mongolia have used trained eagles to hunt for prey. Eagle hunting (*berkutchi*) as a way of life largely died out during the Soviet era, but a few hunters still keep the ancient skills alive. Training the eagle is an extremely labour-intensive exercise, and the resulting relationship between master and bird often lasts for 20 or 30 years. A trained golden eagle once cost as much as five camels.

Hunters hood the young eagles and use a *shyrga* (the skin of a hare or fox filled with straw) to train the bird slowly to hunt anything from marmots to foxes and hares. The other main tool of the trade is the *bardak*, a special wooden prop designed for a saddle and used to help support the weight of the huge birds.

road leads to **Kumtor**, the gold mine that provides 20 percent of Kyrgyzstan's total exports and a remarkable 55 percent of its industrial output. The pass to China is not open to foreigners.

IRKESHTAM ROUTE

The latest international crossing to open between China and Central Asia is at Irkeshtam (Erkech-Tam), one of two routes that now cross into Kyrgyzstan from Kashgar, the other being the Torugart Pass (see page 213). Irkeshtam has quickly become the most popular mountain crossing into Central Asia, largely because it doesn't require the finicky transport arrangements that plague the Torugart crossing. It's a scenically spectacular Silk Road route that offers the most direct way into the Fergana Valley.

The road from the border descends into the Alay Valley, opening up superlative views of 7,134-metre (23,542-ft) Peak Lenin (also known as Koh-i-Garmo, "the Warm Peak"), one of the largest peaks in the Pamir range. At the crossroads village of Sary Tash, travellers have the choice of following

roads south into Tajikistan along the Pamir Highway, west into the Alay Valley or north over the 3,615-metre (11,930-ft) Taldyk Pass to Osh and the Fergana Valley. Homestays are available in Sary Tash, a small town in a beautiful setting well over 3,000metres (10,000ft) above sea level.

The Alay Valley

The incredibly scenic **Alay (Alai) Valley** is located in one of the remotest corners of Central Asia and has more in common with the Pamir region of Tajikistan than with the rest of Kyrgyzstan. For climbers the valley offers easy access to Peak Lenin. The CBT branch at nearby Sary-Moghul can arrange trips to the mountain's base camp at Achik Tash. Extensive mountaineering experience is required to make the climb to the top, as are ice axes and crampons.

Further down the valley is the former fort of Doroot Korgan (Daraut Korgon), from where caravan routes once branched over the Pamir Alai range into the Fergana Valley. The main river through the valley is

At 7,439 metres (24,510ft), Mount Pobedy (Tomur Feng) is the highest peak in Kyrgyzstan. It is located in the Tian Shan range in the far northeast of the country and marks the border with China.

BELOW: Pik Lenin, viewed from Base Camp.

TIP

Authentic eagle hunts only take place in winter, but you can catch summertime hunting displays. The Tourist Information centre in Kadji-Sai and the CBT offices in Karakol and Bokonbaev can arrange hunting displays at Tuura-Suu, Bokonbaev and Kadji-Sai on the southern shores of Lake Issyk-Kul. The August Bird of Prey Festival at Manzhuly-Ata, near Bokonbaev, features demonstration hunts and displays of falconry.

the Kyzyl-Su, which continues into Tajikistan to become the Surkhob. Both names (in Kyrgyz and Tajik) mean "Red River".

KYRGYZ FERGANA VALLEY

In many ways, the settled villages and towns of southern Kyrgyzstan have more in common with the oasis culture of Uzbekistan's Fergana Valley than with the rest of freewheeling northern Kyrgyzstan. With a significant Uzbek population, an Uzbek-style *chaikhana* and bazaar culture and a stronger Islamic identity, it's not surprising that there are occasional clan-based tensions with the more Russian-influenced north of the country. Ethnic tensions simmer close to the surface here; in 1990 violence between local Uzbeks and Kyrgyz left over 300 dead and it spiralled out of control once again in summer 2010.

Osh

With a population of 220,000, **Osh** is Kyrgyzstan's second city and the administrative centre for the entire southern half of the country. The modern city has ancient roots as an early Silk Road city, and in 2000 celebrated its 3,000th anniversary. With the peaks of the Pamir Alai hanging tantalisingly in the distant haze to the south, the city is a starting point for trekkers and mountaineers headed into the high Pamirs.

Osh's main thoroughfare and central statue commemorates Kurmanjan Datka (1811–1907) – the "Empress of the Alay" – who became a rare female governor of the Alay district and oversaw the tricky transition from Kokandi to Russian overlordship. Look for her on the 50-som note.

Osh nestles at the base of the **Takht-i-Suleiman** (Throne of Suleiman), a huge slice of rock that ranks amongst Central Asians as Islam's third-holiest shrine, after Mecca and Medina, thanks to an early appearance by the prophet Suleiman (Solomon). Babur built a personal *chillakhana* (chamber for 40-day retreat) here in 1496, and the small shrine is still known as the Dom Babura (House of Babur). The shrine, which is sadly now no more than a metal hut dating from the mid-1990s, is a favourite among women hoping to conceive. The view across Osh makes the climb worthwhile, particularly at sunrise or dusk.

At the base of the hill is the **Historical Museum** (open 9am–6pm), next to what might well be the world's only three-storey yurt. Exhibits touch on the region's Silk Road history and offer glimpses of the petroglyphs at Saimaluu Tash and other local archaeological sites. Trails lead up from here to the Dom Babura and around the back of the hill, past an Islamic cemetery to the **Historical-Cultural Museum** (open 9am–6pm; admission fee), blasted into the side of the sacred hillside. This is not to be confused with the **Silk Road Museum** (open 9am-6pm; admission fee) at the bottom of the hill, whose range of archaeological and ethnographic displays contain pottery, handicrafts, weaponry and petroglyphs.

BELOW: passing the time of day in Osh.

The other main sight is the huge central **Jayma (Friday) Bazaar**, which lines the churning Ak-Bura (White Camel) River. The lively bazaar, significantly damaged in 2010 but now on the road to recovery, is the one place in Osh that captures the spirit of the city's Silk Road past. It's also one of the best places in the country to buy the white felt Kyrgyz hat known as an *ak-kalpak*. It's the country's quintessential souvenir.

Other sights include the huge new central mosque and the **Lenin statue**, in the south of town by government offices, just one of several examples of Lenin memorabilia that still litter the town.

Around Osh

The best half-day detour from Osh is the 55km (33-mile) trip to **Ozgon** (Uzgen), a largely Uzbek town that is home to a heavily rebuilt 11th century minaret and a trio of ornate Karakhanid (11th–13th-century) mausoleums. The stunningly decorated tombs are noted for their fine incised terracotta decoration and probably provided inspiration for Samarkand's Shah-i-Zindah complex.

The local Ozgon branch of the CBT arranges homestays and horse treks into the **Kara-Shoro National Park** in the mountains above Ozgon. The nearby Kok-Art Pass is a more historically authentic Silk Road pass than either the Torugart or Irkeshtam crossings, but it's not open to international traffic these days.

Another excellent excursion is to **Arslanbap**, where another CBT branch office arranges horse treks through some of the world's largest walnut forests to a series of lovely mountain lakes.

The Uzbekistan border at Dostlyk is only 5km (3 miles) northwest of Osh. Much of the region is a victim of crazy jigsaw borders, delimited by Stalin, that have only gained an international solidity in the last decade. Kyrgyzstan's southern arm hosts several isolated enclaves, pockets of Uzbekistani and Tajikistani territory that are totally surrounded by Kyrgyzstan. The hardening of Uzbekistan's borders in the wake of terrorist activity here in the late 1990s has left much of the region out on a limb.

BELOW: the Ozgon Mausoleum.

YURTS

The nomadic lifestyle requires you to carry your home with you, and the yurt provides the perfect solution.

Along the length of the Silk Road, from the Kazakh steppe to the high Pamir and on into Xinjiang and Mongolia, wherever you find herders you'll see their curious felt houses known as yurts.

Described by travel writer Colin Thubron as resembling "badly done up parcels", yurts are in fact the ideal accommodation solution for any nomad on the move. Relatively portable, warm and spacious and made from raw materials supplied by the herders' own livestock, yurts can be constructed or taken down easily and quickly and carried away on the back of three camels (or more commonly these days, a truck).

It's no surprise then that yurts have been around for over a millennium. Genghis Khan reputedly had a yurt set on wheels and Tamerlane favoured the cosiness of his garden yurts to the cold grandeur of his stone palaces. The khans of Khiva built brick platforms for their winter yurts.

Travellers have the chance to stay in tourist yurts in Uzbekistan, Kazakhstan, Mongolia and parts of Xinjiang, though the most authentic are the yurt-stay programmes of Kyrgyzstan and Tajikistan, and a night in one of these yurts may just be a highlight of your Silk Road travels.

TOP: a yurt, looking like a brown-paper parcel.

ABOVE: the wheel-shaped circular skylight, called a *tunduk*, is depicted on the national flag of Kyrgyzstan.

FUNDAMENTALS OF A YURT

All yurts have inherited a shared structure, though Mongolian yurts are generally bigger than their Central Asian counterparts. The main wooden skeleton of roof poles supports a collapsible concertina-like wooden lattice (*kerege* in Turkic) that forms the inner wall of the yurt. Reed mats form a middle wall, and thick grey or white felt is placed on top. The heaviest sections are the door frame and the circular skylight. The frame is tightened with woven strips and the floor is decorated with appliqué-felt carpets. The key to a yurt's success is felt – warm in winter, cool in summer and surprisingly waterproof.

The interior is divided into sections for the men and women of the yurt. As you walk in the front door, the kitchen is on the left, while hunting gear, horse tack and tools hang from the lattice walls of the men's section to the right. Guests are directed to the place of honour at the back of the yurt, in front of a large pile of bedclothes atop a wooden chest. The hearth and stove form the centre of the yurt, directly below an open skylight, which can be closed in bad weather by sliding a square of felt across the hole. Accessories generally include a shrine and a battery-powered radio.

OVE: a yurt can be assembled in a couple of hours. First comes the rth, then the floor, then the frame, the poles and finally the felt.

T: time spent in a yurt gives you a ringside view of nomad res – churning yoghurt, rolling out noodles, brewing up tea and n nursing sick or very young livestock.

LOW: yurts are known by a variety of local names – *buzoi* in gyz, *kiyizoi* in Kazakh and *ger* in Mongolian – though we actually the English term via the Russian word *yurta*.

TAJIKISTAN

Follow in the footsteps of famous explorers along the Pamir Highway, visit ancient forts and cities that stood astride the old Silk Road, trek in the Fan Mountains, and enjoy the relative comforts of Dushanbe, Tajikistan's attractive capital.

Squeezed between the upper reaches of the Oxus and Jaxartes rivers and bordering the most remote regions of Afghanistan and China, Tajikistan embraces the widest range of scenery of all the Central Asian republics. Most of it is defined by mountains, from the high rolling plateau of the eastern Pamirs to the remote, almost vertical gorges of the western Pamirs and the scenic central ranges of the Fan and Turkestan mountains.

The south is a sun-baked plain of small *kishlaks* (villages) and thirsty cotton fields that has more in common with the plains of northern Afghanistan and southern Uzbekistan than the rest of Tajikistan. The far northern finger of the country reaches into the Fergana Valley, where the bazaars and teahouses resemble those in the great trading centres of Uzbekistan.

History and people

With so many disparate parts, tied together by Soviet nation-building, it was unsurprising that the country imploded during the 1990s civil war. Over 70,000 Tajiks were killed, 500,000 were made homeless and 250,000 fled the country during the first decade of independence. After 10 years of relative peace the contrasts remain, and despite attempts to rebuild a shattered economy, a certain amount of instability persists. Tajikistan is still the poorest of Central Asia's republics.

The Tajiks trace their roots back to the Sogdians and Bactrians, and define themselves as much by their Persian language and heritage than any shared ethnic traits. Ethnic Tajiks make up around 80 percent of the republic's population and consider as kin the Tajik-speaking peoples of northern Afghanistan and the Sarikol region of Tashkurgan in China's Xinjiang province. Many Tajiks live in neighbouring

Main attractions
HIGH PAMIRS
SHOKH-DARA VALLEY
WAKHAN VALLEY
VISHIM QALA
DUSHANBE:
  MUSEUM OF NATIONAL ANTIQUITIES
  BEKHZOD NATIONAL MUSEUM
  BAGH-I-MARKAZI
ISKANDER-KUL
PENJIKENT
FAN MOUNTAINS
KHOJAND:
  QALA
PANCHSHANBE BAZAAR
ISTARAVSHAN

LEFT: Wakhan Valley, near Ishkashim.
RIGHT: modern mural depicting the rites of hospitality, Penjikent.

ENTERING AND LEAVING TAJIKISTAN

Terrible roads, mountainous terrain and a sometimes awkward visa regime make Tajikistan a challenging country to travel in. The Pamir region of the southeast requires a special GBAO permit. (See Travel Tips, page 405, for more information on transport in Tajikistan.)

The border between Daroot-Korgon and Garm is currently closed to travellers, but the Pamir Highway south of Sary-Tash connects **Kyrgyzstan** with Tajikistan's Gorno-Badakhshan province. A special permit and private transport is necessary. A shared taxi service links Batken in southwest Kyrgyzstan with Isfara in northern Tajikistan. Crossing into Tajikistan is normally relaxed and trouble-free, providing your paperwork is already in order.

Tajikistan has a border crossing west of Penjikent that leads to Samarkand in **Uzbekistan** and another further south, just west of Dushanbe. In northern Tajikistan there are crossings at Oybek, west of Khojand, and at Kanimabad to the Fergana Valley. Dushanbe is connected to Termez by a regular rail link, and the circuitous route that links Dushanbe with Khojand also passes through Termez and Samarkand.

Two border crossings exist for **Afghanistan**, both little-used by Western travellers: between Panj-e-Payon and Kunduz, and between Ishkashim and Faizabad. Coming from Afghanistan, to cross at Ishkashim requires a GBAO permit in addition to a Tajik visa.

The Qolma Pass crossing that links Tajikistan's Pamir Highway with **China's** Karakoram Highway is not presently open for use by foreigners.

Uzbekistan, and in fact the towns of Bukhara and Samarkand are largely Tajik cities. Tajikistan's Persian heritage also gives it close ties to Iran.

The region has been at the fringes of empires (the Achaemenid, Kushan, Sogdian, Graeco-Bactrian and Samanid, and the Bukharan Emirate), but at the centre of none. Major branches of the Silk Road have long traversed the region, and the valleys of the Pamirs formed funnels as well as challenges for long-distance caravans. The popular caravan route across the Pamirs from Badakhshan to Tashkurgan was followed by, amongst others, Marco Polo, who described it as the highest place in the world.

Most travellers are drawn to Tajikistan by its spectacular mountain scenery. The tenuous infrastructure is luckily boosted by several excellent community tourism projects, whose homestays, guides and jeeps allow you to travel in basic comfort. Tourism is still very much in its initial stages here, but many people vote Tajikistan the most scenic, hospitable and exciting republic in Central Asia.

The Best-Travelled Man in Asia

The political agent Ney Elias may just be the greatest British explorer of Central Asia that you have never heard of. Dubbed "the best-travelled man in Asia" after a series of epic journeys across Mongolia and the Karakoram, his most impressive achievement was his epic 1885 voyage across the Pamirs, from Kashgar to Badakhshan. His mission was to survey en route the Rang-Kul area and the Shughnan and Bartang valleys in an attempt to define the practical boundaries of China, Russia and Afghanistan. The solo traveller covered 5,000km (3,000 miles) and crossed over 40 passes in his 17-month trip, returning over the Hindu Kush to Chitral and Gilgit. Elias also held political posts in Mandalay, Sikkim, Ladakh and Yarkand, and was consul-general in Mashhad for a time. Francis Younghusband called him "the best traveller there has ever been in Central Asia".

While subsequent travellers to the region, such as Younghusband and George Curzon, shot to fame as imperial heavyweights, the self-effacing and hypochondriac Elias slowly sank into obscurity, and his political reports gathered dust in the locked vaults of the British Indian government, marked "Secret". As his nephew and biographer noted, "Few explorers have done so much and talked so little of what they have done."

THE PAMIRS

Known locally as the Bam-i-Dunya, or Roof of the World, the Pamir region occupies one of Asia's remotest corners. Perched at the high crossroads of China's Xinjiang province, Afghanistan's Wakhan Corridor and Pakistan's Chitral region, the high plateau once marked the furthest reaches of the Russian and British empires.

Chinese travellers such as Sung Yun, Fa Xian and Xuanzang referred to the region as "Pomilo", describing it as the "midpoint between heaven and earth". The Chinese attributed altitude sickness to the wild onions that grew here, going as far as calling the Pamirs "the Congling Shan", or Onion Mountains!

The word Pamir means "high rolling valley", and much of the region is indeed a high-elevation, treeless plateau, almost lunar-like in places, dotted with yurts, livestock and the occasional *tersken* bush. Marco Polo sheep, ibex and yak dominate the eastern half at altitudes of between 3,500 and 4,500 metres (11,500–15,000ft), while the deep, arid valleys, churning rivers and fragile alluvial settlements of the eastern ranges are strongly reminiscent of northern Pakistan.

Little-visited by travellers since the formation of the Soviet Union, the region was ironically one of the most travelled corners of Central Asia in the late 19th century, when the blanks in the map sparked a flurry of expeditions. British explorers like Francis Younghusband and George Curzon concentrated on the upper Oxus and the high passes into British India, while Russian explorers such as Kostenko, Svertsov and Fedchenko explored the Alai ranges and the great peaks of the northern Pamirs. Quintessential Silk Road explorers such as Sven Hedin (in 1894–5) and Aurel Stein (1915) explored the region's historical sites.

Access for today's travellers is via the Pamir Highway, a predominantly tarmac-surfaced version of the Silk Road built by the Soviets between 1934 and 1940 on top of ancient caravan tracks. The region is still widely known by its Soviet name, the Gorno-Badakhshan Autonomous Oblast, or GBAO, and remains a prickly border zone, crossed by Afghan drug-smugglers. For travellers it is simply one of the most scenic and adventurous corners of High Asia.

The High Pamirs

From the remote crossroads of Sary Tash in the Alay (Alai) Valley of Kyrgyzstan, the Pamir Highway swings past close-up views of Pik Lenin (Koh-i-Istiqlal, or Independence Peak), before entering Tajikistan, crossing the Kyzyl-Art Pass and finally descending to the spectacular blue inland sea of Lake Karakul (**Qarokul**). In good weather the lake reflects a radiant turquoise; but it is the overcast waters that give the lake its name "Black Lake" and moved Curzon to describe it as "a splendid spectacle, for its waters toss and boil like a seething cauldron". Formed 10 million years ago by a meteor, the lake is called *chong* (big) Karakul to differentiate from the *kichi* (small) Karakul across the border in China.

TIP

META (Murgab Eco Tourism Association) can organise the logistics of a trip around the Pamirs, from jeep hire and English-speaking guides to both home- and yurt-stay, and they help you obtain the relevant permissions and registration with the touchy local KGB. The associated Yak House organisation supports Kyrgyz craft production by selling felt products to tourists and is well worth a visit.

BELOW LEFT: Ney Elias, explorer extraordinaire.
BELOW: mosque in the village of Karakul.

Behind the lake the high Pamirs rise majestically, concealing the 77-km (46-mile) -long Fedchenko glacier that tumbles off massive Ismoili Somoni (7,495 metres/24,700ft; formerly Pik Kommunizm). East of the lake the highway parallels the Soviet-era double-wire fences that mark the border zone with China. Marco Polo (1274) and the Chinese pilgrim Xuanzang (642) both passed by the lake, the latter believing it to be populated by dragons.

From the southeastern shores the main M41 continues south to Murgab, past a former Russian fort at Muzkol and over the Akbaytal (White Mare) Pass, the highest point on the highway at 4,655 metres (15,361ft).

Murgab

Murgab (**Murghob**) is a scrappy town of around 4,000 people, founded in 1891 by Russian Tsarist officers as a supply post at the furthest reaches of the Russian Empire. The town has a patchy bazaar and even patchier electricity, but it is a good base from which to make excursions to the surrounding high valleys. Most of the region's population is Kyrgyz, who pass the summers in remote herding camps, before moving their yurts down into the warmer valleys during the harsh winter. On a clear day you can see the giant Pamiri peak of Muztagh Ata (7,546 metres/24,901ft) to the northeast across the border in China.

The most exciting excursion from Murgab follows the Aksu River (once considered the source of both the water and name of the River Oxus) into the remotest corner of Central Asia at Shaymak. Less than 84km (50 miles) from the border of China, Afghanistan and Pakistan, and with views over the Mintaka range, this is truly the meeting point of empires. The nearby Nazatash Pass (now closed) was a favourite with Silk Road travellers heading to the Stone Fort at Tashkurgan (Taxorgan), just over the pass to the east. To the south is the Little Pamir and the important Silk Road passes of the Wakhjir (east into China) and the Kilik, Mintaka and Boroghil (south to Pakistan).

It was just southwest of here in August 1891, at Bozai Gumbaz in

BELOW: entrance to the transcaspian bridge on the Oxus.

The Source of the Oxus

By 1872 a border agreement between the Russians and British had settled the Amu Darya, or Oxus, as the demarcation line. The snag was that no one was quite sure where exactly the Oxus was, at least in its upper reaches. As the rival empires inched ever closer, the problem became increasingly acute. A British public that had lapped up the drama surrounding the discovery of the source of the Nile suddenly turned its attention to the Oxus.

John Wood (a Navy officer, of all things!) had made a famous trip in winter 1838 from Ishkashim and Langar up the Pyanj River to Zor-Kul lake, proclaiming it the source of the Oxus and renaming it Lake Victoria after the recently crowned youngqueen. Yet suspicions were soon voiced that the real source lay perhaps in the glaciers dividing Zor-Kul from the Little Pamir to the southeast. The trick was how to define the source of a river – the longest tributary, the highest source or the largest flow?

It was only when George Curzon discovered an ice cave in the Wakhjir region near the border with China in 1894 that the cave and the upper Wakhan River it flows into were agreed on as the true (highest) source of the Oxus. The border was finally demarcated in 1895, fittingly on the shores of Zor-Kul, relegating the debate to an obscure geographical conundrum.

modern-day Afghanistan, that Francis Younghusband was thrown out of the Pamirs by his Russian counterpart Colonel Yanov in one of the remotest flashpoints of the Great Game. The two officers dined on such mountain luxuries as fresh vegetables and Kashgari brandy until the Cossack unit ordered the 28-year-old Younghusband to leave the region, claiming it as Russian territory.

The Chinese trucks you see parked on the outskirts of Murgab are heading to or from the **Qolma Pass** (4,362 metres/14,394ft), now once again an international Silk Road crossing. The pass is currently open to local traffic only, but may conceivably open before long to provide yet another remote border crossing into Central Asia. For the time being the pass is the preserve of Chinese truck drivers and Kashgari entrepreneurs driving Chinese-made minivans across the Pamirs for resale in Dushanbe.

Other excursions lead northeast to the glittering twin lakes of **Rang-Kul** and Shor-Kul, where META offers overnight Bactrian camel trips, or south to see the impressively fresh Neolithic paintings of **Shakhty**. It's possible to continue south by jeep from Shahkty to Jarty-Gumbaz (where you stand an excellent chance of spotting ibex and Marco Polo sheep, particularly during winter and the autumn rut), before continuing southwest to a string of spectacular Pamiri lakes, ending in Zor-Kul (Lake Victoria) at 4,126 metres (13,616ft).

Murgab to Alichur

Back in Murgab, the main Pamir Highway climbs south past a checkpoint to the low Naziatash Pass, to descend into the rich **Alichur Plain**, home to some of the best pasture in the Pamirs. Just past the huge tent-like rock of Chatyr Tash, a side road branches south for 6km (3.5 miles) to the enigmatic mud-brick **Bash Gumbaz tomb**. The main valley west of here is dotted with summertime yurts and the

archaeological remains of past invaders and migrants, including the 11th-century silver mines and 2,000-year-old petroglyphs of Bazar-Dara, a tough day excursion from the main road.

Beyond the uninspiring modern settlement of Alichur, the river meanders through the lush Sumantash Plain while the road detours around a series of high-altitude salt lakes, among them Sassyk-Kul, Tuz-Kul and Yashilkul. You get a great overview of the first two of these lakes as the road climbs to a vantage point.

Just before the viewpoint, a side road branches left to the Wakhan Valley via the Khargush Pass. The main Pamir Highway continues west past a turn-off to the settlement of Bulun-Kul, which offers simple accommodation and a base from which to explore archaeological sites on the northeastern shore of Yashilkul lake. The nearby Mausoleum of Bekbulat marks the furthest extent of Chinese influence in the Pamirs.

Western Pamirs

The main road continues to climb slowly up to the 4,272-metre (14,097-ft)

"The plain is called Pamier and you ride across it for twelve days altogether, finding nothing but a desert without habitation or any green thing, so that travellers are obliged to carry with them whatever they have need of. The region is so lofty and cold that you do not even see any birds flying. And because of this great cold, fire does not burn so brightly, nor give out so much heat as usual, nor does it cook food so effectually."

Marco Polo

BELOW: the Bash Gumbez tomb sits on grazing land off the Pamir Highway.

Koitezek Pass, the watershed that divides the eastern and western Pamirs. On the west side of the pass the mountains of the western Pamirs quickly become dryer and more jagged as the valleys deepen. Settled Pamiri culture replaces the semi-nomadic Kyrgyz lifestyle, and irrigated villages replace seasonal yurt camps. The intense flashes of greenery and the orchards of apricots, mulberries and apples could have been lifted directly from Pakistan's beautiful Northern Areas.

The highway descends past thermal hot springs near Jelondi and then the Gunt Valley enters from the right, draining the waters of Yashilkul lake into the historical district of Shughnan. A cliff above the village of Bogev, further down the valley, hides the ruins of the fire-worshipping centre of Kafir-Qala. Just before Khorog, the road passes a monument to the Pamir Highway in the shape of the first car ever to drive the route.

Khorog

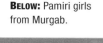

BELOW: Pamiri girls from Murgab.

The straggling administrative centre of **Khorog** (**Khorugh**) is the only town in the Pamirs. It is home to 30,000 locals, as well as government offices, several foreign NGOs and the ambitious new University of Central Asia, a multi-campus project financed by the Aga Khan Foundation. The region's former capital lies across the Pyanj River at Qala-i-Bar Pyanj.

The town is a good place to resupply, relax in one of the many Pamiri-style homestays and arrange your onward transport. The nearby Botanical Gardens are said to be the world's highest. The Regional Museum is worth a visit to see the first piano to arrive in the Pamirs, carried over the mountains from Osh over two months in 1914 for the pampered daughter of a Russian army officer. Also of interest are the recently restored **Central Park** and the actual first car to cross the Pamir Highway, which is kept on a plinth on the outskirts of the town.

Around Khorog

The valleys around Khorog conceal some stunning scenery and interesting archaeological sites, though the

The Mountain Tajiks

Sometimes called "Mountain Tajiks", Pamiris are quite distinct from Tajiks in both language and religion. Speaking a handful of languages that are often incomprehensible even in the next valley, most Pamiris are Ismaili Muslims, followers of the Aga Khan. Local *khalifas* (village headmen) and *rais* (community leaders) take the role of imam, and there are no formal mosques, but rather shared meeting and prayer halls called *jamaat khana*.

If you are lucky you'll get to stay in a traditional Pamiri home. These unique houses have five pillars (representing the five prophets) arranged around a central recessed area, with a skylight (known as a *tsorkhona*) made from four concentric squares, representing the elements of earth, water, fire and air.

roads are bad and transport thin. Sporadically governed in name only by both Afghanistan and the Bukharan emirate, these remote valleys have long preserved their own cultures and languages. Western Pamiri valleys such as Yazgulum and Vanch remain unexplored by all but the hardiest trekkers.

The **Shokh-Dara Valley** to the east has several crumbling forts, at Roshtqala and more impressively further east at Shashbuvad and Deruj, which also has Saka tombs. The views of Engels Peak (6,507 metres/21,473ft) from Javshanguz are unparalleled. In a strong four-wheel-drive vehicle it's possible to continue up the Shokh-Dara Valley onto the plateau of the eastern Pamirs to remote Lake Turuntai-Kul, before joining the main Pamir Highway near the Koitezek Pass.

Equally stunning is the remote and elemental **Bartang Valley**, whose perilous road squeezes between the rocky valley walls and the churning leaden waters. The valley is famed for its music and dance, and you may be lucky enough to hear the strains of a locally made five-stringed *rabob*, accompanied by tambourine and Russian-influenced accordion. The Bartangis are some of the most hospitable people in the Pamirs, and will need persistent persuading not to kill an animal in a visitor's honour.

The best excursion in this valley is to the lovely village of Bardara, 7km (4 miles) off the main road. Beyond here, the main road branches east to the village of Barchadev, where you'll need a special permit to continue the hike up to views of Lake Sarez, the spectacular body of water formed by a huge landslide on the Murgab River in 1911. There are fears that an earthquake could dislodge the plug, causing potentially the largest flood of modern times. An early-warning system was installed a few years ago by Swiss scientists.

The main valley branches northeast to Savnob, a lovely settlement that boasts a ruined *qala* (fortress) and cliffside caves, both built to protect against slave raids by Krygyz, Afghan or neighbouring Yazgulumi

BELOW: the Gunt River flowing through Khorog.

raiders. There's another fort at nearby Roshorv. The main reason to continue further up the Ghudara Valley is for trekking access to the Tanymas Valley and Grum glacier. The upper valleys remain the wild habitat of ibex and snow leopards.

The road south of Khorog passes the **Kuh-i-Lal ruby mine**. Badakhshan has long been famed for both its lapis and rubies, a reputation that even Marco Polo noticed, noting that in "Syghinan" (Shughnan) "the stones are dug on the king's account, and no one else dares dig in that mountain on pain of forfeiture of life". Shortly before the mine is a turn-off marked to the **Garam Chasm** (hot springs), which makes a pleasant diversion en route.

The Tajik Wakhan

The spectacular **Wakhan Valley**, a major branch of the Silk Road, is shared between Tajikistan and Afghanistan, and offers fleeting views up southern side valleys to the snow-capped peaks of the Hindu Kush that form the border with Pakistan. Coming from the east, the poplar trees, well-tended fields and warmer temperatures come as a relief after the rigours of the high plateau.

The valley's main village is **Ishkashim**, which has the only border crossing with Afghanistan open to foreigners. The trade routes from China continued west from here to Faizabad, Kunduz and Mazar-i-Sharif. Marco Polo passed through Ishkashim in 1271 en route to the upper Wakhan, travelling via either Zor-Kul or the upper Sarhad region. A series of new bridges financed by the Aga Khan Foundation have retied many of the Silk Road connections that were severed by the formation of the USSR.

The strategic valley has long been contested by the Afghans, Pamiris, Kyrgyz and even Chinese, and it is dotted with *qalas*, which served to protect, supply and tax the trade caravans headed for Tashkurgan and Badakhshan.

The 2,000-year-old Kaakha Qala is one of the oldest of these forts, dating from the Kushan era and occupied these days by the Tajik army. Nearby is the Ismaili shrine of Shah-i-Mardan Khazrati Ali. East of here, above Darshai village, are some remote rock inscriptions in the 2,300-year-old Kharoshthi script, similar to ones found by Aurel Stein along China's Southern Silk Road.

The most spectacular of the Wakhan's forts is **Yamchun** (Zulkhomor), perched high above the valley floor, a 7-km (4-mile) winding drive off the main road. The massive 3rd-century curved buttresses lead from a narrow and easily defendable entrance into a large castle. The thick, powerful walls, rounded towers and loopholes perfectly fit every child's image of a medieval castle. Aurel Stein visited the fort in 1906 en route to China. The nearby natural hot springs of Bibi Fatima (named after the Prophet Muhammad's daughter) are well worth a visit.

Nearby **Vishim** (**Abrashim**) **Qala**, the "Silk Fort" of Zong, is also

well worth visiting, just 4km (2.5 miles) before Langar, for its stunning views over the confluence of the Wakhan and Pyanj valleys. Paths on the Afghan side continue on to the Sarhad region of the upper Wakhan Corridor. One Silk Road reminder is the 7th–8th-century complex of Buddhist platforms and caves at **Vrang**, which may also have been a Zoroastrian site.

Further up the valley, near the junction of the Pamir and Wakhan rivers, the lovely village of **Langar** is a convenient place to overnight. The local *jamaat khana* acts as a House Museum, opposite the ageless shrine of Shoh Oftabi. Like most Pamiri *oston*, or shrines, it is adorned with ibex horns and holy stones, which the locals kiss while asking for good fortune. Thousands of petroglyphs are said to litter the pastures above town. Across the river on the Afghan side you can still see the hill of the Qala-i-Panj fort, which once controlled entry to the entire lower Wakhan.

Past Langar the road swings north, past the ruins of Ratm Qala and into the deep and dramatic Pyanj River Gorge. The border and customs post at Khargush marks the restricted turn-off east to Zor-Kul. The main road continues north over the Khargush Pass and past the salt lake of Chokur-Kul to the main Pamir Highway.

Khorog to Dushanbe

The 556-km (333-mile) M41 from Khorog to Dushanbe is another dramatic stretch of road that offers a two-day overland alternative to the scenic (but rather scary) hour-long flight back to Dushanbe.

From Khorog the road hugs the Afghan border for hours, following the twists and turns of the Pyanj River past the turn-offs to the **Bartang** and **Vanch** valleys, to arrive in **Kalaikhum** (**Qal'aikhum**), headquarters of the Darvaz district. The valleys of the western Pamir have long been fought over, notably when the Afghan Murad

Beg of Kunduz subjugated the valleys around Shughnan in 1820. The need for protection led to the construction of a string of forts, like those at Kalaikhum, Qala-i-Pyanj and Qala-i-Vomar. Most of the forts were later destroyed by the Russians.

From Kalaikhum there are two routes back to Dushanbe. The more scenic but poorly maintained route winds up to the Sagirdasht Pass before descending into the **Tavildara** and **Karategin** regions. The road is closed in winter as it goes over a high pass and snowfall blocks the way. Some of the worst fighting of the civil war took place in this remote clan-based area, and you can still see gutted tanks and troop transporters abandoned by the side of the road. The **Gharm Valley** joins the main road from the north as the mountains slowly peter out.

The other route choice, and the only wintertime option, is to follow the course of the **Pyanj River** as it makes a huge arc around the border with Afghan Badakhshan. The highway offers excellent views of amazingly remote villages across the river,

BELOW: a veteran of the road.

which are only connected to the rest of Afghanistan by some incredibly stomach-tightening footpaths that sometimes consist of little more than a few planks jammed with stones and suspended above sheer cliffs. The Turkish-built highway passes the lovely villages of Yogd and Zigar, at one stage on a surreal three-lane superhighway, before leaving the Pyanj Valley and climbing over the Shurabad Pass to the uninspiring southern Tajik city of Kulyab. From here it's an easy drive on to Dushanbe.

DUSHANBE

Tajikistan's capital, a city of around 640,000, is an attractive, leafy city, built on a much more manageable scale than either Tashkent or Almaty. The town was known from 1929 to 1961 as Stalinabad, the capital of the Tajikistan SSR. After 1961 the name reverted to the traditional Dushanbe (Monday), named after the ancient weekly market. The emir of Bukhara stopped here briefly in 1920 en route to exile in Afghanistan, and the Turk Enver Pasha captured the town in 1922 as part of his attempts to raise a rebellion against Soviet rule.

There's an air of quiet prosperity in Dushanbe these days, and the streets are full of handsome Mediterranean-looking Tajiks, well dressed in traditional embroidered skullcaps and colourful psychedelic dresses. Most travellers stay only for a day or two, enough to finalise registration formalities and permits for the Gorno-Badakhshan region. Between leisurely lunches and people-watching in the many open-air cafés, there's more than enough to occupy your time.

The city's major points of interest line the main drag, **Rudaki**, named after the Persian poet that Tajikistan (along with Iran) claims as its favourite son. A stroll from north to south passes a statue of Rudaki, a few theatres and embassies and several neoclassical government buildings of salmon pink and canary yellow that remind one more of St Petersburg than inner Asia.

Buildings of note include the Majilsi Oli (Parliament), the Writers' Union Building (decorated with

BELOW: statue of Ismail Samani in Dushanbe.

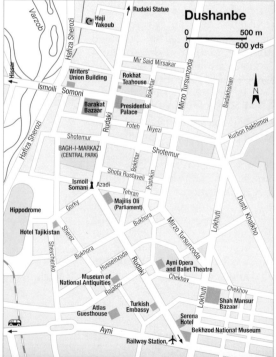

Dushanbe

0 _____ 500 m
0 _____ 500 yds

N

Varzob · Hisser · Hafiza Sherozi · Hafiza Sherozi · Ismoili Somoni · Rudaki · Haji Yakoub · Rudaki Statue · Mir Said Mirsakar · Writers' Union Building · Rokhat Teahouse · Bokhtar · Mirzo Tursunzoda · Badakhshan · Barakat Bazaar · Presidential Palace · Foteh · Niyezi · Kurbon Rakhimov · Shotemur · BAGH-I-MARKAZI (CENTRAL PARK) · Shotemur · Bokhtar · Ismoil Somani · Azadi · Shota Rustaveli · Pushkin · Tehran · Majilis Oli (Parliament) · Hippodrome · Gorky · Bukhora · Mirzo Tursunzoda · Lokhuti · Dusti Khakho · Hotel Tajikistan · Sheroz · Shevchenko · Bukhora · Husseinzoda · Rudaki · Ayni Opera and Ballet Theatre · Chekhov · Rajabov · Museum of National Antiquities · Atlas Guesthouse · Turkish Embassy · Serena Hotel · Lokhuti · Chekhov · Shah Mansur Bazaar · Bekhzod National Museum · Ayni · Railway Station

busts of famous Persian and Tajik writers), the attractive Turkish Embassy and the Ayni Opera and Ballet Theatre. The Oriental-Socialist architecture of the **Rokhat Teahouse** is the perfect place to linger over a pot of green tea.

Dushanbe's main sights are its museums. The star of the **Museum of National Antiquities** (open Tue–Fri 9am–5pm, Sat until 4pm, Sun 10am–2pm, closed Mon) is the 12-metre (40-ft) -long Buddha excavated in 1966 from Adjina Tepe in southern Tajikistan. The 1,600-year-old statue is now considered the largest intact Buddha in Central Asia. Also of note is the ivory carving of Alexander the Great, from Takht-i-Sangin in southern Tajikistan (see below).

Also worth a visit is the **Bekhzod National Museum** (open Tue–Sat 9am–4pm, Sun 9am–3pm, closed Mon), at the southern end of tree-lined Rudaki, home to some wonderful examples of carved wood and Soviet art, alongside the overblown Soviet obsession with mechanised agricultural achievements. The statue

across the road is of Sadriddin Ayni (1878–1954), the famous Soviet Tajik writer.

Lunchtimes at the central **Haji Yakoub Mosque** offer one of city's few visible traces of Islam, as crowds of cloaked and bearded Tajiks stream in for daily prayers. The **Bagh-i-Markazi (Central Park)** is worth a visit at weekends and holidays for its funfair, pilau sellers and a statue of Lenin. The fallen leader's former plinth, a couple of hundred metres south, now houses a **statue of Ismail Samani (pronounced Ismoil Somoni)**, the 10th-century Persian-speaking leader of the cultured Samanid dynasty, who also lends his name to the Tajik currency.

If Dushanbe appears at times disarmingly European, then its two main markets, the Shah Mansur and Barakat bazaars, are 100 percent Central Asian colour and bustle.

Around Dushanbe

The easiest excursion from Dushanbe is to **Hissar (Hisor)**, 31km (18 miles) east, once an important *beglik* and

"Har ki namukht az guzashti ruzgar,Niz namuzad zi hich amuzgar."
"No ordinary teacher will ever reach, Those whom Time has failed to teach."
Rudaki

BELOW: the Haji Yakoub Mosque in Dushanbe.

Intriguingly, the people of the remote Yagnob Valley allegedly still speak a language akin to ancient Sogdian. Colin Thubron describes a visit to the valley in his book The Lost Heart of Asia. Travel agents can arrange treks to the valley via the dramatic kilometre-high cliffs of Margib.

outpost of the Bukharan Emirate. The eroded walls and giant mound of the fort remain, accessed through a restored gate. The fort was occupied by the Basmachi leader Ibrahim Beg until the Red Army destroyed it in 1921. Opposite are two madrassas and the renovated foundations of an early 19th-century caravanserai. Buzkashi tournaments are often held here during Nauroz, the Persian spring equinox festival on 12 March.

Tursanzade to the west is the gateway to Uzbekistan and notable for its huge Soviet-era aluminium factory and for the 11th-century mausoleums of Khoja Durbod and Khoja Nakhshron, outside of town.

SOUTHERN TAJIKISTAN

Amateur archaeologists keen to track down the faintest traces of the Silk Road may want to hire a car and invest a day or two exploring the hot and dusty cotton fields of **Southern Tajikistan**. Once known as Bactria or Tokharia, the scattering of archaeological sites here have revealed traces of a Graeco-Bactrian

culture that incorporated both Greek and Iranian elements in quintessential Silk Road fashion. Unfortunately most finds of importance are housed in St Petersburg's Hermitage Museum.

A short 12-km (7-mile) drive southeast of Kurgonteppa (Qurghonteppa) (about 100km/60 miles south of Dushanbe) is the 7th–8th-century site of **Adjina Tepe** (Witches' Hill), where in 1966 archaeologists unearthed Central Asia's largest surviving Buddha statue. The "Sleeping Buddha" has stylistic elements that have much in common with the Gandharan art of Afghanistan and Pakistan. Wall paintings and sculptures housed in niches once surrounded the central monastic courtyard. The site is currently being restored by UNESCO, though there's not a great deal to see.

The ancient site of Kobadiyan (7th to 2nd centuries BC), further south, is famed as the location for the discovery in 1877 of the **Oxus Treasure**, a stunning 2,500-year-old Achaemenid treasure-trove of 180 gold statues and over 500 coins that now resides in the British Museum, after it was bought piecemeal from Bukharan traders in Rawalpindi. In 2007 President Rakhmonov demanded the return of the treasure, but to no avail. Nearby is the ruined Graeco-Bactrian temple of **Takht-i-Sangin**, where archaeologists unearthed a famous ivory portrait of Alexander the Great, along with sculptures of the Greek god Apollo and an inscription in Greek to the local god of the Oxus.

It was close to here that Alexander crossed the Oxus on inflated hides over five days in 329 BC. These days modern travellers cross the Amu Darya at Panj-i-Payon, from where Afghan roads continue to Kunduz. The crossing was used to supply the Northern Alliance, headed by Tajik commander Ahmed Shah Masoud, during operations in 2001 against the Taliban.

Other sites include the 9th–11th-century baked brick cupolas of the

BELOW: the ruins of Sogdian Penjikent.

Khodja Mashad Sayid Mausoleum and Madrassa in Sayot village, Shahrtuz district. Around 15km (9 miles) outside Shahrtuz are the 44 springs of Jilichor Chashma, a popular pilgrimage and picnic site.

Further east, near Vose, are the excavations of the 9th–11th-century Kulbek (Qulbuk) palace at Kurbanshahid (the ancient region of Kuttal). Inside Kulyab town is the 15th-century mazar of Sufi preacher Mir Sayid Hamadoni (1314–86).

NORTHERN TAJIKISTAN

The north of Tajikistan, cut off from Dushanbe by the towering Hissar, Zarafshan and Turkestan ranges, is in many ways a different country, more Uzbek in its culture and physically closer to Tashkent than to Dushanbe. The scenic drive between Dushanbe and Penjikent or Khojand takes you through some of the region's best mountain scenery.

The main M34 climbs north from Dushanbe past roadside *chaikhanas* and the gleaming villas of Dushanbe's dubiously rich, into the **Varzob Gorge**. As the canyon narrows, side valleys open to offer grand hiking, waterfalls, hot springs and even a ski resort at Takob. Traffic used to have to make the winding ascent to the 3,372-metre (11,128-ft) Anzob Pass, but a new 6-km (3.5-mile) -long Iranian-financed tunnel offers a shortcut through the Zerafshan range in what is viewed as a major attempt to tie the two halves of the country together. The tunnel is not, however, for the faint-hearted as despite being in use it is still incomplete: there are no lights, no proper road surface, and the tunnel regularly floods.

Somewhere in the remote mountains north of here, by the Polytimetus River (which is probably the Zarafshan), is the famed **Sogdian Rock**, where Alexander stormed the Sogdian forces under Spitamenes, his troops using rock-climbing techniques

to capture both the Sogdians and his new wife, Roxanna.

Iskander-Kul

The best detour along this route is to scenic **Iskander-Kul**, a milky-blue mountain lake backed by a sleepy *turbaza* (Soviet holiday camp) and a dacha belonging to the president. Some great treks lead from here into the surrounding Fan Mountains, but it is highly advisable to have a four-wheel-drive vehicle if you plan to drive to the lake itself. Alexander (Iskander) the Great enjoys a cult in Tajikistan, and many lakes, mountains and stories are named after him. The main road follows the rushing river to **Ayni**, home to the heavily eroded 10th-century **Varz-i-Minor Minaret**. From here roads lead west to Penjikent or north over the Shakhristan Pass to Khojand (Khujand, Khojent).

Between Ayni and Penjikent is **Mount Mug**, the site of the Sogdians' last stand against the Arabs in 721 (they lost and their leader Devastich was beheaded). Soviet archaeologists discovered a large cash of Sogdian documents here in 1932.

TIP

Local hiking clubs and travel agencies can arrange hiking trips into the Hissar Mountains around Dushanbe, either to the Payon and Timur Dara lakes in the Karatag Valley or into the side valleys of the Varzob Gorge north of the city.

BELOW: Tajik farmer from Penjikent.

Penjikent

Northern Tajikistan's main archaeological site is the ancient Sogdian city of **Penjikent**, one of the great lost Silk Road cities of Central Asia. This rich, cosmopolitan place thrived on the banks of the Zarafshan River until destroyed by Arab invaders in 722. Silk cocoons were unearthed at the site during excavations.

Like most Central Asian cities, Penjikent consisted of a citadel, or ark, to the northwest, and an inner walled city, or *shakhristan*, which included a palace, temple platforms and streets of shops and workshops. To the south lies a necropolis. Copies of the fabulous Greek- and Iranian-influenced wall friezes, depicting scenes from the *Shahnameh* and local epics, are on display at the site and in the museum in the nearby town, as well as in Dushanbe and St Petersburg. The sensual pillars depicting swaying dancing girls and the Tantric images of the Indian gods Shiva and Parvati riding a buffalo highlight the cosmopolitan range of artistic influences that are so typical of Silk Road art.

The museum displays several *ossuaries*, pots used to store the bones of the deceased after their corpses were eaten by birds, in accordance with Zoroastrian tradition (and similar to Tibetan sky burial).

Just 20km (12 miles) west of Penjikent is **Sarawzm**, one of the oldest settlements in Central Asia, where archaeologists have unearthed a Bronze Age temple complex and the 2,500-year-old grave of a wealthy woman. From here roads continue west along the Zarafshan across the Uzbekistan border to Samarkand.

Fan Mountains

The main launching point for fantastic treks up into the craggy peaks and turquoise lakes of the **Fan Mountains** is the village of Artush, around 60km (36 miles) southeast of Penjikent. Popular trekking routes include to the Alauddin Lakes (four or five days), continuing over the 4,404-metre (14,500ft) Kaznok Pass to Iskander-Kul (total six days); or from the Marguzor Lakes to Iskander-Kul via the Tavasang, Munora and Dukdon passes (six days). Travel

BELOW: the covered bazaar in Penjikent. **BELOW RIGHT:** high up in the Fan Mountains.

agencies in Dushanbe, Penjikent and Tashkent can arrange treks, as can international trekking companies.

Khojand

Khojand (Khujand, Khojent) is one of the oldest cities in Central Asia, though you'd be forgiven for not realising it these days. Alexander the Great founded his ninth city, Alexandria-Eskhate (Alexandria the Furthest), here on the banks of the Syr Darya (Jaxartes), marking the furthest extent of his exploits in Central Asia. The town developed as an important Silk Road depot, guarding and taxing the mouth of the Fergana Valley. The Mongols destroyed it in 1220 after a long siege made difficult by the local resistance leader Timur Malik.

The modern city is the second-largest in Tajikistan, and has more in common with the Uzbek cities of the Fergana Valley than with the Tajik towns of the south. The city (then known as Leninabad) was ceded to Tajikistan from the Uzbek SSR in 1929 solely to help Tajikistan reach the threshold 1 million population it required to become a full republic. The city briefly threatened to secede from Tajikistan during the civil war.

The original 10-km (6-mile) -long city walls are long gone and the military now occupies the old *qala*, whose eastern walls house a small **Museum of Archaeology and Fortifications** (open daily 8am–5pm). The impressive-looking new provincial **Historical Museum of Sughd Province** in the southeast corner of the *qala* has displays on Sogdian history and culture and local hero Timur Malik.

South of the *qala* is the huge **Panchshanbe Bazaar** (Friday Market), built in the 1950s as one of the largest in Central Asia. Across the plaza is the understated tomb-and-mosque complex of Sheikh Muslihiddin, dating from 1394 and a subsequent 16th-century renovation.

Khojand still has several Soviet-era monuments, including one of the largest Lenin statues left in the former USSR, on the north side of the Syr Darya. Look out also for the huge red hammer and sickle beside the bus stop in the centre of town and the bust of Lenin and Marx on nearby Komil Khojandy Street.

From Khojand roads lead northwest to Tashkent and east to Kokand, both in Uzbekistan. If you are heading to Kokand, consider a detour to the 12th-century **Hazrati Bobo Mausoleum** in Chorukh village, near Isfara, a rare wooden mausoleum carved with pre-Islamic symbols.

A worthy excursion from Khojand is to the town of **Istaravshan**, ancient Cyropolis, where you can still visit the citadel stormed by Alexander's forces in 328 BC. The old town conceals some beautiful Islamic tombs, including the Kok Gumbaz Madrassa, whose turquoise dome could have been lifted straight from Samarkand, and the Chor Gumbaz (Four Domes) Mazar, which boasts some lovely interior paintwork. The excellent Istaravshan bazaar is also well worth a visit. The town, known in Soviet days as Ura-Tyube, is 70km (42 miles) south of Khojand.

Khojand is home to one of the largest statues of Lenin still standing in the former USSR.

BELOW: the entrance to the Museum of Archaeology and Fortifications.

UZBEKISTAN

Beyond the fertile Fergana Valley lie the great
cities of Samarkand and Bukhara with their
magnificent Timurid architecture; further west,
near the Oxus River, ancient sites emerge from
desert sands to confront the Silk Road traveller.

For many travellers, Uzbekistan holds the very heart of the Central Asian Silk Road. Its three main historical centres – Samarkand, Bukhara and Khiva – all resonate deeply with the weight of history, and its bazaars and teahouses still carry echoes, albeit faint at times, of its fabulous past.

Uzbekistan – the "Land of the Uzbeks" – is just the latest name used to describe the ancient lands between the Amu Darya (Oxus) and Syr Darya (Jaxartes) rivers. The Greeks called the region Transoxiana; the Arabs knew it as Mawarannahr, the "Land across the River". It is here that the last mountain spurs of the Tian Shan and Pamirs yield to the desolate plains and forbidding desert sands of the Karakum and Kyzylkum deserts.

Cultural legacy

It is also in essence a cultural meeting point: of Turkic and Persian, nomad and settler, Uzbek and Tajik. This desert land, studded with caravan oases and made rich with plunder and trade, is above all the homeland of Timur (Tamerlane), who has bequeathed modern Uzbekistan with some of the Islamic world's most fantastic architecture. The Uzbeks themselves are relatively late arrivals, establishing

themselves in the 16th century. Most of the madrassas and mosques you see in Uzbekistan date from this era.

The teahouses of Uzbekistan are perhaps the best places in the region to soak up Central Asian culture. Factor some time to stroll the bustling modern bazaars, sip green tea on a *tapchan* (tea bed) under the shade of a mulberry tree and dine on *shashlyk* (mutton kebabs) and freshly baked *naan* bread. Uzbeks everywhere wear the *doppi* skullcap with pride, and the fabulously photogenic elders, known

Main attractions

MARGILAN:
  YODGORLIK SILK FACTORY
  KUNTEPA BAZAAR
TASHKENT:
  INDEPENDENCE SQUARE
  MUSEUM OF THE HISTORY OF
  UZBEKISTAN
SAMARKAND: REGISTAN, BIBI
  KHANUM MOSQUE, SIAB BAZAAR,
  SHAH-I-ZINDAH, GUR-I-MIR
SHAKHRISABZ: AK SERAI
BUKHARA:
  THE ARK
  ISMAIL SAMANI MAUSOLEUM
  POI KALON ENSEMBLE
  COVERED BAZAARS
KHIVA: ICHAN KALA
KHWAREZM: TOPRAK QALA

LEFT: view from the Kalon minaret in Bukhara. **RIGHT:** a man and his wares in Samarkand.

ENTERING AND LEAVING UZBEKISTAN

Many visitors arrive first in Tashkent and then fly to Urgench or Nukus before backtracking through the Silk Road cities. (See Travel Tips, page 405, for more information on transport in Uzbekistan.)

The only places to cross to **Kazakhstan** are between Tashkent and Shymkent by road (a main crossing and a smaller crossing primarily for lorries) or between Tashkent and Arys or Nukus and Beyneu by rail. The Nukus crossing involves a long and unpredictable rail journey.

There are several road crossings to **Kyrgyzstan** in the Fergana Valley, although it is necessary to change transport at the frontier. Formalities tend to be more rigorous on the Uzbek side. Daily buses run between Bishkek and Tashkent but require a Kazakhstan transit visa.

A border crossing east of Samarkand leads to Penjikent in **Tajikistan**, and there is another further south that connects with Dushanbe. A further crossing point at Oybek, just south of Tashkent, leads to Khojand in northern Tajikistan, as does a crossing further east in the Fergana Valley just west of Kokand. A regular rail link connects Termiz with Dushanbe.

There are several crossings to **Turkmenistan**: from Bukhara to Turkmenabat, from Urgench to Dashoguz and from Nukus to Konye-Urgench, all of which involve the use of shared taxis to and from each border. Customs formalities at the Turkmen border can be rigorous.

A border crossing into **Afghanistan** exists at Termiz in southern Uzbekistan, although this is not always open to travellers. A tentative bus service is in operation between Termiz and Mazar-e-Sharif.

respectfully as *aksakal* or "white beards", still wear the striped cloaks known as a *khalat* or *chapan*. The women of the region are a riot of colour, dressed in shimmering *ikat* cloth and sporting mouthfuls of gold teeth.

Landscapes are not Uzbekistan's strong point – for those go to Tajikistan or Kyrgyzstan. In fact it has been said that Uzbekistan is two-thirds desert and one-third cotton. Certainly wherever you go in the country you'll pass the endless fields of "white gold" that make Uzbekistan the world's second-largest exporter of cotton. Yet in these fluffy white plants lie the roots of an environmental disaster. Decades of Soviet irrigation schemes has lead to chronic water pollution, soil degradation and the almost complete collapse of the Aral Sea Basin (see page 117). The damaged environment is just one hangover from the 70 years of Soviet rule, whose legacy is apparent everywhere, from Tashkent's Socialist architecture to the mindset of the current authoritarian regime. Defining a new path for independent Uzbekistan remains a huge challenge.

For Silk Road travellers, Uzbekistan is easily the most exciting of the Central Asian republics. It has the region's most fabulous historical sites, its most outrageous architecture and its most stylish accommodations. Don't miss it.

FERGANA VALLEY

After the rigours of the Tian Shan and Pamir mountains, the Fergana Valley must have appeared a paradise to weary travellers and traders. Hemmed in on three sides by the spurs of the Tian Shan, Pamir Alai and Turkestan ranges, the huge and hazy 330-km (200-mile) -long valley is warm, flat and fertile, and its bazaars overflow with fruit and produce.

The valley (known to the Chinese as Dayuan) played a key role in the opening of the Silk Road. Its famed "blood-sweating" horses (believed by the Chinese to be descended from dragons) were in such demand that China forced open the first transcontinental trade routes specifically to gain a supply of the steeds and thus a technical advantage over its marauding nomadic neighbours. The horse trade remained central to the Silk Road long after the secret of silk production had spread to the west.

The valley funnelled Silk Road traffic for centuries, though there's little evidence of this today. Little remains of the Buddhist temple of Kuva, the 7th- to 11th-century ruins of Kasan and Aksiketh outside Namangan and the Zoroastrian tombs of Pap except some neglected and dusty archaeological remnants.

The echoes of the Silk Road ring loudest in the valley's vibrant bazaars and in its crafts – the paper factories of Kokand, the knives from Chust and the blue-and-green ceramics of Rishtan. The valley is one of the world's oldest cultivated areas, and alongside the cotton fields there are orchards, vineyards, walnut groves and, of course, extensive mulberry tree plantations, which supply the valley's

silk factories with their raw material. Cotton and silk milling and the manufacture of chemicals and cement are among the valley's most important industries; along the fringes are deposits of oil, natural gas and iron ore. The region's natural resources contributed to the industrialisation of all Soviet Central Asia.

Home to one-third of Uzbekistan's population, the modern Fergana Valley is the most densely populated part of Central Asia and its most religiously active centre. In recent years the valley has gained infamy as the centre of conservative Islam and of the government's increasingly brutal attempts to stamp its control on the country. Further pressure has been imposed on the valley with the influx of as many as 300,000 refugees from Kyrgyzstan following violence there in 2010.

Andijan

For travellers **Andijan** (Andijon in Uzbek transliteration) is the eastern gateway to the valley, a short hop and a skip from the Kyrgyz border near Osh.

Watermelons from the fertile Fergana Valley.

BELOW: cycling around Fergana.

The city's huge Thursday and Sunday bazaars have been attracting traders for millennia, but these days Andijan is most famous (rather, infamous) for the events of May 2005, when government troops massacred up to 1,000 unarmed demonstrators in the town's central square.

There are several historical sites in town, such as the Babur Literary Museum, a former royal residence, but get advice on the current political climate before exploring too deeply. The Juma Mosque and Madrassa has long been a barometer of the shifting political tides, switching from Soviet-era museum to active madrassa and now back to secular museum.

Fergana Town

In the south of the valley, also within striking distance of the Kyrgyz border, is the city of **Fergana** (Farg'ona in Uzbek). Founded as a Russian garrison town in 1876, it was initially named Skobelov after the Russian commander who subdued Khiva and Kokand and conquered the Turkmen tribes at the battle of Gök-Tepe. The

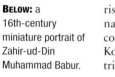

BELOW: a 16th-century miniature portrait of Zahir-ud-Din Muhammad Babur.

blue-hued Tsarist buildings and colonial Russian layout of the town initially seem at odds with the traditional rural architecture of the valley, but the pleasant leafy boulevards, local museum and café-restaurants of the provincial capital make it a good base from which to explore the valley, and there are some good accommodation options, too.

Margilan

Located just 5km (3 miles) to the north of Fergana, **Margilan** (Marg'ilon) was an important stop on the Silk Road. The local mulberry trees have fed silk production for centuries – even during Soviet times – and the economic life of the town is still dominated by the enormous Margilan Silk Factory, which churns out 2.5km (1.5 miles) of silk every day and employs some 15,000 workers. For a fascinating glimpse of traditional production methods, head to the **Yodgorlik Silk Factory** (open daily 8am–5pm). Individual families raise the fussy silkworms on home-grown mulberry leaves,

Babur

A descendant of Timur and grandfather of the Mughal Emperor Akbar, Zahir-ud-Din Muhammad Babur (1483–1530) is an intriguing figure. Born in Andijan in 1483, he was forced out of his beloved Fergana Valley by the rising might of the Uzbek Sheybanids and fled to Afghanistan, conquering Kabul, Kandahar and finally India, where he founded the Mughal Dynasty. Despite his great conquests, he was never able to return to Central Asia, and his major literary work, the *Baburnama*, is infused with wistful longing for his beloved Fergana Valley. Though little-known today, without Babur the Central Asian-inspired architectural genius of the Taj Mahal and numerous other Mughal splendours in Delhi and Lahore might never have come to pass.

before the cocoons are taken to the factory to be steamed and unravelled and the silk woven into thread and then dyed. The result is the *khanatlas* (king of satin) or *ikat*, the brightly coloured blur that clads almost all Uzbek women. Also worth catching is the bustling Thursday and Sunday **Kuntepa Bazaar**, 5km (3 miles) west of the centre. Margilan's atmospheric bazaar was replaced by a giant covered market in 2007. The few architectural remnants in town include the Khonakah Mosque, the Turon Mosque and the Sayid Akhmad Khodja Madrassa.

Namangan

Namangan, in the north of the valley, is the third-largest city in Uzbekistan. It is also known as its most religiously conservative, and its streets contain the highest concentration of veiled women in the country. The many closed madrassas and strong police presence highlight the government's unease with the growth of Islam. If you are passing through the town, the terracotta facade of the Hadja Amin Kabri complex is particularly fine, as are the nearby ruins of Akhsykent, a 1st century AD settlement 25km west of the town.

Kokand

In the west, the Khanate of **Kokand** (Qo'qon in Uzbek) was long Central Asia's third regional centre of power, for centuries jostling for regional dominance with Bukhara and Khiva, until the arrival of the Russians forced them all into irrelevance. At its peak the crossroads city boasted 600 mosques and 15 madrassas, and ruled territory from the Kazakh Steppe to the Pamirs.

Only 19 opulent rooms survive from the original 113-roomed **Palace of Khudayar Khan** (built 1862–72), but it's still worth a look (open daily 9am–5pm). The impressive 100-metre (330-ft) -long *aiwan* of the Juma (Friday) Mosque was built to house

the city's male population during weekly Friday prayers. Nearby is the Amin Beg Madrassa. Fifteen minutes' walk east is the working Narbutabey Madrassa, behind which the royal cemetery houses the Modari Khan and Dakhma-i-Shakhon mausoleums – the tombs of Kokandi Khan Omar, his mother and his wife.

Routes west out of the valley lead naturally from Kokand to Samarkand via Khojand (in Tajikistan; see page 243); but today's convoluted jigsaw borders mean that travellers generally head first to Tashkent, a three-hour drive away over the 2,268-metre (7,484-ft) Kamchik Pass. The newly strategic highway passes endless hairpin turns and snaking lines of crawling truck caravans to cross the Chatkal range, a faint final echo of the mighty Tian Shan.

TASHKENT

Uzbekistan's capital is a huge sprawling city of over 2 million people; the largest in Central Asia and the fourth-largest in the former USSR. As a Soviet-era showcase of orderly

The colourful ikat fabrics worn by Uzbek women are woven from yarns dyed using a resist-dyeing process similar to tie-dye.

BELOW: cloth-seller in Kuntepa Bazaar.

boulevards, museums and monuments it's not a particularly inspiring place but it's worth a day or two's exploration.

The city's roots, at the foot of the Tian Shan, lie in the ancient caravan town that grew up at the border of the settled and nomadic worlds. Known initially as Chach, its name was changed by the Turkic-speaking Karakhanids to Tashkent, or Stone Village, in the 10th century. The Khanate of Kokand absorbed Tashkent in 1809, and in 1864 the Russian Tsarist general Chernaiev took the town with only 1,900 men, disobeying direct orders from his superiors in distant St Petersburg. The Russian military cantonment grew quickly under the first governor of Russian Turkestan, Konstantin Kaufmann.

The city became the capital of the Uzbek SSR in 1930, replacing Samarkand. World War II spurred rapid growth as evacuees and entire communities of deported Koreans and Germans were forcibly relocated here, along with much of western Russia's heavy industry. The modern face of Tashkent (Toshkent in Uzbek) was transformed by the Soviet reconstruction that followed a powerful earthquake in 1966.

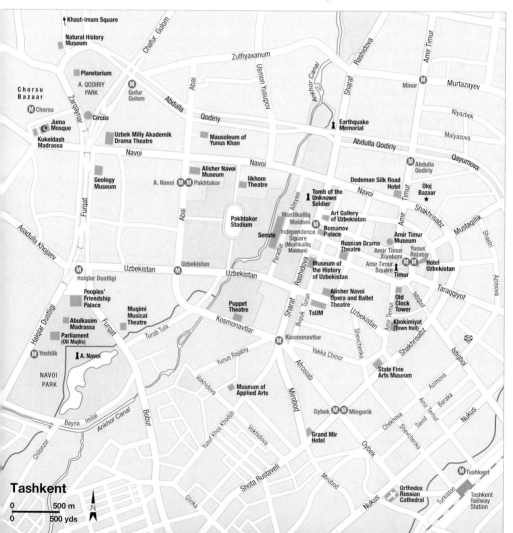

Tashkent

0 — 500 m
0 — 500 yds
N

Central Tashkent

Icons of independence litter the centre of the city. The prime real estate outside the Hotel Uzbekistan, currently known as Amir Timur Square, is occupied by a park with a **statue of Timur** in the centre – the latest in a long line of iconic statues that have included Konstantin Kaufmann, Joseph Stalin and Karl Marx. The pleasant, leafy park is an ideal place to kick off a stroll of the city, dotted with shady glades where locals gather to play chess.

The iconic theme continues in the **Amir Timur Museum**, on the north side of the square. The modern turquoise-domed building, opened on the 660th anniversary of Timur's birthday, is largely an exercise in propaganda, pairing the exploits of Timur with the cult of current president Karimov. The museum collection mainly consists of ancient manuscripts, paintings and engravings, but there are some fine wooden models of Timurid architecture from across Uzbekistan.

Further west, the huge Soviet-era parade ground of **Independence Square** (Mustikalliq Maidoni) was home to the Union's largest Lenin statue until 1992, when it was replaced by a large globe whose only country is an oversized Uzbekistan. The square is the focus of colourful Independence Day celebrations that take place here each 1 September. Surrounding the square is the new senate building, the president's office and various government ministries.

North from here is the **Tomb of the Unknown Soldier**, which commemorates the 400,000 citizens of Uzbekistan who died in World War II. Nearby is the **Earthquake Memorial**, a poignant spot that marks the exact time and date in 1966 that a major earthquake levelled the town and left 300,000 homeless.

Tashkent has the best museums in Uzbekistan, including the Museum of Applied Arts (open daily 9am–6pm) and State Fine Arts Museum (open Wed–Mon 10am–5pm, closed Mon pm), which is based on the private collection of Prince Nikolai Romanov. Most worthy of your time is the **Museum of the History of**

TIP

The best way to get around Tashkent is on the metro, which is worth riding for its stylish stations, dripping in decoration (in particular Kosmonavtlar with its floating cosmonauts). The system opened in 1977. Don't take photos in the metro and watch out for policemen on the make.

BELOW: on the road to Tashkent.

BELOW: Tashkent's ornate Amir Timur Museum.

Uzbekistan (open Tue–Sun 10am–5pm), which houses some 250,000 exhibits including a Kushan-era Buddha statue from Fayaz Tepe, a decorated bronze cauldron from the 4th century BC and an impressive collection of ancient coins and manuscripts. Further west, the **Alisher Navoi Museum** (open Mon–Fri 10am–5pm, Sat until 1pm) celebrates the poet whose major work (*Khamsa*) put Chaghatai Turkic on the literary map in an age when poets generally wrote only in Persian.

Old Town

Tashkent's Old Town (*eski shakhar*) doesn't compare to Samarkand or Bukhara in either scope or style, but it's worth a visit all the same. Start by taking the metro to the **Chorsu** (Four Roads) District and browsing the thunderous local bazaar, easily the city's best, offering the souvenir black-and-white Uzbek skullcaps, colourful mounds of spices, famously sweet melons and huge naan breads served hot out of the *tandur* oven. A short walk to the east

is the traditional-style **Kukeldash Madrassa** and Juma Mosque.

Outside the bazaar is a curious spiral building that houses temporary art exhibitions and is an attractive addition to the Tashkent skyline. Climbing the stairs to the roof (admission fee) gives a perfect panorama of the city.

North from Chorsu, the Soviet boulevards quickly whither to winding alleys of mud-walled houses, and traditional Central Asian culture reasserts itself. Hidden here in the Old Town is the religious heart of the city, the **Khast-Imam Square**, home to the Imam Ismail al-Bukhari Islamic Institute, the highest seminary in the USSR and one of only two that operated in Uzbekistan during the Soviet era. The Mufti of Tashkent (the country's top Islamic cleric) is based in the 16th-century Barak Khan Madrassa to the west.

Next to the nearby Tillya Sheikh Mosque, the affiliated Muyie Mubarek Library Museum (open 9am–4pm) holds an unexpected treasure, the **world's oldest Koran**. The Osman Koran dates from 655, and the blood

of the Caliph Osman still stains several of its deerskin pages. The caliph was murdered while reading from the Koran, an assassination that fuelled the enduring split between the Sunni and Shia branches of Islam.

Back on Navoi Street, and opposite the Literary Museum, is the 15th-century **Mausoleum of Yunus Khan**, grandfather of the Mughal emperor Babur, in the grounds of the Tashkent Islamic University.

Other sights

If you are in Tashkent outside the summer months, try to attend a performance at the lavish **Alisher Navoi Opera and Ballet Theatre**, designed by the same architect who built Lenin's tomb in Moscow. Performances range from Puccini to Uzbek folklore. Check also to see what is playing at the **Ilkhom Theatre**, the most progressive arts venue in the country.

The lonely onion-domed **Orthodox Russian Cathedral** is worth a visit on Sundays for its fine icons. Since independence, large numbers of Tashkent's Russian community have left Uzbekistan for a new life in Mother Russia.

SAMARKAND

More so than any other city in Central Asia, Samarkand's name drips with an exotic romanticism, whose resonance can be largely attributed to the immortal lines of James Flecker's 1913 poem, *Hassan*:

We travel not for trafficking alone:
By hotter winds our fiery hearts are fanned:
For lust of knowing what should not be known
We make the Golden Journey to Samarkand.

Set at a trade crossroads and fed by the Zerafshan River, Samarkand (Samarqand in Uzbek) has been a Silk Road town for around 2,500 years now. Alexander the Great visited in 329 BC, when it was the Sogdian city of Marakanda, part of the Achaemenid Empire. "Everything I have heard about Samarkand is true," he said, "except it is even more beautiful than I had imagined."

The chaos of the Bolshevik Revolution in Tashkent is described by F.M. Bailey in his book Mission to Tashkent. Bailey was in disguise when he passed through the city in 1918, and it must have been a pretty convincing one. At one stage the undercover British spy was given orders by the Russian secret police to hunt himself down!

BELOW: restored tilework in the Khast-Imam complex.

The World's Oldest Koran

You won't be the only one surprised to hear that the world's oldest Koran resides in Uzbekistan, and its journey here was a convoluted one indeed. It is known as the Osman Koran, after the caliph who compiled it in Medina in the 7th century.

In the 14th century Timur brought the Koran to Central Asia, from Basra, to display it on the central marble lectern of Samarkand's Bibi Khanum Mosque. After the Tsarists took the city in 1868, the treasure was carted off to St Petersburg, until Lenin moved it on again, first to Ufa in Bashkaria and then to Tashkent's State Historical Museum. Finally, in 1989, at the height of *perestroika*, the Koran was handed over to Islamic clerics at the Sheikh Tillya Mosque, where it remains to this day.

Deliciously fresh Uzbek bread.

Sogdian wall murals recovered from Afrosiab in the northeast of the city depict the Silk Road heyday, when Tang China craved such exotica as Samarkand's golden peaches. Xuanzang described Samarkand (So-mo-kien) in the 7th century: "The precious merchandise of many foreign countries is stored up here... The inhabitants are skilful in the arts and trades beyond those of other countries."

The cosmopolitan city embraced Zoroastrian fire-worship and even became a Nestorian Christian bishopric until the arrival of the Arab armies changed everything in AD 712. The later invasions of the Khorezmshah and Mongol armies severely diminished the city. Marco Polo reported "a large and splendid city" at the end of the 13th century – but then he never actually saw the city.

Samarkand is, above all, the city of Timur, and it is his turquoise domes and audacious building projects that draw visitors to this day. Timur forcibly relocated artisans from across his empire to embellish his capital, and it was in Samarkand that artisans from Persia, Azerbaijan, Syria and India saw "barbarism turned to beauty". For Timur himself the city was "less a home than a marvellous trophy". Ever the nomad, he preferred

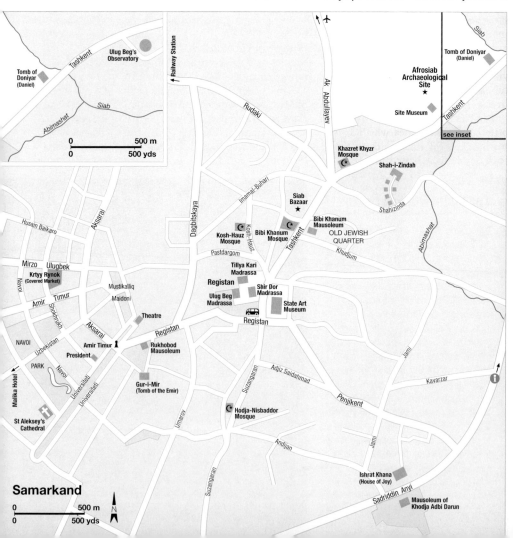

Samarkand

0   500 m
0   500 yds

the tents, camps and gardens outside the city walls to the epic bricks and mortar inside.

Silk Road traffic dried up from the 16th century, and Samarkand gradually took a back seat to Bukhara. The city was taken by the Russians in 1868 and shone briefly as the capital of the Uzbekistan SSR until sinking into obscurity as a remote corner of the Soviet Union.

The Registan

Samarkand's **Registan** (open daily 8am–7pm; admission fee) is without doubt the single most dramatic architectural ensemble in Central Asia. Three towering madrassas, saturated from head to toe in mesmerising tilework, rise around open ground to form an irresistible symmetry. The British MP (and future viceroy of India) George Curzon called it "the noblest public square in the world".

The Registan ("Sandy Place") was originally a market area, where the six roads of the city met in a trade crossroads. It was later used for military parades and public executions, while the Bolsheviks used it for political rallies, trials and veil burnings. Today it has been extensively restored and even offers an evening sound-and-light show, best watched from the neighbouring tea house.

Ulug Beg built the first madrassa here (1417–20), on the west side, flanked by 33-metre (109-ft) -high columns and richly decorated with star designs, *girikh* (geometric) patterns, and stunning mosaic and majolica tilework. If you tip the security guard downstairs, it is possible to climb the right-hand minaret and exit on to the roof, from where there is a superb view across Samarkand. It was a further two centuries before the **Shir Dor Madrassa** (1619–36) was erected to the east as a mirror piece. The madrassa gets its name from the mosaic lions (*shir*) that adorn the corners of the portal – anatomically incorrect, you'll be forgiven for thinking they're tigers. The flouting of the Islamic convention against the depiction of living beings is made doubly heretical by

BELOW LEFT: original tiles on Samarkand's Gur-i-Mir. **BELOW:** the Bibi Khanum Mosque.

Tamerlane the Great

Few individuals shaped the face of Central Asia as much as Tamerlane, a merciless leader who conquered lands from India to Baghdad.

Born into the Barlas clan of Turkicised Mongols only a century after the death of Genghis Khan, legend suggests that Tamerlane's palms were filled with blood, auguring a bloody life. He started his career as a bandit, and at the age of 27 he was shot with an arrow in his right shoulder and hip while rustling sheep. His wounds gave rise to his pejorative Persian nickname Timur-i-Leme (Timur the Lame) and the later Latinised version, Tamerlane.

Timur's ambitions were not easily contained, and by 1370 he had vanquished his former brother-in-law to be crowned ruler of Chaghatai – "Conqueror of the World". He proclaimed, "The world is not large enough for two kings", and for the next 35 years he tried to prove that claim. He defeated the Ottoman sultan Beyazid in Ankara, destroyed the Golden Horde on the Kazakh Steppe, and wrested control of trade routes from Delhi to Damascus.

It has been estimated that Timur's merciless campaigns led to the deaths of 17 million people.

Prisoners in Isfizar in Iran were cemented alive into giant towers. His troops bombarded the Christian armies at Smyrna with cannonballs made from the severed heads of their own knights. He boasted that his troops beheaded 10,000 Hindus in a single hour during the plunder of Delhi. In Baghdad in 1401 his forces killed 90,000 locals and cemented their heads into 120 towers.

Though he remains little-known in the West, his reputation alone was enough to inspire poetry by Edgar Allan Poe *(Tamerlane)*, drama by Christopher Marlow *(Tamburlaine the Great)* and operas by both Handel and Vivaldi *(Il Tamerlano)*. Like all the great nomad leaders, Timur suffered the fate of being chronicled almost exclusively through the jaundiced eyes of his victims.

The man himself is in many ways a contradiction. Islamicised and Turkicised, he was a Muslim, though he never let his religion get in the way of his conquests. He spoke both Persian and Turkic fluently and had a great respect for learned men, yet he himself was illiterate. A nomad at heart who lived on the move, he also created some of the most beautiful urban architecture the world has ever seen. A chess fanatic, he invented a new game that employed twice the number of pieces (including camels, giraffes and war engines). Historians estimate that he had at least 12 wives.

Timur died in February 1405 in Otrar while planning his biggest campaign yet, the invasion of Ming China. His body was "embalmed with musk and rose-water, wrapped in linen, laid in an ebony coffin and sent to Samarkand". His body was interred in the Gur-i-Mir and his howls were allegedly heard nightly for a year after his burial. Perhaps his most fitting epitaph is inscribed on his tomb: "If I were alive," it reads, "people would not be glad."

LEFT: Tamerlane, "Conqueror of the World".
ABOVE: statue of Tamerlane (Timur) in Tashkent.

the beaming Zoroastrian-inspired sun faces painted on the lions' backs.

The ensemble is topped off by the **Tillya Kari Madrassa** (1646–60), wider than the other two and boasting a huge turquoise dome and magnificent gilded interior. The former *hujra* (student accommodation) cells now function as gift shops and you can watch artisans at work. The nearby four-sided Chorsu was once the city's skullcap bazaar.

The **State Art Museum** (open daily 9am–6pm) on the east side of the Registan displays copies of Afrosiab's murals (see below) and the famous Kushan-era Ayrtam frieze (discovered near the Afghan border), as well as Timur's wooden coffin.

Bibi Khanum Mosque

Timur made his true bid for architectural immortality with the **Bibi Khanum Mosque** (open daily 8am–7pm), a monumental building planned on a hitherto unseen scale, along the pedestrian street northeast of the Registan. Financed from the spoils of a recent campaign to Delhi (1398) and built with the labour of 95 imported Indian elephants, the huge 35-metre (116-ft) entry arch was flanked by 50-metre (165-ft) minarets that led into a court paved with marble and flanked with mosques. The mosque was built in too much haste (Timur himself threw gold coins and scraps of barbecued meat to workers to spur them on), and the tottering walls started to crumble almost as soon as they were finished. In the last decade a similarly hasty programme of restoration has rebuilt the three main domes – "a shining blandness", in the words of Colin Thubron, "snuffing out the strange vitality of ruin".

The mosque was built in honour of Timur's chief wife, Saray Mulk Khanum, who was laid to rest in the nearby **Bibi Khanum Mausoleum**. A number of local women still come here to pray, although it is now considered a museum rather than a place of worship. Next to the mosque is the main **Siab Bazaar**, groaning with grapes, fruit and, yes, Samarkand's famed golden peaches. There is a pleasant picnic spot between the mosque and the

"Everything I have heard about Samarkand is true, except it is even more beautiful than I had imagined."

Alexander the Great

BELOW: the Registan in Samarkand.

One of Bibi Khanum Mosque's three domes.

BELOW: unrestored Ishrat Khana has its own special atmosphere.
BELOW RIGHT: column detail in the mausoleum of Khodja Abdi Darun.

market. A short walk north leads to the **Khazret Khyzr Mosque**, named after the pre-Islamic patron saint of wayfarers.

Shah-i-Zindah and around

Samarkand's other great artistic highlight is the **Shah-i-Zindah** (open daily 8am–7pm), a visually absorbing necropolis that ranks as one of the great masterpieces of Timurid art. The street of tombs, accessed from the main road or on foot via the city's modern graveyard, dates from 1372 to 1460 and houses a veritable "Who's Who" of Timurid aristocracy, including Timur's niece Shadi Mulk Aka, sisters Turkhan Aka and Shirin Bika Aka, and wives Tuman Aka and Kutlug Aka.

The tombs' real genius lies in their range of decoration, with carved terracotta and majolica tilework set into complicated floral designs framed with stylised calligraphy, everything saturated in a dozen intense shades of blue. The focus for local pilgrims is the tomb of the Arab leader

Kussam-bin-Abbas, who was beheaded after his attempts to convert locals to Islam and merged into the local pre-Islamic legend of the "Living King" (Shah-i-Zindah). Come shortly before dusk for the most atmospheric experience.

One of the few remnants of the early Silk Road are the ruins of **Afrosiab**, the Sogdian city that flourished from the 6th century BC until the arrival of Genghis Khan in 1220. It was here that the increasingly megalomaniac Alexander the Great killed his favourite general, Cleitus, in a drunken rage. Excavations of the dusty 120-hectare (300-acre) site have revealed Graeco-Bactrian and Kushan roots, Zoroastrian temples and a cult centre dedicated to the local god Anahita, though there's little to see these days except hot dusty trenches and low excavated walls. However, the **museum** (open daily 9am–6pm), housed in the modern Soviet-era building at the site, is fascinating, and guides (some of whom speak English) will provide informative talks on the different periods.

Afrosiab is most famous for its wall murals (long since removed), which feature a royal bridal procession atop a white elephant, a series of bearded ambassadors to the Sogdian court and a ruler in magnificent clothes meeting with silk-bearing Chinese, Turkic and even Korean envoys. Copies of these murals are also on display at the museum. The site is named after the legendary king depicted in Firdausi's epic poem *Shahnameh* ("Book of Kings").

Adjacent to the site is the **Tomb of Doniyar** (Daniel), where a local legend claims that the bones of the Hebrew saint were interred after Timur brought them to Samarkand. It is also worthwhile to visit the **Hazrat Hizr Mosque** next door, an elegant structure with carved wooden pillars and jewel-coloured paintwork.

The most enlightened of the Timurid rulers was without doubt Timur's grandson, the "Astronomer King" Ulug Beg. Ulug Beg's penchant for astronomy, mathematics and science didn't go down well with the conservative court of the day, and he was eventually beheaded by his own

son. In 1908 Russian archaeologists unearthed **Ulug Beg's Observatory**, commissioned in 1428 and destroyed by fanatics 21 years later. The underground chamber was excavated by the Soviets in 1938. You can still see the arc of the great sextant cut into the rock. A poignant inscription outside proclaims: "The religions disperse, kingdoms fall apart, but the work of science remains eternal."

Gur-i-Mir

Samarkand's final "must-see" is the Gur-i-Mir (Tomb of the Emir), the final resting place of Timur. The mausoleum was originally planned for Timur's favourite grandson, Muhammad Sultan (Timur had long wanted to be buried in Shakhrisabz), but Samarkand was deemed a more fitting resting place. The exterior of the building is dominated by a fine entrance portal and the hallmark ribbed turquoise dome that floats like a giant balloon above the central octagonal chamber. It's a beautiful

Ambassador to the Sogdian court depicted on the murals at Afrosiab.

BELOW: Ulug Beg dispensing justice at Khurasan (15th-century miniature).

Ulug Beg

As the ruler of Samarkand, the Timurid ruler Ulug "Mirzoi" Beg (1394–1449), grandson of Timur (see page 256), built several of the city's most beautiful madrassas. However, it is his scientific patronage, and in particular his magnificent observatory, the Gurkhani Zij, for which he is most renowned. Like the Khwarezmian scientist al-Biruni 400 years before him (see page 112), Ulug Beg was the finest astronomer of his age, correctly repositioning 1,018 stars in an astronomical catalogue that was the first of its kind since Ptolemy. Tragically, within two years of his father Shah Rukh's death he was assassinated while on his way to Mecca, a martyr to science, and was laid to rest in his grandfather's tomb, the Gur-i-Mir.

but surprisingly modest monument for the world's greatest warlord. Timur is buried at the foot of his spiritual adviser, Mir Sayid Barakah, under a tombstone that was at the time the world's largest slab of jade. The Persian invader Nadir Shah broke the slab while trying to steal it. The actual graves are in the crypt below, which can usually be visited for a small fee.

Two other tombs are located in the Gur-i-Mir complex: the 14th century **Rukhobod Mausoleum, which** is said to contain a hair of the Prophet, and the unrestored brick-built **Aksaray Mausoleum** on the street behind.

Other sights

Other architectural gems in the Samarkand suburbs include the **Mausoleum of Khodja Abdi Darun**, built by Seljuk Sultan Sanjar and renovated by Ulug Beg, and the nearby **Ishrat Khana** (House of Joy), a refreshingly unrestored pleasure dome built by Timur's wife and later converted into a mausoleum by one of Timur's descendants.

SHAKHRISABZ

South from Samarkand, modern roads follow a side branch of the Silk Road to the Oxus River. The route was popular with invaders and traders, and the latter were taxed at a defile en route known as the "Iron Gates".

The town of **Shakhrisabz**, 80km (48 miles) south of Samarkand over the Takhtakaracha Pass, is most famous as the hometown of Timur, who was born nearby in April 1336. His actual birthplace is in Khoja Ilgar Village, some 13km (8 miles) to the south, where a surprisingly unassuming cairn marks the spot.

Today Shakhrisabz is a charming, traditional Uzbek town, littered with the ruined monuments of its favourite son. The Chinese pilgrim Xuanzang visited when it was known as the Sogdian town of Kesh. Tajik-speakers later renamed it Shahr-i-sabz, the "Green City".

The White Palace

The main sight is the huge ruined complex of the Ak Serai, Timur's "White Palace". Built by slave artisans

Bukhara

0   200 m
0   200 yds

brought here from Khwarezm, the site was planned as a summer residence to complement Samarkand's Kok Serai, or Red Palace.

The restorers have again been hard at work here, trying to recreate the huge 65-metre (214-ft) entry towers that once supported Central Asia's largest portal. The incredible palace was visited in 1404 by the Spanish envoy Ruy González de Clavijo, who described the palace's blue-tiled walls, golden ceilings and the lush surrounding gardens of waterfalls and silk tents that were the site of epic Bacchanalian feasts of wine and horseflesh. By the time Clavijo arrived craftsmen had already been working on the palace for over 20 years.

Today a large statue of Timur dominates the centre of the complex. Here more than anywhere the words of Timur resonate: "Let he who doubts our power look upon our buildings."

Timurid tombs

Other buildings worth visiting as you walk south are the 14th-century Malik Azhdar Khanaga and the Amir Timur Museum, housed in a former madrassa. The impressive blue dome in the south of the town belongs to the **Kok Gumbaz Mosque** (1435–6), built by Ulug Beg as part of the Dorut Tilovat complex. Timur's father Taraghay and his spiritual adviser Shamsaddin Kulyal are both buried in the nearby Timurid mausoleum.

A couple of minutes' walk to the east is the crumbling **Tomb of Jehangir**, all that remains of the Dorus Siadat, a Timurid family memorial that ranked as one of Timur's greatest creations. Timur's eldest son Jehangir and second son Umar Sheikh are both buried here, and Timur himself also planned to be interred here. The intended **crypt of Timur** was discovered nearby in 1943, and you can still see the empty underground marble casket.

From Shakhrisabz, the main M39 road continues southeast to the border city of Termiz, from where the Friendship Bridge leads across the Oxus to the Afghan cities of Mazar-e-Sharif and Balkh, themselves both ethnically Uzbek.

BUKHARA

Known for centuries as Bukhoro-i-sharif (Bukhara the Noble), and the "Dome of Islam", the holy city of Bukhara (Buxoro in Uzbek) is one of the oldest cities in Central Asia, stretching back some 2,500 years. At its peak the city boasted 250 madrassas, 200 minarets and a mosque for every day of the year.

According to the Persian epic *Shahnameh*, the hero Siyavush founded the city after marrying the daughter of neighbouring Afrosiab. The town thrived as a transit spot and a crossroads town, with city gates pointing to Merv, Gurganj, Herat, Khiva and Samarkand.

In the early days Bukhara was eclipsed by great cities now lost in the surrounding deserts. All that

Russian-made Ladas are still a common sight in Uzbekistan.

BELOW: in the shadow of the Kok Gumbaz Mosque, Shakhrisabz.

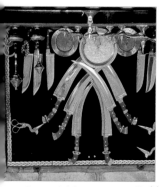

Ceremonial daggers
made by artisans in
Bukhara.

BELOW: a city within
a city: Bukhara's
ancient Ark.

remains of Varakhsha, once the richest caravan stop in the region, are the superb Sogdian murals, now preserved in local museums, of hunters battling leopards and a court scene flanked by winged griffins. The Hephthalite capital of Paikend, another of the great regional trading centres, was destroyed during the Arab invasion.

Bukhara hit its high point in the 9th and 10th centuries under the Samanid Dynasty, when the city became a great centre of Persian culture and science. Thinkers such as al-Biruni, the poet Rudaki and the medic Ibn Sina (Avicenna), Bukhara's grand vizier for a time, enjoyed access to Bukhara's "Treasury of Wisdom", a library surpassed in the Islamic world only by the House of Wisdom in Baghdad.

The city was largely destroyed by the Mongols in 1220. Genghis Khan addressed the trembling citizens of Bukhara with a perverse sense of logic: "If you had not committed great sins," he said, "God would not have sent a punishment like me." When the Moroccan traveller Ibn Battuta arrived in Bukhara a century later in 1333, the city was still in ruins.

The khanate (and later emirate) was revived in the 16th century under the extensive building programmes of Abdullah Khan, but by the Astrakhanid Dynasty the decline of the Silk Road had isolated Bukhara, and the city began a gradual slide into decay and fanaticism.

The 19th century brought intrepid travellers to the city. The great traveller William Moorcroft arrived in 1825 in search of horses but left empty-handed, only to be murdered on the return journey to Balkh. Alexander "Bokhara" Burnes, later to write his classic travelogue *Travels into Bukhara*, visited the city in 1832. The city gained true notoriety abroad when the British officers Connolly and Stoddart were executed in Bukhara in 1839 (see page 273). Bukhara's glory days were coming to an end. Even in the 19th century foreign travellers described the city as wearing "a halo of departed glory".

Today the quiet and largely Tajik town offers plenty of scope for exploration. If you have only one spare day in your itinerary, spend it here. The domes and minarets of the sun-dried city glow golden in the afternoon light, and although a little lacking in spice, exhausted by its long Soviet rule, the city's twisting backstreets still provide plenty of Silk Road atmosphere.

The Ark

The heart of ancient Bukhara is the **Ark** (open daily 9am–6pm), the original 2,000-year-old fortress around which the city formed. Fortified, destroyed and rebuilt many times over the years, the "city within a city" became home to the emirs of Bukhara, evolving into a complex warren of chambers, mosques, reception rooms, servants' quarters, mint, jail and armoury. What remains today is only about 30 percent of the original; peek

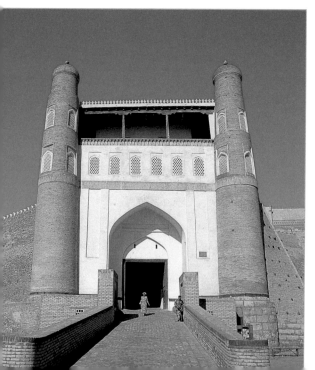

around the back to see the ruins left by the Red Army artillery of General Frunze in 1920.

The main entrance leads up a ramp into the great 18th-century gatehouse, or *darvazkhana*, above which the emir's retinue would watch executions and public events in the square below. The **Bukhara State Art and Architectural Museum** occupies the Friday mosque and the former 17th-century coronation room, and displays 18 permanent exhibitions of paintings, manuscripts, coins and ethnographic items.

Outside the Ark, at the foot of the baked brick walls, is **Registan Square**, home to the city's slave market, parade ground and, when a drumbeat pulsed from the depths of the Ark, its flogging and execution ground. The elegant colonnaded aiwan of the Bolo Hauz Mosque rises to the north.

Around the back of the Ark is the **Zindon**, the former city jail, where important prisoners were held, often for years at a time. You can still see the notorious "Bug Pit" where the British officers Connolly and Stoddart were held for months before being executed.

South of the Registan are the Abdullah Khan Madrassa (1588) and Modari Khan Madrassa (1567), the latter built for the mother (*modar*) of the Uzbek Khan Abdullah Sheybani (1533–97). Further south is the multicoloured Balyand Mosque, noted for its gilded *kundal* paintings.

Samanid Mausoleum

A five-minute walk west of the Ark brings you to Samani Park, which is home to one of Central Asia's great architectural highlights, the **Ismail Samani Mausoleum**. The 10th-century gem houses the tomb of Ismail Samani, founder of the cultured Samanid Dynasty that oversaw Bukhara's cultural highpoint. The genius of the cubed building lies in its elegant basket-weave brickwork, which glows in full glory in the afternoon light.

At the northern end of the park is the **Chashma Ayub** (1380), built around the spring of the Old Testament prophet Job (Ayub in

"A stranger has only to seat himself on a bench of the Registan, to know the Uzbeks and the people of Bokhara. He may here converse with the natives of Persia, Turkey, Russia, Tartary, China, India, and Cabool. He will meet with Toorkmuns, Calmuks, and Kuzzaks, from the surrounding deserts, as well as the natives of more favoured lands."

Alexander Burnes on cosmopolitan 19th century Bukhara

BELOW: the Kalon Minaret and mosque dominate the skyline.

Restoring the Silk Road

War, neglect and an extreme climate have taken a heavy toll on Uzbekistan's architectural gems. By the end of the 19th century, many of Samarkand's domes and Bukhara's minarets had started to collapse. Early Soviet archaeologists painstakingly restored Bukhara's Ismail Samani Mausoleum, and Samarkand's Registan to their former glory, but sadly these monuments are again under threat. A rising water-table is driving salt into Bukhara's brickwork, it's common to see grass growing and birds nesting amongst the tiles, and the clumsy reconstruction of sites like the Bibi Khanum Mosque in Samarkand is damaging Uzbekistan's golden cities. Scaffolding, though essential to repair work, regularly blights domes across the skyline.

The use of all-over brickwork on the Ismail Samani Mausoleum represented an architectural innovation. Its ornate exterior reflects the light in different ways during the day.

BELOW: view of the Kalon Minaret from the Ark.

Arabic). The conical cupola, unique in Bukhara, was designed by artists relocated from Gurganj (Kunya-Urgench) by Timur.

Poi Kalon ensemble

Bukhara's most impressive building is the **Kalon Minaret** (admission charge). Built in 1127 by the Karakhanid ruler Arslan Khan, the tower was probably the world's tallest building at the time of its construction. Even Genghis Khan was awestruck, ordering the building spared from the Mongol destruction. It is the only building of this period to survive in Bukhara.

The minaret rises 48 metres (158ft) through bands of intricate brick patterns. The single turquoise band towards the top is thought to be the earliest example of glazed tilework in Central Asia. The minaret was nicknamed the "Tower of Death" in the 19th century, when criminals were tied in sacks and hurled off the skylight. It's possible to climb the minaret's 105 stairs for glorious views over

the bubbling domes and courtyards of the medieval city.

The attached **Kalon Mosque** (admission charge) was for centuries Bukhara's main Friday mosque, built to accommodate over 10,000 worshippers. The town's first Arab governor built the earliest mosque on this spot. A later 12th-century building was set ablaze by the Mongol forces but was rebuilt in 1514. When Genghis Khan arrived at the holy site he turned the mosque into a stable and uttered "The hay is cut. Give your horses fodder", the signal for his troops to pillage the city. The mosque still has its 288 cupolas, of which the largest is the gorgeous Kok Gumbaz (Blue Dome) at the west end. The mosque was used as a warehouse during the Soviet era.

Across from the mosque are the twin turquoise domes of the **Mir-i-Arab Madrassa** (1535), one of only two such institutions to function in Uzbekistan during the Soviet era. The building was financed by Ubaidullah Khan from the sale of 3,000 Persian slaves and is named after the khan's Yemeni spiritual

adviser (Mir-i-Arab means "Lord of the Arabs"). Both adviser and Khan are buried inside. This is still a working madrassa, and so the fine interior is off-limits to tourists.

To the south of the madrassa is the small **Emir Alim Khan Madrassa**, now a children's library.

To the east is the **Ulug Beg Madrassa** (1417), Central Asia's first madrassa and the prototype for the version that Ulug Beg was to build three years later in Samarkand's Registan Square. Ulug Beg's love of astronomy and science is revealed in the star-shaped motifs and the inscription above the portal that states: "It is the sacred duty of every Muslim man and woman to seek after knowledge." The madrassa was renovated during its 500th anniversary in 1994.

The unrestored **Abdul Aziz Madrassa** (1652) across the road boasts fine Chinese-influenced interior decoration and a woodcarving museum. Both madrassas follow a standard design, with a mosque and lecture hall on either side of an entrance portal and a series of student cells arranged around the inner courtyard.

Bukhara's bazaars

The heart of any Silk Road city lies in its bazaars and Bukhara once boasted 40 of them, along with 24 caravanserais, six *tims* (trading houses) and three *toks* (multi-entried bazaars that straddle major intersections). Though the turbaned traders of old have been replaced by souvenir-sellers, the cool, domed covered bazaars still offer a glimpse of the bones of a medieval Central Asian bazaar. Most of the buildings in this part of town house small exhibitions, craft workshops or souvenir stands, sometimes all three.

The main thoroughfare leads south from the **Tok-i-Zargaron** (1570, Jewellers' Bazaar), which once cornered the local market in lapis and rubies from Badakhshan, past the long-vanished Indian caravanserai to the Abdullah Khan Tim, which once specialised in wool and silk, and now, appropriately, sells carpets.

South of here is the 16th-century **Bazori Cord Hammam**, a bathhouse

"I could have spent months in Bokhara, seeking out fresh memories of its prodigious past, mingling with the bright crowds in the bazaar, or simply idling away my time under the apricot trees in the clear warm sunlight of Central Asia."

Fitzroy Maclean, Eastern Approaches

BELOW: a *chaikhana* (teahouse) in Bukhara's Lyab-i-Hauz District.

BELOW: the bathing pool at the Emir's Summer Palace.

still open for men and tour groups who reserve it in advance. Also here, dominating the five-spoked intersection, is the **Tok-i-Tilpak Furushon**, or Cap Makers' Bazaar, which once specialised in gold-embroidered skullcaps, fur hats and illustrated manuscripts, all of which had to be protected from the glare of the sun. Inside the bazaar is the tomb of holy man Khoja Ahmed I Paran.

To the side, between the two domed bazaars, is the **Magok-i-Attari Mosque**, one of the earliest religious shrines in the city and the site of a former herb, spice and perfume (*attar*) bazaar. Excavations in the depression (*magok* means "in a pit") have revealed a shrine to the local moon god, a Zoroastrian temple, a Buddhist monastery and an Arab mosque, stacked on top of each other in layers of history. To the south is the 12th-century mosque portal, stunningly decorated with incised alabaster *girikh* (geometric designs). A carpet museum occupies the interior, but a portion of the excavations lie revealed in the far corner.

To the west of the Tok-i-Sarrafon is the 16th-century **Gaukushan Madrassa**, now a metal-chasing workshop and named after the slaughterhouse (*gaukushan* means "cow-killer") that used to occupy the site.

Lyab-i-Hauz

With its traditional architecture and ancient mulberry trees set around a central stepped pool, the *mahalla* (district) of the Lyab-i-Hauz ("Around the Pool") is in many ways the town's most attractive. The *hauz* (pool) dates from 1620 and was one of 200 that supplied Bukhara with its drinking water (as well as many of its infectious diseases). The shady poolside chaikhana (teahouse) is a great place to relax over a bowl of *plov* and a pot of green tea, though tourism has forced out most of the *aksakals* who gave the place much of its character.

The *hauz* was commissioned by Grand Vizier Nadir Divanbegi, who also initiated the **khanagha** (pilgrim hostel) and mosque to the west. East of the pool, the **Divanbegi Madrassa** was originally built as a caravanserai,

but when the khan mistakenly inaugurated it as a madrassa it had to be hastily converted (once uttered, the edicts of the khan could never be rescinded). Two mythological birds decorate the portal, grasping white doves in their talons. The Mongol-faced sun recalls the Shir Dor Madrassa in Samarkand. The madrassa hosts a colourful nightly folklore and fashion show in summer, and the nearby puppet show is also worth a visit.

To the south is a statue of Khoja Nasreddin, the Sufic holy fool, whose humorous sayings and anecdotes are much loved throughout the Islamic world. Finishing off the ensemble to the north is the **Kukeldash Madrassa** (1568), the largest in Central Asia, with 160 student rooms.

The town's **Jewish quarter** stretches south from the Lyab-i-Hauz. Legend has it that the Jews were given this land in exchange for the area now known as Lyab-i-Hauz. Bukhara's Jews trace their arrival in Bukhara from the 14th century and they long played an important role in trade with the Khazaria region in the Russian Volga.

The community once numbered 4,000, but since 1991 many have opted for a new life in Israel. It's possible to visit the nearby synagogue and Jewish cemetery.

A few hundred metres east of the Lyab-i-Hauz is the **Chor Minor** (1807), one of Bukhara's quirkiest buildings. This architectural oddity, which resembles an upside-down chair, is actually the gatehouse of a destroyed madrassa. The blue domes of the eponymous four minarets (*chor minor*) were once topped by storks' nests and fell into disrepair but have since been restored by UNESCO. A souvenir seller occupies the ground floor and will allow visitors to climb onto the roof (admission fee).

Suburban Bukhara

If you have a spare few hours, head into the northern suburbs to the Sitorai Makhi Khosa, otherwise known as the **Emir's Summer Palace** (open Wed–Mon 9am–5pm, Tue until 2.30pm). Built by the Russians in 1911, the kitschy half-European, half-Oriental palace was home to the last emir of

BELOW: statue of the mathematician al-Kwarizimi, outside Khiva's city walls.

The Chor Minor once opened into a large madrassa complex. Its name means "The Four Minarets" in Tajik, although its sky-blue turrets have little in common with ordinary minarets.

BELOW: the imposing city walls of Khiva.

Bukhara, Alim Khan, until he fled to Afghanistan in 1920. The first Congress of the Bukharan Soviet was held in the palace that same year, heralding the dramatic political changes to come.

The wedding-cake-like complex leads into an inner courtyard of reception halls, where you'll find the **museums of Applied Arts, National Costume and Needlework**. The examples of gold embroidery and *suzani* (wall hangings) here are particularly fine. The last museum is housed in the former palace harem, where a voyeuristic emir would watch his concubines bathing, before throwing an apple to his passing favourite. The complex is fascinating in its depiction of an emirate straddling the medieval and the modern. The Sitorai Makhi Khosa was the first place in the Bukharan emirate to have electricity.

Around Bukhara

About 12km (7.5 miles) from Bukhara in Kasri Orifon village is the **Bakhauddin Naqshbandi complex**, centred around the tomb of the 14th-century saint who is Bukhara's spiritual protector. With its "wishing trees", holy stones and sacrificial offerings, the site offers a glimpse into Central Asia's brand of popular or "parallel" Islam, which has its roots as much in an animist past as in the formal teachings of Islam. Apart from the saint's tomb, the complex includes two mosques, a huge *khanaga* (1544) and the tombs of two khans, Abdul Aziz and Abdullah II.

The other main Sufic site is the **Chor Bakr**, whose street of tombs is centred around the graves of Sayid Abu Bakr and three brothers (*chor Bakr* means "four Bakrs"). The term sayid denotes a direct descendant of the Prophet Muhammad, and the sanctity this brought the complex made it the preferred burial place of the Bukharan aristocracy. The quiet complex of mosque, pilgrim accommodation, *chillakhanas* (meditation rooms) and *takharatkhanas* (place for ablutions) remains a pilgrimage site and its gardens are a tranquil spot for

picnics. It is 6km (3.5 miles) west of Bukhara.

KHIVA AND KHOREZM

Hidden in the deserts of northwest Uzbekistan, an 18-day journey by camel from Bukhara (or 45-minute flight from Tashkent), the oasis caravan town of Khiva (Xiva in Uzbek) has long been the remotest of the three khanates.

Though local legend has the town founded by Shem, son of Noah, Khiva is not the most ancient town in the region. Like its great brethren the Indus, Nile and Euphrates, the Oxus Delta has long nourished one of Asia's great centres of antiquity. Most of these ancient cities lie neglected, lost and baking in the desert sands, though the former capital of Gurganj (Konye-Urgench) can still be visited in neighbouring Turkmenistan.

Khiva prospered after both the Mongols and Timur flattened Gurganj, and it eventually became the region's capital in 1592. The oasis town provided a vital pit stop for caravans headed to Merv. Trade with the

Russian Volga, particularly Astrakhan, added to its city's wealth and filled its caravanserais with samovars, furs, guns, karakul pelts and Turkestani melons. Isolated and lawless, the city also grew rich on plunder and, importantly, the slave trade.

It was the slave trade, specifically the 3,000 or so Slavic slaves, that gave the Russians the excuse they needed to attack its troublesome neighbour. Things did not go well at first. The first expedition ended in the slaughter of 4,000 Russian troops and the despatch of the expedition's head, literally, back to St Petersburg. The second winter expedition faltered in the frozen desert and never even reached Khiva, with the loss en route of 8,500 camels. In a move typical of the Great Game, the British officers James Abbot and Richmond Shakespear rushed to the city in an attempt to release the slaves and pull the rug from under the Russians' feet. But it was too little, too late. Khiva was living on borrowed time and by 1873 Kaufmann had engineered the absorption of the khanate into the Russian Empire.

BELOW: the unfinished Kalta Minor minaret.

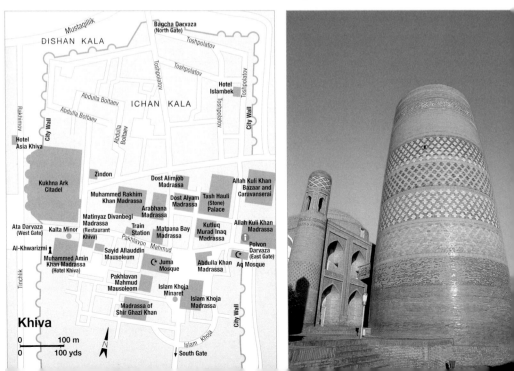

DISHAN KALA

Mustaqillik

Bagcha Darvaza
(North Gate)

Toshpolatov

Toshpolatov

Toshpolatov

Hotel Islambek

Rakhimov

City Wall

Abdulla Boltaev

Abdulla Boltaev

ICHAN KALA

Toshpolatov

City Wall

Hotel Asia Khiva

Abdulla Boltaev

Zindon

Kukhna Ark Citadel

Dost Alimjob Madrassa

Allah Kuli Khan Bazaar and Caravanserai

Muhammed Rakhim Khan Madrassa

Dost Alyam Madrassa

Tash Hauli (Stone) Palace

Matinyaz Divanbegi Madrassa

Arabhana Madrassa

Ata Darvaza (West Gate)

Kalta Minor

Train Station (Restaurant Khiva)

Matpana Bay Madrassa

Kutluq Murad Inaq Madrassa

Allah Kuli Khan Madrassa

Al-Khwarizmi

Pakhlavon Mahmud

Sayid Allauddin Mausoleum

Juma Mosque

Abdulla Khan Madrassa

Polvon Darvaza (East Gate)

Aq Mosque

Tinchlik

Muhammed Amin Khan Madrassa (Hotel Khiva)

Pakhlavan Mahmud Mausoleum

Islam Khoja Minaret

Islam Khoja Madrassa

Madrassa of Shir Ghazi Khan

City Wall

Khiva

0   100 m
0   100 yds

N

Islam Khoja

South Gate

All but one of the columns in the Juma Mosque are carved of black elm wood.

Today Khiva is the most architecturally intact and tightly packed of Uzbekistan's Silk Road cities. Its intense green-and-blue tilework ranks as some of the most opulent in Central Asia, but it also has the feel of a movie set or a museum city, frozen in time and without the lived-in feel that makes Bukhara so fascinating.

The main points of interest are in the **Ichan Kala**, or inner city, encased in 17th-century **city walls** with rounded bastions and punctured by four entrances. These gates were once sealed dusk to dawn to keep marauders out. These days most tourists enter through the western **Ata Darvaza gate**. The city walls sadly no longer rise from the wind-whipped desert sands but rather from a tarmac car park.

The Ichan Kala

As you enter the inner town, on the right (south) is the **Muhammad Amin Khan Madrassa** (1855), the largest in the city and named after one of the city's more impressive khans. The madrassa's 125 *hujra* cells, once housing the madrassa's students, are currently home to the atmospheric Hotel Khiva. Above the main entrance there is an inscription in Arabic calligraphy that reads: "This wonderful building will stay here forever to descendants' joy".

Beside the madrassa is a glowering statue of al-Khwarizmi (783–840), the brilliant Khorezmian mathematician after whom the word "algorithm" is named (he is also considered the father of algebra – another Arabic word, *al-jabr*). Khwarizmi was born in Khiva but spent much of his working life in Baghdad.

Outside the madrassa is the bright green stub of the **Kalta Minor**, commissioned by Amin Khan to be the world's tallest minaret, but abandoned as too costly after the khan was murdered three years later. It is consequently rather squat in appearance.

To the left is the **Kukhna Ark**, the oldest core of the original fortress, whose roots stretch back some 1,500 years. The complex is notable for ice-blue tilework and tall *aiwans* that face north to catch the prevailing summer breezes. The royal rooms include a summer mosque, mint, harem and a throne room where the khan would meet winter guests in a felt yurt erected on a brick base (the yurt was easier to heat than the draughty brick halls of the palace). The Ak Sheikh Bobo citadel offers fine views from the roof. Just outside the Ark is the *zindon*, or city jail.

To the east is the **Muhammad Rakhim Khan Madrassa** (1871), now home to a crafts centre. A museum is dedicated to the khan, who was also known for his poetry, written under the name Feruz Shah. Feruz was the last khan of Khiva. An interesting figure, his notable achievement was to bring the khanate's first telephone from St Petersburg, with little

thought to the fact that there was no telephone line for hundreds of miles in any direction.

One of Khiva's holiest sights is the **Pakhlavan Mahmud Mausoleum**, which commemorates the poet, wrestler and patron saint of Khiva who died here in 1325. The 19th-century tomb contains some of the city's best tilework and also the largest cupola in Khiva. The Soviets spent years trying to dislodge the cult of Khiva's local *pirs* (holy men), but the spot is still madly popular with pilgrims and wedding parties who come here for blessings.

Opposite the tomb is the **Madrassa of Shir Ghazi Khan**, built with the sweat of 5,000 Persian slaves who, sensing that their promised freedom was not forthcoming, lynched the unfortunate khan inside his new building. The inscription on the portal reads stoically, "I accept death at the hands of slaves."

Khiva's tallest minaret, the 45-metre (148-ft) **Islam Khoja Minaret**, is named after the enlightened early 20th-century grand vizier who built several public schools and hospitals before being assassinated by outraged religious conservatives. Built in 1908, it is the last Islamic monument to be built in the city before the arrival of the Soviets. The attached madrassa hosts the city's best museum, featuring some wonderful silk clothing amongst the other applied arts.

If the heat is getting too much, dive into the deliciously cool gloom of the nearby **Juma Mosque** (1788), supported by a dense forest of 213 wooden pillars that are cleverly arranged to allow the entire congregation a view of the *mihrab* (niche pointing the direction to Mecca). Aptly, the mosque holds an exhibition of carved *karagacha* (elm) wood.

Follow the 60-metre (200-ft) -long tunnel of the eastern **Polvon Darvaza** gate (built in 1806) into the main bazaar, where you can pick up one of Khorezm's fantastic hats, brightly coloured *ikat* fabrics and hand-painted ceramics. Be prepared to haggle hard.

Before you leave the old city, don't miss the 19th century **Tash Hauli Palace** (Stone Palace), home to the court of Allah Kuli Khan (1826–42) and a highlight of the city. A secret corridor connects the fabulously decorated inner harem to the reception court (*ishrat hauli*) and law courts. The intricately carved columns are particularly fine, as are the majolica tiles in the harem's inner courtyard.

Excursions from Khiva

Several ruined and crumbling fortresses in the deserts of the Khorezm oasis make for a great overnight trip from Khiva or Urgench. En route to the desert, near the town of Beruniy, the road crosses a rickety pontoon bridge to offer an unassuming glimpse of one of Asia's most historically and geographically important defining points: the Oxus River (Amu Darya). Bled almost dry at this point by the thirsty cotton fields of Turkmenistan and Uzbekistan, the sluggish river is today only a faint echo of its former self.

TIP

The Tourist Information Office in Khiva can supply a car and driver for trips out to Khorezm. A number of options are available.

BELOW: ceiling decoration on the Tash Hauli Palace.

The adobe walls of Ayaz Qala.

BELOW: the ruins of Toprak Qala.

Most popular is the enormous 4th- to 7th-century **Ayaz Qala**, where you can stay overnight in a traditional nomadic yurt. It's also possible to make camel trips from here and even swim in the desert at the nearby Ayaz Lake.

Of most archaeological interest is the Kushan-era **Toprak Qala**, the region's biggest city until the destruction of irrigation canals left it marooned in the desert sands. The Russian archaeologist Tolstov excavated the palace friezes in 1938, unveiling a blend of Classical Roman and Gandharan styles dating from the 2nd or 3rd century AD, a time when the transcontinental Kushan Empire dominated the entire middle leg of the Silk Road.

The other main excursion is to the white salt-caked former shores of the **Aral Sea**, where you can visit the iconic beached fishing trawlers rusting in the sand, 150km (90 miles) away from the nearest water. In what is perhaps the greatest environmental disaster of recent times (see page 117), the dying sea has lost half its area and 75 percent of its volume within a single generation, bled dry by the Soviet obsession with cotton monoculture. A visit to the ruins of the sea and the rusting skeletons of ships is a sobering reminder of the dangers of environmental recklessness.

The trip leads first to **Nukus**, the environmentally blighted capital of Karakalpakstan, where art-lovers should stop at the impressive **Igor Savitsky Art Gallery** (open Mon–Fri 9am–5pm, Sat–Sun 10am–4pm), an unexpected home to one of the finest collections of Soviet avant-garde art from the 1920s and 1930s. Much of the museum's collection, which numbers some 90,000 items, as well as detailed biographies of represented artists, is available to view online at www.savitskycollection.org. The **Karakalpak State Museum** and the **Museum of Amet and Aymkhan Shamuratiev**, a local artist and writer who came to prominence in the early 20th century, are also worth a brief visit.

Connolly and Stoddart

Bukhara was the setting for one of the most notorious incidents in the Great Game, when two British agents held prisoner by Nasrullah "The Butcher" met their fate.

The emir of from 1826 to 1860 was the highly unstable Nasrullah, fondly known amongst his subjects as "The Butcher", a nickname he received when he killed off 28 of his relatives in a bloodstained scramble to become ruler.

In 1837, a British envoy, Colonel Charles Stoddart, arrived at the gates of the emirate in an attempt to build a political alliance between Britain and Bukhara. A soldier rather than a diplomat, he quickly offended the volatile emir with his ignorance of Bukharan protocol and his lack of both gifts and a letter of introduction from Queen Victoria.

Stoddart was thrown into Bukhara's notorious vermin-filled "Bug Pit", a 6-metre (20-ft) -deep subterranean dungeon, accessible only by a length of rope, where he was held on and off for the next two years. Nasrullah played with Stoddart like a cat with a mouse, alternately releasing him and then sending him back into the pit, until Stoddart was convinced he was quite mad. At one point the emir's executioner descended into the pit to behead the British officer on the spot, whereupon the desperate Stoddart converted to Islam in exchange for a modicum of freedom. Amazingly, he managed to smuggle several letters back to his family in which he put on a brave face, despite the ghastly conditions.

Then in the winter of 1841 another agent, Arthur Connolly, arrived outside the gates of Bukhara on a one-man rescue mission. Connolly was certainly well equipped to accomplish the release. A veteran Central Asian political traveller who travelled in disguise under the name Khan Ali, he was the quintessential Great Game player, and is even credited as the first person to coin the phrase.

Connolly was treated cordially at first, but when the British Army was routed in neighbouring Afghanistan it dawned on the unstable emir that he had little to fear from a British reprisal and he once again threw both officers into the pit. The emir was convinced that the men were spies, a suspicion not helped by the British government who had already disowned the two men as "private travellers".

It became clear to the snubbed emir that Queen Victoria was never going to reply to his personal letter. As part of the celebrations over the defeat of his rival the Khan of Kokand, Connolly and Stoddart were led bound into the Registan Square and forced to dig their own graves. Stoddart was beheaded and Connolly was given one last opportunity to convert to Islam, before he too was killed. It was June 1842, and one of the darkest days in the Great Game.

ABOVE: Bukhara palace. **RIGHT:** Emir Nasrullah, the "Butcher of Bukhara".

KAZAKHSTAN

In cutting across just a small part of this huge country, the Silk Road provides a cross-section of its contrasts: from the sophistication of Almaty to the wilds of the nearby mountains; from ancient sites at Turkistan to the rocket-launch site of Baikonur.

Kazakhstan, the ninth-largest country in the world, covers an area greater than that of all the other Central Asian countries added together. Much of Kazakhstan is flat, arid steppe, but the southeast is home to forests and high mountains, and it was this region that was most important during the days of the Silk Road. A northern strand of the trade route passed along the Ili Valley in China through the Dzungarian Gate to continue west between Lake Balkash and the Zailiysky Alatau mountains.

This summer route then followed the Chuy Valley of present-day Kyrgyzstan before reaching Taraz, where branches led southwest to Samarkand, via Shymkent and Otrar.

Kazakhstan has only really existed as a political entity since Soviet times; before that, most of the territory was a sparsely populated buffer zone between Russia and Central Asia. The exception was the far south, which came within the sphere of influence of the main Silk Road settlements of modern-day Kyrgyzstan and Uzbekistan.

The first settlers in the region were probably nomadic Scythians, whose *kurgans* (circular burial mounds) can still be seen dotting the countryside of southeast Kazakhstan and northern Kyrgyzstan. Various Turkic tribes followed, and by the early 10th century the cities of Otrar and Turkistan (known then as Shavgar) were developed in the south of the country. Karakhanid influence superseded that of the Bukhara-based Samanids in the 10th century, but Islam was temporarily replaced by Buddhism when Khitans invaded from Mongolia. The region returned to Islam when it was absorbed into the Khorezmshah Empire in the early 13th century.

As elsewhere, the arrival of Genghis Khan in 1218 would have fateful

LEFT: the vast Kazakh landscape.
RIGHT: *Malus sieversii* is a wild apple native to Central Asia.

consequences. The leader's death in 1227 resulted in his empire being divided between his sons: the younger, Chagatai, inherited the land that included southern Kazakhstan, while the elder, Jochi, took on the territory to the north and the west.

Like the Kyrgyz, to whom they are closely related, Kazakhs have their roots in the Mongol tribes of southern Siberia. They first arrived in modern-day Kazakhstan around the turn of the 16th century, but became subjugated by the Oirats, another Mongol clan, at the end of the following century.

Russian influence in the region was felt for the first time in the early 18th century, and in the 1820s the Kazakhs swore allegiance to the Tsar in order to receive protection from the Kokand Khanate to the south. The Russians, who at that time were active participants in the Great Game, were only too happy to establish a military presence in the region. Slavic settlers poured in throughout the late 19th and early 20th centuries, especially after the Trans-Aral Railway between Orenburg and Tashkent

ENTERING AND LEAVING KAZAKHSTAN

The train network in Kazakhstan is very useful, particularly when travelling east to west, as most of Kazakhstan's Silk Road sites lie on the main route that links Almaty with Moscow. (See Travel Tips, page 405, for more information on transport in Kazakhstan.)

A daily bus service links Yining in Xinjiang, **China**, with Almaty, crossing at Khorgos; a twice-weekly train service operates between Urumqi in Xinjiang and Almaty via the border post at Dostyk.

The route between Almaty and Bishkek in **Kyrgyzstan** has regular bus and shared taxi services that take 3–5 hours. Further bus services link Almaty with Cholpon-Ata at Lake Issyk-Kul in summer.

A major highway leads south from Shymkent, west of Almaty, to Tashkent just across the **Uzbekistan** border. Minibuses and taxis go as far as the border, but it is necessary to cross on foot. A railway link leads south to Tashkent from the junction at Arys, west of Shymkent.

Irregular, un-timetabled ferries link Aktau with Baku in **Azerbaijan**.

A number of crossing points lead into **Russia** along Kazakhstan's northern border: north of Semey; north of Astana via Pavlodar and Petropavlovsk; west of Astana via Kostanai; north of Uralsk and west of Atyrau towards Astrakhan. Long-distance trains link Almaty with Moscow via Aktöbe, and Almaty with Novosibirsk via Semey. Another train line links Almaty and Astana with Moscow via Petropavlovsk.

Origin of the Apple

There is a clue in the name of the Kazakh capital, Almaty, which, in its earlier form, Alma-Ata, translates as "father of the apple". It was originally thought that the 20,000 varieties of the domestic apple known today evolved from the chance hybridisation of several wild species, but recent DNA analysis has revealed that the progenitor of the modern apple is derived from a single species, *Malus sieversii*, that hails from the forests of southeast Kazakhstan's Dzungarian Alatau range, close to the Chinese frontier.

With this knowledge, US scientists are now returning to Kazakhstan to investigate the disease-resistant properties of the domestic apple's forefather. Almaty, it would seem, is a name well-chosen.

was completed in 1906, and Russians continued to arrive during the Soviet period. Even today, Kazakhstan has a considerable Russian population, with just 60 percent of the national total being Kazakhs and the remainder Russians and other races that include Tatars, Uzbeks and Uighurs.

ALMATY

Despite the fact that the country's capital moved to Astana a few years ago, Almaty remains Kazakhstan's largest and most sophisticated city – a metropolis of wide boulevards and leafy parks from where the near 5,000-metre (16,500-ft) -high, snow-capped peaks of the Zailiysky Alatau range loom tantalisingly close to the south. Unlike the brash new capital, Almaty retains a certain old-fashioned charm and resembles a fairly typical Russian city, transported wholesale to remote Central Asia.

The city stands on the site of an old Silk Road settlement destroyed by Genghis Khan's hordes, and the present-day city – originally called Verniy – was established as a Russian

Strolling through Almaty.

BELOW: Zenkov Cathedral.

outpost in 1854. It was badly damaged by earthquakes in 1887 and 1911, and renamed Alma-Ata in 1921. Following the construction of the Turkestan–Siberia Railway, it became the capital of Soviet Kazakhstan in 1927. Deported Koreans and Volga Germans swelled the existing Russian population during World War II and, even today, ethnic Kazakhs have only a marginal majority in a city that still has a very Russian character.

Around town

Most notable is the brightly painted, all-wood **Zenkov Cathedral**, that shines like a beacon through the pines of **Panfilov Park**. The cathedral, as any local will tell you, was constructed in 1904 without the use of nails. With its western tower standing 56 metres (185ft) tall, Zenkov Cathedral is one of the world's tallest wooden buildings, but it is more than a mere museum piece: the place resounds with the rich voices of its Russian congregation each Sunday morning. Panfilov Park is also home to a bold brass **war memorial** and eternal flame that celebrate

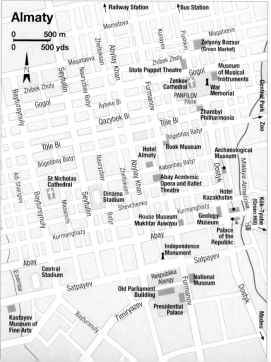

the heroics of General Ivan Panfilov's division during World War II. It is now mainly a popular venue for wedding-party photo shoots.

The **Museum of Musical Instruments** (open Tue–Sun 10am–6pm), located in a curious wooden building near the park's eastern entrance, houses a wide collection of traditional instruments, along with recordings of their sounds. For a taste of rural Kazakhstan a visit to nearby **Zelyony Bazaar** (Green Market), just north of the park, is also recommended.

The **National Museum** (open Tue–Sun 10am–6pm), south of the city centre opposite the Presidential Palace, has displays outlining Kazakhstan's history together with sections on natural history, ethnography and even space flight.

The **Kastayev Museum of Fine Arts** (open Tue–Sun 10am–6pm), west of the centre, has works by Soviet Kazakh and European painters, as well as a collection of Kazakh handicrafts and carpets. Almaty also has a number of fine Soviet-period buildings, including the 1934 neoclassical **Abay Academic Opera and Ballet Theatre**, opposite the Hotel Almaty. Try to catch a bargain-price performance here.

Respublika Alangy, south and uphill from the opera theatre, is the city's most prestigious square, with fountains, an independence monument and more neoclassical buildings. East of here, next to the Palace of the Republic, a cable car climbs Kök-Tyube (Green Hill) to reach a platform that offers sweeping city views.

Around Almaty

The city is pleasant enough, but the picture-perfect Zailiysky Alatau to the south beckon. These mountains, spurs of the great Tian Shan range, offer city-dwellers a place to picnic, walk and escape Almaty's summer heat and pollution.

One easy excursion is to **Medeu**, an Olympic-sized ice rink that has trained generations of Soviet ice stars. Medeu is perfect for skating in winter, and in summer it serves as a good base for walks into the pine-clad foothills that lie immediately above it. There is also the option of a swimming pool just below the ice rink, though it is filled with chilly mountain water! A little further on along the same road, but considerably higher up, the **Shymbulak ski resort** is open from November to April and provides a useful base for hikes during the rest of the year.

East of Almaty, the **Almatinsky Nature Reserve** (Almatinsky Zapovednik) is home to Pik Talgar, at 4,979 metres (16,430ft) the highest point in the Zailiysky Alatau. Snow leopards are present in the reserve, but the likelihood of seeing one is extremely remote; there is a slightly better chance of seeing the arkhar, a large-horned wild sheep native to the region.

West of the city, **Bolshoe Almatinskoe** ("Big Almaty") lake is located high up in the gorge of the Bolshaya Almatinka River. This stunning blue alpine lake lies in the shadow of three towering peaks – Soviet (4,317 metres/14,240ft) to the southeast, Ozerniy (4,110 metres/13,560ft) to

The most fascinating item on display in the National Museum is a replica of the suit of armour worn by the "Golden Man" found in a 5th-century BC Scythian tomb east of the city. Modern thinking suggests that the golden "man" may actually have been a woman.

BELOW: winter in the Zailiysky Alatau

the south and Tourist Peak (3,954 metres/13,000ft) to the southwest – and serves as a starting point for treks into Kyrgyzstan.

SOUTHERN KAZAKHSTAN

The city of **Taraz** (**Dzhambul**) went the way of many former Silk Road settlements when it was destroyed by Genghis Khan's Mongol army in the early 13th century. Hitherto it had been an important Karakhanid settlement. Taraz was eventually rebuilt as a frontier town of the Kokand Khanate before coming under Russian rule in the 19th century. A single Karakhanid monument, albeit a 20th-century Soviet reconstruction, still remains in a park just south of Park Lenina – the mausoleum of an 11th-century khan. The Daudbek Shamansaur mausoleum, built for an important 13th-century Mongol, stands nearby. The city's **History Museum** (open Mon–Sat 9am–6pm) has a collection of *balbals* (Turkic burial stones) and an exhibition on the history of the Silk Road.

The only remnants of ancient Taraz that still stand are to be found 18km

(11 miles) west at Golavachovka, where there is the 12th-century Karakhanid **Mausoleum of Aishi Bibi,** conserved within a protective glass box next to the reconstructed 11th-century **Mausoleum of Babadzi-Khatun.**

Shymkent

Shymkent, an industrial city of half a million people, 200km (120 miles) southwest of Taraz, was yet another Silk Road caravan town that was razed to the ground by invading Mongols. The Kokand Khanate constructed a fort here in the early 19th century, which was subsequently annexed by Tsarist Russia in 1864.

Shymkent's busy bazaar and **Regional Studies and History Museum** (open Tue–Sun 9am–6pm), with its Silk Road exhibit, are the sights of most interest for present-day visitors. For those with an interest in the excesses of the Stalinist period, the **Museum for Commemoration of Victims of Political Repressions** does exactly what its name suggests.

Sayram

Sayram, 10km (6 miles) east of Shymkent, is far older, although there is little hard evidence of its supposed 3,000-year history other than a mention in the Zoroastrian holy book, the Avesta. This small town is best known as the birthplace of Sufi teacher Khoja Ahmed Yassawi (see page 279).

Otrar

Also known as Al-Farabi because it was the birthplace of the famous Islamic scientist and philosopher **Abu Nasr al-Farabi** (*c.*872–950), Otrar has unfortunate associations with Genghis Khan. Following the ill-advised murder of his envoy, the Mongol leader mounted a siege in 1219 that lasted for six months before he finally breached the city walls and slaughtered almost everyone within. Prior to this, Otrar was a collection of oases that together formed one of the most flourishing settlements along the Silk Road.

BELOW: the tomb of Khoja Ahmed Yasavi in Turkistan.

These days Otrar, 170km (102 miles) northwest of Shymkent, is effectively just an archaeological site, although it has UNESCO World Heritage status. Much is still to be excavated, but evidence of bathhouses, kilns, walls and a mosque can all be seen. Close to the site stands the **Mausoleum of Arystan-Bab** (an early tutor of Khoja Ahmed Yassawi), a 20th-century rebuild of an earlier 14th-century structure and an important pilgrimage site. The nearby village of Shauildir has a **museum** dedicated to the life and work of al-Farabi.

Turkistan

This university town on the fringes of the Kyzylkum desert, 60km (36 miles) north of Otrar, is home to Kazakhstan's most important Islamic monument and pilgrimage site: the 14th-century Timurid tomb of the Sufi saint **Khoja Ahmed Yassawi**.

Turkistan, formerly known as Hazrat-e-Turkestan, and as Shavgar or Yassi until the 16th century, was an important Karakhanid trade centre before it came under the rule of the Kokand Khanate in the early 19th century. Khoja Ahmed Yassawi was a Sufi poet and scholar who spent much of his life in the town and died here in 1146. Local Muslims believed that three pilgrimages here were equal in spiritual value to going on Hajj, and so Timur commissioned this impressive mausoleum in the late 14th century at the same time as the construction of his palace at Shakhrisabz. True to form, Timur ensured that he left his mark: inside the tomb, a large bronze cauldron bears the legend, "This is a gift from Timur for having built this mausoleum."

A smaller mausoleum faces the Yassawi tomb, that of **Rabiga Sultan Begimi**, the wife of an Uzbek leader and granddaughter of Timur – a 20th-century reconstruction of a 16th-century original. A restored 16th-century bathhouse stands west of the complex entrance, alongside a mosque. East of Rabiga Sultan Begimi's tomb,

just beyond the gift shop, is the site **museum** (open daily 9am–6pm).

Baikonur cosmodrome

Located far from anywhere, this is where *Vostok 1*, the first manned space flight, piloted by Yuri Gagarin, was hurled into orbit on 12 April 1961. Gagarin led the way for a whole generation of Soviet cosmonauts to take off from here. The cosmodrome, which is central to a closed-off area that measures 90km (54 miles) east to west and 85km (51 miles) north to south, lies on the fringes of the Kyzylkum desert, just north of the garrison town of the same name (formerly Leninsk, but renamed Baikonur in 1995).

With the collapse of the USSR in 1991, Russia was left with the space programme's know-how, and Kazakhstan the prime launch site. An agreement was reached in 1994 in which Baikonur would be leased to Russia for a considerable annual rent – a lease that runs until 2050. Following the conclusion of the space shuttle programme, all flights to the international space station will now depart from Baikonur.

TIP

Visits to Baikonur are possible if organised through a Kazakh or Russian tour company, but these tend to be highly expensive and tangled with red tape. Those fortunate enough to get in can visit the launch pad from where the Soviet cosmonauts rocketed into space, the cosmonauts' "hotel" and a museum that has displays of space food and some personal belongings of Yuri Gagarin.

BELOW: a Soyuz rocket heads for the launchpad at Baikonur.

PAKISTAN

The Karakoram mountains of the Hunza Valley
and Baltistan offer some of the most dramatic
scenery on earth. A branch of the Silk Road
came through here, working its way south to
the ancient capital of Taxila, beyond which lies
the Khyber Pass.

The main Silk Road caravan routes from China headed due east to Central Asia. But there were also routes linking up with South Asia, notably through the Karakoram mountains to present-day Pakistan.

Pakistan is the Land of the Indus, and for millennia this great river that rises in Tibet and then slices through the Karakoram, before spilling onto the plains of Punjab and Sindh, has nurtured a succession of civilisations that have left behind a remarkable cultural legacy. The 5,000-year-old Indus Valley Civilisation centred in the south of the country produced the world's first large-scale urban planning, which can still be seen at Moenjo-daro in Sindh, one of the world's great archaeological sites. Later, the north, always strategically situated between South and Central Asia, found itself at the crossroads of civilisations, where the great city of Taxila became one of the most important centres of learning in the ancient world. Alexander the Great came here after crossing the Khyber Pass in 326 BC, and held philosophical discussions with resident intellectuals before dining in the great hall. Asoka nurtured Buddhism here in the 3rd century BC. Later, under the Kushans, Mahayana Buddhism became the buzzword as monasteries

were created throughout Gandhara, and pilgrims such as Xuanzang (see page 57) took the new ideas north across the Karakoram and into China, where they were further developed and studied in places like Dunhuang (see page 184). The significance of the region as a key player in Silk Road history cannot be underestimated.

In the days of the Silk Road, busy exchanges would have gone on with numerous visitors from foreign lands, something that in recent years modern Pakistan has found hard to emulate.

Main attractions
THE KARAKORAM HIGHWAY
HUNZA VALLEY: BALTIT FORT, ULTAR
  MEADOW
RAKAPOSHI
BALTISTAN
NANGA PARBAT
CHILAS PETROGLYPHS
TAXILA
GRAND TRUNK ROAD
TAKHT-I-BAHI
PESHAWAR
KHYBER PASS

LEFT: Baltit Fort and Ultar Peak, Hunza.
RIGHT: sisters in Shagai, Northwest Frontier Province.

ENTERING AND LEAVING PAKISTAN

Many visitors will arrive at one of the country's three main airports: Islamabad, Karachi or Lahore. Peshawar is also served by international flights from the Gulf. From Islamabad there are daily flights, weather permitting, between Islamabad and Gilgit, and Islamabad and Skardu, both offering superb views of the mountains.

For Silk Road travellers, the journey to or from **China** will be via the Khunjerab Pass on the Karakoram Highway (KKH) from Kashgar. The long flat pass is often snow-covered during the winter and is closed from 15 October to 1 May. Border posts are situated at Tashkurgan on the China side and Sost on the Pakistan side. There are direct bus links along the KKH between Kashgar, Hunza/Gilgit and Rawalpindi.

The main border crossing to or from **Afghanistan** is the Khyber Pass. The road through Pakistan passes through the Tribal Areas, so travellers require a permit and armed guard, obtainable in Peshawar from the Home and Tribal Affairs Office. Coming the other way, from Afghanistan, the permit should be available at the border.

The other main route into Pakistan is from **India**, where the principal border crossing is at Wagah, just to the east of Lahore. This is crossed by the daily Samjhota Express train service and a four-times-weekly bus service operating between Delhi and Lahore. You can enter with a private vehicle providing you have a carnet.

Travellers coming from **Iran** will cross the Pakistan border at Taftan; the nature of the onward journey will depend on the security situation but may require an escort.

The number of tourists had never been that great, but following 9/11 and all the uncertainties posed by media reports of lurking Taliban, the flow virtually dried up. Tourism remains at a low ebb due to ongoing terrorist attacks in Islamabad, Lahore and other prominent locations, and the city of Peshawar on the Khyber Pass is largely out of bounds. Foreigners travelling through Baluchistan are advised to take a police escort. Would-be visitors should take due note of official advice regarding their security and focus their plans on the large parts of Pakistan that are relatively safe. Most Pakistanis are fantastically friendly and welcoming of foreigners.

Karakoram – Hunza Valley

The Karakoram extend right across the Pakistan side of Kashmir, from Baltistan in the east to the **Hunza Valley** region. The range contains the densest concentration of big peaks on the planet, as well as nurturing the longest glaciers in the world outside the polar regions.

The very meaning of the word Karakoram – "black mountain" – conjures up an image of the precarious nature of a journey through this land. Today, following in the footsteps of early pilgrims and merchants, the traverse of the Karakoram is one of the world's great road trips. The Karakoram Highway (KKH), an engineering marvel built by the Chinese and opened in 1986, takes you from China into Pakistan via the Khunjerab Pass, the highest paved road border crossing on the planet. From the top of the Pass it's a gentle downhill journey through scenery that is impressive enough, but it isn't until you reach the fabled Hunza Valley that the Karakoram mountains reveal themselves in all their glory.

Near the north Hunza village of Passu is the snout of the Batura Glacier, a giant river of ice (58km/36 miles) that rises to the west and culminates in the beautiful Passu and Batura

Peaks. On the east side of the Hunza river, a new road bridge provides access to the narrow confines of the remote **Shimshal Valley**, a paradise for trekkers heading for the pastures of Schwert, where the women of the valley tend huge numbers of yaks and goats in the summer. Just to the south, as the KKH veers west towards Central Hunza, are the mighty peaks of Trivor and Disteghil Sar, both of them just shy of 8,000 metres (26,000ft).

With mountains rising steeply on both sides and its tapestry of terraced fields fed by water channelled down from the glaciers, **Central Hunza** is an astonishingly beautiful place. The capital is the town of **Karimabad**, which lies just off the KKH, cowering under the vertiginous flanks of **Ultar Peak** (7,388 metres/24,240ft) that rear up just behind the village, alongside the lower Hunza Peak and aptly named pinnacle of Ladyfinger Peak. The village itself is dominated by the ancient **Baltit Fort** (open 9am–1pm and 2–5.30pm), once the stronghold of the *mirs* (rulers) of Hunza. The hereditary Mir of Hunza is today also the elected governor of the Northern Areas.

For centuries, the *mirs* sat fast in their mountain citadel, dictating the score to anyone with the nerve to pass through, their coffers regularly replenished by booty plundered from caravans plying their trade over the passes to and from Central Asia. The Baltit fort has been restored as a museum of local history and culture. Behind it, a track leads through the Ultar Nullah (ravine) on its way to **Ultar Meadow**, an idyllic spot for camping beneath the ramparts of Ultar Peak. Another good vantage point is the hamlet of Duiker, the so-called **Eagle's Nest**, situated on a knoll high above the valley at 3,200 metres (10,500ft) and offering spellbinding views. Wherever you are in Hunza, the gaze is automatically drawn to the dazzling serried buttresses of **Rakaposhi**, whose sloping northern face is the highest uninterrupted mountain face on earth, rising to a mind-boggling 7,788-metre (25,550-ft) summit straight from its base at only just over 2,000 metres (6,500ft).

From Hunza, the KKH accompanies the Hunza river as it squeezes through rocky defiles on its way to joining the Indus to the south. Just off the highway, the old fort at the village of **Chalt** is a reminder of the presence of the British in the area at the end of the 19th century. The British used Chalt as an important outpost of the Gilgit Agency. The garrison here provided support for expeditionary forces visiting the *mirs* of Hunza and Nagar in a bid to gain allegiances in the face of the much-feared advance of the Russians over the Hindu Kush at the height of the Great Game. The neighbouring village of Nilt was the scene of the final battle in 1891, by which all resistance to the British presence was crushed.

Gilgit

Situated at an altitude of 1,500 metres (5,000ft), Gilgit has always been a

BELOW LEFT: Mount Rakaposhi.
BELOW: Hunza's terraced fields.

TIP

A number of tour operators based in Gilgit will help organise trekking trips to Fairy Meadows and beyond. The most obvious one is Fairy Meadow Tours, based at the Jamal Hotel on Airport Road. It maintains its own chalets and tents on the meadows.

prosperous market town. With the establishment of links to China around 2,000 years ago, it was strategically placed to become an important trading centre along the Silk Road. Today it remains the focal point for the northern region of Pakistan, where the tradesmen of Central Asia and the plains to the south still meet. Since the opening of the KKH the volume of goods and people passing through has increased dramatically; the influx of outsiders has brought much development but also exacerbated long-standing sectarian tensions between Shia and Sunni. The sound of the call to prayer from Gilgit's main mosque has a strange echo in this mountain environment as do the drums and clarinets of the local band attending the afternoon polo game. Polo fans come from across the world to watch Gilgit's team play against their arch-rivals, Chitral, at the **Shandur Pass**, the world's highest polo ground.

Baltistan

Rakaposhi may have the world's highest uninterrupted mountain face, but the Karakoram mountains are at their most unyieldingly dramatic in the region of **Baltistan** to the east, where the giant rock and ice spires of the inner Karakoram culminate in K2, the second-highest mountain in the world at 8,611 metres (28,250ft). No less than five of the world's 14 peaks over 8,000 metres (26,250ft) are clustered here at the head of the thundering Baltoro Glacier. The main centre of Baltistan, **Skardu**, can be reached along the daunting "Skardu Road", which follows the Indus as it recedes eastwards from the KKH just south of Gilgit, slicing its way through some of the most forbidding country on the planet. For more details about the valleys and mountains of Baltistan and how to access them, *see* the *Insight Guide to Pakistan*. Suffice to say here that this region also played a role in Silk Road history. To the west of K2, the Mustagh Pass was an ancient crossing used by local tradesmen crossing from Yarkand to Skardu, from where caravans would continue to Srinagar and Kashmir. Away to the east, out of Pakistani territory in northern

BELOW: polo match at the Shandur Pass.

A Passion for Polo

Polo actually originated in Central Asia and was developed into a competitive sport by the Persians. It spread to southwest Europe, where it eventually died out, and also east to the north of the Indian subcontinent, which is where the British rediscovered it. Polo in the Northern Areas has assumed its wildest and most untethered form. The unbelievably daredevil horsemanship of the players is almost matched by the bravery of the spectators who line the ground atop a low wall from which the ball, hit around at amazing speeds, rebounds into play. The pace of the game is controlled by the music, which increases in pitch as the contest continues. The horses have got to be admired for staying the pace.

The game used to be played all over the Northern Areas, but can now only be seen in those areas still wealthy enough to scrape a team together. It is still played in Gilgit and Chitral and some parts of Baltistan. The only rule seems to be that there are six players to each side, though even this seems to be overlooked on occasion. The first game of the season always comes with the Spring Festival towards the end of March. The old practice of sacrificing a goat and using the head as the ball has all but died out, but judging by the way the ball is hit around the ground it seems that it may still symbolise the skull of the devil.

Ladakh, the Karakoram Pass joined Yarkand with Leh, another important link in the Silk Road network of communications.

Nanga Parbat

The road follows the Indus south from Gilgit until it is forced west by the giant bulk of **Nanga Parbat**, whose 8,125-metre (26,656-ft) summit towers an awesome 7,000 metres (23,000ft) above the river. The huge dimensions of this mountain confirm that while not being quite the highest peak in the world it is undoubtedly the largest. Standing at the very edge of the monsoon belt, Nanga Parbat (Naked Mountain) always receives the final onslaught of the storm. It is the snow, the avalanches, the collapse of ice and the yawning crevasses on its faces that have led to the mountain being renamed the Killer Mountain, as numerous expeditions have found to their cost. Access from the north side is via a rough jeep track from the Rakhiot Bridge, which goes as far as the village of Tato. From there it's a short trek up to the lush pastures of **Fairy Meadows**, where the whole of the North Face confronts the senses in a scene of unrivalled grandeur. For the experienced trekker, the flanks of Nanga Parbat provide unequalled possibilities: at 5,400 metres (17,700ft), the Mazeno Pass provides access to the southern part of the mountain and the Rupal Valley, above which a sheer face soars an awesome 4,500 metres (14,800ft) to the summit.

Rock art

West of Nanga Parbat, the KKH enters the forbidding gorges of Indus Kohistan, but before that, above the river near Chilas, is one of the greatest collections of rock art anywhere in the world. Engraved on boulders, more than 30,000 **petroglyphs** and inscriptions in more than a dozen languages testify to more than 10,000 years of human history, from prehistoric depictions of animals and

ancient symbols, to Scythian merchants and pilgrims from Central Asia, to images of the Buddha and scenes from his life. Sadly, this is all due to be submerged under a huge lake that is to be created by the construction of the massive **Basha Dam** a little further downstream. The dam's foundation stone was laid in 2011 and it is expected to take 12 years to complete. Astonishingly, the dam will straddle the same major tectonic faultline – the collision zone between the Indian and Eurasian continental plates – that has been responsible for making this one of the most geologically unstable places on earth.

Taxila

The KKH continues through Kohistan, reaching the town of Besham before continuing down to the Thakot Bridge and across Hazara to the plains of Pakistan. Just to the west of **Rawalpindi**, the route that took pilgrims and merchants to and from China meets the route that brought invaders via the Khyber Pass to the Indian subcontinent: the Grand Trunk

TIP

If time and security allow, head for the glorious Chitral Valley in the far northwest of Pakistan. Dominated by Tirich Mir, the highest peak of the Hindu Kush, it is popular with trekkers and mountaineers, and just above Chitral Town is the Chitral Gol National Park, one of the most important sanctuaries for the elusive snow leopard.

BELOW: joined by a clear mountain torrent, itself a sizeable river, the mighty Indus slices its way through Kohistan.

Road ("GT Road") as the British came to call it. Persians, Greeks, Mughals, Afghans, as well as the British, all used this thoroughfare for their forays into and out of India.

Just at the intersection of this hugely significant crossroads lies the ancient Gandharan capital, **Taxila**, one of Asia's great archaeological sites, encompassing three major cities and numerous Buddhist *stupas* and shrines dotted around a delightful valley. The first city was Bhir Mound, where streets, lanes and foundations of houses and shops are still clearly visible. The later city of Sirkap was built on a grid layout by the Bactrian Greeks, Alexander the Great's successors, in about 180 BC, and highlights include Greek-style architectural details at the Shrine of the Double-Headed Eagle and the remains of the Royal Palace where St Thomas is said to have stayed in about AD 40 as he began his missionary work in India. There are also several temples in the vicinity with distinctly Greek-style features. Sirsukh dates from the Kushan period, the most frenetic time for

Taxila, when numerous monasteries such as Jaulian were constructed in the valley. The Dharmarajika Stupa, the largest in Pakistan, was reputedly built by Asoka to house the relics of the Buddha himself.

GT Road and Peshawar

Taxila lies close to the present capital of Pakistan. Also planned on a grid system, **Islamabad** represents the modern aspirations of the country, with some striking architecture and pleasant residential zones and shopping centres. To the east of neighbouring Rawalpindi, the GT Road heads towards India. Babur, who founded the Mughal dynasty came this way and proceeded to capture **Lahore**, which subsequently became one of the pearls of the Mughal Empire and is well worth a visit for the Fort, the Badshahi mosque and much else besides. In the other direction lies the ancient city of **Peshawar**, the capital of Gandhara under the Kushans and a place that oozes history. This is one of the great cities of Central Asia, and its bazaars are probably the most authentic along the entire Silk Road. Depending on the latest security advice, take a walk along the Qissa Khawani – the "Street of Storytellers" – and peek into the jewellery shops of Andar Shehr before taking in the colours of the wonderful sabz bazaar (vegetable market) or trying a delicious kebab on the Namak Mandi.

North of Peshawar, on the way to the Malakand Pass, is **Takht-i-Bahi**. This is considered to be the most complete of all the Gandharan Buddhist monasteries, occupying a stunning site on the side of a hill overlooking the plain.

Just west of Peshawar lies the **Khyber Pass** itself. You can hire a car or take the steam train that runs about twice a month. Whichever way you go, it's worth standing at the Khyber, between South and Central Asia, and contemplating the history that has unfolded here.

BELOW: in the Khyber Pass, looking down into Pakistan.

Gandharan Art

It is surprising to find remarkable examples of ancient Buddhist art in the Islamic countries of Pakistan and Afghanistan.

Gandharan or Graeco-Buddhist art is the result of the fusion of Classical and Buddhist cultures in Afghanistan and, to a lesser extent, Pakistan and northern India, created from the time of the conquests of Alexander the Great until the arrival of Islam in the 7th century AD. Initially under the patronage of the Graeco-Bactrian kings (250–125 BC) in Bactria and Sogdiana, and then the Kushan emperors (c.30–230 AD), artists and architects created devotional and municipal works that drew heavily on Buddhist traditions but also had a classical twist. This ancient fusion has created a unique style.

Gandharan art focuses heavily on the person of the Buddha. Episodes in his life, including his childhood, teaching, miracles and death, were exquisitely carved using a variety of media, usually bluish schist or stucco. Although the Buddha was the primary focus in these scenes, there were also supporting appearances from bodhisattvas and Maitreyas.

The living Buddha had explicitly forbidden images of himself. Despite this, the most significant contribution that Gandhara made to the development of Buddhism was the transformation of his image from an abstract symbol to representation in human form, a process that dates to the beginning of the 1st century AD. Early representations of the Buddha as the *chakra*, or wheel (symbolising the wheel of law), and the *triratna*, or trident (symbolising the three pillars of early Buddhism), changed to a new image, that of an idealised teacher.

Cosmopolitan ideas

Gandharan art was very much a result of the confluence of Silk Road ideas in cosmopolitan Afghanistan. The country's historic exports of lapis lazuli, rubies and other precious stones, and also its numerous communications routes to the surrounding countries, made it a veritable trading hub. Patrons and artisans alike were influenced by the latest fashions and developments in style and technique. Thus in Gandharan art we see syncretic depictions where the Indian Buddha, or another local figure, is shown wearing Roman dress and with the hairstyle of a classical general. Gandharan art was transported along the Silk Road to China and Tibet by pilgrims and merchants. It remained little known in the West, until its "discovery" at Dunhuang and elsewhere by European archaeologists following in the wake of the Great Game. Key artefacts are now preserved in the collections of the British Museum, Musée Guimet, the National Museum of Pakistan and Peshawar Museum, the largest such assembly in the world.

Some of the greatest Gandharan artefacts have proved to be too large to remove from the rocks in which they were carved or the cities where they were constructed. The survival of others has been determined largely by chance. Long-abandoned monasteries and stupas have been left to crumble, while the archaeological site of Taxila and the Takht-i-Bahi, both UNESCO World Heritage Sites, have been well-preserved. Numerous other examples have not been so lucky: most famously, the remarkable Buddhas of Bamiyan and Jehanabad were damaged irreparably by Taliban iconoclasts.

RIGHT: Buddhist ruins at the Jaulian Stupa and Monastery, Taxila.

AFGHANISTAN

Sitting astride the Silk Road at the heart of Asia, Afghanistan has an extraordinary cultural heritage: from bustling Kabul to the now ghostly niches of Bamiyan; from the mountains of Badakhshan to the ancient cities of Balkh and Herat.

In recent years Afghanistan has become synonymous with the troubles of the world, from the unfinished business of the Cold War to the "War on Terror". But for most of its history, the country has been referred to as "the crossroads of Asia", a cosmopolitan centre where Central Asia, the Indian Subcontinent and the Middle East all meet.

Afghanistan has played a crucial role in the development of culture and empire, from a crucible for Buddhist ideas under the Kushans, to pride of place in the Timurid renaissance alongside Samarkand and Bukhara. It has also proved a tough nut for other empires to crack, including the British and Russians – only Genghis Khan truly made his mark here.

Modern Afghanistan is struggling to outgrow its history. Newly democratic, the baggage of its recent past violently refuses to let go. Swathes of the south are no-go areas due to the Taliban insurgency, and while the rest of the country tries to move forward out of desperate poverty, anyone planning a visit will need to keep a close eye on events for the foreseeable future.

THE KHYBER PASS

The border post at Torkham (Towr Kham) would be a nondescript sort of a place, were it not for its location at one end of the fabled **Khyber Pass**. The pass is mostly on the Pakistani side, from where you get a sense of the strategic importance of this winding mountain corridor.

The road from Torkham leads to the old Mughal city of **Jalalabad**, famous for its oranges and poetry. The region was important to the Buddhist Kushans, and you can still make out the cliff-side caves that served as monks' retreats on the far side of the Kabul River on leaving town. Near Jalalabad are the ruins of the ancient monastery

Main attractions

KABUL:
  KABUL MUSEUM
  BABUR'S GARDENS
  CHICKEN STREET
  BIRD MARKET
  TIMUR SHAH'S MAUSOLEUM
MINARET OF JAM
HERAT:
  OLD CITY
  FRIDAY MOSQUE
  CITADEL
  SHRINE OF HAZRAT ALI

LEFT: children in the town of Balkh.
RIGHT: *naan* bread at a Kabul bakery.

ENTERING AND LEAVING AFGHANISTAN

It's been a while since Afghanistan was the hub of the old overland trail. Most cross-border routes are fairly straightforward in terms of paperwork, but all require you to check the security situation before attempting. (See Travel Tips, page 405, for more information on transport in Afghanistan.)

The Khyber Pass between Peshawar in **Pakistan** and Kabul is the iconic route into Afghanistan. The road through Pakistan passes through the Tribal Areas, so travellers require a permit and armed guard, obtainable in Peshawar from the Home and Tribal Affairs Office. Across the border at Torkham, plentiful shared taxis rush to Kabul.

A brand-new road means that it's possible to travel relatively quickly from Mashhad in **Iran** to Herat, via the border at Islam Qala, either by shared taxi in stages, or direct buses between the two cities.

The border at Gushgy north of Herat is open, but entering **Turkmenistan** you'll need to be met by an official guide.

The border at Hairatan near Mazar-e-Sharif across the Amu Darya (Oxus) River to Termiz in **Uzbekistan** is open to all travellers holding visas. A new bridge at Shir Khan Bandar makes the **Tajikistan** border crossing north of Termiz a straightforward affair, with onward transport available to Dushanbe. There are two crossings in Badakhshan, at Ishkashim and Khorog. Both lead into Tajik Gorno-Badakhshan, which requires a special permit to travel, which must be arranged at your embassy or in Dushanbe prior to travel. The border at Khorog is not open to vehicles.

of **Hadda**, an important and beautiful pilgrimage site reduced to rubble by Soviet bombardment in the 1980s.

Continuing from Jalalabad, the road rises through the **Tangi Gharu** gorge, before levelling out onto the Kabul Plain, and beginning its approach to the capital.

KABUL

Recently ravaged by war, Kabul has a long history of being fought over. The ancient Persians and Greeks had outposts here, the Kushans turned it into an important trading spur on the Silk Road, while the city was a Hindu outpost for several centuries before the arrival of Islam. It was the Mughal Empire (and in particular its founder, Babur) that made Kabul great, although it took the creation of modern Afghanistan in the 18th century to turn it into a capital.

Modern Kabul remains the vital heart of the country, but it has struggled after the shattering bombardments it suffered during the civil war of the 1990s. Its population has soared, and infrastructure has been unable to

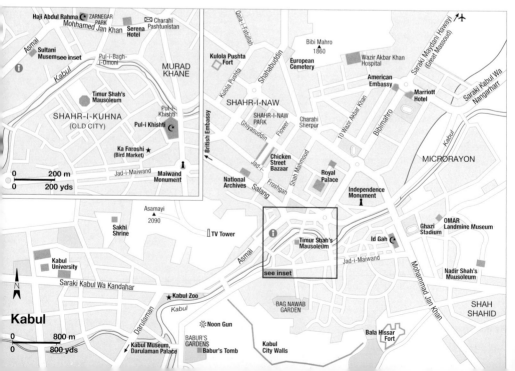

keep pace. There are signs of great poverty and wealth rubbing up against each other everywhere, from begging war widows to the profusion of new glass buildings. Security barriers are a sign of the times, as an often-weary population wonders which direction Afghan politics will carry them next.

Kabul Museum

In the 1970s the **Kabul Museum** (open daily 8am–4pm; admission fee) was one of Asia's best museums, and its diverse collection of artefacts from Greek coinage, Buddhist statuary and Islamic art was almost entirely collected from within the country. During the civil war the museum was looted mercilessly, and virtually razed to the ground. The Taliban smashed much of what remained.

International aid and the dedication of its staff have allowed a modest rebirth. The refurbished building has displays dedicated to several periods of Afghan history, most notably a large collection of wooden statuary from Nuristan. Other items include several Gandharan statues (some recently restored), coins and a huge carved marble mosque basin. Most of the museum's greatest remaining treasures, such as the Bactrian gold hoard from Shiberghan and many of the Bagram ivory carvings, have yet to be exhibited publicly in Kabul, but have toured museums in Europe and the US.

Opposite the museum is the empty shell of **Darulaman Palace**, once the royal residence but gutted during the civil war.

Babur's Gardens

First laid out in the 16th century, the hillside park of **Babur's Gardens** (open daily 8am–sunset; admission fee) is thought to be the world's oldest extant Mughal garden. The emperor Babur (see page 248) was highly enamoured of Kabul, and dedicates much of his memoirs, the *Baburnama*, to descriptions of the city and its gardens.

The garden had been reduced nearly to scrub, and it has undergone a massive renovation project. The old marble channels that send water cascading down the garden's terraces have been restored, and there has been plenty

Afghanistan's eastern border with Pakistan is regarded as illegitimate by many Afghans, who refuse to recognise the 1893 Durand Line drawn by the British that bisected the Pashtun heartland.

BELOW: view over Kabul from the Fort in Shar-e-Naw.

TIP

A particularly idiosyncratic Afghan souvenir is the "war rug". It first appeared after the Soviet invasion, but carpet-makers have twisted traditional designs to incorporate images such as the AK-47, tank, bomber plane and even the collapse of the Twin Towers and arrival of NATO forces.

of replanting. The central terrace holds an old pavilion erected by Ami Abdur Rahman Khan. Above this is a white marble mosque, erected by the Mughal emperor Shah Jahan. Finally, and overlooking all of western Kabul, is Babur's surprisingly modest grave.

Also on the top terrace is the Queen's Palace, used for music and theatrical performances. The slope the gardens sit on is part of the Shir Darwaza mountain ridge that helps split Kabul in two. Above Babur's grave, and slightly to the north, is the **Noon Gun** lookout point, from where you can see most of the city, and also the **City Walls** with similarly remarkable views.

Sultani Museum

Within the grounds of the unremarkable **National Gallery**, the Sultani Museum (open daily 8am-4pm; admission fee) is a private collection housing more than 3,000 well-displayed artefacts. Opened in 2004, the pieces – which include beautifully illustrated Korans, stone-work and gold – were all acquired by gold and antiques dealer Ahmad Shah Sultani while in exile

BELOW: Pendant found at Tillya Tepe.

in London during Afghanistan's civil war. Once security improves, Sultani plans to give his collection to the nation, and those items that came on to the international art market having been looted from the National Museum have already been returned.

Central Kabul

Near the heart of the central Shahr-i-Naw District, **Chicken Street** is Kabul's most famous bazaar street. Once a hub for travellers following the Hippie Trail, its shops can sell you anything from lapis lazuli to carpets and antiques of varying ages.

The occasionally green Shahr-i-Naw Park is just north of Chicken Street, and beyond this is the **European Cemetery** (usually open dawn–dusk; donation requested). Built for the British dead of the Second Anglo-Afghan War, more recent additions include memorials to NATO soldiers killed in Afghanistan since 2001. The celebrated Silk Road archaeologist Aurel Stein is also buried here.

Tucked into the alleys off Jad-i-Maiwand near the blue-domed Pul-i

Scythian Gold

The excavations by Victor Sariandi in 1979 at the Scythian royal burial ground of Tillya Tepe in northern Afghanistan unearthed more than 20,000 gold ornaments, many lavishly decorated with turquoise and lapis lazuli. Yet, with the Soviet invasion looming, archaeologists were forced to hastily abandon the site, without having time to properly catalogue their discoveries. Artefacts were later removed to Kabul and secured in the vault of the National Bank by officials in the late 1980s. The keys to the vault were distributed among a number of trusted diplomats.

In 1996 the Taliban captured Kabul and attempted to force their way into the national vault, but without success. The bank manager even resorted to breaking off his key in the vault door in an attempt to thwart the looters. During the invasion of Afghanistan by US-led forces, the Taliban made one last attempt to get their hands on the treasure by planting bombs on the vault door but were thwarted at the last minute. In 2003, after the Taliban had been expelled from Kabul, the safety of the Bactrian Hoard was finally secured.

A new museum is currently under construction in Kabul to house the Scythian gold and, in the meantime, highlights from the collection have been exhibited in the US, France, UK and Japan.

Khishti Mosque, the **Bird Market** (Ka Faroshi) is one of the few corners of the city where life carries on as if the upheavals of recent history had never occurred. Keeping birds is one of the great Afghan pleasures, and flocks of doves are flown recreationally above the city every evening.

If you continue through the lanes north to the Kabul River, you'll reach **Timur Shah's Mausoleum**. The son of Ahmad Shah Durrani, Timur Shah moved the Afghan capital to Kabul in 1772, and his tomb has been the centre of recent renovation by the Aga Khan Trust for Culture.

Landmine Museum

Sitting near the foot of Teppe Maranjan hill, the OMAR **Landmine Museum** (open daily 8am–3pm; donation requested) is one of the most unusual in Asia. It exhibits mines and ordnance recovered from every corner of Afghanistan, reminding visitors that the country is still one of the most heavily mined in the world. The museum also doubles up as a training centre for mine-disposal experts, and there's a roll call of OMAR staff killed during demining procedures.

Overlooking the museum, **Nadir Shah's Mausoleum** sits broken-faced on the top of Teppe Maranjan. The dilapidated mausoleum is the last resting place not only for Nadir Shah, but also his son, King Zahir Shah, who died in 2007, having returned from exile as "Father of the Nation" after the collapse of the Taliban.

BAMIYAN AND POINTS WEST

Driving north from Kabul to Bamiyan, the highway passes through the wide and fertile **Shomali Plain**, an area famous for its fruit, particularly grapes. Just above the plain is the ancient village of **Istalif**, whose artisans make appealing blue-and-brown pottery.

From the turning off the main highway at Charikar, the Bamiyan road deteriorates considerably in quality but the views, as it winds deeper into the mountains, are increasingly dramatic. Just before entering the Bamiyan Valley, the road meets the confluence of the Bamiyan and Kalu rivers, overlooked by the red fort of **Shahr-e-Zohak**. High on the cliffs, its capture by Genghis Khan from its Muslim Shansabanid rulers was the preface for the Mongol capture of the whole region.

Bamiyan first flourished as a Kushan trading centre in the first centuries of the Silk Road, and reached greater prominence after their eclipse. Under the White Huns in the 6th century, Bamiyan's Buddhist art tradition produced its greatest masterpiece, the two giant **Buddha statues** carved out of the valley's cliff wall. Bamiyan never fully recovered from its devastation by the Mongols, and when its Hazara inhabitants (who claim descent from those invaders) adopted Shia Islam, it placed Bamiyan further from the mainstream of Afghan history.

Destroyed by the Taliban in 2001, the massive empty niches of the Buddhas entirely dominate the town. Known

BELOW: the extraordinary Minaret of Jam.

Around AD 630, the Chinese Buddhist pilgrim Xuanzang passed through Bamiyan. He noted that, at the time of his visit, it was a flourishing Buddhist centre "with more than ten monasteries and more than a thousand monks", while both Buddha figures were "decorated with gold and fine jewels".

BELOW: the Bamiyan Valley and its eerily vacated Buddha niche.

simply as the Large and Small Buddhas, the statues stood 55 metres (182ft) and 38 metres (125ft) high, respectively. The rough figures were cut from the soft sandstone, covered with mud plaster for detailing and finally painted. The faces wore gilded masks, although (like most of the decoration) these didn't survive to the modern period.

A series of passageways, monks' cells and rooms have been dug into the cliffs surrounding each niche. It is possible to climb to the top of the Large Buddha's "head", but it's only for those who have a head for heights.

On one of the hills on the southern edge of Bamiyan there is a scramble to the remains of another fort ruined by the Mongols, **Shahr-e-Gholghola**.

Four hours west of Bamiyan are the mineral lakes of **Band-e-Amir**, a series of five lakes of a nearly magical blue. The most accessible is Band-e-Haibat, held in 10-metre (33-ft) -high limestone walls laid down over millennia to form a natural dam. It's an Afghan tradition to drink the water for its curative powers, and there is a popular lakeside shrine for blessings.

Minaret of Jam

It's possible to traverse central Afghanistan from Bamiyan to Herat by road, although the rough crossing is only for the stout-hearted. Yet virtually in the geographical centre of the country is one of its greatest treasures (and its first UNESCO World Heritage monument), the **Minaret of Jam**.

To reach the minaret takes almost three days of solid driving from Bamiyan through wild mountain terrain, yet its isolation is one of its attractions. Built in the 12th century by the Ghorids, the minaret stands around 65 metres (215ft) high, tucked into the crags of a narrow valley, the last visible symbol of the ancient city of Firuzkoh.

The minaret is a triumph. It has three tapering levels, each decorated in brick arranged into Koranic verses, with one band of blue glazed tile. The lovely views from the top reveal the minaret's hidden location (in a gorge where two rivers meet), which explains why the outside world was unaware of its existence until the 1930s.

An early start from Jam will take you on a long day's drive to Herat.

Demolition Experts

The Bamiyan Buddhas survived for 15 centuries in the remote vastness of the Afghan Hindu Kush. Neither the ravages of time, nor the conquering armies of Islam – not even the scourge of Genghis Khan – had laid them low. Islam first came to Bamiyan with the conquest of the valley by Ya'qub ibn Leys in 871. Subsequently iconoclasts painstakingly cut the eyes and nose off the large Buddha image, but left the figure standing. In the 17th century, the Persian ruler Nadir Shah is said to have "broken the legs" of the larger Buddha, though – this is less clear – the right leg, slightly bent at the knee, remained intact, while the left appeared to have sheared away at the hip.

In its prime, the figure was partly clad in stucco, and cords were draped down the body to simulate the folds and drapes of the robe. Although once brightly painted, time rather than religious vandalism had caused most of the outer coat to fall away, leaving rows of holes which once held wooden pegs to stabilise the stucco. Reports suggest that these very holes were packed with dynamite by the Taliban during their demolition.

By any standards, these towering images formed part of the common cultural heritage of mankind. Viewed in this context their destruction by Taliban was truly a mindless crime.

Make a point of breaking the journey at **Chist** (Chest-e-Sharif) to see the domed Ghorid tombs, contemporaries to the minaret.

Herat

The western city of Herat, near the Iranian border, is a classic Silk Road city. Its roots predate Alexander the Great, and it flourished as a trading city continuously from the Kushans to the modern period, pausing only in the 12th century when the Mongol terror razed it to the ground.

Herat's heyday was during the Timurid Empire. Following Timur's death, Herat became joint capital of the empire with Samarkand. Shah Rukh and his queen Gowhar Shad packed the city with artists, poets and architects, turning Herat into one of the great cities of the age, before the rot of decadence set in. Herat played an early part in the Great Game when it was besieged by the Persians and Russians in 1838. An army mutiny 130 years later, suppressed with Soviet help, was an early marker on the path to full invasion.

The medieval **Old City** forms the core of Herat. Two great monuments are testaments to its history. The **Friday Mosque** (closed to visitors for Friday prayers) is deservedly the most celebrated in the country. The style echoes the Timurid revival, with its massive minarets rising from the ground flanking the great vault of the main prayer hall. The stunning mosaic work is from the mosque's own tile workshop, and restoration is ongoing. On the street running along the northern side of the mosque is a small workshop making traditional Herati blue glass.

A fort has sat on the mound of the **Citadel** (open daily 8am–5pm; admission fee) since Alexander's time, although the current incarnation is Timurid. The complex was a military base until 2005. Now visitors can enjoy the fine views from the massive battlements.

Looking north from the Citadel lets you pick out the tottering minarets of the **Musalla Complex**. This was Gowhar Shad's finest commission, almost completely levelled by the

BELOW: the Friday Mosque in Herat.

In the mountains of Badakhshan.

British in the 1880s to clear a line of fire against a feared Russian invasion. Five minarets, their tiling almost lost, still stand, near the queen's tomb with its distinctive melon-ribbed dome.

An excellent new road leads from Herat to the Iranian border, and work has recently begun on a rail link to Mashhad. The roads northeast to Mazar-e-Sharif (a three-day drive via Meymaneh), or to Kabul via Kandahar, are not safe for overland travel.

ACROSS THE NORTH

In Silk Road days a caravan trail headed across the steppe of Afghanistan's north, via the Wakhan Corridor from China. This thin tongue of land separating Afghanistan from Tajikistan and Pakistan is part of the mountainous region of Badakhshan; a Wakhan permit and permission from the border police are required to go there but can be arranged in half a day in Ishkashim.

Most visitors enter the Wakhan across the border from Tajikistan at **Ishkashim**, where there are a number of small guesthouses and the opportunity to collect a trekking guide. Two of the most popular areas for trekking, though still unfrequented by international standards, are **Noshaq Base Camp**, Afghanistan's highest peak, and routes heading east from **Sarhad-e-Boroghil**, the small town where the Wakhan's only road ends. For the hardy traveller, the Big and Little Pamir ranges offer the greatest – and most remote – scenery, including **Chaqmaqtin Lake**, Curzon's **ice cave** and even the possibility of spotting the elusive snow leopard or Marco Polo sheep in the **Wakhjir Pass.**

It is possible to trek on horseback and also to hire horses and yaks, in addition to human porters, to carry baggage. Accommodation is under canvas, in basic guesthouses or with Kyrgyz families in their yurts at **Bozai Gumbaz**.

Ai Khanoum

From **Ishkashim** the road leads westwards to the regional capital, **Faizabad**, which has a diverting bazaar, and then to **Kunduz**, where some of the country's best *buzkashi*

Lapis Lazuli

The mines of the northeastern province of Badakhshan have been producing lapis lazuli for export for over 7,500 years. Until recently, they were virtually the only known source of this semiprecious stone. Afghan lapis was an important trade good, found in everything from ancient Egyptian jewellery and Tutankhamun's funeral mask to the blue pigments of Michelangelo's paintbox. The Romans even ground it up to use as an aphrodisiac.

More recently, the lapis mines (found at Sar-e-Sang, south of Faizabad) were an important source of hard currency for the *mujahideen* fighting the Soviets, and for the anti-Taliban Northern Alliance. Usually flecked with pyrites and veins of white calcite, the best-quality stone is sold in Kabul and lacks such impurities.

horses come from. An interesting diversion leads north to **Ai Khanoum**, presumed to be the site of Alexandria-Oxiana, founded by Alexander in 327 BC and the easternmost Greek city in the world. On the confluence of the Kokcha and Amu Darya rivers, the site itself was terribly looted during the civil war. The nearby town of Khoja Bahauddin has several Greek column capitals from Ai Khanoum in the town roundabouts.

Mazar-e-Sharif and Balkh

The city of **Mazar-e-Sharif** is the largest in the north, and is dominated by the turquoise domes of the **Shrine of Hazrat Ali**, dedicated to Muhammad's son-in-law, reputedly buried here. Rebuilt many times since the original was erected in the 12th century, the blue shrine has every square inch covered in patterned tiles. The shrine complex is the focus of Afghanistan's Nauroz celebrations every 21 March, and an important pilgrimage site.

Mazar-e-Sharif is a relatively recent city, which has overshadowed the much older **Balkh**, just 20km (12 miles) away, only since the 19th century. Balkh was the home of Zoroaster in the 6th century BC, and hosted Alexander's wedding party three centuries later. It grew rich off the Silk Road, and boomed again after the Arabs (who called it "the Mother of Cities") in the 9th century AD. Despite a Timurid renaissance, Balkh never fully recovered from the violent attentions of Genghis Khan, and is a small town today.

In a park in the centre of Balkh is the 15th-century **Shrine of Khoja Abu Nasr Parsa**, with its distinctive Timurid ribbed dome and delicate painted interior. To the north are the massive ramparts of **Bala Hissar**, Balkh's ancient fort – almost as big as the town itself. The view gives a good idea of the scope of the city walls, sections of which still stretch out to encompass the houses and fields. Down a track on the opposite

side of the main highway in farmland is the 9th-century **Noh Gombad Mosque**, the oldest in Afghanistan. Although it is little more than a handful of columns and walls, the intricate stucco decoration clearly points to the Arabian traditions of the people who brought Islam to the country.

THE ROAD TO KABUL

To the north of Mazar-e-Sharif the road leads to the Uzbekistan border at Termiz. Heading south to Kabul, the road passes through the Shomali Plain before crossing the mountains through the dramatic artery of **Salang Tunnel**, built in the 1960s. North of the pass, before the junction town of Pol-e-Khomri, is Samangan, where the rock-hewn stupa of **Takht-e-Rostam** is Afghanistan's most important intact Kushan site, dating from the 4th century AD. The massive structure has been dug out of the limestone, surrounded by a trench and topped with a carved reliquary. Just below the *stupa*, a series of caves has also been cut from the rock to form airy monks' quarters.

BELOW: tilework on the Shrine of Hazrat Ali, Mazar-i-Sharif.

TURKMENISTAN

Known as the Central Asian hermit kingdom, Turkmenistan is an isolated police state, but one which offers the fascinating ruins at Merv and Konye-Urgench, the burning gas craters at Darvaza and a unique people who still cling to traditional animist beliefs.

Main attractions
MERV
KONYE-URGENCH
ASHGABAT

Turkmenistan is the most isolated of Central Asia's five republics. Largely comprised of desert, a formidable chain of mountains separate it from its southern neighbour Iran. The economy is largely based on oil and natural gas from the Caspian Sea.

An authoritarian dictatorship, Turkmenistan remains largely shut off from the outside world. Media are tightly controlled and speaking against the government a serious crime. Restrictions have been loosened since the death of President Niyazov in 2006, but his successor Berdymuhamedov shows little sign of bowing to international pressure on human rights.

Turkmenistan maintains tightly controlled borders and strict visa regulations and requires that all foreign visitors have an official minder, factors that keep through traffic to a bare minimum. But it wasn't always so: 800 years ago this barren land was at the epicentre of Silk Road trade.

Merv

Merv, located in the southeast, was Central Asia's lynchpin for caravan traffic. Founded in the 3rd century BC, the city changed names several times, at one point being called Alexandria, after Alexander the Great. Invaders also took turns occupying the city but in periods of peace Merv was renowned for its artisans, scholars and religious institutions. Buddhists and Nestorian Christians mixed with practitioners of Manichaeism and Zoroastrianism.

From the 11th century the city was known as Marv-i-Shahjahan – "Merv, Queen of the World." Indeed, it may have been the largest city of this epoch, with a population exceeding 200,000. It all came to a sudden end with the Mongol invasions – the city was ruined and up to 90 percent of its residents put to the sword.

LEFT: the Presidential Palace in Ashgabat.
RIGHT: ruins at Merv.

Little remains at Merv but crumbling walls, toppled buildings and shards of glazed pottery offering a faint reminder of ancient glories.

Konye-Urgench

Konye-Urgench, in the northwest of the country, suffered a similar fate. Located along the northern branch of the Silk Road that travelled towards the Caspian Sea, this was the ancient capital of Khorezm.

In the 12th century Konye-Urgench was renowned for its libraries, mosques and madrassas, but its glory days ended with the Mongol onslaught. After a six-month struggle, the city fell when the invaders diverted the waters of the Amu Darya to flood the streets. The most striking sight among the ruins is the Gutlug Timur minaret, a 60-metre (197-ft) structure. There is an important Sufi shrine, the Mausoleum of Najmuddin Kubra: colourfully dressed pilgrims pray in front of its tilted facade.

From Konye-Urgench the road heads south across the Karakum Desert towards the Turkmen capital Ashgabat. The burning gas craters of Darvaza are a must-see en route. They are best seen at night when the fiery inferno ignites the desert sky.

Ashgabat

Old Ashgabat (Asgabat) was levelled in an earthquake on 6 October 1948 and rebuilt in a thoroughly Soviet manner. But President Niyazov also left a significant imprint on the city, gracing it with lavish government buildings, Las Vegas-style fountains, vast museums and self-glorifying statues. In the evenings visitors can catch a drama, opera or Turkmen concert at one of several marble-domed theatres.

Traditional Turkmenistan can still be found at the delightful Tolkuchka Bazaar, selling everything including fabulous Turkmen carpets and shaggy sheepskin caps. It's also a great place to meet the locals, sip tea and haggle with modern day Silk Road traders.

ENTERING AND LEAVING TURKMENISTAN

To get a tourist visa, visitors must first acquire a Letter of Invitation (LOI), which can be issued by a travel agency. The LOI can take two to three weeks to process. Travellers with tourist visas must be accompanied by a licensed guide while moving about the country – travellers on a transit visa, which typically lasts five days, may not. Pre-arranged guides are required to meet their clients at the border. Visitors on transit visas can take a taxi or public bus from border points to the nearest town, where regular bus services are available.

Domestic air tickets are heavily subsidised so a flight anywhere in the country is never more than US$15; but book as far ahead as possible. A US$25 departure tax must be paid when flying out of Turkmenistan.

Irregular ferry services link the port of Turkmenbashi to Baku, **Azerbaijan**; it is advisable to arrive with one or two days left on one's visa as ferries only sail when full of cargo. Overstaying a visa means a trip back to Balkanabat to apply for an extension.

The southern route runs Bukhara–Merv–Sarakhs. A north-to-south route runs Nukus–KonyeUrgench–Asgabat–Merv–Sarakhs. The Sarakhs exit point has connections to Mashhad in **Iran**.

From Ashgabat the closest border to **Iran** is Gaudan/Bajgiran. There is 20km/12 miles of no-man's-land between the borders. A taxi connects the border posts for around US$4. To leave Turkmenistan at Serkhetabat, walk the 1.5km/1 mile no-man's-land to the **Afghanistan** border. From Torghundi, it's a two-hour drive south to Herat.

WESTERN ASIA

The least visited of the Silk Road sections,
Western Asia nonetheless holds plenty in store
for travellers, from the ancient cities of Iran to
the sensational souks of Aleppo and Damascus.

Traders along the western end of the Silk Road pass over countless layers of history, in a region referred to as "the anvil of civilisation" by historian Sir Leonard Cottrell. This is land touched by ancient Egyptians, Hittites, Sumerians, Assyrians, Babylonians, Greeks, Phoenicians and the later Persians and Romans, who developed and extended skills of warfare, communication and architecture. Despite being best known for the westward trade in silk, there was an equal exchange of goods and knowledge from Western Asia going east, with items including gold and other precious metals, ivory and glass. Add to this the domestication of the camel from Arabia and the flow of Christian and Islamic ideas from the Holy Land, and it can be seen as a true trade of commercial goods and ideologies. The era of the Silk Road was just one of the many historical highlights of the Near East that greatly influenced the world we live in today.

Deserts and rivers

Compared to China and Central Asia, the distances involved are relatively small, yet there is a surprising variety of terrain. Approaching the Mediterranean, the deserts are smaller, the mountains less intimidating, but this is a region where political diplomacy and economic manoeuvring play more important roles.

Any map will show the importance of the two great rivers of Mesopotamia, the Tigris and the Euphrates, which run almost parallel from the Turkish mountains to the head of the Persian Gulf. The Euphrates, in particular, could be exploited by traders, as it virtually connects the Indian Ocean to the Mediterranean Sea. It was a natural waterway that became more important in the later centuries of the silk

PRECEDING PAGES: the Emir Mosque in Isfahan. **LEFT:** a Natura coffeehouse in the Old City of Damascus. **RIGHT:** gateway at ancient Persepolis.

trade, when the sea route from China was more practical than the arduous overland crossing, which often became embroiled in petty disputes for control. Even the Syrian Desert was not as tough to cross as those further east, thanks to natural water springs, particularly at Palmyra.

Stability of empires

Under a series of great warrior-kings in the 5th and 6th centuries BC, the Persian Empire was the largest the world had ever seen. During this period the development

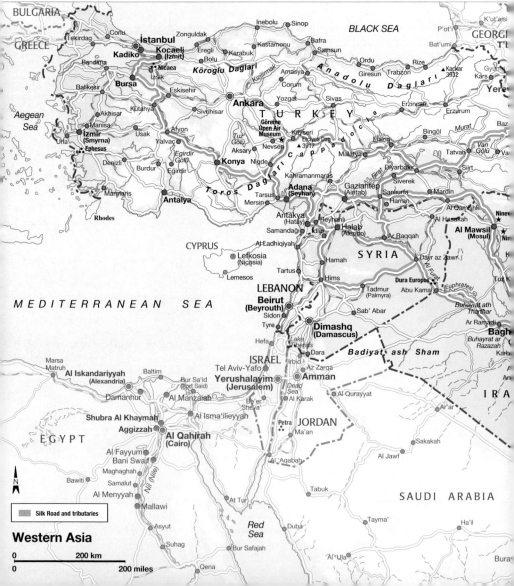

of the Royal Road from Mesopotamia to Turkey literally paved the way for the later Silk Road, but it was the controlled distribution of water into arid areas that was their greatest legacy. The Persian *qanat* system of underground channels, carrying precious water from mountain to desert, was copied throughout Asia and beyond, and was arguably the single most important factor in making the route initially viable and then sustainable for over a thousand years.

Following the collapse of Greek control, the Parthians re-established Persian

authority, and it was they who became the first distant consumers of silken fabric. But once the Romans saw those Parthian silk banners unfurled in battle, a greater market was opened that almost ruined the Roman economy. The stability of the Parthian Empire for 350 years allowed the Silk Road to develop and link China with Rome. This stability and the creation of federations enabling traders to pass safely from one territory to another helped trade. Small independent kingdoms such as Palmyra existed purely because of the trade, and their magnificent desert ruins give us a glorious insight into life and death 2,000 years ago.

Silk routes

Approaching the western end of the Silk Road, traders had to narrow their choice of routes into corridors of trade across northern Iran. Hemmed in by the desolate Iranian plateau on one side and the rugged mountains at the southern end of the Caspian Sea, the route worked its way through to the ancient city of Rey, now a suburb of modern Tehran. From here a seasonal northerly route struck directly towards the Black Sea and Turkey via Tabriz, but was more difficult and only passable in summer. The main highway, however, ran west through the Zagros Mountains, before dropping down into the fertile valleys of the Tigris and Euphrates rivers. More trade goods now appeared from the south, having travelled along the parallel sea route around the Indian Ocean before entering the Persian Gulf, where Palmyrene agents and envoys had established themselves. During its heyday, the desert city of Palmyra controlled all this trade and even became wealthy enough to be the destination of silk in its own right. The ancient cities of Damascus, Aleppo and Antioch were the western crossroads of other trade routes that brought frankincense and myrrh from Arabia and gold from Africa. All this was then shipped around the Mediterranean, from a series of ports stretching from Tyre in the south to Seleucia Piera in the north. The final destination was never a fixed point and Western Asia and the Mediterranean in general were the ends of the Silk Road, at various entrepôts where goods from many destinations were packaged and redistributed.

PRECEDING PAGES: the Euphrates near Dura Europa; a Persian rose.
ABOVE, FROM LEFT: music on the move; carpet in the bazaar. **TOP RIGHT:** Damascus after dark. **RIGHT:** in the souks of Aleppo.

Travel today

With the exception of Turkey, none of these countries is particularly easy to travel through, with negative media images and coverage keeping the majority of tourists well away. However, at the time of writing, it is only Syria that is a no-go area; even parts of Iraq are opening up to visitors. Iran maintains its tough stance against the West, but once inside the country it is possible to travel around relatively freely and follow the route from the Turkmenistan border to Turkey, and almost completely to Iraq. However, the political situation can change rapidly and it is necessary to liaise fully with a local agency in Iran.

With the wonderful vibrant cities of Damascus and Aleppo, Syria should be full of tourists, but political violence paralysed the country in 2011–12, preventing even domestic tourists from enjoying what their country has to offer. There is also a small section of Turkey that lies across the border from Syria, well off the tourist trail despite containing ancient Antioch, that is currently tense due to the influx of Syrian refugees.

Lebanon always seems to have its own completely different set of problems, making travel there uncertain – for months the country is open for business, but suddenly a serious incident occurs, often from beyond its own borders, and everything changes. The situation in Lebanon is improving. This is testified by the flow of foreign investment into Beirut. For most of the time, it is a question of timing your visit wisely and keeping abreast of the current situation via reliable news sources.

IRAN

Ancient cities, some still thriving in the modern age and some abandoned millennia ago, testify to the key role played by this proud land between East and West. Names like Persepolis and Isfahan resonate down the centuries.

The Iranian plateau has effectively controlled the overland Silk Road, with the only other option to go north around the Caspian Sea. Persian rulers, in whatever form, have always had the power to help or restrict this trade. For centuries they produced very little themselves, knowing that luxury goods would pass across their land, from which they could grow wealthy. But it was not just overland trade from the East that made Persian cities prosperous: their unique position meant that they could also benefit from the parallel sea trade.

The Persian Gulf is the closest that the Silk Road comes to the open sea and was often used as a method of bypassing Central Asia completely. From the earliest times even simple boats could navigate along the Indian Ocean coastline into the Gulf and land their goods on Persian shores. Great inland cities such as Isfahan, Yazd and Shiraz developed along these routes linking the Gulf ports with the Silk Road proper, trading in silk and other valuable Eastern commodities such as spices. This trade control has always been envied from outside, making Persia a land to invade and control.

But sometimes the Persians themselves became invaders, using the Royal Road of Darius to stretch their borders to the Adriatic and then east to India. After the short interlude of Alexander and his successors, the Parthians improved roads and water supplies, acting as the linchpin between Rome and China. Sassanids continued to improve the infrastructure, but their constant battles with the late Romans and Byzantium left them too weak to resist the Arab conquest in the mid-7th century. Islam became the dominant religion and Arabic its language.

Main attractions

RIBAT CARAVANSERAI SHERAF
CHESHMEH ALI
SHRINE OF SHAH ABDEL AZIM
TEHRAN:
  CARPET MUSEUM
  GLASS AND CERAMICS MUSEUM
  GOLESTAN PALACE COMPLEX
  TEHRAN BAZAAR
  HOLY SHRINE OF IMAM KHOMENINI
PERSEPOLIS
PASARGADAE
ISFAHAN:
  IMAM KHOMEINI SQUARE
  IMAM MOSQUE
  CHEHEL SOTUN PAVILION
KASHAN
TABRIZ: BLUE MOSQUE

LEFT: Bazaar-e Vakil in the heart of the city of Shiraz. **RIGHT:** detail on the entrance to the Sheikh Lotfollah Mosque in Isfahan.

ENTERING AND LEAVING IRAN

You must have a visa for Iran before you arrive, and visitors will usually be met by a car, driver and guide. You are more likely to have your visa application accepted if it is submitted via an agent. Tourist itineraries must be agreed in advance and overnight accommodation booked by an Iranian agent, but there is nothing to stop you travelling alone for a few days. (See Travel Tips, page 432, for more information on transport in Iran.)

There are two crossings from **Azerbaijan** at Astara and Jolfa. The train from Jolfa can get you to Mashhad and Tehran, via Tabriz, as can the bus, but with no chance of getting out at any of the sites en route.

There is a weekly train from Tehran to Istanbul in **Turkey**, via Lake Van. A Turkish visa can be obtained at the border. Planes, trains or buses can get you to Tabriz, beyond which it is buses or shared taxis to the border at Bazargan, near Maku.

Visitors are not allowed near the Iraq border and will be turned back. It is possible to fly back to Tehran from Kermanshah.

The border crossing to **Pakistan** at Taftan is relatively straightforward. There are regular buses and minibuses from Zahedan to Mirjaveh, from where there are numerous connections to the border.

The border with **Afghanistan** is open on the road between Mashhad and Herat. Crossing is relatively simple.

The main border crossing to Ashgabat in **Turkmenistan** is at Bajgiran. This involves the use of taxis to and from the border.

Turks, Assassins, Mongols and the even more barbaric Timur ravaged Persia for centuries, until the stability of the Ottoman Empire and its Persian counterparts – the Safavids – brought an age of enlightenment, culture and art. But still the invaders came, this time from Afghanistan and Russia, until eventually the British ruled through puppet shahs. The Islamic Revolution of 1979 in part shapes the country as we see it today, but it by no means defines Iran or the Iranian people.

Relations between Iran and the rest of the world remain strained. Ongoing allegations of spying have led to the closure of first the British Council and then the British Embassy in Tehran, though this is most likely to be in retaliation for international pressure and sanctions related to Iran's nuclear programme. President Ahmadinejad remains in power despite widespread allegations of election fraud in 2009 and subsequent protests both in Iran and amongst the Iranian diaspora.

Despite the political tensions, Iran is still a fascinating and largely safe country in which to travel. Historical sites are well-preserved and the museums of Tehran world-class. The Iranian people are cultured, hospitable and often keen to distance themselves from the hardline policies of their government. Visitors are required to show respect for Islam in their dress and behaviour, and avoid criticising the regime, but travel in Iran is nonetheless an exceptionally rewarding experience.

THE BORDER TO DAMGHAN

The modern road from the Turkmen border towards Mashhad is busy with trucks and containers, many carrying expensive stolen cars from Europe and the Emirates across the Persian Gulf to Russia and Central Asia where buyers are less concerned about their provenance. This road follows some sections of the old caravan routes, but eases itself around the rolling hillsides and craggy escarpments. Being traversed on foot and with animals, the old Silk Road was more direct, with many old caravanserais still to be found in the desolate countryside, the first of which is known as **Ribat Caravanserai Sheraf**, one of the largest and most important. This recently renovated *ribat* (meaning "fortified caravanserai"), 6km (4 miles) from the village of Shorlog, lies serenely in a wide valley of barley crops, with the old Silk Road clearly visible through a narrow gorge a few kilometres away. Built in 1140 by the last Seljuk ruler, Sanjar, it is an impressive display of the art of brick construction and decoration, much of which would have been covered by stucco and paint. Inside are vast camel stables, drinking troughs, rooms for fodder and baggage areas, all worked with intricate brick designs and Kufic inscriptions.

This region is home to groups of semi-nomads of Baluchi and Afghan stock, interbred with local families, who sometimes assist with the trafficking of opium from Afghanistan. In spring these gentle mountains are often layered by thin blankets of cloud and completely covered in a haze of vivid reds, yellows and purples from a carpet of wild flowers. This is the time when herders prepare their animals to move into the mountains for three months of grazing, the men living on bread, sheep butter and the occasional hunted boar.

Old and new Silk Road transportation lie side by side where the old caravanserai at Marhee lies ruined and unexcavated alongside the modern railway bridge. This new line was built in 1993 to link Mashhad with Sarakhs and promote trade with Central Asia along the old Silk Road.

Mashhad

Mashhad was a small village called Noqan when the Silk Road passed to the south, but after it became the resting place of Imam Reza, the Eighth Imam, it gained importance. Born in Medina in AD 765, Imam Reza was a direct descendant of the Prophet Muhammad and died in suspicious circumstances while with the Abbasid Caliph Ma'mun. Imam Reza was

The word "paradise" comes from pairi-dis, meaning "a round wall", describing the luxurious Persian walled gardens of pomegranates, almond trees, damask roses and turquoise-tiled pools of water.

BELOW LEFT: the 12th-century Ribat Caravanserai Sheraf.
BELOW: Mashhad and the shrine of Imam Reza.

Persian Carpets

Persian carpets are known around the world for their quality of workmanship, richness of colour and intricate designs.

C arpet-making has been at the heart of Iranian culture for hundreds, if not thousands, of years. Carpets can be valuable documents covering particular periods of everyday life. Persians even wrote love poems about their carpets.

Persians pioneered the art of carpet-weaving, with a history stretching back nearly 2,500 years. The sheep and goats herded by the nomads of the Persian plateau provided the basic materials with which to make carpets. Increased workmanship and quality turned them from simple doorway and floor protection into works of fine art, brought to the attention of kings and rulers, who commissioned more luxurious versions. But unless specifically preserved, an old carpet soon disintegrates, unlike metal plates or coins, so there are seldom remains of carpets from archaeological digs.

Documents from these periods indicate that, for example, the floor of the tomb of Cyrus the Great at Pasargadae was covered with luxurious carpets. A thousand years later Chinese texts mention the amount of carpets looted from Ctesiphon and then later by the Arabs. One of these is the famous Winter Carpet, made for Khosro I (AD 531–79), woven in silk, gold, silver, pearls, rubies and diamonds, and later described by Muslim scholar al-Tabari. It is also known as Khosro's Spring because it represented the most beautiful spring garden, designed to make the king forget about winter. The Islamic garden (*char bagh*) is a popular design for carpets, with weavers replicating their geometric layout and symmetry.

When the Seljuk Turks entered Persia in the 11th century, they introduced the Turkish knot. In East and West Azerbaijan and Hamadan where Seljuk influence was greatest, the Turkish knot is still used to this day. The palace of the Ilkhan leader Ghazan Khan (1271–1304) in Tabriz is reputed to have had paved floors covered with precious carpets. Two of the most famous carpets in the world come from this region and are now in the Victoria and Albert Museum in London and the Los Angeles County Museum. Dated 1539 and known as the Ardebil carpets, the design is typical of Tabriz, when it was still the Safavid capital.

The height of Persian carpet-weaving was during this Safavid Dynasty in the 16th century. Trade with Europe prospered, and the new capital, Isfahan, became one of the greatest cities in the world, with skilled weavers creating wonderful silk carpets with gold-and-silver thread.

Towards the end of the 19th century under Qajar rule, trade with Europe revived and a new period of craftsmanship and carpet-making flourished. Today, carpet-weaving is the most widespread handicraft in Iran and still a huge industry, with the major centres being Hamadan, Isfahan, Kashan, Na'in, Tabriz, Tehran, Shiraz, Yazd, Mashhad and Qom. The Carpet Museum in Tehran (see page 320) has some of the finest examples of the last 450 years.

LEFT: a carpet for sale in Isfahan. **ABOVE:** the Chelsea carpet.

buried next to Ma'mun's father, the famous Caliph Harun al-Rashid, and the shrine became a centre of pilgrimage for Shia Muslims (Mashhad means "place of martyrdom").

Every road seems to lead to the golden minarets and dome of the **Mosque of Gohar Shad**, which lies in the heart of the city. As the holiest site in Iran, any visit must be under strict conditions and tight security – women must wear the *chador* and photography is forbidden. The Foreign Visitors Centre will explain the site to non-Muslims, and a visit is truly memorable. The entrance to the library is a large sculpted piece of artwork showing a gold-and-blue bound Koran sitting upon a pile of books. Inside is a wonderful wooden replica of the first mosque of the Prophet Muhammad – underneath a palm tree in the Arabian Desert. The pure golden entrances to the courtyards are reassuringly dull in lustre, not gaudy, exuding exquisite workmanship of the highest quality. Cream-and-gold tiling creates harmonies with turquoise and dark-blue mosaics that are simply amazing.

The minarets on each side of the mosque are stunning examples of tilework – cream-coloured with small diamonds of dark-blue detail. The light-blue dome is a masterpiece of simplicity with yellow detail spelling out the creed of the faith. The broken mirror work reflects every point of dark blue and purple light from the doorways and countless ornate chandeliers, impossible to focus upon, within the vast shimmering, dazzling landscape. Huge car parks and access roads running below the complex show the massive organisation associated with the shrine. All this is not just paid for by charitable donations, but also the theological colleges, carpet and sugar factories, transport companies, shops and land around Mashhad, under the direction of the clerics.

The village of **Tus**, 18km (11 miles) away, is famous for the tomb of the poet Hakim Firdausi (or Ferdowsi) who lived here in the 10th century. His great poem, *Shahnameh* ("Epic of the Kings"), is still read today after 1,000 years. His tomb takes inspiration from the great Cyrus tomb at Pasagardae,

Many slogans on Iranian buses are variations on "Dear Lord, make this a safe journey for us, praise be upon Muhammad and his tribe".

BELOW: the face of the Ayatollah Khomeini on an Iranian bill.

Caliphs and Imams

These two words appear in many different contexts, and it is often difficult fully to understand their uses. Caliph means "successor" (of the Prophet Muhammad), and as such is the title of a Muslim chief, civil and religious ruler. The Omayyid Caliphate was the dynasty of Sunni rulers based in Damascus just a few years after the death of Muhammad.

An imam can be a religious leader within a mosque or community, or one of the leaders of the Shia sect known as the Twelve Imams, greatly revered in Iran, Iraq, Syria and Lebanon. An *Imamzade* is a shrine or tomb honouring one of the Twelve Imams or one of their descendants. The great split in Islam occurred at Karbala in AD 680, when Caliph Yazid killed Imam Hussein.

but here you can go underground to pay respects amid marble friezes of scenes from Firdausi's poem.

Sang Bast

South of Mashhad, traders heading west along the Silk Road stopped at the caravanserai of **Sang Bast**, now a prison and rehabilitation centre for drug addicts and HIV sufferers. Drug addiction is a growing problem in Iran. Situated on the main road and railway looping around the mountains from Mashhad to Neishabur, Sang Bast also has the remains of a mosque and minaret, the oldest in Khorasan province, and the tomb of Arsalan Jadheb, governor of Tus in the 10th century. This rich agricultural land, all owned and controlled by the clerics in Mashhad, was famous for the quality of its produce, originally irrigated by a system of *qanats* stretching from the continuous line of mountains to the north. But much of this land now lies fallow due to poor rainfall and the illegal drilling of wells, which has reduced the watertable level by some 20 metres (66ft), making the *qanats* useless.

BELOW: a herdsman near Sang Bast.

Nieshapur

One of the most famous locations on the Silk Road used to be **Nieshapur** (**Neyshabur**), but the town is now just a shadow of its former self, having been destroyed and rebuilt many times. Started by the Sassanids under Shahpur I (hence the name), it became a wealthy trading city and thriving intellectual centre, thanks to a good water supply from the mountains. The main caravanserai in the city centre has been heavily restored, offering a glimpse of the past, with a natural history museum, atmospheric teahouse and artisan shops. In the 10th and 11th centuries, as the capital city, it produced some of the finest ceramics and pottery ever made in Persia. Omar Khayyam, one of the world's most famous poets, lived here, working as a mathematician and astronomer, devising an extremely accurate solar calendar called the *Jalali*. He died in 1125, and his modern tomb looks like a giant net being stretched towards heaven. Across the road a new scientific and cultural centre is dedicated to him.

Persian Poets

As Islam spread beyond its Arabian roots, new forms of interpretation and verse appeared in the Persian language, later cherished around the Islamic world for its brilliance, richness and scope. One of the original poets was Firdausi, born in AD 940, who wrote *Shahnameh* (Book of Kings), the national epic of 60,000 couplets.

The 11th-century poet Omar Khayyam is the most renowned of the Persian poets through his work *Rubaiyat*, which is popular in many cultures, while the Sufi *qazals* of Jelaleddin Rumi still resonate with Western followers. Sa'adi became the greatest poet of the medieval period with *Golestan* (Rose Garden), but even he was eclipsed by Hafez in the 14th century, whose great body of work is lovingly quoted today.

Down the road is the tomb of Farid Ud-Din Attar, a 12th-century Sufi mystic who was eminent in the fields of literature and philosophy. This area is Old Nieshapur, of which almost nothing remains, but nearby excavations at Shadyakh have revealed a span of occupation from the Arab conquest. West from here are the wide open plains that catch the full force of seasonal thunderstorms heading towards the distant northern mountains.

Damghan

Damghan was a major trading centre connecting with the route from Hormuz on the Gulf to the Caspian Sea. Not only has it suffered like Nieshapur from invaders, but it is also prone to violent earthquakes. The oldest section of town is Tepe Hessar, with evidence back to Zoroastrian times and the recently discovered body of a woman buried 7,000 years ago. Meanwhile, in the centre of the pleasant town is possibly the second-oldest mosque in Iran, known as the Tarikhaneh (www. tarikhaneh.com), meaning "House of God", which dates

back to the 8th century. The stout columns and simple lines of the prayer hall and courtyard are dominated by the 25-metre (82-ft) Seljuk minaret, of which more is said to be underground, including the original doorway.

SOUTH TO THE GULF

As the main Silk Road passed across the northern Iranian plateau, there is an obvious trade route connection to the south. Before reaching the Mediterranean, the closest that the Silk Road comes to the open sea is the Persian Gulf, connecting with the sea trade running between Asia and Africa. Incense and spices had already been traded around the Indian Ocean for over 1,000 years before silk appeared.

The islands of Hormuz and Qeshm have always been important maritime centres, controlling the entrance to the Persian Gulf through the Strait of Hormuz. Directly inland from Hormuz is the town of **Bam**, an important textile centre from the time of the Arab conquest, with an impressive 2,000-year-old citadel. This mud structure controlled the overland

The Tarikhaneh Mosque in Damghan is one of Iran's oldest mosques. It was built in the 8th century, but its structure reflects earlier Sassanid styles.

BELOW: detail on the tomb of Farid Ud-Din Attar, Nieshapur.

TIP

The Yazd Water Museum documents the digging of *qanats* up to 40km (24 miles) in length and explains the many water systems of the region.

route from southern Pakistan but was badly damaged in the December 2003 earthquake, which killed over 43,000 people. Sympathetic restoration is under way. Skirting around desert and some of the highest peaks in Iran, the difficult route reaches the city of **Kerman**, where the great mosque and the atmospheric Regent's Bazaar are the main attractions. Poor agricultural land has meant that the taxing of trade and weaving carpets have always been the main industries.

Yazd

A look at a map of Iran shows **Yazd** in the centre of the country – a meeting place of trade routes from every corner. Throughout its long history, the inhabitants have prospered from trade and have a great Silk Road tradition. But it has suffered from a less than ideal location on the southern edge of the Dasht-e Kavir Desert, which the main Silk Road skirts to the north.

The large Jama Mosque has the typical Yazd double minarets, cavernous prayer hall, central courtyard and deep *qanat* access. The entranceway is

similar to the remarkable facade of the Amir Chakmaq, used as a grandstand for watching the religious plays during the holy month of Muharram. In this square are also some of the best examples of *badgirs* – wind-towers that catch the slightest breeze to cool houses in the stifling summer temperatures. In recent years, some of the ornate merchants' houses have been modernised into hotels and restaurants and are well worth a visit.

Yazd is the best place in Iran to see the influence of modern Zoroastrianism. Not far from the city centre is the serene setting of the Ateshkadeh (Fire Temple), where the holy flame is said to have been burning for over 1,500 years. The pleasant rose garden is a good place to view the beautiful bright-blue-and-yellow symbolic representation of Ahura-Mazda, above the doorway.

One of the peculiarities of this faith is the ancient method for disposing of dead bodies. In order not to contaminate the earth, air, fire or water, the dead bodies of the faithful are laid out in Towers of Silence – walled areas on hilltops where scavenging birds and animals slowly reduce them to bones. There are two such towers on the outskirts of Yazd beyond the Ateshkadeh. A dome-covered well which received water by *qanat* from the surrounding mountains is one of the buildings at the foot of the hills, where the bodies were initially prepared before being taken up to the top to be torn apart. Restrictions on such practices by the Imams has meant that any of the 25,000 or so Zoroastrian followers of Yazd have to be buried in the modern cemetery nearby. Have a wander and look at a newly prepared grave, to see how the hole is lined with concrete to stop contamination of the earth.

From Yazd there was a longer but easier route to the northwest around the Dasht-e Kavir Desert through Na'in and Kashan (both still important carpet-weaving centres). But the most direct route towards the Caspian

BELOW: intricate tilework on the Jameh Mosque.

Sea and the main Silk Road was heading due north across the inhospitable desert to Damghan, a feasible crossing in spring and autumn.

WEST OF DAMGHAN

West of Damghan lie the southern folds of the rugged Elburz mountains. Routes either climb over some tough terrain near the 5,671-metre (18,605-ft) Mount Damavand (Iran's highest peak) or veer further south along the edge of the Dasht-e Kavir Desert. This strategically important narrow corridor of land between the desert and the Caspian Sea has always physically separated eastern and western Iran, while at the same time linking them together by trade.

Roughly 20km (12 miles) beyond Damghan, a large caravanserai can be seen beside the road at Qodratabad, from where a strange cylindrical mountain rises above the hills to the north. This is Gerdkuh, "the round mountain", as mentioned by early poet Firdausi and site of a famous Ismaili fortress belonging to the Assassins (see page 329).

Shahr-e Qumis

Midway between Damghan and Semnan is Qosheh, from where small mounds can be seen away to the left, generally agreed to be the scant remains of the Parthian capital of **Hecatompylos** (meaning "hundred gates"). Now called Shahr-e Qumis, a restored caravanserai can be inspected along with rough buildings identified as a royal palace and remains of a possible Tower of Silence. Proper excavation in future years might reveal this to be an important centre along the Silk Road.

Leaving these deserted plains, the route passes through the wealthy provincial capital of **Semnan**. Much of the modern success of Semnan comes from mining in the surrounding mountains, mainly the extraction of silicates (insoluble metal salts) needed for the production of cement, brick

and glass. A monumental gateway is all that remains of the citadel, and the Jama Mosque dates from the time of Timur's son Sharokh in 1424.

A restored caravanserai at the foot of a low pass near the village of Lasgerd shows how well protected the traders were. West of here eroded and mined mountains expose their multicoloured bands of striations from creamy browns to rusty purple, beyond which rises Mount Damavand. The pass at Eyvanakey is thought by many experts to be the **"Caspian Gates"** mentioned by classical writers, but for the modern traveller it is notable for a series of reddish-brown bluffs that look like giant heaps of melted chocolate pouring down from the mountains into the meandering streams. The fast highway sweeps into modern Tehran past the new suburbs, but in antiquity the main centre in the region was Rey, 12km (7.5 miles) to the southeast of the capital.

Rey

Below a large isolated mountain, Rey still manages to keep its identity

BELOW: the Silk Road passes Mount Damavand, Iran's highest peak.

An Imamzade is a shrine or tomb honouring one of the Twelve Imams or one of their descendants.

despite the onslaught from the expanding capital. Rey certainly has a long history, with evidence of occupation back to Neolithic times and pottery dated to the 5th millennium BC. These early settlements were centred around the famous **Cheshmeh Ali** water spring (still producing bottled mineral water today), where there is a 19th-century Qajar period bas-relief and a section of early Islamic mud-brick wall, now rebuilt.

This was an important centre for the Medes, and some experts believe that Zoroaster himself was born here in the middle of the 7th century BC. The city appears to have been abandoned

and rebuilt several times, and used by Parthians and Sassanids, before becoming an Abbasid town under Caliph al-Mahdi, whose son Harun al-Rashid was born here in AD 763.

The main attraction today is the Imamzade of three great religious figures, known as the sacred **Shrine of Shah Abdel Azim**. The golden dome is flanked by two golden-topped minarets featuring beautiful spiral tile designs. Gold doors decorated in blue lead straight to the tomb of Hussein, great-grandson of the Second Imam, Hassan, and inside is some of the finest inlaid woodwork to be found anywhere. A series of prayer rooms

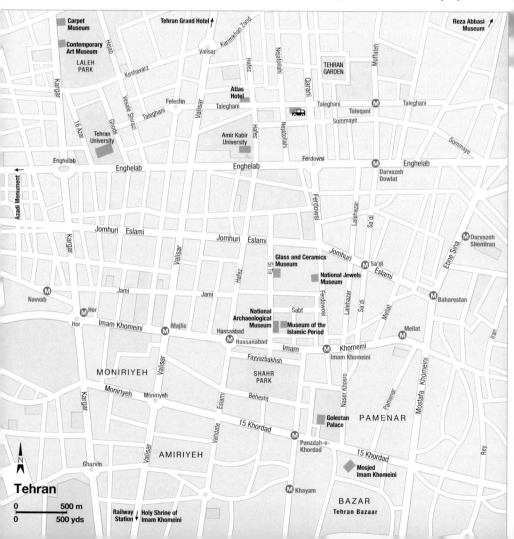

Tehran

0 ____ 500 m
0 ____ 500 yds

and antechambers lead around the complex, each more dazzling than the last. Every step across the marbled floor to the tomb of Taher, a descendant of the Fourth Imam, and Hamzeh, brother of the Eighth Imam, shifts the viewpoint of a million pinpoints of pastel-coloured lights from the fabulous angled mirrors. Muslims come here for a variety of reasons: some are deep in prayer or concentration, while others read the Koran or local newspapers, all in the most ornate of surroundings.

If you are allowed inside, this is a fine alternative to the holier shrines at Mashhad or Qom. Women must wear the *chador* and then have access to their own section. The gateway opposite the main entrance leads into the long covered atmospheric bazaar under a series of brick arches with skylight domes. Across town is the strange bulk of the **Toghrul Tower**, a tower tomb dating from the middle of the 12th century. It might once have had a conical roof, but now, open to the elements, it is like walking into a giant cooling tower.

Away from the centre is a mountain slowly being eaten away by massive mining projects, which once had a Zoroastrian Tower of Silence on top. Below is the 10th-century **Shrine of Bibi Shahrbanu**, a place of pilgrimage especially for women, containing the body of the mother of Sajjad, the Fourth Imam. She was the eldest daughter of the last Sassanid king, Yezdegird III, who was defeated in his series of battles against the invading Arabs. He escaped to Merv and died in 651, whilst his son Firuz is said to have continued east to seek asylum at the court in China. His daughter Bibi Shahrbanu remained behind to become the wife of the Third Imam, Hussein, grandson of the Prophet Muhammad. A nearby cave celebrates the legend that when Bibi Shahrbanu was in danger of losing her life, she prayed to God, who opened the mountain for her to enter for safety, and then closed it behind her.

TEHRAN

The capital, Tehran, has only been a major centre for the last two centuries,

BELOW: the Cheshmeh Ali spring in Rey.

Tehran's futuristic Azadi Monument.

BELOW: the ornate facade of the Golestan Palace.

and here we start to lose the flavour of the East and find more Middle Eastern and Arab influence. The northern suburbs are home to wealthy apartments, exclusive designer shops and restaurants. Higher up the mountainside, they look down on the traffic and smog choking the rest of the city.

Museums

Tehran is the place to see the best items unearthed along the Silk Road in Persia, and most organised tours include city sightseeing, visiting a selection of relevant museums.

The **National Archaeological Museum** (www.nationalmuseumofiran. ir; open Tue–Sun 9am–6pm summer, 9am-5pm winter; admission fee) contains world-class objects from important sites around the country, such as the famous frieze of Darius, fragments of the *Tachra* staircase taken frassanidom Persepolis and the imposing bulk of the 2nd-century BC bronze warrior. Salt was an important commodity, as shown by the discovery of a miner from the 3rd or 4th century BC, in a salt mine near Zanjan.

The **Museum of the Islamic Period** (open Tue–Sun 9am–6pm summer, 9am–5pm winter; admission fee) is nearby and houses both temporary exhibitions and a permanent collection. The illustrated Korans and textiles are particularly fine.

While many world-famous museums display a single Persian carpet, such as the Ardabil carpet in London, the **Carpet Museum** (www.carpetmuseum.ir; open Tue–Sun 9am–5pm; admission fee) has an extensive collection of some of the finest Persian carpets, sourced from weaving centres such as Hamadan, Kashan and Tabriz. The styles of design include Garden of Paradise, Prayer Niche, Tree of Life, Zodiac, Hunting Scenes, Koranic and Historical Figures. Quality is indicated on the label by *radj* – the number of knots over a measurement of about 7cm (3 inches) – and varies between 30 and 120 knots. One of the oldest in the collection is a large blue-and-white carpet from Taft, near Yazd, dating from 1556.

Located downtown in the former Egyptian Embassy, the **Glass and Ceramics Museum** (www.glasswaremuseum.ir; open Tue–Sun 9am–noon and 1–7pm; admission fee) contains another fabulous collection of items from the Silk Road. Behind a beautiful facade and grand staircase are rooms dedicated to pottery, ceramics and glass stretching from the 3rd century BC to the 18th century AD. Here are 11th-century ceramic bowls from Nieshapur; the original 13th-century ceramic tiles from Takht-e Suleiman; and 12th-century pottery from Kashan and Rey decorated with Firdausi poems. The golden age of glass in Iran was around the 12th century, when decorative effects for necklaces, vases and bottles were produced by blowing into the mould, engraving, carving in relief and enamelling.

The **Reza Abbasi Museum** (www. rezaabbasimuseum.ir; open Tue–Sun 9am–5pm; admission fee) has a great selection of items starting with a

wonderful bronze horse bit of the 8th century BC, through to later illuminated manuscripts and folios. On the third floor are the oldest objects including Achaemenid gold plates and beakers, a Parthian gold-and-turquoise necklace, as well as an amazing gold *rhyton* (royal drinking vessel) in the shape of a horse's head. Walking through the display, you can observe the development of simple ancient daggers into elaborate axe heads and finally to beautiful inscribed ceremonial swords of the Sassanid period. The second floor is dedicated to everyday items influenced by the Islamic period – bowls, tiles, figures, vases and plates. On the first floor is the beautiful calligraphy of manuscripts and books decorated with gold and lapis lazuli, and early versions of famous Persian poems such as *Golestan* by Sa'adi and *Shahnameh* by Firdausi.

Not to be missed is the **National Jewels Museum** (open Sat–Sun and Tue 2–4pm; admission fee). The equivalent of the British Crown Jewels are kept in a high-security vault under the central branch of Bank Melli, but only open to the public a few hours each week. Here are some of the most exquisite items in the world, including jewellery and royal regalia of the utmost quality. Of special note is the Darya-e Nur, the largest pink diamond in the world, and the Globe of Jewels, an extraordinary piece of craftsmanship that uses over 50,000 precious stones set into a mounted golden sphere. Oceans are depicted by emeralds, the land as rubies, with certain countries like Iran and England indicated by diamonds. Bands of diamonds show the tropics.

Other sights

One of the city's most pleasant areas is the **Golestan Palace Complex** (www.golestanpalace.ir; open Mon–Wed, Fri-Sat 8.30am–3.30pm; admission fee), which is set around well-kept gardens in the centre of the city. The name translates as "Rose Garden". Not all the

buildings are open to the public and each requires a different entry ticket, but certainly worthwhile is the Marble Throne of Fath Ali Shah, used for the coronation of Reza Shah in 1925. The tall Shams al-Emirah tower, covered with colourful decorative tilework, stands beside art galleries and photographic archives.

Tehran Bazaar, the mother of all bazaars, is more than just a labyrinth of buying and selling. At crucial times in Iran's history, the power of the *bazaris* has helped to support or reject the ruling authority, and it certainly has a great influence over the national economy to this day. With no room to expand, rent at a premium and commuting a nightmare, many wealthy traders are today basing themselves in the more pleasant suburbs and doing all their business on the internet.

The **Holy Shrine of Imam Khomeini**, a newly constructed tomb for Ayatollah Khomeini, is situated outside the Martyrs' Cemetery for those killed in the war with Iraq. This massive building has a golden central dome, four minarets and four

A pottery statue from Lorestan in the National Archaeological Museum in Tehran.

BELOW: schoolgirls outside the mausoleum of Imam Khomeini.

The English word "cummerbund" comes from the Persian kamar-band, meaning waist sash.

outer blue domes. Past the X-ray and security checks is a vast hall with the tomb placed inside a large glass shrine, slowly filling up with money pushed through the panels. The whole area is a vast parkland and a popular place for visiting families and schoolchildren.

The **Azadi Monument** (open Sun–Fri 9am–2pm; admission fee) is a major landmark en route to the airports. This large modern gateway controls the routes to the west. A small museum and viewing platform can be accessed inside.

THE PERSIAN GULF

The Silk Road was not just for the overland transport of goods across Asia, as plenty of routes connected with trade coming by sea. The nearest access was with the Persian Gulf at the easily defended island of **Kharg**, 30km (18 miles) off the Iranian coast. Excavations have shown occupation for at least 5,000 years, and there are two large tombs similar to those at Palmyra in Syria. Kharg Island is still an important trading centre, but as one of the world's largest oil

terminals, access is restricted. To the north of the Gulf, trade also brought prosperity and wealth to a whole string of cities.

Shiraz

A major settlement even before Persepolis existed, **Shiraz** continues to be the great centre of Fars province. It developed after the Arab conquest and became the sanctuary of Iranian poetry and philosophy in the 13th and 14th centuries. The great poet Sa'adi was born here at the end of the 12th century and is said to have lived for over 100 years, during which time he travelled extensively around the Levant as a dervish and was even taken prisoner at one point by the Crusaders in Syria. A man from Aleppo paid for his release on condition that he marry his daughter, which left him far from happy, as retold in his most famous work, *Golestan* (Rose Garden).

Sa'adi is well known in the West – one of his verses even adorns the Hall of Nations entrance of the United Nations building in New York. But in Iran he is not venerated quite as much as the later poet Hafez – a name given to someone who can recite the Koran by heart. Born around 1320, Hafez wrote love verses that endeared him to the Iranian people and are still quoted and interpreted in everyday conversations today. Works of both poets flow lyrically with roses, love and wine – the famous Shiraz grape and wine are named after the city.

The compact **Nasir al-Molk Mosque** and the more central **Vakil (Regent's) Mosque** both have beautiful ceiling designs in the prayer halls. Throughout the day mottled colours sweep across the walls and floors as the sun passes the stained-glass windows. Driving north from Shiraz is probably the best opportunity for observing some of the semi-nomadic tribes, such as the *Qashgai*, who still migrate into the mountains searching out new pastures for their herds of sheep and goats.

BELOW: the prayer hall in the Nasir al-Molk Mosque, Shiraz.

Persepolis

The world-famous site of **Persepolis** (open daily 7.30am–7pm; admission fee) lies 45km (27 miles) northeast of Shiraz on the edge of the Marvdasht Plain. Founded by Darius I after he rejected nearby Pasargadae, it took a further 120 years of continuous building by his successors to cover the site that we see today. While the other capitals of the Achaemenid rulers at Susa, Babylon and Ecbatana were well known to the outside world, Parsa, as it was called at the time, was a secret ritual city. The important ancient Zoroastrian spring festival of *Naurozow Ruz* or New Year, was celebrated here. The entrance to the great city is through the Gateway of Xerxes, perched on the edge of the terrace, flanked by two human-headed bull colossi. Stepping between the colossi, notice the graffiti scrawled by visitors over the past 150 years, notably "Stanley – New York Herald 1870", presumably the year before he found Livingstone in Africa. On the left, now at ground level, are examples of the strange double-headed griffin capitals.

The tall, narrow entrance into the Hall of One Hundred Columns has some of the finest carvings to be seen anywhere; the fine detail on the clothing and footwear is remarkable. The famous **Apadana** staircase shows the conquered nationalities bringing offerings to the king, from Ethiopians and Libyans to Armenians and Indians. An explanation chart nearby helps to identify the peoples and their gifts including kudu, lions and Bactrian camels. The great Apadana, or Audience Hall, is laid out along the massive terrace, designed to accommodate over 10,000 people. Entry was originally through huge wooden doors covered with gold plate leading to a columned portico, and then the central hall of 36 columns with double bull protomes. The roof beams of Lebanese cedar were inlaid with ivory and gold, from which heavy curtains hung, the walls decorated with blue-and-yellow glazed tiles showing lions and bulls.

The compact **Palace of Darius** is decorated with exquisite carvings along the side of the lower courtyard.

SHOP

The bazaar in Shiraz is one of the liveliest in the country, with numerous sections radiating from the Bazaar-e Vakil in the heart of the city, but beware of pickpockets (both male and female) in the crowded thoroughfares!

BELOW: the remains of the Apadana Hall at Persepolis.

The mythological griffin figure known as Homa is the pagan guardian of travellers – and the company logo for Iran Air.

BELOW: relief of a Persian soldier at the entrance to the Hall of One Hundred Columns.

Again there are offerings being brought by conquered peoples, frozen in time, shown climbing the steps forever up to the palace. Returning towards the Apadana, the Tripylon has an excellent carving of Darius on his throne, with his son Xerxes in attendance. On the lower level is the museum, which has a unique collection of items peculiar to this site, such as an extraordinary 2,500-year-old bronze trumpet used in the *Nauroz* ceremonies.

Behind the Royal Treasury is a path up to the two rock-cut tombs overlooking the site. The tomb on the right is for Artaxerxes III, the one on the left for his father Artaxerxes II. Both are set back on a small platform, and each facade is carved with the winged symbol of Ahura-Mazda above the king worshipping before a fire altar. The views from these platforms across the entire terrace and Marvdasht Plain are superb. Having been used for over 200 years, the site was destroyed during Alexander's Persian campaign, but opinion is divided if this was deliberate or accidental.

Naqsh-e Rustam

Darius and his three successors are buried a few kilometres away at a place called **Naqsh-e-Rustam**. Only the Darius tomb has been positively identified, but the others are thought to be, from right to left: Xerxes, (Darius), Artaxerxes and Darius II. Below the tombs are panels of bas-reliefs from later Sassanian times, the most important of which is below the Darius tomb, showing Shapur I holding two captives, thought to be Roman Emperor Valerian and Philip the Arab. The "Cube of Zoroaster" that stands half buried in front of the tombs is probably not a fire temple, but possibly a deposit of holy texts or a resting place of the royal bodies before entombment.

Pasargadae

The earlier Achaemenid capital of **Pasargadae** (open daily 7.30am–7pm; admission fee) lies a further 80km (48 miles) to the north, and was the site of Cyrus' victory over Astyages the Mede in 550 BC. Aurel Stein is mainly associated with his work further east, but

Darius the Great

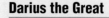

Following a period of unrest, the Achaemenids found their greatest leader in Darius, who ruled from 522 to 486 BC. During this time he extended the frontiers of the Persian Empire to Afghanistan, Ethiopia, Libya and the banks of the Danube. Tributes from all these peoples can be seen on the famous Apadana staircase at Persepolis.

Communications and movement of troops over such a vast territory was facilitated by the building of the Persian Royal Road, running from Persia to western Turkey, sections of which certainly evolved into the Silk Road. Rebellions were frequent and ruthlessly put down, but it is the battles with his Greek neighbours for which he is mainly remembered, for example when he was defeated at Marathon in 490 BC.

he excavated this site in 1934 and concluded that prehistoric communities were settled here at least 6,000 years ago. The most impressive structure is the remarkably well-preserved tomb of Cyrus the Great (559–530 BC), built like a small ziggurat and similar to Lycian tombs found in Turkey. Early historians tell us that the body of the founder of the Achaemenid dynasty lay in a gold sarcophagus on a golden couch, surrounded by treasure. The structure was later developed into a mosque and then a caravanserai.

Some distance away are the remains of the Audience Hall or Pavilion, with fragments of carved mythical animals and a trilingual inscription that reads "I, Cyrus, the King, the Achaemenid". Further still are the heavily supported walls of "Solomon's Prison", maybe a tomb or possibly a fire temple and forerunner of the one at Naqsh-e Rustam. Dominating this area is the citadel, known as the Throne of the Mother of Solomon, whose walls were possibly an early version of the Persepolis stone platforms, upon which a great temple was planned but

never completed. Having been superseded by Persepolis, Pasargadae seems to have retained some importance as a place to confirm a king's coronation. The names of early Islamic prophets like Solomon were sometimes attributed by local people to these ancient structures, in order to avoid destruction by the invading Arabs.

ISFAHAN

Roughly midway between the Persian Gulf and Rey is a highlight of any visit to Iran – **Isfahan** (**Esfahan**), one of the great cities of the world. Its name in Sassanid times was Sepahan (meaning "Place of the Army"), an oasis for caravan trade heading around the Dasht-e Kavir Desert. The fortunes of the city might simply have ebbed and flowed with the passing trade had it not been chosen by Shah Abbas to be his well laid-out capital in 1598. Armenians were brought from Jolfa on the Azerbaijan border to build the mosques and palaces and create the spacious new city. The developing Safavid Dynasty attracted European East India Company agents wanting

BELOW: the incomparable Imam Mosque, Isfahan.

Rose-water is a by-product of rose oil and is highly prized for its perfume. It is used in cosmetics but also as a delicate flavouring in Iranian cuisine.

to influence the court. This zenith of Persian art and architecture lasted for little more than a century and ended abruptly with the Afghan invasions, when Mashhad became the new capital instead. Isfahan slumbered until it re-emerged as the modern centre of the cotton-spinning and wool-weaving industry, and is now the second-largest city after Tehran.

The great open centre of the city is the **Imam Khomeini Square**, around which are the most famous grand buildings. At the southern end is the beautiful **Imam Mosque** with its ornate blue, turquoise and white stalactite work and honeycomb decoration on the porch. Through the imposing portal, the axis shifts by 45 degrees to allow the *mihrab* to be in line with Mecca, before facing the graceful twin minarets and the most beautiful turquoise-blue dome resting on a large circular drum with windows. The space inside this large *iwan* is impressive as is the incredible subdued blue-and-gold decoration on the inside of the cupola. When caught by the sunlight, a beam of golden light breaks the continual circle into a multicoloured peacock's-tail display. Beyond the galleries that surround the courtyard are madrassas, flower gardens and a winter gallery used in cold weather. This masterpiece of Persian art is a testament to the vision and commitment of Shah Abbas, who saw it completed within his lifetime.

On the eastern side of the square is the **Sheikh Lotfollah Mosque**, built at the same time as the Imam Mosque and named after a respected Lebanese scholar. Here the dome is a delicate cream with turquoise, black and white arabesque detail, which sits perfectly on the blue entrance portal. Again there is amazing stalactite work and delicate lettering above the doorway, which leads to a small corridor. There is no courtyard or minaret, just a simple, small prayer hall beneath the double cupola. The decoration is a series of blue–green ellipses receding into the golden centre, and is more harmonious than the Imam Mosque.

The western side is dominated by the tall **Ali Qapu Palace**, initially a monumental gateway into the royal palaces, which once stood behind. It is spread over six floors, and the grandest view is from the open pillared terrace from where the king would watch games of polo in the square. The throne room is full of frescoes, and towards the top of the building is the amazing "music room" whose intricately cut decorations aided the acoustics.

Beyond Imam Square

A couple of blocks behind the Ali Qapu Palace is the tranquil setting of the **Chehel Sotun Pavilion**. Twenty slender wooden columns on lion bases hold up an elaborate wooden ceiling stretching across an open terrace. The name means "40 columns" – which can be seen when the 20 are reflected in the elongated pool in front. Inside the throne room are large historical frescoes and other paintings depicting more intimate themes. A

BELOW: the great hall of the Chehel Sotun Pavilion.

similar ornate pleasure palace called Hasht Behesht (Eight Paradises) is a few blocks further south.

The northern entrance of the Imam Square leads into the maze that is the Esfahan Bazaar, a labyrinth of narrow covered alleys snaking through the suburbs. Here, under the high stone vaults, are some of the finest pieces of work from Persian craftsmen, each in its own section – finely engraved metalwork, gold and silver jewellery, delicate inlaid wood with mother-of-pearl and patterned fabrics.

Seemingly detached from the city-centre bustle is the quiet ambience of the **Friday Mosque** – a place truly to appreciate Islamic art and architecture. The low-key entrance is between a series of fabric shops, which eventually leads to the courtyard with four *iwans*. This is not a Safavid construction, but a sublime piece of work from the 15th-century Mongol–Timurid period that is more associated with destruction. The south porch, with two slender minarets on the left as you enter, has some of the finest mosaic work in the Islamic

world and became a template for later Safavid buildings.

Most of the Zayandeh riverbank area has been turned into pleasant gardens and walkways. A stroll across the **See-o-se Pol** (Thirty-Three Arch Bridge) is a popular evening pastime, as is a drink in the teahouse situated beneath the arches. Built in 1600, the bridge connected the city with the Armenian Christian enclave of Jolfa and its interesting Vank Cathedral. Further downstream are the Khaju Bridge, built in 1650, and the Shahrestan Bridge, with some sections dating to the 12th century. All these old bridges are pedestrianised and illuminated at night, making for irresistible night-time photos.

ISFAHAN TO REY

The old city of **Kashan** developed around the permanent water spring at Fin Gardens – the archetypal Persian Garden with water channels, fountains, pleasure pavilion and a bathhouse dating from the Safavid period. Sialk Hill is the remains of countless settlements at the site dating back at

Many of the wall paintings inside the Chehel Sotun Pavilion depict scenes of Safavid court life.

BELOW: stretching out those limbs at the Zurkhaneh.

The House of Strength

The evening is the time to witness the unique Iranian pastime of a visit to the *zurkhaneh*, or "house of strength". There are many around the country, but those in Isfahan are more used to foreign visitors coming to experience the earthy odours of a bunch of sweaty men being put through their paces by an old man banging a drum and hitting a bell.

Based on Sufi principles, the idea of the experience is to build up the body and mind, within the structure of a group or club of like-minded men. This is achieved through spiritual, mental and physical activity, helping to overcome the difficulties of modern life. Beginning and ending with prayers to Imam Ali, a respected elder leads the younger men in trials of strength and concentration, all to the swaying rhythms of drum and bell. Suddenly it all stops and there is a discussion for five minutes about the application of religion to everyday healthy living or respect for elders. Then all the frantic activity starts again, until another break for a piece of Persian poetry, perhaps.

Some of the elders are 80 years old and former sporting champions, whose fading photos and old patched leather shorts adorn the walls of the *zurkhaneh*. There is nothing quite like it anywhere else in the world, and it is certainly an unforgettable, if somewhat smelly, experience.

least 4,000 years, as proved by important pottery fragments now in the museums of Tehran and the Louvre in Paris. The town grew rich on silk carpet-weaving and became one of the most prosperous towns in Iran. Some merchant's houses and *hammams* have recently been restored and are wonderful examples of local architecture.

Qom

The route from Isfahan to Rey passes through the city of **Qom**, which together with Mashhad are the main sites of Shia pilgrimage in Iran. Non-Muslims must make strict observances to be permitted to the holy site in the centre of Qom – the tomb of Fatima, sister of Imam Reza (buried at Mashhad). Developed by the Safavids as an alternative to the holy sites in Kerbala and Najaf, then under Ottoman control, Imam Khomeini studied here and Qom was always at the forefront of the revolution against the Shah. Today it is the centre of Shia Islamic study, as can be seen by the great variety of nationalities of the many ethnic clerics.

Mausoleum of Oljaitu in Sulteniyeh.

BELOW: locally produced rose-water for sale in Kashan.

Security is high, and photographs are not permitted at the shrine or any of the many seminaries and theological colleges. Women wearing the *chador* and men suitably dressed can enter the shrine complex into a large courtyard with three *iwans*, where there is access for clerics to pray. Beyond this is a beautiful honeycombed ceiling gateway leading to a second and third courtyard with the dazzling mirrored entrance to the shrine itself to the right, and tombs of respected clerics. Fatima is buried below a simple gold dome resting on a high drum with a single band of Islamic text running around the top.

TEHRAN TO TABRIZ

At different times throughout its history, the Silk Road from Rey went north through Tabriz towards Turkey and the Black Sea. Difficult in winter, but feasible in summer, this is the shortest overland route to Constantinople and Italy. Today, the quickest way out of Tehran is on the smart new commuter trains to **Karaj**, running alongside the main highway with forests and the mountains to the north, industrial units to the south.

Qazvin

Qazvin was founded by King Shapur I in the 3rd century AD, and became a later Safavid capital under Tahmasp I. Later still it traded locally produced silk cocoons from the Gilan region along the nearby Caspian coast. A series of earthquakes has destroyed much of old Qazvin, but the Imamzade Hussein (son of the Eighth Imam), Jama Mosque and museum are worthwhile for the Safavid period decorative arts.

Alamut

It can take up to four hours by car and foot to reach the ruins of **Alamut** (**Gazor Khan**), the great centre of Hassan Sabbah. Originally built in 860, the fortress was taken by the Assassins in 1090, who ruled for over

150 years, but it was destroyed by the Mongol leader Hulagu in 1256 and little remains today. The journey should not be undertaken lightly, as the weather can be bad and the castle sometimes closed. This region is the homeland of the Dailamites, a fierce fighting tribe who enlisted into the armies defending Persia against any invader. This strategic location saw them initially fight the Byzantines, who were constantly at war from the 4th to the 7th centuries, and later they strongly resisted the invading Arabs. A few centuries later, many of these fighting Dailamites became Assassins.

Sulteniyeh

The Mausoleum of Oljaitu is all that remains of **Sulteniyeh**, summer capital of the Ilkhanids, descendants of Hulagu. The Spanish ambassador from the court of Henry III passed through the city in the early 15th century and noted that every summer, caravans of camels arrived with many kinds of cloth woven of silk or cotton, brought by ship from China, via Hormuz. Merchants from Genoa, Venice, Turkey, Syria and Baghdad flocked to the city, and in 1318 the pope even established an archdiocese here. This large tomb was originally built for the first Shia Imams, but instead became the tomb of the Sultan in 1316. The brick dome stands 52 metres (172ft) from the ground and is of complex design, modelled after the 1157 tomb of Sultan Sanjar in Merv, serving as the template for all later large mausoleums around the country. Major reconstruction is taking place, but there are glimpses on the interior walls supporting the dome of the beautiful glazed tile and brickwork that once covered the interior.

Further up the valley is the Sassanid-era town of **Zanjan**, with a fine covered bazaar and many caravanserais in various states of disrepair. Metalworking has turned Zanjan into the knife capital of the country, with every type of blade, dagger and sword available.

Takht-e Suleiman

One diversion from here is to the impressive ruins at **Takht-e Suleiman**

BELOW: Alamut, a mountain fortress.

The Assassins

The legend of the Assassins was brought to Europe by the Crusaders and Marco Polo, and popularised by Freya Stark in her book *The Valleys of the Assassins*.

It is thought that Hassan Sabbah was born in Rey around 1040 and possibly studied in Nieshapur with Omar Khayyam. His beliefs and teachings are somewhat obscure as his great library at Alamut castle was destroyed, but he taught his recruits to conceal their particular Shia belief, loosely based on Ismaili principles, and protect their location at all costs. Any Sunni religious or political figures opposing them were likely to be assassinated by his drug-crazed killers, known as the *hashisheen* (hashish-users), from which the word "assassin" derives.

Hassan's method of training involved taking his followers into a garden paradise of wine, honey, music and young maidens, getting them high on hashish before sending them out on their murderous missions – promising them more of the same if they died fulfilling their duty. Hassan died at Alamut in 1124, but the cult spread around the Near East, and at the height of their power there were over 100 Assassins' castles from Gerdkuh in eastern Iran to Masyaf in western Syria. They were forced out of their remote fortresses by the Mongols in 1256 and the majority of their Persian castles were completely destroyed.

(Throne of Solomon), an intriguing site spread around a "bottomless" lake on a sediment plateau. An outer wall with 38 towers dates from the 3rd century, but this was already an important site centuries earlier. Details are obscure, but it may have been the centre of one of the four holy fires for the Zoroastrians, because one of the more substantial ruins is of an ancient fire temple made entirely from fired bricks and lime mortar. It remained a ceremonial centre as Sassanid kings travelled here after their coronation at Ctesiphon to make offerings, and there are later buildings from the Ilkhanid period.

Entry to the site is through the large Ilkhanid gateway, but notice the impressive earlier Sassanid gateway just to the right, which some experts believe influenced Roman arch construction. Follow the outflowing water channel up to the level of the lake from where the site can be viewed. The most striking monument directly across the lake is the Western (Khosro) Gallery, held up by a mass of scaffolding. Foundations and walls have been identified as the fire temple, dining room, hypostyle hall and courtyard, but it is hard to imagine what it could have looked like during any one period. Excavated finds include Sassanid coins and glazed tiles and ceramics, examples of which are in the site museum. The name of the site appears to have nothing to do with Solomon of the Bible; legend says it was invented to stop the invading Arabs of the 7th century destroying the site of one of their early prophets. A few kilometres away is the spectacular volcanic cone known as Zendan-e Suleiman (Solomon's Prison), which was inhabited as far back as 900 BC, and also seems to have been a place of religious significance.

Returning to the road north from Zanjan towards Tabriz, the road climbs a pass to reach Mianeh and then up to Tabriz, set along the Aji Chay Valley below beautiful ranges of mountains, well supplied by *qanat* water.

Tabriz

The Azeri capital of **Tabriz** feels completely different to other major Iranian cities, with Turkey and the Black Sea not far away. Strangely, the Mongols who destroyed many Persian cities treated Tabriz kindly and built a lot of fine buildings under Ilkhan Ghazan. It was the first capital of the Safavids, but suffered from its proximity to the Ottomans and was replaced by Qazvin and then Isfahan, which has also more recently replaced Tabriz as the second-largest city in Iran. Tabriz has regularly been attacked, especially from Russia, as well as suffering from major earthquakes. The climate does not favour its location either, being stiflingly hot in summer and carpeted in snow for long winter months, but it is good for skiing. The majority of the population speak Turkish and have strong ties to the neighbouring countries of Azerbaijan, Armenia and Turkey.

BELOW: aerial view over the fortress, lake and ruins at Takht-e Suleiman.

Built in 1465 by Jahan Shah, the **Blue Mosque** is a masterpiece of Mongol–Timurid architecture and the finest building in the city. Entry is through a great central portal, the only part to survive the earthquake of 1779, and decorated with glazed tile-work of arabesques and intertwined flowers, framed by heavy cable-moulding. The layout is unusual, with the open courtyard covered by a huge dome, probably to combat the severe winter weather. Pass below a small archway of extremely intricate stalactite mosaic work into the second domed chamber, to be dazzled by magnificent cobalt-blue glazed tiles and gilded gold work. Some hexagonal pieces are displayed in a glass case in the centre and are truly exquisite. The Mongols brought Chinese artists with them who added Buddhist influences to the designs such as delicate flower work and strange peacocks. The overall cream, turquoise and cobalt blue is a reminder of the decoration on the two minarets at the holy shrine in Mashhad, on the other side of the country.

Next door is the **Azerbaijan Archaeology Museum** (open Sat–Thur 8am–8pm, Fri 8am–1pm; admission fee), with a fabulous collection of pottery stretching back to 10th-century Nieshapur, rivalling the Glass and Ceramics Museum in Tehran (see page 320). There are Achaemenid *rhytons*, gold necklaces and jewellery from the 1st millennium BC, pottery from the 5th millennium BC and carved stone "hand ingots" (which resemble modern handbags) from the 3rd millennium BC. On the upper floor is the so-called "Chelsea rewoven carpet", which has unsubstantiated claims to be older than the silk and wool Ardebil carpets in London and Los Angeles. Ardebil lies 230km (138 miles) to the east, but the London Ardebil carpet was probably woven here in Tabriz in 1539 and shows Chinese influence with *tchi* cloud bands on the border. This smaller "Chelsea" design is of animal figures on carmine red with dark-blue medallions and, with 462 knots to the square inch, it has over 30 percent more knots than the Ardebils.

As you can imagine, carpets are the main items in the bazaar, and you can find them at every stage of the commercial process – being bought, traded, inspected, cleaned, repaired and ultimately sold. Individuals often wander around with smaller carpets looking for an opportune sale. Ibn Battuta commented in the 14th century that he had never seen such a riotous scene as he did inside the Tabriz bazaar.

Behind the impressive municipality building and clock tower on Shahrdari Square are a few streets of important merchants' houses, about 10 of which have been recently restored, including the wonderful **Ghadaki** and **Behnam houses** now within the Arts Faculty of the university. Nearby is the 160-year-old **Salmasi House**, home to the Sanjesh Measurement Museum, containing instruments for measuring time, distance, volume, weight and

BELOW: a statue of the poet Khaqani outside the Blue Mosque.

Sabzi seeds grown to celebrate Nauroz (New Year).

BELOW: Imam Khomeini Square in Hamadan.

pressure all displayed within fabulous restored rooms of distinct red and white brickwork.

From here the road tackles the mountains to Maku and eventually, after more than 300km (180 miles), reaches the Turkish border at **Bazargan**.

TEHRAN TO IRAQ

From Rey, the route to the Iraqi border follows the ancient Royal Road, used by conquerors and invaders to and from Mesopotamia, and later still by the overland merchants and caravans making straight for the Mediterranean. The route to Hamadan runs through **Saveh**, a town that suffered greatly when the Mongols arrived. But it is associated with a tradition from the times of Marco Polo, that the Magi set out from here and were later buried in three great tombs. True or not, there is nothing to be seen of this today in the modern town. The windswept open plains west of Saveh lead to Mt Alvand (3,571 metres/11,780ft), stunningly snow-capped in winter, with Hamadan nestling at its base.

Hamadan

Modern **Hamadan** is located on top of the ancient trading capital of Hagmatana (meaning "Assembly Point", referring to a free meeting place for the various tribes), called Ecbatana by the Greeks. The history of this important city is as great as any on the entire Silk Road, and dates back to at least the 8th century BC, when it was the capital of the Medes. As power shifted to the Achaemenids, it became the summer capital of Cyrus the Great, while Susa was his winter base. The modern city can be quite disappointing, as almost all traces of its great history have been destroyed or looted by a succession of invaders from Alexander and the Seleucids to the Parthians and Seljuks. But there are wonderful stories, such as the account by Herodotus in the 5th century BC (*Histories* 1.98–9), who describes the Royal Palace and treasure house defended by seven walls, each one taller than the next and painted in different colours, the last two being of silver and gold. It is possible that he was translating an account of a ziggurat, an ancient stepped construction in the centre of the city.

As one city has been destroyed and another built on top, the majority of ancient objects have come from illegal digging rather than supervised excavations. Gold and silver tablets, gold rhytons and jewellery are mainly to be found in the National Archaeological Museum in Tehran (see page 320). But a new museum beside the excavations of old Ecbatana, just to the north of the city centre, is displaying more recent finds, including inscriptions, carvings and a fountain from Safavid times.

The centre of the modern city radiates from Imam Khomeini Square, not far from the tomb of **Esther and Mordecai**, a site of great Jewish historical interest, but of unproven credibility. Esther of the Bible was possibly the wife of Xerxes, who together with her uncle Mordecai sought

permission for the Jews to return to Persia from exile. There are plenty of suggestions as to who is really buried here, but it is still the main place of Jewish pilgrimage.

One of the most ancient sites is at **Ganj-Nameh** (meaning "Treasure Book"), a few kilometres away on the lower slopes of Mt Alvand, where two Achaemenid cuneiform inscriptions list the lineage and conquests of Darius I on the left and Xerxes I on the right. Both are written in three scripts – Old Persian, Elamite and Neo-Babylonian. It is a pleasant summer excursion for city-dwellers, especially on Fridays, who crowd the parks and teahouses.

A later addition in the city centre is the 1950s tomb of the famous Persian philosopher and scholar Ibn Sina, known in the west as **Avicenna**.

Heading west from Hamadan, lush green plains stretch away to distant snowy mountains in all directions. Through this magnificent stark scenery rumble modern traders carrying new commodities – truckloads of cement, fabricated steelwork and oil,

while an optimistic signpost indicates "Kerbala 615km". An early morning sun burns off the overnight moisture, wrapping the fields in thick mist, out of which ghostly figures emerge struggling to control their herds of sheep and goats across the lanes of fast-moving traffic. Beyond a tough mountain pass, often closed by snow in winter, is the largely forgotten site of **Kangovar**, a ruined collection of impressive cut stones and huge columns dominating the surrounding flat landscape. Remains of a temple dedicated to the guardian of water, goddess Anahita, lie on a series of platforms, which have been compared to Persepolis in layout, but this requires a lot of imagination.

It would be only natural that conquering heroes would carve their successes on the spectacular rocky outcrop of **Bisotun**, around which every trader and invader has had to pass for thousands of years. The old main road running along the base of the mountain has thankfully been closed, allowing a safer view of the strange 2nd-century BC reclining statue of Hercules holding a wine goblet.

BELOW: statue of Avicenna.

Avicenna (Ibn Ali Sina)

Avicenna, also known as Ibn Sina, was born in 980 and educated at Bukhara in mathematics, logic and Islamic law. By the age of 20 he had studied the works of Aristotle, Hippocrates and Archimedes and started writing his own theories on philosophy, economics, physics and astronomy. He moved to Rey, where he built up a reputation as a physician and later settled in Hamadan. By the time he died there in 1037 he had completed his *Metaphysics of the Healing* and *Canon of Medicine*, both of which were used as standard textbooks in Europe until the 17th century.

Most of Avicenna's books were written in Arabic, as was the tradition, and it still rankles Iranians that he is usually thought of as Arab, rather than Persian.

A girl dressed up for Nauroz (New Year) in Kermanshah.

BELOW: tilework on the Takiyeh Muavin al-Molk.

Just beyond is a Parthian relief from slightly earlier, but the main interest is to be seen high up on the mountain. On a prepared piece of rock is a carving of Darius (the largest figure, third from the left) standing on his opponent Gaumata, recording that the decisive battle took place here at Bisitun. In front of Darius is a line of eight vanquished rulers paying homage. A ninth figure (in pointed hat at the end) was added after a few years in order to celebrate his later victory over the Scythians. The winged symbol of Ahura-Mazda hovers above the figures and is surrounded by 1,200 lines of text in three languages. So important was this inscription at the time that it was copied and distributed to all the provinces – fragments of it in Aramaic were even found on Elephantine Island at Aswan in Egypt.

Kermanshah

This is the last provincial capital before Iraq, which suffered greatly in the Iran–Iraq War, with an important oil refinery close to the centre of town. Kermanshah, meaning "City of

the Kings of Kerman", was founded in the 4th century around **Taq-e Bustan** (meaning "Arch of the Garden"), a pleasant suburb of garden cafés and a boating lake fed by a sacred spring. To the left of the entrance are archaeological finds from the region, including carved capitals possibly from an unknown temple at Bisitun. Cut into the base of the cliff are two grottoes and a bas-relief panel. The larger grotto is the greatest of the Sassanid period, showing two winged figures, similar to carvings depicting Nike at Ephesus, but here holding the royal diadem. The rear wall is carved in high relief and shows an investiture at the top, whilst below is a remarkable armour-clad king on horseback. The intricate hunting scenes on the two side walls are quite different in style and execution, and would once have been completely coloured. Higher up on the left wall, some colour remains on a much later relief from Qajar times. The older, smaller cave has reliefs of Shahpur III and his relatives soon after the founding of the city. Further along is a bas-relief panel showing the investiture of Ardashir II. Ahura-Mazda is represented by the god Hormizd on the right, with Mithra on the left

On the opposite side of Kermanshah is the **Takiyeh Muavin al-Molk**, an attraction for Shia pilgrims heading for Kerbala. This 19th-century Qajar period celebrates the martyrdom of Imam Hussein in a series of stories depicted in beautiful coloured tilework in both the front courtyard and the rear garden. Some of the themes are unusual, such as the bloody flagellations during the month of Muharram.

The change in scenery is abrupt as palm trees start to appear in marked difference to the Iranian plateau as the highway runs down towards the Mesopotamian plain. The border with Iraq is at **Khosravi**, but access to this whole region is subject to security restrictions.

Magian Spells

Zoroastrian philosophy was the main religious belief system of the ancient Iranians and formed the basis of modern Iranian culture.

I t is uncertain exactly where the early prophet Zoroaster (Zarathustra to the Persians) came from, but it was somewhere in northern Persia, around 1000 BC. He preached that there was just one God, called Ahura-Mazda (Wise Lord) and, pre-dating Judaism, Christianity and Islam, Zoroastrianism is therefore one of the world's earliest monotheistic religions. Ahura-Mazda and his creation represent truth and order and through good thoughts and good deeds his followers can keep chaos at bay. Zoroastrians have faith that Ahura-Mazda will ultimately triumph over Angra Mainyu, the embodiment of evil, the world will end and the souls of the living and the dead will be reconnected with God.

Ahura-Mazda communicated with his devotees in their dreams. The meaning of his messages was not always clear, however, and so the priests of the Median Empire (known as Magi, from the Greek *magoi* or wise men) were required to interpret such dreams. The Greek historian Herodotus, writing in the 5th century BC, records that the Magi had appeared some 200 years previously and were particularly skilled at reading dreams. The historical Magi were part of Persia's elite and valued advisors to their rulers, which gave them the credibility required to successfully spread their faith and other ideas. The Magi tried to explain and understand the world around them by calculating time, developing calendars, understanding tides and studying the early sciences – medicine and alchemy – as well as poetry, art and religion. It has been credibly suggested that the Magi referred to in the Christian nativity story were these same Zoroastrian priests.

Their speciality was studying the night sky, because they believed that whatever they observed in the heavens would be reflected in events on earth. By monitoring movements in the sky, they could make predictions about what would happen below. They developed their own astrology using the twelve signs of the Zodiac that are recognised today. The Magi were not astrologers or astronomers as we would know them today; rather they were "searchers of wisdom" and regarded as scholars in their time.

Today it is estimated that the worldwide population of Zoroastrians is about 200,000, the largest group belonging to India's Parsee community. The population in Iran is significantly smaller, largely having been driven out or converted to Islam during the 7th century. Iran's Zoroastrians are concentrated in Tehran and also in Yazd, where there is still an operational Zoroastrian fire temple (fire being a ritual purifier). Their practice of laying out dead bodies inside Towers of Silence is being restricted, however, and many Zoroastrians are instead buried in concrete-lined graves to prevent the decaying corpse poisoning the earth.

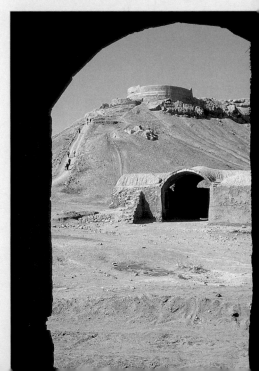

ABOVE: the Azura-Mazda symbol. **RIGHT:** Zoroastrian Towers of Silence, Yazd.

IRAQ

From Baghdad to Babylon, and Ninevah to Nimrud, along the vital conduits of the Tigris and Euphrates rivers, the cultural heritage of Iraq is one of the greatest of the countries along the Silk Road.

Main attractions
BAGHDAD
KARBALA
CTESIPHON
BABYLON
URUK
MOSUL: NINEVAH, NIMRUD

Throughout its ancient history Iraq was known as Mesopotamia – literally "the land between the rivers", referring to the fertile valleys of the Euphrates and the Tigris. As the cradle of the highly developed early civilisations of the Babylonians and the Assyrians, this region has always been envied by neighbouring emerging empires. With the Arab invasion and the spread of Islam, Baghdad became one of its earliest capitals under a dynasty known as the Abbasids. Mongol destruction and Ottoman control eventually led to British rule and reorganisation, until independence in 1932 when it was renamed Iraq.

The monarchy was overthrown in 1958 by a military junta, after which military coups and Ba'ath Party infighting dominated politics until 1979, when Saddam Hussein took control. The fallout from his ousting by allied forces in 2003 is a continuing part of Iraqi and international history, the low point undoubtedly being the destruction of the Babylon archaeological site, but the situation is slowly improving, with visitors being able to visit areas such as Iraqi Kurdistan.

Baghdad

As capital of the country, Baghdad has always been an important trading and economic centre. When the Abbasid Caliphate was based here in the 8th and 9th centuries AD, goods from the Silk Road filled the bazaars and warehouses along the banks of the Tigris. At that time it was the entrepôt of the Middle East, also trading incense and pearls from Arabia; gold and slaves from East Africa; spices and dyes from the Indies. Baghdad became the richest city in the world, with a wealth of Islamic mosques and shrines, including the Kadhimain Shrine, constructed in AD 1515.

The most important Islamic shrines for Shia believers worldwide are to

LEFT: the Kadhimain Shrine in Baghdad.

be found in the holy cities of Kufa, Karbala and Najaf to the south, and Samarra to the north. Kufa (Al Kufah) was the city where Ali, son-in-law and cousin of the Prophet Muhammad and the first Shia Imam, was murdered in AD 661. His tomb in nearby Najaf is a great centre of pilgrimage.

The **Iraq Museum** (www.iraqmuseum.org) housed what was probably the finest collection of Mesopotamian artefacts in the world. About 15,000 items, including 5,000 unique cylinder seals, were looted in 2003, but following the return of some of its most important treasures and an ambitious renovation project, it has since been periodically open to the public. It is hoped the museum will soon reopen permanently and, in the meantime, a large part of the collection is online.

Karbala

Situated south of Baghdad, the holy city of Karbala is where Hussein, the son of Ali, was martyred by the Umayyad Caliph Yazid in AD 680. This conflict over the succession of the Caliphate has distinguished the Shia from the Sunni sects of Islam ever since. Shia followers make pilgrimages here known as *Ashura* ("ten" in Arabic) commemorating the date of Hussein's death. The head of Hussein is said to rest in a shrine inside the Umayyad Mosque in Damascus.

Due to unrest in Baghdad in AD 833, the capital of the Caliphate moved further up the Tigris to Samarra, during which time it was the centre of the Islamic world, until AD 892. It is most famous for its wonderful ziggurat-style spiral minaret, constructed in AD 847. Sadly this unique building was also badly damaged recently when the US military used it as a look-out position, and it became a target for attacks. Samarra also has great significance to Shia Muslims, as the final resting places of the Tenth and Eleventh Imams.

Ctesiphon

Dropping down from the Iranian plateau, the main city established by the Parthians on the eastern bank of the Tigris was Ctesiphon, about 30km (18 miles) downstream from Baghdad. The great arch of the banqueting hall of the Palace of Shapur I (the 3rd-century

BELOW: glazed brick from the Ishtar Gate in Babylon, now in Berlin.

TOURISM IN IRAQ

Over a quarter of a million tourists visit Iraq every year, and have continued to do so throughout the problems of the past decade. The vast majority of these are religious pilgrims visiting the important Shia shrines around the country.

However, tourism is slowly growing in the north of the Republic of Iraq, sometimes referred to as the autonomous Kurdish region of **Kurdistan**, having borders with **Iran**, **Turkey** and **Syria**. The Iraqi Kurds suffered harsh treatment under Saddam and were given protection by the Allies following the First Gulf War in 1991. This period of stability and relative prosperity has allowed Kurdistan to enjoy a higher standard of living than the rest of Iraq. Attempts are now under way to encourage tourism into the area, specialising in cultural and adventure itineraries, including white-water rafting and trekking. The centre of the capital, Arbil, is the huge Citadel, similar to the Citadel at Aleppo in Syria and dating back around 7,000 years. Most of the buildings in the Citadel are decaying mansions from the time when the Ottoman Empire released its grip on the region at the start of the 20th century.

There are two international airports, at Arbil (also known as Hawler) and Sulaymaniyah, with regular flights from Dubai, Amman and Vienna. The massive new airport terminal at Arbil opened in 2010 and has significantly improved communications links in the region.

For the rest of the country, until peace breaks out completely there seems little chance that tourism will develop to any significant extent.

AD Sassanid king carved into the rock facade at Naqsh-e Rustam) is one of the most famous of Iraqi monuments. The slender, fragile arch is thought to be the largest single span ever constructed from baked bricks. Here, the Euphrates and Tigris rivers bend within a few kilometres of each other.

Babylon

South along the Euphrates is one of the most famous ancient cities in the world, Babylon. Most of the buildings to be seen are remnants from the rule of King Nebuchadnezzar II in the 6th century BC. Some of the ruined constructions are said to have been part of the famous Hanging Gardens, one of the Seven Wonders of the Ancient World.

Most prominent are the two palaces of the king, the ziggurat (an early tiered building) and the Ishtar Gate. Dedicated to the goddess Ishtar, the Gate was constructed of blue glazed tiles with alternating rows of bas-relief *sirrush* (dragons) and aurochs; the roof and doors of the gate were of cedar. Through the gate ran the Processional

Baghdad's Stolen Treasure

In just a few days of chaos during April 2003, it was reported that an estimated 170,000 items were looted from the Iraqi National Museum in Baghdad – though still shocking, the true figure was closer to 15,000. Exactly what is missing will probably never be known, as many of the catalogue details have also been lost or destroyed. Some pieces had been stored away safely in advance, but it was not possible to save more in the time available. The Iraq Antiquities Department has now issued identification cards for many of the artefacts and handed them to Interpol. Neighbouring countries such as Syria, Jordan and Lebanon have seized thousands of smuggled items on their borders. Despite an amnesty, however, not all the recovered pieces have been handed back.

Way, which was lined with walls covered with glazed bricks of lions.

The magnificent Ishtar Gate can now be admired in the Berlin Museum, and the black diorite *stele* with the inscribed *Code of Hammurabi* is one of many items to be found in the Mesopotamia Room at the Louvre in Paris.

Recently, American forces used the ancient site as a military command centre named Base Alpha. A helicopter pad was constructed inside the site and vibrations from landings led the roof of one building to collapse.

Uruk

Further south along the old course of the Euphrates are two more important cities. Uruk (also known as Akkad) was the first major city of the Sumerians, and arguably the world's first city. The *Epic of Gilgamesh* celebrates the king of the first dynasty and is one of the first works of literature. Beyond that are the ruins of Ur, close to the modern town of Nasiriya (An Nasiriyah). Mentioned several times in the Bible, Ur has an impressive large ziggurat dedicated to the moon God Nanna.

Mosul

In the far north of the country, the city of **Mosul** (Al Mawsil) is Iraq's second-largest city and a rich mixture of modern Arabs, Kurds and Turkomans. Sadly the regional museum here was looted in 2003. The city has an Umayyad Mosque dating to AD 640, but is primarily the base for visiting two nearby important sites, Nimrud and Ninevah, both on the Tigris River.

Ninevah was an ancient capital of the Assyrians until the death of their last great king, Ashurbanipal, in the 7th century BC, killed by the Medes. Some of the great gateways and walls have been reconstructed, but most of the original bas-reliefs are now held in the British Museum.

Even older are the ruins at **Nimrud**, the previous capital of the Assyrians, known as Calah in the Bible. This was also destroyed by the Medes, with most of the excavated treasures now spread around the museums of the world. Fortunately, pieces of Assyrian gold known as the "Nimrud Treasures", at National Iraqi Museum, were stored in a bank vault and have been saved.

"Dead men, not potsherds littered the way. In the wide streets where the crowds once gathered and cheered, the corpses lay scattered. In the fields where the dancers once danced the dead were heaped up in piles."

Mesopotamian lamentation

BELOW LEFT: Ashurnasirpal II (around 850 BC), depicted in a relief. **BELOW:** the Assyrian palaces of Nimrud, along the Tigris River (restored lithograph).

SYRIA

The ancient cities of Damascus and Aleppo, the evocative desert ruins of Palmyra and imposing Crusader castles such as Krac des Chevaliers: Syria is a microcosm of the Silk Road, packed full of sights.

Syria has always benefited from its unique position at the end of the Asian trade route, controlling overland access to both Europe and Africa. The classic Silk Road reached the Mediterranean after surviving the tough desert crossing via Palmyra, from where goods were sent on to Rome. After Palmyra's demise, the desert crossing became impossible, and so a secondary route became more important which skirted north around the desert by following the Euphrates upstream and then through Aleppo and Antioch.

Until recent national and political divisions, "*Syria*" referred to all the land known as the Levant at the eastern end of the Mediterranean and its hinterland to the Euphrates, of which the modern country is just a small part. Syria is where the world's first written scripts originated, and there is a continuing argument about whether Damascus or Aleppo is the world's oldest city. Damascus is the religious and political capital – aloof and insular – whilst Aleppo bustles with the lifeblood of trade – open and modern.

Syria's central position made it an easy target for any expanding empire, from Hittite and Egyptian to Assyrian and Persian. These and many other ancient civilisations have battered

and rebuilt the country for thousands of years, leaving a rich cultural heritage unlike anywhere else. Buildings separated by centuries lean side by side, ancient ruins recall distant empires, and Bedouins with mobile phones keep society moving forwards, but always with one foot in the past. People continually adapt to the changes around them, and Syrians are some of the best at doing that.

Throughout the latter part of the 20th century, Syria had a no less turbulent time politically. A succession

Main attractions

DURA EUROPOS
PALMYRA
QALAAT IBN MAAN
VALLEY OF THE TOMBS
DAMASCUS:
    OLD CITY
    UMAYYAD MOSQUE
    NATIONAL ARCHAEOLOGICAL
    MUSEUM
BOSRA THEATRE
KRAC DES CHEVALIERS
RESAFEH
ALEPPO: CITADEL, SOUK
APAMEA
QALAAT SEMAAN

LEFT: the ancient ruins of Palmyra.
RIGHT: local farmers in Apamea.

ENTERING AND LEAVING SYRIA

Syria is currently inaccessible to foreigners due to the unstable political situation. Once security improves, however, it should again be one of the easiest countries in which to follow the Silk Road, with minimal formalities and few restrictions. Damascus is the international hub from where all parts of the country can be easily reached, especially as access from Iraq is not possible. The train network is not particularly useful for following the Silk Road, but buses and taxis can get you to most places.

The only chance of following the original direct route, west from Dura Europos across the desert, would be along the supply track of the oil pipeline running from Iraq through Palmyra and Homs to the terminal at Tartus. The modern highway, however, follows the Euphrates to Deir ez-Zor and then strikes west across the desert on new tarmac. (See Travel Tips, page 432, for more information on transport in Syria.)

Buses run regularly along the Euphrates valley to **Turkey**, and some local taxis will get you to the desert sites. There are luxury buses running to Antakya from both Aleppo and Damascus, but quicker and more flexible are private taxis taking three or four people across the border from Aleppo. The train from Aleppo to Turkey does not go west to the Hatay region of Antakya. If returning to Syria ensure that you have a multiple entry Syrian visa.

Buses and taxis run regular services to Beirut, **Lebanon**, but ensure you have a multiple-entry Syrian visa if you intend to return to Syria.

It is not possible for foreigners to travel overland from Syria to **Iraq**.

of military coups and more than 40 years under emergency law effectively suspended the constitution. Disappearances and incarceration without trial were commonplace, and there was no effective opposition to the Assad regime (first Hafez al-Assad and then his son, the Western-educated ophthalmologist Bashar al-Assad).

Simmering discontent came to a head in 2011 when pro-democracy protests (inspired by the Arab Spring) were brutally put down by the government, leading to a virtual civil war between the incumbent ruling Ba'ath party and the opposition, the Free Syrian Army and the Syrian National Council. The government has been accused of firing repeatedly on civilians, many of whom have attempted to flee to Turkey, and the Syrian authorities have been heavily criticised by the UN's High Commissioner for Human Rights. Syria has been suspended from the Arab League and sanctions have been imposed on Assad and other high-ranking officials. As of spring 2012, the country

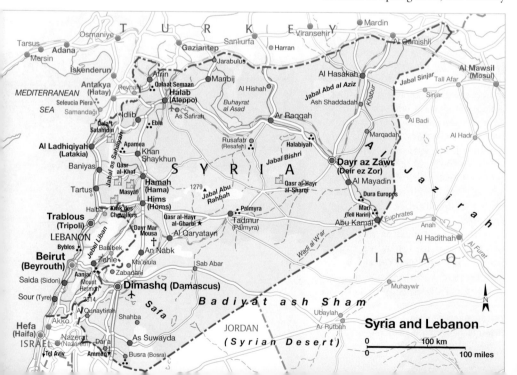

Syria and Lebanon

remains deeply unstable. Tourists are not advised to travel to anywhere in Syria at this time.

NEAR THE IRAQI BORDER

The modern Iraqi border with Syria crosses the Euphrates at Abu Kamal, where the river swings in a more northerly direction. Almost immediately on the western bank is the ancient settlement of **Mari**, at a place called Tell Hariri (meaning "Hill of the Silk-Weaver"). Despite its great importance as an early city-state comparable to Ur in the east and Ebla and Ugarit further west, there is little to see from 6,000 years ago. Excavated items found at the central Palace of Zimri-Lim (now under a protective roof) are in the museums of Aleppo, Damascus, nearby Deir ez-Zor and the Louvre in Paris. A cache of clay tablets in Akkadian script tell us that the city thrived on the tax of passing trade between Mesopotamia and Anatolia around 4,000 years ago. There are confusing outlines of temples and palaces and the remains of possibly the earliest ziggurat, but the only sound to be

heard in this quiet corner of Syria is the hooting of the resident owl.

Dura Europos

Only 15km (9 miles) further north along the highway dotted with mulberry trees is the later developed city of **Dura Europos** (open daily 9am–6pm in summer, until 4pm in winter; admission fee). Dura means "fortress" in Aramaic, hinting at a time before this Hellenistic city became a regional melting pot for East and West, with temples to satisfy all persuasions. Entry is through the substantial Palmyra Gate, from where the Silk Road ran a short distance to its principal trading partner in the desert. Little remains of the important synagogue to the left, but this is where the wonderful frescoes were found that are now reconstructed in the National Archaeological Museum in Damascus (see page 353). Beyond the extensive site are the major buildings spectacularly located on the banks of the Euphrates. To the right is the Strategion Palace and on the left the main citadel. The extent and size of

"I never imagined that my first sight of the desert would come with such a shock of beauty and enslave me right away."

Freya Stark

BELOW: atop the main citadel of Dura Europos, overlooking the Euphrates.

Desert Irrigation

For centuries, desert settlements have relied on underground tunnels to bring water for traders and their animals, and to irrigate crops.

The town of Palmyra owes its existence to the natural Efqa spring (situated near the Cham Palace Hotel) that bubbles sulphurous water to the surface. Without it, it would not have been possible to supply enough water for traders en route to Damascus, and their only choice would have been to travel up the Euphrates Valley.

Without a natural supply, water has to be brought in artificially, and for centuries desert settlements have relied on underground channels, known as *qanats*, to supply the water they need. The history of the *qanat* goes back about 3,000 years to Persia, where the first channels were dug by hand to bring water from the mountains up to 40km (24 miles) away. Vertical shafts allowed for ventilation as well as the removal of silt and stones carried down the channel. The use of this system spread along the early Silk Road routes – east to Central Asia and China, and west to Syria and Jordan. Arab expansion in the 7th century took this same system to the Gulf

States, North Africa and Muslim Spain. Because the *qanats* were so vital, they had to be well protected, especially in times of invasion, as a whole city could easily be taken by cutting its supply of water.

Today, there are an estimated 22,000 *qanats* in Iran carrying water some 300,000km (186,000 miles). These systems require continual skilful maintenance and can soon become blocked and useless if left. Only about 10 percent of Syria's *qanats* are thought to be working, mainly in the mountains around Damascus and the Dead Cities region to the west of Aleppo. Many others were abandoned after Independence in the 1950s, when land reform created large cooperative farms requiring more water than the *qanats* could supply and diesel pumps were introduced.

Ancient *qanats* from Roman and Byzantine times are still being discovered and occasionally repaired. The job of digging and repairing a qanat is highly skilled, requiring nerve and agility to work underground in small tunnels full of dust – skills that are being lost as few people want to do this work.

A method of irrigation popular with the Romans was to have a series of small dams along watercourses and *wadis*, which held rainwater temporarily, but long enough to irrigate fields via canals. These could fill large water cisterns at desert cities such as Qasr al-Hayr al-Gharbi from its dam at Harbaqa. The modern Assad Dam astride the Euphrates does a similar job on a much larger scale. The large waterwheels of Hama are a small-scale solution to water distribution along channels, raised up from the Orontes River.

A consistent and plentiful water supply is still a major concern in these areas today: as the population grows, so too does the amount of irrigated water needed for agriculture. Syria will have problems meeting those demands because of Turkish dam-building projects on both the Euphrates and Tigris rivers, so maybe more 2,000-year-old *qanats* will be brought back to life in the future.

LEFT: the underground cistern at Resfah.
ABOVE: waterwheels at Hama.

the stone blocks is remarkable, indicating the commitment and wealth of the city at this important location. At the far end of the citadel is the **Palace of the Dux Ripae** (meaning "riverbank commander") with the best views across the river and surrounding farmland.

Two main routes then took the silk trade westwards from Dura Europos to the Mediterranean, the first going straight across the Syrian Desert to Damascus via Palmyra. When Palmyra collapsed into the sands its desert trade route was replaced with one continuing up the Euphrates towards Aleppo, which shifted the balance of control to places further north, like Resafeh, leaving Dura Europos to "disappear" until British troops stumbled across it in the 1920s.

ACROSS THE SYRIAN DESERT

The route from Dura Europos to Damascus is the classical route that strikes straight across the Syrian Desert, the route that many people think of as the Silk Road in the Middle East. It passes through the extraordinary city of Palmyra that blossomed briefly in the desert and the imposing city of Damascus.

Roughly midway from Deir ez-Zor (Dayr az Zawr) to Palmyra and about 20km (12 miles) north of the highway is one of Syria's unique sites, Qasr al-Hayr al-Sharqi (Eastern Walled Castle). The 8th-century Umayyad caliphs probably intended it to be a kind of desert pleasure palace-cum-agricultural centre, watered by a dam 30km (18 miles) away. One explanation for the existence of such an eclectic site in this desert wilderness might have been the desire of the caliphs of Damascus to reaffirm their desert roots, within a century or so of the death of the Prophet Muhammad in Arabia. This water supply also naturally attracted overland traders, which could explain the separate caravanserai building to the east of the main site. The two structures stand side by side with a small, square minaret between – possibly the third-oldest minaret in Syria.

Low ridges of hard-packed desert sand alternate with shallow

The tariffs charged on goods arriving in Palmyra was inscribed on a large stone dating from AD 139, now in the Hermitage Museum in St Petersburg.

BELOW: touring Palmyra by camel.

TIP

Upon arrival in Palmyra, go to the museum and confirm one of the set times for accessing the Valley of the Tombs with the guardian. Remember to bring a torch.

depressions of scrub, nibbled by the seasonally wandering goats and sheep under the watchful eye of herdsmen from their tented encampments. The pressures of modern life impinge even here, as the herds are rapidly moved to unexploited grazing sites by huge trucks, which carry the animals, tents and personal belongings hundreds of kilometres.

Palmyra

Images most closely associated with the Silk Road in the Middle East are the evocative vistas of **Palmyra** (**Tadmur**) in the middle of the Syrian Desert. Even today it is still a great adventure to travel to this city spread across the desert sand, whose monuments change shade and texture subtly throughout the day.

A small settlement developed here at a natural water spring almost 4,000 years ago when it was known as Tadmor (a name mentioned in texts from Mari). It grew wealthy by taxing passing traders and charging them for water. After the Romans gained Syria in 64 BC they seemed quite happy to

grant autonomy to places like Antioch and Palmyra – its new name derived from the many date palms. But then the Romans saw the silk banners of the Parthians for the first time and the marvellous new material started to flow to the Mediterranean. By the 1st century AD Palmyra was not just trading silk from east to west, but had become the independent centre of desert routes radiating in all directions to Damascus, Homs, Hama, Antioch, Resafeh, Seleucia (on the Tigris), Dura Europos, Ctesiphon and even Petra.

Through this wealth it became a destination and financial centre in its own right, where luxurious items were bought and resold. Palmyrene merchants arranged much of this trade in advance by setting up agencies in Rome and Egypt, and throughout Mesopotamia. Their presence is recorded on Kharg Island at the head of the Persian Gulf by the great burial tombs they created, almost identical to the sunken mausoleums here in their home city. Rome used Palmyra to defend itself against the Sassanids, but ended up battling the new Palmyrene Empire itself, under the control of Queen Zenobia. Rome retaliated and Palmyra never recovered, losing its silk trade to the Euphrates route towards Aleppo. It was only in the 17th century that the West became aware of this great abandoned city in the middle of the desert.

The first impression approaching the ancient city of Palmyra is the greenness of the palm groves, which adds much-needed colour to the endless dun landscape. If any city developed, blossomed and faded so acutely on the strength of trade, then it is this one.

Palmyra developed its own unique culture, influenced by, but independent of, Rome. It was designed by Roman and Greek architects, which gives the effect of a classical city in the desert, but follows no great plan, as everything fits into the available space. The **colonnaded street** shifted axis to

BELOW: engravings on the entrance to the Temple of Bel.

bend around existing buildings as the city expanded from below the castle towards the modern roadway. One difference from a pure Roman city is the absence of stone paving, apparently to ease the feet of the vast numbers of loaded camels. But all this matters little to the visitors enjoying an evening stroll along the colonnade.

To the left is the small (by Roman standards) restored **theatre**, nowadays the centrepiece for the annual Silk Road Festival. Almost in the centre of the city is a quartet of four-columned structures known as the **tetrapylon**, each one previously containing a large statue. A funerary temple lies at the end of the colonnaded street, with a nearby Temple of Allat and the area known as Diocletian's Camp, installed to reaffirm Roman control after Zenobia's revolt (see panel).

The most substantial of the ruins at Palmyra is the impressive **Temple of Bel** (open daily 8am–6pm in summer, until 4pm in winter; admission fee). Similar in appearance to the religious construction at Baalbek (and dedicated to the same god), the single cella (inner chamber of the temple) is located in a vast compound surrounded by peristyle colonnades inside 15-metre (50-ft) -high walls. Immediately to the left are seven huge columns spanning a small passageway, thought to be the access for sacrificial animals. The floor of the compound is littered with columns, some of which have been sliced and used as a quick fix for broken sections of the north wall.

Between the heavily decorated entranceway and the *cella* are some fallen slabs with wonderful carvings of loaded camels and traders bringing wealth and fame to a city of orchards laden with fruit. Again, things are not quite as they should be, as the door to the *cella* is in effect through the side-wall rather than at one end, with no obvious focus for devotion. A statue of Bel is thought to have been placed on top of the steps to the right, while the opposite end has an earlier sanctuary decorated with signs of the zodiac.

Dominating the city is the distant 17th-century **Qalaat ibn Maan** (Arab Castle), attributed to a Lebanese

In some cases, the silk samples found at Palmyra can even be attributed to individual Chinese workshops.

BELOW: Queen Zenobia honoured on a postage stamp.

Queen Zenobia

Under threat from the Sassanids in AD 256, Rome entrusted Palmyra's defence to family clan leader Odenathus. Upon his death 10 years later, his widow Zenobia assumed leadership, styling herself as "Queen of the East", but she was to become even more troublesome than the Sassanids that she was supposedly protecting Rome from.

A beautiful and courageous woman, she defeated a Roman force sent to subdue her, invaded Egypt and set up her own Palmyrene Empire. Minting coins in Alexandria with herself as "emperor" proved too much for the new emperor Aurelian, who needed to restore Rome's faltering grip on its empire. His forces defeated her army twice and she was captured trying to flee across the Euphrates River.

leader, Fakhr al-Din Mani, who grew wealthy on silk in Ottoman times. His construction is perched on a rocky outcrop, and was probably built upon earlier 12th-century fortifications. From here, the whole precarious position of Palmyra can be viewed along the edge of the Sabkhat al-Moh seasonal salt lake. The building of a new road winding up the back of the castle means that tour groups and local salesmen can easily get to this famous viewpoint, avoiding the lengthy 40-minute climb from the ruins. That in turn has led to the refurbishment of the castle, which has a series of narrow chambers and turrets akin to a mini Krac des Chevaliers (see page 355). Sunrise across the site is often eerily misty.

Valley of the Tombs

One of the most fascinating and unusual sights to be seen today is located a few kilometres from the main site – a series of tombs built both above and below ground. This is where the wealthy merchants of Palmyra constructed great tower tombs for themselves and their families. There are

BELOW: the Tower Tomb of Elahbel.

in fact three main sites of tombs, the southwest and southeast necropolises and the Valley of the Tombs itself.

The impressive **Tower Tomb of Elahbel** is the largest example of this type of construction. Built in AD 103 for a single family, it consists of an early underground chamber and four added floors, totalling 300 burial niches. Each recess for the dead person was closed with a limestone slab on which the features of the deceased were carved in high relief; there are many fine examples of these in museums around the country.

The subterranean **Tomb of the Three Brothers** is a complex of 65 bays with recesses – a popular method of burial in the 2nd–3rd centuries AD. The Hypogeum is reached down a flight of steps leading to a T-shaped chamber, in which are three broken sarcophagi. A vast array of hexagons is painted on the ceiling, but otherwise it is classically decorated. There are frescoes showing the legend of Achilles and the war of Troy, the abduction of Ganymede and portraits of the three brothers in circular frames. An inscription tells us that some of the burial chambers were sold off to other non-family members.

The modern **museum** (open daily 9am–6pm; admission fee) has superb carved heads from funerary tombs, family sarcophagi, fragments of delicate house mosaics and a complete model of the Temple of Bel. Of interest to the Silk Road traveller are the examples of Chinese silk clothing, particularly from the Iamblik Tower Tomb, which dates back to AD 83. The quality of these surviving silk fabrics used for wrapping the mummies is due to the dry desert climate. Imported silk from China was woven on special looms to produce monochrome or polychrome patterns, to which embroidery was sometimes added. As with any valuable commodity, Palmyrene craftsmen were also keen to reproduce these imports and so created local fabrics woven to imitate the more expensive Chinese silks. One display case is labelled "Silk fabrics from China and local imitations 1st–3rd century AD".

Towards Damascus

The most direct route from Palmyra to the Mediterranean is on to Homs and through the Homs Gap, passing close to Krac des Chevaliers, but the most common routing was southwest to Damascus. Inhabitants of Palmyra set up the first trading centre at **Qasr al-Hayr al-Gharbi** (Western Walled Castle) in the 1st century AD. Located within a well-watered area, thanks to the old Roman dam at nearby Harbaqa, it became an early Christian monastery before the Umayyad caliphs turned it into a hunting lodge. It was the counterbalance to their other lodge at Qasr al-Hayr al-Sharqi, but apart from a solid three-storey Byzantine tower, there is little to see here. The two semicircular towers of the gateway were removed and now grace the entrance to the National Archaeological Museum in Damascus (see page 353).

The Silk Road continues in the form of a small tarmac road down a rather inhospitable *wadi* shared only by the railway to Damascus. High in the barren mountains to the right and almost impossible to see from a distance is the remote 6th–15th-century Christian monastery called **Deir Mar Mousa** (www.deirmarmusa.org), named after an Ethiopian St Moses. From here, the Romans controlled their caravans passing along the natural highway through the *wadi* below, and some of the blocks of the present tower are from this time. The small church built in 1058 has interesting Greek frescoes depicting heaven and hell, and St Simeon atop his column. Nowadays the small community is extremely welcoming and offers accommodation and meals in exchange for a donation. There is an evening period of silent meditation, and at 7.30am guests are given the choice of prayers in Arabic, a walk in the mountains or dish-washing!

All roads from here lead to the M1 motorway, which bustles its way through the suburbs to the great capital Damascus.

The National Archaeological Museum in Damascus has reconstructed a complete tomb from Palmyra in its basement.

BELOW: The mummy of a man from Palmyra, over 2,000 years old.

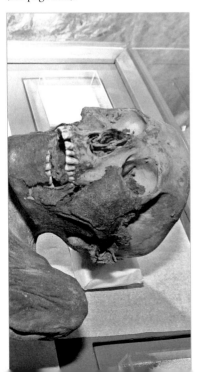

Silk in Mummification

The rows of ornate tower tombs outside Palmyra show the importance of the death ritual in the 1st–3rd centuries AD. All the major organs were removed from the body, which was filled with straw to maintain a natural shape. The brain was extracted in pieces through the nose or removed whole if the head was severed. The head was then replaced and held by wooden clasps at the base of the neck. These organs were then discarded, unlike the ancient Egyptian practice of storing them in canopic jars beside the body. At this stage the bodies were wrapped in layers of fabric such as linen or, in the case of wealthy families, imported Chinese silk.

Each layer of fabric was coated with bitumen, a natural asphalt obtained from the Euphrates Valley, and allowed to dry for up to 70 days. Completed mummies were placed inside family tombs along with their personal jewellery and luxuries, ensuring their continued high status in the afterlife. Examples of the fabrics used to inter the dead are on show at the Palmyra Museum. One of the Chinese silk fragments on display is from the face of a mummy, and is decorated with geometric patterns. An example of silk polychrome design found in the Kilot Tower Tomb of AD 40 has survived with remarkable details depicting Chinese dragons.

DAMASCUS

Along its great length, the Silk Road passes through some famous old centres, but **Damascus** (**Dimashq**) claims to be the oldest continuously inhabited city in the world. Proving this is extremely difficult, as there have been few opportunities to dig through the layers of this ancient city. Tablets from Mari 4,500 years ago mention Dimashq, "well-watered by the Barada River", lying on the way to the early ports of Tyre and Sidon. Egyptians, Hittites, Babylonians and Persians, in fact every civilisation of the region, has needed to take the city to confirm its authority. Early Christian sites are associated with St Paul, and later the emerging Arab civilisation naturally chose the city as its first capital. After ridding the region of the Crusaders in the 12th century, Saladin turned Damascus

The Jesus Minaret of the Umayyad Mosque, viewed from the rooftop Leila's Terrace restaurant.

into an intellectual centre of poets, artists and philosophers.

Despite this rich history, most of what can be seen today dates from Ottoman control, which lasted over 300 years. Generally the city has survived the centuries rather well, as generations of traders have prospered from new opportunities and adapted to the downturns. From the mid-17th century the Ottoman silk-weaving industry boomed in both Aleppo and Damascus, using silk cocoons produced in the nearby mountains.

Though not traditionally considered a target for terrorist attack, Damascus has recently seen a number of clashes between protestors and security forces, including two car bombs and a large explosion in Midan in which civilians were killed. These events are likely linked to the ongoing political unrest in Syria but terror attacks in public places remain a distinct possibility.

The Old City

The area known as the **Old City** has been continually shaped and adapted over thousands of years and yet still

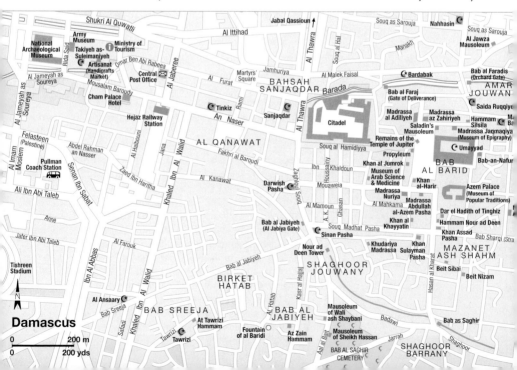

Damascus

0 ——— 200 m
0 ——— 200 yds

retains a unique identity. The area is transforming itself yet again, this time into a tourist destination with a modern infrastructure, as well as important historical sites. The western end of the Old City is essentially a number of parallel streets running towards the Umayyad Mosque. The centuries-old souks are concentrated between Straight Street and the covered thoroughfare known as the **Souq al-Hamidiyya**. A stroll under the bullet-riddled metal canopy in the mornings is quite pleasant, but can be a struggle in the evening crush. The layout of the souks is organised by product, with fabrics and silk generally to the southwest of the Umayyad Mosque, along Mouaweia Street.

The **Khan al-Harir** (Silk Warehouse) contains a fountain and domed ceiling surrounded by countless shimmering wedding dresses. Two centres trying to keep the local silk-weaving tradition alive are the nearby School for Oriental Crafts and the Azem School, built in 1770. Inside the **Azem Palace**, a splendid 18th-century governor's residence, is the **Museum of**

Popular Traditions. Set around a courtyard are themed rooms depicting life in Old Damascus. If you don't get to visit a real bathing house, there is an original *hammam* here.

Away from the souks are more **Damascene houses** in the old Jewish and Christian quarters, some recently renovated into trendy boutique hotels and restaurants. One that is still kept as a private family residence (but open to the public) is the **Dahdah House**, a former Pasha's palace with three graceful *iwans* overlooking a central courtyard. Back on Straight Street are the remains of a **Monumental Arch (Bab al Kanise)** slowly being strangled by the traffic blocking the narrow streets around it. Just before Straight Street reaches the East Gate, Ananias Street leads off to the left to the **Ananias Chapel**, where St Paul's sight was miraculously restored.

Continue following the old walls to the busy **Bab Touma** (Thomas's Gate), an area of modern cafés and bars. To the north of the Umayyad Mosque near Bab al-Faradis (Orchard Gate) is the **Saida Ruqqiyeh Mosque**, a Shia

Fabric woven with raised patterns known as brocade became synonymous with the city. Figured woven material, especially with silk, took its name as "damask".

BELOW: the ablutions fountain in the Umayyad Mosque.

A Christian monk in Bosra is said to have conversed with the young Muhammad while he worked with the camel traders from Arabia, and foretold that he would someday become a great prophet.

BELOW: the basalt theatre of Bosra.

tomb belonging to the daughter of Imam Hussein. The Iranians restored the site in the 1980s in their usual bright style of dazzling mirrors, silver and blue tilework. The combination of cobalt blue, turquoise and gold reflecting from a million sources is stunning. The final climb up to the East Gateway of the mosque can be eased by stopping at one of the traditional cafés. On the left is the **Bab an-Nafura** (Fountain Gate), whose terrace and interior are always crowded with people drinking tea or coffee, or smoking fruit-flavoured tobacco in a *narghile* (hookah pipe), especially in the early evenings when there is sometimes a traditional storyteller.

In the heart of the old city is the **Umayyad Mosque** (open dawn–dusk, closed Fri noon prayers; admission fee), the latest in a long line of religious buildings on this ancient sacred site. There is evidence of worship here from over 3,000 years ago, and each successive civilisation has adapted the area for its own use. In the first century of Islam, a great centre for worship was needed, and negotiations

took place to occupy the site of the church. Despite invasions, earthquakes and fires, the structure has remained remarkably intact and any repairs have been well conducted.

The Umayyad Mosque is usually first viewed from the open space beside the columns of the Western Temple Gate, all that remains of an earlier Roman temple. Enter the vast marble **courtyard** to be dazzled by the gold-and-green mosaics of the prayer hall facade and small octagonal treasury, both of which benefit from really close inspection.

The **prayer hall** is essentially the old Byzantine cathedral, which being aligned to the east was long and narrow. The Muslims placed a *mihrab* (prayer niche) in the southern wall and so the room became unusually short and wide instead. The pretty green-domed marble shrine to the left of the *mihrab* is said to contain the head of **John the Baptist**. Beyond the Dome of the Clocks (which unsurprisingly used to house the clocks of the mosque) is a doorway to the small golden **Shrine of Hussein**, containing

the head of the Third Imam. This is another site of importance for Shia pilgrims from Iran, who have previously visited the Mashhad al-Hussein in Aleppo.

Another famous shrine is through the entrance underneath the Minaret of the Bride, in the centre of the northern wall. The simple tomb in the garden belongs to **Saladin**, the great Muslim warrior and adversary of the Crusaders. His body is in the 19th-century white marble tomb, which replaced the original dark wooden sarcophagus beside it.

National Museum

Many objects are laid out in the garden of the **National Archaeological Museum** (open Wed–Mon 9am–6pm; admission fee) before the imposing entranceway, removed from the site of Qasr al-Hayr al-Gharbi (see page 349), west of Palmyra. Many of the rooms are long and narrow, laid out in a large L-shape, making for a roughly chronological but not very cohesive presentation. The objects themselves are world-class, however, including the

first complete alphabet of 30 cuneiform signs on a small clay tablet found at Ugarit, near Latakia. From the same period (around 1300 BC) is an extraordinary carved ivory inlaid table-top.

There are some direct connections with the Silk Road trade, such as a fresco of a 12th–13th-century man from the Far East fighting a dragon, known as the Raqqa Cavalier. There are also excellent Roman marble sarcophagi and several large mosaics and carvings from Palmyra. Down the steps is the removed Palmyrene burial chamber of Yarhai with individual carved portraits of the deceased. At the far end of the museum is the 2nd-century synagogue removed from Dura Europos, with wonderfully vibrant frescoes showing Old Testament scenes and a painted wooden ceiling of faces.

Across the road is the delightful **Takiyeh as-Suleimaniyeh**, with its two thin Ottoman minarets, built by the architect Sinan, who also designed the Khusuwiye Mosque in Aleppo and Istanbul's famous Suleiman Mosque. It was constructed to aid the passage of

BELOW: modern-day traffic alongside the ancient city walls of Damascus.

TIP

Zabadani and Sirghayya are served by the seasonal and irregular narrow-gauge steam railway, all that is left of the line that once connected Damascus with Beirut.

pilgrims to Mecca, with a hostel area (now the National Army Museum) and madrassa (now an artist and souvenir enclave).

On the outskirts of the city is the **Tomb of Saida Zeinab**, granddaughter of the Prophet Muhammad and another place of pilgrimage for Shia Muslims. It is more modern than the similar Imamzade in Iran, with a large open courtyard and a square blue prayer hall built like a low ziggurat, topped with a squat golden dome. The walls and simple minarets are covered in flowing scripts and flower motifs, but here it is not overdone.

AROUND DAMASCUS

To the south of Damascus, the Hauran landscape is a fertile but stark region of extinct cones and rugged volcanic debris that has resulted in some unusual constructions, such as the black basalt **Bosra Theatre**. The city was known to the ancient Egyptians and Nabataeans because of its position on the route connecting Palmyra with Petra, and was a strategic centre for the Romans. The Arabs swept

in quickly from the south and took Bosra from the Byzantines, in the same year as the death of the Prophet Muhammad.

The almost perfect theatre is the main attraction and is an unusual sight dressed in its black stone. But it certainly has an oppressive feel to it, either with its tight dimensions, or the fact that it is hemmed in on all sides by the modern town, giving it no breathing space whatsoever. Walking around the Old City is like wandering through an old black-and-white photograph of ruins taken a century ago. Piles of desolate carved blocks lie next to lively modern homes created out of ancient structures, and it's uncertain where one stops and the other begins. At the far side is the quaint **Mosque of Omar**, said to have been started by that first wave of Arabs and claiming to be the oldest mosque in Syria, yet what we see today is a 12th-century Ayyubid building.

The language spoken by Christ and the merchants of Palmyra was Aramaic, which is now only used in a few remote villages. One of these is

BELOW: glassware for sale in the old town of Bosra.

Ma'alula, a tight collection of pretty pastel-coloured houses built across a mountainside. Two buildings indicate this to be an early and important Christian centre – the Monastery of St Sarkis, high up on the cliff face (the same Sarkis or Sergius who was martyred at Resafeh), and the lower Convent of St Takla.

Homs

Focus of the current unrest in Syria, the city of **Homs** (**Hims**) developed at the point where the overland route from Palmyra crosses the Orontes River. It grew in importance in Roman times when it was known as Emesa, especially when Emperor Septimius Severus married Julia Domna, the daughter of the local high priest, in AD 187.

Al-Zenar Church (Church of the Virgin's Belt) in the east of the city is of particular interest, but was badly damaged by government forces in 2012. According to the legend, the Virgin Mary died in AD 56, and as the angels were carrying her body to heaven, St Thomas asked for a sign that he could show the other Christians, so she gave him her belt *(zenar)*. Thomas took this with him to India until his relics were returned here, deposited in this church and subsequently forgotten until rediscovered in 1953. The light-beige belt is 74cm (30 ins) long and 5cm (2 ins) wide, and made of wool, possibly with flax and silk. The belt was coiled into a circular reliquary, in its original box, in a small shrine inside the church.

Krac des Chevaliers

Recognised as a UNESCO World Heritage Site since 2006, Krac des Chavaliers was the greatest Crusader castle ever built, controlling the Homs Gap, the easiest and shortest route from Palmyra to the sea. Initially constructed by the Emir of Homs around 1030, it was known as Hisn al Akad – the castle of the Kurds. It was given to the Knights Hospitaller by Raymond II, Count of Tripoli, in 1142 and the Crusaders expanded the structure as part of a line of hilltop castles, while they sought to reclaim Jerusalem from the Muslims.

BELOW LEFT: the ruins of the Assassin castle of Qalaat al-Khaf.
BELOW: Krac des Chevaliers.

TIP

Take a late afternoon stroll along Jdeida's smartly cobbled streets and call at Beit Wakil, Dar Zamaria, Mashrabiya or Yasmeen House for a drink.

Krac des Chevaliers is what every castle should look like – massive, brooding and impregnable, with a surprise round every corner. The fortifications are feats of engineering, and the concentric design allowed defenders to protect themselves on all sides. The distances between the inner and outer walls maximize the accuracy of bow shots, and the angling of the outer walls makes them almost impossible to mine. The earliest extant buildings date from the mid-12th century and it is still possible to walk along the walls and climb original staircases. The vaulted interiors and cloisters are well preserved and so are the cavernous storerooms. It is still possible to see original paintwork and remains of stone carving around the windows and doors in the Great Hall and loggia.

A walk around the castle is tiring, and your lasting impression will depend upon the weather – it is hot in summer and gale-soaked in winter. Few days up here are as pleasant as postcards suggest, but you do get the authentic Crusader experience.

Assassin castles

The Assassins originated in Iran (see page 329), but they had a strong presence in Syria as well. Rashid al-Din Sinan, who was known as the "Old Man of the Mountain", was in charge of the network of 10 Assassins' castles in Syria at the end of the 12th century, all of which controlled lucrative trade and communications routes running to the Mediterranean. As the Assassins' Shia influence in Persia faded and ultimately disappeared, Syria held out for much longer by making allegiances with the Crusaders who were attempting to take Jerusalem by fighting the Sunni Muslims. This Shia/Christian alliance was much to the annoyance of the Ayyubid Dynasty Sunni followers of Saladin. Many of these Assassin fortresses are in stunning locations, but most are now in ruins; the easiest to visit is the imposing fortress at **Masyaf**, whilst one of the most remote is **Qasr al-Khaf**.

TOWARDS LEBANON

At various times the Silk Road from Damascus ran to Byblos, Beirut, Sidon

or Tyre, the last being the easiest route as it went around, rather than over, the Anti-Lebanon range. Today the direct route to Tyre is impossible to retrace due to the ongoing conflict between Israel and Hezbollah.

West of Damascus, each hill reveals another new development tucked into a small valley as the city expands into every tiny parcel of land. Beyond the urban sprawl, a few mulberry trees and conifers have escaped the gnawing of hungry earth-diggers supplying yet more building materials. Heading towards the border, most of the traffic veers north to the pleasant towns of **Zabadani** and **Sirghayya**, closer to Baalbek than Damascus. The quiet road to the border winds through spectacular folded hills, revealing slices of geological history.

ALONG THE EUPHRATES

With the demise of Palmyra, the alternative route from Dura Europos up the Euphrates to Aleppo and Antioch became the main trade route, reducing desert travel to a trickle. The modern road runs through barren desert and is often not close to the river. This is a Bedouin region, where overland trade still continues with neighbouring countries. The Bedouin get certain government benefits; they cannot be prosecuted for speeding and are not obliged to register their trucks and vehicles, hence the lack of number plates.

Resafeh

Resafeh (**Rusafah**) was a relatively small caravan halt between Damascus and northeastern Syria until the Romans withdrew from Dura Europos and re-established their garrison here, building a supply road across the desert from Palmyra. Its location seems strange, being some distance from the river, but this was the route the traders were forced to take, away from the riverbank during times of flood. Unusually, this also became a place of great pilgrimage for early Christians when a Roman soldier by the name of Sergius was martyred here for refusing to make sacrifices to Jupiter. The town became known as

A handmade carpet featuring a traditional design.

BELOW: among the ruins of Basilica A at Resafeh.

Sergiopolis and benefited from lavish gifts of churches, water cisterns and strong walls to defend itself from the desert Arabs.

Highlights of the extensive site are the triple-entrance north gate, the metropolitan church with a curved apse and the impressive underground water cisterns built to supply the desert pilgrims. In the southeastern corner of the site is the beautiful Basilica A, whose original archways were reinforced against continuing earthquake damage by being split into two smaller arches.

From Resafeh, the original course of the Euphrates (now under Lake Asad) swung north, leaving just a 70-km (42-mile) run west to Aleppo. The building of dams across the Euphrates and discovery of oil in the northeast has created a busy superhighway running into Aleppo. A giant electricity plant on the left of the road signals the start of the city's industrial sprawl, with the smoke belching from the five huge chimneys adding to the terrible air pollution and smog that hangs permanently over Aleppo.

ALEPPO

Tucked into the northwest corner of Syria, **Aleppo** (known locally as Halab, a name possibly derived from Aramaic) is one of the oldest cities in the world. Between the Euphrates and the Mediterranean, the city controls access to the sea, Africa and Europe. This strategic centre was coveted, attacked and sometimes destroyed by all the major powers in the region: Egyptian, Hittite, Assyrian, Achaemenid, Greek, Roman, Byzantine, Sassanid, Arab, Turk, Crusader, Mongol, Mameluke, Ottoman and French. With such a colourful and varied history, no wonder the city is a treasure trove of antiquities.

The first thing that strikes you about Aleppo is how lively it is, not just a sterile museum item. Each dog-legged alleyway and all the imposing structures meld into a harmonious, vibrant city, although it has a slightly skewed appearance from all of the earthquakes and invaders that have rumbled through. Today, the centre of the city can be split into new and old, with both sections having many sites of interest.

Jdeida, the New City, was home to many wealthy Christian merchants in the 17th century wishing to live away from the noise, grime and souks of the Old City. One house, with a courtyard, fountain and *iwan*, has been converted into the **Museum of Popular Tradition** (**Beit Ajiqbash**), which shows how people lived in the Mameluke period. This entire area has undergone a remarkable transformation in recent years, and many other residences have been turned into small boutique hotels and trendy restaurants.

On the edge of the Old City is the **National Museum** (open Wed–Mon 9am–1pm and 4–6pm; admission fee), which always seems to be in the middle of a chaotic refit. Eight rooms dedicated to different sites run around a central courtyard, which displays a

BELOW: Aleppo's Citadel.

large wild-animal mosaic and reconstructed underground tomb. Room 2 has the fabulous collection uncovered at Mari, including the wonderful 4,000-year-old statue of an Amorite spring goddess holding a pot from which water once flowed, as well as the strange statue of a bearded man wearing a layered dress of feathers. The Islamic arts room has some interesting Korans and a large model of Aleppo's Old City.

Just to the north of the museum are a few deteriorating streets containing restaurants and hotels, including the venerable **Baron Hotel**. T.E. Lawrence, Theodore Roosevelt, Agatha Christie, Freya Stark and Charles Lindbergh are just some of the famous guests to have stayed here. To the east of the museum is the Clock Tower, surrounded by aromatic streets of coffee-grinders, fruit-juice-makers, nut-sellers and teashops.

The Citadel

Dominating the eastern end of the **Old City** is the formidable **Citadel** (open Wed–Mon 9am–6pm; admission fee), built on a natural mound around which the city has developed. Evidence only goes back to 1000 BC, but it has been the site of countless temples and palaces destroyed and rebuilt by each new conqueror. The moat and sloping stone glacis completely enclose the structure, entered via the 11th-century monumental gateway, ramp and bridge. After negotiating the twists and turns of the secure entry corridor, the area within the walls is laid out like a small town, inside which the early inhabitants of Aleppo could shelter for safety. To the left is the Mosque of Abraham and a bathing complex, ahead is the Great Mosque and café terrace, while on the right are the amphitheatre and beautiful facade of the Ayyubid Palace, with *ablaq* decoration (alternating black and white).

There are usually excellent views across the city, depending on the pollution. Before returning through the gateway, it is well worth climbing up to the Mameluke Throne Room, a real surprise of delicate artwork and design after the heavy masonry outside.

The souk

Traces of the Silk Road still exist inside the souk, which begins immediately outside the Citadel at the **Souq ash-Shouna**, recently renovated into a tourist handicrafts market. In fact this whole area received a facelift when Aleppo became the Islamic Capital of Culture in 2006. At the other end of this ancient shopping mall is the simple design and decoration of the mid-16th-century Ottoman **Khusuwiye Mosque**. Inside are eight black-and-white arches supporting the great dome with a gallery of alternate green and orange windows below. A chandelier hangs from the central motif, otherwise all is in white and simply beautiful. Comparisons can be drawn with the Takiyeh in Damascus and even the Suleiman Mosque in Istanbul, as these were also designed by the architect Sinan.

BELOW: the view from the roof of the Citadel.

A few conical mud houses are still to be found in rural areas south of Aleppo. Known as "beehive houses", the walls are half a metre (1.5ft) thick, keeping the locals warm in winter and cool in summer.

BELOW: one of the many corridors inside the historic souk at Aleppo.

Diving into the narrow alleys, the salesmen become less insistent further away from the Citadel, as the old borders of the 37 sections of the traditional souk become less distinct. The main thoroughfare from the Citadel is the **Souq al-Attarine** (Spice Souk), the bustling heart of this labyrinthine jumble. It is also a great seasonal meeting place for the many tribes scattered across the north of the country.

The **Great Mosque** is almost completely surrounded by the souk, from which there is a rush at prayer times as stallholders and traders take heed of the muezzin. Its minaret has been slightly rocked about by tremors, but amazingly still stands after 900 years as the oldest part of the building. An expansive courtyard leads into the prayer hall, inside which is a *mihrab* towards Mecca and next to it the shrine containing the head of Zacharias, father of John the Baptist.

The mosque was built beside the earlier Byzantine Cathedral of St Helen, and immediately across the alley from the western doorway is the delightful **Madrassa al-Halawiyya**, a Koranic school built out of the 6th-century cathedral. Inside the dusty prayer hall are remnants of the earlier Christian site: a dome supported by Corinthian columns. Look closely at the two outer capitals on the western side to see the acanthus leaves carved as they blow in the wind, an effect also to be seen on the facade at St Simeon's Church. The *mihrab* lies almost unseen along the dark southern wall, but is indicated by the rows of prayer mats. A few locals hang about in the ramshackle rooms off the small courtyard or make ablutions in the pool, but nobody takes much notice of a casual visitor in this forgotten enclave.

About 50 metres further south, following the walls of the mosque, is the **Khan al-Harir** (Silk Warehouse), a 16th-century, two-storey trading centre for silk arranged around a courtyard. This building was the Iranian consulate until the end of Ottoman

Souk Highlights

The Khan as-Sabun (a 16th-century soap warehouse) and the nearby Khan al-Wazir (a 17th-century minister's warehouse), to the east of the Great Mosque, are wonderful examples of trading centres that once acted as hosts to the fully laden camel caravans arriving in the city, and are still important today.

The soap *khan* is today very tranquil, with trails of shady vines drooping from arched terraces and blocks of Aleppo's famous soap still for sale. The crowded shops sell a vast array of fabrics including silk, whose owners are more than willing to talk to anyone interested, especially if it might lead to a sale. As a legacy of the Ottoman period, local silk production has only stopped in the last few years, unable to compete with cheaper imports from the east, mainly China and Korea.

occupation. Continue straight ahead across the many east–west alleys towards the large **Khan al-Jumruk** (Customs Warehouse), originally built for European consuls in 1574 and known as the "English Factory" for almost 300 years. Nowhere typifies the modern usage of these old buildings better than this bustling fabric centre, bulging with sacks and rolls of materials leaning against every possible surface, including the small mosque in the centre.

Continuing east, the main thoroughfare widens slightly, but there is still a high chance of being hit by a fully loaded donkey. At the end on the right is an old mosque, possibly the oldest in Syria, dating to AD 636, with a few reused ancient blocks in its construction. One of its three names is **Al-Tuteh** (Mulberry Tree), perhaps a reflection of the importance of the silk trade, which ferried goods from the old walled city through the Antakya (Antioch) gateway just ahead. Immediately outside are the bus stations, some of which still serve Antakya.

Mashhad al-Hussein

The main road west out of the city is Seif ad-Dawla Street. Turn left after passing beneath the railway bridge, to one of the most important Shia sites in Syria. The 12th-century **Mashhad al-Hussein** embodies the Shia traditions of the local dynasties in Aleppo during the time of the orthodox Sunni rule of the Ayyubids. The shrine contains a piece of marble impregnated with the blood of the Third Imam, Hussein, whose head and those of his 15 followers were carried here from Kerbala in Iraq, where they were martyred in AD 680. The heads were taken on to Damascus, but the stained marble remains here, placed on red silk inside a gold-and-silver shrine venerated by Shia pilgrims from around the world, especially Iran.

AROUND ALEPPO

Named after the Persian wife of Seleucus, **Apamea** became a great military base, with thousands of trained horses and reputedly 500 war elephants imported from India. But the location was not well chosen, as it

The "English Factory" was established at the Khan al-Jumruk by traders of the Levant Company in the 16th century to profit from the annual silk caravans arriving from the Persian Gulf.

BELOW: the delightful courtyard of Madrassa al-Halawiyya.

constantly suffered from earthquakes throughout the Roman, Byzantine, Persian, Arab and Crusader conquests.

From the Antioch Gate, a walk along the mile-long stretch of colonnaded street is a real delight, especially past the row of fluted columns, spiralling in different directions. The effect of these under connecting entablature is mesmerising, even though most of the buildings are quite ruined. One of the final uses for Apamea was as an overnight halt for the Turks en route to Mecca. The 16th-century Ottoman *khan* at the foot of the hill now houses an extensive collection of large mosaics removed from the site. This museum and the nearby theatre are two small disappointments in what is otherwise an atmospheric and beautiful site.

Church of St Simeon

Religious tourism is not a new phenomenon. In the 5th century AD early Christian pilgrims travelled great distances to seek out the ascetic **Simeon the Stylite** (*stylos* is Greek for "pillar"), probably the most famous person in the world during his lifetime, who dedicated his life to the worship of God by rejecting all basic comforts. Seeking solitude, he retreated to the top of an 18-metre (60-ft) -high stone pillar, where he survived for around 35 years, giving daily religious pronouncements. Even after his death, people still visited the site, and this great church was built for worship, unusually centred on the remains of his pillar, rather than the altar. It was the largest Christian building erected for 500 years, until the great cathedrals of Europe. His body was initially buried in nearby Antioch, but was considered to be such an important relic that it was later removed to the Byzantine capital, Constantinople.

The setting of this church, known as **Qalaat Semaan** (Fortress of Simeon) is tranquil, especially after the day-trippers have left, when the orange-tinted weathered limestone starts to glow in the late afternoon sun. Approaching the triple entrance of the church, notice the two capitals holding up the large central arch and the acanthus leaves carved as they blow in the wind, similar to those of the contemporary cathedral

BELOW: herders and their flocks near Apamea.

now part of the Madrassa al-Halawiyya in Aleppo. There are wonderful views across the surrounding countryside down to the village of Deir Semaan (Monastery of Simeon), which became the final stop for pilgrims before climbing up to the church.

TO THE TURKISH BORDER

The rolling landscape of Aleppo's wealthy suburbs gives way to plains of wheat and later a drier, rugged terrain of olive groves interspersed with vines. This is the region of the so-called **Dead Cities**, over 700 sites of occupation between the 1st and 8th centuries AD, now mainly abandoned. The completeness of the stone buildings, including entire villages, has puzzled experts for years, but it would seem that the reason for the sudden exodus was a downturn in olive oil demand, traded through Antioch. Following the collapse of this lucrative market to the Roman Empire, farmers were immediately forced to grow grains in the more fertile river valleys to become self-sufficient. The most impressive Dead Cities to visit

are Serjilla and Al-Barah to the south of Idlib.

Forty kilometres (24 miles) beyond Aleppo is one of the most amazing stretches of Roman Silk Road to be seen anywhere. At a small village by the name of Tal al-Karamah, just inside the province of Idlib, the main road to the border crests a small hill and cuts through a section of ancient paved **Roman road**. The shiny limestone blocks meander ahead through some modern housing, whilst the surface makes a reasonable soccer pitch for the local children.

In the opposite direction (back towards Aleppo) the road twists down and around a small wood before finally disappearing into a field after about 400 metres. Some of the massive blocks are misplaced, but it is remarkably intact and even possible to discern the ruts made by wheeled carts rumbling towards Antioch almost 2,000 years ago. It is a most unlikely reminder of the journey being made. The terrain becomes more rugged towards the border, which is located in a small dry valley.

BELOW: carved acanthus leaves on the Church of St Simeon.

LEBANON

Lebanon is a land so imbued with silk that it even has its own Silk Museum, harking back to a time when great cities traded across the Mediterranean.

Main attractions
AANJAR
BAALBEK
B'SOUS SILK MUSEUM
BEIRUT: NATIONAL MUSEUM,
    AUB MUSEUM
TYRE: AL-BASS, AL-MINA

Long before silk arrived in Tyre, the Phoenicians traded from these ports all around the Mediterranean. Beirut was never as important as Tyre and Sidon in the south, or Byblos to the north, but it did become a centre for intellectual thinking, law and philology, with no equal in Roman times. Chinese silk dyed in purple from Tyre became the most sought-after luxury garment in Rome, at the culmination of this epic Silk Road overland journey.

Encouraged by the Byzantines, silk-weaving became a major industry, whose skills were passed on to Greece and Sicily. Arabs and Crusaders took control and then moved on, until the Ottoman silk industry boom in the mid-19th century, which transformed the mountainous hinterland.

War-torn and battered through the 1970s and '80s, Lebanon emerged briefly in the late '90s with new hope and enthusiasm for the future. Sadly it has descended back into armed conflict both internally and with its two neighbours, Israel and Syria. Hezbollah and Amal forces seized western Beirut in 2008 following the government's declaration that Hezbollah's communications network was illegal, and 62 people died in the ensuing violence. The government came under pressure once again in 2011 after 10 ministers resigned due to tensions resulting from the Special Tribunal for Lebanon, which was expected to indict Hezbollah for the murder of Prime Minister Rafik Hariri in 2005. Political infighting followed, the Hezbollah-led opposition March 8 Alliance gained a parliamentary majority, and their candidate, Najib Mikati, became the latest prime minister of this sadly troubled land.

SYRIAN BORDER TO BEIRUT

Leaving the border, the landscape changes completely, from the dry, rugged Anti-Lebanon Mountains of

LEFT: the ruins of the Great Mosque at Aanjar.
RIGHT: view towards Beirut from B'sous.

Syria to the well-watered southern Bekaa Valley. Almost immediately you come to the ruins of **Aanjar**, an 8th-century Omayyid town built to control the caravan trade along this route from Damascus. Interestingly, it was the only ancient trading centre in Lebanon to be inland and it also doubled as a summer hunting lodge for the caliph. The town is laid out as a perfect square, divided into quarters by two main central roads with gateways at each end. At the upper part of this quiet site is the famous restored palace with graceful arches on two storeys.

Baalbek

Only 35km (21 miles) away up the Bekaa Valley is Lebanon's greatest Roman site at **Baalbek**, a name taken from the worship of the Phoenician god Baal in the Bekaa. The site seems to have been continuously inhabited for about 4,000 years, with traces of Phoenician, Greek (when it was known as Heliopolis), Byzantine and Arab dynasties, as well as the major Roman buildings to be seen today. The temples of Jupiter and Bacchus are two of the largest in the world, which dominate the site with the scale of their columns, entablatures and carvings. Nearby is the smaller Temple of Venus and unusual Hexagonal Court.

Getting to the coast means climbing out of the Bekaa up a southern spur of the Lebanon Mountains, twisting around some of the old abandoned sections of rack-and-pinion railway from Damascus. The views back across the southern Bekaa to Mount Hermon (Jebel al-Sheikh to the locals) can be stunning in good weather.

Silk Museum

High in the hills above Beirut in the village of **B'sous** is a small museum in a converted silk mill dedicated to the manufacture, trade and use of silk. Follow the signs, from the main Damascus road through the village of Aley, marked "Musée de la Soie", or ask for *mathaf harir*. The **Silk Museum**

ENTERING AND LEAVING LEBANON

It is best to obtain a Lebanese visa before arrival in Lebanon. The southern border with Israel is closed, as, for the time being, is the border with Syria. (See Travel Tips, page 432, for more information on transport in Lebanon.)

When it is open, the main border crossing from **Syria** is at Masnaa. From here, continue with your bus or taxi to Beirut, or get out to visit Aanjar and Baalbek. During any period of unrest within Lebanon, the Bekaa Valley, with its Hezbollah strongholds, is usually one of the first sites to become out of bounds, so choose your visit carefully. There is plenty of public transport on to Beirut, but during the summer of 2006, Israel bombed and destroyed many of the strategic bridges and main roads in this mountainous region, which still causes traffic chaos. The situation is further complicated by the current unrest in Syria.

From Beirut, it is possible to travel on to Tyre further south, a journey that can easily be undertaken by taxi or hire car. The route south along the coast passes many Palestinian refugee camps that can be potentially problematic and even out of bounds. Roadblocks will stop you if there is a problem, and travel south of the Litani River along the Israeli border is severely restricted. Tyre, only 80km (48 miles) south of Beirut, is still being fought over today.

There is also a crossing at Aarida, north of Tripoli, which leads to Latakia in western Syria. The border crossings at Aabboudiye and Al-Qaa both lead to the troubled Syrian city of Homs.

(open May–Sept Tue–Sun 10am–6pm; admission fee) was founded in 2001 by George Asseily and his wife Alexandra. Despite the lack of tourists, the small team strive to preserve the silk legend with an informative video presentation. The museum deals with Silk Road history as well as highlighting the 19th-century Lebanese silk industry, which used this mill and many others, when Mount Lebanon was known as the "Mountain of Silk". There is even a selection of live silkworms, from tiny grubs to fully grown caterpillars gorging themselves on tender, locally grown mulberry leaves, until starting to spin a cocoon around themselves.

The route down to the Mediterranean coast is a thrilling descent through picturesque scenery.

BEIRUT

Beirut (Beyrouth) has an amazing early history that has seen the headland protect fleets of Phoenician biremes, Greek triremes, Roman galleys and Ottoman galleons. Once the hotspot for famous celebrities in the 1960s, Beirut is just a shadow of its former self, but despite many difficulties, it is striving yet again to be a top resort and a financial centre for the region. Reminders of the unrest are everywhere – from the bombed-out shell of the old Holiday Inn to streets still lined with tanks and armoured cars. Beirut has become synonymous with the troubles in the Middle East, an image that it is struggling to shake off, but on a calm day there is nowhere better to have a sumptuous meal with magnificent views, promenade along the Corniche and party till the early hours.

The **National Museum** (www.beirut nationalmuseum.com; open Tue–Sun 9am–5pm; admission fee) suffered as much as any building during the civil war, being located right on the Green Line separating the warring factions. An unnerving video presentation shows how the collection was protected during this time.

Of particular interest are the objects from Tyre, including 2nd-century BC marble sarcophagi, one with fabulous details of Greek battles and another known as the "Drunken Cupids". The "Legend of Achilles" is decorated with amazing figures on the frieze carved

BELOW: weaving at the Silk Museum.

Silk Industry in Lebanon

The Silk Museum in B'sous is located inside one of the many redundant silk factories on the Lebanese hillsides. Mulberry trees grow easily here, and silk production was the major activity during Ottoman control in the Middle Ages, employing people of all age groups from the peasant farming communities.

By the late 19th century, there were over 3 million mulberry trees growing in the area. In the industry's heyday, silk accounted for half the income from the Mount Lebanon region, traded through Beirut and Tripoli. Many investors came from France to set up cocoon-reeling factories for the export of yarn to Lyon. Some of the old silk factories, such as Deir al-Qamar and Beit Eddine, have become famous sites in their own right.

almost in the round. A much earlier connection with ancient Egypt is the black basalt stele of Pharaoh Ramses II from the 13th century BC – an example of the strict formality that ruled art here until the arrival of the Achaemenids in the 6th century BC. The 5th-century BC capital with bull protomes found at Sidon would not look out of place at Persepolis. The Anthropoid Sarcophagus, found in Sidon, shows all the cultural influences of the great empires in the region – Egyptian, Persian and Greek.

Reopened in 2006 after extensive renovation is the impressively modern **American University of Beirut** (AUB) **Archaeological Museum** (www.aub.edu.lb/museum_archeo; Mon-Fri 9am-4pm; free) in Hawra District, which originally opened in 1868. Of interest is a section about purple dye from Tyre, a small loaded camel statue from the Achaemenid period and a great photo of Lebanon from space showing the major archaeological sites and trade routes. Notice the number of sites directly inland from Tyre, indicating the route used from Damascus around the Golan Heights. Guided tours and audio tours are available on request.

SIDON

It is only 40km (24 miles) from Beirut to Sidon (Saida), an important trading and shipbuilding centre from Phoenician times, which reached prominence under the Persians, for whom it became a renowned glass-making centre. Most of what can be seen dates back to Crusader times, including the quaint Sea Castle, built to defend the harbour using blocks pillaged from nearby Roman buildings.

TYRE

For more ancient sites covering the period of silk trade, we must head for the ultimate destination on our journey, the port of Tyre, now called Sour. Tyre has been shaped by all the major civilisations of the region – Egyptians, Phoenicians, Assyrians, Greeks and

Romans. It lent its name to the royal purple dye, created from the tiny sea shells found off the shore, that graced the silk garments worn by some of the greatest leaders the world has ever known. A pile of ancient shells, known as Murex Hill, has survived from this trade inland from the harbour.

The **Al-Bass** site contains the large hippodrome and a vast Roman necropolis with fine examples of carved marble sarcophagi covering an 800-year span from the 2nd century BC, even though some of the tombs have obviously been reused. The triumphal arch and hippodrome are similar to those at Leptis Magna in Libya.

The coastal **Al-Mina** site is located on a promontory overlooking the Egyptian harbour, facing south. A colonnaded road, an agora and a wonderful line of columns stretch towards the sea. The Roman baths are a reminder of the site of Carthage in Tunisia. Such reminders of distant Carthage and Leptis Magna across the Mediterranean are understandable, as both were wealthy Roman cities based upon earlier Phoenician harbours.

TIP

The Mouawad Museum, centrally located downtown inside the secure zone, has many ancient objects placed around the garden.

BELOW: smoking *nargiles* on Beirut's Corniche.

TURKEY

The last leg of the 10,500-km (6,500-mile) journey from China to Europe often meant heading into Asia Minor, either to the port of Antioch or across Anatolia to the magnificent city of Istanbul.

O nce they crossed into Anatolia – in modern Turkey – the weary travellers on the Silk Road may still have had hundreds of kilometres to go. They might take the northern route west, threading along the Black Sea coast via Trebizond (Trabzon) to reach the Byzantine and Ottoman capital of Constantinople, which was to become Istanbul. Another way of reaching the city's fabulous bazaars was by continuing right across the central Anatolian plains, following the Persian Royal Road and avoiding the steep mountains to the north and south, heading to the major cities where they could trade along the way – Diyarbakır and Mardin, Konya and Bursa.

The east

Entering Turkey from the east, specifically from modern Iran, Armenia and Georgia, is now easier than it has been for decades. Far from the standard tourist trail there are also a number of significant sites, not least among them **Mount Ararat**.

The Ararat massif is 40km (25 miles) in length and includes the highest peak in Turkey: Mount Ararat itself. Known most widely as the place where Noah's ark came to rest, the mountain is also the national symbol of Armenia, featuring on the country's coat of arms and bank notes. A climbing permit

and certified guide are required should you wish to climb the peak.

15km (9 miles) to the southwest of Ararat is Dogubeyazit, the unprepossessing town that marks the border with Iran. Two things make Dogubeyazit worth a visit, however: the views of Ararat (5137m/3192ft), Little Ararat (3896m/2421ft) and Tendurek Dagi (3533m/2195); and the spectacular **Ishak Pasha Palace** (admission fee). Begun in 1685 by Colak Abdi Pasha and completed a century later by his grandson Ishak

Main attractions

ANTAKYA
MARDIN
URFA: HARRAN
CAPPADOCIA
KONYA: MEVLÂNA TEKKE MÜZESI
EGIRDIR
BURSA
IZNIK
ISTANBUL: GRAND BAZAAR

LEFT: interior of the Blue Mosque, Istanbul.
RIGHT: time for lunch in Antakya.

ENTERING AND LEAVING TURKEY

Turkey is a very easy country in which to travel. Most nationals can buy their visas at the airport or land border on arrival, and the roads are good and reasonably well signposted. But distances are long, and you may want to consider taking some internal flights – the network of local airports is excellent – or take the train along limited sections of the route such as Istanbul–Ankara. There are good coach services and plenty of taxis or shared taxis (*dolmuş*) for local travel. (See Travel Tips, page 432, for more information on transport in Turkey.)

There are many crossing points along the long border with **Syria**, with the main one on the road between Antakya and Aleppo. Turkish visas are available (and much cheaper) if you buy them on arrival at the border with hard cash. Get Syrian visas in advance. Some smaller crossings close or charge a fee at night.

The border between Turkey and **Iraq** (Silopi/Zakho) is open and busy with freight traffic. Turkish visas can be bought with hard currency on the border; Iraqi visas are theoretically available at the border but it is probably worth getting one in advance from an embassy. There are likely to be long delays. Check the security situation before travelling.

The border crossing between Turkey and **Iran** is near Dogubeyazit at the foot of Mt Ararat. With plenty of freight traffic and rail connections between Istanbul and Tehran, it works well, but get Iranian visas in advance. As with border crossings from other countries, Turkish visas are available on arrival.

(Isaac), the palace and administrative complex is one of the most impressive examples of Ottoman architecture. The vast entranceway, courtyards, mosque and harem are well preserved and the site is rarely crowded.

The inland routes

Inland, the Silk Road effectively followed the same route for much of its distance as the Persian Royal Road, which connected Ephesus and İzmir on the Aegean seaboard through Zeugma, crossing the Euphrates near Gaziantep to Babylon, as early as the 5th century BC. In later Roman times, there were military camps every 30–40km (20–25 miles), where travellers were welcome to rest in safety, while the later Byzantine Empire spaced its camps out every 50km (30 miles). But it was the Seljuks who really went to town on travellers' facilities.

By the 12th century, when the sea routes were in the hands of the West, the Seljuks enticed traders to use the land routes by offering foreign merchants guarantees that they would be free from robbery. These were the world's

The Seljuk Turks

First mentioned in Chinese writings in 1300 BC, the Turks are people of Central Asia, their language belonging to the Ural-Altaic family of languages, which includes an eclectic selection from Finnish, Hungarian, Japanese and Korean. Traditionally they married outside their tribe, and, as renowned horsemen, were hired as mercenaries by empires from the Mongols to the Abbasids. In the mid-11th century, a small Turkoman tribe, the Seljuks, recent converts to Islam and in the service of the Abbasid caliph, set up a state in Iran, with their capital in Isfahan. Impatient for greater power and with evangelising zeal, they decided they were the true heirs to all the lands once conquered by the Prophet Muhammad and set off to fight, negotiate and buy their way to an empire.

At the Battle of Manzikert in 1071, the Seljuks won a decisive victory against Byzantine Emperor Romanus IV Diogenes, who was captured and ransomed in exchange for much of eastern Anatolia. From here they built themselves an empire and a civilisation, but it came to an abrupt and untimely end in 1243 when they were themselves destroyed in battle by Genghis Khan and his Mongol hordes, in spite of help from the Byzantine emperor, leaving the field clear for the rising power of the Ottomans.

first insurance deals, and, to ensure the safety of the travellers, tax was levied only in areas where crimes occurred – no crime, no tax. So it was in local interests to keep the neighbourhood clean. Good roads were built, with caravanserais no more than a day's travel apart. Some 200 of these magnificent *hans* (travellers' inns) survive in varying states of decay and restoration across Turkey, some now back in business as hotels, restaurants, nightclubs and museums, and others in ruins or used as barns.

Just across the Syrian border, **Mardin** rears up from the Mesopotamian plain, a city of mellow, pale golden stone known for its filigree jewellery, pistachio nuts and as the home of popular Turkish TV series *Sıla*, a glamorous family drama.

The town, whose magnificent warren of old stone houses and alleys cascades down the cliff like golden lace in the evening light, began to thrive in the 3rd century AD with the arrival of the Syriac Christians, who built numerous monasteries and churches and lived on trade and as jewellery-makers. The last of them emigrated

to Sweden in the 1980s, leaving only a few priests to man the cavernous churches. There are five former inns and caravanserais.

From here the road heads north. This whole vast area of southern Turkey is part of the GAP Project, a massive feat of water engineering that is creating a sequence of dams along both the Tigris and Euphrates rivers for hydroelectric power and irrigation.

If the Kurds had a capital, it would be solid, black **Diyarbakır**, about four hours' drive north of Mardin. The Old Town of this grimly workaday city on the Tigris lies behind vast charcoal-black basalt walls 5km (3 miles) long, with a ring of 82 defensive towers, built during the reign of Constantinus but frequently restored over the centuries, with numerous inscriptions, geometrical and animal designs. It is possible to climb some of the towers and walk some sections of the wall, from where there are fine views across the city and the Tigris Valley.

Known in classical times as Amidiya, the city was annexed to Islamic rule in AD 639 when it

BELOW LEFT: Seljuk palace at Ani, northeast Anatolia. **BELOW:** detail of a mosaic from the Hatay Regional Museum in Antakya.

became the property of the Arab clan of Baqr (hence the name "abode of the Baqr", or Diyarbakır). Within the walls are a number of mosques and ancient Orthodox churches, the grandest of them the Ulu Camii (Grand Mosque; İzzet Paşa Caddesi), which is the oldest in Anatolia and once the Syriac Cathedral of Mar Touma (St Thomas). Stripy black-and-white Syrian-style architecture is found in many of the city's public buildings, not least the huge Hotel Grand Kervansaray, built in 1521 as a *han* for travellers on the Silk Road with 72 rooms, 17 shops and stabling for 800 camels. It is once again working as a hotel and restaurant, though without the camels.

Birthplace of Abraham

The main route now heads southwest, along the Euphrates Valley and past what is now the huge **Ataturk Dam**, centrepiece of the whole GAP Project, to reach the ancient city of **Sanlıurfa**. Some scholars believe that Sanlıurfa, or Urfa, was the biblical town of Ur, but Iraqis have a similar claim. Here not only are you swept straight back

into the Old Testament, with references to prophets abounding, but far beyond, to the dawn of civilisation. The world's first domesticated grains (dating back to c.9500 BC) were recently found here, while the world's oldest known temple stands on a windswept hillside overlooking the plains of Harran at Goblekitepe, about 20km (12 miles) out of town.

According to Islamic tradition, it was in Urfa that Abraham was catapulted off the cliff into the fire, to be saved by God, who turned the fire into water and the logs to fishes – both sacred pool and fishes still survive beneath the citadel and are a place of pilgrimage and great beauty in the town centre. The cave where Abraham was supposedly born is in the same park.

To the south of the city, the green, irrigated Mesopotamian plains are littered with ancient history, much of it as yet unexcavated. Of all the villages, the most important is **Harran**, an ancient city and site of the original Temple of Sin, now buried deep beneath centuries of other archaeological gold. Known throughout the

BELOW: Mardin at night.

ancient world for its astronomers and savants, it was here that Ruth poured water for Jacob, and where the Roman emperor Crassus supposedly died by having liquid gold poured into his mouth.

About three hours' drive further west, **Gaziantep** (formerly Antep) dates back to the Hittite period. Home of pistachios, copperware, *lahmacun* (meat with dough) and the best *baklava* in Turkey, it is a thriving industrial city and a major producer of silk and cotton textiles. A fine 6th-century Byzantine fortress, remodelled by the Crusaders, tops an artificial mound near the city centre, and there are numerous fine old houses, mosques and caravanserais in the winding city streets. The **Archaeological Museum** (Istasyon Caddesi; open Tue–Sun 8.30am–noon, 1–5pm; admission fee) has a few of the many magnificent mosaics rescued from the rising dam waters at nearby **Zeugma**. The major crossing point of the Euphrates on the eastern edge of the Roman Empire, Zeugma was a city of enormous wealth, as these world-class mosaics attest. Half the site has been flooded by the new

lake, but archaeological excavations continue on the other half.

Antakya, ancient Antioch

Many travellers would also arrive in the northwest corner of Syria and head for the nearby city of Antioch, now Antakya, in Hatay, a finger of Turkish territory between Syria and the sea. The Turkish border post at **Reyhanlı** is continually being extended to deal with the rapid increase in overland trade between the two countries and also, for the time being, the flood of refugees fleeing violence in Syria. Beyond the hills that form the border, the land flattens into an endless panorama of wheat fields. The dark outline of the Amanus Mountains looms ahead, but the ancient traders took an easier route south along the base of the mountains following the Asi (Orontes) River, itself having run across the border from Homs and Hama. Long before any towns are visible, there are the unmistakable pencil-thin Ottoman minarets piercing the landscape.

The modern town of **Antakya** (ancient Antioch) lies astride the

BELOW: rock formations at Göreme, Cappadocia.

pleasant Asi (Orontes) Valley a few miles from the sea. It is fitting that, with the spread of Christianity along the Silk Road, there is a direct link from this western end, where St Peter resided a few years after the death of Christ. His simple grotto church, known as **Sen Piyer Kilisesi** (open Tue–Sun 8.30am–noon, 1.30–7pm; admission fee), overlooks the town from the side of Mount Staurion ("Cross Mountain") and is worth a visit for this view alone. One of the first secret prayer places for followers of Christ, this was possibly the first church where the disciples were called "Christians". Drops of water seeping into the cave serve for baptism and are believed to have special properties.

The houses, mosques and bazaar in the Old Town are interesting, but there is little to see from antiquity, other than in the excellent **Hatay Regional Museum** (open Tue–Sun 8.30am–noon, 1.30–5pm; admission fee) by the banks of the river, where the vast range of high-quality mosaics is well presented.

This branch of the Silk Road ends at the coast near **Samandağı**, at the ruins of the old harbour of Seleucia Piera, the port of Antioch. History has been swallowed by sand and overgrown by coastal vegetation, but it is an interesting, if forgotten area. Near the village of Çevlik, the large, white, stone walls creating field barriers are parts of the old harbour wall.

Road signs indicate the "Ancient City of Seleucia Piera and Cave City" behind a seaside restaurant. The site map shows the extensive area stretching inland, but the main sites are the tunnel and caves, an easy 90-minute walk away. The route is along the floodwater channel (Titus Tunelı) built by Emperors Titus and Vespasian in the late 1st century AD. The most remarkable section is where the sky becomes a thin slit of light, until finally a square tunnel the size of an underground railway cuts through solid rock. It is extremely dark, but a good adventure. Retrace your steps to the small bridge, and follow the signs to the Bezikli Megara, leading to the area of limestone rock-cut tombs, some dating from the 1st century AD.

BELOW: whirling dervishes.

Cappadocia

Far to the northwest, **Kayseri** is one of the oldest cities in Anatolia and was always an important Silk Road centre at the junction of a number of historic routes. It was the capital of the Graeco-Roman province of Cappadocia from 380 BC to AD 17, and, from 1071, a Seljuk city. Many fine Islamic monuments remain, and the 1,500-year-old castle, built initially by the Romans, still stands at the central square of the city. Nearby, the **Karatay caravanserai** (see panel) is one of the finest restored caravanserais in the country.

Kayseri is the gateway to **Cappadocia**, an otherworldly and impossibly beautiful landscape of twisted limestone towers, crevasses and canyons. Dominated by Erciyes Dağ (ancient Mt Argaeus), the third-highest mountain in Anatolia (3,917m/12,848ft), the whole area was covered in soft limestone when the mountain erupted millions of years ago, since when the weather has carved it into these tortuous shapes, seen at their most fantastic in the fairy 'chimneys' of Zelve and the towering rock citadel of Üchisar.

There are also troglodyte houses, cave churches and huge underground cities seven and eight storeys deep. There are over 400 of these, the largest and most spectacular at Derinkuyu and Kaymaklı (both open daily 8am–5pm, to 6pm in summer; admission fee), once capable of housing up to 20,000 people. But perhaps even more fabulous than the cave houses are the churches, of which there are some 3,000 known so far. The best are in the Ihlara Valley, with over 60 churches in the walls of the 10-km (6-mile) -long gorge, and in the fabulous **Göreme Open Air Museum** (open daily 8am–6pm, to 5pm in winter; admission fee with additional fees for Buckle Church and Dark Church), which encloses over 30 of the finest churches in Cappadocia, most dating from the 9th–11th centuries. The villages of Ürgüp, Ortahisar and Göreme are where most tourists stay.

Seljuk capital

For the medieval traveller, arriving in **Konya** was like arriving in New York or London. From 1071 to 1308, it was

BELOW: the main portal to the ruins of Karatay Caravanserai.

Karatay Caravanserai

The certificate of foundation of the Karatay Caravanserai, built in 1237 near Kayseri, offers a fascinating glimpse into how these institutions operated. No matter what time they arrived, travellers were welcomed, given a place to wash (with soap), stable and feed their animals, store their goods safely and sleep. Food and medical services were provided, shoes mended or new shoes given if the old ones were too worn. Animals were re-shod, oil and candles were provided for light and firewood for heat. And all this was completely free of charge. In the morning, once everyone had packed and was satisfied that all was present and correct, the manager would ceremonially throw open the doors and send them on their way with the blessing "Bismillah" (in the name of God).

the capital of the Seljuk Empire and a vastly important political and commercial hub. Overlooking the city's many Seljuk monuments is a huge mound, Alâeddin Tepesi, on top of which stand the last remaining walls of the Sultani Sarayı (Palace of the Seljuk Sultans) and the Alâeddin Camii (12th and 13th centuries); some of the world's oldest carpets were found here, dating from the 13th century.

Of far greater importance, however, is the **Mevlâna Tekke Müzesi** (Kısla Caddesi; open daily 9am–5pm, Mon from 10am; admission fee), the monastery and **tomb of Mevlâna Jelaleddin Rumi**, an Afghan-born Islamic mystic who wrote mystical poetry in Persian (the court language of Seljuk Konya) and founded the Sufi monastic order of Dervishes who aimed to achieve mystical union with God through music and dance. The Whirling Dervishes still pray in stately pirouettes, although you can see the *sema* (ritual dance) performed at tourist shows. The monastery is a place of pilgrimage, also supposedly housing hairs from the Prophet Muhammad's beard

as well as a magnificent collection of art, ancient manuscripts and rare 13th-century *kilims* (woven carpets). The wonderful Karatay Medresi, an Islamic school built in 1251, now houses a fine **Ceramics and Tile Museum** (Hastane Caddesi, Alâeddin; open daily 9am–noon, 1–5pm; admission fee).

From Konya, some traders would turn south to the coast at Antalya to trade through the port, but most would trudge on to the west, heading towards **Eğirdir Gölü**, the second-largest freshwater lake in Turkey. The pretty town of **Eğirdir** on its shores became a regular stop for travellers, with a fine collection of old Greek and Ottoman houses, the ruins of an old Seljuk fort and a 15th-century Ulucamii (Great Mosque). St Paul gave his first sermon at **Yalvaç** (ancient Antioch ad Pisidiam; open 9am–5pm; admission fee), up the eastern shore of the lake.

Centre of the silk industry

Bursa was supposedly founded by the Bithynian King Prusias I Cholus "the Lame" (r.228–185 BC), who chose

the site, in the shadow of 2,554-metre (8,377-ft) Uludağ, with the help of the great Carthaginian general Hannibal. However, the city really came into its own in 1326, when it was conquered by Orhan Gazi, described by 13th-century traveller Ibn Battuta as "the greatest of the Turkmen kings, and the richest in wealth, lands and military forces".

Bursa became the Ottoman capital upon the fall of Constantinople in 1453. From the first, it was a trading centre – Orhan issued his first coins here in 1327 and set up a bedesten (combination inn, market and secure lock-up) in 1340. Today, it is the fifth-largest city in the country, and its lovely architectural heritage is slowly being submerged beneath a sea of concrete.

The Çarsı (Bazaar) is still the commercial centre of the city; the Bedesten, built by Sultan Beyazıt I on the site of Orhan Gazi's earlier building, is still used for storing and selling gold and silver jewellery. Around it stand a group of *hans* (inns), each built round courtyards shaded by trees and cooled by fountains, the rooms used as shops, storage and dwellings. The earliest of them was the Emir Han, the grandest the Koza Han, today the centre of the Turkish silk industry, with vivid bolts of cloth festooned over counters and piled high against the walls of the tiny shops. You can buy silk shirts, suits, ties and scarves or even have your dress made, for a fraction of what you might pay elsewhere.

Profits from the bazaars went to support a network of mosques and charitable institutions, many of which are architectural masterpieces.

Outside the city centre, three of the early emperors have fine complexes and, just to the south of Çekirge Caddesi, the Muradiye Külliyesi (1425–6) has several royal tombs, including the tomb of Murat II (1421–51). Nearby are the 17th-century **Ottoman House Museum** (open Tue–Sun 9am–5pm; admission fee), and the **Hüsnü Züber Müzesi**

(Uzunyol Sok 3, Kaplıca Caddesi; open Tue–Sun 10am–5pm; admission fee), a restored Ottoman guesthouse, built in 1836.

Tile town

There was one more significant stop en route: **İznik** (formerly **Nicaea**), 80km (50 miles) northeast of Bursa, was founded in 316 BC by Antigonus I (the One-Eyed) and renamed Nicaea in 301 BC by Lysimachus, after his deceased wife. An important Roman city, it was here that Constantine convened the First Ecumenical Council in AD 325, which formulated the Nicaean Creed, the expression of faith still used by most Christians. A Byzantine refuge during the 13th-century Crusader occupation of Constantinople, it was conquered by the Ottomans in 1331. Potters brought in from Tabriz in Persia created the ceramic industry, which sent magnificent İznik tiles across the empire.

Beyond İznik the route lay around the shores of the Sea of Marmara, and to the Bosporus – the edge of Asia.

In the sema – the dance ceremony of the Whirling Dervishes – dancers whirl symbolically, their right arm stretched towards heaven, their left pointing to the earth, so God's grace can flow through them to humanity. The hat represents a tombstone, the cloak the tomb, and the white skirt is the funeral shroud.

BELOW: the distinctive green minaret of the Mevlâna Tekke Müzesi in Konya.

On the far side, over 2,500km (1,500 miles) after crossing the Syrian border into Anatolia at Mardin, after a journey that would take even a modern tourist with a good car at least two days, the footsore camel caravan stood at the gates of one of the greatest cities on earth.

Istanbul

Whether it is called Constantinople or **Istanbul** depends on the date, but it still has one of the most tumultuous bazaars the world has ever known. This is the prize for which the weary travellers have quite literally crossed a continent. The domes and spires of Aya Sofia (Hagia Sophia in Greek), the Blue Mosque and Topkapı Palace rising above the Bosporus remain a stunning, welcoming site. Step across this remarkable waterway and you step from Asia to Europe.

At the city's ancient heart is Sultanahmet, between the Bosporus and the Golden Horn, centred around At Meydanı, the Hippodrome. Nearby is Aya Sofia, the Church of the Holy Wisdom, constructed in AD 632–7

on the orders of Emperor Justinian, turned into a mosque and made a national museum in the 1930s, when its beautiful medieval mosaics were uncovered. Its splendid design has been followed by mosque-builders ever since. The Blue Mosque opposite dates from 1616. With six minarets, 260 windows, madrassa, caravanserai and kitchen, it was a complete social centre. In front of the Blue Mosque is the **Museum of Turkish and Islamic Arts** (open Tue–Sun 9am–5pm; admission fee), which specialises in textiles, particularly carpets.

The extraordinary underground water cistern, **Yerebatan Sarayı** (open daily 9am–5pm; admission fee), should not be overlooked, nor should the **Archaeology Museum** (open Tue–Sun 9am–5pm).

Most intriguing of all is **Topkapı Sarayı** (Topkapı Palace; open 9am–7pm, in winter until 5pm; admission fee). Here, among the courtyards and kiosks, libraries and gardens, sultans reigned in glory. And the harem and its incumbents were swathed in the finest silks that money could buy.

BELOW: the stunning skyline of Istanbul.

The Grand Bazaar

The end of the Silk Road was the fantastic warren of Istanbul's bazaar, where anything could be sold or bought – and can still.

By the time of Mehmet I's conquest, Constantinople was a sorry place – the real money had been in Ottoman hands for decades, while the Byzantine emperors cowered fearfully behind the city walls. What the city and the empire needed was a hard injection of cash, and that would come from trade. By 1461, building was under way, just beside the old Forum of Constantine, the commercial centre of the city since it was built in the 4th century AD. A trading centre fit for an empire began to take shape, with *bedestens*, *hans*, restaurants, water fountains and teahouses, banks, storerooms, workshops, mosques, a bathhouse, school and literally thousands of shops. It even had its own fire brigade.

Today, the Grand Bazaar remains one of the largest buildings in the world, with 22 gates leading to 61 streets covering 31 hectares (76 acres). No one knows exactly how many shops there are, and even though some have combined into larger spaces, there are estimated to be up to 4,500 shops and 30,000 traders working in the bazaar at any one time, attracting more than a quarter of a million shoppers and visitors each day.

Right at the centre, the İç Bedesten is the oldest building in the bazaar, adapted to be the market's first lock-up and also used for slave auctions. It is still used for the bazaar's most precious sales, from fine jewellery to antiques and icons. The silk market is the 15th-century Sandal Bedesten in the southeast corner. Beneath a roof of 20 brick domes, there is still a silk auction here every Wednesday at 1pm. A silk carpet is a fitting souvenir.

Around the *bedestens*, the grid of streets is named after the craftsmen and traders who once plied their trade there – silk-thread makers (*kazazcilar*), fur-makers (*kürkçüler*), slipper-makers (*terlikçiler*), shoemakers (*kavafçilar*), mirror-makers (*aynacilar*), fez-makers (*fesçiler*), quilt-makers (*yorgancilar*), polishers (*perdahçilar*) and jewellers (*kalpakcilar basi*). Although few names still reflect their origins, with every alley piled with *lokum* (Turkish delight) and chess sets, leather bags and stained-glass lanterns, gleaming copperware and twinkling inlaid wood, the Jewellers' Street, on the south side of the bazaar, still burns with polished gold and silver, the sparkle of diamonds and the deep lure of sapphires. The finest carpets are found deeper into the maze or in some of the 40 former hans, such as Zincirli Han.

And if the vast array within the covered market is insufficient, the streets around are crowded with stalls, leading to the Book Bazaar near the university, down through the very workaday market of plastic buckets and cheap saucepans, to the water's edge at Eminönü, where the Mısır Çarsısı (Egyptian or Spice Market), built in the mid-17th century, is the place to buy every kind of spice and herb.

ABOVE: no two carpets are identical. **RIGHT:** in the heart of the Grand Bazaar.

✖ INSIGHT GUIDE — TRAVEL TIPS

THE SILK ROAD

TRANSPORT

GETTING THERE AND GETTING AROUND

By Air

On arrival, passengers from international flights must fill out arrival cards, and customs and health declarations. On departure, passengers must fill out a departure card. Some airports levy a departure tax (see below).

Beijing

Beijing's modern Capital Airport, 25km (16 miles) from the centre, connects China to the world's major cities and the city to all parts of China (for details see, www.en.bcia.com.cn). The journey into the city centre takes 30 minutes if the traffic is light but can take an hour at busier times. Airport bus services (16 Rmb) operate regularly to downtown Beijing, and many of the leading hotels offer limousine or minibus services.

Taxis can be found between international and domestic arrivals; ensure that the meter is turned on and ignore the hordes of taxi touts who wait inside the terminal building: these taxis are illegal.

You must check in at least two hours before departure for an international flight, as security measures in China are now very tight. Hotels usually have flight booking services, and most major airlines have offices in Beijing.

Hong Kong

Hong Kong is a major international air-traffic hub for the region, so there is no shortage of flights. Hong Kong's international airport (www.hongkongairport.com) is at Chek

Departure Taxes

There is a departure tax of around HK$120 (US$15) to be paid on flights from Hong Kong, and 90 Rmb (US$12) on flights from Shanghai. For passengers departing from Beijing, the airport tax is now included in the price of the ticket.

Lap Kok, a small island to the north of Lantau Island and about 34km (21 miles) from Central (the main shopping and banking area).

The Airport Express (AEL) is a comfortable train service that runs every 12 minutes and takes 24 minutes into town; it offers the most convenient and cost-effective way to get to and from the airport (the journey by road via taxi or bus takes around 40 minutes and costs about HK$240 to Kowloon, HK$330 to Hong Kong Island).

There are numerous buses linking the airport to the city and to destinations in Guangdong. The Airbus services (prefixed "A") run at regular intervals from 6am to midnight and cost HK$35–45. Slower commuter buses are prefixed "E", and there are shuttle buses to Tung Chung MTR station. There are also direct ferry services from the airport to Macau and Shenzhen.

Flying out, you can check in at the AEL Central and Kowloon stations 90 minutes before departure.

Kashgar (Kashi)

The airport is located 11km (7 miles) north of the city. There is a shuttle bus between the airport and the CAAC office on 95 Jiefang Nanlu (tel: (0998) 282 2113). China Southern Airlines

and Hainan Airlines have daily flights between Kashgar and Urumqi, and seats are not usually difficult to come by.

Lanzhou

The airport is at Zhongyuan, 70km (44 miles) north of Lanzhou. CAAC (tel: (0931) 888 9666) runs an infrequent shuttle bus (30 Rmb) to and from its office at 520 Donggang Xilu. Unfortunately, there are no fixed times for the buses; they vary according to departing and arriving flights on any given day, so be sure to check with the office ahead of time.

Taxi drivers charge around 200 Rmb for the trip. As with most things in China, bargaining is in order. Beware of taxi drivers who mill around the CAAC office and offer to take you to the airport for significantly less. Travellers with early-morning flights may want to spend the night before at one of the airport hotels, such as the Zhongchuan Hotel (tel: (0931) 841 5926).

Shanghai

Shanghai is one of China's main transport hubs, connected to a number of foreign destinations and almost all domestic locations, and is one of only two cities in China to have two airports (Beijing being the other). Most domestic and some international flights use the old airport at Hongqiao (tel: (021) 5260 4620), about 15km (9 miles) west of the city centre. The international airport (tel: (021) 9608 1388) in Pudong is 70km (44 miles) east of downtown. It is still not at full capacity (it is expected to be fully operational by 2015), but the number of destinations served is steadily increasing.

From Hongqiao Airport it can take from 30 minutes to an hour to the city. Most hotels have shuttle buses available. Otherwise, plenty of taxis are available right outside both terminals. Don't hire drivers who tout their services at the terminal entrances; their cars don't have meters, and they will try to charge you exorbitant rates. To get into the city, most drivers use the expressway that connects to the Ring Road. Expect to reimburse the driver for the toll.

From Pudong a taxi will take you approximately an hour (reckon on 130–160 Rmb) to the city, but the new high-speed maglev train can rocket you to Longyang Road underground station in Pudong in under eight minutes for 50 Rmb (single fare). There are eight airport bus lines. Airport Shuttle No. 1 connects Hongqiao and Pudong airports. The No. 2 metro line will eventually run east–west between Hongqiao and Pudong airports, and numerous stops in between, but it is yet to be completed.

If leaving on an international flight, you are expected to arrive at the airport two hours before takeoff.

Urumqi

The airport (tel: (0991) 3804322) is 17km (11 miles) north of the city. China Southern Airlines has its main office at 62 Youhao Nanlu, tel: (0991) 451 4668, and is open 7am–5pm daily. The airline has a number of booking offices around the city.

A taxi to the airport will cost around 30–40 Rmb, or you can take either the airport bus (20 Rmb) or bus No. 51 (5 Rmb).

Urumqi is connected via international flights to Almaty (Kazakhstan), Bishkek (Kyrgyzstan), Islamabad (Pakistan), Novosibirsk and Moscow (Russia), Tashkent (Uzbekistan) and Tehran (Iran). Foreign airlines in Urumqi include Siberian Airlines (tel: (0991) 2864327) and Kyrgyzstan Airlines (tel: (0991) 231 6333).

Border Crossings

Western China shares international frontiers with Mongolia, Kazakhstan and Kyrgyzstan, as well as shorter international frontiers with Russia, Tajikistan, Afghanistan, Pakistan and India. At time of writing, international land crossings are only possible between Xinjiang and Kazakhstan, Kyrgyzstan and Pakistan. See individual Places chapters for information on entering and leaving China.

ABOVE: the Karakoram Highway in Xinjiang.

Xi'an

The airport is about 40km (25 miles) northwest of Xi'an at Xianyang. Most major hotels offer limousine or bus transfers, which have to be arranged ahead of time. China Southern Airlines runs a shuttle bus (6am–6pm) between the Melody Hotel (86 Xi Dajie), just to the west of the Bell Tower, and the airport, which is timed to its arriving and departing flights.

Otherwise, a taxi will cost around 100-120 Rmb to go into the city, but you may have to bargain hard as overcharging is common. The trip takes around 50 minutes.

Xi'an's airport connects it to most of the big cities in China, as well as to Nagoya and Hiroshima in Japan. In Xi'an, China Southern Airlines has a number of ticket offices dotted around the city. One of its main offices is located at the corner of Laodong Nanlu and Xiguan Zhengjie, 1km (¾ mile) outside the west gate of the old city (tel: (029) 8870 2299). Other airlines flying to Xi'an daily include Air China, China Eastern Airlines, Hainan Airlines and Shanghai Airlines.

Overland Routes

See also Central Asia Travel Tips, page 404, and Entering and Leaving panels in each chapter.

Kazakhstan

There is a daily bus service and a twice-weekly train service between Urumqi and Almaty in Kazakstan (you will need to obtain a visa in advance).

Kyrgyzstan

Although it is, in theory, possible to take a bus from Kashgar to Bishkek in Kyrgyzstan over the Torugart Pass,

foreigners are not permitted to do so. You can travel as far as the border but must arrange private transport on the other side. You need to obtain a Kyrgyz visa in advance.

Pakistan

It is possible to travel the Karakoram Highway between Kashgar and Islamabad. Visas are required for entering Pakistan and cannot be obtained at the border for either Pakistan or China. Officially the border is open between April and October, though even those dates are weather-dependent. During this time there are daily buses, weather permitting, going from Kashgar to Tashkurgan (five hours), which is the last outpost in China where immigration and customs checks are performed. The bus stops here overnight before continuing over the Khunjerab Pass to Sost. In summer there are daily departures for the two-day, 500km (310-mile) trip. On both the Pakistani and Chinese sides of the border the roads may be blocked by landslides, and you may have to walk a fair distance, carrying your luggage. Accommodation en route is relatively modest, and closed completely out of season.

GETTING AROUND

By Air

Flying within China is a quick and relatively cheap way of getting around the country. There are more than 175 airports in the country, and the number of regional airlines connecting these airports has grown dramatically over the last few years. Two of the larger domestic carriers,

China Southern (CZ) and China Eastern (MU), cover most destinations throughout the Shaanxi, Gansu and Xinjiang regions.

Xinjiang is China's largest province, and there are regular air links from its capital, Urumqi, to cities across China, including Beijing, Chengdu, Chongqing, Guangzhou, Hong Kong, Kunming, Lanzhou, Shanghai and Xi'an.

Xi'an, the capital of Shaanxi province and eastern terminus of the Silk Road, is a major Chinese city and is readily accessible by air from most provincial capitals as well as from Beijing, Chengdu, Guangzhou, Shanghai and Urumqi.

There are regular flights from Lanzhou and Dunhuang in Gansu province to destinations including Beijing, Guangzhou, Urumqi and Xi'an.

By Train

China's rail network covers 74,400km (46,200 miles) and includes numerous destinations along the Silk Road. There is no first or second class on Chinese trains, but four categories or classes: *ruanwo* (soft-sleeper), *ruanzuo* (soft-seat), *yingwo* (hard-sleeper) and *yingzuo* (hard-seat). The soft-seat class is usually only available for short journeys. Long-distance trains normally only have soft-sleeper or hard-sleeper facilities. The soft-sleeper class has four-bed compartments with soft beds, and is recommended, particularly for long journeys. The hard-sleeper class has open, six-bed compartments. While you can reserve a place for the first three classes (you always buy a ticket with a place number), this is not always essential for the hard-seat category.

BELOW: street life in Khotan.

Train Travel along the Silk Road

One of the most romantic ways to travel over large distances is by train, for which the Silk Road is particularly well suited the further east you go. Almost half of the length of the Silk Road is within China, and it is an unforgettable train journey across the vast open expanses from Xi'an to Urumqi and Kashgar, via Lanzhou, Jiayuguan and Turpan. However, some of the ancient Silk Road sites are not along the modern railway. For Dunhuang the nearest station is Liuyuan, whilst the station for Turpan is actually Daheyan, about 30km (19 miles) away.

Reservations can be made at ticket offices in the town centre, through travel agencies or at your hotel. Be on time, as trains tend to be punctual.

As a rule of thumb, train services tend to operate less frequently but take less time than buses to reach their destination. The excellent website http:/trains.china.org.cn provides up-to-date train timetables and seat prices for all inter-city routes, though tickets can unfortunately not yet be booked online.

By Bus

Overland buses are the most important means of transportation in many parts of China where there is no railway line. All travel along the southern section of the Chinese Silk Road can conveniently be achieved using the regular bus services between the towns. Distances are not too great, and reasonably comfortable buses ply these routes. Buses are the cheapest means of transport, but are also correspondingly slower. There are regular breaks during journeys. Many overland buses have numbered seats, and it is advisable to book a ticket well in advance. Modern air conditioned buses are usually available between the larger cities.

Kashgar (Kashi)

The long-distance bus station is on Tiannan Lu, just south of Renmin Lu. There are daily buses from Kashgar to Korla, Kuqa, Aksu, Hotan, Daheyan, Urumqi and Yengisar.

Lanzhou

The south bus station is on Langongping Lu, and from here there are several buses serving Linxia, but only three direct buses to Xiahe each day. The main long-distance bus station on Pingliang Lu serves Tianshui, Wuwei and Zhangye. The west bus station is at the western edge of town on Xijin Xilu, where buses depart regularly for the trip to Binglingsi.

Urumqi

Urumqi is the hub of bus travel throughout Xinjiang. The south bus station is some way south of the city and serves destinations including Hami, Hotan, Korla, Kashgar, Kuqa and Turpan. The north bus station on Heilongjiang Lu serves Yining and other points north and northwest.

Xi'an

There are three major bus stations scattered around the city. The most convenient, the long-distance bus station, is located opposite the main train station just off Jiefang Lu.

By Taxi

Taxis are certainly the most comfortable form of transport, and drivers will agree a fixed rate for longer journeys and excursions, with prices usually starting at around 300–400 Rmb. Taxis are plentiful in all cities, and if you don't speak the language, it is a good idea to carry details of your destination written in Chinese.

Be wary of people offering taxis away from taxi ranks. Before setting off in a taxi, agree on a price for the journey, or ensure that the driver agrees to use the meter.

ACCOMMODATION

HOTELS AND GUESTHOUSES

Choosing a Hotel

China's large cities have numerous modern hotels, most of them at the high end of the market, including many of world-class calibre. Many belong to international hotel chains, and their management and staff have been trained abroad. The prices of these better hotels are in line with hotel prices in the West. Tour groups are usually accommodated in well-appointed tourist hotels. Except in the first-class hotels, take caution with laundry services, particularly with delicate clothes.

Booking rooms at hotels in the middle and lower price ranges can sometimes be difficult, particularly during Chinese New Year (a week or two in January or February) and during the May and October holiday periods, when hotels are often completely full.

Rates at all but the cheapest hotels are subject to 10–15 percent service surcharge. Rates for each price category are shown in the yellow boxes in the listings and are for a standard room.

Guesthouses

Some guesthouses or simple hotels refuse to take foreign guests, usually because of rules imposed by Chinese travel agencies or the local police, who often determine where foreigners may stay.

However, individual travellers may be able to find lodgings in guesthouses in smaller towns off the tourist track. They usually have rooms with two or more beds, or dormitories, shower and washing facilities, and are recommended for those on a budget.

Other Accommodation

It is difficult for foreigners to find accommodation outside of hotels and guesthouses, although some universities and institutes have guesthouses where foreign visitors can find good, cheap lodging. In 2006 YHA China joined the International Youth Hostels Federation, with online booking at www.hihostels.com.

If you are going on a long trip or hike in the countryside, especially in Tibet or in areas around the sacred mountains of China, you will probably come across various types of "long-distance travellers' lodgings". It is advisable to carry a sleeping bag.

In Beijing and some provinces, restrictions have been eased as to where foreigners can stay. Not all hotels are aware of the ruling, however, and may still shun foreigners. It is to be hoped that a more relaxed regime will eventually cover the whole of China, so that tourists are no longer restricted to the more expensive hotels and barred from countless budget options.

SHAANXI

Xi'an

Bell Tower Hotel (Zhonglou Fandian)
110 Nan Dajie
Tel: (029) 8760 0000
Good-value hotel within walking distance of Xi'an's Drum Tower, the Great Mosque and Beiyuanmen Street ("Islamic Walking Street"). Rooms overlooking the street can be a bit noisy, but this is compensated for by the views of the Bell Tower, which at dusk are especially excellent. The buffet breakfast is

extra. A business centre, minimarket and CITS office are all on the premises. **$$**

City Hotel (Chengshi Jiudian)
70 Nan Dajie
Tel: (029) 8721 9988
www.cityhotelxian.com
Centrally located near the Bell Tower, this is one of Xi'an's better budget options. Clean if simple rooms with amiable staff; internet access and cable TV are standard. Located down a small side street off

Nan Dajie, the rooms are relatively quiet. **$$**
Grand Mercure
319 Dongxin Street
Tel: (029) 8792 8888
www.mercure.com
Attractive modern hotel within the historic city walls. The Grand Mercure overlooks the pagodas of Renmin Square, has a pleasant restaurant, and there is Wi-fi in every room. **$$**
Hantang Inn (Hantang Yi)
211 Xi Dajie
Tel: (029) 8723 1126

www.hostelxian.com
A good budget option, this clean, comfortable and friendly establishment offers cable TV and internet access as well as (surprisingly) a tennis court. Well located for Xi'an's Muslim

PRICE CATEGORIES

Price categories are for a double room with breakfast/tax.

$ = less than US$50
$$ = 50–150
$$$ = over US$150

Quarter, it's close to the Great Mosque, as well as to numerous restaurants and food stalls serving Chinese and Hui Muslim cuisine. **$**

Howard Johnson Ginwa Plaza Hotel
18 West Section, Huancheng Nan Lu
Tel: (029) 8842 1111
www.ginwaplaza.com
Close to the ancient South Gate, this perfectly comfortable hotel is well placed for discovering the Old City and other nearby attractions like the Small Wild

Goose Pagoda. Guest rooms are large with a modernist feel. One of Xi'an's better breakfast buffets is included in the price. Internet, English-speaking staff. **$$$**

Hyatt Regency Xi'an (Xi'an Kaiyue Fandian)
158 Dong Dajie,
Tel: (029) 8769 1234
www.xian.regency.hyatt.com
Located within the old city walls, this excellent five-star hotel with a spectacular interior attracts tour groups. All bedrooms include

wireless internet access. Other facilities include a tennis court, spa, fitness club and pizzeria. Breakfast is not included. English-speaking staff. **$$$**

Shangri-La
38B Keji Road
Tel: (029) 8875 8888
www.shangri-la.com
Luxury hotel in Xi'an's business and technology district. The Shangri-La offers four world-class restaurants, a health club and spa, and an attentive level of service. **$$$**

Sofitel Hotel
319 Dongxin Street
Tel: (029) 8792 8888
www.sofitel.com/China
Located in central Renmin Square, the Sofitel Hotel is one of Xi'an's most luxurious hotels. Rooms are attractively decorated and offer internet, good views and all modern conveniences. As well as Chinese and international fare, there's a good Japanese restaurant. Helpful, English-speaking staff. **$$**

GANSU

Tianshui

Dongan Fandian
Yima Lu
Tel: (0938) 261 3333
Tianshui is divided into two sections, Beidao by the railway station to the east and Qincheng (which is more upmarket) to the west. Dongan Fandian is located near the railway station and offers excellent value, clean rooms and easy access to several nearby restaurants. **$$**

Golden Sun Hotel
19 Zhonghua Lu
Tel: (0938) 827 7777
The best option in the western part of town, located in a pedestrian zone (and therefore relatively quiet). Clean, friendly, with a reasonable restaurant, and conveniently located for the long-distance bus station. Unusually for Tianshui, some English is spoken. **$$**

Lanzhou

Grand Hotel Soluxe
428 Qingyang Road
Tel: (0931) 460 8888
www.grandsoluxehotel.com
Large and centrally located hotel owned by PetroChina. Ostentatious decor prevails throughout the building, but the rooms are large and well-equipped, and there are restaurants, a swimming pool, gym and spa on site. **$$**

JJ Sun Hotel (Jinjiang Yangguang Jiudian)
589 Donggang Xi Lu
Tel: (0931) 880 5511

www.jinjianghotels.com
This 24-storey, three-star hotel is situated in the city's busy commercial district and is well placed for some of Lanzhou's best restaurants. Guest rooms are pleasantly furnished and offer cable TV, internet access, minibar and refrigerator. **$$**

Lanzhou Hotel (Lanzhou Fandian)
434 Donggang Xilu
Tel: (0931) 841 6321
Pleasant, reasonably priced establishment set in a recently renovated Soviet-style building. Well located for both the train station and long-distance bus station. Facilities include internet and a travel agency for onward bookings. **$$**

Lanzhou Legend Hotel (Lanzhou Feitian Dajiudian)
599 Tianshui Lu
Tel: (0931) 852 2888
www.lanzhoulegendhotel.com
Probably the best hotel in Lanzhou, with modern facilities including internet, cable TV, several good restaurants, a money exchange and English-speaking staff who can arrange sightseeing trips and onward reservations. Well located for the train station and the long-distance bus station. **$$**

Linxia

Hehai Mansion (Hehai Dasha)
50 Hongyuan Lu

Tel: (0930) 623 5455
Linxia is somewhat off the beaten track and does not have any luxurious four- or five-star hotels, but Hehai Mansions is solid, dependable, relatively clean and reasonably priced. **$**

Linxia Hotel (Linxia Fandian)
9 Hongyuan Lu
Tel: (0930) 623 0080
Similar in standard and price to Hehai Mansion. Facilities are adequate, but not great. **$**

Xiahe

Labrang Baoma Hotel (Labuleng Baoma Binguan)
Renmin Xijie
Tel: (0941) 712 1078
www.labranghotel.com
Well-run and friendly Tibetan-oriented establishment, with pleasing decor and two restaurants serving good Sichuan and Tibetan food. It's reasonably priced, and for travellers on a tight budget also offers tolerably comfortable dormitory beds. Services available include bicycle hire, an ideal way to explore Xiahe and Labrang Monastery. **$**

Overseas Tibetan Hotel (Huaqiao Fandian)
77 Renmin Xijie
Tel: (0941) 712 2642
www.overseastibetanhotel.com
Situated right next door to Xiahe's major attraction, the Labrang Monastery, this hotel has seen steady

improvement in its general facilities, to the point where the rooms are now really quite comfortable. However, some guest rooms don't have their own bathroom. **$**

Wuwei

Tianma Binguan
2 Jianguo Jie
Tel: (0935) 221 5170
The Tianma is adequate but far from spectacular. Popular with tour groups, it's centrally located by the Bank of China and within easy walking distance of the Luoshi Pagoda and the Bell Tower. The upper floors offer the quietest rooms. **$–$$**

Zhangye

Huachen International Hotel
Dong Jie
Tel: (0936) 824 5088
www.huachenhotel-hangzhou.com
A new establishment offering the best value in town, and clean and friendly service. Close to Zhangye's Marco Polo statue, Ganquan Park, the main Western Bus Station, and – most importantly – Minqing Jie Food Street. **$$**

Zhangye Hotel
56 Xianfu Jie
Tel: (0936) 821 2601
Long-established, unspectacular but reliable, this recently renovated hotel offers clean rooms with all basic amenities. Located in the southwestern part of town, it offers easy access

to CITS, the Bank of China, Xilai Si, Mu Ta and the main bus station. **$$**

Jiuquan

Jiuquan Binguan
2 Cangmen Jie
Tel: (0937) 261 5591
A useful standby for budget travellers staying overnight in Jiuquan rather than – as is more usually the case – in nearby Jiayugan. It's basic, adequately clean, and offers a choice of private rooms or dormitory bedding. **$–$$**

Jiuquan International Hotel
33 Jiefang Lu
Tel: (0937) 261 8000
The best accommodation in town, offering more facilities than you might expect in Jiuquan, including a business centre, fitness centre,

casino, coffee shop and sauna, as well as well-appointed rooms. **$$**

Jiayuguan

Great Wall Hotel (Changcheng Binguan)
6 Jianshe Xilu
Tel: (0937) 622 6306
Vast compound of buildings loosely modelled on Jiayuguan's famous fort and well positioned for the Great Wall Museum. Outstanding amenities include a beauty salon, snooker parlour, sauna, bicycle rental service and a reasonably proficient tour operator. **$$**

Taihe Shanzhuang
Jiayuguan Fort
Tel: (0937) 639 6622
Quiet, out-of-the-way establishment located at Jiayuguan Fort, about 5km (3 miles) from Jiayuguan

City. Comfortable and clean rooms designed to look like a Ming Dynasty house. **$$**

Dunhuang

Feitian Hotel
Mingshan Lu
Tel: (0937) 882 2008
www.feitianhotel.com
Clean and friendly hotel close to the long-distance bus station. Private bedrooms and dormitory accommodation available. No restaurant, but right next to the best selection of English-language menus in Dunhuang on either side of downtown Mingshan Lu. **$$**

Grand Sun Hotel (Taiyang Dajiudian)
5 Shazhou Beilu
Tel: (0937) 882 9998
Friendly, hospitable and doubtless the pre-eminent place in downtown

Dunhuang. The new wing's rooms are very good, but more expensive than those in the old wing, which although not as well maintained do have a certain character. Tours can be arranged at the hotel's tour desk. **$$**

Silk Road Dunhuang Hotel (Dunhuang Shanzhuang)
Dunyue Lu
Tel: (0937) 888 2088
www.duanhuangresort.com
Located in an incredible setting amid the giant sand dunes south of town. All bedrooms and suites are elegantly decorated and sport warm desert colours. Certain guest rooms even copy the long-established Silk Road caravanserai style of accommodation. Activities arranged by the hotel include camel-riding, sand sledding and archery. **$$**

XINJIANG: THE NORTHERN ROUTE

Hami (Kumul)

Jiageda Fandian
Aiguo Beilu
Tel: (0902) 223 2140
The best (and most expensive) accommodation in Hami, with comfortable, rooms and pleasant views overlooking downtown Renmin Park. Conveniently close to the long-distance bus station, and not far from Hami train station. **$$**

Turpan (Tulufan)

Grand Turpan Hotel (Tulufan Dafandian)
20 Gaochang Lu
Tel: (0995) 855 3668
www.xjturpanhotel.com
Probably the most comfortable budget option in town. The newer guest rooms have minibar, satellite TV and internet. The friendly tour desk can arrange all manner of local tours. **$–$$**

Jiaotong Hotel
230 Laocheng Road West
Tel: (0995) 853 1320
Renovated in 2010, the Jiaotong is centrally located and reasonably priced. Dormitories as well as private rooms are available, making it an attractive budget option. **$–$$**

Oasis Hotel (Luzhou Binguan)
41 Qingnian Beilu
Tel: (0991) 852 2491
www.the-silk-road.com
Part of the Silk Road chain. A unique feature is the Central Asian-style rooms with kang beds, originally heated by internal flues, though here they are just for style. Internet café, sauna room and an excellent Muslim restaurant serving Xinjiang specialities. **$$**

Turpan Hotel (Tulufan Binguan)
2 Qingnian Lu
Tel: (0995) 852 2301
Long-established budget-traveller favourite, with a choice of private rooms and dormitory beds. Near the enduringly popular John's Information Café (closed in winter months) offering bicycle rental, local tours and Western breakfasts. Uighur song and dance shows each evening during the summer season. **$–$$**

Korla (Ku'erle)

Bayinguoleng Binguan
Renmin Donglu
Tel: (0996) 202 2248
Reasonably priced and

comfortable alternative to the Silverstar Hotel, with rooms and dormitory accommodation. Two restaurants serve Muslim and Chinese food. **$–$$**

Silverstar Hotel
36 Renmin Donglu
Tel: (0996) 202 8888
Perhaps Korla's best hotel, and certainly one of its newest. Services include car hire and tour booking, plus swimming pool, tennis courts and three restaurants serving Chinese, Muslim and Western cuisines. **$$**

Kuqa (Kuche)

Kuche Fandian
Tian Shan Dong Lu 8
Tel: (0997) 723 3156
Popular with tour groups, this large complex has a variety of rooms, some of which are rather better than others. **$$**

Kuqa Hotel (Kuqa Binguan)
Jiefang Lu
Tel: (0997) 712 2901
Kuqa's main hotel is centrally located, with private rooms (clean and well appointed) and dormitory accommodation. **$$**

Aksu (Akesu)

Hongfu Jinlan
32 Dongdajie Lu
Tel: (0991) 588 1588
Probably the best place to stay in Aksu, with all the usual four-star facilities such as a business centre, beauty parlour, fitness centre, bars, restaurants and cafés. **$–$$**

Kashgar (Kashi)

Chini Bagh Hotel (Qiniwake Binguan)
144 Seman Lu
Tel: (0998) 282 2103
Unattractive but functional hotel built in the grounds of the old British Consulate. Rooms in the old wing are cheaper than in the new wing. Facilities include internet, sauna and a rather run-down karaoke lounge. Western breakfasts and other dishes are available at John's Information

PRICE CATEGORIES

Price categories are for a double room with breakfast/tax.

$ = less than US$50
$$ = 50–150
$$$ = over US$150

Café in the hotel grounds. **$–$$**

Qianhai Hotel (Qianhai Binguan)
48 Renmin Xilu
Tel: (0998) 282 2922
Peaceful, relaxed, if somewhat anonymous hotel with two pretty good restaurants. Rooms include refrigerators, essential in the hot summer season. Occasionally the service can be a little lacking, but the staff try their

best to make an impact. **$–$$**

Seman Hotel (Seman Binguan)
337 Seman Lu
Tel: (0998) 258 2150
www.semanhotel.com
Set in the grounds of the old Russian Consulate. Offers fairly comfortable rooms; the best are in the old consulate building. By no means the best lodgings in Kashgar, but it

does still manage to radiate a little 19th-century Great Game charm. **$–$$**

Wen Zhou Mansion
17 West Renmin Road
Tel: (0998) 280 8889
Large and modern hotel within walking distance of People's Square. The hotel restaurant serves both Han and Uighur cuisines, and there is a business centre, beauty salon and souvenir shop on site. **$$**

Tashkurgan (Tashiku'ergan)

Crown Inn
87 Seman Road
Tel: (0998) 342 2888
www.crowninntashkorgan.com
This foreign-run hotel has superb views across the Pamirs and is a haven for overland travellers and trekkers. The hotel can also arrange permits and transport for onward travel. **$$**

XINJIANG: THE SOUTHERN ROUTE

Charklik (Ruoqiang)

Tianranju Binguan
Near Charklik Bus Station
Tel: (0996) 710 5566
The best option in town, this new establishment offers clean standard rooms with en suite bathrooms and TV. **$$**

Xin Xin Binguan
Next to Charklik Bus Station
Clean if basic double rooms above a simple Sichuan restaurant. **$**

Cherchen (Qiemo)

Kunyu Binguan
Junction of Sichou Lu and Tuanjie Lu
Tel: (0996) 762 7666

The newest and most modern accommodation in town. **$$**

Muzitage Binguan
Yingbin Lu
Tel: (0996) 762 2687
A little way north of town, close to the airport. Adequate facilities. Staff can arrange trips to the ruins at Qiemo Gucheng. **$$**

Khotan (Hetian)

Hetian Binguan
Wulumuqi Nanlu
Tel: (0903) 251 3564
Close to the Bank of China and the local CITS office. One of the best places to

stay in town, with good breakfasts. Restaurants on the premises serving both Uighur and Chinese food. **$$**

Jiaotong Binguan
Taibei Xilu
Tel: (0903) 203 2700
Long-established standby next to the long-distance bus station. Offers reasonably priced and clean rooms and dormitory accommodation. **$**

Karghalik (Yecheng)

Yecheng Dianli
500 metres (550 yds) east of Karghalik Bus Station
Tel: (0998) 728 9800

The best accommodation currently available in Karghalik; cleaner and more friendly than the Jiaotong Binguan at the bus station, though the latter serves as a well-located fallback for travellers obliged to stay in this small town. **$**

Yarkand (Shache)

Shache Binguan
4 Xincheng Lu
Tel: (0998) 851 2365
The best accommodation currently available in Yarkand, and also the establishment officially favoured by the local PSB. **$–$$**

XINJIANG: THE DZUNGARIAN ROUTE

Urumqi (Wulumuqi)

Bogda Binguan
10 Guangming Lu
Tel: (0991) 282 3910
This reasonably priced three-star option is clean, friendly, and within easy walking distance of City Square and the bustling area around Zhongshan Lu and Minzhu Lu. **$$**

Hoi Tak Hotel (Haide Jiudian)
1 Dong Feng Lu
Tel: (0991) 232 2828
This centrally positioned hotel is a genuine five-star option. The upper floors provide wonderful views of the Tian Shan mountains. Oddly, the facilities include an eight-lane bowling alley. Other amenities include snooker tables,

sauna and whirlpool. **$$$**

Hongfu Hotel (Hongfu Dafandian)
26 Huanghe Lu
Tel: (0991) 588 1588
www.hongfuhotel.com
Mainly a business hotel, but offers some great bargains on its excellent four- to five-star rooms. Amenities include an indoor pool, spa, sauna and massage rooms. **$$$**

Sheraton Urumqi
669 Northern Youhao Road
Tel: (0991) 699 9999
www.starwoodhotels.com
20 minutes from Urumqi airport, the Sheraton is one of Urumqi's newest hotels. With five restaurants and nearly 400 rooms, the hotel is vast, well-appointed and

equipped with all mod-cons. **$$$**

Xinjiang Fandian
107 Changjiang Lu
Tel: (0991) 585 2511
Situated some way from downtown Urumqi, this is perhaps the best budget option in the city. It's also well located for nearby Urumqi Train Station. Popular with Pakistani travellers. **$–$$**

Yining (Gulja)

Ili Hotel
Yingbing Lu
Tel: (0999) 802 3126
A rambling place right next to the Night Market in the eastern part of town. **$–$$**

Tianshan Binguan
Shengli Lu
Tel: (0999) 782 2304

Friendly, clean budget accommodation, no frills but very reasonably priced. Centrally located, just north of Hongqi City Square. **$**

Youyi Binguan
7 Stalin Jie
Tel: (0999) 782 3111
The best accommodation in Yining, with well-appointed rooms and friendly staff. Not far from the main restaurant area between Feijichang Lu and Jiefang Lu. **$$**

PRICE CATEGORIES

Price categories are for a double room with breakfast/tax.

$ = less than US$50
$$ = 50–150
$$$ = over US$150

EATING OUT

RECOMMENDED RESTAURANTS AND CAFES

What to Eat

Eating along China's Silk Road is surprisingly varied and good. Most visitors would agree that the choice and quality of cuisines available between Xi'an and Kashgar are markedly superior to those available elsewhere in Central Asia, and travellers heading westwards along the Silk Road will have to wait at least until Iran, and probably until Turkey, to find a comparably sophisticated choice of cuisine.

In large part this is, of course, due to Chinese culinary influence dating back at least two millennia. In the two decades since China began its gradual but inexorable opening to a free-market economy, even relatively remote areas like Gansu and Xinjiang have become more prosperous than ever before, and restaurants serving all China's great schools of cuisine – but most especially Sichuan – are to be found in every major city and oasis town between Xi'an and Kashgar. Even night stops for truckers in transit points like Anxi and Hami spell out regional specialities in neon lights, encouraging drivers to patronise this Northeastern diner or that Cantonese dim sum establishment.

Nor is Chinese culinary influence limited exclusively to Chinese cuisine. Most visitors to Xinjiang would agree that Uighur food is superior to any other indigenous Central Asian tradition. From the delicious flat breads and rich, locally grown fruits, to the unusually succulent lamb and noodle stews, Xinjiang leaves the various "Stans" standing.

Other cuisines available along the Eastern Silk Road include Tibetan fare, mainly along the Gansu–Qinghai frontier, and Mongolian – the latter

not terribly sophisticated, but quite acceptable in an Urumqi hotpot restaurant (especially in winter), if less so at an isolated Mongol yurt erected somewhere in the endless Gobi steppe. The latter is no place for vegetarians!

Uighur and Hui Cuisine

The Northwest differs from other regions of China in that pork – though still popular among Han Chinese and widely available in Han Chinese restaurants – is not the staple it has become elsewhere in China. Gansu province, with its substantial Hui Muslim population, tends to favour beef as an alternative to pork, and Xinjiang is definitely mutton country.

Uighur food features the usual Central Asian specialities, combined with some South Asian elements derived from the region's Mughal past and current Pakistani influence. The difference from the various countries of former Soviet Central Asia is that Uighur food seems to be fresher, better-quality, better-cooked, spicier and more varied.

The staples of Uighur cuisine are **mutton** (or beef, or chicken) **kebabs**, served with delicious *naan* breads baked in a tandoori oven and sprinkled with fennel, poppy seeds, sesame, garlic or onion. They vary in size, shape and flavour from oasis to oasis, but are uniformly delicious and make excellent long-distance snacks, especially when eaten with local grapes, melon or other luscious fruits with which Xinjiang abounds in season.

Also enduringly popular are **pilaf**, known locally as *polo*, *chuchura* (**dumplings**) and *samsa* (**samosas**) stuffed with minced meat and vegetables). Uighurs are great noodle

cooks (and eaters), specialising in "hand-pulled" *laghman* **noodles** (*lamian* in Chinese) served with a rich stew of mutton, peppers, tomatoes, aubergines, garlic and spring onions. Noodles fried with meat and vegetables are called *suoman*. The vegetarian variant is called *suoman gush siz* – nutritious and delicious.

Uighurs sometimes end their meals with locally made **ice cream**, sweetened sticky rice desserts or fresh or dried fruits – it's even possible to dry strips of Hami melon in the hot, arid summer months.

Hui (Chinese-speaking) Muslim cuisine is much closer to Han Chinese than to Uighur, but is always halal, never using pork or other forbidden foodstuffs. As Han Chinese can eat in Hui Muslim restaurants (but it is much less usual for Hui Muslims to eat in Han restaurants), Hui restaurateurs have traditionally dominated much of the culinary scene in Xi'an, Gansu and Xinjiang, as well as being enduringly popular further afield in Beijing, Shanghai and other great cities of eastern China.

Where to Eat

Chinese meals are generally better shared between several people who can dip into a variety of dishes placed in the centre of the table. Most better-quality hotels have a variety of restaurants that offer good food at reasonable prices. Chinese snack foods such as noodles, dumplings and dim sum are readily available at stalls in night markets or near bus and train stations. Chinese (including Hui Muslims) generally eat using chopsticks.

The main oases in Xinjiang, notably Turpan, Korla, Kashgar and

Khotan, all have good speciality Uighur restaurants. Similarly, better hotels in Xinjiang often have a Muslim restaurant offering *halal* food to Muslim guests, as well as a Chinese restaurant and a restaurant serving international dishes. Finding Uighur food at the plethora of street stalls in and around bus and train stations and in local bazaars is simplicity itself, as these stalls are found just about everywhere. Uighurs don't usually eat with chopsticks, but may employ fork, knife, spoon and of course fingers – though only of the right hand, which is reserved for communal eating, while the left hand is considered "impure" and used for ablutions.

Drinks

Bottled **water** is available everywhere at reasonable prices. Most hotel rooms (as well as railway sleepers) provide thermos flasks filled with hot water and a small selection of bags of black and green **tea**. Chinese also drink lots of **hot water**, which is surprisingly refreshing and good at quenching thirst. Chinese **beer**, in dozens of different brands, is available everywhere – even in the most Muslim of towns like Linxi and Khotan; cheap, plentiful and low in alcohol content, it makes an excellent accompaniment to both Chinese and Uighur food. Better yet, especially around Dunhuang and Turpan, are

the excellent **wines** made from locally grown but nationally celebrated grapes. One of the best brands is Loulan, named for the ancient lost city at the heart of the Lop Desert. Sorghum, barley and millet are widely grown throughout the Northwest, and from these, as well as from rice, a surprisingly large choice of Chinese **spirits** are on offer – try, for example, the 55 percent wheat and sorghum spirit called *maotai jiu*. Imported spirits, wines and beers are increasingly available across the Northwest. Drinking alcohol – even in front of Muslims, far from all of whom are teetotallers – is acceptable behaviour. Being drunk or rowdy in public is not.

SHAANXI

Xi'an

Azur
319 Dong Xin Street
Tel: (029) 8792 8888
Inside the Sofitel is Azur, a pleasant restaurant with a Mediterranean menu and an open kitchen so you can watch the food being prepared. Dishes are tasty and well-presented, if a little pricy. **$$–$$$**

Defachang Dumpling Restaurant
1 Xi Dajie,
Zhonggulou Square
Tel: (029) 8721 4065
This huge restaurant located near the Bell and Drum Towers is an excellent place to discover dumplings. With more than 100 different choices of pastry-wrapped dumplings (*jiaozi*), the selection can be overwhelming. Try the Dumpling Feast, a *jiaozi* banquet, with fillings

including duck, fish, savoury chive and shrimp. There are even sweet walnut marzipan dumplings. **$$–$$$**

Green Molly
Gaoxin Road
Hidden behind the Bank of China, Green Molly is an eclectic fusion of Italian pizzeria and Irish pub. It's a combination not to be missed. First-time visitors should ring the bell for entrance; thereafter entry is via members' swipe card. **$$**

Hui Muslim Quarter
Dapi Yuan, Damaishi Jie
This is an excellent area to explore for Muslim food stalls and street food. Cheap, reasonably clean and often delicious dishes to look for include *fenzhengrou* or minced mutton wok-fried with ground wheat; *roujiamo* or spicy fried pork or beef in a pitta-like roll; *rouchuan* or

kebabs; and the Xi'an Muslim speciality, *yangrou paomo* or mutton soup served with strips of bread. **$**

Lao Sun Jia
364 Dong Dajie, Beilin District
Tel: (029) 8721 4438
A firm favourite with Xi'an's Muslim community, this family-run restaurant's speciality, *yangrou paomo* (mutton soup), is a well-known Xi'an favourite. The rich soup is filled with soft mutton, and glass noodles and pieces of steamed bread are soaked in the stew. **$$**

Shang Palace
Shangri-La Golden Flower, 8 Chang Le Xi Lu
Tel: (029) 8323 2981
A top-class hotel restaurant, the Shang serves Cantonese specialities along with various traditional Chinese seafood dishes. There is also an exceptional wine list. **$$–$$$**

Tang Dynasty Theatre Restaurant (Tang Yuegong)
75 Chang An Lu

Tel: (029) 8782 2222
www.xiantangdynasty.com
An overpriced dinner theatre, the Tang Dynasty provides an exquisite set fusion menu. Quirky dish names include Willow's Melody (taro and water chestnut dessert) and Heart of the Dragon (crispy king prawns). Enjoy your food while watching a colourful and creative 90-minute floorshow. At lunchtime try the good Cantonese buffet. **$$$**

Xi'an Restaurant
298 Dong Dajie
Tel: (029) 8768 0618
Built in 1929, this is one of Xi'an's oldest restaurants and is justly celebrated for its superb Shaanxi cuisine. The waiting staff speak English and can help you with your choice of dish, although they will usually point you in the direction of the set menus, which offer good value for money. **$$**

BELOW: "eight treasure pudding" vendor in Xi'an.

GANSU

Tianshui

Beidao Food Street
Erma Lu
In Beidao, the grittier and less up-market east side of Tianshui, Erma Lu, just south of Tianshui Railway Station, also offers a wide variety of snack foods and

cheap but tasty meals served in small streetside restaurants or from mobile food stalls at very reasonable prices. **$**

Golden Sun Hotel
Zhonghua Lu
Tel: (0938) 827 7777

This establishment has one of the best hotel restaurants in Qincheng, the western side of Tianshui, serving local and regional Chinese specialities and international fare. English-language menus are available, and staff are friendly and helpful. **$$**

Qincheng Food Street
Xiaochi Jie
In the western part of Tianshui, on the appropriately named Xiaochi Jie or "Snack Street'", there are literally dozens of small restaurants and streetside stalls selling every kind of Chinese snack food. **$**

Lanzhou

Boton Coffee Shop
Nongmin Xiang and Tianshui Lu
Conveniently located next to the Lanzhou Hotel, this is a place to go if you're seeking Western food and desserts, ranging from pizza through steak to BLTs and pancakes, together with excellent coffee, an English menu and friendly service. **$–$$**

Fengshan Jiudian
Nongmin Xiang
Tel: (0931) 653 2108
The Fengshan, near the CITS office, serves some excellent local Gansu dishes, including desserts such as stuffed melon or steamed lily. **$**

Hezheng Lu Night Market
Tianshui Nanlu
An excellent and extensive night market with a bewildering selection of small restaurants and street stalls selling Han Chinese, Hui Muslim and Uighur foodstuffs and dishes of all kinds. **$**

Mingde Gong
191 Jiuquan Lu
Tel: (0931) 466 8588
In a town of good restaurants the Mingde Gong stands out. Each of its four floors offers more sophisticated, and consequently more expensive, dishes than the one below. The *jincheng baita*, a dish intended roughly to approximate the shape of Lanzhou's famous White Pagoda (*Baita*) is worth discovering. **$–$$**

Paris Keting
819 Gannan Lu
Tel: (0931) 845 4395
Open until 1.30am, Paris Keting is a great place for a late-night bite. The large restaurant draws a mixture of local and foreign clientele and has an eclectic menu incorporating everything from peperoni pizza to Japanese fish dishes. Live music and singing regularly accompany dinner. **$$–$$$**

Linxia

Bei Dajie Food Street
Minzhu Square
All along Bei Dajie there are food stalls selling a variety of Hui, Han and Tibetan food. On either side of the Jiefang Lu intersection there are two small Muslim restaurants, the **East Happy Bridge** and **West Happy Bridge Restaurants**, serving roast chicken, noodles, mutton soup and green tea. For a taste of the local alcoholic speciality, try *huang jiu* or "yellow wine", served at the nearby **Fang Jia Huang Jiudian** or **Fang Family Yellow Wine Shop** on the west Qianheyan Donglu, or the nearby **Xu Family Yellow Wine Shop** on the east side of Qianheyan Donglu. **$**

Hehai Mansion (Hehai Dasha)
50 Hongyuan Lu
Tel: (0930) 623 5455
Linxia isn't known for its fine restaurants or Chinese Muslim haute cuisine, but the Hehai Mansion restaurant serves generous portions of tasty Gansu food at reasonable prices. **$–$$**

Xiahe

Everest Café
Renmin Xijie
Tel: (0941) 712 2642
Attached to the Overseas Tibetan Hotel, this Nepali-run establishment offers good Western and South Asian breakfasts, Nepali curries with *naan* or *chapatti*, sizzling steak dishes, Tibetan specialities and, of course, chilled local beer. Good value and friendly staff. **$**

Snowland Restaurant (Xuecheng Canting)
Renmin Xijie
Tel: (0941) 712 2856
The Snowland caters to Westerners with its delicious desserts and good Tibetan cuisine. Try the *momo* (dumplings) and the *tsampa* (yak butter and barley), washed down with a refreshing glass of *chang* (barley beer). They also serve some standard Chinese, Western and international dishes. **$**

Tsewong's Café
Renmin Xijie
Tel: (0941) 712 5842
This is an enduringly popular Xiahe choice offering an eclectic mixture of Tibetan, Muslim and international travellers' fare at very reasonable prices. Favourites include pizza, kebab, *momo* dumplings and sweet pancakes. **$**

Wuwei

Liangzhou Binguan
68 Dong Dajie
Tel: (0935) 226 5999
Part of the centrally located Liangzhou Hotel on downtown Dong Dajie, this restaurant serves perhaps the best Chinese food in town. **$**

Nan Dajie Food Stalls
Nan Dajie north of Nanmen (South Gate)
There are several food stalls on the southern section of Nan Dajie, a short walk from the Liangzhou Hotel and Wenhua Square. Here, especially in the early evening, stalls sell every kind of food, from Chinese to Hui Muslim and Uighur. Tasty *lamian/laghman* noodles served with beef and vegetables are particularly popular. **$**

Zhangye

Mingqing Jie Food Street
Mingqing Jie
Zhangye's most popular eating institution, this recently refurbished street – a predominantly pedestrian zone named "Ming-Qing Street" after the two dynasties (1368–1911) it is meant to represent architecturally – offers a huge array of Chinese and Muslim street food and snacks, especially in the evening. **$**

Shibazhe Meishilin
Mingqing Jie
Located on the east side of Mingqing Jie, not far from Ganquan Park and the Marco Polo statue, this is one of the best restaurants in town, offering a good selection of local *huoguo* or hotpots and stews (ideal for colder weather) and an eclectic mix of Chinese and Muslim dishes. **$**

Jiuquan

Jiuquan International Hotel
33 Jiefang Lu
Tel: (0937) 261 4211
The best hotel in town also has what is probably the best restaurant, serving good Gansu Chinese cuisine, as well as popular specialities from across China, and a limited range of international dishes. Jiuquan means "wine spring", and certainly some local and imported wines are available. **$–$$**

Jiayuguan

Fuqiang Market (Fuqiang Shichang)
Fuqiang Donglu
The nearest thing to a "food street" in Jiayuguan is Fuqiang Market, where a good number of stalls sell a selection of Chinese, Hui Muslim and Uighur snacks, and there are casual benches and tables scattered about to sit at. **$**

Liuyuan Jiudian
34 Xinhua Nan Lu
Tel: (0937) 628 6918
The Linyuan, opposite the bus station, is popular with locals, possibly because there are so few good places to eat in town. Ask for the English menu and you'll find a list of regular Cantonese and Sichuan favourites: nothing great, but certainly acceptable. **$**

PRICE CATEGORIES

Prices are for a meal per person:

$ = under US$10
$$ = US$10–25
$$$ = over US$25

TRANSPORT

ACCOMMODATION

EATING OUT

ACTIVITIES

A – Z

LANGUAGE

Dunhuang

Charley Johng's Café
Mingshan Lu
Tel: (0937) 883 3039
There are a few good Western-style cafés in Dunhuang, and they all serve similar dishes, including Chinese favourites like sweet and sour pork (gulu rou) and spicy tofu (mala doufu), plus breakfast standbys such as banana fritters, muesli with local fruit, often with better coffee than you'll find at the hotel restaurants. As well as being a café, Charley Johng's provides help with bus, train and air tickets,

plus bicycles for hire. **$**
Feng Yi Ting
Silk Road Dunhuang Hotel,
Dunyue Lu
Tel: (0937) 888 2088
Feng Yi Ting means "Chamber of Grandeur", and that's certainly what this excellent restaurant is. It serves a bewildering number of Cantonese and Sichuan specialities. Striking red lanterns decorate the large dining area, and between July and September, the main tourist season, traditional dancers perform nightly in the restaurant's courtyard. **$$–$$$**
John's Information Café

(Yuehan Zhongxi Canting)
22 Mingshan Lu (beside the Feitian Hotel)
Tel: (0937) 882 7000
A branch of the budget-travel chain, which has other outlets further west in Turpan and Kashgar. They serve many old travellers' favourites, banana pancakes, fruit shakes, Western breakfasts and first-class coffee. The café will arrange a variety of trips into the desert and mountains, and it is also an excellent source of travel information. Closed during the winter months. **$**
Oasis Coffee House
Fanggu Shanye Yitiao Jie

American-owned Oasis has a committed following of expats, largely due to the excellent milkshakes and filter coffee on offer. The pizzas and hamburgers are reasonable and offer a taste of home. **$**
Shazhou Night Market
Off Yangguan Donglu
A really good night market selling Han, Hui and Uighur food in a pedestrian area just to the south of Yangguan Donglu in the northern part of town. The numerous Hui Muslim places are obvious from the white caps of their owners and the ubiquitous aroma of mutton. **$**

XINJIANG: THE NORTHERN ROUTE

Hami (Kumul)

Hami Hotel
Yingbin Lu
Tel: (0902) 223 3140
The Hami has two pretty good restaurants, one serving Chinese food, and the other various Muslim dishes, both Uighur and Hui. **$–$$$**
Hami Night Market
Off Aiguo Lu
Centrally located and open in the afternoons and evenings in the warm summer months. Features the usual extensive collection of food stalls selling Chinese, Hui Muslim and Uighur food. It's very fresh – especially the fish, which are usually kept alive in tanks – and reasonably priced. **$**
Maixiang Yuan
Aiguo Beilu
About as "international" as the cuisine gets in Hami, this small establishment, not far from the long-distance bus station, serves a selection of sausages, burgers, steaks and rather sweet cakes. **$–$$**

Turpan (Tulufan)

John's Information Café
(Yuehan Zhongxi Canting)
2 Qingnian Lu
Tel: (0995) 852 4237
Similar to the other two branches in Dunhuang and Kashgar, and serving pretty much the same Chinese

and Western dishes. Also has internet facility and bicycle rental. A good place for breakfast – most Westerners find the local naan bread goes very well with eggs and coffee. **$**
Turpan Bazaar (Shi Maoyi Shichang)
Off Laocheng Lu
Numerous food stalls selling local Muslim cuisine and variants of Chinese cuisine from distant provinces in China proper. It's reasonably priced, friendly and fun to visit. For those desperate for a break from Sino-Uighur fare, there's a branch of **Best Food Burger** more or less opposite the bazaar on the north side of Laocheng Lu. **$**
Xin Shiji
Xinzhan Dingzi Lukou
Tel: (0995) 855 1199
The Xin Shiji is a great place to sample an Uighur banquet, and it's also famous for its "cook your own" kebabs and sangshen jiu (mulberry wine). It's also a lively favourite for group tours and locals out for an evening of Xinjiang-style entertainment. The staff are attired in traditional costume, and energetic dancers make this the ideal place to relax after a hard day's sightseeing or a lengthy period in the desert. **$–$$**

Korla (Ku'erle)

Bayinguoleng Binguan
Renmin Donglu
Tel: (0996) 202 2118
This establishment has two in-house restaurants serving, respectively, Muslim and Chinese food. **$**
Silverstar Hotel
36 Renmin Donglu
Tel: (0996) 202 8888
This is perhaps Korla's best hotel, and certainly one of its newest. Centrally located, it offers three restaurants, serving Chinese, Muslim and Western cuisines. **$$**

Kuqa (Kuche)

Meile Chuancaiguan
Wenhua Lu
A popular Sichuan establishment serving the usual spicy dishes at very reasonable prices. **$**
Xinhua Lu Night Market
Near junction of Xinhua Lu and Youyi Lu
A bustling collection of food stalls and streetside restaurants offering Chinese, Hui Muslim and especially Uighur dishes. **$**

Aksu (Akesu)

Hongfu Jinlan
32 Dongdajie Lu
Aksu's premier hotel has restaurants offering Chinese, Uighur and international dishes. **$–$$**

Kashgar (Kashi)

Caravan Café
120 Seman Lu
Tel: (0998) 298 2196
The café serves good Western breakfasts and good coffee. Other potentially interesting diversions from endless kebabs and mutton include pizzas, sandwiches, cinnamon rolls and fresh yoghurt. The friendly staff can help with most travel enquiries, and they will arrange trips into the Taklamakan Desert, to Tushuk Tagh and elsewhere in the vicinity of Kashgar. **$**
Jiefang Beilu Night Market
Jiefang Beilu
A busy and picturesque night market opposite the central Id Gah Mosque, offering all kinds of foods, but especially local Uighur specialities, at very reasonable prices. **$**
John's Information Café
(Yuehan Zhongxi Canting)
337 Seman Lu
Tel: (0998) 258 1186
www.johncafe.net
Yet another in Western China's beloved chain, John's serves a range of popular Chinese dishes and Western favourites. The pancakes are good and the apple pie delicious. There's also a variety of sundaes and cold beer. The café offers free travel information and will arrange trips to just about anywhere in the vicinity.

Internet access and bicycle rentals round up what is a very helpful operation. **$**

Karakoram Café
87 Seman Lu
Proper coffee and western breakfasts draw an unending stream of backpackers to the Karakoram Café.

Food is tasty and reasonably priced, and many of the staff speak English. **$**

Lao Chayuan Jiudian
251 Renmin Xi Lu
Tel: (0998) 282 4467
Regarded by locals as the finest restaurant in Kashgar, this place offers a variety of

Uighur food, including the fabled *polo* (an Uighur rice speciality), lamb shish kebabs and beef noodle soup. **$**

Tashkurgan (Tashiku'ergan)

Laochengdu Canting

East of Tashkurgan Bus Station
Good Chinese food and cold beer in an area with several Chinese and Muslim eateries aimed at the long-distance bus traffic on the Karakoram Highway. **$**

XINJIANG: THE SOUTHERN ROUTE

Charklik (Ruoqiang)

Xinchuanzhao Daisuo
The best Chinese restaurant in town, with an extensive menu (in Chinese) and friendly staff. There are several Uighur places near the bus station. **$**

Cherchen (Qiemo)

Lao Huimin Dapan
Wenhua Lu
Simple but clean noodle restaurant run by Hui Muslims. **$**

Pakdiyar
Sichou Lu
Well-run and friendly restaurant specialising in Uighur dishes. **$**

Niya (Minfeng)

Bashu Yuzhuang
Bosetan Lu
Clean and tasty Chinese restaurant offering private rooms located in the basement of the

Luzhou Binguan building. **$**

Niya Gongyu
Off Highway 315
Good Chinese food in the Niya Gongyu Hotel. **$**

Keriya

Buihalqam
North side of Highway 315
Uighur specialities. **$**

Manzilgah Tiz
South side of Highway 315
Uighur specialities. **$**

Khotan (Hetian)

Huimin Fanguan
Beijing Xilu
As the name suggests, a Hui Muslim restaurant serving halal dishes that seem to appeal to all palates, Uighur, Hui, Chinese and Western. **$**

Ilqi
Ying Bin Lu
You may be surprised to find a seafood restaurant so far from the sea, but Ilqi's

numerous tanks of live fish ensure their offering remains fresh right up until it hits your plate. **$$**

Lokman
Zhong Nan Hai Lu
The best Uighur food in Khotan is probably to be found at Lokman. The laghman washed down with pomegranate juice is particularly good. **$**

Maixiang Yuan Bakery
Tuanjie Square
Western-style fast-food place serving bread, cakes, pizza, pasta, fresh coffee and iced beer. Centrally located. **$**

Tuanjie Square Night Market
South of Tuanjie Square
The usual reliable collection of food stalls and streetside restaurants serving all the local Uighur favourites, as well as Hui Muslim and Chinese dishes. **$**

Karghalik (Yecheng)

Yecheng Dianli
500 metres (1,650ft) east of Karghalik Bus Station
The "Electricity Hotel" offers reasonably priced local food, but Karghalik (a junction town with Highway 219 leading south to Tibet) is really just a large truck stop with food stalls and simple restaurants. **$**

Yarkand (Shache)

Meraj Restaurant
Laocheng Lu
Arguably the best restaurant in Yarkand, serving a wide range of Uighur specialities including roast pigeon. **$**

Yengisar (Yingjisha)

Yengisar Bazaar
There are plenty of small food stalls selling Uighur snacks and fresh naan around the town centre and scattered among the shops of the knife bazaar. **$**

XINJIANG: THE DZUNGARIAN ROUTE

Urumqi (Wulumuqi)

Fubar
Gongyuan Beijie
Tel: (0991) 584 4498
Urumqi's very own sports bar, with regular live football, rugby and cricket coverage from around the world, as well as a pool table and darts. The friendly management (Irish and Japanese) are perhaps the best source for information on travel in Xinjiang for Western travellers. **$–$$**

Kashgari's
168 Xinhua Beilu
Tel: (0991) 281 8788
Part of the Xinjiang Grand Hotel and consequently the

prices are quite high. Dishes are comparable to those found in surrounding markets, but the general presentation and quality of ingredients is far superior. **$$–$$$**

Texas Café
55 Ma Shi Xiang
Home of the Lone Star State in China. Look out for the giant cowboy boots and Stetson above the door, and tuck in to burgers, steaks and surprisingly cheesy pizza. **$$**

Urumqi Night Markets
Eating on the street in China can always be a risk, but if you are bold enough then

why not try some of the Muslim restaurants on Xinhua Lu, and if you're truly daring, the night market on Changjiang Lu with its lamb kebabs, naan, *laghman* (noodles in a thick stew) and *samsa* (samosas). **$**

Yining (Gulja)

Ili Hotel
Yingbing Lu
Tel: (0999) 802 3126
This establishment has good Chinese and international restaurants. **$–$$**

Naren Canting
Xinhua Xilu
Tel: (0999) 803 2434
A bit of a Kazakh touch

here, with horse meat to eat and mare's milk to drink, as well as accompanying *naan*, salads and yoghurt. **$**

Yining Night Market
Yingbing Lu
Immediately to the west of the Ili Hotel, this large and bustling market offers the usual range of Uighur, Hui and Chinese specialities, all at very reasonable prices. **$**

PRICE CATEGORIES

Prices are for a meal per person:

$ = under US$10
$$ = US$10–25
$$$ = over US$25

TRANSPORT

ACCOMMODATION

EATING OUT

ACTIVITIES

A–Z

LANGUAGE

ACTIVITIES

THE ARTS, FAIRS, FESTIVALS, OUTDOOR ACTIVITIES AND SHOPPING

THE ARTS

Concerts and Theatres

Shaanxi

Tang Dynasty Theatre Restaurant
75 Chang'an Lu
Tel: (029) 8782 2222
www.xiantangdynasty.com
One of Xi'an's top attractions –
particularly popular with visiting
Chinese tourists – is the elaborate
floor show at the Tang Dynasty
Theatre Restaurant (Tang Yuegong).
A glitzy, somewhat over-the-top
"re-creation" of the elaborate
entertainments available in Old
Chang'an, it features a mix of
traditional dancing, music and
song performed by a large cast in
spectacular costumes. Explanations
are in English as well as Chinese. It
doesn't come cheap, but you won't
find anything else like it for the length
of the Silk Road.

Shaanxi Song and Dance Theatre
165 Wenyi Lu
Tel: (029) 8785 3295 / 8785 3304
The Shaanxi Song and Dance Theatre
(Shaanxi Gewu Juyuan) is more
authentic and less touristy, offering
nightly shows that include traditional
song and dance, Tang Dynasty operas
and lantern festival shows. It's a very
professional theatre that tours in
China and internationally. Their opera,
Zhang Qian recreates the story of the
opening of the Silk Road more than
2,000 years ago.

Gansu

Lanzhou Theatre
237 Zhongshan Road
Tel: (0931) 846 4057
Lanzhou is not widely celebrated for

its nightlife or cultural activities, but
the Lanzhou Theatre stages operas
featuring Qing (Shaanxi) Opera, Long
(Gansu) Opera, Yu (Henan) Opera and
Beijing Opera on a weekly basis.

**Linxia Nationalities Song and
Dance Troupe**
27 Bei Dajie, LinXia
Tel: (0930) 621 3023
The Linxia Nationalities Song and
Dance Troupe features cultural shows
celebrating local cultural traditions
of the region's Hui, Dongxiang and
Tibetan minorities.

Xinjiang

In Turpan the Turpan Hotel (Tulufan
Binguan, 2 Qingnian Lu, tel: (0995)
8568 888) hosts an Uighur song and
dance display most evenings, except
in winter, in a covered area behind the
main hotel. Accompanied by kebabs,
Xinjiang beer and local wine, it can
be great fun, but closes by 10pm at
the latest.

Urumqi's main theatrical
entertainment venue is the Xinjiang
Erdaoqiao International Bazaar
Theatre on Xinhua Nanlu, specialising
in glamorous and elaborate displays
of song and dance by all Xinjiang's
nationalities, but especially the Uighur
(whom the dominant Han consider to
love "song and dance" above all else).

FAIRS AND FESTIVALS

Holidays such as National Day and
International Labour Day are fixed
on the modern calendar, but most
traditional festivals and events are
determined by the lunar calendar,
which means the date varies slightly
from year to year. Each region has its
own special days and events.

ABOVE: cable cars at Heavenly Lake
near Urumqi.

Muslim Festivals

The main festivals specific to Xinjiang
and other predominantly Muslim
areas along the Silk Road are Eid
al-Fitr (Turkish: Bayram, the "Festival
of the Breaking the Fast"), held
at the end of the Muslim fasting
month of Ramadan; and Eid al-Adha
(Turkish: Kurban, the "Festival of
the Sacrifice"), held to mark the
culmination of the Hajj pilgrimage to
Mecca. Since the Muslim calendar,
like the traditional Chinese, is lunar,
these festivals fall on different dates
each year. It's worth noting that the
fasting month of Ramadan – which is
observed by many Muslims in China
– is easier on the non-Muslim visitor
than it would be, for example, in Iran

John's Information Café

In 1988 John Hu set up the first café and travel service for Western tourists in Kashgar. Today there are several branches of **John's Information Café** (www.johncafe. net) conveniently spread along the Chinese section of the Silk Road. They are excellent places to pick up the latest information on all forms of transportation and organise a bewildering number of treks and tours, especially out of Kashgar. Onward travel arrangements can

also be arranged.
Dunhuang
22 Mingshan Lu (next to the Feitian Hotel)
Tel: (0937) 882 7000
Turpan
2 Qingnian Lu (next to the Turpan Hotel)
Tel: (0995) 852 4237
Kashgar
337 Seman Lu (next to the Seman Hotel)
Tel: (0998) 258 1186

or Saudi Arabia, as Han Chinese restaurants, at least, remain open everywhere.

Buddhist Festivals

Labrang Monastery, at Xiahe in Gansu, is the most important Tibetan monastery in China outside the Tibetan Autonomous Region. Between approximately 14–17 January and 26 June–15 July (according to the lunar calendar), major festivals are held here each year involving merit-making, sutra-chanting and devil-dancing. The most important festival of all, known as Monlan or "Great Prayer", falls sometime in February or March, with pilgrims dressed in their finest clothes visiting from all over the Tibetan-speaking world.

The most important festival time is the Lunar New Year, or Spring Festival, which usually falls in late January or early February. Public buildings are festooned with coloured lights, people from all over China travel to reunite with family and friends, debts are settled and food is consumed. In recent years, a more relaxed atmosphere has brought the revival of old Spring Festival traditions, such as giving *hongbao* – small, red envelopes containing money – to children and young adults. Temple fairs feature martial arts demonstrations, stand-up comedy and home-made toys.

On the 12th day of the third lunar month, at the beginning of April, the Chinese honour their deceased ancestors by observing Qingming, sometimes referred to as the "grave-sweeping" day. It is much less impressive nowadays, as people are cremated instead of buried. Qingming is a time for remembering ancestors, but also for revelling in a warm spring day.

The Mid-Autumn Festival usually takes place around mid-September.

Shops do great business in "moon cakes" – pastries filled with gooey sesame paste, red-bean and walnut filling. *Tang yuan*, glutinous rice-flour balls with sweet fillings in sugar syrup, and *yue bing*, a cake baked specifically for this occasion, are also eaten. In the tradition of poets, this is the time to drink a bit of wine and toast the moon.

OUTDOOR ACTIVITIES

Trekking and Mountaineering

Shaanxi

The most popular trekking destinations in Shaanxi are the many paths around Mount Huashan, 120km (72 miles) east of Xi'an, though some of the climbs are very steep and not suitable for the unfit. The best walking trails are between Jade Fountain Temple and North Peak, and south across Green Dragon Ridge to Yangtian Pool and South Peak. The scenery is spectacular, and both food and accommodation are available.

Gansu

An interesting and not too arduous hike associated with the ancient Silk Road runs between Binglingsi and the Tibetan monastery at the head of Binglingsi ravine. More difficult, but still accessible to the amateur walker, is the hike between Mati Si (near Zhangye) and the nearby rural Yugur communities, where it is possible to enjoy horse riding and stay in yurt accommodation. It's possible to follow the Great Wall for considerable distances, especially near Shandan and the Longshou Mountains, but remember to take adequate drinking water even for a short hike, as it is an arid and hot area.

Xinjiang

There are so many opportunities for walking and mountaineering in Xinjiang that it's invidious to attempt to list them all. The most readily accessible areas are around Urumqi, where it's easy and safe to arrange trekking in the Tian Chi (Heavenly Lake) area, though climbing nearby Bogda Feng (5,445 metres/17,960ft) requires special permission and very professional mountaineering qualifications – otherwise it's better to hike around Tian Chi and maybe stay overnight in a Kazakh yurt. Also near Urumqi, the lovely "Southern Pastures" at Baiyang Gou make readily accessible and great trekking. Both can be arranged through travel agents in Urumqi.

Kashgar, too, offers some fantastic trekking and mountaineering possibilities, though the latter often requires special permission, and peaks in frontier areas, especially to the south near the Pakistani and Indian frontiers, are off-limits except for Beijing-sanctioned expeditions. Still, for the enterprising or enthusiastic amateur, a one- or two-day visit to Shipton's Arch, the highest natural arch in the world, is an outstanding experience. Most travel agents in Kashgar will be able to arrange trekking in the area, whether to the nearby Tushук Tagh Mountains, or the equally close-by Taklamakan Desert. Neither should be undertaken lightly, however, and a local guide is essential, as these are hard, dry and dangerous terrains where the inexperienced visitor could easily die of thirst or exposure in a matter of hours.

Another beautiful hike is around Lake Karakul, just off the Karakoram Highway. It's possible to stay in rather touristy Kazakh yurts near the highway, or in somewhat less touristy accommodation at the Kazakh village on the southeastern shores of the lake some distance away. Allow at least a couple of days, particularly if you are intending to visit the glacier fields on nearby Muztagh Ata (7,546 metres/24,900ft). The setting is truly spectacular, but a local guide is always advised. A sudden snowstorm or drop in temperature could prove dangerous or even fatal.

Organised Tours

There are countless travel agencies within and outside China that handle domestic travel arrangements. Agencies may also have business interests extending beyond simply arranging tours and bookings; they may own or partly own hotels. An agency that arranges a tour may do so by contacting agencies in places you will visit, and asking them to deal with local bookings. If you go direct to an agency in the area you are visiting, savings may be possible.

Sometimes agencies such as CITS may hold tickets for rail journeys, operas, acrobatic performances and concerts, even when such tickets are sold out at the stations or venues.

It is also quite possible nowadays to travel in China without the services of any agency. Note that within China, agencies have nothing to do with visa extensions or other passport matters. For these services you will need to visit one of the many Public Security Bureaux (see Visas, page 400).

China International Travel Services (CITS; www.cits.net) have offices in most cities and can help with most travel-related enquiries. An English-speaker is usually available.
Beijing
28 Jianguomenwai Dajie
Tel: (010) 6515 8587
Kashgar (Kashi)
Chini Bagh Hotel (Qiniwake Binguan)
Tel: (0998) 298 3156
Lanzhou
Tourism Building, Nongmin Xiang
Tel: (0931) 883 5566
Shanghai
1277 Beijing Xilu
Tel: (021) 6289 8899
Urumqi
38 Xinhua Nanlu
Tel: (0991) 282 1428

SHOPPING

Many of the larger towns will provide ample opportunity for shopping. Xi'an in particular is full of antique, handicraft and souvenir shops. It is worth looking for local products in the smaller towns or in places where ethnic minorities live, as these will be difficult to find anywhere else.

Antiques that date from before 1795 may not be legally exported. Those that can be taken out of China must carry a small red seal or have one affixed by the Cultural Relics Bureau. All other antiques are the property of the People's Republic of China and, without the seal, will be confiscated without compensation. Do not buy "antiques" that the vendor claims are over 100 years old, as they are probably fake.

What to Buy

Xi'an

Shuyuanmen, also known as Arts Street, runs between the South Gate and the Forest of Stelae Museum. It's a collection of Ming- and Qing-style buildings with shops selling all manner of items including calligraphy, jade ornaments, the infamous Terracotta Warrior reproductions and ink paintings. Prices are a little higher than other shopping areas in Xi'an.

BELOW: traditional embroidered hats for sale.

The **Rongshengzhai Tourist Shopping Centre** (42 Chang'an Lu; tel: (029) 8222 9903) is a huge showroom offering an array of handicrafts, including furniture, paintings, tapestries, jade and calligraphy. The **Kai Yuan Shopping Centre**, Dong Dajie (East Street; tel: (029) 8723 5340), near the Bell Tower intersection, is a good place to find clothes, with a wide range of brand-name items.

Kashgar

Laocheng Shichang (Old Town Bazaar), on Jiefang Beilu and the surrounding streets, offers a multitude of shopping opportunities, with Uighur-style carpets, shoes, clothing, spices, herbs and many, many other items. Heavy competition among traders means you ought to be able to find some bargains, but make sure you haggle hard.

Xingqitian Shichang (Sunday Market), across the river from central Kashgar, and off Aizirete Lu, is the town's main attraction, a huge market selling everything from clothing, knives, household goods and food to a variety of domestic animals. Furs are widely available, and some of them are high quality, but be wary of purchasing skins from endangered animals.

Turpan

Turpan Shichang (Turpan Bazaar), on Laocheng Lu, is a modest affair in comparison to other cities in the Xinjiang region. It's mainly an Uighur market selling an array of fancy hats and clothing, as well as silk. Most of the market, however, sells fresh produce, with a variety of exotic fruits, dried fruits, spices and nuts.

Urumqi

Erdaoqiao Shichang (Erdaoqiao Market), between Xinhua Nanlu and Jiefang Lu, is Urumqi's largest bazaar. Look out for traditional handicrafts, hats, clothing and silk. Fine-quality silk carpets from Xinjiang and other parts of Central Asia are found on the second floor.

Xiahe

Xiahe's **main street** is overflowing with shops and stalls selling all manner of Tibetan items, including prayer wheels, bells, silver ornaments, handicrafts, hats and shawls. Bargaining is essential. It's a great place to browse and to watch the continuous flow of Tibetan pilgrims searching for the perfect item to take back to their homes in Tibet.

A – Z

A HANDY SUMMARY OF PRACTICAL INFORMATION, ARRANGED ALPHABETICALLY

B

Budgeting for Your Trip

Travelling in China remains relatively cheap for foreign travellers as the Chinese government controls the renminbi exchange rate, ensuring it stays competitive for exports. In a country as vast as China prices still vary considerably, however, not only between city and countryside but also between provinces. For budget travellers, daily costs including accommodation and food (but excluding transport) range from US$25 to US$40 per day. Travellers wishing for a higher degree of comfort should allow US$40–75 per day. Travellers planning to stay in top-end accommodation should allow US$75–200, although, increasingly, the sky is the limit, especially in Xi'an, Lanzhou, Dunhuang and Urumqi.

Remember that if you are travelling with your own vehicle in China, you will require incur not only the fee but also the travel, food and accommodation expenses of your government-approved guide, significantly driving up your costs.

C

Climate

Chinese Central Asia, which includes not just Xinjiang, but also the neighbouring provinces of Gansu and Qinghai, as well as nearby Tibet and Inner Mongolia, is an area of climatic extremes, being very hot in summer and often well below zero, even at midday, in winter. **Shaanxi** is marginally warmer in winter, but more humid and uncomfortable in summer, when **Xinjiang** and **Gansu** can be very hot but with dry heat. Another climatic problem unique to the Northwest within China is dust. All of the Northwest, but Xinjiang in particular, can suffer from blinding, choking sandstorms, especially in spring and early summer. Rainfall is virtually non-existent for most of the year – but when the heavens do open, the downpour can be heavy.

Crime and Security

There is still less crime in China than in many countries, but crime is an increasing problem. Take the same precautions applicable anywhere, on the street and with valuables in hotels and on public transport. Pickpockets and bag-slashers can be a problem, especially on crowded trains and buses, and in stations.

The **Public Security Bureau** (gongan ju) is the ever-present police force. They are usually friendly towards foreigners. With serious travel-related disputes – for example, with taxi drivers or hotels – they are usually able to resolve the problem.

Customs Regulations

On arrival each traveller must complete a health declaration form. Tourists can freely import two bottles of wine or spirits (four bottles if you staying more than six months), 400 cigarettes and a reasonable amount of perfume, as well as foreign currency and valuables for personal use without restrictions. The import of weapons, ammunition, illicit narcotics and pornographic

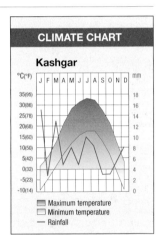

CLIMATE CHART

Kashgar

literature is prohibited. On departure, antiques such as porcelain, paintings, calligraphy, carvings and old books must be certified by an official antique shop, or they may be confiscated.

D

Disabled Travellers

Only in recent years have the needs of disabled people received attention in China. Now, regulations regarding rooms and other facilities for the disabled will be met in the new hotels. In general, though, towns, institutions, public transport and sights offer little accessibility.

Travelling in a group for the disabled certainly reduces these problems considerably. The China National Tourist Offices and CITS have information about special trips for the disabled.

E

Embassies and Consulates

Beijing

Australian Embassy
21 Dongzhimenwai Dajie Sanlitun, tel: (010) 5140 4111, www.china. embassy.gov.au
British Embassy
11 Guanghua Lu, Jianguomenwai, tel: (010) 5192 4000, www. ukinchina.fco.gov.uk/en
Canadian Embassy
19 Dongzhimenwai Dajie, Chaoyang District, tel: (010) 5139 4000, www. beijing.gc.ca
Irish Embassy
3 Ritan Donglu, tel: (010) 6532 2691, www.embassyofireland.cn
New Zealand Embassy
1 Ritanlu Dongerjie, tel: (010) 8532 7000, www.nzembassy.com/china
US Embassy
55 An Jia Lou Lu, tel: (010) 8531 4200,
http://beijing.usembassy-china.org.cn

Shanghai

Australian Embassy
22/F, CITIC Square, 1168 Nanjing Road (W), tel: (021) 2215 5200, www.shanghai.china.embassy.gov.au
British Embassy
Shanghai Centre, Suite 301, 1376 Nanjing Rd (W), tel: (021) 3279 2000.
Canadian Embassy
Shanghai Centre, Suite 604, 1376 Nanjing Rd (W), tel: (021) 3279 2800, www.shanghai.gc.ca
New Zealand Consulate989 Chang Le Rd, tel: (021) 5407 5858, www. nzembassy.com/China
US Embassy
1469 Huaihai Rd (C), tel: (021) 6433 6880, www.shanghai.usembassy-china. org.cn

Hong Kong

Australian Embassy
21–24/F, Harbour Centre, 25 Harbour Road, Wan Chai, tel: (0851) 2827 8881, www.hongkong.china. embassy.gov.au
British Embassy
1 Supreme Court Road, Admiralty, tel: (0852) 2901 3000.
Canadian Embassy
11/F, Tower One, Exchange Square, 8 Connaught Place, Central, tel: (0852) 3719 4700, www.hongkong. gc.ca
US Embassy
26 Garden Road, Central, tel: (0852) 2523 9011, www.hongkong. usconsulate.gov

Electricity

The electricity supply is 220 volts, 50 cycles AC. Supplies in outlying areas can be erratic, but the larger towns and cities are usually well powered. There are a number of different plugs used in China, but generally you'll find either the three-pronged angled pins or the two-pronged flat pins in hotels. It's a good idea to carry a conversion plug with you, especially if you are travelling with a laptop computer or mobile phone.

Emergencies

If you have a mobile phone with roving capacity, you may be able to SOS. Check with your service provider. If you have an accident, emergency services are called by dialling **110** for police, **119** for fire services, or **999** for the ambulance service (**120** if you are in Beijing or Shanghai) .

Etiquette

The dominant **Han** culture is very self-confident. Chinese can be polite as individuals, but sometimes seem collectively impolite to visiting Westerners. Concepts of maintaining face and level tempers are highly valued. Belching, shouting loudly into mobile phones, smoking and spitting are all openly frowned upon by the Chinese authorities, who are doing their best to reform such "outdated, antisocial" behaviour. Time will tell!

G

Gay and Lesbian Travellers

In the past two decades gay people of both sexes have increasingly reasserted their presence and rights, especially in such big and go-ahead cities as Shanghai, Beijing and Guangzhou. In western Xinjiang, where Central Asian Islamic mores are more apparent, homosexuality may be more readily accepted but is still not flaunted.

H

Health and Medical Care

A yellow fever vaccination certificate is required if coming from an infected area less than six days prior to entering China. Vaccinations for hepatitis A and B, diphtheria, tetanus, typhoid and polio should be up to date.

The most frequently reported health problem in China is diarrhoea. The best prevention is to ensure maximum hygiene while travelling, especially in restaurants and road-side snack bars. Never eat raw, uncooked or partially cooked food, including salads, other than in the top hotels. Animal or human excrement is still frequently used as fertiliser, so bacteria on uncooked vegetables can easily be ingested. It is also suggested if travelling outside a tour group, to acquire chopsticks and a tin bowl with lid for train journeys and meals in small road-side restaurants. Drink only boiled or bottled water, even though the tap water is drinkable in some places, and reduce exposure to insects as far as possible.

There is a big difference in China between urban and rural medical services. If travelling in the countryside, there may be no appropriate medical services beyond primary health care, which is good in China. Some hospitals in cities have special sections for foreigners where English is spoken. Many of the large hotels have their own doctors. Payment must be made on the spot for treatment, medicine and transport.

I

Insurance

Travel and medical insurance is essential, including evacuation cover. Bring copies of documentation and all necessary phone numbers with you.

Internet

Internet cafés are to be found just about everywhere. Even the smallest towns on the Silk Road have their own cafés, usually close to the centre, and rates are very reasonable. One word of warning: they can be smoky and noisy, and often unpleasant to sit in for too long. Most four- and five-star hotels have their own business centres with internet access, but rates can be considerably higher than the ordinary cafés.

M

Maps

A significant number of English-language maps have been produced for China in recent years, which is a real boon for tourists. City maps, provincial maps and regularly updated road maps are all readily available abroad, and can also be purchased from English-language bookshops and tourist centres in major Chinese cities.

Media

An English-language newspaper, the China Daily, is published every day except Sunday. It is often obtainable from the big hotels for free. Same-day editions are available only in large cities; elsewhere, it'll probably be several days late. International newspapers and magazines can usually be found in the larger hotels.

Money

The Chinese currency is called the renminbi or "people's currency", usually abbreviated to Rmb. The basic unit is the yuan (colloquially, kuai). Ten jiao (colloquially, mao) make one yuan; ten fen make one jiao. Thus, 100 fen make one yuan. Notes are currently issued for 1, 2, 5, 10, 20, 50 and 100 yuan. Coins come in 1 yuan, 5 jiao, 1 jiao and 5 fen.

Major currencies are accepted in banks and hotels. Global network-connected ATMs (Cirrus, Plus) can be found in major cities – try branches of the Bank of China.

Don't expect to use credit cards much outside of Xi'an, except in the very top hotels. Also, most transport costs (e.g. domestic air and train tickets) are paid in cash. Cash advances may be obtained from major branches of the Bank of China in Xi'an, Lanzhou, Kashgar and Urumqi.

O

Opening Hours

Shops are open every day, including public holidays. Opening hours are usually 8.30am or 9am to 8pm. Government offices and banks are usually open Mon–Fri, 8.30am to 5.30pm, with a lunch break from noon to 1.30pm. Note that these times can vary slightly from place to place. In Xinjiang and parts of Gansu, for example, offices often open later as they are on Beijing time, rather than the local unofficial time.

P

Photography

Taking photographs or videos of bridges, government buildings, military installations and railway stations is strictly prohibited. As in other countries many museums, palaces or temples will not allow photographs to be taken, or will charge a fee. At other times, photography is allowed, but without using either a flash or a tripod. A good example of this is the Terracotta Warriors in Xi'an: photography was banned completely until a recent easing of restrictions. No special permit is necessary for a video or movie camera, as long as it is clearly not for professional use.

Photographic film, memory cards and batteries are widely available in China, but professional slide film is increasingly hard to find in a digital age.

Postal Services

Express mail (EMS) is available to the majority of international destinations, as are private international courier services. Note that large parcels must be packed and sealed at the post office.

For general delivery and poste restante services you should visit the central post office.

Public Holidays

In addition to China's national holidays (see above), 1–7 May and 1–7 October are week-long public holidays for the majority of Chinese. It is not advisable to plan a trip during these times. Most shops are open during holidays. School holidays in China are between 1 August and 30 September. This also applies to universities.

Don't plan on travel or border crossings during holidays unless

National Holidays

1 January New Year's Day
January/February Chinese New Year (lunar)
8 March International Women's Day
1 May Youth Day (4th May Movement)
1 June Children's Day
1 July Founding of the Chinese Communist Party
1 August Founding of the People's Liberation Army
1 October National Day

reservations have been made and confirmed a long time in advance. It is especially wise not to make any travel plans during the Spring Festival, which is three days long and is the period when everyone is travelling to their hometown.

R

Religion

The various Muslim peoples of the Northwest are – with the exception of a handful (39,000) of isolated Shia Ismaili Tajiks in the high Pamirs – uniformly Sunni Muslims of the moderate Hanafi school, much given to trade and commerce and little interested in fundamentalism. Visitors are welcome to enter mosques and religious schools, but should dress modestly and remember to remove their shoes.

Officially, the People's Republic encourages atheism. However, there are Buddhist and Daoist temples and places of worship throughout the country, as well as mosques in the Muslim areas and in all large cities, which have regular prayers at the prescribed times. Catholic and Protestant churches can also be found in most big cities.

T

Telecommunications

Domestic long-distance calls are cheap; international calls are relatively expensive. Local calls in China from hotels are usually free of charge, but international calls made from hotels typically have high surcharges added to China's already high IDD rates. IP (Internal Phone) cards are the cheapest way to phone abroad; these can be purchased at news-stands and hotels in the larger cities. The international dialling code for China is +86.

Domestic Area Codes

Add 0 to the codes below if dialling from within China:
Beijing 10
Dunhuang 937
Hotan 903
Kashgar 998
Kuqa 997
Lanzhou 931
Tianshui 938
Turpan 995
Urumqi 991

TRANSPORT

ACCOMMODATION

EATING OUT

ACTIVITIES

A – Z

LANGUAGE

Time Zones

The whole of China officially runs on Beijing time (GMT + 8 hours), although Xinjiang time is unofficially GMT + 6 hours.

Xi'an 29
Zhangye 936

Tipping

Tipping is still not common in the majority of restaurants and hotels, although it is accepted in the top-class ones. Note that as part of the ritual any gift or tip will, at first, be firmly rejected.

Toilets

Public toilets in China are usually best avoided. Squat toilets are the norm, privacy cannot always be counted on, toilet paper is rarely provided and standards of sanitation are generally low. Some international fast-food chains provide Western-style facilities, but by far the best option is to head for a good hotel.

Tourist Information

The **China National Tourist Office** (www.cnto.org.uk) is a useful source of information on travelling in China and has 15 offices in several countries across the world.
Some of these include:
Australia
19th Floor, 44 Market Street, Sydney, New South Wales, 2000.
Tel: +61 (2) 9252 9838.
Canada
480 University Avenue, Suite 806, Toronto, Ontario, 91203.
Tel: +1 (416) 599 6636.
United Kingdom
4 Glentworth Street, London, NW1 5PG.
Tel: +44 (20) 7935 9787.
United States
370 Lexington Avenue #912, New York, NY 10017.
Tel: +1 (212) 760 8218.
France
15 Rue De Berri, 75008, Paris.
Tel: +33 (1) 5659 1010.

V

Visas

All foreigners must acquire an entry visa before arrival in China. If you are part of a group, the tour operator

will often obtain this. Individual travellers can apply at any Chinese embassy or consulate. The process is straightforward, taking about five days depending on current regulations and on your own country's regulations for issuing visas to Chinese nationals. A 30-day single-entry visa is usually issued. Your passport must be valid for six months after the expiry date of the entry visa.

If your visa expires while you are in China, it can be extended once (or sometimes twice) by the local Public Security Bureau (gongan ju). It is essential to apply for an extension before your current visa expires, or you risk paying a substantial fine.

Public Security Bureaux

Beijing
9 Dongdajie, Qianmen.
Tel: (010) 8402 0101.
http://www.bjgaj.gov.cn/web/
Kashgar (Kashi)
111 Youmulakexia Lu.
Tel: (0998) 282 2048.
Lanzhou
482 Wudu Lu.
Tel: (0931) 871 8114.
Shanghai
1500 Minsheng Lu.
Tel: (021). 2895 1900.
Urumqi
Jiefang Beilu.
Tel: (0991) 282 4629.
Xi'an
136 Xi Dajie.
Tel: (029) 8675 1111.

W

Weights and Measures

China uses the metric system.

What to Bring and Wear

Nowadays it's increasingly easy to buy just about anything you require in China, and not only in great cities like Beijing, Shanghai and Xi'an, but also in lesser provincial centres like Lanzhou, Urumqi and Kashgar. That said, it's a good idea to bring your own medication (the Chinese traditional pharmacopoeia is extensive but very different), tampons etc. Travellers might also consider bringing a small torch and a multiple adaptor for three-pin sockets.

In the summer months, take light cotton clothes that are easily washed and not too delicate. For winter in the Northwest, take some really warm clothes – insulated thermal

Websites

The following websites are a useful source of information on China and the Silk Road.
http://china.blogs.time.com Daily commentary about China, written by correspondents at Time magazine.
http://idp.bl.uk/idp.a4d The International Dunhuang Project run by the British Library.
http://depts.washington.edu/silkroad Silk Road Seattle Project, sponsored by the University of Washington.
http://www.orgs.muohio.edu/silkroad/ The Miami University Silk Road Project.
www.wildcamels.com The Wild Camel Protection Fund.

underwear and warm socks are a good idea – as well as gloves and a hat, though the latter are readily available at reasonable prices locally. Much of the Eastern Silk Road runs through arid country where rain rarely falls, but an umbrella (together with a hat) will shield you from the very powerful sunlight. Good walking shoes are essential for visiting ancient cities and Buddhist cave temples.

When to Go

Given the climatic constraints of Chinese Central Asia, the best times to visit the Chinese sections of the Silk Road are late spring and early summer (approximately April–June), as well as late summer and early autumn (approximately September–November). In midwinter passes are often snowed-in or iced-up, travel is difficult and many restaurants and hotels close for the duration of the cold season.

Women Travellers

Women travellers are, generally speaking, remarkably safe travelling in China. The usual precautions have to be taken, especially in remote areas or rough districts of large cities, but no more so – indeed rather less so – than in many Western countries. Xinjiang, especially among the Uighur and other Muslim minorities, is a little different. Here excessive displays of female independence, revealing clothing and sexually explicit talk can lead to trouble, though to a far lesser extent than in neighbouring India or Pakistan. In all instances, it's better to dress discreetly, especially when visiting temples or mosques, and to avoid noisy behaviour and public tipsiness.

LANGUAGE

UNDERSTANDING THE LANGUAGE

Mandarin Chinese

Mandarin is a collection of dialects spoken across north and southwestern China. With more than 1 billion speakers, it has more native speakers than any other language in the world.

Mandarin relies on word order and participles to provide information such as person, number, tense and case. The basic word order of subject-verb-object is generally used but there are regional variations, in particular preceding the direct object with the indirect object. Post-verbal participles denote the aspect of the action, but again there is variation in their usage.

The vocabulary of Mandarin is vast and it includes loan words from other languages with which Mandarin has interacted, notably Mongolian and Manchurian. New words are commonly formed with the addition of prefixes and suffixes or by compounding two words with similar meaning.

Pronunciation of Mandarin tends to terrify non-native speakers. Syllables are comprised of an initial consonant, followed by a glide, a vowel, a final and a tone, and there are several hundred syllables in regular usage. Tones vary between regions but regardless of the area in which they are spoken, they tend to fall into four tonal categories: the level tone, rising tone, falling tone, and a final stop.

Key phrases

Hello. 你好。 *Nǐ hǎo.*
How are you? 你好吗？ *Nǐ hǎo ma?*
Fine, thank you. 很好, 谢谢。 *Hěn hǎo, xièxie.*
Please. 请。 *Qǐng.*
Thank you. 谢谢。 *Xièxiè.*
Excuse me. 请问 *Qǐng wèn.*

I'm sorry. 对不起。 *Duìbùqǐ.*
I can't speak Chinese. 我不会说中文。 *Wǒ bú huì shuō zhōngwén.*
Is there someone here who speaks English? 这里有人会说英语吗？ *Zhèlǐ yǒu rén huì shuō yīngyǔ ma?*
Help! 救命！ *Jiùmìng!*
I'm lost. 我迷路了。 *wǒ mílù le.*
Goodbye 拜拜。 *Bai-bai.*

Uighur

Uighur is a Turkic language with an estimated 10 million speakers, who are split largely between Xinjiang and Kazakhstan. It was first written down in the 5th century and is usually written in Perso-Arabic script, though you will occasionally also see Uighur in Latin or Cyrillic script.

Uighur grammar has a number of interesting features. Whilst the word order is subject-object-verb as in many European languages, there is no difference in inflection for masculine and feminine nouns, and six different cases. Verbs are conjugated for both tense and mood.

Although the core Uighur vocabulary is Turkic, Uighur also features a number of loan words. Kazakh, Uzbek and Chagatai are dominant donors due to the geographical proximity of their speakers as well as their linguistic similarity, but words of Arabic, Persian and Tajik are also prominent due to the spread of their respective literatures (including religious texts) in areas where Uighur is spoken.

Key phrases

Hello. (Greeting) *Ässalamu aläykum*
Hello. (Response) *Wä'äläykum ässalam.*
How are you? *Yakshimasiz?*
Fine, thank you. *Yakhshi.*
Thank you. *Rakhmat.*
You're welcome *Tuzut Qilmang!*
I'm lost! *Man ezip Qaldim.*
Can you help me? *Manga yardam Qlarsizmu?*

BELOW: example of chinese script on black bamboo

FURTHER READING

History

Foreign Devils on the Silk Road by Peter Hopkirk, John Murray (2006). Thoroughly readable account of Stein, Hedin and other explorers' search for the lost treasures of Central Asia.

Life along the Silk Road by Susan Whitfield, John Murray (1999). A fascinating and erudite collection of historical "short stories" based on characters – the merchant, the soldier, the courtesan etc. – chiefly based on first-hand information derived from the archives and murals of Dunhuang.

Silk Road: Monks, Warriors and Merchants on the Silk Road by Luce Boulnois, Odyssey Publications (2003). Lavish, well illustrated and researched account of the Silk Road.

Southern Silk Road: In the Footsteps of Sir Aurel Stein and Sven Hedin by Christoph Baumer, Orchid Press (2003). Account of the exploration and identification of lost cities along the Southern Silk Road between Kashgar and Dunhuang.

The Silk Road: 2000 Years in the Heart of Asia by Frances Wood, British Library Publishing (2003). The story of the Silk Road in its broadest possible scope, with illustrations taken largely from the collections of the British Museum and British Library.

The Travels of Marco Polo translated by Ronald Latham, Folio Society (1990). Tried and tested English translation of Polo's Il Milione, including travels in Xinjiang and along the Eastern Silk Road.

Travel Writing

Danziger's Travels: Beyond Forbidden Frontiers by Nick Danziger, Harper Collins (1988). An overland journey via Turkey, Iran and Afghanistan to Xinjiang, Gansu and Tibet.

From Heaven Lake: Travels through Sinkiang and Tibet by Vikram Seth, Phoenix (1993). In this well-written travelogue Seth describes his unusual journey through remote areas of China, Tibet and Nepal.

In Xanadu: A Quest by William Dalrymple, Flamingo (1990). An overland journey approximately following the tracks of Marco Polo from the Middle East, through Xinjiang, to Mongolia.

News from Tartary by Peter Fleming, Birlinn Ltd (2001). Travels in the 1930s across Northwest China and Xinjiang.

Shadow of the Silk Road by Colin Thubron, Harper Collins (2007). Sublime account of a journey from Xi'an in China to Antakya in Turkey, with plenty of detail on Gansu and Xinjiang.

The Road to Miran: Travels in the Forbidden Zone of Xinjiang by Christa Paula, Harper Collins (1994). Intrepid and ultimately successful attempt by an art historian to reach the (then) forbidden city of Miran near Charklik.

Send Us Your Thoughts

We do our best to ensure the information in our books is as accurate and up-to-date as possible. The books are updated on a regular basis using local contacts, who painstakingly add, amend and correct as required. However, some details (such as telephone numbers and opening times) are liable to change, and we are ultimately reliant on our readers to put us in the picture.

We welcome your feedback, especially your experience of using the book "on the road". Maybe we recommended a hotel that you liked (or another that you didn't), or you came across a great bar or new attraction we missed.

We will acknowledge all contributions, and we'll offer an Insight Guide to the best letters received.

Please write to us at:
Insight Guides
PO Box 7910
London SE1 1WE
Or email us at:
insight@apaguide.co.uk

Other Insight Guides

Other **Insight Guides** that highlight destinations in China include: Beijing, China, Hong Kong and Shanghai. Insight's **Step-by-Step** series includes titles on Beijing, Shanghai and Hong Kong. These books pack information into an easily portable and convenient format. Arranged in handy A–Z sections, the comprehensive listings allow the visitor to make their own decisions about where to go and what to see. Insight **FlexiMaps** are designed to complement our guidebooks. They provide full mapping of major destinations, and their easy-to-fold, laminated finish gives them ease of use and durability. The range of titles features the following destinations: Beijing, Guangzhou, Hong Kong and Shanghai.

TRANSPORT

GETTING THERE
AND GETTING AROUND

GETTING THERE

By Air

Central Asia's main hubs are Almaty (Kazakhstan), Tashkent (Uzbekistan), Bishkek (Kyrgyzstan) and Karachi (Pakistan). Although there are some direct flights from Western Europe, many stop over at Moscow, Istanbul or Dubai en route. There are few direct transatlantic flights to the region, so a transfer is necessary in London, Istanbul, Moscow or Dubai. It is possible to reach Central Asia from the US West Coast by flying west via Tokyo or Seoul. The best approach for travellers from Australasia is via Bangkok.

Kyrgyzstan

Bishkek is close enough to Almaty, in Kazakhstan, to use it as a gateway, but the Kyrgyz capital has direct flights to London with British Airways, to Moscow with Aeroflot and to Istanbul with Turkish Airlines. KLM provides a free transport service to Bishkek for its Almaty-bound flights. The national carrier, Kyrgyzstan Airlines, flies to over a dozen destinations, which include Delhi, Urumqi and Moscow. China Southern Airlines flies to Urumqi, which is useful if you are connecting to other destinations in China.

Departure Taxes

With the exception of Afghanistan, departure taxes are included in the price of the air ticket. Passengers flying from Kabul airport will be charged a departure tax of US$10.

Tajikistan

Dushanbe has few connections outside Central Asia other than regular flights to Moscow. Rossiya-Russian airlines flies to Dushanbe from St Petersburg, and these sometimes connect with London flights. It may be more convenient to take a regional flight from Bishkek or Tashkent. The national carrier, Tajik Air, currently flies to 15 destinations, including Sharjah, Urumqi, Istanbul and Tehran, but its poor safety record prevents it flying to Europe.

Uzbekistan

Tashkent is reasonably well connected, although British Airways no longer flies there from London. Uzbekistan Airways has flights to European destinations that include London, Rome, Frankfurt and Istanbul, as well as various Asian destinations.

Kazakhstan

Almaty has regular flights to London and other European cities with British Airways, Lufthansa, KLM and Turkish Airlines. The Kazakhstan national carrier Air Astana also flies direct to London Heathrow and Frankfurt, and to Asian destinations including Delhi, Bangkok and Seoul. Air Arabia links Almaty with Sharjah (UAE) twice a week and Air China flies to and from Urumqi, in Xinjiang, most days of the week.

Pakistan

Most flights arrive at Karachi, but PIA, British Airways and Qatar Airways all operate direct flights to Islamabad from London and Manchester on an almost daily basis. There are also direct flights to Lahore. Emirates, Gulf Air and Etihad Airways fly from

London to a variety of destinations in Pakistan via Dubai, Bahrain and Abu Dhabi.

Afghanistan

The refurbished Kabul International Airport is the main way of getting in and out of Afghanistan, and there are a surprising number of flights each day, including to neighbouring capitals. Ariana, the national carrier, flies to Frankfurt, Istanbul and Dubai, but for most international connections you need to fly via Dubai, from where there are several flights a day to Kabul.

By Bus

International bus routes connect **Kazakhstan** with Xinjiang province in China. A daily morning bus service runs in both directions between Yining (Ili), in China, and Almaty, in Kazakhstan, crossing at Khorgos. This takes 10–12 hours, including a minimum of two hours at the border where luggage has to be unloaded and X-rayed. It is also possible to take an overnight sleeper bus to the Khorgos border from Urumqi, cross on foot and then pick up Almaty-bound transport on the other side.

To reach **Kyrgyzstan** from China by bus there is just one option, via the Irkeshtam Pass. This route is fairly straightforward, as there is an overnight bus service between Kashgar in Xinjiang and Osh in southern Kyrgyzstan. However, timetables are sporadic, and the bus runs infrequently during the winter months. The journey takes around 18 hours as long as there are no breakdowns or delays at the border. To cross the 3,752-metre (12,381-ft)

Torugart Pass further north requires the hire of private transport, as foreigners are not allowed to use the public bus that runs between Kashgar and Naryn. Tour agencies in Kashgar can arrange Chinese transport as far as the pass and for a Kyrgyz vehicle to be waiting on the other side for onward travel to Naryn.

There is a through service between Kashgar in China and Gilgit in **Pakistan** along the Karakoram Highway, via the Khunjerab Pass. This is open from 1 May to 31 October for groups and to 15 November for individual tourists. It takes about five hours to travel from Tashkurgan (the last town in China) to Sost (the first village in Pakistan) – not including the time taken for the formalities at the border. Bus, van and jeep services from Tashkurgan to Sost are run by the PTDC (Pakistan Tourism Development Corporation) and NATCO (Northern Areas Transport Corporation).

There is a direct daily bus service between Mashhad in Iran and Herat in **Afghanistan**, which takes about seven hours.

By Car

For the experienced and strong-stomached motorist, driving to Central Asia can be a rewarding challenge. There are four main overland routes to reach Central Asia. Crossing Russia, motorists require both a visa and a "Green Card", which is proof of motor insurance. This costs about $110 if purchased at the border but is cheaper bought in advance. An international driving permit and translations of your documents into Russian will speed up any encounters with traffic police or border officials. Driving from Moscow to the Kazakh border takes two days (more if you plan to enter Kazakhstan further east) and four border crossings are open: those at Uralsk, near Kostanai, at Petropavl and at Omsk.

Approaching from the southwest, a *carnet de passage* is required for both Turkey and Iran. The cost of the carnet is dependent on the value of your vehicle, and the fee is non-refundable. UK nationals should request a carnet from the RAC (www.rac.co.uk), and other nationalities can get one from the equivalent motoring club in their country of residence. The Iranian border with Turkmenistan is open between Mashhad and Ashgabat, and, for those unable or unwilling to pass through Iran, an alternative route exists from eastern Turkey through the Caucasus and by boat across the Caspian Sea, entering either into Turkmenbashi in Turkmenistan or Aktau in Kazakhstan. The ferry from Baku (Azerbaijan) to either destination is unscheduled, but departures take place approximately twice a week. It is not possible to make a reservation in advance as vehicles and passengers take lower priority than cargo. Sailings typically take 14–16 hours and cabins are allocated on a first-come-first-served basis.

Driving into Central Asia from China is challenging and expensive. Although a carnet is not necessary, you must apply for a foreign vehicle permit in addition to your visa. You will also require an official guide or escort for the duration of your trip, and must pay not only his salary but also his transport (if there is no space in your own vehicle) and accommodation. Allow at least $50 a day. If your visa application is accepted but your vehicle permit is declined, it is sometimes possible to arrange to ship your vehicle to the border as "goods in transit". This is, however, time-consuming and costly as you must travel separately from your vehicle. The main crossing from China into Kazakhstan is Khorgos near Almaty, and there are also open borders further north at Bakhty and Maikapshagai. The Irkeshtam and Torugart Passes both permit foreign tourists to enter Kyrgyzstan by private vehicle, though resolving red tape at the latter can take as much as eight hours. China's border crossing with Tajikistan is not currently open to foreigners.

Afghanistan

Motorists require a Ministry of Foreign Affairs vehicle import permit from an Afghan consulate ($100). An additional $100 may also be payable at the border for a Ministry of Finance vehicle permit. The quality of roads in Afghanistan is extremely poor, meaning that driving speeds rarely exceed 20km/h (12mph) away from highways. Motorists can enter Afghanistan from Tajikistan at Ishkashim, or from Uzbekistan at Termiz. The road into Iran via Herat is also open though less secure.

Pakistan

Motorists must have a valid carnet or pay import duty. The Khunjerab Pass into China is closed in winter but a relatively straightforward drive from April through October. It is not advisable to enter Afghanistan or Iran from Pakistan without a police escort.

Kyrgyzstan

No permit or import duty is payable. There is, theoretically, a three-month import period for foreign vehicles, after which you must get foreign plates, but in practice this is usually overlooked. The main border with Kazakhstan is at Kordai and it is also possible to enter past Taraz. Sary Tash serves as the main entry point when driving to Tajikistan and, when open, Dostlyk is the main border crossing with Uzbekistan.

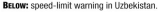

BELOW: speed-limit warning in Uzbekistan.

Kazakhstan

No permit or import duty is payable. A Russian translation of vehicle documents is highly advisable. Expect a thorough vehicle check by customs. Allow at least four days to drive north to south across Kazakhstan. Failure to present all vehicle documents on request by the police may result in a fine.

Uzbekistan

No permit or import duty is required, but expect to pass through quarantine as well as customs and immigration. Until recently, the only border with Kazakhstan officially open to foreigners was Shymkent. This appears to have changed, with the lorry crossing at Ahay also open to foreign cars, but this may not be permanent. The land borders with Kazakhstan and Kyrgyzstan may be shut without warning. Fuel shortages are common. When leaving Uzbekistan, motorists must get an exit stamp costing $4.

Tajikistan

Motorists pay a temporary import fee on arrival. The exact cost seems to be dependent on the customs official in charge, but is approximately $50. You must keep this receipt or you will be charged again on departure. There is a $10 vehicle exit fee. Fuel shortages are common and it is almost impossible to get spare vehicle parts unless you are driving a Toyota. Road conditions are exceptionally poor, as is the standard of driving.

By Train

Train is an interesting way to reach Central Asia for those happy to contemplate the Kazakh steppe for days on end. Coming from the west, Moscow is the main departure point, and Russian and Kazakhstan transit visas are necessary.

The most convenient train is probably the **Moscow–Almaty** service (train number 8, Kazakhstan), which leaves Moscow every other day and takes approximately 77 hours to reach the Kazakh capital. This route comes via Orenburg in Russia, and Aralsk and Kyzylorda in Kazakhstan. A longer route runs down to Almaty from the Trans-Siberian route to the north at Novosibirsk.

The twice-weekly **Moscow–Bishkek** direct service (train number 18, Kirgizia) follows the same route through Kazakhstan and takes around 74 hours.

Tashkent is best reached on the thrice-weekly train number 6 (Uzbekistan), which takes a branch line south of the main Moscow–Almaty route just west of Shymkent. The overall journey time is 69 hours.

Train classes are based on the Russian system in which *spalny vagon* is a sleeping compartment with two beds, *kupe* is a four-berth sleeping carriage and *platskartny* an open-plan carriage with dormitory-style bunks. Kupe is adequate in most circumstances. Precise train times and days of running can be found at www.poezda.net.

Coming from China, a twice-weekly "Zhibek Zholy" (Silk Road) service runs between Urumqi and **Almaty**, which takes around 36 hours, including a lengthy bogie-changing procedure at the Kazakh frontier in which the carriages are winched above the tracks. A daily train service links Urumqi with Beijing. There is a monthly express train from Zahidan in Iran to **Quetta** (via Taftan) in Pakistan, which takes 30 hours or more.

GETTING AROUND

By Air

Given the often poor road conditions, air travel in the region is a viable option, especially for long distances. **Kyrgyzstan** has connections that link the capital with a handful of towns with Kyrgyzstan Airlines (www.air.kg), Eastok Avia and Itek Air (www.itekair.kg). Most useful is the regular service between Bishkek and Osh, which reduces a 14-hour road journey to less than an hour and costs little more than a place in a shared taxi. Similarly, in **Tajikistan**, Tajik Air's (www.tajikair.tj) Dushanbe–Khorog service, a spectacular mountain-skimming one-hour flight, does away with the need for an exhausting 24-hour overland journey. Tajik Air also has a service between Dushanbe and Khojand in the north of the country.

Uzbekistan has a fairly efficient national network with Uzbekistan Airways (www.uzairways.com) that stretches across the country from Tashkent to far-flung destinations like Nukus and Urgench.

Kazakhstan is well covered by Air Astana (www.airastana.com), whose network centres on Almaty, and to a lesser extent, Astana, which link the main cities with domestic

destinations like Aralsk and Semey. Scat Air (www.scatair.kz) also operates domestic flights. The price of some airline tickets is subsidised by the Kazakh government.

Flying within **Pakistan** is a quick way of getting around the country, and is often very cheap. Shorter journeys are subsidised by the government, so a flight to Gilgit on the Karakoram Highway from Islamabad is not that much more expensive than taking the bus. PIA (www.piac.com.pk) produces a timetable listing all its flights. Apart from PIA, there are several other internal air services, notably Air Blue (www.airblue.com), Aero Asia, Bhoja Air and Shaheen Air, though these are not as extensive as PIA's.

Afghanistan's two airlines – Ariana (www.flyariana.com) and Kam Air (flykamair.com)– offer domestic services from Kabul to major cities, including Herat and Mazar-i-Sharif (there are also connections between these two cities). There are no flights to Bamiyan. Many foreign embassies ban their staff from flying on Afghan airlines owing to safety concerns. The UN operates more reliable flights and, although primarily for NGO staff, remaining seats may be sold to other travellers.

By Train

Central Asia's rail network is a Soviet legacy and operates in much the same way as the current Russian system. Rail is a useful means of getting around in Uzbekistan and Kazakhstan, but hardly registers as an option in Kyrgyzstan and Tajikistan. There is no functioning passenger railway in Afghanistan.

Kyrgyzstan has almost no domestic services, apart from very slow holiday services between Bishkek and Kaindi, and Tokmok and Balykchy on Lake Issyk-Kul. **Tajikistan's** Dushanbe–Moscow service no longer runs, although irregular trains link Khojand with Samarkand, and Dushanbe with Termiz in southern Uzbekistan. There is also a limited rail service from Dushanbe to Kurganteppa and Kulyab in the south.

Uzbekistan has a reliable rail service that links Bukhara and Samarkand with Tashkent – slower than shared taxis but cheaper and more comfortable. The website www.seat61.com lists the current timetables for Uzbekistan's internal rail routes as well as international services. In **Kazakhstan**, where vast

ACCOMMODATION

EATING OUT

ACTIVITIES

A - Z

LANGUAGE

distances separate the major centres, overnight train travel is the only real alternative to flying, and the rail services that link Almaty and Astana with Moscow are useful for long-distance east–west or north–south travel.

The trains in **Pakistan** are slow but convenient, serving the major towns and sites of interest.

By Bus

Buses vary enormously in Central Asia, ranging from comfortable **long-distance** coaches to decrepit **regional** services. The former mostly run between larger urban centres and the latter between country towns and villages, where they tend to stop on demand. Long-distance bus stations are commonly located some distance from the town centre and often require a minibus or taxi ride to reach them. Long-distance tickets are usually bought from the station office or an agent prior to travel, whereas fares are normally collected by a conductor on local buses. On long-distance buses luggage is normally stored in the baggage compartment or on a roof-rack, while on local services it usually has to go inside the vehicle along with the sacks of vegetables.

Kyrgyzstan has a limited number of buses running long-distance routes from the capital, mostly east to Lake Issyk-Kul, and a fair number of local services connecting Bishkek with the towns of the Chuy Valley. Those buses donated by China Aid (clearly marked with the donor's logo) tend to be the newest and therefore most reliable. Most people travel by minibus (see below) or shared taxi. There are no bus services between Bishkek and Osh because of tunnel restrictions at the Töo-Ashuu Pass. In the south of the country there are limited bus services for destinations like Batken and Kyzyl-Kiya, but nothing that goes beyond the border into Uzbekistan.

Tajikistan has a limited bus service that mostly operates between Dushanbe and the south of the country, though the service is at best erratic. Given the mountainous terrain and terrible roads, shared taxis and minibuses (see below) are a more practical means of transport, though breakdowns and blown tires are an inevitability.

In **Uzbekistan**, the state bus service is in decline, and many routes have been taken over by private bus companies that offer a more comfortable service. These usually do not leave until full, which can mean a lengthy wait. Shared taxis are a swifter option, particularly if you are prepared to pay for un-filled seats to get the vehicle moving.

Long-distance, inter-city buses are most common in eastern **Kazakhstan**, particularly between Almaty, Astana and the cities of the southeast. Western Kazakhstan generally relies more on rail services.

In **Pakistan**, private operators run regular air conditioned coach services between towns and cities, often referred to as "big buses". Daewoo Intercity is highly recommended. NATCO (Northern Areas Transport Company) runs more decrepit buses up the Karakoram Highway (KKH) to Gilgit and beyond. A good new addition to Northern Areas transport is the Silk Route Bus Service, air conditioned coaches that ply direct routes between Rawalpindi and Kashgar via Hunza.

There are no organised bus companies in **Afghanistan**, rather a collection of small operators with mainly minibuses plying the routes between cities.

By Minibus

Minibuses – usually referred to as marshrutki or marshrutnoe – run on fixed routes throughout Central Asia, often following a bus route but providing a faster service at a slightly higher price. Other routes ply where bus services do not exist at all. Minibuses usually leave when full, and it can be hard to pick them up midway between destinations because of lack of seats. They usually operate from outside bus stations but may sometimes have a separate stand. The minibuses typically have a poor safety record due to a combination of lack of maintenance and bad driving, so try to get a seat rather than standing if you have the option.

By Taxi

Taxis fall into two categories: **private taxis** hired for a specific journey and **shared taxis** that run on fixed routes. With private taxis it is imperative that a price is agreed before setting off, as well as details regarding tolls to be paid and charges for waiting time. Long-distance private taxis are most useful in **Kyrgyzstan**, where costs are low and few alternatives exist to reach off-the-beaten-track destinations. Shared taxis are an important mode of transport

Border Crossings

Very few bus services cross international boundaries in Central Asia, and so it is a matter of taking local transport to a border point, walking across and then looking for onward transport. See individual Places chapters for information on entering and leaving.

throughout much of the region, especially in **Uzbekistan**. They run on regular routes between cities and leave when all seats are full. It is always possible to leave earlier by buying all of the remaining seats.

In **Pakistan**, Suzuki pick-ups, three-wheeled scooter rickshaws and private taxis are the most common transport options in towns.

Driving

Self-drive car hire is available in some of the larger cities like Almaty, Tashkent and Islamabad, which have local agencies or international franchises. However, insurance may be difficult to arrange, and this, coupled with poor roads and erratic driving standards, is probably enough to put off most would-be drivers.

Hiring a vehicle with driver is an altogether better option. It does not cost that much more (with the exception of Tajikistan), and the driver, who will know the region and the road conditions, can sometimes also act as a guide. The Community Based Tourism (CBT) organisation in **Kyrgyzstan** can provide knowledgeable local drivers at a fixed per-kilometre rate.

In **Afghanistan** it is not possible to hire a car without also hiring a driver – Afghan roads are not for the faint-hearted anyway. Paved highways are a rarity, there are no road signs, few road rules, but plenty of police checkpoints. The Kabul–Kandahar–Herat road passes through Taliban country and is highly dangerous. Large hotels can usually offer cars with drivers, or contact tour operators in Kabul.

In **Pakistan**, cars with drivers can be hired from some larger hotels. Though more expensive, they may be worthwhile, as the drivers usually speak some English. Avis has offices in Karachi, Islamabad and Lahore (www.avis.com.pk) and Europcar has an office in Islamabad (www.europcar.com).

ACCOMMODATION

HOTELS, B&BS AND HOMESTAYS

Hotels

There is a wide range of accommodation in Central Asia, from simple B&Bs to five-star hotels. Hotels fall into three categories: Soviet-period hotels whose designated star-rating may demand something of a leap of faith; modern, **international-style** hotels with standards similar to those anywhere else in the world; and smaller **boutique** hotels that offer character and a more personal touch. **Soviet-style** hotels may be the only choice in towns that lie off the beaten track, especially in **Kazakhstan** and much of **Tajikistan**. Although these are sometimes reasonable, more often than not they fulfil all the stereotypes of the former USSR, with bleak, anonymous rooms and grumpy staff who welcome guests with a scowl. Most hotels in this category follow the Soviet system of having a woman *(dezhurnaya)* responsible for each floor whose job it is to look after room keys and ensure that guests do not get up to any mischief.

Uzbekistan probably has the best options in terms of variety and comfort, particularly in the Silk Road cities of Samarkand, Bukhara and Khiva. **Kazakhstan** is mostly geared towards business visitors, and away from Almaty and Astana, Soviet-style hotels may be all that is available.

There is a good range of hotels in Bishkek, **Kyrgyzstan**, some of which can be booked online at www.bishkek-hotels.net, and new places have opened for business in provincial centres like Karakol, Naryn and Osh in recent years.

In smaller towns and villages, often the only option is to stay with a local family. Fortunately there is an excellent network of homestays under the auspices of the CBT programme *(see below)*.

Tajikistan is probably the least geared up for visitors, with mostly run-down Soviet-period accommodation and just a few private hotels outside of Dushanbe. There is, however, a fledgling Community-Based Tourism (CBT) programme in operation that offers basic homestay accommodation in the remote Gorno-Badakhshan region of the southeast.

Pakistan has some excellent up-market hotels, including the home-grown Avari (www.avari.com), Pearl Continental (www.pchotels.com) and Serena chains (www.serenahotels.com), in both the cities and smaller tourist centres. In addition, there are some beautiful hotels run by the PTDC (Pakistan Tourism Development Corporation), as well as numerous recommendable options in out-of-the-way places – particularly in the north.

Along with affordability, the most important consideration in **Afghanistan** is security. The best accommodations operate to the UN's Minimum Operating Security Standards (MOSS), offering the most secure environment – particularly important in Kabul.

Homestays

For those willing to rough it a little, homestays offer a viable alternative to hotels, and in some areas may be all that is available. Found mostly in **Kyrgyzstan** and **Tajikistan**, homestays are generally fairly basic, and have facilities that usually include a shared living area, an outside toilet and makeshift shower. This offers simple but comfortable accommodation for a very reasonable price – an excellent choice for backpackers and independent travellers.

The Community-Based Tourism (CBT) organisation coordinates and monitors homestays throughout Kyrgyzstan, but there are others that work outside these networks. Homestays in Tajikistan, mostly in Gorno-Badakhshan, tend to belong to META, the Tajik equivalent to CBT.

The homestay experience is one of the joys of travelling in the region as it enables the traveller to get close to the everyday life of the country. English is not generally spoken, and so it requires an effort from both host and guest to make each other understood. Having to clean one's teeth in the garden and share a squat toilet is a small price to pay for a memorable experience, fierce hospitality and tasty home-cooked food.

Yurt Camps

Yurt camps can be found throughout the region, but they are by and large a Kyrgyz speciality. In **Kyrgyzstan**, yurt-stays may be arranged with Bishkek tour companies, local CBT groups or informally with local Kyrgyz willing to rent out a spare yurt. Yurt camps are found in various upland areas, most notably at Lake Song-Kol, around Lake Issyk-Kul and at Tash-Rabat.

In **Tajikistan** there are yurt camps in the Pamir region of the southeast; in **Kazakhstan**, in the mountains of the southeast near the Chinese border; and on the edge of the Kyzylkum Desert in **Uzbekistan**.

Most yurt camps are simple affairs where guests sleep on bedding on the floor and make use of a basic toilet and washstand outdoors. There are more luxurious ones, too, with proper beds, flush toilets and high-class cuisine.

Turbazas

These Soviet-era holiday camps are still a popular choice with some Central Asians. They are usually found near water (Lake Issyk-Kul, Kyrgyzstan) or at beauty spots with a reputation for fresh mountain air (Arslanbob, Kyrgyzstan; Iskander-Kul, Fan Mountains, Tajikistan).

Despite the professed health benefits of a *turbaza* stay, the routine, for many Central Asian men at least, often revolves around lengthy vodka and karaoke sessions rather than bracing mountain hikes.

Camping

Wild camping is the only option in mountainous areas of **Kazakhstan**, **Kyrgyzstan** and **Tajikistan**. It is sometimes possible to camp next to a *turbaza* or yurt camp and make use of the facilities. Some of the more well-trodden trekking routes in Kyrgyzstan and Kazakhstan have

basic campsites scattered along the trail, but these tend to be cramped and litter-strewn.

Camping is part and parcel of the trekking scene in the Karakoram and Hindu Kush in **Pakistan**, with some dramatically situated sites in the Hunza Valley. The same applies in the Wakhan Corridor, where a tent may be your only accommodation option. There are two designated campsites (both signposted but without electricity and a water tap) but otherwise be prepared to pay a small fee direct to the landowner if camping in a field. All camping equipment should be brought with you.

KYRGYZSTAN

Bishkek

Ak-Keme
Mira 93
Tel: (0312) 540 143
www.akkemehotel.com
This 15-storey business hotel south of the city centre, formerly the Pinara, has been fully renovated by a Kyrgyz-Malaysian joint venture. Some rooms have mountain views to the south. **$$$**

Alpinist Guesthouse
Panfilov 113
Tel: (0312) 441 522
Centrally located hotel with just 19 rooms that caters for trekking and climbing groups (hence the climbing wall) but is open to all. All rooms have air conditioning and cable TV. **$$**

Asia Mountains Guesthouse
Tugolbai Ata 1a
Tel: (0312) 694 075
www.asiamountains.co.uk
Small, comfortable guesthouse close to the railway station, with air conditioning and satellite TV. Often used by tour groups but available to independent travellers. **$**

Bishkek Guesthouse
Ulatalieva 165
Tel: (0555) 119 489
http://bishkekhouse.ucoz.com
Bishkek's prime backpacker option. Dormitory beds and private rooms in a brand new location. Staff speak English and there is Wi-fi. **$**

Dostuk
Frunze 429b
Tel: (0312) 433 888
www.dostuk.kg/en
Every Soviet-built city seems to have a Hotel Dostuk, and they largely look the same. Fortunately this particular property has been recently renovated and now boasts all modern conveniences. No disabled access. **$$$**

Holiday
Abdrakhmanov 204a
Tel: (0312) 902 900
www.holiday.kg
Centrally located and with pleasant staff, the Holiday is one of Bishkek's better mid-range options. No parking on site. **$$**

Hyatt Regency
Abdrakhmanov 191
Tel: (0312) 661 234
www.bishkek.regency.hyatt.com
Bishkek's top hotel, centrally located close to the State Opera and Ballet Theatre. Large, luxurious rooms with internet access, plus swimming pool, banqueting hall and fitness centre. **$$$**

Park Hotel
Orozbekov 27
Tel: (0312) 665 518
www.parkhotel.kg
Aimed primarily at business travellers and equipped with conference facilities, the Park Hotel is Bishkek's newest hotel. Decor is neutral throughout. **$$$**

Shumkar Asia Guesthouse
Osipenko 34
Tel: (0312) 671 141
Small new guesthouse complete with sauna, swimming pool and bar. **$$**

Silk Road Lodge
Abdumomunov 229
Tel: (0312) 661 129
www.silkroad.com.kg
Modern tourist hotel with helpful, English-speaking staff close to the centre and many clubs, bars and restaurants. Complimentary airport transfers are included in the tariff. The hotel is owned by Celestial Mountains, a British-run travel company. **$$$**

Karakol

There are over 20 **CBT** homestays in Karakol, all of which provide comfortable accommodation and excellent food; a full list can be provided by the local CBT office (Abdrakhmanov 123; tel: (03922) 555 00) or the nearby Tourist Information Centre (Abdrakhmanov 130; tel: (03922) 234 25).

Amir
Amanbaev 78
Tel: (03922) 513 15
www.hotelamir.kg
New hotel aimed at tour groups with a sun terrace and a restaurant serving Kyrgyz and European dishes. Rooms are clean and staff pleasant. **$$**

Green Yard Hotel
Novostrika 14
Tel: (03922) 298 01
Centrally located, family-run hotel in pleasant surroundings. **$$**

Marzey's Guesthouse
Korolkova 86
Tel: (03922) 555 54
Email: marzy@nomansland.ch
Small guesthouse with just four rooms, run by an Iranian woman. The guesthouse has a lovely garden and is situated in a quiet part of town. **$**

Neofit Guesthouse
Jamansariev 166
Tel: (03922) 206 50
www.neofit.kg
A central guesthouse run by the Neofit trekking company. Most rooms have private facilities and TV. **$**

Yak Tours Guesthouse
Gagarin 10
Tel: (03922) 569 01
A fairly basic place that has more the atmosphere of a backpacker's hostel than a traditional guesthouse. The owner, Valentin, can organise treks and arrange guides, transport and equipment hire. **$**

Kochkor

The **CBT** office just off the main road at Pionerskya 22a (tel: (03535) 223 55; www.cbtkochkor.com) can arrange accommodation in one of around 20 homestays in the town.

Naryn

Naryn has more than a dozen homestays, mostly in Soviet-period apartments, that can be arranged through the efficiently run **CBT** office: Lenina 33, apartment 8; tel: (03522) 508 95. There is also a yurt camp on the edge of the town.

Ala-Too
Lenina 18
Tel: (03522) 521 89
This large, central hotel is a grim throwback to the Soviet era, although the premium "lux" rooms are reasonable enough. **$–$$**

Celestial Mountains Guesthouse
Razzakova 42
Tel: (03522) 504 12

www.celestial.com.kg
Small, well-run hotel next to a park, also known as "The English Guesthouse". Eleven comfortable double rooms plus lower-priced yurt accommodation in the garden. Price includes meals. **$–$$**

Satar Yurt Inn
Airport road
Tel: (03522) 503 22
Located at the eastern end of town on the way to the airport, this is popular with tour groups. Facilities include hot showers, heating in the cooler months and a yurt bar. **$–$$**

Osh

CBT homestays (mainly in city apartments) can be

organised through the office at Kelechek Plaza (tel: (0772) 574 940).

Alay
Kurmanjan Datka 230
Tel: (03222) 577 29
Email: palvan@yandex.ru
Cavernous and functional, this Soviet-era hotel offers basic rooms at low rates. Some rooms have been refurbished. The hotel is unmarked. **$**

Kristall
Navoi 50a
Tel: (03222) 204 47
New hotel right next to the bazaar that would be good value if it did not have a two-tier pricing system – foreigners pay double. **$–$$**

Osh Guesthouse
Kyrgyzstana 8

Tel: (03222) 306 29
Cheap hostel popular with backpackers. Dormitories are available, though often crowded and not particularly clean. **$**

Sara
Kurmanjan Datka 278a
Tel: (03222) 225 59
Small hotel on the road leading to Solomon's Throne. Clean, fairly basic rooms, some of which are en suite. **$–$$**

TES Guesthouse
Say-Boyu 5
Tel: (03222) 215 48
Email: afc-osh@mail.kg
Small guesthouse located south of the centre that is popular with foreign NGOs and gets booked up well in advance. **$–$$**

TAJIKISTAN

Dushanbe

Atlas Guesthouse
Mirzo Rizzo 63
Tel: (0372) 264 628
Small, up-market guesthouse with internet access and all modern conveniences. **$$**

Avesto
Rudaki 105a
Tel: (0372) 211 175
Typical of its type, with variable rooms and unpredictable plumbing. Next to a mosque. **$$**

Dushanbe
Rudaki 7
Tel: (0372) 221 2357
Soviet-era three-star hotel with no-nonsense rooms and pleasant mountain views. The good-value mini-lux rooms have air conditioning and hot water. **$–$$**

Hyatt Regency
Ismoili Somoni 26/1
Tel: (048) 702 1234
http://dushanbe.regency.hyatt.com
Large and immaculately presented business hotel with excellent views across the city. Staff are attentive and there is a bureau de change and ATM on site. **$$$**

Marian's Guesthouse
Shotemur 67
Tel: (0372) 223 0191

A popular choice with NGO workers that gets booked up well in advance. **$$**

Mercury
Lev Tolstoy 9
Tel: (0372) 244 491
www.hotel-mercury.tj
New hotel with modern facilities located a 20-minute walk from the city centre. Large, tidy rooms, helpful staff and a pleasant outdoor seating area. **$$**

Serena
Rudaki
Tel: (048) 701 4000
www.serenahotels.com/serenadushanbe
Opened in autumn 2011, this property is the latest addition to the Serena chain. Designed, built and maintained with meticulous attention to detail, this is the finest place to stay in Dushanbe. **$$$**

Tajikistan
Shotemur 22
Tel: (0372) 216 262
Fairly standard, four-star hotel recently taken over by the Best Eastern group. Cable TV and air conditioning in some rooms. **$$**

Khojand

Ehson
Rudaki 171

Tel: (03422) 669 84
"Rooms" in this modern apartment block are actually four-room apartments, which are bare but adequate and certainly spacious. **$**

Khujand
Mavlonbekov 1
Tel: (03422) 659 97
Close to the Museum of Archaeology and park with just five large comfortable rooms. **$–$$**

Vahdat
B. Marvazi 22
Tel: (03422) 651 01
The Hotel Khujand's neighbour, with similar rooms and rates. **$–$$**

Khorog

MSDSP Guesthouse
Lenina 50
Tel: (035220) 227 19
A simple guesthouse located on the main street behind the museum. **$**

Pamir Lodge
Gagarin 46,
UDP Microrayon
Tel: (035220) 265 45
www.pamirlodge.com
Simple but friendly B&B run by a Tajik couple, 15 minutes from the town centre. Good-value meals cooked to order. Best place to hook up with

travelling companions. **$**

Serena Inn
Tem Microrayo
Tel: (035220) 232 28
www.serenahotel.somc
This relatively new guesthouse built in traditional Pamiri style by the Aga Khan Development Network is the best hotel in all of Gorno-Badakhshan. 6 km (3.5 miles) north of Khorog on the Dushanbe road. **$$**

Penjikent

The only official accommodation is the old Intourist **Hotel Penjikent** (tel: (03475) 545 09), which is very run-down and does not have running water. The local representative of the Pamir Travel tour agency (tel: (03475) 531 34/550 88, www.pamir-travel.com) may be able to arrange homestay accommodation.

PRICE CATEGORIES

Price categories are for a double room with breakfast/tax.

$ = less than US$50
$$ = 50–150
$$$ = over US$150

ABOVE: Soviet block: the Hotel Uzbekistan in Tashkent.

UZBEKISTAN

Tashkent

Dedeman Silk Road
Amir Timur C4 7/8
Tel: (071) 120 3700
www.dedeman.com
Four-star international
hotel, run by the Turkish
Dedeman group, located
close to the Amir Timur
Museum in the city centre.
Comfortable rooms, good
service and a choice of res-
taurants that serve
European and Asian food.
$$$

Grand Orzu
Makhmud Tarobi 27
Tel: (071) 120 8877
www.orzu-hotels.com
Located in downtown
Tashkent close to the
Israeli Embassy, the Grand
Orzu is a medium-sized
three-star hotel popular
with business travellers
and tourists. **$–$$**

Gulnara's Guesthouse
Azad 40
Tel: (071) 144 7766
Family home in a typical
Uzbek courtyard style, popular with backpackers and
five minutes from Chorsu
Bazaar. Tasty evening meals
provided on request, and
airport transfers can be
arranged with the English-
speaking owner. **$**

Malika
Chupon-Ata 53a
Tel: (071) 152 4200
www.malika-tashkent.com
Challenging to find, but
worth the effort. The Malika
has large, well-equipped
rooms and a pleasant gar-
den. Breakfast is included.
$$

Hotel Poytaht
Movarounnahr 4
Tel: (071) 120 86600
Central, modern hotel with
comfortable, air conditioned
rooms at reasonable prices.
Its two restaurants serve
European, Japanese and
Korean food. **$$**

Rovshan
Mirabad 118
Tel: (071) 150 3020
www.rovshan-tashkent.com
The Rovshan is a fairly new
middle-range hotel close to
the centre. All rooms come
with air conditioning and
satellite TV. The hotel has a
rooftop café and a shady
garden. **$**

Tashkent Palace Hotel
Buyuk Turon 56
Tel: (071) 120 5800
www.tashkent-palace.com
Formerly Le Meridien
chain, this recently renovated international hotel is
in a stylish historic building
opposite the Opera House.
Facilities include swimming
pool, sauna, gymnasium
and three restaurants.
$$$

Hotel Uzbekistan
Musakhanov 45
Tel: (071) 120 7777
This startling edifice from
the Soviet era is where
many tour groups stay.
Conveniently located by
Amir Timur Square. **$$**

Samarkand

Antica B&B
Iskandarov 56–8
Formerly known as
Muhandis, this up-market
B&B close to the Gur-i-Mir
and Rukhabad mausoleums
has a range of comfortable
rooms decorated with
antique textiles, all opening
onto a shady courtyard.
$–$$

Bahodir B&B
Mulokandov 132
Tel: (0662) 385 529
This backpacker's favourite
close to the bazaar has a
range of rooms, some with
private facilities. The communal evening meals are
excellent value and a good
opportunity to meet other
travellers. **$**

Furkat
Mulokandov 105
Tel: (0662) 358 812
Pleasant small hotel that
caters for both tour groups
and independent travellers.

The location, close to the
Registan and the bazaar, is
excellent. **$**

Malika
Khamraev 37
Tel: (0662) 330 197
www.malika-samarkand.com
Part of the popular Malika
chain, this modern hotel is
centrally located and well
maintained. Rooms are
comfortable and air conditioned. There is a restaurant, business centre and
parking on site. **$$–$$$**

President
Shokhrukh 53
Tel: (0662) 332 475
www.uzhotelpresident.com
This is a popular choice with
tour groups. Centrally
located with very comfortable rooms and some VIP
apartments, this modern
hotel also has a fitness centre, souvenir shop,
exchange office and busi-
ness centre. **$$–$$$**

Sherdor
M.Koshgari 91
Tel: (0662) 333 633
www.sherdor.com
Central, three-star establishment, built in traditional
Uzbek style in 2004, aimed
at both tourists and business travellers. There is a
pleasant courtyard where
music and dance perfor-
mances are sometimes
staged. **$–$$**

BELOW: Sasha and Son Hotel, Bukhara.

Zarina
Umarova 4
Tel: (0662) 350 761
www.hotel-zarina.com
Small modern hotel close to the Registan – a reliable choice. Air conditioned rooms come with bathroom and satellite TV. Uzbek and Tajik food served in the courtyard. **$–$$**

Bukhara

Amelia
Bozor Hoja 1
Tel: (065) 224 1263
www.hotelamelia.com
Located close to Lyabi-Hauz, this family-run boutique hotel, formerly a merchant's house, has real atmosphere and rooms decorated in traditional Bukharan style. Uzbek, Tajik and European food is served on a traditional Uzbek dining platform in the courtyard. **$–$$**

Bukhara Palace
Navoi 8
Tel: (065) 223 0024
http://hotelbukharapalace.com
Bukhara's only four-star hotel, with amenities such as a swimming pool, conference hall, sauna and jacuzzi, and the only late-

night club in the city. **$$**

Emir B&B
Husainov 17
Tel: (065): 224 4965
www.emirtravel.com
Emir is another cosy place near the Lyabi-Hauz complex. All 13 air conditioned rooms have modern bathrooms. **$–$$**

Grand Nodirbek B&B
Sarrafon 10
Tel: (065) 224 3446
Located close to a former synagogue, this is simpler and less expensive than most, but still a comfortable and convenient place to stay. **$**

Lyabi House
Husainov 7
Tel: (065) 224 2484
www.lyabi-house.com
One of Bukhara's more established B&Bs, right next to Lyabi-Hauz. The 19th-century dining room has been tastefully restored, and the courtyard has a traditional dining platform available for tea-drinking and relaxation. **$**

Sasha & Son
Eshoni Pir 3
Tel: (065) 223 3890
www.sacholga.narod.ru

This 16th-century Jewish merchant's house has charming rooms decorated in Bukharan style with antique carpets and locally crafted fittings. Frequent musical evenings are staged with traditional Uzbek food. **$–$$**

Khiva

Arkanchi
Pahlavan Mahmud 10
Tel: (06237) 52 230
This well-established, rather sprawling hotel is close to the mausoleum of Pahlavan Mahmud. All rooms are large, with air conditioning, heating and en suite bathrooms. **$**

Asia Khiva
Kadir Yakubova
Modern three-star hotel just outside the south gate of the Ichon-Qala, with air conditioned rooms with bath and satellite TV. **$$**

Islambek
Toshpulatov 60
Tel: (06237) 53 023
www.islambekhotel.nm.ru
Close to the east gate of the old city, this relatively new hotel has courteous staff and good heating. Good

views from the upper balconies. **$**

Khiva
Pahlavan Mahmud 1
Tel: (06237) 54 945
This hotel is actually a converted madrassa, as is the restaurant next door. The rooms are former student's cells and therefore fairly small. **$$**

Fergana

Akbarov Guesthouse
Djambul 1b
A small family guesthouse in a Fergana suburb with a shady patio for relaxing. **$**

Asia Fergana
Navoi 26
Tel: (0732) 45 221
Modern three-star hotel in the southern part of town. Reasonable air conditioned rooms have satellite TV. There is an outdoor swimming pool and a restaurant serving Uzbek and European food. **$–$$**

Club Hotel 777
Pushkin 7a
Tel: (0732) 43 777
A pleasant modern hotel with rooms arranged around a courtyard and an open-air swimming pool. **$–$$**

TURKMENISTAN

Ashgabat

Grand Turkmen Hotel
Georogly 7
Tel: (012) 512 050
One of the better hotels in Turkmenistan, but distinctly average by international standards. The location is central but rooms are shabby and the

staff generally unhelpful. **$$$**

Hotel President
Archabil Shayoly 54
Tel: (012) 400 000
Elaborate business hotel with marble floors, chandeliers and a decent-sized swimming pool. Wi-fi is available in all rooms. **$$$**

Sofitel Ashgabat
Bitarap 231
Tel: (012) 449 500
www.sofitel.com
A genuine international five-star hotel that has all the expected facilities and standards, including three high-quality restaurants. Undoubtedly the best place to stay in Ashgabat. **$$$**

Hotel Turkmenistan
Neutral Turkmenistan 19
Tel: (012) 350630
One of Ashgabat's few mid-range options, Hotel Turkmenistan is clean and comfortable, if not terribly exciting. The hot water and air con usually work. **$$**

KAZAKHSTAN

Almaty

Alma-Ata
Kabanbay Batyr 85
Tel: (0727) 272 0070
www.hotel-alma-ata.com
Opposite the neoclassical Abay State Opera and Ballet Theatre, this Soviet-era hotel offers reasonable value for money. **$$**

Ambassador
Zheltoksan 121
Tel: (0727) 250 8989
www.ambassadorhotel.kz
Almaty's first boutique hotel with 54 comfortable and character-filled rooms. All rooms have cable TV, internet access and air conditioning. **$$$**

Intercontinental Almaty
Zheltoksan 181
Tel: (0727) 250 5000
www.intercontinental.com
Comfortable, well-equipped hotel primarily servicing business travellers. Close to Republic Sq. **$$$**

Kazakhstan
Dostyk 52
Tel: (0727) 291 9101

A large, 26-storey hotel just south of the city centre, with

PRICE CATEGORIES

Price categories are for a double room with breakfast/tax.

$ = less than US$50
$$ = 50–150
$$$ = over US$150

renovated rooms and top-floor café with excellent views over the city. The golden crown atop Hotel Kazakhstan is a key part of Almaty's skyline. **$$**
Otrar
Gogol 73

Tel: (0727) 506 830
Up-market hotel centrally located opposite Panfilov Park, with views of Zenkov Orthodox Church. All rooms come with air conditioning, satellite TV and minibar. **$$$**

Hotel Turkistan
Makataev 49
Tel: (0727) 266 4135
Popular budget option close to Green Bazaar. Rooms are clean and there is a sauna in the basement. **$–$$**

Hotel Zhetisu
Ablai Khan 55
Tel: (0727) 250 0407
www.zhetysuhotel.kz
Comfortable, centrally located budget hotel in a Soviet block. Dormitory beds are available. **$–$$**

PAKISTAN

Islamabad

Best Western
6-Islamabad Club Road
Tel: (051) 2277 4608
www.bestwebernisb.com
Well-maintained, trusted hotel located in the heart of Islamabad, with all the usual amenities, albeit lacking in flair. Ample parking, good security and above-average restaurant on site. **$$**
Islamabad Marriott Hotel
Agha Khan Road F-5
Tel: (051) 282 6121
www.marriott.co.uk/Islamabad
Conveniently located, close to all the government buildings, parliament and the Presidential Palace. Has a weekend disco. Favourite for high tea, its Nadia coffee shop is the busiest in town. **$$$**
Serena Hotel Islamabad
Khayaban-e-Suharwardy, opposite Convention Centre.
Tel: (051) 111 133 133/287 4000
www.serenahotels.com

The most luxurious hotel in Pakistan, set in 2½ hectares (6 acres) of land-scaped gardens beneath the Margalla Hills, within walking distance of the diplomatic enclave. Excellent service and three different restaurants with an open-air barbecue. It also has a swimming pool. **$$$**

Rawalpindi

Blue Sky Hotel
Committee Chowk, Murree Road
Tel: (051) 596 0918-23
The Blue Sky Hotel offers well-furnished rooms for budget travellers. Situated in the heart of the city, near to Raja Bazaar. Rooms are air conditioned. **$**
Kashmir Inn Hotel and Restaurant
B 55/5 Bank Road,Rawalpindi Cantt
Tel: (051) 556 3742
For the budget traveller who wants to be near Saddar. This is a quiet place with clean rooms. **$**

Pearl Continental
The Mall
Tel: (051) 556 6011–20
www.pchotels.com
Pindi PC, as it is commonly known, is Rawalpindi's poshest hotel, centrally located on Mall Road. Food is excellent: the Bukhara restaurant is famous for its barbecue. **$$$**

Peshawar

In addition to these hotels, travellers can try a wide range of guesthouses in the University Town area.
Khan Klub
New Rampura Gate, Old City
Tel: (091) 2214802
Occupying a renovated Sikh *haveli* (mansion) in the heart of Peshawar's Old City, Khan Klub has just eight rooms, each fittingly named after a precious stone. There's a feeling of personable luxury that is found at no other hotel in the country. The central well is occupied by a delightful lounge, and there's an airy breakfast room on the top floor. In the downstairs restaurant, diners are seated on cushions and carpets, Pathan-style. Needless to say, there's an excellent menu. **$$$**
Khanis
Fakht-e-Alam Road
Tel: (091) 5277 512
Clean, well-run and friendly hotel, an ideal choice for budget travellers not wanting to stay in the Old City. **$**
Pearl Continental
Khyber Road
Tel: (091) 5276361
www.pchotels.com
Peshawar's poshest hotel, complete with swimming pool. The service is good, and so is the food. The hotel also offers a bar for

non-Muslim foreigners and a health club. **$$$**
Spogmay Hotel
Namak Mandi
Tel: (091) 5213255
In the heart of the Old City, this is a favourite for travellers on a really tight budget. **$**

Hunza Valley

Diran Hotel
Minapin, Nagar
Tel: (05821) 58149
Beautiful hotel on the edge of Minapin village, dominated by the mighty Rakaposhi. A variety of rooms available in the main building or annexes. Wonderful orchard, great food and even a pool for a refreshing dip. Treks can be organised with local guides to Hapakun and Rakaposhi Base Camp. **$**
Eagle's Nest
Duikar
Tel: (05821) 57074
Magnificently situated at the hamlet of Duikar high above Karimabad and Altit. The Eagle's Nest has pleasant rooms and an excellent restaurant. **$$**
Hunza Embassy
Tel: (05821) 57001-2
www.hunzaembassy.com
The former Mountain View hotel under new management. Well sited up the hill but just below the village itself, it has been renovated in a traditional style with nicely decorated and furnished rooms. Fine views of Rakaposhi, Diran and Golden Peak. **$$**
Hunza Marcopolo Inn
Gulmit
Tel: (05822) 546107
Its proximity to the KKH makes it a convenient stopover for travellers on their way to Khunjerab Pass. Mr

BELOW: Peshawar's elegant Khan Klub.

Hussain Raja is a worthy man to talk to about the history of Hunza. **$$**

Passu Ambassador Hotel
Tel: (05822) 5003 ext 36
Situated past Passu Village right on the Karakoram Highway, this is a good place to stay overnight just before leaving for China. Sixteen rooms with en suite bathrooms. **$$**

Passu Inn
The original hotel in Passu and a good place to organise porters and guides. **$**

PTDC Motel
Aliabad
Tel: (05821) 57069
On the KKH, between Karimabad and Aliabad, with great views of Rakaposhi. It has pleasant and comfortable rooms, many with balconies. Adequate food. **$$**

PTDC Motel
Sost, Pak-China Border
Tel: (05823) 51030
Right on the KKH, the PTDC's convenient location makes it a popular resting place for weary travellers heading north or south. Closed in winter. **$$**

Silk Route Lodge
Tel: (05822) 50229
Has 20 clean rooms with hot and cold water and several facilities to make your stay comfortable. Offers tour services and jeep rental. Excellent view towards the impressive rock spires of Mt Topopdan (Cathedral). **$$**

World Roof
Tel: (05821) 57129
Fairly new hotel featuring mainly double rooms with private balconies and magnificent views. Rooftop barbecue. **$**

Gilgit

Gilgit Serena
Jutial
Tel: (0581) 155 894
www.serenahotels.com
This hotel offers luxurious rooms and fine facilities, plus magnificent views of the mountains. It's also famed for its all-you-can-eat buffet in its Dumani restaurant. **$$$**

PTDC Motel Chinnar Inn
Babar Road
Tel: (05811) 54262/52562
Ideal location near the river offering friendly service, clean rooms and excellent value. **$$**

Riveria
River View Road
Tel: (05811) 4184/53093
Located near the river, this is a pleasant, secluded hotel, with most rooms overlooking the large lawn. Very professional staff and good food. **$$**

AFGHANISTAN

Kabul

Gandamack Lodge
Charahi Sherpur
Tel: (0700) 276 937
www.gandamacklodge.co.uk
Owned by ex-BBC cameraman Peter Jouvenal, this top-notch guesthouse with pleasant garden is run to very high standards, has a good restaurant and even a replica English pub (The Hare and Hounds), in the basement. **$$**

Heetal Plaza
Wazir Akbar Khan
Tel: (0799) 159 697
Email: heetalkabul@yahoo.com
This new hotel with small rooms is built in the style of a caravanserai and has a popular Mexican restaurant. **$$**

Kabul Intercontinental
Bagh-i-Bala
Tel: (020) 2201 321
www.intercontinentalkabul.com
Long-standing hotel that's hosted everyone from Soviet soldiers to wine-cellar-smashing Taliban. Recently refitted, just outside Kabul centre. **$$$**

Kabul Serena
Jad-i-Froshgah
Tel: (0799) 654 000
www.serenahotels.com
Centrally located, Kabul's luxury hotel option. Excellent rooms and service with popular restaurants, and increased security following an attack on the hotel in early 2008. **$$$**

Maple Leaf Inn
Street 3, off Jad-i-Kolola Pushta
Tel: (0799) 321 401
www.mapleleafinn.ca
Efficient and high-walled modern hotel, with good rooms and sports and business facilities. **$$**

Mustafa Hotel
One block from Chicken Street, near Flower Street
Tel: (0700) 276 021
www.mustafahotel.com
Slightly down-at-heel and exposed, but this old journalists' haunt offers perennially good service. **$$**

Safi Landmark Hotel
Kabul City Centre, Shahri Naw
Tel: (020) 220 3131
wwww.safilandmarkhotelsuites.com
All rooms overlook the inner courtyard of Kabul's only mall. This upscale hotel has a decent Indian restaurant on the top floor. **$$$**

Bamiyan

Bamiyan Hotel
Teppe Baba Shah
Tel: (0799) 212 543
One of the few remaining government-run hotels. Has a garden with several musty yurts for visitors in addition to regular rooms. **$$**

Roof of Bamiyan Hotel
Sir Asyab
Tel: (0799) 235 292
Decent hilltop hotel, with spectacular views over the Bamiyan Valley and good rooms. **$$**

Herat

Ishkashim

Aria Guest House
46 Alfath Guzar
Tel: (0799) 178661, (0799) 372449
Located at the top end of the bazaar. Western-style guesthouse, with five bedrooms (though more are currently being built) and hot water available. **$**

Juma Guesthouse
Tel: (0795) 770104
Pleasant guesthouse with an immaculately maintained garden, courteous host and secure parking. **$**

Marco Polo Hotel
Jad-i-Badmurghan
Tel: (040) 221 944
Email: heratmarcopolo@yahoo.com
A favourite of independent travellers, the hotel has air conditioning in many rooms, although they can be cramped. Small internet café downstairs. **$$**

Mazar-i-Sharif

Barat Hotel
Chowk-i-Mukharabat
Tel: (0700) 502 235
On the corner of the square overlooking the Hazrat Ali Shrine. Well-run and friendly hotel, although bathrooms are shared. **$$**

Royal Oak Hotel
Darwaza Bagh Road, opposite Indian Consulate
Tel: (0700) 276 021
Email: afghanistan@raints.com
Run by a logistics company, this guesthouse behind high walls is comfortable and unobtrusive. **$$**

Wakhan Corridor

There are official, well-marked guesthouses in and throughout Qazideh, Khandud, Qala-e Panj, Kret and Sarhad-e Broghil. Visitors should just turn up as most villages lack mobile coverage and phone lines. Virtually all guesthouses cost $25–30 per person per night, which includes freshly prepared meals. Guests should expect a clean bed in a shared, single-sex dormitory. Bathrooms are basic, but hot water can usually be arranged in buckets. English is rarely spoken. **$**

PRICE CATEGORIES

Price categories are for a double room with breakfast/tax.

$ = less than US$50
$$ = 50–150
$$$ = over US$150

EATING OUT

RECOMMENDED RESTAURANTS AND CAFES

Where to Eat

In the larger cities there is a choice of restaurants to suit all pockets and tastes, from expensive international-standard restaurants to cheap kebab places. Away from the major centres, the choices will be fresh and tasty Central Asian or Russian dishes, although Korean food can sometimes be found in the most unlikely places. Written menus will usually be in the local language and/or Russian.

In a region where the fat-tailed sheep is king, vegetarians may have a hard time finding something suitable, vegans even more so, as some sort of meat finds its way into most dishes, even salads. Homestays and guesthouses more familiar with Western ways are sometimes able to provide vegetarian meals on request.

A *chaikhana* is traditionally a place that serves only tea but they often have a *shashlyk* (kebab) griddle out the front and may serve a couple of other dishes. The more traditional ones are characterised by *takhta* – low tables on raised platforms around which customers sit cross-legged. *Chaikhanas* are found throughout the region, but most commonly in Uzbekistan, Afghanistan, southern Kyrgyzstan and northern Tajikistan. Shoes should be removed before sitting down.

If hygiene appears to be dubious it is wise to avoid salads or food that has been inadequately reheated. Kebabs, piping hot from the griddle, and freshly boiled noodles are invariably safe.

What to Eat

Mutton is by far the commonest meat, beef less so. Chicken is sometimes available, while pork, forbidden to Muslims, is served mostly in Russian restaurants. Horse meat is common in some areas, especially Kazakhstan, where *chuchuk* (horse-meat sausages) are seen as the ideal accompaniment to vodka. As ubiquitous as mutton dishes is *plov*, an Uzbek speciality that is a sort of rice pilaf made with carrots and stock.

Laghman – chunky noodles with chunks of mutton and a spicy stock – is another very common dish, although the best is undoubtedly made by Uighurs in Chinese Xinjiang. *Shorpo* – a thick soup of boiled mutton and root vegetables – is also very popular, particularly in Kyrgyzstan. Other Kyrgyz staples include *samsa*, baked pastry-like parcels stuffed with fatty mutton, and *manti*, steamed dumplings. *Beshbarmak*, made from flat noodles and a spicy mutton sauce, is a dish for special occasions in Kazakhstan and Kyrgyzstan and is not usually sold in restaurants.

Russian dishes that are commonly served in the region are *pelmeni* (small ravioli in broth), *blini* (pancakes) and *borscht* (beetroot soup). Most Russian dishes usually come served up with a dollop of *smetana* (soured cream) and a dill garnish.

Pakistan shares its culinary heritage with India, so menus overlap, although the food is generally less hot than traditional Indian fare. Classic dishes include *korma* (meat in spicy yoghurt gravy) and *roghan gosht* (garnished meat). Meals are usually accompanied by breads such as *naan*, *kulcha* and *paratha*, which are sometimes stuffed with minced meat or vegetables.

Afghan cuisine relies on a handful of dishes that, while individually tasty, can become quickly monotonous. The two main dishes are *pulao* (rice cooked with lamb or beef, usually with raisins and carrot), and kebabs with bread. A popular northern dish is *mantu*, a steamed ravioli with yoghurt sauce. Vegetables can be thin on the ground, but there is usually a surfeit of excellent fruit, including grapes, melons, pomegranates, apples, cherries and nuts.

Drinks

Chai (tea), both green and black, is found everywhere. Drinking either is an excellent way to hydrate cheaply and safely. Unboiled tap water is best avoided, but bottled water is usually easy to find.

As in the rest of the former Soviet Union, vodka is a way of life for some in Central Asia, despite Islamic prohibition, and the notion of "just a small glass" is an alien one. Once a bottle is opened it is meant to be finished, and to stop drinking once a session is under way is seen as very bad form. Beer is very popular, and Russian Baltika of varying strengths is widely available. In Kyrgyzstan and Kazakhstan, *kymyz*, slightly alcoholic fermented horse milk, is the tipple of choice in mountainous areas. Other popular drinks include *bozo*, made from millet, and *maksym*, from wheat. In Uzbekistan, *katyk*, a thin yoghurt drink, is common, and in drier parts of Kazakhstan *shubat*, fermented camel's milk, is the local equivalent of *kymyz*.

Non-Muslim visitors who wish to drink alcohol in Pakistan require a permit that enables them to buy alcohol from hotels or authorised vendors. Similarly in Afghanistan, alcohol is only available at restaurants catering to foreigners, almost all in Kabul.

KYRGYZSTAN

Bishkek

Adriatico Paradiso
Chui 219
Tel: (0312) 614 609
A cosy Italian trattoria that serves excellent pasta dishes and has live piano music some nights. **$$**

Beta Gourmet
Chui 150
Located above the Beta supermarket, this busy canteen serves a variety of tasty Turkish and continental dishes. **$**

Jalal-Abad
Kievskaya/Togolok Moldo
Tel: (0312) 362 619
Unusual for cosmopolitan Bishkek, this traditional Uzbek restaurant gets crowded at lunchtimes. A variety of Uzbek dishes are served, including shashlyk, but no alcohol. **$**

Metro Bar
Chui 168
Tel: (0312) 310 710
Sometimes referred to as the "American Pub", this is both an American-style bar and a restaurant serving American and Tex-Mex dishes. Very popular with foreign expatriates, especially Americans. **$$**

Navigator
Moskovskaya 103
Tel: (0312) 665 151
A bar-restaurant popular with embassy staff that serves Mediterranean-style food with plenty of vegetarian choices. **$$**

Old Edgar (Stari Edgar)
Panfilov 273
Tel: (0312) 624 408

Located next to Panfilov Park with a pleasant outdoor dining area. European dishes served, including excellent pizza, and live music most nights. **$$**

Steinbrau
Gertzena 5
Tel: (0312) 432 144
An enormous German beer cellar that brews its own excellent beer and serves hearty German and Austrian dishes to mop it up. **$–$$**

Karakol

Arzu Café
Kushtobaev 17
Tel: (03922) 239 99
Popular café with a variety of snacks, including vegetarian options. **$**

Kalinka
Abdrakhmanov, junction with Koenkozova
Tel: (03922) 588 88
This restaurant looks like a Siberian log cabin from the outside. True to form, its menu lists a selection of Russian favourites like blini and borscht. **$–$$**

Kench
Telmona, near junction with Gebze
Considered by some to be the best restaurant in town, Kench has an indoor dining room and an outside terrace. The English-language menu has a good range of Russian and European dishes. **$–$$**

Kochkor

The best food is served in the CBT homestays. There

are a few basic cafés along Orozbekova, the main street, like **Café Visit** and **Babar-Ata**, and food yurts close to the market.

Naryn

Anarkul
Sagynbay Orozdak Uulu, near the junction with Kyrgyzskaya
A large, sprawling restaurant with several dining rooms, a bar and a reasonable choice of Kyrgyz and Russian dishes. **$**

Ayana
Sagynbay Orozdak Uulu
Just behind the Ala-Too hotel, this pleasant, down-to-earth place has all the standard Kyrgyz and Russian dishes. **$**

Korona
Kulumbaeva/Lenina
Tel: (03522) 502 94
Currently Naryn's top place to eat, this restaurant has a cavernous interior and a high ceiling. The extensive Russian-language menu lists a good range of Kyrgyz, Russian and Chinese dishes, at very reasonable prices. The staff are courteous and helpful, and the atmosphere convivial. **$**

Nuur
Lenina
Small but popular café with a pleasant outdoor seating area and a range of cheap snacks. **$**

Osh

There are several Uzbek restaurants on Kyrgyzstana

near the new mosque and bazaar, serving good shashlyk and plov. Jayma Bazaar also has a number of no-nonsense eateries.

Aphrodite
Lenina
A Kyrgyz novelty: a Greek restaurant. Salads and grilled meats are the focus of the menu, but they're tasty and served with a smile. **$**

Greenwood
Lenina
This pleasant café-bar, set back from the main road near the post office, does decent pizzas and salads and has a quiet outdoor area. **$–$$**

Istanbul Café
Navoi 22
A café and patisserie serving light meals and Turkish pastries. **$**

Kara Alma
Alisher Navoi, junction with Kurmanjan Datka
Opposite the Hotel Alay, this café with a large outdoor terrace serves Kyrgyz dishes at low prices. **$**

Rich Men Café
Kurmanjan Datka 60
Tel: (03222) 24 303
As its name implies, this place south of the centre is a cut above the competition and one of the nicest places to dine in the city. The English-language menu lists a wide range of international dishes, plus a choice of Georgian, Moldovan and Romanian wines. **$–$$**

TAJIKISTAN

Dushanbe

Café Merve
Rudaki 92
A modern café with a wide selection of Turkish dishes and snacks including pide, kebabs and Turkish tea. Good Turkish breakfasts of bread, cheese and olives. **$**

Delhi Darbar
Rudaki 88
Tel: (0372) 218 863

This branch of the Indian chain serves surprisingly good Indian cuisine and vegetarian thalis. **$–$$**

Eurasia
Rudaki 81
Tel: (0372) 233 994
A little hidden away on the western side of Rudaki, this has European and Tajik food that includes good steaks and some vegetarian options. **$**

Georgia
Rudaki 29
Pleasant and relaxed café-bar, although the food is just an approximation of Georgian cuisine. **$**

Rokhat
Rudaki 84
Tel: (0372) 217 654
A modern, Tajik-Persian chaikhana serving plov, samsa and shashlyk. **$**

Khojand

Khojand has few formal restaurants, but the bazaar area has several decent chaikhanas. Other good places to

PRICE CATEGORIES

Prices are for a meal per person:

$ = under US$10
$$ = US$10–25
$$$ = over US$25

TRANSPORT
ACCOMMODATION
EATING OUT
ACTIVITIES
A – Z
LANGUAGE

eat include the **Turk-Tajik** café on Lenina that serves light meals and cakes, and the friendly bar-restaurant on the right-hand side of

Lenina a few hundred metres north of the Hotel Ehsan.

A branch of the Indian restaurant chain **Delhi Darbar** opened here in early 2008. Otherwise, there is little choice apart from a chaikhana in

Central Park, a few food stalls at the bazaar and a couple of cafés on Lenina close to the museum.

UZBEKISTAN

Tashkent

For authentic and cheap Uzbek food there are many excellent local courtyard restaurants in the old part of town close to Chagatai Bazaar. Head north from Tinchlik subway station, along Obid Sadikov towards Chighatoy Bazaar and the junction with Forobiy. Just follow your nose, as the restaurants are unsigned.

Baron
Makhsumova 72
Tel: (071) 233 9301
Sophisticated European food cooked under the guidance of a German chef. Live music on most nights.
$$–$$$

Caravan
A. Kakhar 22
Tel: (071) 152 7464
Close to the Grand Orzu Hotel, this has three dining halls centred on a courtyard. The food is Uzbek–European fusion, and the restaurant is decorated with a range of regional artefacts. An attached gift shop sells Uzbek crafts.
$$

Central Asia Plov Center
Corner of Ergashev and Abdurashidov
The best plov in the region is found at the Central Asia Plov Center. Vast portions of fresh plov are served up with hardboiled eggs, fresh bread and plenty of tea. Open at lunchtime only. **$**

Omar Khayyam
Movarounnakhr 33
Tel: (071) 132 2151
Almost opposite the Arts Museum, this serves Middle Eastern cuisine in rooms decorated in caravanserai style. A good-value business lunch is served during the week. **$$–$$$**

Persia
C-5, Khurshid 57
Tel: (071) 234 1661

European and Iranian cuisine. **$$**
Turkuaz
C4 Amir Temur 7/8
Tel: (071) 120 3700
Located at the Dedman Silk Road Hotel, the Turkuaz kitchen dishes up a variety of Turkish, Uzbek and international dishes. Live piano music at dinner. **$$$**

Samarkand

Afrodita
Orzu Mahmudov 4
Tel: (0662) 335 870
Elegant, old-fashioned restaurant serving European cuisine. **$$**
Istiqlol
Amir Temur 157
Traditional restaurant serving Uzbek favourites like plov and manti, with two indoor dining rooms and two outdoor courtyards. **$**
Karim Bek
Gagarin 194
Tel: (0662) 212 756
Stylish place serving Uzbek and European dishes. **$–$$**
Lyabi Gor Chaikhana
Registan 6
Traditional Uzbek restaurant is popular with tour groups at lunchtimes. Tasty shashlyk and plov, washed down with plenty of green tea, and the balcony offers a great view over the Registan. **$**
Oasis Beer Restaurant
Gorky Park
Tel: (0662) 333 754
http://oasis-samarkand.com
Restaurant in southern corner of park with outdoor seating, European and Uzbek fare and draught Czech beer. **$**
Platan
Pushkin 2
Tel: (0662) 338 049
Small restaurant with great ambience a little away from the centre. The menu includes vegetarian dishes and the food is excellent.
$–$$

Regina
Amir Temur 65a
Tel: (0662) 335 788
Modern bar-restaurant serving European food. **$**

Bukhara

The most enjoyable places to eat in Bukhara are the outdoor chaikhanas that surround the Lyabi-Hauz pool. There are more chaikhanas on either side of the road to the west of the Bolo-Hauz Mosque on the northwestern side of the city.
Bella Italia
B. Naqshbandi 125
Tel: (065) 224 3346
An Italian restaurant to the east of Lyabi-Hauz in the new town. Live jazz at weekends. **$**
Doston House
Kalon 5
Uzbek restaurant in a traditional 19th-century merchant's house, which frequently stages folklore shows for tour groups. **$**
Lyabi Hauz
Lyabi-Hauz complex, B. Naqshbandi
Tel: (065) 224 5070
One of several restaurants here that serve Uzbek and European dishes. **$**
Minzifa
Dome 1, Old Town
Minzifa's location in the heart of the old town and views over the bustle of the city set it apart from all other restaurants. The menu focuses on lamb dishes, but the vegetarian options are also reasonable.
$–$$
Sezam
B. Naqshbandi 153
Tel: (065) 225 0577
East of the city centre in the new town on the airport road, this is an Ali Baba-themed restaurant serving Uzbek and European food.
$

Silk Road Tea House
5 Halim Ibodov Street
Tel: (065) 224 2268
Situated in a heritage building renovated in 2009, this family-run teahouse combines Bukharan history with modern service. Herbal teas and cardamom coffee are highlights of the menu, as are traditional sweets. **$**

Khiva

Ata Darvoza
Ichon-Qala West Gate
Tel: (06237) 58 204
Just outside the city wall, facing the West Gate, this is a fairly typical Uzbek chaikhana serving all the standard dishes. **$**
Khorezm Art Restaurant
Madrasa Allah Kulikhan
Tel: (06327) 57 918
Large and lively restaurant that is particularly popular with tour groups. **$**
Parvoz
Rakhimov
Tel: (06237) 53 579
Just north of Ichon-Qala across the main road, this is more up-market than most of the other chaikhanas and has a wider selection of dishes. **$**

Fergana

There are several chaikhanas around the market serving Uzbek staples, and the restaurant at the **Hotel Asia** has a variety of pizzas and pastas as well as familiar Uzbek and Russian dishes.
Askiya
Opposite Hotel Ziyorat
Tel: (0732) 44 807
Pleasant café-restaurant in the city centre. **$**

PRICE CATEGORIES

Prices are for a meal per person:

$ = under US$10
$$ = US$10–25
$$$ = over US$25

KAZAKHSTAN

Almaty

Dastarkhan
Shevchenko 75
Tel: (0727) 272 5427
www.dastarkhan-almaty.kz
Popular with both Almaty natives and expatriates, this restaurant serves Kazakh and international dishes at reasonable prices. **$$**

Govinda's Krishna Restaurant
Abylay Khan 39
Tel: (0727) 271 0836
Not far from Almaty-II train station, this is that Central

Asian rarity: a vegetarian restaurant. Run by members of the Hare Krishna sect, it serves vegetarian *thali* meals and a variety of spicy Indian dishes. **$**

Mad Murphy's Irish Pub
Tole Bi 12
Tel: (0727) 291 2856
A fairly typical Irish pub that serves American-style fast food and Irish and Russian beers. **$$**

Teatralnoye
Zhambyl 51A
Immediately opposite the

Opera House is this elegant restaurant, which bravely attempts a classical interior. The cuisine is predominantly French and can be eaten in the garden in summer. **$$$**

Zheruik
Seifullina 500
Tel: (0727) 263 9828
Advertising itself as a restaurant-museum, its name means "The Promised Land". With lots of museum-like exhibits and a yurt in the banqueting hall, dining

here is an enjoyable, slightly over-the-top experience. The food is traditional Kazakh, with plenty of horse meat and offal. **$$$**

Zheti Khazyna
Ablai Khan 58A
Tel: (0727) 273 2587
A Middle Eastern doorway (think *1001 Nights*) greets customers at what is otherwise a traditionally decorated Central Asian restaurant. Kazakh and *Uighur* dishes feature prominently on the menu. **$$$**

PAKISTAN

Islamabad

Most of Islamabad's best restaurants and cafés are found in the commercial areas: the Blue Area, Jinnah Supermarket etc. The hotels all have restaurants, too; most have several and some of them are superb.

Bolan Saltish
In the trendy Blue Area strip Famous Baluch restaurant serving authentic dishes. Try its delicious leg of lamb *(sajji)*. **$$**

Jahangir Bar-Be-Que
Moscow Plaza, Blue Area
Islamabad's busiest Pakistani restaurant, famous

for its chargrilled lamb ribs and brain masala fry. **$$**

Kabul
College Road, Jinnah Market
Superb Afghan restaurant popular among diplomatic and other expat communities. Reasonably priced barbecue dishes served with roti, yoghurt, rice and salads. **$$**

Ye Olde Hang Out
Kings Arcade, Jinnah Supermarket
Pakistan's first-ever sheesha bar and restaurant, favoured by the young and trendy for its lively music and excellent food. **$$**

Peshawar

Peshawar is no place for vegetarians. Pathans like their meat to the extent that a vegetable pilau may contain meat. So in Peshawar, kebabs are a must. There are many stalls along the streets; Namak Mandi and Shoiba Bazaar are notable for Afghan food. There are also some excellent bakeries in Saddar.

Charsi Tikka Carrai
Namak Mandi
A small but famous restaurant. Serves a variety of kebabs and tikkas. Nice

atmosphere with upstairs room. **$**

Khan Klub
New Rampura Gate, Old City
Beautiful Pathan food served in the traditional surroundings of an old Sikh *haveli* in the Old City, with guests sitting on cushions at low tables. **$$$**

Northwest Heritage
Firdaus Chowk
Traditional barbecue on rooftop; great views of the old fort and walled city. **$$**

Salateen Restaurant
Namak Mandi
Serves spicy mutton karahi and lovely *seekh* kebabs. **$**

AFGHANISTAN

Kabul

Le Bistro
Off Chicken Street
Tel: (0799) 598 852
As French as the names suggests, and the in-house bakery makes this a good draw, especially for breakfasts and brunch. Holds regular art and crafts exhibitions. **$$**

Cabul Coffee House
Street 2, Qala-i-Fatullah
Tel: (0752) 005 275
As much a place for excellent American-style burgers as for fresh coffee and thickly filled sandwiches. Hosts music and poetry events. **$$**

Flower Street Café
House 57 Street 7, Qala-i-Fatullah
Tel: (0700) 293 124
Great hamburgers and sandwiches. Not actually in Flower Street, but loved by embassy staff and NGO workers nonetheless. **$$**

Heart
Shahr-i-Naw Park
Busy blue-fronted corner restaurant, packing diners in with Afghan staples, a large selection of grilled meats and sweet desserts. **$**

Sufi
Street 2, Qala-i-Fatullah
Tel: (0799) 337 193

Excellent Afghan food, with dishes ranging far beyond kebabs and *pulao*. Pleasant garden and live Afghan music on Wednesdays. **$$**

Taverna du Liban
Lane 4, Street 13, Wazir Akbar Khan
Tel: (0799) 828 376
One of the oldest post-Taliban restaurants still in business, this restaurant has a small garden and a wide variety of Lebanese dishes. Diners can enjoy a continual succession of *meze*. **$$**

Herat

Arghawan
Chowk-i-Cinema

Tel: (040) 221 919
Very good traditional Afghan restaurant, with raised carpeted areas with cushions to dine in. **$**

Mazar-I-Sharif

Delhi Darbar
Doh Sad Bistar
Tel: (0700) 505 417
Probably north Afghanistan's only Indian restaurant, and it's a good one. You can dine in the garden, alcohol is served and there is a wide selection of vegetarian dishes. **$$**

ACTIVITIES

THE ARTS, FAIRS AND FESTIVALS, NIGHTLIFE, SPORT, OUTDOOR ACTIVITIES AND SHOPPING

THE ARTS

Art Galleries

Kyrgzstan is home to the Gapar Aitiev Museum of Applied Arts in Bishkek, which features mostly Kyrgyz art, while the Bekhzod National Museum in Dushanbe, **Tajikistan**, has a surprisingly good collection of Soviet art. In **Kazakhstan**, Almaty's Kasteyev Museum of Fine Arts has a good collection of Russian and European art.

The **Uzbekistan** capital, Tashkent, has two major collections – the Fine Arts Museum of Uzbekistan, with a comprehensive pre-Soviet collection, and the Museum of Applied Arts. The rather forlorn city of Nukus is the unlikely home of the **Igor Savitsky Art Gallery** – a glorious collection of banned paintings from the Soviet period. Many consider this to be the second-best art collection in the former USSR, after St Petersburg's Hermitage Museum.

Painting is an important art form in **Pakistan**. Budding artists tend to turn up at houses and show their work to the occupants in the hope of making sales. Works of art are also displayed on the walls of some of the luxury hotels and restaurants and may be for sale.

The National Gallery in Kabul, **Afghanistan**, has a permanent exhibition. There are regular art and photographic exhibitions – see Afghan Scene magazine for details.

Cinemas

Many English-language films are shown in Central Asian cinemas,

but they are often badly dubbed into Russian. Russian movies are more popular, and the occasional Kazakh- or Uzbek-language film also sometimes makes it onto the big screen. Pakistani cinemas show imported films from various sources, including blockbusters from the West, and home-grown Lollywood movies are growing in popularity. There are only a couple of cinemas in Kabul, mainly showing Bollywood-style films to exclusively male audiences.

Concerts and Theatres

Many of the Central Asian capitals have concert halls and opera and ballet theatres that date from the Soviet period. As these are state-subsidised, tickets are invariably inexpensive. The Abay State Theatre of Opera and Ballet in Almaty, the Alisher Navoi Opera and Ballet Theatre in Tashkent and the Philharmonia and State Opera and Ballet Theatre in Bishkek are all worth checking out.

The Foundation for Culture and Civil Society holds regular concerts in Kabul of Afghan music, poetry recitals and the occasional theatrical production, including performances at the restored Babur's Gardens.

FAIRS AND FESTIVALS

The spring equinox festival of Nauroz (also known as *Nauryz, Nooruz, Nawroz* or Navrus), widely celebrated in the region, is an excuse for traditional games like *buzkashi* and much partying. Horse game fairs are also staged in the

summer *jailoos* (seasonal pasture) of **Kyrgyzstan**, in particular the annual Central Asia Horse Festival.

In **Pakistan**, there are a great many *melas* (festivals), jolly occasions with fairs, circuses, pilgrimages, religious frenzy, people in catatonic trances, beating of drums and bagpiping. The most exciting religious *melas* are those marking the *urs* of the Sufi saints. The dates for most of these *melas* depend on the sighting of the moon and therefore vary from year to year. Most of them, however, occur during the spring period.

Two important festivals in **Afghanistan** are the Gul-e Sorkh International Music Festival, in Mazar-e-Sharif in March, and Kabul's AgFair Agriculture Festival in October.

NIGHTLIFE

There is little nightlife outside the capitals, but Almaty, Bishkek and Tashkent all have raunchy nightclubs where the emphasis is on drinking, dancing and spending hard currency. Vodka is the beverage of choice.

Pakistan is officially dry, but there are clubs serving foreigners and the young elite, and some five-star hotel venues have music and dancing. Recent years have seen the growth of a thriving underground music scene, which, combined with the staging of more mainstream pop and rock concerts, has helped to make the cities much more lively places. Returning to your hotel can sometimes be problematic, as taxis and rickshaws tend to disperse after nightfall.

There is no nightlife in **Afghanistan**. Kabul's expat community has attempted to recreate a semblance of one through the restaurants and bars serving alcohol – something of concern to many Afghans. Its health is entirely dependent on the security restrictions of the day.

SPORT

Spectator Sports

The king of Afghan sports is *buzkashi*, something akin to rugby played on horseback using a dead calf for a ball. It's wild and exciting, and played across northern **Afghanistan** (and sometimes in Kabul) throughout the autumn and winter months until the Afghan New Year celebrations (21 March). The Kyrgyz version, *ulak-tartysh*, is popular in **Kyrgyzstan**, southern **Kazakhstan** and parts of **Tajikistan**. Games can be seen at Independence Day celebrations or at organised games put on by the CBT organisation. Other typical Kyrgyz horse games include at *chabysh* (long-distance race), jumby atmai (shooting at a target whilst galloping), *oodarysh* (horseback wrestling) and *kyz-kumai* (literally "kiss the girl" – a ritualised horse chase involving riders of both sexes).

Street cricket may form the most prominent element of **Pakistan**'s sporting life, but there is a vast array of other sports, including traditional polo, which are alive and kicking in the Northern Areas, especially in Gilgit and Chitral. Polo clubs in the major cities follow international rules and contrast sharply with the hair-raising variety in the mountains.

OUTDOOR ACTIVITIES

Trekking

The most popular areas for trekking in **Kyrgyzstan** are the Lake Issyk-Kul area (especially the valleys south of Karakol), the valleys south of Bishkek like Ala-Archa, and the lower reaches of the Central Tian Shan. The whole country has enormous potential for outdoor activities, and areas such as the Chatkal Valley and the Fergana range offer great opportunities for adventurous trekking.

Low-lying **Uzbekistan** has less to offer, although hiking excursions are a possibility in the Uzbek enclave of Shakhimardan, which lies stranded within Kyrgyzstan's Batken province. The Chatkal range north of Tashkent offers further possibilities. In trekking terms, **Tajikistan** has it all – that is, apart from a viable infrastructure. One of the most rewarding areas is the Fan Mountains east of Penjikent. The country's other exceptional trekking area is the Pamir region in the remote southeast, which requires a special permit.

In **Kazakhstan**, the most fruitful region for trekking is the Zailiysky Alatau range around Bolshoe Almatinskoe Lake and Malaya Almatinskaya Gorge. Long-distance trekking is also possible between Kazakhstan and Kyrgyzstan, provided that the necessary paperwork can be sorted out.

In the Karakoram, **Pakistan** has probably the most dramatic mountain scenery on the planet. The main areas are the Hunza Valley, dominated by the Ultar Peaks and Rakaposhi; Baltistan, notably the Baltoro Glacier trek leading to K2 and the Hushe Valley; Nanga Parbat (from both the north and the south)

and Chitral. The trek closest to the line of the old Silk Road through the Wakhan Corridor in Afghanistan leads from northern Hunza via the Chilinji, Karumbar and Shah Jinali passes, taking about two weeks.

The Wakhan Corridor is **Afghanistan**'s premier trekking spot, high and remote. It's also the best place to spot wildlife – including the Marco Polo sheep and snow leopard if you're lucky. Other interesting areas such as wooded Nuristan are strictly off-limits due to security concerns. A significant landmine risk exists throughout the country.

Mountaineering

The Central Tian Shan range that stretches across the borders of **Kyrgyzstan**, **Kazakhstan** and Chinese Xinjiang provides the greatest draw for experienced climbers, having the forbidding peaks of Khan Tengri and Pik Pobedy. The other main area is the Pamir range of northern **Tajikistan** and southern Kyrgyzstan, which has challenging summits such as Pik Lenin. Elsewhere in Kyrgyzstan and Tajikistan there are lower, yet still challenging peaks, many of which remain unnamed and unclimbed.

K2 and Nanga Parbat in **Pakistan** are the ultimate goal of many

BELOW: Tajikistan's Fan Mountains.

TRANSPORT

ACCOMMODATION

EATING OUT

ACTIVITIES

A – Z

LANGUAGE

ABOVE: in the market in Penjikent.

mountaineers, but there are five peaks over 8,000 metres (26,000ft) altogether, as well as scores just below that height. They include the beautiful Rakaposhi in Hunza and Tirich Mir in Chitral.

Organised Tours

A large number of tour companies operate out of Central Asia. As well as organising tours, they can also help with transport, visas and permits.

Kyrgyzstan

Asia Mountains
Tugolbai Ata 1a, Bishkek
Tel: (0312) 694 073
Trekking in the Central Tian Shan and mountaineering in the Pamirs.
Celestial Mountains
Kievskaya 131-2, Bishkek
Tel: (0312) 31 18 14
www.celestial.com.kg
Can arrange individual travel and give expert advice on crossing the Torugart Pass to China.
Central Asian Tourism (CAT)
Chui 124, Bishkek
Tel: (0312) 663 665 / 665 692
Organises tours, provides ticketing and arranges LOI for visas.
Ecotour
46-A, Donskoy Pereulok, Bishkek
Tel: (0312) 660 894 / 772 802805
www.ecotour.kg
Various tours including activities such as birdwatching and photography.

Neofit
Jamansariev 166, Karakol
Tel: (03922) 5 58 50 / 5 58 02 www.neofit.kg
Experienced local trekking company.
Novi Nomad
Appartment 10, Togolok Moldo 28, Bishkek
Tel: (0312) 622 381
www.novinomad.com
Various treks and mountain bike tours, as well as arranging visas and overland travel to China.
Tien Shan Travel
3/1 Bakinsy Lane, Bishkek
Tel: (0312) 466 034 / 490 180
www.tien-shan.com
Mountaineering and high-altitude trekking specialists.
Turkestan Travel
Toktogul 273, Karakol
Tel: (0543) 911 452 / (0550) 234 911
www.karakol.kg
Adventurous tours and treks to Central Tian Shan region.

Tajikistan

Central Asian Tourism (CAT)
Tel: (0312) 663 664 / (0312) 663 665
www.cat.kg/en
See Kyrgyzstan, above.
Pamir Adventure
Tel: (0372) 234 424
www.pamir-adventure.com
Trekking specialist based in Dushanbe that offers bespoke treks and jeep and horseback tours of Pamir region.

Uzbekistan

Asia Travel
Chilanzarskaya 97, Tashkent
Tel: (071) 173 5107
Mountain expeditions, trekking and heli-skiing trips.
Dolores Tour
M. Tarobi 27, Tashkent
Tel: (071) 120 8883
www.sambuh.com
Various historical tours across Uzbekistan, plus visa support.
Sairam
Movarounnakhr 16a, Tashkent
Tel: (071) 233 7411
www.sairamtourism.com
Wide range of tours in Central Asia.
Salom Travel
49 Sarrafon Street, Bukhara
Tel: (0652) 244 148
www.salomtravel.com
Wide range of Silk Road tours in the region. They also offer visa support.
Sogda Tour
Registan 38, Samarkand
Tel: (066) 235 3609 / 235 1320
www.sogda-tour.com
Cultural and eco-tours in Uzbekistan and beyond.

Kazakhstan

Central Asian Tourism (CAT)
Seyfullin 537, Almaty
Tel: (3272) 501070
Almaty branch of Central Asian Tourism (see Kyrgyzstan, above).
Stan Tours
Konaev 163/76, Almaty
Tel: (0705) 118 4619
www.stantours.com
Experts in running tours throughout the region and dealing with red tape. They also have an office in Ashgabat.

Pakistan

Adventure Travel
PO Box 2062, 15 Wali Centre, 86 South Blue Area, Islamabad
Tel: (051) 2260 820 / 2252 759
www.atp.com.pk
Jeep safaris and trekking/ mountaineering expeditions in the north, plus boat safaris on the Indus.
Cox & Kings Pakistan (Pvt) Ltd
163-C, Bank Road, PO Box 1605, Rawalpindi
Tel: (051) 552 9473 / 9474
www.coxandkings.com.pk
Branch of the venerable tour operator, established in Pakistan in 2001.
Hindukush Heights
Chitral
Tel: (0344) 9700 800/(0300) 8521 887
www.hindukush.com.pk
Run by the owners of the Hindukush

Specialist Tour Operators

There are a number of international tour operators who specialise in tours to Central Asia, sometimes arranging group visits to specific countries, others focusing on overland trips along the Silk Road. They fall predominantly into two categories: adventure/overland tours and luxury tours.

UK

Audley Travel
Tel: 01993 838000
www.audleytravel.com
Bespoke itineraries including 19-day escorted tours taking in the highlights of Central Asia.
Dragoman Overland
Tel: 01728 826 317
www.dragoman.com
Truck-based journeys for those with an adventurous spirit. Facilities are basic but with routes such as the 11-week trip from St. Petersburg to Beijing get right to the heart of the Silk Road.
Explore Worldwide
Tel: 0845 291 4541
www.explore.co.uk
Overland tours with programmes that include aspects of both culture

and adventure. The 11-day Golden Road to Samarkand is a particular favourite.
Go Russia
Tel: 020 3355 7717
www.justgorussia.co.uk
Go Russia specialises in tours to the former Soviet Union, but also has inspiring itineraries combining the "Stans" with China and Mongolia.
Secret Compass
www.secretcompass.com
Secret Compass runs expert-led expeditions to largely unexplored regions. Whether you want to climb mountains in northern Iraq or trek your way across Afghanistan, this is the way to do it.
Wild Frontiers
Tel: 020 7736 3968
www.wildfrontiers.co.uk
Small-group tours to the Silk Road's cultural sites but also off-the-beaten-track destinations, including three distinct tours in Afghanistan. Tours can also be tailor-made.

US

40 Tribes Backcountry Adventures
Tel: 0305 552 6034
www.fortytribesbackcountry.com

Package tours and bespoke itineraries with a focus on sports and the great outdoors. The skiing and fly-fishing options are particularly popular.
Geographic Expeditions
Tel: 0415 922 0448
www.geoex.com
Overland tours, treks and expeditions including trips across western China and Kyrgyzstan. Customised programmes also available.
Red Star Travel
Tel: 0206 522 5995
www.travel2russia.com
Tours to all parts of Central Asia, also visas, flights and train bookings.

Australia

Intrepid
Tel: 03 9473 2626
www.intrepidtravel.com
Multicountry tours, including trips to Kyrgyzstan.
Russian Passport
Tel: 03 9500 0444
www.russia-rail.com
Numerous road and rail tours including a 22-day programme from Beijing to Moscow.

Heights Hotel. Expeditions in Chitral, including classic treks and jeep safaris, plus pony trekking on mountain ponies from Badakhshan.
Karakurum Treks & Tours
PO Box 2803, Hotel Metropolitan, 21-B, G-9 Markaz, Islamabad
Tel: (051) 226 4876 / 225 0317
www.karakurum.com.pk
The first company to organise treks and mountaineering expeditions in the Northern Areas. Also runs cultural and sightseeing tours, and jeep safaris along the Indus.
Sehrai Travels & Tours
Saddar Road, Peshawar Cantt
Email: sehrai@brain.net.pk
Peshawar's oldest tour operator. Its main speciality is the Khyber Steam Safari, but it also runs historical, cultural and archaeological tours, including one of Gandharan sites.
Sitara Travel Consultants (Pvt) Ltd
Waheed Plaza, 3rd Floor,52 West Jinnah Avenue, Blue Area, PO Box 1662, Islamabad
Tel: (051) 287 3372-75/227 4892-93
www.sitara.com
Well-established company focusing on tours to Silk Road countries. Run by Mr Shiraz M. Poonja; also

maintains an office in Tashkent.
Travel Walji's Ltd
10 Khayaban-e-Suhrawardy, PO Box 1088, Islamabad
Tel: (051) 287 0201-9
www.waljis.com
Pakistan's oldest tour company, offering tours for the adventurous and culture vultures alike.

Afghanistan

In the current climate, visiting Afghanistan independently is less preferable than using a local tour operator with ground experience and access to current security information.
Afghan Logistics & Tours
106 Ansari Square, Street No. 1, Shar-e-Now
Tel: (0798) 44 22 11/(0707) 44 22 11
www.afghanlogisticstours.com

SHOPPING

What to Buy

Both Bukhara and Samarkand in **Uzbekistan** have an enormous number of gift shops that sell a range of items including traditional clothing,

wall hangings, pottery and leather goods. **Kyrgyzstan** has less choice, but *shyrdaks*, the felt carpets used in Kyrgyz yurts, are widely available. There are other felt goods besides *shyrdaks* that may be purchased, such as slippers and wall hangings.

Traditional hats make good, inexpensive souvenirs: the white felt *kalpak* worn by Kyrgyz men, the square *doppi* of Uzbekistan or the well-known woollen *pakol* caps of **Pakistan** and **Afghanistan**.

In the bazaars of Islamabad, Rawalpindi and Peshawar you will find silverware, woodwork, embroidered items, *namdah* rugs (made from chain-stitch embroidery on felt with colourful designs), kaftans, Kashmiri shawls, *salwar kameez* and woollen *weskits* (waistcoats). One item to look for is Peshwari chappals – sturdy and comfortable men's sandals.

Afghan carpets are deservedly famous, from the richly decorated Bokhara styles of the Turkmen north to the tribal Baluchi style. Chicken Street is Kabul's most famous shopping address and sells wool or silk embroidered *suzani* bedspreads, carved lapis lazuli, *pakol* hats and pottery from Istalif. Herat is famous for its handmade blue glass.

A – Z

A HANDY SUMMARY OF PRACTICAL INFORMATION, ARRANGED ALPHABETICALLY

B

Budgeting for Your Trip

Flights to and from, and the numerous visas and permits required to travel across, Central Asia drive up the cost of travelling in what is otherwise a relatively inexpensive part of the world. Local incomes tend to be low, and this is reflected in the cost of the most basic accommodation, food and transport options.

Capital cities and also the oil towns of Turkmenistan and Kazakhstan are atypically expensive, however. Hotels and restaurants are aimed at expats and business travellers, all of whom are using their expense accounts, and so double rooms start at around $120 and rocket up from there. Likewise, a meal in a reasonable restaurant, excluding alcohol, will set you back at least $30 per person. If you plan to drink alcohol, remember that imported brands are markedly more expensive than local ones because of the import taxes.

If you are travelling on a more modest budget and in remoter areas, it is usually possible to find homestay or guesthouse accommodation for $10–15. Afghanistan is the notable exception, where bed and breakfast will set you back around $25. Eating where the locals eat – usually road-side stalls – is cheap providing you can live on *shashlyk*, *shorpo* and tea, and supermarkets and corner shops tend to stock a range of affordable local brands. Shared taxis or minibuses are cheaper than private cars; even if you are hitchhiking you will be expected to contribute towards the cost of fuel.

C

Climate

Extreme continental: Uzbekistan can get very hot – above 40°C (104°F) – in the summer months, while the mountainous areas of central Kyrgyzstan can dip to −25°C (−14°F) in the dead of winter. The Central Asian capitals, which are all relatively low-lying, are warm and humid in summer (30–35°C/85–95°F) but often sub-zero in the winter months. Astana in Kazakhstan has the greatest temperature swing. Spring receives the highest precipitation, which may fall as snow as late as April.

Crime and Security

Most of Central Asia is generally safe for travellers. The Islamist insurgencies that took place in southwest **Kyrgyzstan** a few years ago now appear to be a thing of the past, though communal violence is not uncommon. The greatest threat of robbery tends to be in the big cities, especially at night outside bars and nightclubs in Bishkek and Almaty, and also while travelling by public transport. If you lose any items, contact the police. Crooked officials pose less of a problem than they used to, although there are still a few who attempt to extort money from foreigners. This is particularly true of the transport police. Keep calm, make sure you have copies of all important documentation (including your driving license), and try to avoid handing over money on the street. Ask to be taken

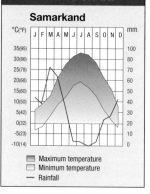

CLIMATE CHART

Samarkand

to the nearest police station, and always demand a receipt.

Afghanistan is a somewhat different country to the other destinations in this guide. The ongoing Taliban insurgency in the south and east continues to affect the country profoundly, while the weakness of the Afghan government and rule of law in general add further to instability. Even the areas we cover in this guide are not immune from trouble, and Kabul in particular has been the target of repeated Taliban terror attacks, including suicide bombings. The British government advises against non-essential travel to Afghanistan, though this warning is reduced for the Wakhan Corridor. Even if conditions permit a visit, we advise against independent travel in favour of using a Kabul-based tour operator (or local operator in the case of the Wakhan), who will have access to current security information, risk assessments and contingency planning.

In **Pakistan**, there is a risk from random terrorist attacks on the northwest frontier, due to the recent problems in Baluchistan and the fallout from the "war against terror", which has spawned Taliban activity in NWFP and certain areas outside it. It is therefore advisable not to venture beyond Quetta in Baluchistan, and one should check with local officials before venturing out in West Punjab – or indeed anywhere in Federally Administered Tribal Areas (FATA) of NWFP. Except for people arriving overland from Iran by car, the authorities are unlikely to provide police escort to ordinary tourists. Local and intelligence officials are also very suspicious of cameras (video, especially), and Western documentary filmmakers have been locked up for months. As for the rest of Pakistan, it should be pretty safe, and that includes Peshawar and the Settled Areas of NWFP. Inevitably, one explosion in Karachi or a shooting in Gilgit leads to stern travel advisories being issued by foreign governments (they seem to pick on Pakistan more than elsewhere), with the result that the whole local tourism industry collapses for several months. Note these advisories by all means, but also bear in mind that sectarian violence in Gilgit and Karachi is nothing to do with tourists, and they are therefore never targeted. When trouble does occur, visitors are protected rather than threatened.

Statistics show that Pakistan is a very safe place to travel for foreigners; visitors are much less likely to get mugged here than in London or New York. However, you should still keep your personal belongings on your person or lock them in the hotel safe. Some hotels request that you deposit your valuable articles like jewellery and cash with the receptionist.

Customs Regulations

There are no major restrictions other than for weapons, drugs and the export of artefacts, which require an export licence. The import of liquor into Pakistan is not permitted, though foreigners can drink in hotel bars. Customs declaration forms need to be filled out when entering some of the countries in the region and presented when leaving. Cash is also supposed to be accurately accounted for, so anything undeclared is best stashed away in case an over-vigilant customs officer wants to count it.

Electricity

220 Volts AC, 50 Cycles. Countries in Central Asia use European-style two-pin rounded plugs. Power cuts are the norm and generators ubiquitous.

D

Disabled Travellers

Little concession is made to disabled travellers in the region outside the top hotels and, sadly, wheelchair access is extremely problematic. In the former Soviet "Stans", disabled children have typically been left in the care of the state, and attitudes are slow to change.

E

Embassies and Consulates

Kyrgyzstan
British Honorary Consulate
2nd Floor, Ibraimova 115, Bishkek, tel: (0312) 584 245, http://ukinkz.fco.gov.uk/en/
A British Embassy will be opening in Bishkek in 2012 but it will not have a consular department.
US Embassy
Prospect Mira 171, Bishkek, tel:(0312) 551 241 , http://bishkek.usembassy.gov

Tajikistan
British Embassy
Mirzo Tursunzade 65, Dushanbe, tel: (0372) 242 221/241477, www.ukintajikistan.fco.gov.uk
US Embassy
Ismoili Somoni 109A, Dushanbe, tel: (0372) 292 000, http://dushanbe.usembassy.gov

Uzbekistan
British Embassy
Gulyamov 67, Tashkent, tel: (071) 120 1500, www.ukinuzbekistan.fco.gov.uk
US Embassy
Moyqorghon 3, 5th Block, Yunusobod, Tashkent, tel: (071) 120 5450, http://uzbekistan.usembassy.gov

Kazakhstan
Australian Embassy
Al-Farabi 5/2A, 9th Floor, Almaty, tel: (0727) 777 879.
British Embassy

6th Floor, Kosmonavtov Street 62, St. Chubary District, Astana, tel: (07172) 556 200, www.ukinkz.fco.gov.uk
US Embassy
Ak Bulak 4, Str. 23–22, building #3, Astana, tel: (07172) 702 100, www.usembassy.kz

Pakistan
Australian High Commission
Constitution and Ispahani, Diplomatic Enclave, No. 1,Sector G-5/4, Islamabad, tel: (051) 835 5500, www.pakistan.embassy.gov.au
British High Commission
Diplomatic Enclave, Ramna 5, Islamabad, tel: (051) 201 2000.
US Embassy
Diplomatic Enclave, Ramna 5, Islamabad, tel: (051) 208 0000, http://islamabad.usembassy.gov

Afghanistan
Australian Embassy
Serena Hotel, Froshgah Street, Kabul, tel:. (0799) 654 840
British Embassy
15th Street Roundabout, Wazir Akbar Khan, Kabul, tel: (0700) 102 000, www.ukinpakistan.fco.gov.uk
Canadian Embassy
House 256, Street 15, Wazir Akbar Khan, Kabul, tel: (0799) 742 800, www.afghanistan.gc.ca
US Embassy
The Great Masoud Road, Kabul,tel: (0700) 10 8001 , http://kabul.usembassy.gov/

Emergencies

It is advisable to carry the telephone number of the nearest embassy (see above) or honorary consul of your country at all times. Emergency numbers for ambulance, fire and police are respectively **01**, **02** and **03** in **Kazakhstan**, **Uzbekistan** and **Tajikistan** and **101**, **102** and **103** in **Kyrgyzstan**.

Emergency services in **Pakistan** are contacted by dialling **15** plus a local number for police, **16** plus a local number for fire services, and **115** plus a local number for the ambulance service. Of course, you need to get the local number.

There are no country wide emergency numbers in **Afghanistan**. In Kabul, dial **100** for the police, **0799 357 049** for ambulance and **020 210 1341** for the security department.

Etiquette

Although not always on the surface deeply religious,the Central Asian countries are socially conservative and predominantly Muslim, particularly in more rural areas, and visitors should therefore behave sensitively. Particular in the former Soviet states you may well see the young, urban population skimpily dressed, but this is not recommended for foreigners as it may be seen to be disrespectful by older generations. In Afghanistan, men must wear long trousers and long-sleeved tops. Women should wear tunic-style blouses that cover their body shape, and a headscarf. The same dress code should be applied when visiting mosques and other religious sites in the region.

Handshaking is a widespread ritual, often accompanied with a gesture to the heart, and it is common for men to continue holding hands as they talk. Women do not usually shake hands, but foreign women may be invited to do so with Central Asian men. Do not take offence if your hand is declined.

Shoes should be removed whenever entering a home or a mosque. In more conservative areas, particularly in Afghanistan and Pakistan, homes are strictly divided by sex and male guests will not encounter female members of the family. Foreign women have a hybrid status and are sometimes allowed to participate in both male and female spheres.

Eating is always done with the right hand, especially when sharing a communal bowl, as the left hand is used for washing oneself and therefore is considered dirty. Bread is considered sacred and should never be discarded on the floor. Hospitality is of prime importance, even in the poorest communities, so you should always show gratitude to your host and bring a gift or an item of food if invited to share a meal.

G

Gay and Lesbian Travellers

Male homosexuality is legal in Kyrgyzstan and Kazakhstan, but illegal in Uzbekistan, Tajikistan, Pakistan and Afghanistan. Female homosexuality is not sanctioned either way, presumably because it is not considered an issue. Because of social mores, public displays of affection between same-sex – and also straight – couples is best avoided. There is a nascent gay scene in Almaty but otherwise the Soviet rhetoric that homosexuality is a mental disorder is widely accepted.

H

Health and Medical Care

A yellow fever vaccination certificate is required if coming from an infected area less than six days prior to entering Kazakhstan or Pakistan. Vaccinations for hepatitis A and B, diphtheria, tetanus, typhoid and polio should be up to date for all countries.

A malaria risk exists across all non-mountainous parts of Afghanistan and parts of Pakistan. There is also a slight risk in southern Uzbekistan and Tajikistan in summer. Diseases such as leishmaniasis and brucellosis, common in some local populations, are rarely contracted by travellers to the region. Rabies is present, but only poses a risk to those spending long periods in rural areas. HIV and STDs are fairly widespread.

However, despite the risks listed above, diarrhoea is the illness visitors are most likely to suffer from.

Air pollution in large cities can cause severe problems to anyone suffering from breathing difficulties, so remember to bring inhalers and suitable medication.

I

Insurance

Travel and medical insurance is essential, including evacuation cover. Check before purchasing, however, as some insurers won't cover for travel to Afghanistan. Bring copies of documentation and all necessary phone numbers with you.

Internet

Internet cafés are widespread throughout the region, although connections can be slow. Many of the better hotels offer Wi-fi access.

M

Maps

Good maps of Central Asia are frustratingly hard to come by. The Soviets did produce detailed topographical maps of the region but they do not tend to be commercially available, even in the countries themselves. The same applies to trekking maps, which should be purchased abroad, if indeed they are in print.

Hotels and tourism offices in capital cities and towns with a significant inflow of tourists often produce maps of their local area. These may be photocopies of print-outs from Google, but they are often all that is available.

Media

Kyrgyzstan, Tajikistan, Uzbekistan and **Kazakhstan** have a range of newspapers in Russian and the national language. Kazakhstan

BELOW: Traditional Pakistani buses

National Holidays

Kyrgyzstan
1 January New Year's Day
7 January Christmas (Russian Orthodox)
8 March Women's Day
21 March Nauroz
9 May Victory Day
5 May Constitution Day
31 August Independence Day

Tajikistan
1 January New Year's Day
7 January Christmas (Russian Orthodox)
8 March Women's Day
21 March Nauroz
1 May Labour Day
9 May Victory Day
27 June National Unity Day
9 September Independence Day
6 November Constitution Day

Uzbekistan
1 January New Year's Day
7 January Christmas (Russian Orthodox)
8 March Women's Day
21 March Nauroz
9 May Victory Day
1 September Independence Day
8 December Constitution Day

Kazakhstan
1 January New Year's Day
7 January Christmas (Russian Orthodox)
8 March Women's Day
21 March Nauroz
9 May Victory Day
10 June Capital Day
30 August Constitution Day
25 October Republic Day
16 December Independence Day

Pakistan
23 March Pakistan Day
1 May Labour Day
1 July Bank Holiday
14 August Independence Day
6 September Defence of Pakistan Day (commemorating the Indo-Pakistan War of 1965)
11 September Anniversary of the death of the Quaid-e-Azam, M.A. Jinnah
9 November Iqbal Day (anniversary of the birth of Allama Iqbal)
25 December Anniversary of the birth of Quaid-e-Azam
31 December Bank Holiday

Afghanistan
21 March Afghan New Year (Nauroz)
28 April Victory Day
1 May National Labour Day
4 May Remembrance Day for Martyrs and the Disabled
19 August Independence Day
9 September Ahmad Shah Massoud Day

2,000, 5,000 and 10,000 tenge, and 1, 2, 5, 10, 20, 50 and 100 tenge coins.

Afghanistan's currency, the afghani, has bank notes of AFA5, 10, 20, 50, 100, 500, and there are coins of AFA1, 2 and 5. Pakistan's unit of currency is the rupee, with 100 paisas to a rupee. Notes are in denominations of Rs1,000, 500, 100, 50, 10 and 5. Coins are in denominations of Rs2 and 1, and 50 and 25 paisa.

By far the best currency to carry is US dollars as sterling and euros are a struggle to exchange. Dollars used for exchange must be in pristine condition and preferably of high denominations, otherwise they will be refused. Traveller's cheques are generally more trouble than they are worth. ATMs are relatively numerous in the towns and cities of Kazakhstan. In Kyrgyzstan, they are currently only found in Bishkek, Osh and Jalalabad. Tajikistan has very few, mostly in Dushanbe, and in Uzbekistan they are unreliable, even in Tashkent. There are a limited number in Kabul accepting Visa and MasterCard, and increasing numbers in Pakistan.

Credit cards are usually accepted for payment in top hotels and some up-market restaurants and shops, except in Afghanistan, where US dollars or afghanis are preferred.

O

Opening Hours

Opening hours are normally Monday to Friday from 9am until 5pm or 6pm. Banks are normally open from 9am to 4pm, except in Pakistan where they close at 1pm. Shops often stay open later, until around 8pm or 9pm.

Friday is the official holiday in Afghanistan. Museums and galleries are usually closed on one day of the week, often on Mondays. Restaurants tend to close early outside the larger cities. Shops and businesses may change their opening hours during Ramadan, particularly in Pakistan and Afghanistan.

P

Photography

Avoid taking photos of military installations, bridges and airports, especially in Uzbekistan, Pakistan and

---

has the English-language *Almaty Herald* and *Kazakhstan Monitor*, and Kyrgyzstan the *Bishkek Observer* and *The Times of Central Asia*, which covers all of Central Asia. Neither **Uzbekistan** nor **Tajikistan** has any English-language print media.

In **Afghanistan**, newspapers are sold in the cities. The international press can be hard to find even in Kabul, although the *Kabul Times* is published in English. *Afghan Scene* is an English-language monthly aimed at expats.

In **Pakistan**, there are many Urdu publications, and also publications in regional languages. The major Urdu newspapers are *Nawa-i-waqt*, *Jang* and *Wafaq*. International newspapers and news magazines are available in the cities, at bookshops and in the foyers of high-class hotels. English-language newspapers, such as *The Nation*, *The News* and *The Leader*, are published in the major cities.

Television and radio are tightly controlled in **Uzbekistan** but more liberal in the rest of the region, with privately owned channels

supplementing state-controlled ones.

In **Afghanistan**, local television and radio broadcasts are mainly in Dari and Pashto, but the BBC World Service broadcasts on FM in Kabul, and across the rest of Central Asia. International English-language satellite channels are provided for guests at many hotels throughout the region.

Money

The **Kyrgyzstan** currency is the som, which comes in notes of 1, 5, 10, 20, 50, 100, 200, 500 and 1,000 som and a few rarely used coins.

In **Uzbekistan**, the official currency of sum comes in notes of 1, 3, 5, 10, 25, 50, 100, 200, 500 and 1,000, but because there are currently around 1,300 sum to the dollar, smaller denomination notes are rarely seen. **Tajikistan**'s currency, the somoni, has notes of 1, 5, 10, 20, 50, 100 somoni and coins of 5, 10, 20, 50 diram and 1, 3 and 5 somoni.

Kazakhstan uses the tenge, which comes in notes of 200, 500, 1,000,

ABOVE: colorful paper kites for sale in a market in Pakistan.

Afghanistan. In general, it is unwise and unkind to photograph people unless they give their consent. Do not attempt to take photos of women in the street in Afghanistan. Women visitors might have the opportunity of taking photos of Afghan women, in an all-women environment.

Ensure that you bring sufficient photographic materials, including film/memory cards and batteries.

Postal Services

Kazakhstan, Kyrgyzstan and Pakistan probably offer the most dependable services. For important parcels and documents it is probably best to make use of an international courier service like DHL. There is a Datapost service from Pakistan to some countries, including the UK and US. All items sent by this service are registered and covered against loss. In Afghanistan, use only postal services in Kabul, Herat and Mazar-i-Sharif.

Public Holidays

Islamic holidays are based on the Hejiri calendar. The months are lunar months, so the year is 13 days shorter than the Western calendar. Thus dates of certain holidays may vary from year to year. It is best to find out whether any of these dates fall within the time period of your projected visit. In Afghanistan and Pakistan, Ramadan or an Eid (religious feast) will mean that places are closed at certain times and that food may not be readily available because everyone else is fasting.

The two main holidays, **Eid al-Fitr** and **Eid al-Adha**, are also observed throughout Central Asia, but other

Muslim holidays are mainly observed in Pakistan and Afghanistan.
Eid al-Fitr, three days marking end of Ramadan (fasting month)
Eid al-Adha, four days at the end of Hajj
1st of Muharram, Islamic New Year
9th of Muharram, Ashura
12th of Rabe'a al-Awwal, Prophet Muhammad's birthday

R

Religion

In **Kyrgyzstan**, **Tajikistan**, **Uzbekistan** and **Kazakhstan** most people are Sunni Muslim, nominally at least, while many Russians follow the Orthodox Christian faith. Uzbeks from the Ferghana Valley tend to practise a more conservative Islam, while the Pamir region of Tajikistan has many Ismailis, a unique and tolerant sect of Shia Islam that follows the Aga Khan. Many people, particularly Kyrgyz, observe a syncretic version of Islam that is suffused with elements of shamanism.

Islam is the main religion of **Pakistan**. Some 97 percent of the total population are Muslims, with less than 1.5 percent Hindus and about the same number of Christians, and considerably fewer Sikhs. The Muslim population is divided mainly between Sunnis (77 percent) and Shias (20 percent).

Afghanistan is almost entirely Muslim, with 85 percent of the population being Sunnis. The Shia minority includes the Hazaras. There are small numbers of Sikhs and Hindus in urban areas.

Weights and Measures

Countries in Central Asia use the metric system.

T

Telecommunications

The best place to make international calls is the local telephone office, as surcharged hotel rates tend to be sky-high. Phonecards are available in Pakistan and can be used to make cheap overseas calls. The landline network in Afghanistan is extremely limited but mobile coverage is reasonable. Main post offices have international phone facilities, otherwise look for PCOs (Public Call Offices) or phone stands – a guy with a phone, stopwatch and calculator. Calls between neighbouring Central Asian countries are considered to be international and charged accordingly.

Many Western mobile phone networks have roaming arrangements in Central Asia but these are quite costly. Buying a local SIM card is a good idea if staying for any length of time.

International Dialling Codes

Kyrgyzstan +996
Tajikistan +992
Uzbekistan +998
Kazakhstan +7
Pakistan +93
Afghanistan +92

Tipping

Tipping is not common in Central Asia, except in larger cities where a 10 percent service charge may be added to your restaurant bill.

Toilets

Modern, sit-down toilets are found in most hotels and restaurants, with squat toilets elsewhere. In rural areas, even quite wealthy private homes will often just have a hole-in-the-ground earth toilet. Carry your own toilet paper.

Tourist Information

The websites of tour and trekking companies operating in the region are a good source of information. KCBTA (tel: +996-312-443 331; www.cbtkyrgyzstan.kg), **Kyrgyzstan**'s community-based tourism coordinators based in Bishkek, can give helpful advice on Kyrgyzstan.

The **Pakistan** Tourism Development Corporation (PTDC; www.tourism.gov.pk) has information offices in every city and can help organise trips and transport. The provincial governments also have their own tourism bodies, which offer similar assistance as well as running their own trips. The Afghan Tourist Organisation in Kabul (tel: +93-20-2300 008) is eager, but offers little of practical use to visitors.

V

Visas

This is a complex area that is continually in flux. Visas are necessary for all of the Central Asian republics, although some are more difficult to obtain than others, and some embassies require a "letter of invitation" (LOI) before they will issue a visa. An LOI can be obtained by post or email from a reliable Central Asian agency.

In terms of difficulty, a visa for **Kyrgyzstan** is the easiest to obtain at the current time. A one-month tourist visa can be obtained by posting a downloaded application form to a branch of the embassy (www.kyrgyz-embassy.org.uk or www.kgembassy.org), or by buying one on arrival at Bishkek Airport. Visas for **Kazakhstan** are a little more difficult, and the embassy (www.kazembassy.org.uk or www.kazconsulny.org) may want to see an LOI, although this requirement appears to have stopped for the time being for British and EU passport-holders.

Uzbekistan visas are relatively easy to obtain (see www.uzbekembassy.org or www.uzbekconsulny.org) but an LOI is currently necessary for British passport-holders. It is usually possible to get a **Tajik** tourist visa on arrival at Dushanbe airport, but applying in advance at a Tajik embassy (www.tajikembassy.org) may be a more reliable option.

A visa for **Pakistan** can be obtained from one of its embassies or consulates, and an application form can be downloaded from www.phclondon.org or www.embassyofpakistanusa.org .

All visitors to **Afghanistan** require a valid passport and an entry visa, which should be obtained prior to departure, from Afghan consulates

and embassies. More details and a downloadable visa application form can be found at www.afghanembassy.co.uk, or www.travcour.com. Single-entry visas are valid for one month.

W

Websites

Some useful websites:
www.times.kg The Times of Central Asia.
www.eurasia.net Regional news.
www.helvetas.kg General information on Kyrgyzstan.
www.uzbekistan.com General information on Uzbekistan.
www.tourism.uz Tourism in Uzbekistan.
www.pamirs.org Travel and trekking in the Pamir region.
 www.pakistan.gov.uk Official website of the government of Pakistan.
www.kabulguide.net Useful site for those staying long-term in Kabul.
www.kabulcaravan.com General travel information.
www. Afghannews.tv Good news website.
www.iwpr.net Institute for War and Peace Reporting.
www.fco.gov.uk UK Foreign Office advice.

What to Bring and Wear

A torch (flashlight) is handy for power cuts and late-night trips to the bathroom. Bringing photocopies of your passport, visas and essential documents is a wise precaution, and a supply of passport photos will be necessary if applying for visas.

Comfortable, hard-wearing clothing is best. Loose-fitting clothes are ideal for most of the year, but be prepared for extremes of temperature, especially if trekking. Visitors to the more conservative countries should respect

religious sensibility. Sun lotion and sunglasses are essential and if you are a spectacle-wearer, bring along a spare pair of glasses just in case.

When to Go

Central Asia is a seasonal destination whose upland areas (much of **Kyrgyzstan** and **Tajikistan**) are best visited between late May and October. Because of blistering summer temperatures, lowland areas such as **Uzbekistan** and much of **Kazakhstan** are best visited between April and June and September to early November.

The northern mountains of **Pakistan** can be visited from spring through to autumn, although in high summer the heat in the valleys can still be oppressive.

Spring and autumn are the ideal times to visit **Afghanistan** as summers can be brutally hot, and the winter freeze brings whole areas of the country to a standstill. The warm seasons are shorter in the mountains, with winter arriving early and snow melting late.

Women Travellers

Women travellers do not face any particular problems, although those travelling alone will come across examples of unapologetic sexism from time to time. It is advisable to dress and behave modestly and avoid situations that may turn out to be compromising. When travelling by public transport it is best to seek out fellow Western or local female travellers for company.

Women can have a difficult time in Afghanistan, however, and will find travelling with a male companion will help avoid unnecessary hassles. Non-revealing clothes to cover your body shape are essential, along with a headscarf.

BELOW: Tajikistan is best visited between late May and October.

TRANSPORT

ACCOMMODATION

EATING OUT

ACTIVITIES

A – Z

LANGUAGE

LANGUAGE

UNDERSTANDING THE LANGUAGE

Central Asia has a *smorgasbord* of languages, with each community championing its own tongue and literature. Russian, however, remains the *lingua franca* for inter-ethnic communication in the "Stans", and English or a smattering of Persian will serve you well in Afghanistan and Pakistan.

Russian

Russian is a Slavic language spoken by an estimated 300 million people in Russia and the former territories of the USSR. It is written in the Cyrillic alphabet.

Russian grammar is challenging, but native speakers recognise this and will be understanding if you get it wrong: it is the vocabulary and pronunciation that is most important. Nouns and adjectives have six cases (which are dependent on their grammatical function in a sentence) and verbs are conjugated on the basis of gender (masculine, feminine or neuter) and tense. Pronouns are often omitted in the present and future tenses.

Syllables in Russian can be hard or soft and this largely (though not always) depends on the following vowel. Russian is thankfully phonetic (ie words are pronounced how they are spelled), though putting the stress in the wrong part of a word can change the meaning.

Key Phrases

Hello Привет. *pree-VYEHT*
How are you? Как дела? *kak dyeh-LA?*
Fine, thank you Хорошо, спасибо. *kha-ra-SHO spa-SEE-ba*
Please Пожалуйста. *pa-ZHAL-sta*
Thank you Спасибо. *spa-SEE-ba*

Yes Да. *da*
No Нет. *nyet*
Excuse me Извините. *eez-vee-NEET-yeh*
I can't speak Russian Я не говорю по-русски *ya nye guh-va-RYOO pa ROO-skee*
Do you speak English? Вы говорите по-английски? *vi ga-va-REE-tya pa ahn-GLEES-kee?*
Help! Помогите! *pa-ma-GEE-tyeh!*
I'm ill (man) Я болен *ya-BOH-lyen*
I'm ill (woman) Я больна *ya-bahl-NAH*
I need a doctor Мне нужен врач. *mnyeh NOO-zhen vrahch*

Dari/Tajik

Dari and Tajik are both closely linked to Persian, and speakers of either

language can easily understand the other. Although Tajik is sometimes written in Cyrillic, both languages are normally written using the Perso-Arabic script due to their largely Islamic cultural heritage. Perso-Arabic scripts are written from right to left. You will find speakers of Dari and Tajik not only in Afghanistan and Tajikistan but also in large numbers in Uzbekistan: Bukhara and Samarkand were once both Tajik literary centres.

Key Phrases

Hello سلام *Salaam.*
How are you? چی حال داری؟ *Chi hal dari?*
Fine, thank you خوب تشکر *Khob, tashakor*
Please. لطفاً *Lotfaan*
Thank you تشکر *Tashakor*

BELOW: Quran showing Urdu text

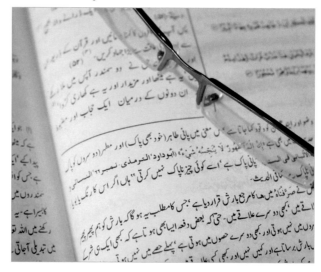

Kazakh

Kazakh is a Turkic language closely linked to Nogai and Karakalpak. Approximately 10 million speakers live within the borders of Kazakhstan itself, and there are another million east of the Altai in Xinjiang. Today the language is written in Cyrillic, though it has historically also been written in Perso-Arabic and Latin.

The greatest proponent of literature in Kazakh was Abay Kunanbayev (1845-1904), who wrote extensively about folk culture as well as producing his own poems. Many Kazakh streets are named in his honour.

Key Phrases

Hello Сәлем. *sa-lem.*
How are you? Қалыңыз қалай? *khaly-ngyz-qalai?*
Fine, thank you Рақмет, жақсы. *rakh-met, jaq-sy.*
Thank you Рақмет. *rakh-met.*
Yes иә. *ee-ah.*
No жоқ. *joq.*

Kyrgyz

Kyrgyz is a Turkic language that is similar enough to Kazakh for speakers to understand one another. Originally written in Turkic runes, then Perso-Arabic and, for a short period, Latin, the Cyrillic alphabet has been in use since the 1940s. There are an estimated four million Kyrgyz speakers spread between northern Afghanistan, eastern China and Uzbekistan, though the majority are in modern Kyrgyzstan.

Nouns in Kyrgyz take one of six cases, and this is shown in their endings. There are eight possible pronouns (including variations for formal and informal addresses), which can be declined in all six cases, and a possible 42 morphemes indicating those same people!

Key Phrases

Hello *Salam*
How are you? *Kandaisiz?*
Fine, thank you *Jakshuh, rakhmat*
Please *Suranych*
Thank you *Rakhmat*

Turkmen

Turkmen is yet another Turkic language, but also heavily influenced by Persian due to being spoken in not only modern Turkmenistan but also northeastern Iran and parts of northwestern Afghanistan. Turkmen today is written in a variant of the Latin script known as *Täze Elipbiý*, or the "New Alphabet". The political opposition, however, continues to use Cyrillic.

The structure of Turkmen is characterised by vowel harmony: words of native origin consist either entirely of front vowels or of back vowels, and this is dictated by the infinitive form of the verb. Prefixes and suffixes take the same pattern as the words they are attached to, but foreign loanwords are unaffected by this grammatical quirk.

Key Phrases

Hello *Salam*
How are you? *Ýagdaýyňyz niçik?*
Fine, thank you *Bolýar*
Please *Baş*
Thank you *Sag bol*

Urdu

Urdu is an Indo-European language that is akin to Hindi but takes the majority of its loanwords from Persian rather than Sanskrit. It is spoken by as many as 70 million people across Pakistan and northern India, as well as amongst the South Asian diaspora. Urdu's grammatical structures are relatively easy to learn, though the tendency to miss out vowels when writing the Perso-Arabic script can make it tricky to read for beginners.

The long interaction between Urdu and English in colonial

ABOVE: Detail from an Uzbek stamp

India has created a large shared vocabulary: listen out for familiar words such as bungalow, pajamas, polo and Raj.

Key Phrases

Hello سلام *salaam*
How are you? آپ کیسے ہیں؟ *Aap kaise hain?*
I am fine میں ٹھیک ہوں *main theek hoon*
Please براۓ مہربانی *barai mehrbaani*
Thank you شکریہ *shukriya*

Uzbek

Uzbek is a Turkic language written in the Cyrillic script. There are approximately 25 million native Uzbek speakers, who live not only in Uzbekistan but also across the rest of Central Asia and in western China. Its vocabulary and grammar are closely linked to Uighur, but Persian, Arabic and Russian have also had a significant influence on the language's development and its modern usage.

Uzbek has a number of different dialects originating in different regions. The dialects you are most likely to hear are those used in Afghanistan, Fergana and Khorezm.

Key Phrases

Hello *Salom*
How are you? *Qalay siz?*
Fine, thank you *Yakshi, rakhmat*
Please *Markhamat*
Thank you *Rakhmat*

FURTHER READING

History and Culture

Asia Overland: Tales of Travel on the Trans-Siberian and Silk Road by Bijan Omrani, Odyssey Publications (2010).
A History of Inner Asia by Soucek Svat, Cambridge University Press (2000). Accessible introduction to the history of Central Asia.
Everyday Life in Central Asia: Past and Present by Jeff Sahadeo and Russell Zanca (editors), Indiana University Press (2007).
Afghanistan: A Companion and Guide by Leeming and Omrani, Odyssey Publications (2011). A richly illustrated history of Afghanistan and its peoples, authoritative and written with flair.
The Great Game by Peter Hopkirk, Oxford University Press (1990). A gripping account of the exploits of young soldiers and other players engaged in a shadowy struggle along distant frontiers.
Younghusband by Patrick French, Harper Collins (1995). A superbly researched biography of Sir Francis Younghusband, last of the great imperialists and key player in the Great Game.
Where Three Empires Meet by Knight, E.F. Longman (1894). Travels in Kashmir and the British invasion of Hunza and Gilgit, 1891.

Modern History

Beyond the Oxus: The Central Asians by Monica Whitlock, John Murray (2003). An incisive look at the region from a former BBC correspondent.
The New Central Asia: The Creation of Nations by Olivier Roy, I.B. Tauris (2007). An analysis of the emergence of national identities in post-Soviet Central Asia.
Murder in Samarkand by Craig Murray, Mainstream Publishing (2006). The memoirs of a British ambassador fired after drawing attention to human rights abuses in Uzbekistan.
The New Great Game: Blood and Oil in Central Asia by Lutz Kleveman, Atlantic Books (2004). An investigation into the international struggle for dominance over the region's oil and gas reserves.

Tamerlane's Children: Dispatches from Contemporary Uzbekistan by Robert Rand, Oneworld Publications (2006). A short but perceptive look at modern-day Uzbekistan.
Taliban: Militant Islam, Oil and Fundamentalism in Central Asia by Ahmed Rashid, Yale University Press (2001). The Lahore-based journalist's authoritative account of the causes and effects of the Taliban's rise to power.
Afghanistan: A Modern History by A. Rasanayagam, I.B.Tauris (2005).

Art and Architecture

Kyrgyzstan by Klavdiya Antipina and Rolando Paiva, Skira (2007). A lavishly illustrated book about the costumes of nomadic Kyrgyz.
Monuments of Central Asia: A Guide to the Archaeology, Art and Architecture of Turkestan by Edgar Knobloch, I.B. Tauris (2001).
Three Women of Herat by Veronica Doubleday, Jonathan Cape (1988). A musician's account of her experiences in 1970s Afghanistan.

Fiction

Tales Told in Tents: Stories from Central Asia by Sally Pomme Clayton and Sophie Herxheimer, Frances Lincoln Children's Books (2006).
Jamilia by Chingiz Aitmatov, Telegram Books (2007). A love story set in the Caucasus.
The Railway by Hamid Ismailov, Vintage (2007). An imaginative portrayal of the fortunes of a fictional Uzbek village.
The Kite Runner by Khaled Hosseini, Bloomsbury (2003). A captivating story of friendship and betrayal in 1970s Kabul.
Earth and Ashes by Atiq Rahimi, Vintage (2003). A tale of three generations of an Afghan family during the Russian occupation.
The Far Pavilions by M.M. Kaye, various editions. A good old romance with a kick at the end and a grand account of the Second Afghan War.
Kim by Rudyard Kipling, Macmillan (1899); various editions. Classic novel, not just for children.

Travel Narratives

Out of Steppe by Daniel Metcalfe, Arrow Books (2010). A vivid travelogue combined with a sensitive discussion of Central Asia's declining minorities.
Silk Dreams, Troubled Road by Jonny Bealby, Arrow Books (2003). A fascinating account of an epic journey along the Silk Road on horseback.
A Game of Polo with a Headless Goat by Emma Levine, Andre Deutsch (2003). An interesting book about the game of buzkashi and other traditional Asian sports.
The Lost Heart of Asia by Colin Thubron, Vintage (2004). The inimitable travel writer's account of his journey through Central Asia in the early 1990s.
In Search of Kazakhstan: The Land That Disappeared by Christopher Robbins, Profile Books (2007). A fascinating insight into this vast and varied country.
A Ride to Khiva by Frederick Burnaby, Cosimo (2007). A classic Victorian travelogue.
Eastern Approaches by Fitzroy MacLean, Penguin (2009). This new edition reveals to a new generation the real-life Soviet adventures of super-spy MacLean, the original inspiration for James Bond.
The Road to Oxiana by Robert Byron, Penguin (1937). Byron's classic account of his travels in Persia and Afghanistan in search of the region's architectural treasures.
The Sewing Circles of Herat by Christina Lamb, Harper Collins (2002). A fascinating glimpse into life under the Taliban and the heroic resistance of a women's sewing group.
A Short Walk in the Hindu Kush by Eric Newby, Macmillan General Books (1997). Newby's account of his journey with a friend from London to the wild mountains of the Hindu Kush. One of the best travel books ever written.

Other Insight Guides

Other **Insight Guides** that highlight destinations in and near Central Asia include India, Russia and Estonia, Latvia & Lithuania.

TRANSPORT

GETTING THERE
AND GETTING AROUND

GETTING THERE

By Air

Iran

The national airline, Iran Air, flies direct from many European and Asian cities to Tehran. British Airways, Lufthansa, Austrian Airlines, KLM, Turkish Air and Gulf Air also fly to Tehran. Tehran's aged airport at Mehrabad is located only 10km (6 miles) west of the city centre, but the new Iman Khomeini Airport south of Tehran is now handling more international flights.

Syria

The international airport at Damascus is surprisingly small, with relatively few flights each day. Larger European airlines including Air France, Turkish Airlines and British Airways fly here, but often not daily. Services from the Middle East are better. Aleppo is the other international airport, with less choice, and it could be the same plane calling to/from Damascus.

Lebanon

Rafik Hariri International Airport to the south of Beirut is the home of

Departure Taxes

There is a departure tax of around US$13 to be paid on flights departing Syria. Departure taxes for flights from Iran and Lebanon are usually included in the price of the ticket. There is no departure tax for non-nationals flying from Turkish airports.

Middle East Airlines (www.mea.com. lb). It operates flights to Europe, the Middle East and Africa. Some European airlines, including British Airways and Air France, also fly into Beirut.

Turkey

Air transport is excellent and cheap, with regular scheduled international flights into Istanbul, Ankara and Antalya, several low-cost carriers serving both Istanbul and Antalya, and numerous charter flights into Antalya in summer.

By Bus

The days of the "hippie trail" which wound its way from Europe to Afghanistan, via Iraq and Iran, are long gone, but theoretically it is still possible to follow a similar route. Turkey and Turkmenistan would be the modern entry and exit points, and some overland tour buses and trucks still manage to make the crossings. If entering and departing across these land borders, the maximum length of a transit visa is 10 days, which can normally be extended in the major cities. All visas and paperwork should be completed in advance of reaching the Iranian border.

Iran

Express coaches run almost daily between Tehran (and Tabriz) and Istanbul, Ankara and Erzurum in Turkey. There is also a daily service into Azerbaijan.

Syria

The bus links with Turkey are particularly good, with Aleppo and Damascus being directly linked

with Antakya, Ankara and Istanbul. Check timings in case departures are at inconvenient times as, for example, the two buses going from Damascus to Antakya leave at 10pm daily from the Harasta terminal. There are express bus services from Damascus to Amman. In addition to buses to Beirut, it is also possible to travel there by minibus or taxi (see below).

Lebanon

The bus and taxi links between Damascus (Syria) and Beirut are fast and reliable. The taxis that run between Lebanon and Syria are usually the old, large American gas-guzzlers.

Turkey

There are coach services across Europe to Istanbul with Eurolines (www.eurolines.co.uk), plus coaches linking Antakya with Damascus (Syria), and towns in the far east of the country with Georgia, Armenia and Iran.

By Train

Many of the countries of Central and Western Asia are keen to promote the idea of rail travel along the Silk Road, but any serious journey soon gets bogged down in impracticalities. Irregular and uncertain train services (some only for freight or non-foreigners), not to mention different gauges and border restrictions, mean that crossing between countries can be extremely difficult. Having said that, rail travel within each country can be a real delight. The overnight trains through Uzbekistan are always great fun, and if you can get tickets, the ride

ABOVE: travelling in style in Isfahan, Iran.

across northern Iran is great value. There are two weekly train services leaving Tehran that are useful. The Trans-Asia Express goes to Istanbul and another goes to Aleppo, both via Tabriz and Lake Van. See www.seat61.com for more information and timetables.

Iran

The only passenger railway connection operates across the Turkish border from Tehran to Lake Van and beyond.

Syria

The romance of international train travel still lives on with a weekly service from Istanbul, in Turkey, to Aleppo and Damascus, in Syria, which takes a couple of days. However, at the time of writing this service was suspended. There is theoretically a twice-weekly service along the old Hejaz railway from Damascus to Amman, but it takes double the bus time and is not very comfortable.

Turkey

There are rail links to Istanbul from Europe via Bulgaria, and the famed Orient Express passenger train (www.orient-express.com) even goes back there once or twice a year. There is a weekly service onwards to Aleppo and Damascus in Syria from Istanbul, which takes a couple of days. Rail Europe can provide timetables and tickets for travel in Turkey. In the UK, contact (08448) 484 064 or www.raileurope.co.uk; in the US, contact (1-800-622 8600) or www.raileurope.com.

GETTING AROUND

By Air

Iran

Iran Air (www.iranair.com) operates internal services to Ahvas, Bandar Abbas, Isfahan, Mashhad, Shahrekord, Shiraz and Tabriz among other destinations. These and many other destinations are also served by newer, smaller airlines such as Caspian Air, Iran Aseman (www.iaa.ir), Taban (www.tabanair.ir), Saha Air, Eram Air, Qeshm Air (www.qeshm-air.com) and Mahan Air (www.mahan.aero). Many Iranians use the internal airlines as their primary means of transport over longer distances, so flights are often booked up well in advance. Be aware, however, that international embargoes have had a detrimental impact on the upkeep of Iranian aircraft and, consequently, Iran's air safety record.

Syria

Distances are not so great that flying is essential. Syria Air (www.syriaair.com) operates internal flights between Damascus, Aleppo, Lattakia, Qamishli and Deir ez-Zor, all at reasonable prices.

Lebanon

There are no internal flights in Lebanon due to the small size of the country.

Turkey

There is a wide network of domestic flights operated by

Turkish Airlines (www.thy.com), Onur Air (www.onurair.com.tr), Atlas Jet (www.atlasjet.com) and Fly Air (www.flyair.com.tr).

By Train

Iran

The railway service is not extensive, and all lines radiate inconveniently out from Tehran. The services generally run on time and are at least comparable with express coach journey times. Men and women are sometimes in separate compartments, but mixed tourist groups are allowed. The two metro lines running underneath Tehran may also be useful.

Syria

Syria's limited train network operates quite well, although it is not particularly useful for destinations on the Silk Road. Railway lines on maps do not always mean passenger services, as some are just for freight or minerals, such as the line towards Palmyra. Even between the large cities of Damascus, Homs, Hama, Aleppo, Raqqa, Deir ez-Zor and Qamishli the train will take at least double the time of a bus.

Lebanon

There is currently no rail network in operation in Lebanon.

Turkey

The train network in Turkey is limited, with few lines and infrequent services, although these do happen to coincide with some Silk Road destinations. Inter-rail, Eurodomino and Balkan Flexipass tickets are valid in Turkey; Eurail passes are not. A cheap 30-day Train Tour Card (www.tcdd.gov.tr) offers unlimited travel throughout the country.

By Bus and Minibus

Iran

Express coaches serve many towns and cities and are a popular, quick and reliable way to get around the country. Bus stations are usually located along ring roads on the outskirts of towns, which often require a taxi journey into the centre. Tehran has several huge bus terminals in the suburbs, generally located in the direction of travel. In rural areas men and women are sometimes seated apart, but on longer coach journeys both sexes sit together.

Border Crossings

Travel between Western Asian countries is generally straightforward, although it is advisable to organise visas in advance, particularly if crossing the border from Syria into Lebanon because of the unpredictable political situation. See individual Places chapters for information on entering and leaving Western Asian countries.

Syria

Damascus is the international hub from where all parts of the country can be easily reached, especially as access from Iraq is not possible.

Distances within the country are quite small and easily covered by a bus in a day, with comfort stops every few hours. Competition is fierce between the companies, and prices are excellent value. Several companies like Kadmous, Omar and al-Rayan organise inter-city "Luxury" bus travel in modern air conditioned coaches. Next come the older government-owned Karnak fleet, followed by the slightly cheaper, noisier and slower "Pullman" service, which often departs from a different bus terminal.

Buy your tickets a day in advance if possible. Most large bus companies have offices in the city centre as well as at the terminal. In Damascus double-check where the bus is departing from and allow plenty of time to get through the traffic.

Smaller towns and villages are served by private minibus services

BELOW: a battered Merc in Yazd.

that follow reasonably set times and leave from yet another terminal.

Lebanon

Distances are small and easily covered in a day. Buses and minibuses are good options around the towns and cities.

Turkey

Coaches are the main form of long-distance inexpensive travel in Turkey, and every town and city has a bus station. With every competing company running its own booking kiosk, it's probably easier to go via a travel agent who will book you onto the service that fits with your timings.

Taxis

There are plenty of taxis in all larger towns and cities. Try to get the meter activated, but as many drivers will refuse to do so it is best to agree the fare beforehand. No journey within a city should cost more than a few US dollars, except in Turkey where fuel is more expensive. If visiting out-of-town sights, don't forget to arrange for the return trip as well or you could get stranded.

Shared Taxis

These are great fallbacks should you fail to get a bus ticket or miss a departure. The large taxis leave (usually not far from the bus station) when they are full and are faster, but more expensive. If the waiting proves too much, you can offer to pay the set fare for the "empty" seats to get it moving. Within cities, shared taxis run along set routes, picking up and dropping off as they go. Should you be the last person in the taxi, the drivers will sometimes take you direct to your destination, such as a hotel.

Driving

Vehicles can be brought into all the countries in this region with the correct paperwork, or hired through international companies like Hertz, Europcar, Avis and Sixt. Drivers must be at least 21 years old and hold an International Driving Permit and national driving licence.

However, unless you are staying for an extended period, speak and read good Arabic, Farsi or Turkish, and know exactly where you are going, it makes more sense to hire a car and driver for about the same rate as a self-drive car.

Iran

Vehicles can be brought in and driven around Iran, but this is a serious undertaking in such a dangerous traffic-accident country. Some of the major car-hire companies advertise at arrivals halls, but these would tend to be for Iranian or Arab nationals rather than Western tourists. Europcar advertises through Iran Tour (www. irantour.org), but the prices include a driver. To drive in Iran you would need an International Driving Permit (check which sort), national licence and suitable insurance cover.

Syria

Vehicles can be rented through Hertz, Europcar, Sixt and Avis. Local car-hire companies include Middle East Travel Service (www. victoria-syria.com) and Marmou (www. marmou.com). However, unless you are staying in the country for an extended period, speak and read good Arabic and know exactly where you are going, it makes more sense to hire a car and driver for about the same rate. There are good signposts in Arabic and English along the highways and to the major sites, but it is often difficult to find a remote site, and so a local Syrian guide/ driver is invaluable.

Lebanon

All the major international car-hire companies and many local ones will rent vehicles to foreigners.

Lebanon is a small country with all the major routes radiating from Beirut. The main highway is along the coast, from where roads reach inland to the mountains. During periods of unrest in Lebanon you might be stopped at roadblocks along the coast road, which passes close to the many Palestinian refugee camps.

Turkey

You can hire a car through Hertz, Europcar, Sixt and Avis or any number of local companies. Car hire is not particularly cheap, and fuel is extremely expensive (diesel is cheaper than petrol).

The condition of the roads in Turkey is usually reasonable, although if you can avoid driving at night, you would do well to do so. The roads are not well lit, nor well enough signposted, so it is advisable to drive defensively. It is also a good idea to have your address written down to help when asking passers-by for directions.

ACCOMMODATION

HOTELS AND B&BS

Choosing a Hotel

The tourist infrastructure in **Iran** is still undeveloped, with a few four- and five-star hotels, basic hostels for local travellers and not much in between. In many cases the choice of hotel will have already been made for you as part of a tour package. The lack of good quality two- and three-star accommodation means that most organised tours are either quite expensive, limited in the itineraries they offer or stay in hotels that might not come up to Western standards. Experienced tourists acknowledge that the standard of a five-star hotel in Iran is not quite the same as in Europe or the US.

While tourism tries to establish itself, hotel facilities such as room service or the quality and range of breakfast might be less than visitors expect because staff are relatively inexperienced and do not speak much English, so be patient and flexible.

Large hotel chains in **Syria** like Sheraton, Four Seasons, Meridien and locally owned Cham offer standard international rates for rooms and facilities. There are also numerous first- and second-class hotels throughout the country charging US$100–250 per person per night. Small hotels and apartments near universities are good value outside term time.

A recent development is the conversion of palaces and houses in the old cities into small boutique hotels (US$40–175 per person per night). This started in Aleppo with the wonderful Beit Wakil (www.beitwakil. com), and now there are many similar. Damascus followed with the Beit al-Mamlouka (www.almamlouka. com) and others, aimed at the long-

weekend holiday traveller.

Lebanon can be a popular tourist destination, with a range of hotels from five-star luxury to rural B&Bs. Luxury hotels and resorts are concentrated in and around Beirut, along the coast and at the main ski centres. Most hotel staff speak fluent English, French and Arabic.

In **Turkey** there is a huge selection of excellent hotels in Istanbul and Cappadocia, from international chains to delightful historic boutique hotels. Elsewhere along the route the choice is strictly limited. In many places, however, there are restored historic houses that offer excellent accommodation, some with restaurants, at prices of around US$75–250 per night for a double room.

A Turkish *pansiyon* is somewhere between a simple hotel and a bed and breakfast, popular with Turkish holiday-makers. They can be lovely places to stay, especially if run by a family. The more expensive will have en suite facilities in every room.

Hostels

There are no youth hostels in **Iran**. There are basic hostels, known as *mosaferkhunehs*, for local travellers, but these do not always permit foreigners. A better option for budget travellers is to stay at one- and two-star hotels, some of which are decent and reasonably priced.

Youth hostels and student dormitories are available during the summer season in Damascus, Aleppo and Latakia, in **Syria**.

One of the main developments in **Lebanon** over the past few years is the rise of eco-tourism and the opportunity of spending a few nights

in local communities. Some families are opening their homes to visitors on a B&B basis (typically US$10–40) to offer an authentic Lebanese experience.

Accommodation is so reasonably priced in **Turkey** that there are very few youth hostels as such. It is possible, out of term-time, to stay in empty student dormitories or halls of residence or in teachers' accommodation *(ogretmen evi)*, but the rooms will be spartan and often no cheaper than the cheapest ordinary *pansiyon (see above)* or hotel.

Camping

The authorities in **Iran** are not keen for tourists to stay too far off the beaten track, and certainly not in tents. Iranians have recently taken to camping, and now take every opportunity of pitching a tent on any piece of open ground. If camping is a part of your tour, then this will be arranged through your tour operator, who will get the necessary permits.

There are few official campsites in **Lebanon**, but there are some on the outskirts of cities and at summer resorts in **Syria**. On the coast there are numerous seasonal tourist camping sites and chalets of various categories and prices.

You can actually camp anywhere in **Turkey** except designated historic or natural sites, provided you don't damage farmland or light fires in forests. For most trekking activities camping is necessary. The best camping areas are close to the seaside resorts, and have all the necessary facilities, including showers, shops, restaurants and activities. They generally cost around as much as staying in a cheap hotel.

IRAN

Tehran

Canary
168 Sommaye Avenue, between Forsat and Moffateh Avenues
Tel: (021) 882 5616-7
www.hotel-canary.com
Excellent-value, modern downtown hotel with a great restaurant downstairs. **$$**

Enghelab
50 Taleghani Avenue, between Hafez and Valiasr Avenues
Tel: (021) 8893 7251-5
www.enghelab.parsianhotels.ir
Imposing high-rise building in city centre, popular with conferences. Café and three restaurants. **$$**

Ferdowsi International Grand Hotel
20 Kooshk e Mesri street, Ferdossi Avenue, north of Imam Khomeini Square
Tel: (021) 6672 7026-31
www.ferdowsihotel.com
Good hotel ideally located close to the bazaar and the National Museum. There are 185 rooms and facilities include satellite TV, plus a coffee shop and several restaurants. **$$**

Iranshahr
75 Southern Iranshahr Street , between Sommaye and Enghelab Avenues
Tel: (021) 8831 0995-9/8884 6650-1
www.hotel-iranshahr.com
Pleasant smaller hotel with 48 rooms, well located downtown. Facilities include a coffee shop and restaurant. The owner is the head of the Tehran Hotels Association. **$$**

Laleh
Dr Fatemi Avenue, north of Laleh Park
Tel: (021) 8896 6021-9
www.lalehhotel.com

Luxury hotel with French and Polynesian restaurants, swimming pool and sauna. Located to the north of the city, close to the National Carpet Museum. **$$$**

Naderi
572 Jomhuri Avenue, between Ferdowsi and Hafez Avenues
Tel: (021) 6670 86106670 1872/6672 0791
Small hotel and café located near the British Embassy. **$**

Tehran Grand
2 Valiasr Avenue, on corner of Motahari Avenue
Tel: (021) 8871 9610
www.tehrangrandhotel.com
Large hotel with 200 rooms, in a 20-year-old tower block situated to the north of the centre. Also has traditional and self-service restaurants. **$$**

Isfahan

Abbasi
PO Box 81465, Charbagh Avenue, Amedgah Street
Tel: (031) 1 222 6010-9
www.abbasihotel.ir
Classic, luxury hotel with 230 rooms, swimming pool, library and own museum, all in the heart of Isfahan. Modern facilities within an 18th-century caravanserai with beautiful Safavid architecture, renovated in 1967. **$$$**

Ali Qapu
Chahar Bagh Avenue
Tel: (031) 1 222 7929
www.aliqapuhotel.com
Good, centrally located hotel with 104 rooms, coffee shop, restaurants and swimming pool. **$$**

Hasht Behesht
Tel: **(031) 1 220 0967**
www. ehbhotel.webs,com

A welcoming, family-run apartment hotel with helpful, English-speaking staff and clean bathrooms. Great location. **$–$$**

Safir
Amedgah Street
Tel: (031) 1 222 2640/9412
www.safirhotel.net
Centrally located modern hotel with coffee shop, restaurant and sauna. **$$**

Shiraz

Arg
Takhti Street
Tel: (071) 1 222 8989
www.arghotel.ir
Smaller hotel near centre with restaurant and internet. **$**

Homa Hotel
Meshkinfam, next to Azadi Park
Tel: (071) 1 228 8000
www.homahotels.com
Comfortable hotel set in beautiful surroundings. The staff can arrange tours to Persepolis and Pasargadae. **$$**

Parse
22 Bahman Street
Tel: (071) 1 222 6600
New hotel with 70 rooms, a coffee shop and a restaurant. Located near the city centre. **$$**

Yazd

Silk Road
5 Tal-e Khakestary Alley, close to Jama Mosque
Tel: (035) 1 625 2730
www.silkroadhotel.ir
Beautifully converted traditional house around central covered courtyard, in Old Town. **$**

Tabriz

Azarbayjan
North Shariati Street

Tel: (041) 1 555 9051-3
Good-value modern place with 47 rooms in the centre of the city. **$**

Gostaresh
Imam Khomeini Street, just at Azadi Square
Tel: (041) 1 334 5021-4
www.gostaresh-hotel.com
Large and somewhat uninspiring hotel about 3km (2 miles) from the city centre. **$$**

Mashhad

Ferdowsi Grand
20 Modarres Blvd
Tel: (051) 1 221 6162-6
Email: mashhad_ferdosi_grandhotel@yahoo.com
New 14-floor hotel on the edge of the city centre with coffee shop and restaurants. **$$**

Pars
Vakilabad Blvd
Tel: (051) 1 868 9201
Up-market hotel complex 8km (5 miles) west of the centre. Rooms are spacious and very clean, but the location is too far away from Mashhad's main sites if you don't have a car. **$$**

Salam
6 Pasdaran Street
Tel: (051) 1 851 8950-8
Email: salam_hotel@yahoo.com
A new smaller hotel situated in a quiet area about 2km (1 mile) from the centre. **$**

Hamadan

Azadi Parsian
Eram Blvd
Tel: (081) 1 825 2001-4
www.azadihamedan.parsianhotels.ir
Good food and rooms on outer ring road, part of the Parsian International Hotels chain. **$$**

SYRIA

Damascus

Afamia
Behind the main post office off Jamhuriya Street, PO Box 5565
Tel: (011) 222 9152/222 8963
www.afamiahotel.com
Popular with small tour groups and offers good value

in the middle of the city. Forty-two air conditioned rooms. **$**

Al-Iwan
Bahasa Street, PO Box 6759
Tel: (011) 232 1476
www.hoteliwan.com
Centrally located 100

metres north of Martyr's Square, off Al-Ittihad Street. Good value, with 57 rooms spread over eight floors. **$$**

Beit al-Mamlouka
Al-Qaimariyeh district of the Old City near Bab Touma
Tel: (011) 543 0445-6

www.almamlouka.com
Just off a narrow alley near Bab Touma, this is a beautiful conversion of a 17th century Damascene house set around a small courtyard. The owner, May Mamarbachi, holds a PhD in Islamic architecture from SOAS in London, and supervised the entire operation and redecoration. There are only eight bedrooms (two singles, two doubles and four suites), with terraces and private patios. It also features an old stable, converted into a gallery, restaurant and bar. **$$$**

Fardoss Tower
Fardoss Street, PO Box 30996
Tel: (011) 223 2100-3
www.fardosstower.com
Tower-block hotel with 100 rooms near Yusef al-Azmeh Square. Popular with European tour groups, it offers two restaurants, piano bar and night club. **$$**

Four Seasons
Shukri al-Quwatli Street, PO Box 6311
Tel: (011) 339 1000
www.fourseasons.com/Damascus
The new luxury hotel and distinctive landmark in the middle of the city. All the facilities as expected, including DVD players and internet access in rooms, spa, gym and outdoor pool. **$$$**

Salam
Halbony, PO Box 10443
Tel: (011) 221 6674/9764
Email: salamhotel@mail2world.com
On a side street almost opposite the Tekkiye near the museum. Close to the university, which means it is full during term, but offers good value in holidays. **$**

Talisman
116 Tal El-Hijara Street, off Straight Street in the Old City near the Roman Arch
Tel: (011) 541 5379
www.talismanhotels.com
This old Jewish palace, built on a quiet side street, has been restored in the most authentic tradition of an Arab house. Sixteen rooms

surround the central garden with fruit trees and a small swimming pool. Delightful. **$$$**

Aleppo

Baron
Baron Street
Tel: (021) 211 0880-1
Email: hotelbaron@scs-net.org, hotelbaron@mail.sy
Not many hotels have streets named after them, but this is the famous hotel where Lawrence of Arabia, Agatha Christie and many others have stayed since 1911. Thirty-five classic rooms, recently renovated with air conditioning. The old travel posters and bar are a throwback to the glory days of the Orient Express. **$$**

Beit Wakil
Al-Hatab Square, Sissi Street, Jdeida
Tel: (021) 211 9776
www.beitwakil.com
Owner Habib Bassous was the first to renovate one of these beautiful 16th-century Aleppine palaces, keeping the 16 rooms as authentic as possible. Good restaurant, atmospheric cellar bar and tunnels that are said to go to the Citadel. **$$**

Dar Zamaria (Martini)
Just east of Al-Hatab Square, Jdeida
Tel: (021) 363 6100
www.darzamaria.com
Two larger restored 17th-century houses linked by a bridge across an alleyway. Fifty rooms and a courtyard, plus a restaurant, bar and

rooftop terrace open in summer. **$$**

Ramsis
Baron Street, PO Box 5097
Tel: (021) 211 1102/211 1040-2
www.ramsishotel.com
Centrally located five-storey hotel completely renovated in 2003. Good value, with 28 rooms and eight suites, streetside café and rooftop restaurant with excellent views over the city towards the distant Citadel. **$$**

Palmyra

Orient (al-Sharq)
Palmyra town centre
Tel: (031) 910131
Just off the main road in the centre of town with many similar hotels around, popular with smaller tour groups. Good views from the rooftop restaurant. **$**

Tadamora Palace
Main Entrance Road
Tel: (031) 5915 701
www.sixsenses.com
Luxurious hotel and spa complex within walking distance of the Roman Temple of Bel. Rooms and bathrooms are large and attractively decorated. Free internet access.

Deir Ez-Zor

Ziad
Abu Bakr as-Saddiq Street
Tel: (051) 227338/(051) 214596
www.ziadhotel.com
Clean, friendly hotel close to the centre of town beside a pleasant canal leading to the Euphrates river, about 1km (0.6 mile) away. **$**

BELOW:the courtyard at Hotel Biet Wakil in Aleppo.

LEBANON

Beirut

Cedarland
Abdel Aziz Street, Hamra
Tel: (01) 340 233
www.cedarlandhotel.com
Comfortable budget hotel ideally situated in heart of the lively Hamra District. Air conditioned rooms, laundry service and satellite TV. **$**

Intercontinental Le Vendome
PO Box 13, Ain Mreysseh
Tel: (01) 369 280
www.levendomebeirut.com
Smaller luxury hotel with 73 rooms, located right on the coast. Spacious rooms have satellite TV and DVD players and free broadband internet. **$$$**

Intercontinental Phoenicia Hotel
Rue Fakhr ed-Dine
Minet al-Hosn
Tel: (01) 369 100
www.ichotelsgroup.com

Renovated pre-war hotel with a lavish interior. All the facilities you would expect from an international-standard hotel. **$$$**

Palm Beach
Ain Mreysseh
Tel: (01) 372 000
www.palmbeachbeirut.com
Recently renovated four-star hotel with 87 rooms. Facilities include a rooftop restaurant and a swimming pool and gym. **$$$**

Hotel Riviera
Corniche el-Manara
Tel: (01) 373 219
www.rivierahotel.com.lb
Mid-range hotel situated away from the centre, along the beach, with on-site yacht club facilities. Has 105 air conditioned rooms with internet access and satellite TV. Friendly hotel staff can arrange transport and sightseeing tours. **$$**

TURKEY

Diyarbakir

Class Hotel
Gazi Caddesi 101
Tel: (0412) 229 5000/213 7787
Not particularly exciting, but a good safe bet – a comfortable four-star business hotel in the city centre, within walking distance of all the main sights. **$$**

Mardin

Erdoba Evleri
1 Cadde 135
Tel: (0482) 212 7677/213 7787
www.erdoba.com.tr
Magnificent restored mansion in the Old City with a terrace overlooking the ramparts, and a café-restaurant. **$$**

Antakya

Grand Antakya Hotel
Ataturk Caddesi 8
Tel: (0326) 213 5858
www. buyukantakyaoteli.com
Comfortable, modern hotel with large, light rooms and three restaurants, one with a terrace. **$$**

Savon Hotel
Kurtulus Caddesi 192
Tel: (0326) 214 6355
www.savonhotel.com.tr
An elegantly restored 19th-century soap and olive oil factory, now a charming boutique hotel with a restaurant and fountain courtyard. **$$**

Cappadocia

Esbelli Evi
Esbelli Sok. 8, 50400 Ürgüp
Tel: (0384) 341 3395
www.esbelli.com
Several connected old houses, comfortably furnished with antiques and run with laid-back charm. Eight rooms. **$$**

Les Maisons de Cappadoce
Belediye Meyd. 28 ,50240 Üçhisar
Tel: (0384) 219 2782
www.cappadoce.com
Luxuriously architect-restored village houses, with kitchens and gardens. Minimum stay of four nights. Two apartments and six houses available. Cash payment only. **$$**

Serinn House
Esbelli Sokak 36, Ürgüp
Tel: (0384) 341 6076
www.serinnhouse.com
Five-room luxury cave hotel with city-chic design, superb views and friendly hosts. **$$**

Konya

Hotel Balıkçılar
Mevlana Karøısı 2, Karatay
Tel: (0332) 350 9470
www.balikcilar.com
Comfortable if dull hotel overlooking the Mevlana, with all the facilities, including a hammam (bathing house), restaurant, bar and roof terrace. **$$**

Afyon

Orucoglu Thermal Resort Hotel
Kutahya yolu 14 km, Afyonkarahisar
Tel: (0272) 251 5050
www.orucoglu.com.tr
Major spa resort with 330 rooms, 14km (8 miles) from the centre of Afyon. Facilities include recreational and therapeutic spa treatments, waterslides and mud baths, plus gardens, pools, restaurant and bar. **$$–$$$**

Bursa

Hotel Çelik Palas
Çekirge Caddesi 79, 16070
Tel: (0224) 233 3800
www.celikpalasotel.com
A grand 1930s spa hotel, combined with a modern five-star hotel, with a sumptuous hammam (bathing house). **$$$**

Otantik Club Hotel
Botanik Parkı, Soganli
Tel: (0224) 211 3280
www.otantikclubhotel.com
A restored Ottoman house with 29 rooms and traditional decor, situated in the park. Facilities include spa, indoor swimming pool, garden, restaurant and bar. **$$–$$$**

Istanbul

Basileus
Sehit Mehmet Pasa Sok. 1, Sultanahmet
Tel: (0212) 517 7878
www.basileushotel.com

ABOVE: typical accommodation at Les Maisons de Cappadoce.

Charming boutique hotel in an old house in the centre of Sultanahmet. Rooms are large, linens are crisp and the buffet breakfast delicious. Highly recommended. **$$**

Divan
Asker Ocağı Caddesi 1Tel: (0212) 315 5500
www.divan.com.tr
A relatively small, first-rate hotel with 169 rooms and 11 suites, and one of the most distinguished restaurants in Istanbul. A few rooms have private terraces. **$$$**

Four Seasons Hotel
Tevkifhane Sok. 1, Sultanahmet
Tel: (0212) 402 3000
www.fourseasons.com/Instanbul
An Ottoman prison in the Old City, now one of Istanbul's finest hotels, with one of the city's best restaurants, a superb rooftop view and a health club. **$$$**

Hotel Hanedan
Akbiyik Caddesi, Sultanahmet
Tel: (0212) 516 4869
www.hotelhanedan.com
Sultanahmet's best budget hotel is central and with excellent staff and delicious breakfasts. Rooms on the upper floor have views out to the Marmara Sea. **$**

Mavi Ev (Blue House)
Dalbastı Sokak 14, Sultanahmet
Tel: (0212) 638 9010
www.bluehouse.com.tr
Pretty blue restored Ottoman house behind the Arasta Bazaar and Blue Mosque – great location

and superb views, friendly staff, attractive furnishings and a rooftop restaurant. **$$$**

Merit Antique
Küçük Ayasofya Caddesi 17, Sultanahmet
Tel: (0212) 5160 997
www.hotelantique.com
This lovingly restored early 20th-century apartment complex in the heart of the old city is now a charming hotel with 274 rooms. Superb Chinese, Turkish and Kosher patisserie, wine bar and health club. **$$$**

Sarniç Hotel
Küçük Ayasofya Sok. 26, Sultanahmet
Tel: (0212) 518 2323
www.sarnichotel.com
One of the cheaper special hotels in the Old City, with simple but pretty decor, cookery classes, its own masseur and a Byzantine cistern in the basement. **$$**

Sumahan on the Water
Kuleli Caddesi 51, Çengelköy
Tel: (0216) 422 8000
www.sumahan.com
A beautifully converted raki factory on the Asian shore of the Bosphorus, with fabulous views and a magnificent seafood restaurant. **$$$**

PRICE CATEGORIES

Price categories are for a double room with breakfast/tax.

$ = less than US$50
$$ = 50–150
$$$ = over US$150

EATING OUT

RECOMMENDED RESTAURANTS AND CAFES

What to Eat

Other than the major hotels in **Iran** there are surprisingly few restaurants to choose from, even in a large city like Tehran. A few offer Persian dishes like the excellent *fesanjan* (chicken or duck in rich pomegranate and walnut sauce), and some specialise in international fare such as Indian, Korean, Chinese or Lebanese. Most Iranians socialise with their family and apart from business meetings would eat at home, so there is little trade to keep many restaurants in business. Persian food is generally very good and healthy, with many regional specialities prepared from fresh ingredients consisting of rice, meat, nuts, fruits, vegetables and herbs. For convenience, many of your meals are likely to be variations of lamb, mutton or chicken kebabs, which Iranians know how to prepare and cook very well.

Visitors to **Syria** will usually find something to their liking as Syrian cuisine is well known for its variety, but the quality differs tremendously. Try to find a restaurant that has as few items on the menu as possible and is popular with the locals. Stick to the basics – fish along the coast, meat in the mountains, pasta and rice in the desert, and you won't go far wrong.

However, finding a local place with excellent food can be a real highlight. Some of the old Damascus and Aleppo houses converted into restaurants have amazing atmosphere and great food. *Meze* is a range of small starters. There are almost 20 varieties of *kibbeh*, small pastries with different fillings. The Syrian Academy of Gastronomy has its own website with information and recipes (www.gastrosyr.com/eng).

In **Lebanon**, Beirut is well served with high-quality restaurants, and its food is rightly famous around the world as a blend of Western and oriental flavours. Despite recent problems, top restaurants in the Central District remain fully booked, especially over weekends. Along the coast are many local places specialising in fish and countless others offering a wide range of Western and Middle Eastern dishes. The area of Achrafiye has many trendy restaurants, while the coastal views over Pigeon Rocks at Raouche are popular sunset eateries.

A typical quick breakfast in Syria and Lebanon is a bowl full of *foul madames*, consisting of beans, olive oil, lemon and herbs. In the city centres there are countless fast-food outlets ranging from sliced *shawarma* (meat served with salad in local bread) and *falafel* sandwiches to Western burgers, fries and pizzas. Also look for *börek* (savoury pastries), *gözleme* (pancakes, usually served with a tomato sauce), and *lahmacun* (thin pizzas).

Everything is on offer in **Turkey**, from grand palaces to modern chic restaurants and backstreet cafés. A *restoran* will usually specialise in either *et* (meat) or *balık* (seafood); all offer a wide range of *meze* with salads and dips, such as *hummus*, which can be a meal in themselves. Fish costs at least twice as much as meat. Lower down the scale, the *lokanta* can be anything from a cheerful self-service cafeteria to an atmospheric brasserie.

Drinks

Tea *(chay)* is undoubtedly the national drink of **Iran**, and always served hot, black and strong. Some of the most memorable places are the atmospheric teahouses, known as *chaykhanes*. Coffee beans are an expensive import, and the local replacement coffee mixtures are unlikely to stimulate much appreciation, apart from thick, rich Turkish coffees. Delicious fruit and vegetable juices, milkshakes and yoghurt drinks are all freshly made throughout the country. Alcohol is strictly forbidden, though it is permitted for religious purposes, such as communion wine in churches, and to non-Muslims with special permission, but not tourists.

Most people prefer to drink bottled water produced from the many natural springs in **Syria**, especially in the mountains between Damascus and Aleppo. Beer and wine is available in some restaurants, but not all. There are a few bars and alcohol shops, generally in Christian areas.

Lebanon's café and bar scene rivals that of any major European city. The recently restored Beirut Central District and Gemmayzeh area are usually buzzing with activity well into the night with lively music and theme bars. Here the Mediterranean aniseed drink is called *arak*, to be sipped with a splash of iced water, while the Lebanese climate is perfect for making high-quality wines. Traditionally, at the end of the meal, black Turkish coffee is offered.

Bottled water is freely available in **Turkey**, which also produces reasonable beer and wine, although they are not available in all restaurants. There are plenty of bars in main cities and tourist centres, but elsewhere, the tea (*çay*) shop is the social centre. There are also excellent fresh fruit juices, according to season.

IRAN

Tehran

Akbar Mashti Bastani
Shahid Bahonar Avenue
The most famous ice cream parlour in Iran has been keeping Tehranis happy since the 1950s. **$**

Azari Teahouse
Valiasr Ave
One of the most popular meeting places in the south of the city is this attractive restored teahouse where musical performances enliven the evenings. **$**

Canary
92 Sommaye Avenue, between Forsat and Moffateh Avenues
Tel: (021) 882 5616-7
Popular modern Persian food restaurant, part of the Canary Hotel. **$$**

Chinese
3 Abdo Street, off Valiasr Avenue (opposite Fatemi Avenue)
Tel: (021) 8890 0714/8880 0163
Ideal if you want a few different spicy flavours. **$$**

Ghazakadeh Sonnati
Karimkhan Zand Blvd, 7 South Aban Street
Tel: (021) 8880 5868
Mobile: (912) 154 7248
Email: sonnatiaban@yahoo.com
Owner Medi lived in England for many years and provides traditional Persian food, including fesanjan. **$$**

Lounge
17 Erfani Alley, Mojdeh Street, Niavaran Avenue
Tel: (021) 2271 5953
One of the many new eateries in the plush northern suburbs around Tajrish. Narrow room, cool decor, tasty menu and trendy clientele. **$$$**

Shabestan
Nejatollahi Street, near Taleghani Avenue
Tel: (021) 8880 9766/8891 1951
Folklore music and Persian food served in this traditional restaurant. **$**

Taj Mahal
29 Mollasadra Avenue
Tel: (021) 8803 5444
Lively curry house with a wide selection of vegetarian dishes. **$–$$**

Isfahan

Bastani
127 Chaharsogh Maghsod Bazaar, Imam Khomeini Square
Tel: (031) 1 220 0374-5
Wonderful service and traditional food in a corner of the main square close to the Imam Mosque. **$**

Shahrzad
Abbas Abad Avenue, just off Chahar Bagh Avenue
Tel: (031) 1 220 4490
Very popular, ornately decorated place in good location offering Persian and Western food. **$$**

Shiraz

Sharzeh
Near Vakil Mosque
Tel: (071) 1 224 6648
Popular restaurant on the edge of the bazaar. **$$**

Yurd
Tel: (071) 1 625 6774
This open-air restaurant 8km (5 miles) northwest of Shiraz offers a real evening

ABOVE: freshly brewed *chay* in a teahouse in Isfahan.

adventure in the countryside and the opportunity to sample local food and music in a traditional tent. **$$**

Yazd

Khan Teahouse
Ghiam Street
Atmospheric teahouse with vaulted ceilings inside a former bathhouse. **$**

Malak o'Tojar
In the bazaar area off Qeyam Street
Tel: (035) 1 626 1479
Eat outside in the covered central courtyard of a restored house. **$$**

Tabriz

Baliq
Golshahr
Fabulous fish in 101 guises. Enjoy watching the fish in the tanks as you tuck in to their brethren on your plate. **$$**

Parvini
North Shariati Street
Tel: (041) 1 554 4965
Simple kebab restaurant serving high-quality food, just outside the bazaar. **$**

Mashhad

Bagh-e Sabz
Junction of Imam Khomeini Street and Modarres Street
Tel: (051) 1 222 2433
Long-established family restaurant with English-speaking staff. **$**

Hezardestan
Jannat Mall
Tel: (051) 1 222 2943
Newly built traditional teahouse with good food in a pleasant basement and live music at 9pm. Gets crowded after 11pm. **$$**

Hamadan

Payvand
Shariati Street (opposite side to Esther and Mordecai tomb)
Good-quality local food about 400 metres from Imam Khomeini Square. **$**

SYRIA

Damascus

Jabri House
Al-Sawaf Street
Tel: (011) 541 6254/544 3200
www.jabrihouse.com
Large covered courtyard restaurant serving many local dishes in a 1737 house, which has been in Raed Jabri's family for the last century. Extremely popular. **$**

Leila's
Kabakbieh Street, on the southeast corner of the Omayyid Mosque
Tel: (011) 9456
www.crmonline.info
Restaurant in covered courtyard (food only) and fantastic roof terrace (open 9pm, alcohol and drinks only) below Jesus minaret of mosque. Perfect place to wind down in the evening. Stunning. **$**

Omayyid Palace
Southeast of Omayyid Mosque in a narrow alley
Tel: (011) 222 0826
Large palatial downstairs restaurant, set buffet popular with tour groups. Extensive menu, music after 9pm. Their beautiful "cave bar" is a few doors down the alley. **$**

Whispers
Omayad Hotel, 1 Brazil Avenue
Tel: (011) 223 5500 ext. 30
www.omayad-hotel.com
Quality restaurant, part of the Swiss International Hotels Group, doubles as a lounge bar. **$$$**

Aleppo
There are several restaurants located in converted

PRICE CATEGORIES

Prices are for a meal per person:
$ = under US$10
$$ = US$10–25
$$$ = over US$25

old houses in and around Al-Hatab Square, in Jdeida District.

Al-Mir
Tel: (021) 211 6880
Beautiful interior arched sections. **$**

Beit Wakil
Tel: (021) 211 7083
www.beitwakil.com
Part of the Hotel Beit Wakil, with a taverna and "cave bar". **$$**

Cantara
Tel: (021) 225 3355
Italian specialities served in an open courtyard setting. **$**

Dar Zamaria
Tel: (021) 363 6100
www.darzamaria.com
Larger setting for courtyard restaurant, bar and roof terrace. **$$**

Mashrabia
Tel: (021) 211 5249
Small pub restaurant. **$**

Yasmeen House
Tel: (021) 222 5562
Local and Arabian specialities. **$**

Palmyra
Main Square, opposite Museum
Large and airy covered

eatery with plenty of shade, ceiling fans and attentive waiters. Serves alcohol. **$$**

Laylaty
Main Street, in front of the Commercial Bank of Syria
Tel: (051) 229 648/226 388
Italian food, mainly for a lively younger crowd, with fantastic decor. Stunning Art Deco design, with pastel ziggurats and starbursts, that has been in the family of boss Ismat Ayash since it was a cinema in the 1920s. No alcohol. **$**

ABOVE: dining in Damascus.

Lebanon

Al-Sultan Brahim
Minet el-Hosn, Starco Area, Downtown
Tel: (01) 989 989
www.sultanbrahim.com
Specialist high-quality fish and seafood restaurant,

with three other branches in Antelias, Aley and Ashrafieh. **$$$**

Café d'Orient
Ain Mreysseh
Tel: (01) 366 222
Email: cafedorient@idm.net.lb
Fish and seafood restaurant

in a fine period building overlooking the sea. **$$$**

La Piazza
Sodeco
Tel: (01) 339 449
One of several modern restaurants near Monot Street in Sodeco area. **$**

La Posta
287 Rue Maarad, Downtown
Tel: (01) 970 597
www.laposta-beirut.com
One of the many lively eateries near the Nejmeh Square clock tower. **$$**

Turkey

Hotel Büyük Kervansaray
Gazi Cad. Mardin Kapi Deliller Hani
The Seljuk caravanserai is still doing business as a hotel and restaurant – a bit chaotic as a place to stay, but great for a meal. **$$**

Antakya Evi Restoran
Silahli Kuvvetli Cad
Tel: (0326) 214 1350
Traditional Antakya mansion serving spicy eastern Turkish food in a maze of family-style rooms. **$$**

Old Greek House
Mustafapasa
Tel: (0384) 353 5345
Delightful frescoed house, just outside Ürgüp, with home-cooked food and a *hammam*. **$**

Haci Sukru
Devricedid Mah. Cem Sultan Caddesi

Fabulous *tandir* and kebabs cooked and presented in a traditional Konyan style. **$–$$**

Mevlevi Sofrası
Civar Mahallesi Nazimbey Caddesi 1- A, Karatay
Tel: (0332) 353 3341
Pleasant restaurant near the Mevlana offering traditional local cuisine. **$–$$**

Cumcurul
Çerkirge Cad
Tel: (0224) 235 3707
A restored Ottoman house in suburban Çekirge, with several rooms and a delightful garden; serving grilled and baked fish. **$$$**

Amedros
Hoca Rüstem Sokak 7, off Divanyolu
Tel: (0212) 522 8356
Perfectly positioned, just off Sultanahmet Square, this friendly café-restaurant is open all day, serving anything from a cup of coffee to a full meal. **$$**

Asitane
Kariye Oteli, Kariye Cami Sok. 18, Edirnekapi
Tel: (0212) 534 8414
Excellent restaurant near the Kariya Camii serving exotic Ottoman court cuisine, using recipes taken from the kitchens of Topkapi Palace. Outdoor courtyard and classical Turkish music. **$$$**

Feriye Lokantasi
Çiragan Caddesi 40, Ortaköy
Tel: (0212) 227 2216/7
Fashionable restaurant on the Bosporus serving Ottoman cuisine, including charcoal grills and an excellent Sunday brunch, with a fabulous waterfront setting. Booking ahead advisable. **$$$**

Havuzku Lokantası
Gani Çelebi Sokak 3, Kapalı Çarşı
Tel: (0212) 527 3346
Probably the best of several simple restaurants actually inside the Grand Bazaar, serving kebabs and meze on cast-iron coal ovens. Open Mon–Sat noon–4pm, lunch only; get there early. **$**

Kumkapi
Sahil Yolu, between Yenikapi and Sultanahmet
A former Byzantine fishing harbour, now surrounded by some 50 fish restaurants with wandering gypsy musicians; great food and atmosphere. **$$**

Leb-i-Derya
Kumbaraci Yokusu 115/7, Tünel, Beyoglu
Tel: (0212) 293 4989
Fashionable restaurant with cocktail bar, international cuisine, live music and a tiny roof terrace. **$$$**

Tria Elegance
Akbiyik Caddesi
The best Ottoman food in Istanbul comes from the kitchens of Tria Elegance. The *meze* includes delicious vegetarian dishes. **$$**

Prices are for a meal per person:

$ = under US$10
$$ = US$10–25
$$$ = over US$25

ACTIVITIES

THE ARTS, NIGHTLIFE, SPORT, OUTDOOR ACTIVITIES AND SHOPPING

THE ARTS

Art Galleries

There are art exhibitions at universities and museums in **Iran**, such as the Museum of Contemporary Art and Golestan Palace in Tehran. Paintings and sculptures by local artists are sometimes exhibited in private galleries in the cities. In a similar vein is the exquisite work of the miniature artists, most notably at Isfahan.

Artistic and cultural events are held throughout the year in **Syria**, with art exhibitions at universities, museums and cultural centres. Paintings and sculptures by local and foreign artists are exhibited in private galleries in the cities. Check the Ministry of Culture website (www.moc.gov.sy) for details.

There are several private galleries in **Beirut**, with one of the more stylish being Espace SD on Charles Helou Avenue (tel: (01) 563 114).

In **Istanbul**, you will find many small galleries tucked into the ground floor of office headquarters. There are also small commercial galleries, some of which double up as bars or cafés. Current exhibitions will be featured in city-guide magazines, such as *The Guide*.

Concerts and Theatres

Traditional music is played in some local restaurants and teahouses in **Iran**. There are Iranian pop bands, but these are not appreciated by Iranian youth who prefer more famous international musicians. There are occasional classical and operatic performances at the Vahdat Concert Hall and Rudaki Hall in Tehran, but these and

other cultural events are strictly monitored by the Ministry of Culture and Islamic Guidance. The Tehran Symphony Orchestra plays at official engagements. Plays by national and foreign writers are sometimes performed at the Sangalaj Hall in Tehran, on Behesht Street, opposite Shahr Park.

The Dar al-Assad Theatre with its new opera house is **Syria**'s most recent attempt to boost its arts and culture scene and bring international performances into the country.

The Al-Qabbani Theatre is one of the oldest in the city, presenting serious shows of world literature, while local plays and musicals are performed by Syrian folk groups at the Workers Union Theatre. Information on cultural events can be found at www.opera-syria.org.

Lebanon was a centre for Arab drama, dance and music through the 1960s, and despite the recent problems, art groups try to offer regular performances. Details of events can be found at www.lebweb.com.

In **Turkey**, the huge Atatürk Kultur Merkezi (Atatürk Cultural Centre) on Taksim Square (tel: (0212) 251 5600) is home to Istanbul's symphony, opera and ballet and also host to the Istanbul Arts and Culture Festival. For what's on elsewhere in the city, get hold of the English-language *Turkish Daily News*. Outside Istanbul, there is relatively little along the route of the Silk Road – ask at the local tourist offices.

Cinemas

Cinema screens in Western Asia are dominated by Hollywood blockbusters, although home-grown dramas and comedies are occasionally shown.

Iranian films and their directors often hit the headlines at the major film festivals, but these art films are of little interest to Iranian audiences, who prefer more high-action films. Some Western films do get released in censored form and there is a steady trickle of acceptable Iranian movies.

NIGHTLIFE

Nightclubs and Bars

Iran

There is precious little nightlife in Iran by Western standards, but there are always films to watch at the cinema (see above), or games of billiards or pool. Otherwise it is endless rounds of tea and drags on the *qalyan* water pipes.

Syria

Damascus and Aleppo have large hotels offering nightclubs and discos, sometimes with live music. They tend to start late (around 10pm) and are often part of a set meal with drinks. The art of storytelling has all but disappeared, but a few places keep the tradition alive: try the An-Nafura Café just outside the eastern gate of the Omayyad mosque in Damascus. City-centre bathing houses (*hammams*) are open until midnight, but check the opening times for men and women.

Lebanon

For many years Lebanon was known as the nightspot of the Middle East. While it has struggled to maintain this image over the past decades, it still has a healthy nightlife. Bars and nightclubs are spread throughout the city, catering for almost every taste in music and activity.

Turkey

Istanbul is a major international city with the nightlife to go with it – fabulous restaurants, chic clubs, serious money, high culture and everything else. Beyond that, the options shrink rapidly to toe-curling hotel discos and traditional teahouses, although Cappadocia's resort hotels generally lay on a cabaret. City-centre bath houses (*hammams*) are open in the evenings.

SPORT

Spectator Sports

Football draws the big crowds, either to the stadiums or in front of the television to follow the national teams. Other popular sports include wrestling, basketball, volleyball, handball and judo. One peculiar spectator sport to go and watch in Iran is at the *zurkhaneh* (see page 327).

Participant Sports

Large cities have sports complexes for keen athletes, and some individuals have excelled at international level, like Ghada Shouaa who won Olympic gold for **Syria** in 1996 in the women's heptathlon. Tennis and boxing are popular, and there are many pools for single-sex swimming. In **Iran**, most sports are segregated between the sexes and include swimming, badminton, table tennis and bowling.

Some large hotels have pools and some resort hotels have tennis courts. Istanbul and Ankara in **Turkey** both have golf courses, but the country's golfing mecca is Belek near Antalya, on the south coast.

Fairs and Festivals

Most celebrations are connected to Islamic holidays (see Public Holidays, page 448). Others include:

Iran

February Fajr Film Festival, Tehran
March 21 Nauroz (New Year)
October Tehran Short Film and Iran International Documentary Festival

Syria

April/May International Flowers Fair (Damascus)
May–June Palmyra Festival
July Vine Festival (Suweida), Cotton Festival (Aleppo)
August Damascus International Fair
September Desert Festival (Deirezzor and Palmyra), Bosra Festival (every two years), Silk Road Festival

October Damascus Cinema Festival (every two years)
November Theatre Festival (Damascus; every two years)

Lebanon

February Al-Bustan Festival
July/August Baalbek Festival, Beiteddine Festival, Byblos International Festival, Tyre Festival, Aanjar Festival

Turkey

June traditional Kirkpinar Oil Wrestling Tournament (Edirne)
June–July Istanbul Arts Festival
September International Grape Harvest Festival (Ürgüp)
Sept–Nov Istanbul Bienal (odd-numbered years)
December Mevlâna Commemoration Ceremony (Konya)

OUTDOOR ACTIVITIES

Trekking

Day-walking is a popular activity in **Iran**, especially close to the main cities, such as around Darakeh and Darband along the lower slopes of the Alborz Mountains north of Tehran. More adventurous treks lasting several days would be in the remote regions around Tabriz or in the Zagros Mountains of central Iran, where the opportunities are endless. Treks to the Assassins' castles north of Qazvin, going from one village to another, offer amazing views if the weather is good. It is often cold and wet in the mountains even late into the spring, so autumn tends to be the best trekking season.

The mountainous region inland from the **Syrian** coast is perfect for trekking, amid ruined castles and dramatic scenery. But with no proper detailed maps, signs or routes, each hike along a track or footpath would certainly be an adventure. Similarly in **Turkey**, there are many excellent areas for trekking, but relatively few properly waymarked paths. Middle Earth Travel (see page 443) are pioneers in the field, setting up and managing long-distance footpaths; they also operate trekking holidays.

Mountaineering

The most established climbing routes are in the Alborz and Zagros ranges, which contain most of the highest mountains in **Iran**. The beautiful Alborz Mountains run in an arc along the southern edge of the Caspian Sea. At the eastern end is the 5,670-metre (18,700-ft) -high volcanic cone of Mt Damavand, the highest peak in Iran. Several specialist companies offer climbs to the summit. There are also many other peaks over 4,000 metres (13,000ft), many with mountaineering facilities. The website of the Iran Mountaineering Federation (http://msfi.ir/) and www.mountainzone.ir are useful sources of information on climbing. Climbing trips can be organised through Alpine Ascents (www.alpineascents.com/iran.asp).

There are also two climbing walls in Iran – the Bandyakhcall Wall, near the Shervin Hut, outside Tehran, and

BELOW: a riverside teahouse in Isfahan, Iran.

the Osson Wall, near the Osson Hotel just north of Darband Square.

Other Activities

Western Asia offers some excellent routes for mountain-biking and horse riding, such as near the Army Hospital, east of Darabad in **Iran**, and in Cappadocia, **Turkey**. The vast deserts of Iran make it possible to enjoy four-by-four trips over the sand dunes or explore the desert riding camels, and camping out at night.

In summer, the beaches of **Syria** and **Lebanon** are crowded with people involved in the many water sports including water-skiing, windsurfing and jet-skiing. Snorkelling, scuba-diving and fishing are also popular.

Some of the most popular sports in **Lebanon** in the winter months are skiing and snowboarding, and there are winter sports centres and resorts in the mountains. There is also skiing outside Bursa in **Turkey**.

For lovers of white-water rafting and canoeing there are some great runs in **Iran**, down the wild rivers running into the Caspian Sea, and in Cappadocia in **Turkey**.

Organised Tours

Iran

Given the visa and entry restrictions, most visitors will have to book on an organised tour simply to visit Iran. Many itineraries are similar, usually limited to Tehran, Isfahan, Shiraz and Yazd. The more adventurous will add on Hamadan, Kerman and maybe Tabriz. The Caspian coast is an interesting option through the summer months. Religious tourism covers the holy cities of Mashhad and Qom. For a personal itinerary contact one of the tour operators to see what they can offer, but it will be expensive to pay for your own vehicle, driver and national guide.

Tours can be booked through the Iranian tourism association's website (www.irpedia.com), or through **Iran Travel** (www.irantravel.biz) or Iran Tour (www.irantour.org). Here are some of the better Tehran-based operators:
Arg-E-Jadid
296 Motahari Avenue
Tel: (021) 8883 3583
www.atc.ir
Azudi International Tourism Organisation
37, 8th Street, Bokharest Avenue
Tel: (021) 8873 2191
www.aitotours.org
Caravan Sahra
29 Ghaem Magham-e-Farahani Avenue

Tel: (021) 8864 0481
www.caravansahra.com
Magic Carpet Travel
Tel: +44 1344 622832
www.magic-carpet-travel.com
Sarvineh Parvaz Co.
1919/2, Shariati Avenue
Tel: (021) 2272 4930/31/32
www.holidayiran.com

Syria

Most tour operators and large hotels offer organised tours to the main sites and are reasonably flexible. The following recommended tour companies are based in Damascus:
Atlas Tours DMC
PO Box 4304, Fardos Street
Tel: (011) 221 5275
www.atlas-tours.com
Dawn Creative Tours
PO Box 2764, Dar al-Mouhandesseen Building, Maysaloun Street
Tel: (011) 224 1127
www.dawncreative.com
Syriana Travel and Tourism
PO Box 7814, Ahmad Mareiwd 36 Street
Tel: (011) 331 3612/5381
www.syriana.com

Lebanon

Specialist tour operators in Lebanon include:
Nakhal Travel and Tourism
Ghorayeb Building, Sami el-Solh Avenue, Beirut
Tel: (01) 389 389
www.nakhal.com.lb
Rida Travel Agency
5th floor, Arz centre, Jal al-Dib, Beirut
Tel: (01) 4718 790
www.ridaint.com.lb
TLB Destinations
Rue Principal, PO Box 197, Antelias
Tel: (01) 441 4697/9848
www.tlb-destinations.com
Organises cultural and adventure tours, and also tours in Syria and Jordan.

Turkey

Reliable tour operators include:
Peten Tours
Halaskargazi Cad. 345, Helal Apt, Daire 7, Istanbul
Tel: (0212) 248 9636
www.petentour.com
Plan Tours
Cumhuriyet Caddesi 131/1, Elmada, Istanbul
Tel: (0212) 234 7777 / 230 2272
www.plantours.com
Middle Earth Travel
Gaferli Mah. Cevizler Sok. 20, Göreme, Nevsehir
Tel: (0384) 271 2559
www.middleearthtravel.com

SHOPPING

What to Buy

Iran

Persian handicrafts include silks, gold, silver, brassware, ceramics, hand-blown glass, inlaid wood and carved or painted miniatures. Carpets and *kilims* are always good value, especially in Hamadan, Isfahan, Kashan, Na'in, Tabriz, Tehran, Shiraz and Yazd. Saffron, caviar and pistachios also make good gifts.

Syria

Syrian handicrafts represent an ancient tradition of skilled workmanship. Items to be found in the souks of Damascus and Aleppo include hand-woven silk brocades, embroidered tablecloths, carpets, engraved brass and copper, leather goods, glass vases, hand-printed cotton garments, jewellery, furniture inlaid with mother of pearl, as well as preserved fruit and Turkish delight.

Lebanon

Locally produced goods include carpets, brassware, silver jewellery, pottery and fossils.

Turkey

Turkish bazaars are a shopper's paradise, filled not only with traditional crafts but chic modern design. Carpets and cushions are of course king, but other items include leather, cotton, silk, jewellery, ceramics and inlaid chessboards. Edible gifts include saffron, nuts and Turkish delight.

BELOW: silk in Shiraz, Iran.

A – Z

A HANDY SUMMARY OF PRACTICAL INFORMATION, ARRANGED ALPHABETICALLY

B

Budgeting for Your Trip

Iran is a good-value destination, where eating out is cheap by Western standards, as are most transport costs. If on a group tour, accommodation and travel costs will already be covered, so it is just extras like additional food and drink, further sightseeing and souvenirs that you will need to pay for. Meals in local restaurants should cost no more than US$10 per day, or about US$20 in better hotel restaurants. Remember that there are no ATMs or credit/debit card facilities in Iran: you must bring all your money with you in cash, ideally as US dollars.

International flights and accommodation costs will be the largest items to budget for in **Syria**; travel and food within the country are relatively cheap. **Lebanon** is slightly more expensive, around US$50–75 a day, particularly for eating, drinking and accommodation.

In **Turkey** you can set your budget where you want to (within limits) with low-cost airlines, buses and pensions offering low-cost options, and five-star deluxe hotels and private chauffeurs catering for higher budgets. Allow a minimum of US$75 a day, then work upwards to your required level of luxury.

C

Climate

Summer can be very hot (as high as 50°C/122°F) in the south and central

CLIMATE CHART

Damascus

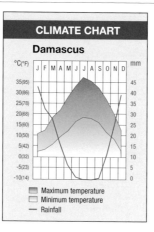

- Maximum temperature
- Minimum temperature
- Rainfall

regions of **Iran**. Northwest Iran is always about 10–15°C cooler than the rest of Iran, and winters can be very cold. The wettest months almost everywhere are March and April.

Syria has a moderate Mediterranean climate with four distinct seasons. Temperatures in autumn and spring range from 20°C to 25°C (70–77°F), but the weather can be changeable, especially in the mountains along the coast. Winter is generally moderate, but wet in the coastal region and cold inland: 5–15°C (40–60°F). Summer is hot everywhere (around 35°C/95°F), dry inland, humid on the coast and scorching in the desert.

Lebanon's Mediterranean climate enjoys 300 sunny days per year. Winters are moderate on the coast and cold in the mountains, with snow covering the highest peaks. Summer is hot and humid along the coast, but refreshingly cool in the mountains.

Turkey has three distinct climatic regions – the Mediterranean coast, the Anatolian plain and the Sea of Marmara. The Mediterranean remains relatively mild in winter, although there is snow on the mountains, with hot dry summers. Inland, the winters can be bitterly cold and the summers searingly hot. In the Istanbul region, the weather tends to be damp and grey in winter and warm in summer.

Crime and Security

Most of the concern about visiting **Iran** will be before actually arriving. But once inside the country, the visitor soon realises how friendly most Iranians are, compared with the vision conjured up by the Western media. With such strict Islamic penalties for even minor offences, most visits are trouble-free, but there are still opportunists in every bazaar and market. Beware pickpockets (both local males and females) who seek out solo tourists by jostling them in crowded places while reaching into bags and pockets, especially in the bazaars of Shiraz, Isfahan and Tehran. The authorities take allegations of spying and drugs possession particularly seriously, and it's these rules where foreigners tend to fall foul.

Due to the current political situation as of February 2012, it is not safe for tourists to visit **Syria**. Most foreign embassies have closed and withdrawn their staff. Should Syria again become accessible during the duration of this edition, tourists should be vigilant for potential terrorist attacks and remember that the death penalty is enforced for drug trafficking.

Security is a constant worry for those visiting **Lebanon**. In Beirut, as in other towns and villages, streets are generally safe day and night, and the culture encourages the community to watch out for all locals and visitors alike.

Crime is very low in **Turkey**, although there is inevitably some pickpocketing in the cities. Sadly, terrorism is a risk, but most visits are trouble-free. The police go out of their way to be polite to Westerners, but will deal harshly with drugs offences.

Customs Regulations

Alcohol is prohibited in Iran, but you are allowed to import 200 cigarettes and 50 cigars duty-free. Books and magazines might be inspected, and any unsuitable literature will be confiscated. DVDs and videos can be seized if the officials suspect that they may contain offensive or pornographic material.

Elsewhere, alcohol and cigarettes are usually limited to 200 cigarettes and 1 litre of wine or spirits. Expensive electrical equipment such as laptops, DVD and MP3 players, digital and video cameras could be of interest to customs and might be written into your passport, ensuring they depart with you. DVDs and tapes might be viewed for content.

D

Disabled Travellers

There are few concessions for disabled travellers, who unfortunately have to get by as best they can. Hiring an extra carer to look after a disabled traveller would not be expensive, and it is advisable to alert hotels and destinations well in advance.

Some museums and newer buildings are equipped with ramps for wheelchairs, but most of the ancient sites are not, so there are still many steps, staircases and rough surfaces to be negotiated. Local blind people are often accompanied.

Electricity

220 Volts AC, 50 Cycles. Countries in Western Asia use European-style two-pin rounded plugs. Some remote areas still get power cuts, but often these are confined to the early hours of the morning.

E

Embassies and Consulates

Iran

Australian Embassy
No. 2, 23rd Street, Khalid Islambuli Avenue, Tehran, tel: (021) 8386 3666, www.iran.embassy.gov.au
British Embassy
198 Ferdowsi Avenue, Tehran, tel: (021) 6405 2000, www.ukiniran.fco.gov.uk/en
Canadian Embassy
Shahid Sarafraz 57, Ostad Motahari Avenue, Tehran,tel: (021) 8152 0000, www.iran.gc.ca
Irish Embassy
Bonbast Nahid Street 8, North Kamranieh Avenue, Tehran, tel: (021) 2280 3835, www.embassyofireland.ir
New Zealand Embassy
1, 2nd Park Alley, 34 Sosan Street, North Golestan Complex, Aghdasiyeh Street, Niyavaran, Tehran, tel: (021) 2612 2175, www.nzembassy.com/iran
US Embassy
The Swiss Embassy (Africa Avenue, Farzan-e-Gharbi 59, Tehran, tel: (021) 2254 2178) has a US Interests section.

Syria

British Embassy
Kotob Building, Mohd Kurd Ali Street, Malki, Damascus, tel: (011) 339 1513, http://ukinsyria.fco.gov.uk
Canadian Embassy
Lot 12, Autostrade Mezzeh, Damascus, tel: (011) 611 6692, www.dfait-maeci.gc.ca/syria

US Embassy
Abou Roumaneh, 2 Al-Mansour Street, PO Box 29, Damascus, tel: (011) 339 4444, http://damascus.usembassy.gov

Lebanon

Australian Embassy
Embassy Complex, Serail Hill, Beirut, tel:, (01) 961 600, www.lebanon.embassy.gov.au
British Embassy
Serail Hill, Beirut Central District, Beirut, tel: (01) 990400, www.britishembassy.gov.uk/lebanon
Canadian Embassy
43 Jal Al-Dib Highway, Coolrite Building, 1st floor, Jal Al-Dib, Beirut, tel: (01) 713 900, www.lebanon.embassy.gov.au
US Embassy
Awkar facing the Municipality, PO Box 70-840, Antelias, Beirut, tel: (04) 542 600, http://lebanon.usembassy.gov

Turkey

Although the embassies are in Ankara, the consulates in Istanbul handle visa and passport matters.
Australian Embassy
MNG Building, Ugur Mumcu Caddesi 88, 7th Floor, Gazi Osman Paşa, Ankara, tel: (0312) 459 9550, www.turkey.embassy.gov.au.
British Embassy
Sehit Ersan Addesi 46/A, Çankaya, Ankara, tel: (0312) 455 3344, www.ukinturkey.fco.gov.uk
Canadian Embassy
Cinnah Caddesi 58, Çankaya, Ankara, tel: (0312) 409 2700, www.turkey.gc.ca
Irish Embassy
MNG Binasi, B Blok Kat 3, Ugur Mumcu Caddesi 88, Ankara, tel:

BELOW: signs often appear in English at popular tourist sights.

(0312) 459 1000,
www.embassy of Ireland.org.tr
South Africa Embassy
27 Filistin Street, GOP, 06700,
Ankara, tel: (0312) 405 6861, www.
southafrica.org.tr
US Embassy
110 Atatürk Blvd, Kavakıdere, 06100
Ankara, tel: (0312) 455 5555, http://
turkey.usembassy.gov

Emergencies

In **Iran** the initial call should be to the
police on **110**. Explain (in Farsi only!)
what has happened and they will then
alert any other emergency services if
needed. Otherwise, you can contact
services directly on **115** (ambulance)
or **125** (fire). No payment is required
for any medical assistance provided
by an ambulance, but a hospital or
clinic would need payment. Obtain
a receipt for claiming against
insurance.

The Ministry of the Interior Public
Relations Department in **Syria**
has dedicated 24-hour telephone
numbers for tourist advice and
assistance: tel: (011) 221 1001/2.
Dial **110** for general emergencies,
112 for police and **113** for fire
service.

The following emergency numbers
are used in **Lebanon**: police **160**,
internal security forces **112**, Red
Cross **140**, civil defence **125**.

The general emergency telephone
number in **Turkey** is **115**. Others are:
Police **155**, Ambulance **112**, Fire **110**.
In major tourist areas there are also
specialist tourist police (Istanbul, tel:
(0212) 527 4503 and Ankara, tel:
(0312) 384 0606).

Etiquette

Iran is a deeply religious country that
follows Islamic code. For both men
and women, it is best to cover up as
much as possible. In an effort to be
friendly, the male tourist will often
extend a hand of friendship, which
will be warmly accepted by an Iranian
man, but politely refused by an Iranian
woman. Always be aware that shoes
need to be removed, not just inside
mosques, but also some tombs,
mausoleums, madrassas and private
homes. In holy places like Mashhad or
Qom, women must wear the *chador*,
which can be obtained from the site
guardian.

The days when an unmarried
couple were not allowed to sleep in
the same room seem to be over, but
there may still be some small local
hotels (particularly in holy centres)

where this could be a problem. Men
and women, even if they are married,
should not show affection for each
other in public. Most Iranians will
politely indicate if a visitor is doing
something unacceptable, albeit
something unknowingly.

Whilst more moderate than Iran,
Syria, **Lebanon** and **Turkey** are
still Muslim countries, and visitors
should respect religious sensitivity,
particularly in the matter of dress
and public conduct, and when in
the towns and away from the beach.
Eating, drinking and smoking in public
during the holy month of Ramadan
should be avoided.

G

Gay and Lesbian Travellers

Homosexuality is illegal in **Iran**, **Syria**
and **Lebanon** (although there is a
lively gay scene centred on a few
bars in and around Beirut). However,
both male and female travellers
will not have any problems, as long
as there are no outward signs of a
gay relationship. As in many Middle
Eastern countries, local men might
well hold hands in the street, but this
is usually just a sign of friendship.
Istanbul has a more open gay scene,
and details of the latest fashionable
locations will be in the press and
online.

H

Health and Medical Care

No vaccinations are compulsory,
but there are recommendations for
protection against tetanus, typhoid,
hepatitis B, rabies, cholera and polio.
Consult a travel clinic for advice
about prophylaxis against malaria,
which can be a problem in southeastern
Iran between March and November
and northeastern Syria between
May and October. A yellow fever
certificate is required if entering
from an infected area. For latest
advice consult a doctor or visit www.
fitfortravel.nhs.uk.

Large towns and cities on the
tourist trail are well served by
hospitals and clinics. Doctors are
generally well qualified and most
medical personnel speak English
or French. For minor ailments
and problems, such as breathing
difficulties due to air pollution, refer

to one of the pharmacies in all towns
and cities. The pharmacist can often
speak a European language and will
advise treatment. A useful website in
Iran is www.daroyab.com, where typing
a known prescription or drug name
into the search reveals alternatives
in Farsi.

Intense heat and sun can cause
problems during the summer months,
so ensure you take sun protection for
skin, eyes and head and drink plenty
of bottled water.

I

Insurance

Every traveller should have some
form of travel and medical insurance.
Small medical costs should be paid
direct and reclaimed, but for a major
medical problem consult the 24-hour
emergency number. Bring all your
details of insurance cover.

Internet

Modern **Iranians** are proud to tell
you that Farsi is the fourth most
widely used language on the internet,
indicating just how much they have
taken to the service, with internet
cafés all over major cities.

Internet facilities in **Syria** only
began after President Bashir
al-Assad came into office in 2000,
and even now still have some way to
go. Even Damascus and Aleppo do
not have many internet cafés and
they will need to be searched out.
Access is good value but slow, with
some sites and addresses no-go
areas, but it is getting better. There
are many internet cafés in the main
centres in **Lebanon**.

The **Turks** love the internet and,
unusually, almost every hotel offers
free broadband.

M

Maps

Good maps of Iran are hard to
obtain, and very few of these have
detailed information. The vast
majority of visitors arrive as part of a
group through local tour operators,
who often give away free maps of
Iran upon arrival. Tourist cities such
as Tehran, Isfahan, Shiraz and Yazd
have good street maps indicating the
main points of interest, obtainable

free at hotels or tourist information offices.

Apart from those of major national highways, no two Syrian road maps are alike. Various maps show alarmingly different routes, with well-established roads being omitted, dirt tracks elevated to super highways and others purely imaginary (or yet to be built).

Good-quality maps of Lebanon and Beirut are available from larger bookstores in the capital. Tourist information offices can also provide free, but less accurate, maps.

Maps and signs in Turkey are fairly clear, but it is difficult to get hold of decent street maps of towns and cities outside Istanbul before you get there.

ABOVE: Turkish newspapers for sale in Istanbul.

Media

The media in **Iran** is firmly in the control of the ruling authorities, with many previously independent publications and websites forced to close over recent years. Print media seem to offer a vast choice of almost 30 newspapers and 80 magazines, but they are mainly variations on the official line. Several newspapers are in English, with some offering better coverage of overseas news or international sport. See www.iran-daily.com and www.tehrantimes.com but beware that both sites are periodically blocked or suspended.

State television runs two government channels as well as dedicated religion, news, science and sports channels. There is also a local TV channel for each province.

The more up-market hotels have (theoretically illegal) satellite dishes with access to BBC, CNN and Euro News channels. Some TV channels and internet sites are occasionally blocked due to perceived outside bias in the reporting (such as the BBC Persian-language website www.bbcpersian.com), but radio signals, including the BBC World Service, from around the world remain intact. Illegal satellite dishes are installed on most rooftops, and the general population has an informed view of international politics.

Arab and local newspapers and magazines are sold everywhere in **Syria** and **Lebanon**, while foreign newspapers are found at the international hotels. The *Syria Times* (www.syriatimes.com) is a daily government English-language newspaper. The *Daily Star* (www.dailystar.com.lb) is the English-language newspaper in Lebanon. Local television and radio broadcasts mainly in Arabic, but there are some wildlife programmes in French and English. Satellite dishes can access all the major international news channels, provided by all the top hotels.

Sabah and *Hürriyet* are **Turkey**'s best-selling national newspapers, while the left-wing *Cumhuriyet* is considered the most serious newspaper. *Milliyet* is a well-established liberal paper. The English-language Turkish *Daily News* (www.turkishdailynews.com) provides coverage of local and international events. International newspapers and magazines can be bought at news-stands and bookshops in tourist areas. Turkey has over 12 television channels, plus additional regional channels, the majority of which are privately owned. Satellite and cable channels are available in major hotels.

Money

Iran

It will take a few days to get used to the incongruities of the Iranian currency, because even though notes and coins indicate rials, most prices are written and spoken as tomans (1 toman = 10 rials). So initially, the confusion of so many zeros is heightened by exactly which price is being referred to. A bottle of mineral water costing 3,000 rials (about 30 US cents) could be indicated as 300 tomans or even a verbal or finger sign for "3", leaving you to figure it out. Most sellers are genuinely

National Holidays

Iran

1 January New Year's Day
6 January Army Day
11 Feb Victory of Islamic Revolution
20 March Oil Nationalisation Day
1 May Labour Day
14 July National Day
17 July Republic Day
8 August Ceasefire Day (End of Iran–Iraq War)

Syria

1 January New Year's Day
8 March Revolution Day
21 March Mothers' Day
17 April Independence Day
1 May Labour Day
6 May Martyrs' Day
6 October Liberation Day

Lebanon

1 January New Year's Day
9 February Mar Maroun Feast
1 May Labour Day
6 May Martyrs' Day
15 August Assumption of Mary
22 November Independence Day

Turkey

1 January New Year's Day
23 April National Sovereignty and Children's Day
19 May Youth and Sports Day
30 August Victory Day
29 October Republic Day
The dates for religious holidays (which change from year to year as they are based on the lunar calendar) are available at www.god web.org/IslamCalendar.htm

honest and will rectify any mistakes or misunderstandings.

Exchanging money can be a problem, especially off the main tourist trail. In the main cities, exchange offices and some souvenir/carpet shops speedily change cash in major currencies, but banks can be choosy about what currencies they take and are often slow. Credit cards and traveller's cheques are not generally accepted, except for some tourist shops in large cities, so travellers should carry US dollars to cover their needs.

Syria

The Syrian pound (lira) has banknotes of 5, 10, 25, 50, 100, 200, 500 and 1000 liras, and there are coins of 1, 2, 5, 10 and 25 liras. As usual, US dollars are the best currency to bring, as traveller's cheques can be difficult to change. ATM machines are appearing, but check beforehand for your particular card. Credit and debit cards are useful for larger purchases, top-class hotels, air tickets and car-hire deposits.

Lebanon

The official currency is the Lebanese pound, but US dollars are widely used. Many shops, hotels and restaurants accept credit cards and there are many ATMs. Traveller's cheques can be exchanged at some banks.

Turkey

The yeni (new) Turkish lira (YTL) notes come in denominations of YTL 1, 5, 10, 20, 50 and 100 notes and YTL1 coins. YTL1 is split into 100 kurufl. Make sure you have plenty of small change and small denomination notes, as people rarely seem to have change. ATMs are plentiful if you need to top up. Most tourist shops take credit cards and are prepared to deal in US dollars, euros or sterling.

O

Opening Hours

Friday is the official holiday in **Iran** and **Syria**, where government and bank official hours are roughly 8am–2pm Saturday to Thursday. In **Lebanon** many offices close early on Friday, and bank hours are 8.30am–12.30pm Monday to Saturday. Banks in **Turkey** are open Monday to Friday 8.30am–noon and 1.30–5pm, and a few larger branches also open Saturday

morning; all have 24-hour cash dispensers. Most places are closed on Sunday.

Shops and stores in Iran and Syria are open 9am–1.30pm and 5–8pm, later in summer. In Lebanon and Turkey stores tend to remain open all day, but shut at around 6pm. Museums are usually closed one day of the week – either Monday or Tuesday. Historical sites are open every day, and sometimes stay open later in summer.

The fasting month of Ramadan and the two-week New Year holidays are rules to themselves, but generally places are open in the mornings.

P

Photography

Photographers should take care of exactly what their camera is pointing at, especially outside the main tourist sites. It is forbidden to take photos of any government or official building, police station, military site, airport, harbour, dam, train station or any place deemed to be strategically important. Avoid taking shots of anything that has a uniformed presence outside, or aerials on top. Photography is banned in some religious sites in Iran, such as Mashhad and Qom, although many locals do not seem to be aware of this.

Taking photographs of individuals also requires caution; whilst most local men seem agreeable, almost all women are not. Women visitors might have the opportunity of taking photos of local women in an all-women environment. Observe any signs where photography is

forbidden and certainly do not attempt to photograph any police, soldiers or other security forces. Some mosques and most museums allow photography while others charge an extra camera fee. Bring as many memory cards as you need, as the quality of local supplies is limited.

Postal Services

Every town and city has a main central post office, and stamps can also be bought at some tobacco kiosks. Post office hours generally follow official opening hours (see above), but some main post offices stay open late.

Public Holidays

Islamic holidays are based on the Hejiri calendar. The months are lunar so the year is 13 days shorter than the Western calendar. Thus dates of certain holidays may vary from year to year. It is best to find out whether these fall within the time period of your projected visit. Ramadan or an Eid (religious feast) will mean that places are closed at certain times and that food may not be readily available because everyone else is fasting. The ancient Iranian New Year celebration called Nauroz (also Now Ruz) starts on 21 March and lasts for two weeks, during which time many people are absent from work. Christmas and Easter are also celebrated in Western Asia, and each country has its own national holidays.

Islamic Holidays

Eid al-Fitr three days marking end of Ramadan (fasting month)
Eid al-Adha Four days at the end of Hajj

BELOW: PTT the logo for Turkey's Post Office.

1st of Muharram Islamic New Year
9th and 10th of Muharram Ashura – martyrdom of Imam Hussein
12th of Rabe'a al-Awwal Prophet Muhammad's birthday
27th of Rajab Ascension of Prophet Muhammad

R

Religion

Iran

Iran is the only country where Shia Islam is the state religion. Almost 99 percent of the population are Muslims, with only a small percentage belonging to the Sunni sect. Followers of Sunni Islam live along the coast of the Persian Gulf, with many links to the Sunnis of UAE. Three minority religions are officially recognised – Zoroastrianism, Judaism and Christianity – and each is concentrated in certain traditional centres.

There are Zoroastrian temples in Yazd, Isfahan and Tehran. For thousands of years, Jews have traded in the region, and since the time of Cyrus the Great have settled as artisans. There are still Jewish synagogues in Tehran, Hamedan and Isfahan. Christian churches are mainly from the Armenian branch and are found in all main towns and cities, with especially strong communities around Tabriz. Religious minorities that are not recognised include Buddhists, Sikhs and Baha'is (whose founder came from Shiraz). For these followers there can be no outward sign of community or places of faith, so worship is carried out in the privacy of the home.

Syria

Almost 90 percent of Syria's population are Muslims, with the majority being Sunni. This also includes many Kurds, whose homeland straddles the Turkish and Iraqi borders. There are small concentrations of Shia, Druze, Ismaili and Alawite. Syrian Christians make

Time Zones

Iran is GMT +3.5 hours from 22 September to 21 March and GMT +4.5 hours from 22 March to 21 September. Syria, Lebanon and Turkey are GMT +2 from November to April and GMT +3 from May to October.

up about 10 percent of the total and are also split into many diverse groupings.

Lebanon

Around 60 percent of the population are Muslims, of which Shia are the majority, followed by Sunni and Druze. Christians make up approximately 39 percent and are also split into many diverse groupings, and the remaining 1 percent are classified as "other".

Turkey

Almost 99 percent of the population are Muslim. Turkish Islam is generally moderate, and the country prides itself on its secular government, but religious sentiment should still be respected.

T

Telecommunications

International 24-hour phone and fax services are available in most hotels in **Iran**. The use of mobile phones is also spreading fast, but as of yet there are no international roaming agreements.

Elsewhere in Western Asia, there is good mobile phone coverage, and many networks have international roaming agreements, albeit at costly rates. If staying for a long time, consider buying a local phone and SIM card offering better rates. International calls from hotels can be extremely expensive. Telephone booths offer local and international calls with payphone cards bought from post offices and kiosks. Some post offices have good-value international phone facilities but short opening hours, while nearby there is usually an enterprising shop or café owner with a phone and calculator.

International Dialling Codes

Iran +98
Syria +963
Lebanon +961
Turkey +90

Tipping

In **Iran**, restaurant staff expect a small gratuity from tourists, around 10 percent, and hotel staff should be tipped small notes for any help they give. Try to keep as much small change as possible for taxi drivers, porters and toilet attendants too.

As tourism increases and more people depend on it for their living, **Syria** is heading in the same direction as Egypt as regards the *baksheesh* culture. This is especially true during downturns in tourist numbers, when everyone will expect an additional payment. Restaurants and guides will expect at least 10 percent. In **Lebanon**, it is customary to tip 10–15 percent in restaurants, plus service charge.

If there is no service charge (*servis dahil*), leave 10 percent in restaurants in **Turkey**; if there is a service charge, leave a little small change. Allow YTL1–2 for porters and about YTL5 per day for the room cleaners in hotels. *Hammam* attendants will generally expect up to 25 percent of the price. Do not tip taxi drivers.

Toilets

There is absolutely no problem in using the toilets belonging to a hotel or restaurant even if you are just passing by, but try to leave a tip for the attendant. There are some toilets in public parks, service stations and modern shopping malls. It should always be possible to use the toilets in a mosque if necessary, but remember to carry toilet paper at all times.

Tourist Information

In **Iran**, tourism falls within the duties of the Ministry of Culture and Islamic Guidance, but the best you can hope for are maps and smiles at a few tourist offices. Most of the active promotion comes from the private tour operators, who supply guides, transport, maps and itineraries for their incoming tour groups.

There are some official tourist offices in **Syria**'s main cities, but they are of limited help, offering just a few city and regional maps. Information for the Ministry of Tourism can be found at www.syriatourism. org. Most tourism promotion is within the private sector, and many tour operators have good information and travel advice on their websites.

The main **Lebanese** tourist office is on Rue Banque du Liban in Beirut's Hamra District, and can provide maps and information. The Ministry of Tourism's website (www. lebanon-tourism.gov.lb) is also a useful source of information. Much of the tourism promotion is done by the many tour operators, who have good information and travel advice on their websites.

Almost every town with anything to offer tourists has a small tourist office or kiosk in **Turkey** and, in most, the person behind the counter will have a rudimentary grasp of English. Whether they have any useful information depends on what you are asking. Try the Ministry of Culture and Tourism website (www.goturkey.com) as a first step.

V

Visas

To get a visa for **Iran** you must first be invited into the country by an Iranian company or institution or, in the case of tourists, an approved Iranian travel agent. They will take your personal details to the Ministry of Foreign Affairs in Tehran, who issue an authorisation number, which will be faxed to the Iranian consulate in your country. At this point you get a visa application form from the consulate and lodge your passport, photographs (women must wear a headscarf in photos), letters and application forms with the visa number they give you. It may take up to five days for the consulate to issue your visa, and the whole process might take three to six weeks. Passports must be valid for at least six months. A transit visa lasts for a maximum of 10 days, but extensions can be obtained once inside Iran. See www.travcour.com for more details.

All visitors to **Syria** require a valid passport and an entry visa, which should be obtained prior to departure, from Syrian consulates and embassies. Syria will not grant a visa or entry permit to anyone with a passport showing evidence of a visit to Israeli-occupied territory, including the border crossings of Araba, Sheikh Hussein, Rafah and Taba. More details and a downloadable visa application form can be found at www.syrianembassy.co.uk , or try www.travcour.com. Don't forget to obtain a multiple-entry visa if you intend travelling in and out of Syria. Make sure you receive an entry card at immigration, and keep this with your passport until departure or extending your visa beyond a 15-day visit. Passports are often kept at reception for your first night at a hotel.

Visitors to **Lebanon** are advised to obtain a visa in advance from the nearest embassy or consulate. Some tourists can obtain visas at Beirut Airport or at the Syrian border, but

check details. For updates on visa information, contact the Lebanese embassy or consulate in your country. Passports must be valid for at least six months. Travellers with passports containing visas or entry/exit stamps for Israel are unlikely to be allowed into Lebanon.

All visitors to **Turkey** require a valid passport and an entry visa, obtained at the airport on arrival – keep hard currency handy: UK (£13), Canada (US$60), Australia (US$20), USA (US$20) and Ireland (E15). It's more expensive if you get it in advance.

W

Websites

Some useful websites:
www.iranchamber.com Iranian history, art and culture.
www.chnpress.com/tourism Cultural Heritage News agency.
www.tourismiran.ir/ Official tourism website.
www.cafe-syria.com General information.
www.ecotourismsyria.com Environmental information relating to Syria.
www.made-in-syria.com General information on Syria.
www.travel-to-lebanon.com A traveller's guide to Lebanon.
www.lebanon.com General website with hotel and restaurant listings.
www.mfa.gov.tr Turkish Foreign Ministry
www.istanbul.com Official Istanbul tourist office website.
www.kultur.gov.tr Turkish Ministry of Culture and Tourism.
www.turkeytravelplanner.com Definitive US-run website.

What to Bring and Wear

Be sure to bring appropriate clothing if travelling in **Iran**. Men should wear shirts and long trousers, but shorts are not acceptable. Women must not draw attention to the shape of their body or expose any flesh except their face and hands. At its simplest, women should arrive in a pair of loose trousers, long shirt and compulsory headscarf, then see what the local fashion is and buy accordingly in the shops. Elsewhere in Western Asia, women should not wear short or revealing clothing in mosques or souks.

Between October and May, winter clothing is recommended – at least

Weights and Measures

Countries in Western Asia use the metric system.

a fleece and waterproof jacket. The desert can be freezing in winter, as are sites in the higher mountains, and you'll need to keep warm and dry. In the summer (May–September), clothing should be light and loose-fitting. Always bring sunglasses, suncream and a hat. Mosquito repellent, plasters, a torch (flashlight), camera and an extra bag to take home your shopping complete the kit.

When to Go

Spring (April–June) and autumn (September–November) are the best times to visit Western Asia, when it is hopefully not too hot or cold, with warm days and pleasant evenings. Try to avoid Easter, however, when hotels can be fully booked with tour groups, and Ramadan, when everything slows down a bit. Skiers should plan a visit between November and March.

It can be unbearably hot in southern **Iran**, so a winter/spring tour of the southern half of the country is ideal, but not for the main Silk Road sections of the north, where winter weather can be severe. The route from Mashhad across the north of Iran to Reyy is good apart from the winter months, and the northern route through Tabriz is best undertaken from late spring to early autumn. Rain can be a problem at any time of the year in the north.

Women Travellers

As long as you are prepared to observe the strict codes of female behaviour and dress, most women have no problems travelling around **Iran**. But it is always advisable to keep to well-lit and busy parts of towns and cities. As an "honorary man", a woman tourist is accepted in public places such as teahouses, but can also go into female enclaves of a private house, which are forbidden to men. If you can overcome the communication barrier, most local men are extremely helpful, and the women will be interested about your life and family.

The same applies to Syria, Lebanon and Turkey, although women may be gazed at. Turkish men are great flirts, but if in doubt, shout and every man in the vicinity will rush to your rescue.

LANGUAGE

UNDERSTANDING THE LANGUAGE

Western Asia has a rich linguistic heritage that encompasses everything from Aramaic, Assyrian and Babylonian through Latin and Greek, Kurdish, Armenian and classical Persian. While not all of these languages are spoken today, you will see their inscriptions in archaeological sites and historic manuscripts, and their grammatical structures, words and literary ideas have significantly influenced three of the modern languages widely spoken in the region today: Arabic, Persian and Turkish.

Arabic

Arabic is a Semitic language, closely related to Hebrew, and its various dialects all stem from the Classical Arabic of the 6th century AD. Today's written Arabic (Modern Standard Arabic) is derived from the Arabic of the Koran and is the official language of 26 states, even though their various spoken dialects can be mutually unintelligible.

Arabic verbs are marked for person, gender and number, and conjugated for the past or non-past, an active or passive voice, and one of five different moods. Nouns have three grammatical cases, three numbers (singular, dual or plural), two genders and three states (indefinite, definite and construct). Adjectives are marked for case, gender, number and state but interestingly, non-human nouns are always combined with a singular feminine adjective.

Arabic has three short vowels (a i u), three long vowels (ā ī ū) and two diphthongs (aj and aw). A vowel at the end of a word is often not

pronounced. Consonants can be plosive or fricative, and either voiced or unvoiced.

Key phrases

Hello مرحبا. *marhaba*
How are you? كيف حالك؟ *Kayfa Haaluka?*
Fine, thank you شكرا, بخير *bi-khair Shukran*
Please من فضلك. *min faDlak*
Thank you شكرا *shukran*
Yes نعم *na`am*
No لا. *laa*
Excuse me لو سمحت *min faḍlak*
Goodbye مع السلامة *ma`a as-salaamah*
Do you speak English? هل
تتكلم الانجليزية *Hal tatakallam al-ingliziyyah?*
Help! مساعدة! *Musaa`adah!*

Persian

Persian (often also referred to as Farsi) is an Indo-Iranian language and so has close grammatical and structural links with European languages such as Latin and French. It has around 110 million native speakers who reside across modern Iran, Afghanistan and Tajikistan, and it has significantly influenced the structure and vocabulary of other regional languages including Hindi, Urdu and Armenian.

Persian grammar is pleasingly straightforward. Normal sentences

BELOW: in the market in Penjikent.

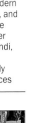

ABOVE: Taxi rank in Turkey

are structured with the subject-object-verb word order and, if the object is specific, it precedes a prepositional phrase. The declension of verbs expresses the tense and aspect of an action, and they agree with number and person of the subject.

The Persian vocabulary has been significantly widened through the compounding of existing words and also the addition of prefixes and suffixes to the stems of verbs and also to nouns and adjectives. Persian has also adopted loanwords from a variety of sources: Mongolian and Turkic words are present in large numbers due to the political role of successive Turkic dynasties in Persian history; French and Russian words (and their adaptations) were absorbed into Persian in the 19th and early 20th centuries; and English is also now making its presence felt, particular in technical vocabulary.

Persian has six vowels (three long and three short) and 23 consonants, of which two are nasal. The majority of consonants are labial (pronounced on the lips, for example m, p, b) or alveolar (pronounced with the tongue just behind the top teeth, for example n, t, d). Only j is spoken with the tip of the tongue on the palate. Syllables always begin with a consonant sound, and it is usually the last syllable of a word that is stressed.

Key Phrases

Hello. سلام *Salâm*
How are you? چطورید *chetorid?*
Fine, thank you خوبم، خیلی ممنون *xubam, xeyli mamnun*
Please لطفاً *lotfan*
Thank you مرسی *mersi*
Yes بله *bale*

No نه *na*
Excuse me ببخشید *bebaxšid*
Goodbye خداحافظ *xodâhâfez*
Do you speak English? میتوانید انگلیسی حرف بزنید؟ *Mitavânid Engelisi harf bezanid?*
Help! کمک *komak!*

Turkish

Turkish is the native language of more than 80 million people, not only in modern Turkey but also in parts of Cyprus, Iraq, Greece and Bulgaria. The language originated some 1,300 years ago in Central Asia, but the standard version spoken today is known as Istanbul Turkish because of the region in which it is primarily spoken. As late as 1928 Turkish was written in the Perso-Arabic script, but Ataturk introduced a variant of Latin script so that Turkey would be more

closely aligned with Europe and also to break with the country's Ottoman past.

In Turkish the standard word order is subject-object-verb, though this can be altered to stress the importance of a specific word or phrase. Nouns do not have a specific gender, but there is an extensive use of honorifics and second-person pronouns (with their respective verb endings) to denote the status of the person and also the level of familiarity the speaker has with the subject.

The Turkish alphabet has 29 letters, seven of which have been modified from their original Latin forms. There are eight vowels (a, e, i, ı, o, ö, u, ü), and no letters for q, w and x. Turkish words never contain two vowels next to each other, so if you do see two vowels together you know that it's a loanword from another language. The language is entirely phonetic, which definitely aids pronunciation.

Key Phrases

Hello Merhaba *mehr hah bah*
How are you? Nasılsınız? *na suhl suhn uhz*
Fine, thank you İyiyim, teşekkürler. *ee yee yeem teh shek ür lerr*
Please Lütfen *Luet fen*
Thank you Teşekkür ederim *teh shek uer eh der eem*
Yes Evet *eh vet*
No Hayır. *Hah yuhr*
Excuse me Bakar mısınız? *bah kar muh suh nuhz*
Goodbye Hoşçakalın. *Hosh cha kaluhn*
Do you speak English? İngilizce biliyor musunuz? *Eengleez jay bee lee yor muh suh nuhz*

BELOW: mosque door with Persian text.

FURTHER READING

History and Culture

The Heritage of Persia by Richard N. Frye, Weidenfeld & Nicholson (1962). Academic analysis of Persian civilisation, history and art.

Damascus: Hidden Treasures of the Old City by Brigid Keenan, Thames and Hudson (2000). A tour through the wealth of Roman, Christian and Islamic relics of the Old City.

Monuments of Syria by Ross Burns, I.B. Tauris (1992). In-depth descriptions of all the major historical sites.

Travellers History Turkey Chastleton Travel (2006). A potted guide to the history of one of the oldest and most complicated countries in the world.

Byzantium by John Julius Norwich, Penguin, 1996. Three-volume definitive guide to the magnificent Byzantine empire.

Lords of the Horizons: A History of the Ottoman Empire by Jason Goodwin, Vintage (1999). A concise but lively run through the Ottoman period.

Storm on Horseback: The Seljuk Warriors of Turkey by John Freely, I.B. Tauris (2008). Book about the original Turks by one of the great writers on Turkey.

Istanbul, The Imperial City by John Freely, Viking (1996). Illustrated introductory biography of the city and its social life through 27 centuries.

Lives and Letters

Portrait of A Turkish Family by Irfan Orga, Eland (2002). Haunting autobiography of childhood life in Turkey at the birth of the Republic.

The Imperial Harem of the Sultans: The Memoirs of Leyla Hanımefendi by Leyla Hanımefendi, Peva Publications (1995). The only contemporary account of daily life at the Çiragan Palace in the 19th century and a vivid portrait of this hidden world.

The Turkish Embassy Letters by Lady Mary Wortley Montagu, Virago (1995). Lively and intelligent letters, written in 1716 when the writer's husband had just been appointed ambassador.

Letters from Syria by Freya Stark, John Murray (1942). Personal memoirs from her travels in the late 1920s.

Daughter of Persia: A Woman's Journey from Her Father's Harem Through the Islamic Revolution by Sattareh Farman-Farmaian, Corgi (1993). With honesty and humour, Farman-Farmaian describes her upbringing in the home of a Persian prince and her ringside seat on the turbulent political events of Iran's 20th century.

Modern History

Persian Fire by Tom Holland, Little Brown (2005). Good coverage of the Persian Empires in the first few chapters.

Behind Iranian Lines by John Simpson, Robson Books (1988). Views of the Islamic Revolution from inside Iran.

Out of Iran: A Woman's Escape from the Ayatollahs by Sousan Azadi, Irwin (1987). A westernised Iranian woman's account of life under the ayatollahs.

The Truth about Syria by Barry Rubin, Palgrave Macmillan (2007). Placing ancient Syria in the political jigsaw of the modern Middle East.

Hedjaz Railway by R. Tourret, Tourret Publishing (1989). All you ever needed to know about the railway that Lawrence of Arabia blew up.

Pity the Nation: Lebanon at War by Robert Fisk, Oxford University Press (1990). Continually updated accounts of Lebanon's political problems both internal and external.

Art and Music

Islam: Art and Architecture edited by Markus Hattstein and Peter Delius, Konemann (2000).

Introducing Persian Architecture by Arthur Upham Pope, Oxford University Press (1972).

A History of Ottoman Architecture by Godfrey Goodwin, Thames and Hudson (2003). Comprehensive and definitive, covering every kind of building all over Turkey.

Fiction

Fragments of Memory by Hanna Minah, Interlink (2004). A look at the changing silk industry a century ago.

The Prophet by Gibran Khalil Gibran (1923). A guide to life by Lebanon's most celebrated author.

The White Castle, **The Black Book**, **The New Life**. Novels by Orhan Pamuk, translated by Güneli Gün (Faber). Three of many books by introspective, perceptive, sometimes over-complex Nobel-prize-winning Turkish writer.

Modern Syrian Short Stories by M.J.L. Young, Three Continents Press (1988). A view of life in the changing Syria of the 1980s.

Travel Narratives

Adventures in Persia by Reginald Teague-Jones, Gollancz (1990). Amazing account of a car journey through Persia in 1926.

The Valleys of the Assassins: And Other Persian Travels by Freya Stark, John Murray (1940). Wonderful descriptions of all the major sites as seen in the early 1930s.

The Hills of Adonis by Colin Thubron, William Heinemann (1968). The famous travel writer witnesses the Lebanon of the 1960s.

A Fez of the Heart by Jeremy Seal, Picador (1996). Travels around Turkey in search of a real fez, the red felt hat banned in 1925; a perceptive, alternative view of modern Turkey.

Istanbul: Memories and the City by Orhan Pamuk, Faber (2006). An evocative biography of the city, drawing upon Pamuk's own childhood and a rich understanding of its history.

Other Insight Guides

Other **Insight Guides** that highlight destinations in Western Asia include Jordan, Israel and Turkey. Discover Istanbul's hidden corners with the award-winning **Select Guide to Istanbul** – a stylish guide to the city, offering a selection of unusual and quirky ideas to suit your mood. Insight **FlexiMaps** are designed to complement our guidebooks. They provide full mapping of major destinations, and their easy-to-fold, laminated finish gives them ease of use and durability.

ART AND PHOTO CREDITS

AFP 279
akg-images 33B, 35, 62, 63, 64, 67, 336, 338
Alamy 80/81T, 81TR, 92/93T, 93ML, 95, 146, 163, 175, 176T, 188, 210, 214T, 220, 222, 277, 278, 287, 289, 292, 293, 294, 296T, 299, 317
Art Archive 68T, 339
Bigstock 273T, 400/401B
Bradley Mayhew 145, 216, 226/227T, 227TR, 227TR
Brice Minnigh/Apa Publications 21B, 30B, 400/401T
Bridgeman Art Library 36, 39, 44, 48, 54, 59, 65, 68B, 69, 70B, 71L, 81BL, 81ML, 94, 97, 98, 100
British Library 75, 84, 111
British Museum/British Museum Images 50, 55
ChinaFotoPress 2/3, 155
Chris Bradley/Apa Publications 3, 4B, 5, 6ML, 7MR, 10BL, 11B, 26, 31T, 31B, 32, 33T, 34, 42, 47, 53, 57, 92ML, 99, 102MR, 103MC, 106, 108, 302, 303, 304, 305, 306B, 306T, 307T, 307B, 308, 310, 311, 312B, 312T, 314, 315B, 315T, 316, 319, 320B, 320T, 321T, 321B, 322, 323, 324B, 324T, 326, 327T, 328B, 328T, 331, 332T, 332B, 334B, 334T, 335T, 335B, 340, 341, 343, 344B, 345, 346, 348, 350/351B, 350T, 352, 353, 354, 355L, 355R, 357T, 357B, 358, 359, 361, 362, 363, 364, 365, 366, 369, 371, 430/431, 432, 436, 438, 439L, 440, 441, 442, 443L, 445L
Corbis 12/13, 22, 23, 24, 27, 45, 80BC, 87, 90, 91, 120/121, 162B, 349
Croquet-Zouridakis 7TL, 82/83, 92BR, 103TR, 211, 213, 214B, 217, 226BR, 226MC, 227B, 300/301, 309, 406/407
David Henley/CPA 6TR, 7TR, 8BR, 10TR, 11T, 20, 25, 28, 41, 46, 56, 61, 70T, 77, 128, 129, 130, 131, 132B, 133, 134, 135, 136, 140, 141T, 142, 144, 148, 149B, 149T, 150B, 150T, 151, 152B, 152T, 153,

154T, 154B, 156, 158T, 159, 160, 164, 165, 166, 169, 170, 171, 172, 173, 174, 176B, 177T, 177B, 178, 179, 180, 181TR, 181BR, 181BL, 182, 184, 185, 186, 187, 189, 190T, 190B, 191, 192, 193T, 193B, 194, 195, 196T, 196B, 197, 198TL, 198B, 198/199B, 200, 201, 245, 380, 381L, 382, 384/385, 390, 394B, 396, 396/397
Dreamstime.com 427, 428B
Elmira Aleynikova 93TR
Flickr/Retlaw Snellac 132T
Getty 14/15, 218, 329
ImagineChina 109, 161
iStockphoto 4T, 6B, 7ML, 7BR, 8M, 16/17, 29, 30T, 66, 85, 86, 89, 92MC, 93BR, 96, 102ML, 102BL, 102/103T, 112, 113, 114, 119, 125B, 125T, 139, 141B, 143, 157, 162T, 183, 212, 215, 219T, 219B, 223, 226ML, 257, 275, 276B, 284, 291, 296B, 298, 313, 325, 344T, 347, 360T, 360B, 367, 372, 373, 374, 375, 376, 377, 402, 402/403, 407, 424, 426, 428T, 429L, 430
Kenneth Garrett 79
Kunst Staatliche Museen zu Berlin 76
Laurence Mitchell 224, 225, 228, 231, 233, 234, 235, 237, 238, 239, 243T
Maison Cappadoces 437L
Mary Evans Picture Library 37, 40
Michael Grimsdale 49T
Natalie Behring 49B
Pete Bennet/Apa Publications 368, 379T
Jon Martin yoyoboom@yahoo.com 276T
Rebecca Erol/Apa Publications 21T, 378, 447L, 448
RMN/RÉunion des MusÈes Nationaux 78, 80MR
RMN/Thierry Olliver 73
Robert Harding 147, 158B, 167, 236, 274, 288, 295, 297 330, 370
Royal Geographical Society 72, 74
Superstock 7MR, 115, 116, 117, 118, 122/123, 124, 137, 207B, 280, 327B, 333, 380

Tony Halliday/Apa Publications 1, 7BL, 8ML, 9BL, 9BR, 9TR, 10MR, 18, 19, 51, 52, 101, 103B, 105, 168, 202/203, 204, 205, 206, 207T, 229, 240, 242L, 242R, 243B, 244, 247T, 247B, 249T, 249B, 251, 252, 253, 254, 255R, 255L, 256T, 258TL, 258BL, 258BR, 259T, 261T, 261B, 262B, 262T, 263, 264B, 264T, 265, 266, 267, 268T, 268B, 269, 270TL, 270/271B, 270BL, 272T, 272B, 281, 282, 283, 285, 286, 379B, 388/389, 394T, 404, 410B, 410T, 412, 414, 418, 419, 420, 422, 433, 434, 444
Topfoto 71R, 104, 110, 232, 248, 273B
Topham Picturepoint 230, 259B
Walter Callens 221, 241
Werner Forman Archive 43, 58, 60, 80ML, 107, 138, 337
4Corners Images 256B

PHOTO FEATURES

Bazaars
Chris Bradley/APA 102CR, 103C; **Croquet-Zouridakis** 103TR; **Tony Halliday** 103B; **iStockphoto** 102TL, 102BL, 102/103T

Silk Production
Alamy 92/3T, 93BL; **Elmira Aleynikova** 93BR **Chris Bradley/APA** 92TL; **Croquet-Zouridakis** 92BR; **iStockphoto** 92BL, 93T

Treasures of the Silk Road
Alamy 80/81T; **Bridgeman Art Library** 81C, 81B; **Corbis** 80B; **CPA** 81TR; **RMN/Ravaux** 80CR; **Werner Forman Archive** 80TL

Yurts
Croquet-Zouridakis 216CL, 216BR, 217B; **iStockphoto** 216TL; **Bradley Mayhew** 216/217T, 217TC, 217TR

INDEX

Main references are in bold type

Silk Road